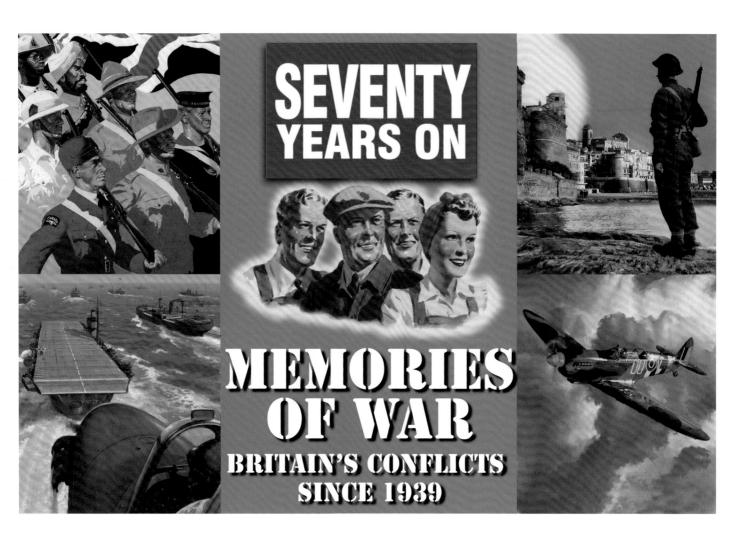

SEVENTY YEARS ON

MEMORIES OF WAR
BRITAIN'S CONFLICTS SINCE 1939

"I see the world being slowly transformed into a wilderness,
I hear the approaching thunder that, one day, will destroy us
too, I feel the suffering of millions. And yet, when I look up
at the sky, I somehow feel that everything will change for
the better, that this cruelty too shall end, that peace and
tranquility will return once more."

ANNE FRANK

Born 1929.
Betrayed to the Nazis in August 1944.
Died in Bergen–Belsen Concentration Camp, March 1945.

SEVENTY YEARS ON

FOREWORD & INTRODUCTION
DAME VERA LYNN on page 5
EDITOR DAVID ARNOLD on page 6

Steps to War

Aftermath of the Great War. Hitler and the Nazi rise to power. R J Mitchell's Spitfire: Birth of a Legend. Japan and Russia clash in the summer of 1939. A compact digest of the whole of the World War 1939-1945. **8**

CONTENTS

1939-1940

Unholy alliance: Hitler and Stalin seize Poland. The Phoney War. Finland rattles Russia. Norway and Denmark capitulate. Holland, Belgium and France cave in. Miracle evacuation for BEF at Dunkirk. RAF win the Battle of Britain. Heavy civilian casualties as the Blitz on London begins. **21**

1941

Defeat for Italy at sea and in Africa. Britain aids Greece. The *Bismarck* is sunk. Britain loses in Greece and Crete. Rommel's Afrika Korps arrive. Hitler turns his armies against Russia. War with Japan. USA now in the fight but badly hurt by surprise attack on Pearl Harbor. **65**

1942

Japan seizes British colonies. Singapore falls and Burma is invaded. U-Boats endanger our Atlantic lifeline. After winter reverses, Germany resumes offensive in Russia but is defeated at Stalingrad. Japanese carrier fleet sunk at Midway. German retreat from El Alamein. **91**

1943

Malta holds out. Afrika Korps defeated by Eighth Army and US forces in Tunisia. Allied invasion of Sicily. Red Army wins gigantic tank battle at Kursk. Mussolini deposed; Italy changes sides as Allies invade mainland. U-Boat menace is diminished. US troops 'over here'. **125**

1944

Allies held at Cassino and unable to advance at Anzio. Allied bombers range over Germany and Occupied Europe in invasion build-up. Russians steadily advance on the Eastern Front. Rome liberated 24 hours before D-Day. Paris and Brussels freed. Hitler's Ardennes Offensive. **153**

1945

Allies push forward over the Rhine. Advances in Italy. Red Army moves into Berlin. Death of the Dictators. Victory in Europe. Successes in Burma and the Pacific. Atom Bombs on Japan end World War II. Even so, Britain faces many more military conflicts in the next seven decades. **347**

2

Tales of Their Times

As well as telling the story of the Second World War and recounting Britain's military conflicts since 1945, *Seventy Years On* is laced with scores of fascinating eyewitness reports and experiences gathered from a host of veterans, civilians and people who grew up in wartime. Some of the stories are humourous and some are harrowing. All are true. A montage of photographs appears here to give a flavour of the contents. A full index of the individual stories can be found at the back of the book starting from page 412.

> Happy and Glorious,
> One between four of us,
> Thank God there's no
> more of us,
> Hallelujah, Amen!

3

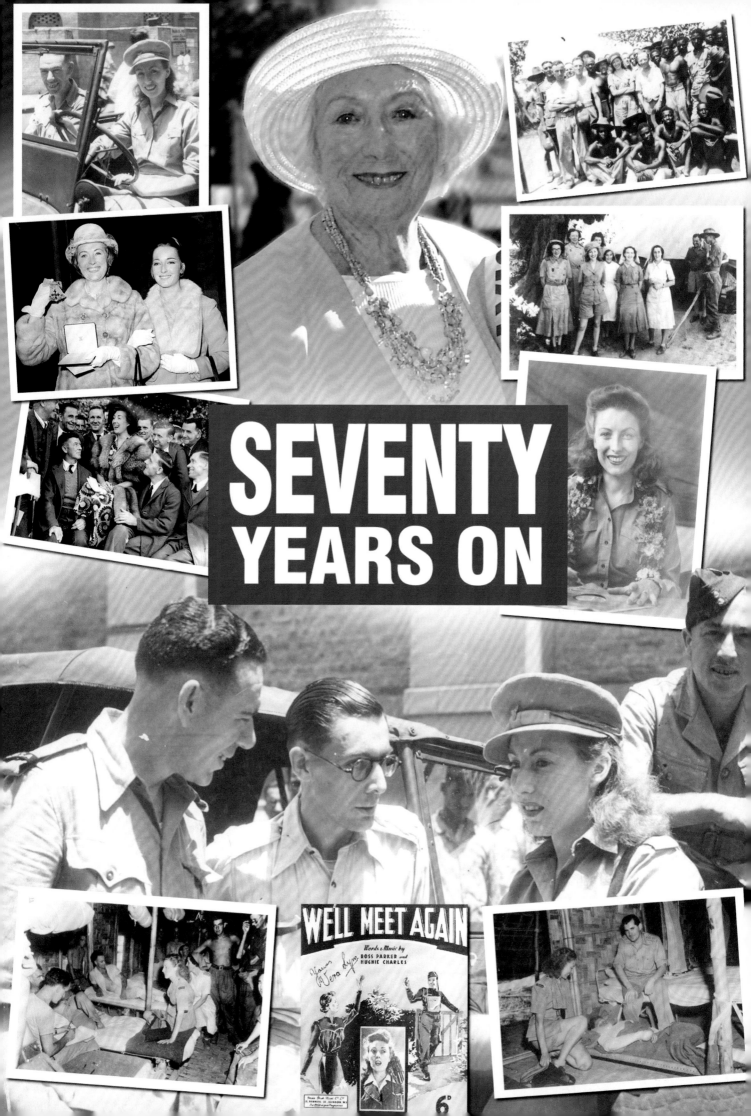

SEVENTY YEARS ON

WE'LL MEET AGAIN

Words & Music by
ROSS PARKER and
HUGHIE CHARLES

6ᴰ

A Need To Remember

My lifetime has seen destiny shaped by two all-consuming wars. The First World War was dubbed the 'war to end all wars', yet just 21 years later saw the outbreak of the Second World War, a conflict that would swiftly escalate into the most destructive war in history.

Dame Vera Lynn and her good friend, singer Hayley Westenra, plus military escort at the launch of a recent Poppy Appeal.

It seems that since the end of that war hardly a year, or even a day, has gone by where we have not been involved in some form of confrontation or conflict. In the process, friends have become enemies and former enemies have become friends; a sure testament, if ever it were needed, to the futility of war.

I have witnessed the pain and anguish endured by families and loved ones at home in the face of the sacrifices made by so many of our young men and women on active service. I witnessed for myself the terrible civilian toll of deaths and injuries incurred in the bombing Blitz on Britain and the later V1 and V2 rocket attacks. I visited the jungles of Burma in 1944 and met servicemen and women serving in the most inhospitable and difficult circumstances.

The pages of this book, *Seventy Years On*, tell the story of those tumultuous war years but also bring us on a journey through time that encompasses Britain's many conflicts since 1945. I do believe my experiences of some seventy years ago are echoed today when we see entertainers and public figures visiting Afghanistan to show their support for Britain's armed forces. We do not have to approve of a war or a military campaign in order to wish the very best for our boys and girls and a safe return home when they can meet again with their loved ones.

We have been given the gift of memories that may be happy or sad or reflective. Others have experienced the despair of losing someone close or have faced up to sharing the future with a loved one terribly injured by a bomb or bullet or is a victim of the simple bad luck that is the ever-present and heartless companion of war.

The children of yesteryear have paved the way for the children of today. Our simple legacy must be to always remember the sacrifices that have been made and are still being made. We must also ensure that the children of future generations learn of our history so they too can pay their respects and take forward the flame of remembrance.

Vera Lynn

Dame Vera Lynn DBE LLD

A Corner of a Foreign Field...

Royal Scots Fusilier George 'Geordie' Kane was killed at Anzio on 18 April 1944. At 28 years of age, Geordie was a veteran who had survived the Dunkirk evacuation and another four years of soldiering before taking part in the Italian Campaign. At the time of the Anzio landings in January he was with the British forces along the Garigliano river, some 80 miles south of the beach-head. The Second Battalion of the Royals Scots Fusiliers were withdrawn from the Minturno area in late February 1944, reformed and then sent by sea to reinforce the Allied forces who had suffered many casualties. By 9 March the whole Battalion had disembarked at Peter Beach, north of the port of Anzio, and were in position along the left flank of the beach-head.

The exact circumstances of Geordie's death are unknown to his family, shellfire being the most likely cause. He is buried in the Beach-Head War Cemetery at Anzio, as are many fellow servicemen. Geordie left a widow in Ayr, Scotland, together with three children, the youngest of whom he was never to see for the soldier was posted before the birth of his last daughter.

For over 45 years no member of Geordie's family had ever been to Anzio to visit his grave. Not at all an unusual thing in the aftermath of a war in which so many died. But then in 1988, Geordie's older sister Elizabeth Huxley of High Hurstwood in East Sussex began to talk more and more of Geordie. His picture had been on display in her house for decades past. In the spring of that same year,

Mrs Huxley's daughter Barbara was able to take a weekend break in Rome. She and her husband hired a car and drove out of the city for an hour or so until they came to Anzio. There they located the Beach-Head Cemetery and found the grave of Fusilier Kane, maintained wonderfully well as if Geordie had died just weeks before and not four and half decades ago. Barbara was able to bring home photographs for her mum showing the headstone and cemetery, together with the story of how Geordie's memory is preserved in such a peaceful setting in that far-off corner of a foreign land. Geordie's sister Elizabeth herself died just a few months later.

However, that journey to Anzio achieved more than serve to revive the memory of Geordie and bring some comfort to his sister Lizzie's last days. For out of that poignant visit came also the ultimate inspiration for

Above: This is the War Cemetery at Cassino. It holds 4267 British and Commonwealth casualties. They almost certainly include some men who would have been known to Geordie because the Royal Scots Fusiliers were in the line in that area of Italy early in 1944 before going to Anzio.

Left: The sign for the German Military Cemetery at Cassino. It's an ironic twist of fate that Geordie's widow would marry a released German POW after the war.

Seventy Years On. You see, Geordie's niece, Barbara, is my wife.

There is an ironic and sad postscript to Geordie's story. After the end of the war his widow married a released German POW who had no wish to return to a devastated Germany. He became stepfather to Geordie's children.

Soon after the predecessor to this book *Seventy Years On* was published, my wife Barbara and her sister Margaret paid a visit to Ayr to visit their Mum's family for the first time in several decades. They discovered that Geordie's widow's husband had died almost in the same week that the earlier book was published. Isn't life strange?

Life gets even stranger when you consider a further tragedy that visited Geordie's extended family nearly three decades after his death at Anzio. Three young off-duty Royal Highland Fusilier soldiers murdered in Northern Ireland by the IRA in early 1971 were related to him. One of the lads was just 17. The three are remembered in the National Memorial Arboretum. Their story is told in more detail on page 398 of this book.

How odd to think that Catholic Geordie could die in the Allied crusade against Hitler's tyranny far away on the coast of Italy yet less than 30 years later related folk from Scotland could be murdered in peacetime in cold blood near Belfast, a place in Britain less than 90 miles distant from his home town of Ayr.

Barbara at her Uncle Geordie's grave at Anzio, Italy, Easter 1988.

NATIONAL MEMORIAL ARBORETUM

Barbara's uncle lies in a grave in a pristine cemetery established by the Commonwealth War Graves Commission. We have visited it on several occasions since 1988 and it's always a pleasure to see how beautifully maintained the place is. Indeed, I find it hard to reconcile the sight of the lovely flowers and immaculate lawns with the terrible death and destruction visited on the area in 1944.

There is a parallel with the National Memorial Arboretum in Staffordshire. Until recently the site was a flat and featureless riverside plain that had been excavated for sand and gravel and left looking much like a Great War battlefield.

Part of the Royal British Legion Group, the Arboretum has been fashioned into a most beautiful place; a haven of peace where trees, wild flowers and varied wildlife thrive. It is described as 'Britain's living and growing tribute to the service and sacrifice of so many for our freedom' and there are plots and monuments to scores and scores of organisations and institutions including a grove of willow trees dedicated to those who have lost their lives in Iraq and Afghanistan.

In the heart of the Arboretum is the striking Armed Forces Memorial bearing the names of every man and woman who has died in the service of their country since 1945. On a recent visit, Barbara and I looked for and found two names in particular. The first was that of Vincent Scott. 'Vinny' was the son of my brother Derek's sister-in-law, Marie. A soldier with the Lancashire King's Regiment, he was murdered in terrible circumstances in Northern Ireland in 1990. The second name was that of Reg Gliding who was the uncle of our sister-in-law, Marina. He was one of the Glorious Glosters who died on the Imjin River in Korea in 1951. We also looked for and found the name of Dennis Moppett in the Arboretum's Far East Pavilion. Dennis was the brother of a late neighbour of ours, Felicity. He died in Japanese captivity in 1945. I have been pleased to include the stories of all three of the above-named in *Seventy Years On*.

Sad to say, there is room for many more names on the walls of the Armed Forces Memorial.

SEVENTY YEARS ON

The secret is out. *Seventy Years On* has ancestors. Following a poignant visit made to the grave of my wife's uncle at Anzio, Italy, in the spring of 1988, I had an idea – no, it was more of a nagging thought – that I must do something to help people tell their wartime stories before time took its toll.

The result was *Fifty Years On*, a bi-monthly partwork published in 1994. It concentrated on the years 1944–45 and was well received by those folk who managed to find it hidden away on the bottom shelves of a limited number of newsagents. Producing the partwork was a struggle. I had a young family and a demanding full-time job as a magazine editor.

Even so, I owe much to *Fifty Years On*. It introduced me to the remarkable Ron McGill. Barely a teenager when war broke out, Ron was a Telegram delivery boy by 1944 and had a host of adventures, some that were desperately sad, others hilarious. A talented artist, Ron is also a gifted writer and in later life had found the time to record his memories. Though *Fifty Years On* was not a financial success, I became an immensely richer person in spirit for having met him. To this day he offers me unstinting support and encouragement and his contributions are always of the highest calibre.

Stories from every age group

Move on nearly 10 years. I was still in that same full-time job. It entailed editing *Motoring & Leisure*, the magazine of the Civil Service Motoring Association. Yet I still experienced those nagging thoughts about older folks and the need to record their stories. So in January 2004 I started a series within the magazine. Of course, it had to be called *Sixty Years On*. The response was astounding. I was overwhelmed with a deluge of enthralling material. Not just from older people; sons, daughters and even grandchildren sent me stories galore, mainly concerned with the years 1944–45. Indeed there was enough to fill a book; and so, thanks to CSMA underwriting the cost, a book duly appeared. *Sixty Years On* came out in 2005 and in a very short time sold nearly 10,000 copies, in the main to *Motoring & Leisure* readers. It certainly was a financial success – but not for me as I had forgotten to secure a royalty deal!

David and Barbara Arnold. It was taken at a black tie 'do' in the Imperial War Museum so makes this particular picture feel somehow appropriate.

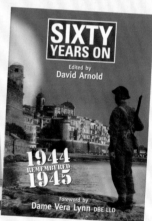

Move on to 2008. The history bug still hadn't gone away. Then, after 29 years as Editor, I had the chance to take early retirement. It seemed the perfect opportunity to devote myself to another incarnation of that aspiration that first took root in Anzio Beach-Head Cemetery way back in 1988. Only this time the book would be bigger than ever, encompass the whole of the Second World War and include a timeline of tales involving Britain's many small wars and conflicts that have flared up from 1945 right up until the present day.

Dear reader, I give you *Seventy Years On*. If you enjoy this book please tell your friends to buy a copy. I've spent my pension lump sum on producing it!

David Arnold, Editor

The book *Seventy Years On* was first published in Great Britain by Crown Publishing Ltd, 14 St John Street, Lewes, East Sussex BN7 2QE. Tel: 01273 478513. Email: david.arnold@me.com

Printed by Butler Tanner & Dennis Ltd.
Repro and Origination by Marion Hughes.

Steps to War

The origins of World War Two are to be found in the aftermath of the 1914-1918 Great War. Germany felt aggrieved at the peace terms imposed by the French and British victors and their allies. The punitive Treaty of Versailles, signed on 28 June 1919, limited the size of the German army to 100,000 men and restricted the navy to 36 warships. At the same time it imposed territorial penalties with France regaining Alsace-Lorraine, which the Prussians had taken from her in 1871. Poland was also granted a strip of German land; the 'Polish Corridor' gave the Poles access to the Baltic at Danzig, which was made a League of Nations trust territory. Germany was also required to pay massive war reparations.

This humbling of the Fatherland was deeply resented by the German army generals. Many of them took the view that they had, in fact, not actually been defeated by the French,

Epitaph to the Great War 1914-1918. Nearly 10,000,000 soldiers, sailors and airmen from all the countries involved were killed in battle and some 6,000,000 crippled or invalided for life. Countless thousands of civilians also died. When it was over the League of Nations vowed 'never again'. Twenty one years later the world went once more to war. How did it happen?

plebiscite resulted in part of Upper Silesia being given to Poland. Political weakness coupled with a dire economic climate created the conditions where a strong character with a simple message of national ambition would be sure of an eager audience.

Adolf Hitler strode onto Germany's political stage in 1923. With a group of right wing, thuggish supporters he made a first attempt to seize power in 1923 in what became known as the Beer Hall Putsch. It failed and Hitler was sent to gaol for nine months. In prison he wrote *Mein Kampf* (My Struggle), his blueprint for the future of Germany and its place in the world. Anti-Semitism and the policy of *Lebensraum* – Germany's right to take 'living space' by force from its eastern neighbours – were enshrined in the book.

For the next 10 years Hitler slowly but surely gathered support for his National Socialist Party

British and United States armies. The war had ended with an armistice, a poorly negotiated one in the German military view, and not an unconditional surrender.

Even so, Germany remained the biggest economic power in Central Europe, a position reinforced by the post-war disbanding of the Hapsburg's defeated Austro-Hungarian Empire. A new country, Czechoslovakia, was sanctioned as a direct result and part of its territory, the Sudetenland, was dominated by a population of German origin.

Germany's continuing importance was also reinforced through the effects of the Treaty of Brest-Litovsk. Signed in March 1918, this document saw the Bolsheviks withdrew from the war. Even though the Treaty was

repudiated within eight months, territorial concessions prevailed and these included independence for Poland and Finland. The latent might of Russia was marginalized.

Versailles also led to the foundation of the League of Nations, an international forum where nations could settle their problems by mutual agreement rather than war. Unfortunately, the League lacked the will and the power to influence world affairs right from the start, a situation not improved by the failure of the USA to join. Instead, the most powerful country on earth withdrew into isolationism, leaving Europe and the rest of the world to fend for itself.

Economic disaster

In the early Twenties, economic disaster struck Germany. The fastest and most disastrous monetary inflation ever known destroyed the value of the German currency and plunged millions of citizens into poverty almost overnight. It required millions of Marks simply to purchase a loaf of bread.

Germany's Weimar Republic of the time was a coalition government that had replaced the autocratic rule of the Kaiser. It proved ineffective and its unpopularity was not helped when a League of Nations-imposed

– the Nazis. The Great Depression that hit the world's stock markets in October 1929 gave him a big boost; Hitler's promises to bring full employment and make Germany militarily strong again found broad appeal in a country where a third of working men were without jobs.

By 1932 the Nazis had won 230 seats in the Reichstag parliament. On 30 January 1933 the respected but ageing President Hindenburg felt obliged to offer the Chancellorship of Germany to Hitler. Though he had achieved power via the ballot box he was determined that he would never lose it through the same process. When Hindenburg died in 1934, Hitler declared himself President as well as Chancellor, assumed command of Germany's military and called himself 'Fuhrer', leader of the Third Reich and its people.

Hitler was not the first dictator to emerge in Europe in the years following the Great War. Benito Mussolini had led the Italian Fascist party to power in 1922 after marching on Rome and demanding that the king appoint them to govern the country. Mussolini did indeed embark on a major public works programme and famously made 'the trains run on time'. But he too harboured ambitions of empire and in 1935 he sent an army across

Left: Adolf Hitler is the man most responsible for provoking World War II. Here he is reviewing a parade of his infamous 'Brownshirts' at a Nazi rally in Nuremberg in 1927. The name Nazi was derived from letters contained in Nationalsa Zlatstiche Deutsche Arbeiter Parteir (National Socialist German Workers Party). The Swastika is a very old, sacred symbol with links to the Hindu and Buddhist cultures. In his book Mein Kampf, *Hitler wrote of the device, 'In the red we see the social idea of the Nazi movement, in the white the Nationalist idea and in the Swastika the vision of the struggle for the victory of the Aryan man.'*

Germany's rising power

This striking promotional photograph taken in 1936 depicts Germany's growing technical dominance both on land and in the air with a Mercedes-Benz 500K Special Roadster and the Graf Zeppelin *Hindenburg* hovering overhead.

Not long after in 1937 disaster would strike when the gigantic dirigible exploded while landing at Lakehurst, New Jersey. At the time the airship was filled with highly inflammable hydrogen but in fact Dr Hugo Eckner, chairman of the Zeppelin company, had originally intended to inflate the *Hindenburg* with the non-flammable gas helium. Unfortunately for Zeppelin, the US Government had control of the only natural deposits of helium in the world and were reluctant to release any to a Germany under the sway of Hitler's increasingly aggressive Nazi regime.

The *Hindenburg* was a marvel of design. The space the fully inflated airship occupied was about the equivalent of the *Titanic*, another doomed construction of gargantuan size.

Oddly enough, the *Hindenburg* was fitted with a room for smokers. It had an anti-chamber airlock to keep any flames from spreading. The room was lined with asbestos and just a single lighter sat at a central table. Once all other lighters were confiscated from passengers and locked away, this was the only source of flame available to light a cigarette on the whole of the airship.

Though there would be no place for obsolete Zeppelin bombers in the rapidly expanding Luftwaffe, Mercedes-Benz and parent company Daimler were absolutely key to giving the German armed forces the mobility and technical cutting edge essential to the waging of Blitzkrieg.

Photo from: Daimler & Benz - The Complete History

the border from Italian Somaliland into independent Ethiopia.

Militarist Japan

Meanwhile, on the other side of the world, the Empire of Japan was on the march. Lacking in natural resources on their home islands, a militarist creed held sway with influential politicians and senior officers. Japan invaded Manchuria in 1931 and in 1932 changed the country's name to Manchukuo; it had become a Japanese colony. A Chinese boycott of trade with Japan resulted in an attack on Shanghai. Incidents and annexations of parts of China continued in the following years until, in July 1937, the Japanese decided they must overthrow the Chinese Nationalist leader, Chiang Kai-shek, and conquer the whole of China.

In the previous year, 1936, it came as no surprise to some observers – including Winston Churchill – when Germany and Italy first established the Rome – Berlin Axis of Fascist States. A few months later, Hitler concluded a treaty – the Anti-Comintern Pact – with Japan. The three most militarily aggressive countries in the world were thus in alliance and bent on pursuing their individual territorial aims at any cost.

Hitler was now pushing his luck and testing the resolve of the French and British. In 1935 he had reintroduced conscription and brought in extensive rearmament programmes. All German soldiers, sailors and airmen had to swear an oath of personal loyalty to him as their Fuhrer. In 1936 the *Wehrmacht* marched into the Rhineland, de-militarised under the Treaty of Versailles. France and Britain took no steps to punish Hitler's action. But both countries were now looking at their own armaments situation and discovering serious shortcomings.

Civil War broke out in Spain in 1936 when General Franco led a Fascist revolt against the newly democratically elected Government. The latter did not cave in and a bitter conflict ensued that polarised the divisions between right and left. Hitler and Mussolini sent troops and aircraft to aid Franco and took advantage of the opportunity for a dress rehearsal of the far, far bigger war to come. The Soviet leader Stalin sent aid for the Republican side who were also bolstered by the arrival of volunteers from all over Europe, especially Britain. Unfortunately,

part of the cost of Stalin's help was political infighting between the different Communist factions and left-wing bodies that resulted in many deaths. The war ended with a Franco victory early in 1939 but so war-wracked and exhausted was Spain by then that the Generalissimo wisely adopted a neutral stance as the war clouds gathered elsewhere in Europe.

For his part, Stalin had already hamstrung his own armed forces in Russia with a deadly purge of the most senior generals and officers. He was paranoid of plots, real or imagined, against his total control of the Soviet Union.

On 12 March 1938 Hitler ordered *Anschluss*, the annexation of Austria, a mission accomplished in two days. He next turned his attention to Czechoslovakia where the Sudetenland border area was already an issue, being populated in the main by ethnic Germans; its transfer to Germany had been imposed only in 1918.

The British attempted to negotiate the problem but Hitler held firm. At a crucial meeting in Munich, British Premier Neville Chamberlain felt he had extracted the best deal possible with Hitler. He returned to Heston Airport with that infamous piece of paper and the words, 'Peace in our Time'.

Sudetenland occupied

There was no peace for the Czechs. The Germans marched into the Sudetenland. Within a short time, Poland and Hungary took the opportunity to occupy smaller parts of Czechoslovakia where a majority of Poles and Magyrs were resident.

Hitler next demanded German control of the rest of the country. In March 1939 he made his move. German and Hungarian forces took control of the remaining Czechoslovakian land. On 16 March Hitler himself went to Prague to proclaim Bohemia and Moravia as

German Protectorates.

Now it was Poland's turn to take centre stage. Britain and France tried to enlist Russia's aid in guaranteeing military assistance for Poland in the event of a German attack. When Russia asked for a similar pact for themselves, they were astonished when Chamberlain refused. Put simply it meant that Britain and France wanted Russia's help if an attack on Poland led to Germany being at war with them but the two western countries were not prepared to side with the Soviet Union in the event of a German attack on Russia. The problem was that Britain and France were suspicious of Stalin and believed that the long term aim of the Soviets was to spread Communism and revolution.

Next occurred one of the great *volte faces* in history. Unable to reach an agreement with Hitler's adversaries, the Russians concluded a pact with the Nazis. Signed on 23 August 1939, the deal effectively sealed Poland's fate; both Hitler and Stalin had agreed on the partition of that country following an imminent invasion by the Germans that was to be followed up by a Soviet move into the eastern part.

On 25 August the British Government signed a Treaty of Mutual Assistance with Poland. Hitler paused for a week during which he demanded that the Poles give up territory or face war. The Poles refused. The Luftwaffe commenced the bombing of Warsaw on 1 September. Britain's latest ally was under attack. The House of Commons demanded that Chamberlain send an ultimatum to Hitler. It was duly despatched as was a similar one by the French. The British ultimatum expired at 11am on 3 September. The furious German assault on Poland continued unabated. That same day Britain and France found themselves at war in Europe, just 21 years after the end of the Great War, the war that was supposed to end all wars.

Hitler pleased his supporters with the launch of the Volkswagen (the 'people's car'), declaring that every German worker should possess one. The world's biggest motor plant was built near Wolfsburg. With the onset of war the factory was at once turned over to armaments production. Under the Third Reich, not a single Volkswagen was ever delivered for civilian use.

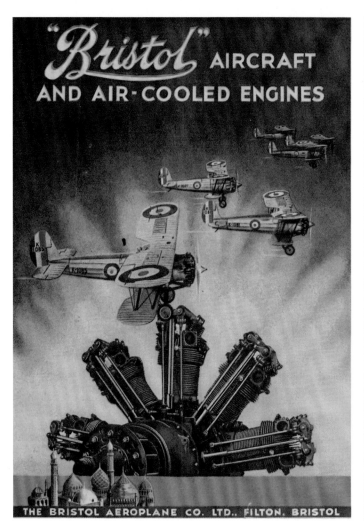

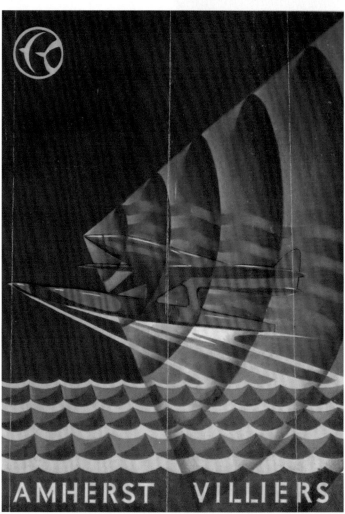

We are grateful to the Solent Sky Aviation Museum in Southampton for making these images available. Visit: www.spitfireonline.co.uk

BIRTH OF A LEGEND

The Spitfire is the most iconic aircraft of World War II. It played a crucial role in 1940 when the RAF victory in the Battle of Britain ensured this country's survival and ultimately led to the defeat of Nazi Germany. The Spitfire went on to serve with distinction in all theatres of conflict. But were it not for the genius and dedication of one man and the patriotism of a very wealthy widow the Spitfire might never have flown.

Reginald J Mitchell cut his aviation design teeth in the sport of air racing. His streamlined S5 and S6 seaplanes had successfully competed in the international Schneider Trophy races of the Twenties. But in 1931 the British Government decided to withdraw their financial support and it looked as though an RAF entry could not be mounted.

Step forward Lady Lucy Houston. When this wealthy widow, a noted eccentric said to be an admirer of the Italian dictator Mussolini and reputed to be the richest woman in the world, heard the news she donated the required £100,000. Consequently Mitchell was able to further improve his aircraft and on 13 September 1931 at Spithead in the Solent the S6B flew the course at an average speed of 340.08mph. As this was a third British win his reward was to win the Schneider Trophy outright for Great Britain. Ironically, Mitchell's entry was the only one that year but it didn't deter a vast crowd turning up to cheer on pilot Flt Lt J N Boothman.

Streamlined for fast flight

A couple of weeks later, with its Rolls-Royce engine boosted to 2600hp, the S6B became the first aircraft to exceed 400mph. Mitchell knew his streamlined design was the future for fast flight and when he turned his attention to fighter planes he drew on his air racing experience. Learning that the Germans were experimenting with sleek monoplane machines, Mitchell looked at the fabric-covered biplanes that were then Britain's frontline fighters and felt increasing unease. He and a dedicated team set to work on the Supermarine Type 300; Mitchell was spurred on even more when he learnt he was suffering from an incurable cancer.

Left: Advertisements from the official programme of the 1931 Schneider Trophy race. Even at this time Spitfire designer R J Mitchell believed that biplanes lacked sufficient speed to serve as fighter aircraft in modern aerial warfare.

Right: 'The First of the Few' is the famous aviation artist Frank Wootton's depiction of the 1936 test flight of the first production Spitfire Mk1, K9787, reproduced here with the kind permission of Mrs Virginia Wootton.

On 5 March 1936 the prototype aircraft made its first flight from Eastleigh Airport in Hampshire. The results were highly encouraging and on 3 June of that year the Air Ministry ordered 310 of the aircraft. A week later the Air Ministry reluctantly approved the new fighter's name as proposed by Supermarine Chairman Sir Robert McLean. The choice of 'Spitfire' found no favour with Mitchell, either, who described it as 'bloody silly'.

Clearly influenced by Mitchell's designs, Sir Sidney Camm had meanwhile been working on what was to become the redoubtable Hawker Hurricane. In fact, production of the latter overtook that of the Spitfire due to manufacturing complications.

Air speed record lasted 30 years

The Germans had also been working apace on their own fighters. They'd had the advantage of testing their aircraft in action with Franco's fascist forces during the Spanish Civil War. On 26 April 1939 a prototype Messerschmitt Bf 209R flown by Fritz Wendel took the official world air speed record of 469.22mph (755kmph). His achievement would stand for 30 years.

However, in the Battle of Britain just over a year later it was the Spitfires and Hurricanes of the RAF that proved superior to the Luftwaffe fighters. But getting the British machines and their pilots ready for war had been - to echo the words attributed to Wellington after Waterloo - a damn close run thing.

R J Mitchell didn't live to see his Spitfire triumph in the air war. The cancer claimed him in 1937 when he was aged just 42.

Japan and Russia Clash

In the summer of 1939, Japan and the Soviet Union went to war in the Far East. The Japanese suffered a stinging defeat. As a direct consequence Japan set out on a course that would eventually lead them to Pearl Harbor.

The clash between Russia and Japan concerned their respective influences in Mongolia and Manchuria, the northeastern-most part of China. In the Great Depression, as trade dwindled and unemployment grew, an ultra-nationalist clique within the Japanese military looked to simply seize the raw materials Japan so desperately wanted. The Kwantung Army, set up in Port Arthur in 1919, was quasi-independent and advocated Japanese expansion in China. Various 'provocations' were stage-managed to justify their aggressive incursions into Manchuria. In 1932 the Japanese proclaimed the puppet state of 'Manchukuo'. By the second half of 1937 the Japanese had captured Peking (Beijing) and most of the other major cities of China. But the Chinese did not surrender.

Even so, many in the Japanese military saw the Soviet Union as an equally important enemy. When in 1936 the Soviets proclaimed the Mongolian People's Republic (MPR) they were highly alarmed. As a result in 1937 there were 33 armed clashes along the 3000 mile frontier separating the Soviet Union from Manchukuo. Russia and Japan were fighting an undeclared war via their two client states.

Zhukov takes command

On 1 January 1938 talks took place in Berlin about a possible German-Japanese alliance. Hitler was eager to expand the Reich in Europe and it would benefit him to keep the Soviets preoccupied. He also had a secret longer-term intention to invade Russia and a Japanese ally on the Soviet eastern border could prove very useful. No agreement was reached but this would not deter Japan from confronting Russia.

In early July of 1938 the Japanese demanded that the Soviets evacuate disputed territories along the Manchurian border. In July and August 1938 the two powers clashed in another disputed area between Siberia and Japanese-controlled Korea. The result was inconclusive. However, the Kwantung Army leadership was still willing to gamble. The Japanese believed the typical Russian soldier to be weak-willed and lacking in spirit. They also knew that thousands of experienced

officers had been purged on Stalin's orders. In consequence they developed an ambitious plan to expel the Russians from the Far East and push them back beyond Lake Baikal.

On 11-12 May 1939 small units of Manchurians and Mongolians fought each other to a standstill at the village of Nomonhan near the Khalkin Gol river. Japanese and Red Army troops then became involved in a see-saw battle. On 28 May a Japanese thrust over the Khalkin Gol was repulsed. The Kwantung Army escalated affairs. Their air force made a surprise attack on the main Soviet air base in Mongolia. Then on 1 July they sent tanks and infantry against the Russians dug in east of the river and pushed them back.

China fought against Japanese aggression for the longest time of any of the Allied nations. This poster reminded the US public of China's key role in the war with Japan. China was the also the catalyst for the conflict between Russia and Japan in 1939.

Now a new figure emerged in the Red Army. General Georgi K Zhukov, 42, had taken command of the Russian forces in June. Learning of the Japanese penetration, this dynamic and aggressive officer launched a three-pronged armoured counter-attack. Zhukov quickly retook all the lost ground.

Heat, dust and disease

By 25 July 1939 the Japanese had sustained some 5000 casualties. Russian losses were higher, but the Red Army had greater manpower. Zhukov also proved to be a master of logistics, keeping his army well supplied; the Japanese were poorly served by comparison. Both sides were fighting in hot, dusty and inhospitable terrain where disease was rife. By early August there were 75,000

Japanese and Manchurian troops in the fight and the Kwantung Army prepared to attack again. Meanwhile, alarmed at Hitler's threats against Poland, Stalin wanted to be freed up from distractions in the Far East; he ensured Zhukov was heavily reinforced.

At 6am on 20 August, Zhukov was the first to strike; 100,000 Russian and Mongolian troops moved forward along a 48-mile front, supported by 500 tanks and 216 artillery pieces. Surprise was total. Soviet artillery easily outgunned the Japanese and blew apart their dugouts. Over 200 bombers gave air support. On the ground, the Soviet tanks bested the weak Japanese armour. In savage fighting the Soviets destroyed an entire Japanese division near Nomonhan. By 31 August the Japanese had been defeated. Of 60,000 Japanese troops involved nearly 45,000 were killed. The Red Army suffered around 16,000 killed or wounded.

At this point Manchuria was at mercy of the Soviets. But instead of invading they halted at Mongolia's original border. The Soviets had a highly effective spy ring operating in Tokyo headed by Richard Sorge. He had revealed that the Japanese in Tokyo wanted to rein in the Kwantung Army and end the fighting. As early as 22 August, Moscow had offered a ceasefire.

'Strike South' faction takes over

On 23 August the Soviets signed a Non-Aggression Pact with Nazi Germany, agreeing to divide Poland. On 16 September, as German tanks closed in on Warsaw, a ceasefire between Russia and Japan took effect. Even as war engulfed Europe, Stalin knew his eastern border was safe, leaving him free to seize a slice of Poland and demand territory from Finland and Rumania.

In the event of a war with Germany, Stalin realized that in Zhukov he had an exceptionally able commander to call on, moreover one who had been tested in the art of mobile warfare on the plains of Nomonhan. The Soviets would also improve their weapons; the robust and efficient T34 tank was one result.

The Japanese took pains to avoid provoking Russia again. Even when they finally signed the Tripartite Pact with Germany and Italy in March 1941, they quickly concluded a non-aggression pact with Moscow as well.

Japan's bitter war with China would go on but the 'Strike South' faction now came to the fore. Led by the Imperial Navy, this lobby advocated Japan expanding into South East Asia and the Pacific to seize the rich colonies held by Britain, France and the Netherlands. Sometime in the not too distant future, the United States, too, might have to be dealt with.

A PROMISE TO THE NATION

With the onset of hostilities, British artists and designers were rapidly recruited by the various Ministries who required morale-boosting posters and information leaflets. The example above is by Pat Keely who, as a civilian artist, did a lot of work for the railways. This poster depicts a Great War infantryman behind a machine-gunner who may well be serving with the BEF in France just as the British Army did in 1914-18. The clear message is to encourage the British public's faith in their armed forces. This is the original concept complete with hand-fashioned lettering (National Archives – The Art of War).

The War 1939-45

In *Seventy Years On* we attempt to tell the whole story of the Second World War in words and pictures. Though we endeavour to adhere to a month by month timetable of key events, it is impossible to record everything in the order it happened, particularly as so many of our contributors were on active service throughout all or much of the conflict. To aid greater understanding of how the war unfolded, here and on the following pages we present a chronological digest of all the significant events and campaigns.

Poland fought hard for three weeks before her poorly-equipped army and obsolete air force were finally overwhelmed. At this point the Russians moved into eastern Poland, largely unopposed. They took into captivity some 200,000 Polish servicemen. A number of these would live to fight another day either with the Red Army or with the Western Allies, where their bitterness at the fate of their country and knowledge of the privations visited upon their families would turn them into dauntless airmen and soldiers of the highest calibre.

In Britain the period following the subjugation of Poland became known as the 'Phoney War'. Anticipated German air attacks spreading bombs and lethal gas amidst British cities did not materialise. Children were evacuated, a black-out was imposed and rationing entered the lives of everyone.

It was different at sea. German submarines began sinking British warships and merchant vessels. In October 1939 a U-Boat penetrated the defences of Scapa Flow in the Orkneys and sank the battleship *HMS Royal Oak* with tremendous loss of life. Two months later the Royal Navy hit back and chased the German pocket battleship *Graf Spee* into Montevideo harbour in neutral Uruguay where her captain scuttled the ship rather than risk a fight.

Outside of Britain and France, for much of Europe the war became very real indeed. Despite his unlikely pact with the Nazis, Stalin knew he could not trust Hitler. Consequently he sought to strengthen the Soviet borders by taking back into the Kremlin's fold, by force if necessary, those countries that had been given

their independence and freedom some two decades earlier by the Treaty of Brest-Litovsk, ironically a peace arrangement concluded with Germany.

The Baltic States of Estonia, Latvia and Lithuania were pressured into granting rights of occupation to the Red Army. Then, on 30 November 1939, the Russians attacked Finland after the Finns had turned down the former's demands for territory and strategic bases that they considered vital for the protection of the city of Leningrad.

In the course of the 'Winter War' the Finns, outnumbered by more than two to one, nevertheless gave the Russians a bloody nose before being finally forced to give in to Russian demands on 13 March 1940. British public opinion had been firmly on the side of the gallant Finns. Germany gave more tangible support to the Finnish commander, General Mannerheim, in the form of arms and war materiél. Ironically, the Red Army learnt a lot of lessons about the right way to fight in the snow and frozen mud, lessons that would prove invaluable in the years ahead.

Hitler strikes north

Less than a month after the end of the Winter War, Hitler struck north and invaded Denmark and Norway. Denmark had no chance of offering serious resistance and reluctantly gave in without a fight. German troops landed at Oslo on 9 April 1940 and, despite counter-landings by the British Army and Navy and a serious naval reverse to the Kriegsmarine at Narvik, were able to occupy the country.

By early May the mood of the House of Commons was very much against the

Conservative Neville Chamberlain continuing as Prime Minister. A coalition government was required in the face of tribulation. Though Winston Churchill was also a Conservative it was the Labour Party that sealed the appointment of him as Prime Minister on 9 May.

The last British units withdrew from the north of Norway on 8 June but by then momentous things had occurred in mainland Europe. Hitler had ordered a simultaneous Blitzkrieg attack against France, Belgium and Holland. The defenders included the relatively small but powerful British Expeditionary Force (BEF) who were equipped with a significant proportion of Britain's operational tanks, artillery and transport. The RAF were present in force as well.

The German assault in the West began in the early hours of 10 May 1940 with parachute troops capturing key objectives in Holland and Belgium. Then the German panzer armies erupted out of the Ardennes, a region that the vaunted French Maginot Line of 'impregnable' fortifications did not extend to. One of the panzer commanders was Erwin Rommel, demonstrating the audacity and panache that would later make him such a dangerous adversary in North Africa.

Miracle of Dunkirk

The speed and fury of the German attack threw the French and British into confusion. Holland and Belgium quit the fight in the early stages. The huge French army found itself split by the German columns and unable to function as a cohesive force. Just one French commander, Charles de Gaulle, who had long warned of the German menace, was able to put in a serious counter-attack. It failed.

The BEF at first rushed north into Belgium, according to pre-arranged plans. When the Germans reached the English Channel at Abbeville on 20 May the British turned around and headed for the Pas de Calais region. With the French in disarray and much of their army isolated from the battlefield, the BEF commander Lord Gort realised the British were trapped with their backs to the coast. Evacuation by sea offered the only escape if things continued to go badly.

Now came the 'Miracle of Dunkirk'. On 26 May Lord Gort was given permission to evacuate the BEF from France to England. Next day a perimeter was formed around Dunkirk and evacuations also commenced out of Calais and Boulogne. For some reason, three days earlier Hitler had ordered his panzers not to press home the assault and although the infantry and Luftwaffe remained very active, *Operation Dynamo* saw 338,226 British and French troops saved to fight another day.

As France went down under the German onslaught there was one remarkable lifeline thrown by Churchill; the serious proposal of an act of union between Paris and London that would bind the two countries as tightly together as that which bound England, Scotland, Wales and Northern Ireland. But it was too late for gestures, however well-intentioned.

Hitler danced a jig of delight in Paris to celebrate his crushing victory in mainland Europe. Now in the summer of 1940 Britain faced the very real prospect of a German invasion. The majority of the BEF may have escaped capture but most of their tanks, artillery and heavy weapons were destroyed or left behind. The Navy had sustained heavy losses in the course of the evacuation and anyway the narrow confines of the English Channel, across which the German troopships must come, would put the bigger British warships at great risk from air attack. Only the RAF remained largely intact.

Battle of Britain

In the face of the debacle in France, the Head of RAF Fighter Command, Air Marshal Sir Hugh Dowding, had insisted on keeping a significant pool of squadrons in reserve in Britain. His foresight gave the RAF the chance to deny air superiority to Luftwaffe; without this an invasion was unlikely to succeed. Fortunately the RAF had excellent aircraft in the shape of the Spitfire and Hurricane. Coupled with an efficient chain of radar stations and the closer proximity of their airfields, the RAF had just enough advantages to weather the aerial storm that opened in earnest early in August. They would win the Battle of Britain.

The turning point came on 7 September when Hitler ordered his bombers to hit London in reprisal for an earlier RAF night raid on Berlin. In consequence, attacks on RAF fighter stations lessened. London and other British cities bore the brunt of the subsequent Blitz and thousands of civilians died. But Hitler's invasion never came.

The new peril for Britain was the U-Boat. Ranging out into the Atlantic and Caribbean, they exacted a growing toll of merchant shipping. The Battle of the Atlantic would last for years and the casualty rate for the civilian crews of both the ships and the U-Boats were pro rata the highest in any theatre of war. Through improved submarine detection techniques on warships and aircraft and the cracking of the German Enigma code, the Allies would eventually overcome the U-Boat threat.

A consequence of the Fall of France was the entry of Italy into the war. In the summer of 1940, Britain and Italy squared up in the Mediterranean and on the North African shore. The British held Egypt while Italian forces were based in their colonies next door in Libya and farther west. The Royal Navy got in the first decisive blow with a devastating air attack on the Italian fleet at anchor at Taranto on 11 November. Half of Italy's fleet was sunk at a cost of two Swordfish aircraft.

Within months the triumph at sea was mirrored by a brilliant victory for General Wavell's 30,000 British and Australian troops who captured 130,000 prisoners and around 400 tanks for the loss of 500 men. The Italians would have been pushed right out of Africa but for ominous German movement in the Balkans where Mussolini's men invading from Albania were being bested by the Greek army.

Greece and Crete

Hitler was not prepared to see his Axis partner humiliated. He sent his army into Yugoslavia and also set out to conquer Greece. Wavell sent a large force to the aid of the Greeks but it was not enough to stem the German advance and an evacuation became inevitable. A stand by Greek, British and New Zealand troops on the island of Crete was

"NEVER WAS SO MUCH OWED BY SO MANY TO SO FEW" THE PRIME MINISTER

ended by an audacious German airborne assault in May. The Royal Navy also lost nine ships. To add to the British troubles, a familiar foe now appeared in North Africa as General Erwin Rommel's Afrika Korps took to the offensive and immediately made major gains in territory recovered from the weakened British and Commonwealth forces. The desert war would now see saw backwards and forwards for the next 18 months.

Unknown at the time, but of immense importance to the outcome of the war, was the fact that Hitler's excursion into the Balkans had cost him a delay in the launching of his next massive military gamble; *Operation Barbarossa*, the invasion of the Soviet Union. This began on 22 June 1941 when three million Germans, supported by numerous satellite armies including those of the Finns and Rumanians, launched a surprise attack on a vast front. The Germans met with dizzying early success and rounded up huge numbers of prisoners caught in a series of encircling movements. Vast tracts of land were conquered and Hitler's panzers seemed unstoppable as they moved up as far as Leningrad in the

north, close to the gates of Moscow itself in the centre and beyond the city of Kharkov in the south. Stalin's greatest ally now came to the rescue as the harsh Russian winter set in to cripple the German Army's ability to wage war. The Red Army, on the other hand, was equipped for the conditions and received substantial reinforcements from Siberia. The Germans were forced to retreat and the prize of Moscow slipped through their grasp. If Hitler had been able to attack in May instead of June, those extra weeks of summer campaigning could have damaged the Russian colossus beyond recovery.

Stalin's decision to bring soldiers from Siberia was made possible because of the actions of one man. Richard Sorge was a German newspaper correspondent in Tokyo who was familiar with both the German and Russian ambassadors to Japan. He was also a Russian spy. Late in 1941 the Kremlin received information from Sorge to the effect that the Japanese had decided to go to war with the United States and Britain in the Pacific and Far East. The Soviet Union would not be a target.

War with Japan

'The Day of Infamy' came on 7 December 1941 with a surprise air attack on the US Pacific Fleet at Pearl Harbour in the Hawaiian Islands followed by attacks on US bases in the Philippine Islands and the invasion of European colonies and possessions in South East Asia. For good measure, within days Hitler declared war on America. Now it was truly a World War.

Pearl Harbour was a devastating blow to the US Navy. However, by good luck, on the day of the attack no US aircraft carriers were in the port and they were spared destruction. The Japanese and the Americans both knew that air power was going to be the key to winning a war in the Pacific; whichever side could sink more of the enemy's ships must have a winning hand.

Ironically, it was the Japanese who demonstrated this point most graphically at an early stage. Two days after Pearl Harbour, the battleship *HMS Prince of Wales* and battle cruiser *HMS Repulse* were bombed and sunk when they were caught without air cover off the coast of Malaya. The British had failed to learn their own lesson from Taranto, an operation that had been studied in depth by the Japanese commander of the Pearl Harbour attack, Admiral Yamamoto.

In the opening months of 1942, the Japanese tide of conquest seemed unstoppable. Hong Kong, Malaya, Singapore, the Philippines and most of Burma were quickly occupied and the British, Australians and Americans were in retreat everywhere and thousands of Allied servicemen and women became prisoners of the Japanese. The latter's military creed did not recognise the notion of surrender and horrendous cruelty and hardship was meted out on their unfortunate captives. Darwin in Australia was bombed and Japanese submarines raided Sydney.

However, it quickly became clear that the Japanese had vastly underestimated the resources of their enemies and over-stretched their own ability to sustain and supply their armed forces who were now spread out in battlefields ranging from the Chinese mainland to thousands of miles away in far-flung South Pacific archipelagos. They were also fighting the British army in Burma, close to the frontier with India from which country upwards of a million volunteers were coming forward to join the Allied fight. On the giant islands of New Guinea and Borneo, tough Australian troops were proving more than a match for the Japanese in jungle fighting.

In early April five Japanese aircraft carriers ventured into the Indian Ocean, threatening the British naval and air bases in Ceylon. Though the Royal Navy lost two cruisers and the aircraft carrier *Hermes* it was an inconclusive engagement that eventually saw the Japanese withdraw never to return to the area in strength. The turning point in the Pacific war came in early June 1942. Thanks to good intelligence of Japanese intentions, the Americans destroyed all the carriers in an enemy fleet that sought to capture the island of Midway. The Imperial Navy's power was broken for good in a battle fought exclusively by aircraft and where the opposing ships never got within sight of each other. The war against Japan in the Pacific now became a process of slowly grinding down the stubborn and fanatical enemy and retaking one by one the islands they'd occupied and fortified.

Afrika Korps retreats

The last quarter of 1942 saw a significant reverse for the Germans in North Africa. The Afrika Korps was in Egypt, facing the British Eighth Army near the little town of El Alamein, a halt on the rail line that hugged the North African coast from east to west. A new British commander, General Bernard Law Montgomery, had instilled enormous confidence in his men. They had received copious new armaments and were backed by a powerful air force. In October, Montgomery's 'Desert Rats' struck. Even though Rommel was absent on sick leave in Germany, his Afrika Korps and their Italian comrades fought back hard but in the end were forced to retreat. All the way to Tunisia.

On 8 November 1942 *Operation Torch* began with a combined Anglo-American landing on the Atlantic and Mediterranean shores of French North Africa. The Germans were caught by Allied advances from east and west but instead of escaping back to Europe, Hitler sent reinforcements, even switching 400 precious aircraft from the Russian Front to Tunisia. The fighting in North Africa continued until 13 May 1943. The war in the desert had cost the Germans and Italians almost one million killed, maimed or captured.

After the extreme rigours of the Russian Winter and the Red Army's resurgence, Germany regained the initiative in the spring and summer of 1942. The siege of Leningrad continued. In the south the Wehrmacht scored

some spectacular victories of encirclement and spilled across the vast Russian plains until it approached the banks of the Volga river at Stalingrad and threatened the Caucasus and the vital oil towns of Baku, Tiflis and Maikop. The Germans didn't have the strength to both take Stalingrad and seize the oilfields. Hitler had to choose one or the other. He chose to take Stalingrad and in doing so committed a major strategic blunder.

Battle for Stalingrad

Like a deadly magnet, the long thin city on the west bank of the Volga drew the German Sixth Army into what became an urban death trap for the Wehrmacht. The Russians had their backs to the river and nowhere to go. Accordingly they defended with a ferocity and intensity that shocked their

enemy. More and more German units were brought up and Stalingrad was reduced to a mass of broken buildings and rubble in which the Russians clung on.

Meanwhile, the Red Army had been massing new forces on the flanks of the Sixth Army where they faced mainly Rumanian and Hungarian troops. On 19 November 1942 the Russians attacked in massive strength. Within days the lines of the Axis allies were broken and it was the turn of the Red Army to win a battle of encirclement; the entire Sixth Army of a quarter of a million men became surrounded in Stalingrad.

The Germans held out until 2 February 1943 when Field Marshal von Paulus was forced to surrender his remaining 91,000 soldiers. Hitler's hopes of defeating Stalin died along with so many of his best soldiers in and around the city on the Volga.

Battle of the Atlantic

What Winston Churchill called the Battle of the Atlantic was waged for most of the war. German surface ships and U-Boats menaced the vital convoy routes from America to

Britain. When massive aid was despatched by sea to Russia these convoys too were attacked by the Kriegsmarine and Luftwaffe. The U-Boats had the advantage of bases on the Atlantic coast of France.

Allied and German fortunes in the war at sea ebbed and flowed. At times the U-Boats dominated – they reached their nadir in March 1943 when 'wolf packs' totalling 40 submarines sank 21 merchant ships from two convoys. After this, advances in Allied radar and anti-submarine tactics began to take their toll. RAF Coastal Command became increasingly effective; they had aircraft equipped with the 'Leigh Light' that could illuminate surfaced U-Boats at night. Also absolutely crucial were the 'code breakers' of Bletchley Park who had learnt to read the German Enigma code signals and could accordingly let the Allied navies and air forces know where the U-Boats were gathering. Ultra Intelligence revealed many more war-winning secrets.

The Battle of the Atlantic was considered won by the opening months of 1944. By the end of the war over 30,000 British merchant seamen had lost their lives. They were considered civilians by the War Office.

Malta was also crucial to the Allies winning in North Africa and the Mediterranean. Just 70 miles from Sicily, this tiny island was relentlessly battered from the air from the middle of 1940 through to the middle of 1943. At times it seemed it would be starved out as food, fuel and ammunition convoys failed to make it through the swarms of U-Boats and enemy bombers ranging under and over the central Med. But hold out it did to become an invaluable base from where the Allies could mount offensive operations against the Axis.

Invasion of Italy

Stalin had been urging the US and British armies to open a Second Front in northern Europe at the earliest opportunity to relieve pressure on the Red Army. At this stage of the war, the Western Allies were simply not strong enough for such an undertaking. However, from their positions along the North African shore, it was but a small step to take the war to the land of Germany's prime Axis partner. On 10 July 1943 *Operation Husky*, the invasion of Sicily, began. Within a few weeks it led to the downfall of Mussolini who was deposed by his own Fascist Grand Council and arrested. Even without their dictator, the Italians stayed in the war but looked to secure advantageous peace terms with the Allies.

The new Prime Minister Marshal Badoglio signed a secret act of surrender on 3 September, the same day that the Allies crossed the Straits of Messina to land on the mainland of Italy. Five days later when news of the surrender was broadcast, the Germans reacted quickly to occupy Rome and pour troops into the south of the country. The Germans knew that the long 'boot and heel' of mountainous Italy favoured a defensive war and that's exactly what they proposed to fight. An Allied outflanking landing at Salerno on 9

September came close to being pushed back into the sea and was saved only by the intervention of naval gunfire and massive air support. The able German General Kesselring was charged with making the Allies pay dearly for any advance up the Italian peninsula. He withdrew just to the north of Naples and set up the Gustav Line, a defensive position defined by fast-flowing rivers, high, steep mountains and valleys where attackers could be easily detected and fired upon. The line hinged around the town of Cassino which was dominated by an ancient Benedictine monastery set high above on the top of a mountain. The mountain was Monte Cassino.

Fighting in Burma

In Burma the British had not had a good start to the year 1943 with the failure of their first real offensive against the Japanese. This took place on the stretch of coast beside the Bay of Bengal known as the Arakan. A military disaster was averted when Lieutenant-General William Slim was asked to take command of the defeated British and Indian troops; he conducted an efficient withdrawal to the India – Burma border. Slim was later appointed commander of the newly-created Fourteenth Army, under Admiral Lord Louis Mountbatten's South-East Asia Command (SEAC). Even with this reorganisation of the command structure, there would be no major British offensives in the region for the rest of the year, although the RAF remained active and Chinese forces – backed by some American units – probed with little real effect into Northern Burma late in 1943.

After the massive defeat at Stalingrad, the Germans were forced to retreat along most of the length of the Russian Front, until better weather in the spring enabled his generals to stabilise the situation. Hitler also managed to maintain the siege of Leningrad throughout the whole of 1943. In July he was able to mass one more army, equipped with new and more heavily armoured tanks, and mount a major offensive to erase a Russian salient at Kursk in the centre of the front. Kursk turned into the greatest tank battle in history. It was another disaster for the Germans as they failed to make any substantial advance and exhausted themselves battering in vain against vast belts of minefields and Russian artillery concentrations. Tank for tank, the Germans found that the Russians too had new machines, the equivalent or better of their own.

As 1943 closed, it was estimated that nearly 20,000,000 Russians had died since the war began in 1941. Hitler and his Nazi henchmen now knew they could not beat the Red Army. Their only hope was to contain the Allies in Italy and defeat the Western Allies when the inevitable invasion of Northern Europe occurred. This would free troops to be sent to reinforce the Eastern Front and stem the Russian advance. Meanwhile, German scientists were feverishly working on secret weapons that ranged from revolutionary jet fighter aircraft to devastating rocket bombs. The Nazis hoped that at least one or more of their projects

would prove to be a war-winning invention.

The year 1944 opened with a surprise German bombing offensive over Britain that was to last until the early spring. The attacks were really no more than nuisance raids and sometimes comprised lone aircraft hitting random targets around London. By comparison the Allies own bombing campaign was massive and ranged over Germany, Italy and almost the whole of Occupied Europe.

In Italy the winter weather along the Gustav Line made it wet and miserable for the soldiers of both sides. A US attack across the Rapido river was repulsed with heavy casualties. The Eighth Army was also stalled. In a bid to break the stalemate an Allied landing was made at Anzio, well behind German lines and just 40 miles from Rome. A fast and furious German reaction prevented

lend a hand with the potato harvest at a farming holiday camp

OCT AND NOV FREE TRAVEL AND REDUCED ACCOMODATION TERMS

the Allies from exploiting the initial surprise of the landing. It would be late May before the British and Americans would break out of their beach-head and advance on Rome.

Red Army advances

Offensive operations began early for the Red Army. On 6 January they advanced across the pre-war border and entered Poland. By the end of the month the 900-day siege of Leningrad was declared over. Around half of the city's three million civilian population had died, mainly from starvation and the cold, since the siege began in 1941.

In the Pacific the Americans were engaged in bitter fighting for island after island. The eventual goal was Japan itself although General McArthur insisted on first liberating the Philippines rather than bypassing this huge island nation. Kwajelein in the Marshalls was secured on 4 February at the cost of 372 US dead. Just 130 Japanese out of an original garrison of 8000 men survived. On New Guinea in early February, Australian troops linked up with American forces to put pressure on the Japanese.

In Burma there was fighting in the Arakan area again as the Japanese sought unsuccessfully to push back British and Empire forces. In early March three brigades of Chindits were airlifted 200 miles behind Japanese lines in central Burma. Within days, however, a major Japanese offensive was mounted with the aim of invading India and seizing the key supply centre of Imphal in the border state of Assam. Enemy troops entered Indian territory on 21 March 1944 but Japanese hopes of a popular uprising against British rule by the Indian population proved in vain.

Russians enter Rumania

After Finland sought to conclude a peace treaty with the Soviets, Hitler became very wary of further defections by his allies. In the middle of March German forces entered Hungary and arrested the country's leader, Admiral Horthy. Some 50,000 Germans also moved into Rumania to protect the vital oilfields at Ploesti. By 1 April Russian tanks crossed Rumania's eastern border and within two weeks they had closed to within 150 miles of Ploesti.

Meanwhile in Britain the massive build-up of forces continued as the Allies prepare for the long-awaited invasion of France. In April and May country roads and parks became crammed with military vehicles of all kinds and vast stands of tanks and artillery. Airfields filled up with transport planes, gliders, bombers and fighters. A huge bombing programme was directed at road and rail communications centres in mainland Europe. Unfortunately, as a result there were a large number of civilian casualties, particularly in France.

Whilst the Japanese were clearly losing the air and sea war in the Pacific they still retained the power to launch a big land offensive in China in the middle of April. At the same time on the Burma – India frontier, Japanese forces all but surrounded the hilltown of Kohima. General Slim's Fourteenth Army put up a fierce resistance and ultimately repulsed the Japanese, ending Tokyo's ambitions of challenging British rule in India.

By the middle of May 1944 the Russians had overcome the resistance of the last German and Rumania troops in the Crimea. The Red Army continued to move westwards along the entire front. Also in May another ferocious Allied assault was mounted against Cassino, lynchpin of the Gustav Line in Italy. By 18 May Polish soldiers finally captured the ruined monastery at the summit of Monte Cassino; the Germans began withdrawing rapidly northwards. Within days the troops in Anzio began to break out – they linked with the soldiers advancing from the south on 25 May. On 5 June the Allies entered Rome.

D-Day: Invasion of Normandy

Next day one of the war's most momentous events unfolded. D-Day, 6 June: The invasion of Normandy. For a while at Omaha Beach it was touch and go but everywhere else the Allied forces landed by air and sea secured a foothold. The euphoria of D-Day would wear off in the following few months when a battle of attrition was fought amidst the hedgerows and sunken lanes of Normandy. The first of Hitler's 'Vengeance' weapons – the V1 rocket – started to fall on England bringing civilian deaths and devastation.

It was August before the Allies could break out in Normandy but once they did the speed of advance was breathtaking. Paris and Brussels were swiftly liberated and the Allies pushed on into Holland. Allied forces landed in the South of France and swiftly rushed north. In Italy, Florence was liberated on 22 August.

In the middle of September the audacious *Operation Market Garden* was mounted. A carpet of airborne forces landed along a corridor in Holland that led over the Rhine and would allow the Allies to debouch into Germany's industrial Ruhr region. But hopes of an early end to the war were dashed when the British 1st Airborne Division found itself outnumbered and surrounded on the wrong side of the Rhine at Arnhem. Most of the men were killed or captured. It was indeed, 'A Bridge Too Far.'

The Allies closed up to the German frontier and prepared for a hard winter's fighting. In October in Warsaw, Polish freedom fighters rose against the Germans in a bid to liberate their capital by themselves before the Red Army moved in. The uprising failed.

In November the Red Army's advance was halted 40 miles from Budapest in the face of heavy rain and stiffening German resistance. The lights went on in Britain as the blackout was lifted even though the terror from the air persisted with V1 rockets now joined by the even more deadly V2 missile. There was better news for the Allies on the logistics front when the port of Antwerp opened on 28 November. Now it was just a 60-mile drive to the British troops facing the Germans along the River Maas.

The Allies in Italy were once again bogged down by the onset of winter although on 4 December the Eighth Army moved into Ravenna.

In the Pacific in the same month the Americans were moving into the Philippines where they encountered a new and desperate Japanese tactic – Kamikaze suicide air attacks. In Burma the Fourteenth Army steadily pushed back the Japanese.

Battle of the Bulge

Hitler shocked the Allies in Europe when the Germans launched a fierce offensive in the inhospitable snow-bound Ardennes region of Belgium. They had amassed a reserve of panzers and fresh troops and met with some initial success in this weakly-held sector of the front. Bad weather also grounded the Allied air force. The attack created a dangerous bulge in the front line but there was never any real likelihood that the Germans would reach their objective of

Antwerp and isolate the Allied forces in Holland. As the skies cleared in January, Allied air superiority dictated the course of the battle. This last major offensive cost the Germans dearly in men and material. At the same time the Red Army had built up its strength for a big offensive aimed at Berlin. By the end of the month the German capital was less than 100 miles behind the front line and Russian forces were actually fighting on German soil.

In the Far East the Fourteenth Army laid siege to Mandalay and captured it after 10 days of close quarter fighting. Next they advanced on Rangoon, Burma's capital. The Americans took the island of Iwo Jima after a terrific battle with the Japanese garrison who died almost to a man. Next target in the US sights was Okinawa, considered a 'home

island' by the Japanese. Meanwhile, following the liberation of Manila, US troops aided by Filipino guerrillas gradually wore down the remaining Japanese on the Philippines.

The massive bombing offensive against Berlin and other major German cities in the rapidly shrinking Reich was maintained at high intensity in March and April. The Allies stormed across the river barrier of the Rhine in two places on 22 and 23 March 1945. Germany was being squeezed from two sides in a military vice that was inexorably tightening.

At the beginning of April the largest amphibious landing of the Pacific campaign took place on Okinawa. Half a million US service personnel were involved. On 5 April Moscow repudiated its neutrality pact with Japan, a sure sign that when the war in Europe was over, the Soviet Union would enter the war in the Far East. Despite a change of Government in Tokyo there was no indication of a Japanese willingness to surrender.

On 12 April Germany's Nazi leaders were cheered by news of the death of President Roosevelt. But Harry S Truman was at once sworn in as President and he made it clear it

was very much business as usual in prosecuting the world war. At this time the Russians were only 40 miles from Berlin and had just captured Vienna. Meanwhile the advance of the Western Allies was revealing the unimaginable full horror of the Nazi Death Camps. In the north of Italy the German army was in full retreat and anxious to escape into Germany and Austria.

Hitler takes to his Bunker

In mid-April Hitler took refuge in his bunker as bombs and shells rained down on Berlin. By 21 April Soviet troops were probing into the suburbs and next day reported being within three miles of the city centre. On 28 April Mussolini was detained by partisans. The former Italian dictator had been attempting to flee to Switzerland. He and his mistress, Clara Petacci, were later executed.

On 30 April Hitler and his new bride, Eva Braun, committed suicide in his Berlin bunker. The 'Thousand Year Reich' was crumbling away. Just over a week later, Hitler's chosen successor, Admiral Donitz, authorised the unconditional surrender of all German land, sea and air forces in Europe. At 3pm on 8 May, British premier Winston Churchill, speaking in the House of Commons, proclaimed the end of the war in Europe.

In Burma the Japanese continued their retreat while on Okinawa the fighting raged on. The island was not considered subjugated until 21 June. By then an estimated 130,000 Japanese had died with just 7400 taken prisoner. The Americans suffered 13,000 dead and 36,000 wounded. The US Navy's losses, mainly incurred through Kamikaze attacks, were even greater than those incurred at Pearl Harbor. Japan itself was now just 350 miles away; Allied leaders steeled themselves for a million casualties should they have to invade.

An intense bombing campaign had been waged against Japanese cities for many months with aircraft based on the islands captured by the Americans. On 6 August a bomb of exceptional and terrible power was dropped on the seaside city of Hiroshima. This explosion of the first atomic bomb to be used in anger exceeded the force of 20,000 tons of TNT. Around a third of the city's 300,000 population was killed. Two days later Russia invaded Japanese-held Manchuria, fielding over one million troops supported by 4000 aircraft.

With no indication of a Japanese surrender, on 9 August a second atomic bomb was dropped, this time on the city of Nagasaki. Despite the awful potency of the new bomb, the Japanese did not agree to lay down their arms until 16 August when their Emperor Hirohito made a radio broadcast to the country's armed forces.

Fighting went on in Manchuria and New Guinea and the last Japanese forces in the Philippines and in Burma did not formally surrender until 30 August. The Second World War had finally ended.

From Phoney War to the Blitz

1939-40

WAR DIARY 1939

Sunday 3 September 1939: Half an hour after the war begins at 11.15am, Britain receives her first air raid warning. In a few minutes the 'All Clear' is sounded. Later the Air Ministry say that the sirens were activated because a strange aircraft had been observed approaching the south coast.

President Roosevelt says that the USA will remain neutral in the conflict now embracing much of Europe.

As dusk falls on the first day of the war, a German U-Boat claims the first British shipping casualty. The liner *Athenia* was en route from Belfast to Montreal with 1400 passengers.

4 September: RAF bombers open the air war with a raid on the German fleet in its harbours at Wilhelmshaven, Cuxhaven and Brunsbuttel at the entrance of the Kiel Canal. Hits on major German ships are claimed and it is admitted that some of the British bombers failed to return.

8 September: The evacuation of schoolchildren and others out of London to rural areas and country towns deemed unlikely to be the targets of German bombers continues. In the past four days, 650,000 have left. Other cities too are emptying of youngsters in a carefully planned mass exodus.

An Irish newspaper reports that the last of 10,000 horses bought by Germans in Eire have arrived at Hamburg. Many of the horses were selected by members of the German Jumping Team who attended the Dublin Horse Show in August.

9 September: Millions of leaflets are being dropped over Germany by the RAF. The German people are urged to reject Hitler and seek peace. Belgian fighter planes attack two British bombers who stray over Belgian territory. One Belgian plane is shot down and both British planes are forced to land. The British Government apologizes for the incident.

German Field Marshal Hermann Göring gives a speech at a German munitions factory: 'We will have our Nazism and the Russians their Bolshevism, but we are both people who want peace and we are not going to be so silly as to smash in each other's heads for Britain.'

10 September: Canada declares war on Germany and joins Australia, New Zealand, South Africa and the British Empire in the fight against Hitler. Arabs and Jews in Palestine – where there is a British mandate – are amongst the many territories that offer support.

17 September: A U-Boat sinks *HMS Courageous*, the Navy's first wartime loss. The ship was a cruiser that had been converted into an aircraft carrier.

Polish forces are being battered by the Germans who now control about a third of the country. Poland's fate is sealed today when Stalin's Red Army invades at a number of points between Latvia in the north and Rumania in the south. It is clear that the Russians and Germans have reached an accommodation to divide Poland between them.

21 September: The Premier of Rumania, Armand Calinescu, is assassinated by pro-Nazi members of the Iron Guard. German radio reports: 'This bloody deed was England's work.' The terrorists are caught as they later attempt to seize Bucharest radio station and summarily executed. King Carol seeks to suppress fascism in his country but he himself is effectively a dictator.

25 September: The French air force bombs a Zeppelin base at Friedericshafen. Germany had led the world in airship development in the Great War and in the Thirties but they had already decided against their deployment in this new conflict. However, it is believed they are experimenting with captive balloons that can be exploded from the ground and destroy near-by aircraft. The German navy also has an aircraft carrier called the *Graf Zeppelin*.

KEEP CALM AND CARRY ON

Millions of copies of this 'Keep Calm and Carry On' poster were printed on the eve of World War II, but never displayed. With war against Germany on the horizon, the Ministry of Information commissioned three posters with the aim of boosting civilian morale. All topped by the crown of King George VI and set against a bright red background, the trio of posters featured the words: 'Freedom is in Peril', 'Your Courage, Your Cheerfulness, Your Resolution Will Bring Us Victory', and 'Keep Calm and Carry On'. Two-and-a-half million copies of the latter were printed, only to remain in storage throughout the war. Just two copies of the original posters are known to survive, the rest were pulped. However, in recent years reproductions of the poster have found huge demand amongst people eager to embrace the spirit of another time; this simple message that suggests no situation is quite as bad as you think it is or may become. It's a message that could have helped people live with the prospect of the Blitz or, in our troubled present day, equally, could help people live in a world of economic chaos and ongoing conflict in distant lands.

Daily Mail

FOR KING AND EMPIRE

**CHURCHILL
IN BRITAIN'S
WAR CABINET**

NO. 13,529   MONDAY, SEPTEMBER 4, 1939   ONE PENNY

BRITAIN & FRANCE AT WAR WITH GERMANY

We meet a challenge which would be fatal to civilised order—THE KING

OUR NEW WAR CABINET

GREAT BRITAIN AND FRANCE ARE AT WAR WITH GERMANY.

At nine o'clock yesterday morning Germany was informed that unless Britain received satisfactory assurance by 11 a.m. that Germany had stopped aggressive action in Poland "a state of war would exist as from that hour."

At 11.15 Mr. Chamberlain announced to the nation that "no such undertaking has been received and this country is at war with Germany."

France delivered a similar ultimatum to Germany at noon, to expire at 5 p.m. At that hour she considered declaration of

Churchill as First

The King's Message

BROADCASTING to the Empire last night, the King said: "In this grave hour, perhaps the most fateful in our history, I send to every household of my people both at home and overseas this message, spoken with the same depth of feeling for each one of you as if I were able to cross your threshold and speak to you myself.

"For the second time in the lives of most of us we are at war.

"Over and over again we have tried to find a peaceful way out of the differences between ourselves and those who are now our enemies. But it has been in vain.

"We have been forced into a conflict. For we are called with our allies to meet the challenge of a principle which, if it were to prevail, would be fatal to any civilised order in the world.

Pursuit of Power

"It is the principle which permits a State in the selfish pursuit of power to disregard its treaties and its solemn pledges; which sanctions the use of force or threat of force against the sovereignty and independence of other States.

"Such a principle stripped of its

Poles Launch Counter-attack

POLAND yesterday launched her counter-attack. She struck at East Prussia in the Deutsch Eglan sector. After violent fighting the town of Zbaszyn, taken by the Germans on Saturday, was recaptured.

The Polish attack suggests that a German claim on Saturday that their forces driving east and west across the neck of the Corridor had made contact was unfounded.

In the south violent fighting was reported around Czestochowa, the Lourdes of Poland. The Germans claimed that the town had fallen, and the Poles admitted that it was in flames.

North of Czestochowa, the Germans claimed to have captured the town of Wielun, after crossing the River Warthe. Polish sources said the town's municipal h... during the attack, ... miles from the G... Eastern front.

Polish radio ... night that W... camp in Dr... resisting Ge... and sea.

The camp ... times, was ... cruiser...

GE...

POLES SMASH WAY INTO EAST PRUSSIA

Warsaw, Sunday.

Officials in Warsaw to-night state that the Polish Army has smashed a way across the northern border into East Prussia, after driving the Germans from several Polish towns in bitter fighting.

On the northern front the Poles are reported to have defeated the German effort to drive a barrier across the upper part of the Corridor by driving the Germans back across the border.

The Poles say they have broken through the German fortifications as far as the railway terminus of Deutsch Eylau. One of the most important towns recaptured is stated to be Zbaszyn.—British United Press.

CONVOY AGAIN...

The...

THE STORM BREAKS

Below: Map from News Review, 21 September 1939

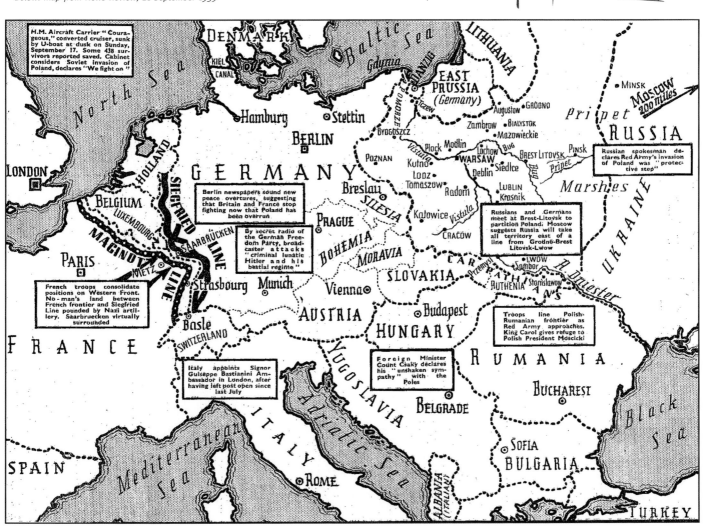

WAR DIARY 1939

" 27 September. Germany and Russia sign a treaty in Moscow by which Poland is completely abolished. The two countries jointly declare that the war should now cease... **"**

27 September: In bomb-ravaged Warsaw, the Poles announce that they will surrender. Two days later the Foreign Ministers of Germany and Russia sign a treaty in Moscow by which Poland is completely abolished and new and permanent Russo – German frontiers established. The terms include a denial of the right of interference by any Third Power and a declaration that the war should now stop.

30 September: People in London and Paris carry their gasmasks as they go about their daily business. Both cities are 'blacked out' as are the capitals of all the belligerents. French and British women are rapidly taking on many jobs previously undertaken by men; the latter are subject to general mobilisation.

1 October: The last bastion of Polish resistance at Hela surrenders to the Germans. There are reports that the Russians are executing captured Polish officers who display an anti-Soviet attitude. Whilst lots of Polish servicemen will eventually fight with the Red Army against Germany, there are a substantial number of Polish pilots, sailors and soldiers determined to join the British and French forces in the West.

5 October: Hitler is in Warsaw to review a triumphal march of Nazi troops.

7 October: There are regular artillery exchanges on the Western Front but no large-scale fighting has taken place. British troops are steadily arriving in France.

14 October: U-47 evades the defences of Scapa Flow, an important anchorage in the Orkneys for the British Home Fleet, and puts two torpedoes into *HMS Royal Oak*. The battleship sinks with great loss of life.

On **16 October** German bombers attack the Royal Navy off Rosyth. RAF fighters close with the enemy and later claim to have shot down four Heinkel 111's, the first German aircraft to be destroyed over Britain since 1918.

21 October: *War Illustrated* reports that Britain's First Lord of the Admiralty, Winston Churchill, has been elevated to 'Nazi Enemy Number One' on German radio. The magazine says: 'Churchill's political knowledge, his eloquence and his resolution are all assets of incomparable value to Britain and Britain's cause.'

28 October: The first German aircraft to come down on British soil crash lands on a hillside near Haddington, east of Edinburgh.

There is speculation in the British press as to why the Italian dictator, Mussolini, has remained neutral in this new war. It had long been assumed that when Hitler declared war, Mussolini would follow suit.

4 November: The US lifts its embargo on the export of arms. In theory all the warring nations are put on an equal footing; Germany has the equal right to buy along with France and Britain. But with the latter two largely controlling the seas so far as surface warships go, it means that they have an immense advantage over their enemy in being able to obtain US military materials. The Speaker of the House of Representatives has also declared: 'You cannot place an embargo on man's mind and heart ... Thank God, we're still entitled to express our views and our preferences for the democratic liberties of France and Britain to the rule of the concentration camp and the firing squad.'

8 November: In a speech in the Buergerbraeu beer cellar, Munich, Hitler violently attacks on Britain. Twenty minutes after he leaves, a bomb explosion takes place in the cellar killing nine people and injuring more than 60. In the days to come, thousands of suspects, including many Jews and members of the Gestapo itself will be arrested.

9 November: A clandestine radio station called 'German Freedom' declares: 'In Germany the first bomb against German Dictatorship has exploded. Many more will follow.' Even so, there is speculation in Britain that the bomb may have been a self-inflicted Nazi ruse to whip up war-fever amongst the German public.

11 November: After taking control of Estonia, Latvia and Lithuania, the Soviet Union has turned the Baltic into a virtual 'Red Lake'. Now Stalin is turning his attention to Finland and making territorial demands of this Scandinavian country.

It is Armistice Day and thousands of poppies are distributed to British troops to wear in memory of the fallen of the Great War. Tanks and artillery pieces are hung with poppies while every one of the British cemeteries in France also received the artificial flowers.

18 November: The evacuation of 220,000 inhabitants from Strasbourg is complete. The city is just two miles from the Kehl Bridge that spans the Rhine. Many other towns and villages on both sides of the frontier have also been emptied of people.

21 November: Germany has been laying newly developed magnetic mines in the open sea without disclosing their positions as required by the Hague Convention of 1907. Ironically, among the first victims are ships belonging to two powers who are sympathetic to the Nazi cause, firstly the Italian steamer *Gazia* and then, today, the crack Japanese liner *Terukuni Maru*. Both went down off the east coast of Britain.

22 November: A German magnetic mine lands in mud off Shoeburyness, Essex. It is recovered, stripped, and evaluated by a team from *HMS Vernon*, revealing the secret of its magnetic polarity. The underwater mine is activated when subjected to a magnetic field of 50 milligauss. British ships will now be able to install degaussing systems to make them invisible to the mines.

23 November: This afternoon the armed merchant cruiser *Rawalpindi* clashes with the German pocket battleship, *Deutschland*, in the North Atlantic to the east of Iceland. A second, unidentified, Kriegsmarine warship supports the battleship. Despite obviously being greatly outgunned, the *Rawalpindi* refuses to surrender when a shot is put across her bows. A 40 minute fight ensues in which the British ship's guns are all put out of action and she begins to go down in flames. Just a handful of her crew of 300 survive. The German ships steam away from the scene at the approach of a British cruiser.

28 November: The Germans and the Allies are fighting a war of words. The former have made numerous claims that major British warships have been destroyed when they are demonstrably still afloat. One broadcast asserts that *HMS Kestrel* has been sunk when in fact the name is given to a Fleet Air Arm training establishment in Hampshire.

30 November: Just days after accusing Finland of mounting provocative actions against their border defences, Soviet forces attack their northern neighbour by land and air. At 9.15am, Russian aircraft begin bombing the Finnish capital, Helsinki. The Finns are not expected to resist the onslaught for very long. There is in existence a pact of non-aggression between Finland and the USSR and it is not due to expire until 1945.

4 December: Pamphlets dropped by British aircraft over Germany are dubbed 'clergymen's bombs' by the Nazi press.

9 December: Many RAF and Royal Navy personnel have died since the war began on 3 September. But today sees the first death in action of a British soldier. Corporal Thomas William Priday is killed while leading a patrol on the Western Front.

WAR DIARY 1939

This sketch-map of Europe shows the main changes that occurred in 1939 as a result of German and Soviet territorial ambitions.

14 December: The Soviet Union is expelled from the League of Nations following her attack on Finland and earlier annexation of eastern Poland and the Baltic states of Estonia, Latvia and Lithuania. A few days earlier, Lord Halifax had addressed the House of Lords: 'The Russian attack ... seems to me to be a direct consequence of German policy. By the agreement which he thought would give him a free hand to attack Poland it would seem that Herr Hitler bartered what was not his property to barter – the liberties of the Baltic peoples.'

18 December: Winston Churchill makes a broadcast in which he details major recent successes by the British submarine fleet that includes the sinking of a Koeln class cruiser by the *Ursula* and the damaging of two others by torpedoes fired from HM Submarine *Salmon*. Churchill also praises the Royal Navy for their recent South Atlantic action that resulted in the scuttling of the damaged pocket battleship *Admiral Graf Spee* in the estuary of the River Plate, Uruguay

Canadian troops are arriving in England.

21 December: Stalin's birthday is celebrated in Moscow newspapers with fulsome praise of the Soviet leader. The Russian High Command also expected to be able to announce a 'glorious victory' in the central zone of the Finnish front. Instead the Red Army has been rebuffed by fierce Finnish resistance. Forced to retreat, the Russians have lost around 20,000 men, dead and wounded, and the Finns have captured masses of machineguns, artillery and armoured vehicles.

25 December: The British steamer *Stanholme* is sunk without warning by a U-Boat not far from the coast of South Wales. Among the survivors is Mrs Jenvy, wife of the Chief Engineer. She later tells the press: 'We rushed on deck as the vessel began to heel over and a second explosion shook us. My husband ran to the lifebelts, put one over my head and threw me into the water. That was the last I saw of him, for he went down with the ship.'

Below: British public interest in Hitler was stoked up by a plethora of books, including the German leader's own Mein Kampf *('My Struggle').*

27 December: A massive earthquake strikes the Anatolia region of Turkey. Aftershocks and terrible floods will contribute to the estimated 35,000 dead with hundreds of thousands made homeless.

The Finns continue to give the Russians a bloody nose. Today they claim to have brought down 23 Soviet aircraft. In places the Finns have advanced into Russian territory.

31 December: Hitler's Deputy, Herman Goering, issues a New Year's Eve proclamation that warns of the 'enormous and most formidable tasks that lie ahead for the German people in the year to come.' Fresh sacrifices would be inevitable, but their motto remained: 'If the Fuhrer commands, we will follow.'

HITLER's MEIN KAMPF
Unexpurgated – Illustrated
PART 2 6ᵈ
(Ready Today)

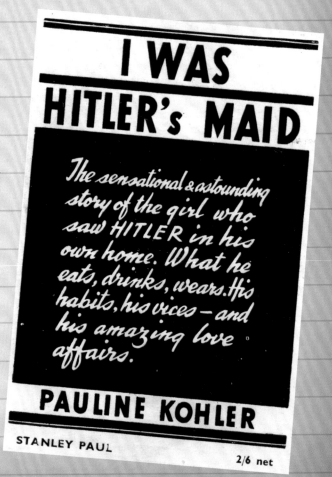

I WAS HITLER's MAID

The sensational & astounding story of the girl who saw HITLER in his own home. What he eats, drinks, wears. His habits, his vices – and his amazing love affairs.

PAULINE KOHLER

STANLEY PAUL

2/6 net

U-BOAT
The threat surfaces...

Sinking of HMS Courageous

The Royal Navy's first wartime loss came with the sinking of the aircraft carrier *HMS Courageous* by a U-Boat on the night of 17 September 1939 while engaged in anti-submarine activities off the south west coast of Ireland. Over 500 of the ship's crew died when she was torpedoed by U-29. The casualties included Captain W T Makeig-Jones RN; eye witnesses said he went down with his ship while saluting the flag.

One of the youngest survivors was Bugler R D Emerson of the Royal Marines. Aged just 15 and only five feet tall, when the ship was struck he went on the flight deck, took off his bugle and tied it to the ship's rail. Then he undressed, clambered down the starboard side and struck out for a raft. The youngster told *The Daily Telegraph* that he saw British destroyers dropping depth charges and he was convinced that the U-Boat was blown up: 'The conning tower broke one way and the stern the other and oil shot up from the water. We all cheered. As we paddled away the men sang, "Heigh ho, heigh ho, it's off to work we go." We had not gone far when the *Courageous* went down.' The 741 survivors were eventually brought home on Lord Louis Mountbatten's ship, *HMS Kelly*.

Passenger liner is first victim

At 7.30pm on Sunday 3 September, Britain's first night of the war, the first ship to be sunk by the German U-Boat fleet was torpedoed some 200 miles out in the Atlantic beyond Ireland. *SS Athenia* was en route from Glasgow to Montreal under the command of Captain James Cook. She'd set sail on 1 September and then called at Liverpool and Belfast. The ship carried 1418 civilian passengers. They included 300 Americans who had cut short visits to London or Paris in order to return home before the anticipated bombing of the cities began. There were also many refugees.

The Germans struck as dusk fell. A torpedo crashed into the ship which shivered from the blow. Most passengers did not realize the cause of the explosion but all proceeded to their lifeboat stations. Some survivors later reported seeing the sinister silhouette of a submarine emerging from the waters; it turned its gun on the ship and fired at her wireless. Fortunately, the ship's SOS was picked up by many vessels, including three Royal Navy destroyers. The Norwegian merchantman, *Knute Nelson*, was first to arrive followed by the *Southern Cross* at

around 2.30pm on the Monday afternoon. The *Athenia* had sunk some four hours earlier but the sea was dotted with lifeboats and rafts that had sustained the survivors through the dark night and on into the morning hours. Some were dangerously overcrowded and were swamped; a Russian Jewish couple, hoping to start a new life in the United States, saw their two young sons drown when their boat capsized at the stern. Eyewitnesses spoke of seeing a great school of whales that at one point were plunging all around the lifeboats. Despite the horror of the sinking, survivors praised the crew for their conduct and they in turn said the passengers had displayed heroism and maintained perfect morale in harrowing circumstances.

The Germans were signatories to an agreement that non-combatant ships should be subject to stop and search before being attacked and also that their crews and passengers must be given the chance to disembark safely into lifeboats. Embarrassed at causing the death of 128 civilians, the German authorities denied that one of their U-Boats had sunk the *Athenia* and instead claimed it must have been a British submarine.

...and HMS Royal Oak

On 17 October Winston Churchill reported on the sinking of *HMS Royal Oak* to a shocked House of Commons: 'The battleship was sunk at anchor in Scapa Flow at approximately 1.30am on Saturday 14 October. When we consider that during the course of the whole of the last war this anchorage was found to be immune from such attacks, on account of the obstacles imposed by the currents and net barrages, this entry by a U-Boat must be considered as a remarkable exploit of professional skill and daring...I deeply regret I have to inform the House that upwards of 800 officers and men have lost their lives.'

The *Athenia* sinking.

First rescue by seaplane in naval history

October 1939 newspapers reported how the 34 survivors of the sinking of *SS Kensington Court* by a U-Boat's gun were rescued by three RAF flying-boats. It was the first such air-sea operation ever attempted. The 4863-ton ship had made her way from Argentina and was near the English coast en route for Birkenhead when a U-Boat surfaced and took the unarmed vessel under fire. Five shells hit home before Captain Schofield gave the order to abandon ship but not before a radio SOS had been transmitted. With the ship sinking, the U-Boat left the scene. The crew of the *Kensington Court* were amazed when three RAF flying-boats subsequently arrived and landed on the sea to pick up the men. Captain Schofield told the *Daily Telegraph*: 'It was all very remarkable to us. It was the modern method of rescue and we had never had any experience like it. When we got on board the planes we were treated to cups of tea and cigarettes.'

U-Boat lands Greek survivors in Eire

Earlier in the same month, 28 survivors of the neutral Greek steamer *Diamantis*, sunk by U-35 about 40 miles off the Cornish coast, were picked up by the German submariners and allowed to go ashore on an isolated part of the Kerry coast of Eire. The U-Boat closed within 50 yards or so of the shore before allowing the Greeks to board a collapsible boat and row to land. The Greeks made their way by ferry to Holyhead in Wales where the ship's captain reported his opposite number on the submarine had spoken good English and treated him and his men with the greatest courtesy.

By coincidence their landing place in a small bay near Dingle was near the spot where Sir Roger Casement, the Irish rebel, was landed by a German submarine in 1916.

First Air Raid

At around 2pm on the afternoon of Monday 16 October 1939, the gardens that run through the heart of Edinburgh were crowded with people reading their newspapers and enjoying their paper-bag lunches in the warm autumn sunshine.

Suddenly a strange clatter in the sky drew all eyes upward. The blue panoply was speckled with little white bursts and in the distance there was the muffled bark of guns. The first German air raid on Britain in World War Two was in progress. Twelve enemy bombers were headed up the Firth of Forth, their target being Royal Navy warships at anchor in the area of the mighty Forth Rail Bridge and the naval dockyard at nearby Rosyth. The ships included *HMS Hood*.

Train on the Forth Bridge

Spitfires of the *City of Edinburgh* Squadron 603 had been quickly scrambled to intercept the raiders. Two German machines were spotted over the Isle of May in the outer estuary and chased away. Two others were shot down, one near Crail where its crew were picked up by a fishing boat, *Dayspring*. The pilot showed his gratitude at being rescued by presenting his wedding ring to the boat's skipper.

The rest of the aircraft flew up the river as far as the Forth Bridge. In the little town of Queensferry in the shadow of the bridge, despite the air raid siren having sounded, locals gathered in the open to watch the action unfold. A train had been halted at Dalmeny Station above Queensferry but when the driver thought he heard the all-clear it set off across the bridge. Passenger Edward Thomson later posted his eyewitness account on the BBC WW2 *People's War* website:

'I was a passenger on the Dundee section of an Edinburgh to Aberdeen train. The next stop was to be Leuchars Junction at the northern end of the bridge. I was in the corridor with an older boy called Jack Thomas from Edinburgh. We were trying to identify some of the fleet at anchor below the bridge. Suddenly there was a giant waterspout as high as the bridge alongside one of the capital ships and a barge tied up alongside; it seemed to fly up in the air! In later life I discovered the ship was *HMS Southampton*. There were two or three other explosions further off and one of the ships was actually struck. The German bombers were in plain sight only a short distance away flying parallel to the bridge. Meanwhile the train stopped briefly and as it did so the painters and riggers who'd been working on the bridge scrambled from the scaffolding and made for shelter. Luckily the train carried on without further incident. Very soon the RAF fighters became involved and drove the raiders out to sea.'

The Germans targeted three ships; *HMS Edinburgh*, *Southampton* and the destroyer *HMS Mohawk*. The *Southampton* was hit but it was the *Mohawk* that came off worse with 15 sailors killed (including her Captain) and nine injured. The Home Fleet admiral's barge and a small steam pinnace that happened to be alongside the *Southampton* were sunk. Two more of the Luftwaffe raiders were shot down as they flew away towards the North Sea.

Edward Thomson added a postscript: 'My Uncle William Thomson was with the British Red Cross at Edinburgh Castle and that's where the captured German aircrew were first taken. He told me later that the airmen seemed certain the war would be over in a matter of weeks.'

TOGETHER

The King's Christmas Message

Extracts from King George V's broadcast from Buckingham Palace on Christmas Day 1939:

We feel in our hearts that we are fighting against wickedness, and this conviction will give us strength from day to day to persevere until victory is assured.

To all who are preparing themselves to serve their country, on sea or land or air, I send my greeting at this time. The men and women of our far-flung Empire working in their several vocations, with the one same purpose, all are members of the great Family of Nations that is prepared to sacrifice everything so that freedom of spirit may be saved to the world. Such is the spirit of the Empire; of the great Dominions, of India, of every Colony, large or small. From all alike have come offers of help, for which the Mother Country can never be sufficiently grateful. Such a unity in aim and effort has never been seen in the world before.

...A new year is at hand. We cannot tell what it will bring. If it brings peace, how thankful we shall all be. If it brings us continued struggle we shall remain undaunted.

Left: The poster 'Together' is reproduced courtesy of the National Archives.

Battle of the River Plate

Admiral Graf Spee was the newest of Germany's pocket battleships – her sister ships being the *Deutschland* and *Admiral Scheer*. She left Germany on 21 August 1939 and made for the South Atlantic. Here the warship could regularly rendezvous with supply ships and the tanker *Altmark*. On 26 September the *Graf Spee* was ordered to commence operations against British and French merchant shipping.

Ranging as far east as the Indian Ocean, the warship sunk nine British ships before being sighted off the coast of neutral Uruguay on 13 December by the cruiser *HMS Ajax*. The *Graf Spee* had bigger guns but was slower than *Ajax* which closed in until both ships came into range and opened fire. The flash of guns could be observed from the shore. Then a second British cruiser, the *Exeter*, appeared over the horizon, followed by a third, *HMS Achilles*, which also entered the fray. In the ensuing battle the *Exeter* sustained serious damage and slowed down but the *Graf Spee* was herself hit by a number of eight and six-inch shells and temporarily crippled. The German ship – under orders not to risk a naval engagement – limped away to the River Plate and the neutral harbour of Montevideo.

Battleships and aircraft carriers

Under the Hague Convention of 1907, the *Graf Spee* could not remain in the port for more than 24 hours. In addition, under the same convention, the vessel had to give British merchant ships 24 hours start if they left port. The British Consul arranged for the merchant ships in port to sail at 24 hour intervals, effectively locking the *Spee* in the harbour. At the same time stories were spread about a vast fleet of British warships, including battleships and aircraft carriers, racing to the area. In fact just one more Royal Navy vessel would arrive. On 14 December, under British pressure and believing the ship to be seaworthy again, the Uruguayans announced that if the *Graf Spee* did not sail within a set time limit, she would be interned.

The *Graf Spee's* Captain was Great War veteran Hans Langsdorff. His first action upon entering Montevideo was to release the 62 crew of the merchant ships he'd recently sunk.

The *Graf Spee* pictured before the war.

All of them spoke highly of both their treatment and of Langsdorff, who spoke perfect English. On 15 December, the *Spee's* 36 crew who had been killed in the naval action were buried with full military honours in the German cemetery in the city. Many officers of the sunken merchant ships attended the service.

At 6.15pm on 17 December 1939, the German warship left Montevideo harbour. Three British cruisers were waiting nearby in international waters, expecting to do battle. But surprisingly, instead of trying to fight through the blockade, the *Graf Spee* sailed just outside the harbour; at 7.52pm there was a terrific explosion and when the smoke cleared the battleship was seen to be low in the water, resting on the bottom of the estuary.

Captain Langsdorff clearly expected to lose in any battle with the British and did not wish to risk unnecessarily the lives of his crew. He committed suicide three days later by shooting himself, perhaps an ultimate gesture to prove that he had not acted out of fear for his own life.

Back in Britain news of the ignominious end of the *Graf Spee* was greeted with much public rejoicing and the Royal Navy's reputation was boosted enormously.

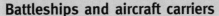

The *Graf Spee* scuttled.

Hugh Thomas tells the story of Peter Ayerst DFC, a remarkable airman who flew with the RAF from the start to the finish of World War II and beyond.

Few RAF pilots flew operationally from 1939 and the start of the war right up until the end in 1945. Fewer still can claim to have taken part in the 'Phoney War', the Battle of France, Battle of Britain, El Alamein, the Battle for Normandy and *Operation Market Garden*.

In the course of six intense years of war Peter Ayerst would survive being shot down in North Africa, hit by flak, chased by more than two squadrons of German aircraft and flying a dangerous secret mission behind enemy lines!

Peter joined the RAF in 1938 on a short service commission and went to France at the beginning of September 1939 as part of the Advanced Air Striking Force.

On 6 November 1939, he was alone at an airfield in France on aerodrome defence, sitting in his Hurricane. At around 2.30pm Peter looked to his right, over to the little road and the early warning post. The Poilus were waving their red flags, signalling an alarm.

He looked up at the sky and saw a little dot, travelling in a westerly direction – it was the enemy aircraft he was supposed to chase. The Rolls Royce Merlin engine roared into life and Peter hurtled over the grass. It took him about 10 minutes to match the enemy aircraft in height. Operationally inexperienced, Peter was

The DECOY

intent on chasing the raider – a Dornier bomber. But what he omitted to do in all the excitement was to keep an eye on his compass. Suddenly he realised that by flying in an easterly direction for so long, he had strayed well into German airspace.

Without delay he turned back on a reciprocal heading, making for France. As the Hurricane turned, he looked down over his starboard side. Inside his turn – and below him – were nine aircraft, in line astern formation, turning in precisely the same direction. Peter tacked onto the end of the line with the other aircraft at 18,000 feet. But something didn't seem quite right. They looked unfamiliar. Were they Hurricanes? No. These aircraft had ugly black crosses painted on either wing. Messerschmitts! Peter gave a quick squirt from his guns towards the tail-end Charlie and shoved the stick forward so that the Hurricane flew into a very steep dive towards some broken cloud about 4000 feet below. He kept the aircraft on a westerly course.

Nine Me-109s with black crosses peeled off and began to chase him. The Hurricane was fitted with a special booster operated by a 'tit' on the throttle. To increase speed, a tiny wire had to be broken which allowed the pilot to pull the engine booster and obtain extra thrust. Heart pulsating, throat dry, eyes wide, Peter broke the wire and pulled the booster tit.

27 ME-109s in pursuit!

What he didn't know at that time (but was told by witnesses later) was that there were another 18 Me-109s on patrol in the area that same November day. Having seen nine of their comrades peel off after something, they, in turn, decided to investigate. So, in effect, there weren't just nine on Peter's tail, but no less than 27 enemy aircraft!

At this point Peter confesses to feeling more than a little scared, although his RAF training warded off outright panic. He tucked himself in the Hurricane seat, ducking in front of the armour plate that protected the back of his head. Darting and nipping in between the broken cloud, he kept an ever-watchful eye on the direction bearing of the compass. It still pointed west.

There were no radio or directional aids to assist Peter. He saw one of the landmarks that Allied pilots used to look for in evaluating their location; factories with window glass painted blue by the French. So now he knew he was back over France, but didn't have the foggiest as to precisely where.

Left top: The winter of 1939-40 was exceptionally cold with lots of snow. Here a British soldier stands guard beneath a grounded RAF fighter.

Left: Scramble! Reims, 1940. Peter Ayerst is third from the left.

At this point 27 Me-109s were still chasing one under-powered Hurricane flown by one green and very nervous pilot. Peter prefers to think of it as one Hurricane leading 27 Messerschmitts towards a group of French fighter aircraft. Never had Peter been more relieved to see a bunch of Moraine-Saunier 406s and Curtiss P-40 Hawks. Salvation had arrived. This was to be the first genuine dogfight of the Second World War, with dozens of aircraft scrapping high over the French frontier. Nine Me-109s were shot down by the French.

If the enemy aircraft weren't enough to contend with, Peter was confronted with another problem. His fuel was very low. He had to find somewhere to land – and soon. Far away to the distance he could see aircraft circling. The needle on the fuel gauge rested on the bottom. Unable to afford the luxury of flying a circuit before he landed, Peter went straight in on the grass airstrip, finished his landing and turned off, aiming to taxi to the active side of the airfield. But as he turned off the engine cut. He had run out of fuel. The airfield he touched down on, with literally a drop of petrol to spare, was Nancy.

Unwitting decoy

The following morning Peter left Nancy for the short hop to his base at Rouvres. All Peter had to do was to keep heading north, in order to make the final side of the triangle. The greeting he received from his No 73 squadron groundcrew at Rouvres was less than effusive – he hadn't noticed that bullets had damaged his tail-plane, which could easily have come adrift.

What had happened on the previous day was the largest air battle of the Second World War to date, and Peter had been right in the centre of it. For evading the 27 Messerschmitts, he was dubbed 'Decoy' by the boys in the squadron. Moreover, he had now invaluable experience of fighting with the enemy. Experience was the key for a fighter pilot; the more you had, the better your chance of survival. The magnitude of this episode was played upon by the press and one account was accompanied by a dashingly portrayed double-spread illustration by the artist, C E Turner.

War Illustrated wrote: 'A fact in which the RAF may feel justifiable pride is that the French success was the outcome of a British pilot finding himself far over the line, after pursuing a German reconnaissance machine and actually joining up with a Messerschmitt formation. The enemy pilots did not recognise the British machine at first. When they did, the pilot was able to escape and led the Germans into the arms of the French.'

The event was also featured in daily newspapers in Britain, especially *The Daily Mail* and *Daily Mirror*. It also made the *Southend Standard*: 'Westcliff airman's busy day – Chased by 27 planes. Westcliff Officer in thrilling escape – an unwitting decoy.'

The rest of 1939 was all about patrols although frays with enemy aircraft were increasing. The New Year of 1940 provided a respite from flying; pilots could catch their breath because the snows were heavy and cold that winter. It was impossible to move so the Hurricanes stayed grounded, dormant under a

white blanket – a situation that applied to the enemy as well.

In January an epidemic of German Measles ran riot through the area. Peter was one of two pilots to catch it. His companions speculated that as the Luftwaffe hadn't managed to bomb them, so they had resorted to other ideas. The two were packed off to convalesce in a requisitioned chateau in Epernay, the town of champagne fame. Once mended, the pair had the chance to explore for a few hours whilst awaiting their transport back to Rouvres. They came across a plaque on the wall of another chateau; it read Moet et Chandon. Intrigued for obvious reasons, the two went inside and asked if they could look around. They were duly welcomed in and were taken into the cellars that went on for miles and miles below ground. Peter remembers the millions and millions of bottles on wooden racks. The word got around that two RAF airmen were in the building and the managing director summoned them to his office where champagne was duly produced for a toast. It was certainly the best medicine the pair had received over the past fortnight. Of course, one drink was never going to be enough; Peter vaguely remembers them being driven back to the airfield while laid out on stretchers in the back of an ambulance.

Peter's first kill came in April 1940. His logbook records: 'I clobbered my first Me-109 and damaged another.' The squadron was flying a lot of patrols again and he says he had to get one sooner or later. For many fighter pilots, getting that first kill was a defining moment, not just in their career, but also in their life. It was a life-changing experience. Peter says he didn't feel like that at all. It was more a case of 'got you, you bastard!'. The incident on 7 April was later reported by *Daily Mail* correspondent Noel Monks.

On 21 April Peter was part of a patrol that ran into around 30 Me-109s and Me-110s. He shot down another 109. Pilots had learnt not to hang around to watch as their 'prey' crashed to the ground. If they did they risked themselves falling victim to other enemy aircraft. Most attacks came from behind and

One student Peter instructed at Hawarden was Brendan 'Paddy' Finucane; he would go on to attain legendary status as a fighter pilot and became the youngest-ever RAF Wing Commander. By the time he died on 15 July 1942 having crashed into the English Channel after being hit by ground fire over France, he had 26 confirmed victories, six shared and eight probables.

pilots always had to watch their tail; Peter says he would spend three-quarters of the time looking behind and the remaining quarter looking to the front.

The face of the RAF

Around about this time the pilot found himself featured on the front page of a recruiting pamphlet beside a slogan that read: 'The Royal Air Force need men like these NOW!' The picture had been taken by the *Daily Mirror's* Stanley Devon and was a classic image of a fighter pilot. Evidently this was a view shared by the RAF publicity department, who saw the shot of this 19-year-old as something to whom aspiring pilots could relate. Peter had become the face of the RAF.

By late April things were hotting up and then came the German breakthrough at Sedan and the retreat of the BEF towards Dunkirk. No 73 Squadron were to pull back to the relative safety of Reims airfield. Peter was grounded having contracted a virus that gave him a very high temperature. He was asked to make arrangements for the withdrawal of the unit. Ground crew and vehicles had to be speedily evacuated. The Hurricanes soon disappeared,

bound for Reims. After a week they moved again, this time to a grass-strip at Gaye, near the town of Troyes. An instruction had been received from AASF HQ that all pilots who had flown in France since September 1939 were to be sent back to Britain. The situation was confused. Peter recalls that the general train of thought among them was along the lines of 'Christ, what the hell is going on?'

Peter and some fellow pilots made their way to Paris by train. He says that the city's nightlife still seemed to be in full swing although there was a black-out. They had been told to evacuate out of the port of Cherbourg but getting there was going to be a problem; the trains had stopped running and the country roads were filling with refugees. Peter was lucky to hitch a lift on the back of an old open-topped potato lorry that took him all the way. Bombing by Ju 87 Stukas restricted the number of ships entering the port but Peter managed to get aboard a packed vessel and get safely home to Southampton. His batman, Ashley, was not so lucky. He became one of several thousand casualties when the *Lancastria* was bombed and sunk outside St Nazaire on 17 June. It was the worst maritime disaster of the war involving a British merchant ship.

First flight in a Spitfire

Peter was given 48 hours leave. Then he was to report to RAF Digby, his original RAF station. On the Saturday morning train from Southampton to Waterloo Peter couldn't believe what he saw as he travelled through the pleasant Hampshire countryside; white clad figures playing cricket on immaculate village greens. It was as if nothing had changed, almost as if England was oblivious to what was happening on the other side of the Channel.

At Digby, for the first and only time in his RAF career, Peter met Trafford Leigh-Mallory who told him and the other assembled pilots they were to report to some newly formed units. Peter was to become an instructor in an Operational Training Unit. By 6 July he was at Hawarden in North Wales with No 7 OTU. He was able to fly a variety of machines including the Gloster Gladiator, Harvard and Fairey Battle.

Peter in his Hurricane, France, March 1940

He climbed into a Spitfire at Hawarden for the first time on 6 July 1940. Thereafter, having flown his first trip, he was then instructing pilots on it. Five days later on 11 July, he carried out his first defensive operational Spitfire patrol. Peter was still only 19 and most of his pupils were much older than him.

One of the unique aspects of Peter's service record is that he flew combat missions for the whole of the war, even when his posting to Hawarden was considered non-operational. On 14 August his logbook notes a kill whilst on an operational patrol. Peter was in one of three Spitfires scrambled to attack a German bomber raiding RAF Sealand, not far away. The trio shot and hit the lone Heinkel 111 and Peter followed it down. One spectator to the action was the future bandleader Syd Lawrence, then a 16-year-old boy standing in Salisbury Street, Shotton, as the bomber flew across the bottom of the road, 20 feet in the air, closely followed by Peter's Spitfire. It was an unforgettable sight for the people on the ground.

The Heinkel actually made a safe landing and the crew all survived. Forty eight years later Peter met the four of them in less confrontational circumstances. He says there was no doubt that the Heinkel pilot Artur Wiesemann was a skilful and brave man.

In 1942 Peter sailed in a convoy that took him to Freetown, Sierra Leone. From there he flew via Lagos in a Dakota to Cairo. Here he stayed in a transit camp in a block of flats in the city. The adjutant was Flt Lt Arthur Howard. He would appear after the war in the popular TV series *Whacko!* with Jimmy Edwards. Howard's brother Trevor also took up acting and starred in the film *Brief Encounter*.

Crash landing in minefield

Peter would go on to have a hectic time in North Africa where he took part in the Battle of El Alamein. On 4 November he claimed a 109 destroyed and one damaged. On this same day his aircraft was hit by light ack ack and he was forced to crash land his Hurricane in the desert. Once down he came under German small arms fire and dived for shelter behind his aircraft. After dark he was about to set off in the direction of the Allied lines when he heard the noise of a lorry. Peter was highly relieved when its occupants turned out to be Australians. They had seen his aircraft come down but had to wait for darkness before they could venture out to rescue him. Peter also learnt that the area all around was full of minefields!

Peter spent Christmas Day 1942 in an RAF rest-house at St Paul's Bay, Malta, having been on ferry duty flying a Hurricane from North Africa to the beleaguered island. The rest-house was run by the same Flt Lt Arthur Howard whom Peter had earlier encountered in Cairo.

In 1943 Peter was sent with other instructors to South Africa, going by Shorts flying boat via Khartoum, Kenya and Mozambique. Hearing how the build-up for the invasion of France was proceeding apace in Britain, Peter applied to return. He pleaded his case on being an operational squadron pilot with great experience. The upshot was that Peter stepped back on English soil on 24 April 1944.

Once home he joined No 124 (Baroda) Squadron. His D-Day was a quiet one; being stationed at Manston, Kent, he was a long way from the Normandy beaches. His patrols took him over the northern coast of France. Post the invasion his missions included escorting bombers searching for V1 flying bomb sites and another force that bombed German troop and armour concentrations in the forest around the Normandy town of Villers-Bocage.

On 10 August, Peter and the boys of No 124 moved to Westhampnett, a satellite airfield to Tangmere (it's the present-day Goodwood airfield). In the middle of September he participated in *Operation Market Garden*, escorting glider-towing and supply aircraft over Holland.

Drinks with Major Cain VC

Two months later and now back at Manston, Peter and a friend, Jimmy Melia, took Major Robert Cain on a visit to the Three Compasses in Canterbury. The family of Peter's fiancée, Betty, ran the pub. Cain had been awarded the VC for his bravery with the First Airborne at Arnhem and was staying at Manston. The three of them chatted about flying escort missions and the problems the RAF were facing. Peter remembers it as an amiable evening. When the bell rang for last orders the bar stayed 'open' in honour of Cain's achievement. An account of Major Cain's brave exploits appears on page 401 of this book.

In February 1945 Peter joined Vickers-Armstrong as a test pilot working with the famous Alex Henshaw.

Castle Bromwich was then the biggest aircraft factory in the country. At the peak of production, 330 Spitfires were built each month, in addition to the completion of 30 Lancasters.

In May 1945, Peter was flying Spitfire Mk IXs. He took his last European wartime flights at Vickers on 7 May, flying three different machines; Peter climbed into the cockpits of TD 406 (twice), TE 181 (once) and TE 232 (twice). The entries in his logbook record that the flights were routine and uneventful. And then the declaration of peace in Europe came.

Right: Peter, his wife Betty and their daughter Jane on the beach at Tankerton in 1948.

Above: Pilots of 238 Squadron at El Adem, November 1942. Tom Phillips (in white), Roy Marples and Peter.

Victory bells

Peter didn't fly again until 11 May. Many people know precisely where they were on 8 May – VE Day. Peter can't remember in detail how he celebrated this momentous event, but thinks he must have gone in to work as normal, only to be told by Alex Henshaw that the pilots should take a few days off. There was only one place where he wanted to celebrate – and that was with his fiancée, Betty, in The Three Compasses in Canterbury. While the bells rang out across Britain, Peter was doing a 'dirty dart' to Kent!

Peter continued to fly with the RAF until 26 April 1973. He was aged 53 when the wheels of his English Electric Lightning XS 459 touched down on the runway at RAF Wattisham, Suffolk, for the last time with Peter as the pilot. His flying career had truly been the stuff of Biggles.

Hugh Thomas is a freelance writer. He wrote a biography of Peter Ayerst DFC – Spirit of the Blue – that was first published in 2004 by Sutton Publishing and has been reprinted several times since then. The book's foreword is by Alex Henshaw.

Glorious Glowworm

The finest tradition of the Royal Navy was upheld in the course of the Norwegian campaign in an astonishing engagement between a single British destroyer and a strong detachment of the Kriegsmarine. *HMS Glowworm* had left her place in the escort for the battleship *HMS Renown* to search for a man swept overboard. On the morning of 8 April 1940 *Glowworm* was on her way to rejoin the *Renown* when she encountered two German destroyers in heavy fog at around 8am. The destroyers were part of a German force led by the heavy cruiser *Admiral Hipper* en route to land invasion troops at Trondheim.

Siren's banshee wail

A skirmish broke out and the German destroyers fled, signalling for help. *Admiral Hipper* responded. Although hopelessly outgunned, *Glowworm* accepted the fight and, while receiving several heavy hits, fired torpedoes at the German cruiser. They missed and, in a final desperate effort to sink her opponent, *Glowworm* moved to ram *Admiral Hipper*. An enemy shell struck home and set off the British ship's siren. To the soundtrack of a banshee wail the ships collided; *Admiral Hipper* suffered major damage, sustaining a large underwater gash in her bow. With the two ships locked together, *Glowworm* fired one last shot at point-blank range into the *Hipper*. *Glowworm* was pushed under the cruiser's bow and her entire fo'c'sle was sheared off up to the bridge. For several minutes she drifted on fire, before capsizing and sinking; 111 of the ship's company were killed and 39 were taken prisoner. The *Hipper* departed the scene and limped off to Trondheim.

Captain won the VC

The *Glowworm's* commanding officer, Lieutenant Commander Gerard Roope, killed when she sank, was posthumously awarded the Victoria Cross thus becoming the first VC recipient of the Second World War. The award was justified, in part, by the recommendation of Captain Hellmuth Heye of the *Admiral Hipper*, who wrote to the British authorities via the Red Cross, giving a statement of the valiant courage Lt Cdr Roope had shown when engaging a far superior ship in close battle.

NAVAL ACTION

In February 1940 the British public thrilled at the story of the Royal Navy's rescue of 299 captured merchant seamen from a German prison ship that had taken refuge in Norwegian territorial waters. The *Altmark's* human cargo were survivors from ships sunk by the pocket battleship *Graf Spee*, the last of them being taken aboard in the South Atlantic on 6 December. The ship had then headed home for Germany by way of Icelandic waters before turning south and hugging the coast of Norway.

Anxious to avoid upsetting the Nazis, the Norwegian authorities allowed the ship to proceed towards Germany, despite the *Altmark's* captain refusing a request for his ship to be searched. However, spotted by aircraft of Britain's Coastal Command, the *Altmark* slipped into Joessing Fjord and waited for darkness and the chance to escape into the Skagerrak and then make the short dash home.

British destroyers were sent to intercept the prison ship. First on the scene was *HMS Cossack* under Captain Vian. He found several Norwegian warships present and proposed that the *Altmark* should be put under a joint Anglo-Norwegian guard and taken to Bergen for examination. The Norwegians refused, saying that the *Altmark* was unarmed and as far as they were concerned had no prisoners on board.

Captain Vian withdrew. Then came the Admiralty agreement for him to go in and

get the prisoners that same evening. On 16 February 1940 with searchlights blazing, *Cossack* glided into the fjord. Approaching the Norwegian ship, *Kjell*, the British again requested that the *Altmark* should be escorted to Bergen with a joint Anglo-Norwegian guard. The request was again refused.

Grappling irons thrown across

Meanwhile the *Altmark* began working her engines. The *Cossack* came alongside; grappling irons were at once thrown across and a boarding party leapt the gap. Hand-to-hand fighting broke out before the British took control of the ship. With shouts of 'The Navy's here!', hatchways and doors were flung open and hundreds of cheering British seamen were released. Soon they had transferred to the *Cossack* and other waiting British destroyers and by the next afternoon were ashore at Leith in Scotland.

Seven Germans died and several were wounded in the operation. The British sustained just one severely wounded casualty. Norway protested the action and Germany was indignant at the boarding of 'a peaceful merchantman in neutral waters... and the brutal murder of German seamen'. The British Government was unperturbed. Especially when it became clear that public opinion in the United States enthusiastically supported the Royal Navy's action.

Above: The Altmark *pictured in Joessing Fjord, Norway.*

Germany Strikes North

April 1940. Norway and Denmark are two more neutral countries that went out of their way not to upset the Nazis but still found themselves on Hitler's shopping list of countries he covets.

Germany's war machine was dependent upon iron ore from Sweden that was shipped to the Reich in the main by way of Narvik in northern Norway. The latter country was determined to remain neutral; indeed she was even prepared to turn a blind eye to German ships entering her territorial waters to escape encounters with the Royal Navy.

But Hitler was determined to occupy Norway. He felt he could not risk the Allies stepping in to cut off the vital supply of ore. Further, taking possession of Norway's long coast would allow German aircraft to more easily reach targets in the northern British Isles. Allied ships maintaining the blockade of Germany would also have to pull back in the face of the air threat. Finally, the Norwegian ports would be safe havens for German warships and U-Boats who would be much

closer to the Atlantic shipping lanes upon which Britain depended for her food and war material coming out of the USA and the Caribbean in increasing quantities.

Swastikas suddenly fly

The Germans struck north on 9 April 1940. Little Denmark was in no position to resist and within 12 hours the whole country was occupied. At the same time, the Luftwaffe swarmed into Norwegian skies and all but destroyed Norway's air force in a few hours. Troop transports were already secretly at sea. Bad visibility meant they went largely undetected by both the Norwegian coastguards and British reconnaissance aircraft and soon German troops were rushing ashore at Narvik, Trondheim, Bergen and Kristiansand. Merchant vessels in Norwegian ports ran up the Swastika and revealed themselves as supply ships for the invaders.

An attempt to force a passage up the Oslo Fjord was repulsed by Norwegian coastal defenders; a German cruiser, the *Blucher*, was sunk by guns firing from the island fortress of Oskarsborg. But German paratroopers were successful in capturing the airfields at Oslo and Stavanger. A fleet of 500 transport planes then began ferrying in troops and equipment to quickly outnumber the Norwegian army. With command of the air

and efficient motorised transport, the Germans swiftly moved to occupy most of the country.

Britain and France already had contingency plans for the mining of Norwegian waters and the landing of troops at strategic ports – moves that were intended to deter a German invasion and cut off the Swedish ore supply. If the proposed actions had been taken before the Germans invaded then it may even have resulted in a state of war between the two Scandinavian countries and the Allies. However, the German aggression settled the issue and Norway welcomed Allied intervention who quickly landed troops halfway up the coast above and below Trondheim and at Narvik, much farther to the north.

Reindeer to the rescue

RAF Gladiators flying in from aircraft carriers attempted to operate from the surface of a frozen lake near Trondheim where 3000 reindeer helped trample the snow down into a compressed mass six inches thick. But a combination of cold, lack of fuel and faster and much more numerous German fighters doomed the move from the start. The Central Norwegian operation was abandoned and by 2 May all Allied troops had been evacuated.

At Narvik it was a different story. Near the port, between 10 and 13 April, the Royal Navy had bested the German navy in a sharp series of engagements, sinking in one day seven enemy destroyers. The town is 400 miles north of Trondheim and within the Arctic Circle and road communications with southern Norway were very poor in 1940. The distance meant that the Germans were unable to mount a big air offensive and they were only able to insert a relatively small body of troops to occupy the area. British and French forces landed in the vicinity and after a series of engagements finally took the town on 28 May.

Given momentous events unfolding elsewhere in Europe, it proved a hollow victory and within two weeks the Allies withdrew from Norway. Even so, before leaving the Allies destroyed Narvik's port facilities so thoroughly that no iron shipments left the town for Germany until January 1941.

German troops probe warily into a Norwegian town.

This Viking emblem was chosen to mark the British Fifth Army Corps service in Norway 1940.

Magnetic Mine Menace

DORNIER Do.18 FLYING BOAT WITH 2 JUNKER DIESEL ENGINES

D

A

B

C

This diagram appeared in *The War Illustrated* in December 1939. It shows how German flying boats laid magnetic mines in Britain's sea lanes and river estuaries. A: Mines being released.
B: Note the parachutes that prevent the mines from landing too hard. C: Mines are coupled in pairs.
D: Decoy enemy aircraft fly at a great height while the mine-laying machines fly just above the sea.

By the spring of 1940 a means of defeating the mines had been developed by British scientists. A de-Gaussing coil fitted to a ship neutralizes the vessel's magnetic effect, making her quite safe from magnetic mines.

HOW MAGNETIC MINES ARE LAID FROM FLYING BOATS

DETAIL OF APPARATUS

Ship's Dynamo

Casing

Coils of Insulated Wire

Normal Magnetic Field with N & S Polarity which is set up by Ship's Hull

Magnetic Mine on Sea Bed

When the Opposite Polarity of the Electro Magnet is used, the Normal Magnetic Field of the Ships is neutralized

Mine is then useless

Finland defies the Bear

March 1940. Blue swastikas are painted on RAF aircraft as Britain prepares for war with Russia!

Following the Red Army's seizure of eastern Poland in September 1939, Stalin and Hitler reached an understanding concerning the spheres of interest of Germany and the Soviet Union. Moscow wanted Finnish territory in order give the city of Leningrad more space in which to construct defences in depth.

What became known as the Winter War began when Russia attacked Finland on 30 November 1939. Germany had agreed not to intervene in the war but much of the world was outraged resulting in the Soviet Union being expelled from the League of Nations on 14 December.

Russia had four times as many soldiers as the Finns, 30 times as many aircraft and 218 times as many tanks. Further, the Red Army had recently fought a successful war against the Japanese in Russia's Far East (see page 14). So it came as a shock to the Russians when the Finns not only fought back ferociously in the winter snows but also inflicted a whole series of major defeats on the Red Army, winning the admiration of the free world in the process.

Allied forces on standby

France and Britain did not want to see Finland occupied by Russia. An army of 50,000 French soldiers and a large British naval and air force prepared for action; on 11 March, Prime Minister Neville Chamberlain announced that the Allies were ready to 'proceed immediately to the help of Finland, using all available resources'.

The prospect of Allied intervention alarmed Norway and Sweden, who feared becoming a battleground where the Allies would fight with Russia on the Finnish front and inevitably tangle with Germany in the Baltic. As it happened, the Finns were forced to yield to overwhelming Russian force before the Allies could intervene. But it's intriguing to speculate on what course history might have taken if Britain had gone to war with

Russia in 1940!

A number of RAF aircraft were painted with striking blue swastikas in readiness for action. But the Finnish blue swastika had no Nazi connection. It was originally the symbol of luck of Count von Rosen. He had donated the Finnish 'White Army' its very first aeroplane during the country's War of Independence with Russia in 1918. It was adopted as the official marking of the Finnish armed forces. Only after the Nazis made it their official emblem in the Twenties did it acquire a sinister significance. By a further coincidence, Finnish soldiers were also issued with German-style 'coal scuttle' helmets.

These Finnish soldiers are counting down the minutes before making an attack.

Stalin demonised in the West

Finland fought well but was eventually worn down by the massive Russian military machine. The day after Chamberlain's offer of help, a peace treaty was signed in Moscow. Finland had to surrender about a tenth of its pre-war territory and a fifth of its industrial capacity and also give Russia an island in the Baltic. The Finns lost nearly 25,000 killed while Soviet losses were estimated at 48,000 dead. Moscow's reputation was greatly damaged and Stalin and the Soviet system were demonised in the British press.

When Hitler turned on the Soviet Union in 1941, Finland allied herself with the Nazis and with the help of thousands of German troops, managed to eject the Russians from the territory they'd occupied in 1940. Though the Finns showed no real heart for invading Russia proper, it was inevitable that Finland would attract strong criticism from the Allies who now counted Stalin as a friend.

As the fortunes of war swung again in 1944, and faced with another Soviet invasion, Finnish troops turned on the Nazis, forcing them out of the country. At the end of the war Russia reclaimed her Winter War territorial gains and extracted massive war reparations from Helsinki.

After the war the Finns abandoned the disreputable swastika in favour of a blue and white roundel. In 2007, the 80,000 members of the Finnish War Veterans Association were offered commemorative rings featuring the swastika. They pointed out that originally the symbol was a Hindu mark of peace.

Christopher Lee was a volunteer who went to aid the Finns

The Winter War attracted thousands of foreigners eager to help democratic Finland. One British volunteer who managed the difficult journey was Christopher Lee who would later find fame as an actor. Lee – like most of the volunteers – was never allowed into battle. He later joined the RAF and in North Africa he served as an Intelligence officer with the Long Range Desert Group. As a Cipher Officer for No 260 Squadron RAF he accompanied the unit through Sicily and Italy. Additionally, he saw service with the Special Operations Executive (SOE). Lee retired from the RAF with the rank of Flight Lieutenant. His subsequent acting career saw him star in a host of films, most famously the Hammer horror movies. He also appeared in the cult film *The Wicker Man* and is pictured here with frequent co-star Ingrid Pitt. Ingrid's own wartime experiences begin on page 82.

Early in 2009 Christopher Lee received a knighthood.

WAR DIARY 1940

3 January: This evening the German submarine U-25 secretly moors next to the German merchant ship *Thalia* in the neutral Spanish port of Cadiz where she will refuel and restock.

4 January: Figures released today show that the lifeboats of the RNLI have been launched over 400 times since war began. The lifeboatmen have already saved over 1000 lives and regularly go out to rescue the crews of ships that have struck mines or been torpedoed by U-Boats.

12 January: The 'Winter War' between Finland and Russia continues. The Finns are clear masters of the art of fighting in the snow and have a large number of ski troops in white snow capes who move swiftly through the forests to ambush Soviet columns moving on the few tracks passable for motorised vehicles.

Britain is experiencing the severest winter since 1894. At one time the Thames froze over for the first time in 45 years; an icebreaker was required to keep the flow of water clear at Teddington Lock. Ice has formed on the sea in many places.

20 January: Bad weather means it is a quiet month for ground and air activity although the mine menace and U-Boat threat continues unabated. Men from Newfoundland – Britain's oldest colony – have been arriving to support the war effort.

24 January: British merchant ships are being sunk on a daily basis by mines and U-Boats. The *Newhaven* and *Parkhill* were announced lost today with all hands.

29 January: The East Dudgeon lightship stationed off Wells, in Norfolk, is machine-gunned and bombed. John Sander of Great Yarmouth is the only survivor of the crew of eight.

5 February: Helsinki announces that the Russian 18th Division of up to 20,000 men has been almost entirely destroyed near Lake Ladoga. The Finns call their petrol bombs in bottles 'Molotov Cocktails', so-named after the Russian Foreign Minister.

9 February: There is speculation in the British press that the Nazis are urging Stalin to attack British interests in the Near East. One report suggests there may be as many as 800,000 Russian troops massing on the Soviet border with Afghanistan threatening to advance on the north west frontier of India. As alternatives, incursions into Iran (Persia) or Turkey have been postulated. However, the Red Army's poor showing in battle against the Finns does not do much to support the case for such adventurism.

14 February: It is estimated that the Russians have lost 40,000 men in their recent attack on Finland's Mannerheim Line. The defensive position is named after the country's military leader. International volunteers are serving with the Finnish forces and it is reported that the actress Greta Garbo has given £1250 to the Swedish fund in aid of Finland.

Opposite page: With the British and French lack of military success in early 1940, this poster points at leaked secrets being a likely culprit (National Archives).

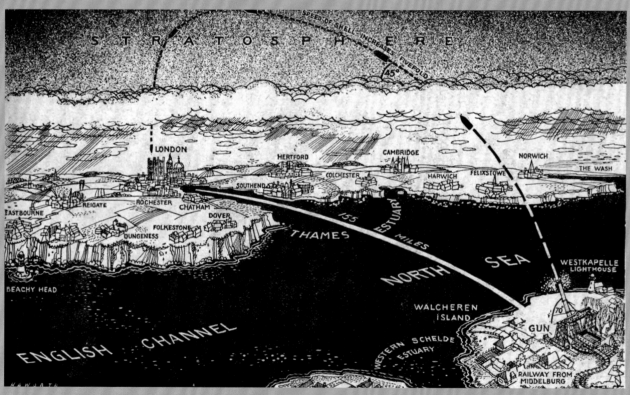

Will Hitler's Big Gun Target London?

In World War One the Germans had a huge gun – Long Bertha – that was able to throw shells a distance of 75 miles from Laon to explode in the streets of Paris. In the spring of 1940 there were newspaper suggestions that the Nazis had developed an even bigger gun with a range of 155 miles. Projectiles from the super-gun would rise to a height of 37 miles and enter the stratosphere where their velocity would be quintupled. If fired from German soil, the gun would menace most of the important Dutch and Belgium cities. However, if Germany occupied Holland and placed the weapon on the island of Walcheren then London would come within range. *The War Illustrated* comments: 'From a military standpoint, the new gun must be unwieldy and erratic in use, though against this valuation we must set Hitler's addiction to the spectacular and unorthodox. For centuries no enemy has laid hands on Britain's capital and it is not difficult to imagine what devastating play Dr Goebbels would make with the story that London was at long last at the mercy of German guns.'

TO THE BRITISH TROOPS

"I want to know where your unit is stationed —so that I can bomb you and drop parachute troops to machine-gun you. This information I will get from you and your friends—please continue to give your friends military details. I shall hear." *Lieutenant-General Schultz.* GERMAN INTELLIGENCE.

WAR DIARY 1940

23 February: The Government is stimulating increased production of home-grown food and announces that 25,000 women and girls have now joined the Women's Land Army. The Ministry of Agriculture has called for an additional 1,500,000 acres of grass in England and Wales to be ploughed and planted in time for the 1940 harvest. It is said that at present home-grown food supplies would last Britain from breakfast on Sunday until midday dinner on Wednesday; for the rest of the week the country must rely on food from overseas.

1 March: The overwhelming strength of the Red Army is at last beginning to wear down the Finnish forces who admit they have been forced to retreat in places in the Karelian Isthmus.

10 March: Tonight Finnish delegates fly to Moscow to commence negotiations on a peace agreement to end the Winter War.

11 March: It is believed that German submarines and a number of merchantmen are hiding out in the Russian port of Murmansk, afraid to venture out to sea because of the threat posed by Royal Navy ships waiting in ambush.

13 March: Finland concludes a peace agreement with the Soviet Union. On every front the Finns agree to cede territory including the Karelian Isthmus and the whole shore of Lake Ladoga. Indeed, the Finns will lose more land than was originally demanded by Stalin before the war began. The Finnish Foreign Minister says: 'our army fought with all its might, but we are only a small people.'

16 March: Nearly half a million Finns are hastily evacuating the land ceded to Russia under the terms of the peace treaty signed just a few days ago.

At dusk this evening German bombers attack Scapa Flow. Some planes bomb the village of Bridge of Waith in Scotland, killing James Isbister. He is the first British civilian killed in the war.

20 March: French and British ships are tightening the maritime blockade of Germany. At the beginning of the war, only ships of any nation carrying goods going into Germany were stopped but as a reprisal for the indiscriminate sowing of magnetic mines, the Allies now stop and seize up to an estimated half of seaborne exports coming out of Germany. At the same time, the Allies are suffering daily losses through mines and U-Boat actions. In consequence the German word 'ersatz' is frequently used in the British press. It means 'substitute' and refers to the artificial products replacing foodstuffs and raw materials now in short supply as a result of the war. They include substitute rubber, textiles, petrol, soap, tea and coffee.

26 March: There is a new Government in France led by Paul Reynaud. The new Premier assures the nation that the objective of the war remains the same – 'to vanquish the enemy'.

30 March: Winston Churchill makes a broadcast in which he warns people to expect an intensification of the war and also warns neutral nations that Germany would have no respect for their desire for peace.

2 April: After 25 years the Anzacs (Australian and New Zealand Army Corps) are once more marching to the aid of the Mother Country. They occupy practically the same desert camp in Egypt that their fathers used in 1915.

5 April: German aircraft are attacking Britain's herring fleets. RAF planes assigned to protect the boats have been nicknamed 'Kipper Kites' by the press.

9 April: Hitler's forces invade Denmark and Norway. As early as 3am today, large numbers of German troops were coming ashore in southern Norway. By 3pm the Germans will have already occupied Oslo. In the course of the day the Germans also take complete control of Denmark.

Why Quisling was a Commander of the British Empire

From the start of the German attack on Norway, a number of Norwegians emerged as fifth columnists, openly assisting the Germans in their conquest.

These traitors would become known as 'Quislings', so named because of the Norwegian fascist politician, Vidkun Quisling, who declared himself the new leader of Norway. Ironically, Quisling had been made a Commander of the British Empire in 1929 for his role in 'maintaining the interests of the British Government in the Soviet Union'.

Norway's King Haakon and his Government refused to surrender to the Germans. Instead they chose to go into exile on 7 June when *HMS Glasgow* ferried the party to Britain. After the war, Quisling refused a state offer to flee Norway; in October 1945 he was executed for his treachery.

10 April: The British destroyers *HMS Hardy* and *Hunter* are sunk early today while attacking German naval forces close inshore to the northern Norwegian port of Narvik. The Germans also lose several warships.

13 April: *HMS Warspite* and a flotilla of destroyers enter the waters around Narvik and sink seven German destroyers to break Nazi sea power along the coast of northern Norway.

16 April: British forces land on the Faroe Islands. Officially Danish territory, the islands have been put under British protection.

18 April: The submarine *Spearfish* returns to port. On 11 April she had torpedoed and sunk the German pocket battleship, *Admiral Scheer*.

4 May: Japanese bombers strike at Chungking in China causing a 48 hour firestorm amidst the flimsy wooden houses. One fifth of the city is destroyed and around 10,000 civilians die.

7 May: Prime Minister Neville Chamberlain has been explaining the background to the Norway campaign to the House of Commons. It triggers a fiery response from Admiral of the Fleet Sir Roger Keyes, naval hero of an attack on Zeebrugge docks on 23 April 1918. Keyes says that the failure to take Trondheim was '...a shocking story of ineptitude, which ought to have never happened. If proper steps had been taken immediately, and carried out with resolution and speed, the situation could have been retrieved by immediate naval action. As Nelson said 140 years ago: "I am of the opinion that the boldest measures are the safest," and that advice still holds good today.'

Collapse in the West

Above: A wounded French soldier is aided by his enemy, perhaps the man who shot him.

Churchill becomes Prime Minister

On the very day that the Germans struck against the Allies in the West, Neville Chamberlain tendered his resignation as Prime Minister. He advised the King to send for Mr Winston Churchill who immediately answered the call. Next day *The Daily Telegraph* hailed the appointment: 'Mr Churchill takes up the duty of national leadership at a great hour in the life of our country. By the inspiration of a bold and fertile genius, by long study and aptitude for war, by unrivalled experience in administration, and above all by force of will and hearty understanding of that stubbornness and fire which have made the British Nation great in arms, he has the qualities to make his arduous task glorious. He will be able to command support from the leaders of the several parties making easy the establishment of a Government completely representative of the nation and uniting the ability and energy which will bring forth the utmost power of the country and direct it to the swiftest and greatest advantage.'

Blitzkrieg! The Wehrmacht and the Luftwaffe sweep all before them as they crash into Holland, Belgium and France in early May 1940.

At 2.41am on 10 May 1940 anti aircraft guns in Amsterdam opened fire on German aircraft caught in the probing beams of searchlights. Twenty minutes later German troops began to cross the frontiers of Holland, Belgium and Luxembourg. Shortly after 4am the first parachute troops descended on the dark countryside of the Netherlands. There had been no warning and no declaration of war before Hitler's biggest Blitzkrieg so far was unleashed.

The German victories in Poland, Denmark and Norway had filled the dictator with

41

FRANCE 1940

The drawings on this page were the work of a German artist who accompanied the *Wehrmacht* on their lightning conquest of France in May and June 1940. They were published in a book that was, ironically, printed in Occupied Paris during the following year. What is noticeable in the book are the large number of horses that feature and the fact that there is just one sketch of a panzer. This reflects the fact that the German Army at this early stage of the war was still very reliant on horses for moving artillery, ammunition, food supplies and baggage.

The French and British outnumbered the Germans in the numbers of tanks they possessed but it was the German generals who had developed the concept of Blitzkrieg - concentrating their armour on a narrow front to achieve a local breakthrough that could quickly be exploited, regardless of any danger to their flanks. It was a concept perfect for rendering impotent the powerful fixed defences of the Maginot Line.

The wrecked bridge below is close by Chateau Amboise in the Loire Valley. It was blown up by the French themselves.

confidence that his armies and air force could brush aside any Dutch and Belgian resistance and easily vanquish the Allied forces of France and Britain. He had two million men under arms for the attack in the West plus 3900 combat aircraft.

Numerically, the Allies far outnumbered the Germans in men and the machines of war. But in the air they were much weaker with just 1100 planes based on French soil. Moreover, the Wehrmacht had learnt how to concentrate their forces, particularly the fast-moving panzer formations that were backed up by swarms of dive-bombers; they wanted to wage a war of movement. By contrast the French – always conscious of the terrible losses they had sustained in the Great War – had embraced a strategy based on fixed defences best illustrated in the Maginot Line. This was a massive chain of forts and redoubts that began just to the east of Sedan and ran all the way to the Swiss border.

German troops found Holland's waterways no obstacle.

get close to the shore.

The British and French conducted a fighting retreat into a perimeter around Dunkirk. Some days before, British forces had been hurriedly landed at Boulogne and Calais and these conducted a spirited defence as the Germans poured past them heading north. Eventually the Germans decided to attack the two ports. Boulogne fell first but Calais held out until 26 May having diverted panzer and troop forces away from adding pressure against the Dunkirk perimeter.

Faced with disaster, Churchill knew he would have to put more planes into the fight. Their role would be to prevent the Luftwaffe from destroying the British army on the beaches, but also to protect the hundreds of Royal Navy and civilian vessels of all sizes rushing from Britain to rescue the armies at Dunkirk.

Initiative with the Germans

The British and French had another problem. They knew Hitler would not respect neutral Holland and Belgium but neither country was willing to invite the Allies in because they feared it would provoke a German attack. So the initiative was very much in the hands of Hitler's generals. They grasped it with alacrity. Holland was subjected to indiscriminate bombing and key bridges and towns were swiftly seized. On 14 May 100 Heinkel He 111s attacked Rotterdam even as a Dutch delegation was on its way to discuss surrender terms. The Germans tried to abort the raid but only about half the aircraft received the radio messages or spotted the red flares fired by ground troops; 815 Dutch civilians died in the subsequent bombing.

A series of well-planned assaults were directed at Belgium strongpoints. The Eban Emael fort, linchpin of the Belgian defence system and thought to be impregnable, fell to a daring assault spearheaded by airborne troops who actually landed on the ramparts. Stormtroopers seized bridges across the Albert Canal.

Following their previously agreed plan, the British Expeditionary Force (BEF) and French troops hurried north into Belgium to confront the Germans as best they could. While this was happening the Germans did the unexpected; a mass of tanks and mechanised columns erupted out of the rugged and lightly defended Ardennes. The Maginot fortress line was way to the south of this location and very quickly the Germans were

across the River Meuse and pouring through a 50-mile hole in the Allied line. Air attacks on the enemy's heavily defended pontoon bridges over the Meuse were unsuccessful. The Germans headed for the Channel coast and as they did so the British and French forces in the north became cut off from the rest of France.

Rommel leads spearhead

While the RAF found their Hurricanes to be effective fighters the French air force fared poorly and was almost completely destroyed by the time the German spearhead – led by General Erwin Rommel – reached the sea at Abbeville. The French pleaded for RAF reinforcements; some were sent but as the situation on the ground worsened, Churchill and the British Government knew they had to hold back sufficient forces to defend Britain itself should the unthinkable happen and France fall.

When the Belgians surrendered on 28 May the Germans were left free to attack from the north and the Allies in Flanders found they were surrounded and feeling the full force of Blitzkrieg. Thousands of refugees clogged the roads and compounded the chaos and confusion. The Allies fell back towards the Channel ports even as a plan was evolved – *Operation Dynamo* – to evacuate as much of the BEF and French army as possible. The port of Dunkirk's location close to the Belgian border made it the natural site for the evacuation, especially as there were wide, sandy beaches nearby where small craft could

Hitler halts the panzers

Not for the first time in the war, Hitler now read the situation wrongly. Convinced by his air chief Herman Goering that the Luftwaffe alone could smash the Allies trapped in the Dunkirk perimeter, Hitler halted his panzers and reined in his ground troops. The Nazi leader's decision may well have been swayed by the widespread destruction wrought from the air he had seen for himself in conquered Poland.

From 28 May to 2 June, Hurricanes and Spitfires engaged in a terrific air battle that raged over the North Sea, English Channel, French coast and the flat lands of Flanders. The anxious Allied troops lining up in the port and on the Dunkirk beaches couldn't see much of the fight due to smoke and distance and many thought they'd been abandoned by the RAF. But the latter's intervention meant the armada of ships great and small – many crewed by civilians – was able to steadily pick up men and transport them back to British ports.

In the end around 225,000 British troops and 113,000 French and Belgian soldiers were saved to fight another day, though they had lost most of their bigger weapons, armour and transport. The evacuation was dubbed the 'Miracle of Dunkirk'. But it was a miracle made possible by the courage of the sailors who braved time and again the dangers of air attack in the Channel and the RAF pilots who held the Luftwaffe at bay.

On 5 June the Germans resumed their ground attacks into central France even as Allied troops were being landed at various

French ports in the west of the country. The British 51st Highland Division found itself trapped in the small port of St Valery-en-Caux, under fire from Rommel's panzers on the nearby cliff and unable to evacuate by sea. On 12 June some 8000 officers and men surrendered. A German victory on the Continent became inevitable. The heart had gone out of the French; their Maginot fortresses proved to be concrete illusions against the reality of the terrifying mobile warfare waged by the Germans.

Petain seeks an armistice

Despite Churchill proposing a binding Anglo-French union, the Government of Paul Reynard gave way to a new leader, the aged Marshal Henri Petain, a hero of the Great War. Petain immediately sought an armistice. On 25 June France surrendered to Germany. The surrender document was signed in a forest clearing at Compiegne, in the same railway carriage where Germany had signed her own armistice with the Allies in 1918.

Petain believed he had done the right thing for France. A large part of the country would remain under French control from a government based at Vichy. The French fleet and the French colonial empire also remained intact for now.

But not all Frenchmen were prepared to acknowledge defeat. One intensely patriotic officer, Charles de Gaulle, would not give in. He had fought with distinction during the Battle of France and had evaded capture. Now he was preparing to rally free Frenchmen all around the world to the Allied cause.

Below: They made it home from Dunkirk.

Meanwhile, the British army and air force, back on British soil, could pause for breath. Heavy weapons and transport were in short supply. The RAF had lost 959 planes from 10 May up until the capitulation of France – that was about 40% of their strength. The obvious question was would there be enough fighters left to meet the inevitable German air onslaught that would be the precursor of an invasion of England.

The Battle of France was over. The Battle of Britain was about to begin. On 19 June Churchill spoke to a hushed House of Commons: 'Let us brace ourselves to our duty, and so bear ourselves that, if the British Commonwealth and Empire lasts for a thousand years, men will still say, "This was their finest hour".'

Left: *Allied ack ack guns left disabled on La Panne beach, Dunkirk. The BEF lost just about all of its transport, tanks and heavy weapons.*

Above: *General Erwin Rommel pictured with General Fortune, captured commander of the British 51st Highland Division at St Valery en Caux.*

Le Havre to the Cocos

Royal Engineer Jack Walter's war began with the BEF in France in 1940. Five years later, the end of hostilities found him serving in the garrison of a group of tiny but top secret coral islands in the Indian Ocean.

Above: Jim and Jack Walter (right) with their mother Annie in 1940.

Below: Jack pictured recently at his family's villa in Thailand.

B ut for a bitter sweet accident of history, Sussex born and bred Jack Walter would most likely never have been born, let alone attain the age of 89 and these days be living in a luxury air conditioned villa in the beautiful Krabi region of Thailand.

Jack's father and sister and other family members all decided to emigrate to Canada in search of a new life a decade or so into the start of the 20th century. The family wanted to sail across the Atlantic together but there was not enough space to accommodate them on the ship they wanted to travel on. So it was that Jack's newly-wed aunt and uncle took a berth on one vessel while the rest of the family found places on another liner. Tragically for the honeymoon pair, the ship they sailed on was called the *Titanic*; the White Star liner was on its maiden voyage and heading for a rendezvous with an iceberg. Sadly, Jack's aunt and uncle were not numbered among the lucky survivors.

The family's move to Canada didn't work out and two years later they returned to Sussex and settled in High Hurstwood, a village between Uckfield and Crowborough on the fringe of the Ashdown Forest. It's where Jack was born on 3 July 1920. Although christened William John he became known as Jack at a very early age.

Blowing up bridges

With the outbreak of World War II, Jack and his brother Jim volunteered for the Royal Engineers, enlisting at Brighton on 25 January 1940. Jack was a concreter and Jim a bricklayer and the pair served together

Right: An RAF maintenance squad pose beside a partly stripped Spitfire on the Cocos in 1945. Jack and Jim helped construct the runway after clearing away island jungle.

until the end of hostilities. They hadn't had much training before they crossed from Dover to Calais in March 1940 to join the BEF.

When the German breakthrough threatened to encircle the British forces in May, Jack's unit found itself isolated away from the main BEF force that was eventually hemmed into the Dunkirk perimeter. They withdrew southwards. At one time they were sent to a bridge under orders to blow it up. With the charges in place, the men saw a vehicle approaching and assumed it was the enemy. The plunger was pressed but nothing happened – which was rather fortunate because the 'enemy' vehicle turned out to be a friendly bren gun carrier that was able to cross the bridge and escape the advancing Germans.

Later they blew up a much bigger bridge and Jack remembers how the whole structure lifted high into the air before crashing back into the waterway in a buckled 'v' shape. They also speedily constructed a casualty clearing station near Le Havre in Normandy.

It was at Le Havre that the soldiers saw their transport disabled. The pair had no idea if they would evade capture until they were ordered to board what Jack describes as 'a bloody old tub'. The thick clouds of smoke from burning oil installations gave them cover from German bombers but they did witness the shooting down of a French fighter plane that crashed into the sea close by their vessel. The two engineers eventually landed at Southampton, rifles in hand. They had escaped from Le Havre alongside some 11,000 British troops in the course of *Operation Cycle*, a successor to *Dynamo* at Dunkirk.

Long walk home

Jack has still got his Army paybook and in it is an annotation: 'June 1940. Ex BEF 48 hours leave with Free Warrant.' He took the opportunity to go home but he could only get a train as far as Tunbridge Wells and had to walk the remaining 15 miles to High Hurstwood.

That summer there was the threat of a German invasion and the air war steadily intensified. Jack remembers the white contrails in the sky as the Battle of Britain began. He and Jim went to work constructing air raid shelters in London in preparation for what would become the Blitz. Then they went north to build more shelters; on one occasion they were caught up in a big air raid on Halifax. It was while he was up north that Jack met Yorkshire lass Dorothy, a bus conductress in Leeds. The two were destined to marry in June 1943.

Jack and Jim next went up to Scotland to build a POW camp near Edinburgh. Later they helped build airfields to support the growing Allied bomber offensive against Hitler's Fortress Europe. But the winds of war were set to take the two engineers much farther than over the Channel. Earmarked to go to Singapore, their move was cancelled when the Japanese seized the island early in 1942.

It was well into 1944 before they were finally shipped out in convoy to the Far East. With the Mediterranean by then dominated by the Allied navies and air forces, the convoy went via Su*ez*. Jack remembers sinking a few beers in Bombay before sailing on to Ceylon. Their eventual destination was the Cocos (Keeling) Islands in the middle of the Indian Ocean almost midway between Australia and Ceylon. The islands were a vital communications link for the Allies but were extremely vulnerable to a Japanese strike from their bases in Java and Sumatra. For this reason the existence of the island base was kept top secret. Even so, it is very surprising that the Japanese did not mount an invasion in 1942 when they were ascendant in that part of the world and Britain feared potential invasions of Ceylon and even Madagascar. In fact the Japanese threatened the Cocos only once when, on Christmas Day 1942, the submarine I-166 surfaced and bombarded the islands but caused no damage.

Two Spitfires collided

Jack and Jim were engaged in building an airfield and the infrastructure needed to support over 10,000 servicemen that were eventually stationed on these islands which in peacetime had a population numbered in mere hundreds. Jack says the aircraft on the Cocos were mostly American with a couple of Dutch squadrons. On one occasion two Spitfires collided; one crashed into the sea

while the second made a belly landing off the end of the runway. Miraculously, both pilots survived. Not so fortunate were the nine out of 14 Canadian crew members of Catalina JX435 that crashed in Cocos lagoon on 27 June 1945.

Jack's memorabilia includes a leaflet intended for Japanese troops that advised them to surrender. He's also got a *Health Memorandum for British Soldiers in the Tropics*. It states: 'Our aim should be real cleanliness and not "eyewash". Good discipline and method are a great help in attaining real cleanliness.' The 20-page guide concludes with the motto: *Mens Sana in Corpore Sano* – 'A Sound Mind in a Sound Body.'

At the end of the war, Jack returned to Britain by way of India. He got back to his wife Dorothy in Yorkshire on 3 May 1946 when he saw his 10-month-old daughter, Sandy, for the first time (later the couple had a second child, Stuart). Jack's Soldier Release Book (stamped 2 May 1946) describes him as a hardworking and industrious NCO who displayed exemplary conduct.

Jack's back in the Tropics!

I have known Jack Walter for nearly 40 years. But it wasn't until I visited him and his daughter Sandy and son-in-law Mick in their home in Krabi, Thailand, early in 2009 that I learnt for the first time of his fascinating wartime experiences. Jack's wife Dorothy died in 1991. He'd also suffered a serious stroke.

'After six decades Jack returned to the Tropics and now lives in air-conditioned luxury in Thailand. Once a week he catches an open air bus to town for a therapeutic massage!'

But when Sandy and Mick asked if he wanted to accompany them to Thailand where they were building a retirement home, he leapt at the opportunity, despite the fact that he had not left England for much more than a day trip to France since coming home from the war! Five years later and he is enjoying his life in the air-conditioned luxury villa. Once a week he even catches an open air bus to the nearby town of Amphoe Muang for a massage and treats the girls to lunch.

Jack's wartime *Health Memorandum* for soldiers states: 'Only one case of typhoid occurred in the BEF in France up to the time of evacuation…' So it was ironic that Jack should have caught it a few years ago in Thailand! However, good health treatment in the town of Krabi effected a cure and speedy recovery.

DAVID ARNOLD

Cocos visitors include Charles Darwin and a Great War German warship

The first European to discover the then uninhabited Cocos Islands was Captain William Keeling in the course of a voyage from Java back to England in 1609.

On 1 April 1836, *HMS Beagle* anchored off the Cocos to take soundings establishing the profile of the atoll. Young naturalist Charles Darwin was on the ship. Just as he would later in the ship's survey expedition when exploring the Galapagos Islands, Darwin studied the natural history of the Cocos and collected specimens.

The islands were annexed to the British Empire in 1857. Later a wireless telegraph station was set up and it became a vital link in communications between Great Britain, Australia and New Zealand.

On 9 November 1914, the islands became the site of the Battle of Cocos, one of the first naval encounters of the First World War. The German light cruiser *Emden* arrived to destroy the wireless station but soon afterwards was herself surprised and sunk by the Australian cruiser, *HMAS Sydney*.

Parts of the *Emden* were salvaged by the Cocos islanders and fashioned into various artefacts offered for sale to visitors. Jack Walter still has in his possession a knife made of *Emden* steel together with a wooden sheaf, a unique souvenir of his time on the islands.

Mutineers executed

Prior to Jack's arrival, on the night of 8–9 May 1942, 15 members of the island garrison – men from the Ceylon Defence Force – mutinied in protest at what they considered to be unfair treatment on the part of their British officers. One non-mutinous soldier was killed and an officer was wounded before the mutineers were arrested. After a trial, three of the mutineers were executed, including the leader, Gratien Fernando. It was the only time in World War II that British Commonwealth soldiers faced capital punishment for mutiny.

The Cocos (Keeling) Islands today is a territory of Australia. Only a few hundred

Australian air force jets flying over the Cocos Islands.

people – mainly Malaysian Muslims – live there all year round but plenty of tourists visit, drawn, in the main, by the superb diving opportunities and the sheer isolation of the islands. Though the Cocos were fully in the path of the 2004 Indian Ocean tsunami, the islands were spared devastation due to the exceptionally deep waters close to shore.

A fortune in precious metal apparently awaits discovery on the seabed somewhere off the Cocos. In June 1690, a Spanish ship en route from Mexico to Manila in the Philippines came to grief on a reef. One chest of silver was recovered but it is believed that silver coins and a haul of ceremonial silver swords worth millions still sit at the bottom of the Andaman Sea, close to the Cocos.

WAR DIARY 1940

10 May: Hitler's long-awaited offensive in the West opens today with attacks by land and air on Holland, Belgium and Luxembourg.

11 May: The situation in Holland is critical but it is becoming clearer that there are two other main enemy thrusts. One is aimed through the rough and wooded terrain of the Ardennes and the other, further north, is headed for Maastricht and Brussels beyond.

British and French forces land on the Dutch West Indian islands of Curacao and Aruba to safeguard important oil refineries. Two days later the Dutch royal family will arrive in London.

12 May: Five obsolete Battle aircraft from No 12 Squadron – the 'Dirty Dozen' – are lost in an attack on bridges across Belgium's Albert Canal seized by the Germans. The airmen have some success; later the action will result in the first RAF VC's of the war when Flying Officer D E Garland and Sergeant T Gray are posthumously given the awards.

14 May: According to plan, British and French troops have been moving into central Belgium to meet what was thought to be the main German route of attack. But now it becomes clear that a massive force of German troops and tanks have erupted out of the rugged forests of the Ardennes when they cross the River Meuse at Sedan and Mezieres, in France.

16 May: British troops are fighting a fierce battle in and around the Belgian town of Louvain.

21 May: The German Blitzkrieg across France has created a 50-mile wide corridor behind the main British and French armies. Today the spearhead of the advance – panzers led by General Erwin Rommel – reach Abbeville on the Channel coast and wheel north in the direction of Boulogne and Calais.

26 May: BEF commander Lord Gort is given Cabinet permission to 'operate towards the coast forthwith in conjunction with the French and Belgian armies'. The British are drawn towards the coastline around the port of Dunkirk. This evening an evacuation of Allied troops begins in earnest. All heavy weapons and transport are being left behind.

28 May: Hitler has halted his panzers. He has ordered the Luftwaffe to bomb the soldiers trapped inside the Dunkirk perimeter into submission. But the RAF is proving a formidable adversary even though their Hurricanes and Spitfires are rarely seen by the troops crowded on the beaches and in the port.

29 May: The evacuation of the BEF from Dunkirk continues apace but the Royal Navy is sustaining heavy losses. Today about 40 miles north-west of La Panne, the British destroyer *Wakeful* is hit by a torpedo, splits in half, and sinks in 15 seconds, killing about 100 soldiers. Elsewhere in the English Channel, a U-Boat torpedoes the destroyer *HMS Grafton*, also damaging the destroyer *HMS Comfort*. The destroyer *HMS Lydd* rams *Comfort* in error, cutting the ship in half. Off the French coast, the destroyer *HMS Gallant* strikes a mine, killing 55 of the crew, but the ship survives. Close by the Dunkirk beaches the destroyer *HMS Grenade* is bombed and sunk.

2 June: Just before midnight, Admiral Bertram Ramsay – organiser of the massive rescue by sea – receives a welcome signal from Dunkirk: 'BEF evacuated'. Some 225,000 British troops have been saved to fight another day.

3 June: Over 250 Parisians die in the first bombing raid on the city.

4 June: The last of 113,00 French and Belgium troops are ferried across the Channel as *Operation Dynamo* comes to an end. Around 35,000 French and Belgians have to be left behind to surrender.

7 June: Tonight a single French aircraft flies over Berlin and drops bombs in the suburbs of the German capital. Two nights

Loss of the Lancastria

On 17 June 1940 Britain's worst-ever maritime disaster occurred off the port of St Nazaire on the Atlantic coast of France. The Cunard liner *Lancastria* was loaded with between 5000 and 9000 British soldiers and airmen of the BEF being evacuated home. Five German aircraft dive-bombed the heavily over-laden ship and sank it with enormous loss of life; as many as half of those on board died. Winston Churchill, who had proclaimed only days before that the entire BEF had been withdrawn through Dunkirk, ordered that the event be kept secret. The ship is pictured below after it had rolled over. Though some British newspapers did report the story after it had broken in the US press some weeks later, the full facts will not be known until 2040 when the Royal Navy files on the sinking will be declassified.

later the same aircraft bombs the Heinkel aircraft factory at Rostock.

10 June: Italy declares war on Britain and France. Hostilities will commence at midnight.

As Allied forces withdraw from northern Norway, the Royal Navy today loses the aircraft carrier *HMS Glorious*, two destroyers and an oil tanker as they head for Britain.

11 June: Eight RAF Whitley bombers fly from Britain to bomb the Fiat works in Turin, having refuelled in the Channel Islands.

Italian bombers make the first raid on British-held Malta situated to the south east of Sicily. In the course of the war, the small island will become the most bombed location of anywhere in the world.

19 June: Spain's dictator Francisco Franco makes a secret offer to join the Axis at war in exchange for French Morocco, the Oran region of Algeria, an expansion of Spanish Sahara and Spanish Guinea, and substantial economic and military provisions. Adolf Hitler makes no commitment.

De Valera's Eire Wakes Up To Danger

Speaking in Dublin on 16 June 1940, Eire's Prime Minister, Eamon de Valera announced: 'The nation is in danger; the danger is more menacing as the hours pass by.' This was the time, he went on, to prepare quickly for whatever might befall them. It was no time to merely talk when their neighbour's house was on fire and the sparks were falling on Eire's roof.

De Valera was responding to German remarks to the effect that with the de facto fall of France: 'Our U-Boats are already blocking the southern and northern ends of the Irish Sea and Eire is now in reach of our air force.'

Thousands of men from Eire have joined the British military and another 50,000 have joined Eire's Local Security Corps to augment the country's small army and navy. In his speech, de Valera said it was sad to think there should be an Achilles in the tent. An observer wrote: 'All his hearers knew that he was referring to that irreconcilable element in the nation's life represented by the Irish Republican Army. Proscribed and driven underground as it was, this revolutionary organisation still continued to exist in skeleton shape and was still inspired by that bitter hatred of England and all things English that had ever been its inspiration and support. In the IRA any German invaders might well find a potential Fifth Column.'

WAR DIARY 1940

22 June: France formally surrenders to Germany. The signing ceremony is held in the Forest de Compiègne, in the same rail car in which Germany had surrendered to France in 1918.

24 June: The Armee de l'Air flies its last operational sortie before the Armistice comes into effect. French casualties from the campaign total 90,000 soldiers killed and 200,000 wounded. In the coming weeks 1.5 million members of her armed forces will be marched into captivity.

28 June: The British Dominions Secretary informs the Australian Government that with Italy in the war and France out, Britain could not send a fleet to the Far East. Britain asks Australia for troops and two squadrons of aircraft for the defence of Malaya.

Soviet troops occupy Bessarabia and north-east Bukovina.

The British Government recognises Charles de Gaulle as leader of Free Frenchmen.

29 June: The Spanish border with France is closed.

30 June: German Major General Alfred Jodl writes a memorandum stating that if a strike on Britain fails, the next best place to defeat Britain is in the Mediterranean.

This month the total U-Boat toll of merchant shipping in the Atlantic amounts to 58 ships.

1 July: Winston Churchill writes to Josef Stalin, warning him of Adolf Hitler's intentions for an invasion of the USSR.

2 July: The passenger liner *Arandora Star* is torpedoed off the coast of Ireland, carrying 1500 German and Italian aliens from Britain to camps in Canada; 175 Germans and 486 Italians are killed. Canadian destroyer *St Laurent* rescues 857 survivors.

Hitler decides that a landing in England is possible, provided air superiority is attained. He orders the armed forces to prepare for an invasion.

The Bank of Canada in Montreal receives £30 million in gold bars and £200 million of marketable securities for wartime safekeeping. The transfer from the Bank of England was made via the battleship *HMS Emerald*. It's the largest single transfer of wealth in world history to date.

3 July: British troops seize French ships in British harbours. A British naval group arrives at Oran and Mers-el-Kebir in Algeria, requesting the surrender of the French fleet. The French refuse, and the British ships open fire. The battleship *Bretagne* blows up, *Dunquerque* is run aground, *Provence* is beached and the torpedo cruiser *Magador* explodes. 1300 French sailors die.

4 July: A French Court Martial sentences Charles de Gaulle in absentia to four years in prison for treason.

5 July: Near the south-west coast of Ireland, a submarine torpedoes and then shells the Canadian merchant ship *Magog*. The crew abandon ship.

> *That period in 1940 was one of sharp contrasts; of the pleasure of being alive and with friends in the gentle Sussex summer evenings; of visits from Diana, when we would dine and dance in Brighton, or sit long on the balcony outside the Old Ship Inn at Bosham watching the moon on the water and listening to the tide lapping against the wall beneath us. And memories of tearing terror when, at the end of a dogfight, I found myself alone with 50 miles of hostile sky between me and the Channel coast and the hungry 109s curving in to pick off the straggler.*

THE BATTLE OF BRITAIN REMEMBERED BY TANGMERE SPITFIRE ACE, FLYING OFFICER 'COCKY' DUNDAS

9 July: Twelve British Blenheim bombers attack aircraft at Stavanger. Some 30 Me 109 and 110 fighters attack them. Only four British planes survive, badly damaged.

10 July: Sixty four German aircraft attack southern England. Five RAF squadrons fly to intercept them. Twelve German planes are shot down, at a cost of three British fighters. The Battle of Britain has begun.

12 July: Units of the 1st Canadian Division land at Brest, France, and head toward Laval and Le Mans. Within days they will make a hasty retreat back to Britain.

16 July: Hitler issues Directive No 16 concerned with preparations for invading Britain. The landing would be on a wide front from Ramsgate to west of the Isle of Wight. First, the RAF must be defeated and the Royal Navy must be contained in the North Sea and Mediterranean. The Straits of Dover are to be sealed off with minefields on both flanks. The invasion's codename is *Seelöwe* (Sea Lion).

17 July: Under Japanese pressure, Britain agrees to close the Burma Road to China for three months.

Secret plans are being formulated for a joint German – Spanish attack on Gibraltar.

18 July: Prime Minister Winston Churchill makes his 'This was their finest hour' speech in Parliament.

19 July: In the Gulf of Athens, British warships sink the Italian light cruiser *Bartolomeo Colleoni*.

24 July: A Chance Voight 156 dive bomber of US manufacture but with Luftwaffe markings is shot down over England. It must have been captured from the French.

Left: A group of Local Defence Volunteers at the ranges are receiving instruction in rifle shooting. By the end of June 1940 - with the threat of a Nazi invasion looming large - nearly one million men of all ages had responded to the LDV appeal. Later they would be renamed as the Home Guard.

WAR DIARY 1940

For the first time in her history England is being shelled from French soil. The German guns target coastal convoys in the Channel but can also hit Dover. British guns return fire...

2 August: Fast German motor torpedo craft known as E-Boats are being used to attack British convoys in the Channel.

In recent weeks British bombers have been attacking any concentrations of barges observed in German-occupied ports and waterways along the coast from Holland to Normandy. The air strikes are aimed at disrupting Hitler's preparations for an invasion.

7 August: An explosion occurs on the Norwegian steamer *Lista* and the ship beaches in flames in New York harbour. FBI 'G-Men' believe the blast is an act of sabotage and are hunting for Nazi agents. It is reported that 16,885 cases of suspected sabotage have been investigated since the European war broke out.

13 August: For the first time in her history England is being shelled from French soil. The German guns are aimed at Allied ships in the Channel but can also hit Dover. British guns return fire and the RAF bomb the enemy batteries.

14 August: It is stated that Rumanian exports of oil to Germany in July totalled about 180,000 tons – enough to keep 6000 enemy aircraft fully fuelled for more than a month.

19 August: The evacuation of British forces with most of their equipment from Somaliland across the Red Sea to Aden is successfully completed. However, it is admitted that British prestige in East Africa has greatly suffered.

22 August: A regiment of the French Foreign Legion is included in General de Gaulle's Free French Army. The unit had served alongside the British at Narvik and fought in the Battle of France before escaping to England. Their ranks include Germans and Italians.

25 August: There is one civilian death as German aircraft bomb the Scilly Isles.

29 August: General de Gaulle announces that the Free French flag is flying over the whole of French Equatorial Africa and French Cameroons as well as the Territory of the Chad. Soon the Society Islands (including Tahiti) and the Marquesas as well as Martinique and Guadeloupe will embrace de Gaulle's rallying cry.

30 August: An evacuee ship en route to Canada is torpedoed in the Atlantic. Fortunately all 320 British children on board are rescued.

Rumania – a country largely created under the Versailles settlement at the end of the Great War – is being broken up under pressure orchestrated by Hitler and Stalin. The Soviets took over the regions of Bessarabia and Bukovina on 28 June, Bulgaria took southern Dobruja on 22 August and today Hungary has been awarded two thirds of Transylvania. King Carol of Rumania had earlier repudiated a British guarantee of support in the hope that Hitler would not interfere with his kingdom.

3 September: President Roosevelt addresses Congress in respect of the Anglo-American Naval Agreement which sanctions the transfer of 50 vintage destroyers to the Royal Navy in return for the British concession to the USA of naval and air bases in the Atlantic and Caribbean.

7 September: King Carol has abdicated the throne of Rumania and is seeking refuge in Switzerland. Pro-Axis General Ion Antonescu has been appointed Dictator.

9 September: Italian aircraft bomb the Jewish coastal town of Tel Aviv in Palestine; 111 civilians die. Four of the raiders are downed.

French India consists of five enclaves, the largest of which is Pondicherry at 196 square miles holding 300,000 people. Today the enclaves have rejected Vichy and declared for de Gaulle.

13 September: Marshal Graziani's Italian army of invasion crosses the frontier from Libya into Egypt. The defending British and Commonwealth forces are outnumbered five to one.

16 September: A Spanish delegation visits Berlin for negotiations on Spain's joining the Axis in war. Germany wants one of the Canary Islands, a German base in French Morocco (if gained by Spain), and influence in Spain's economy. The terms are unacceptable.

23 September: General de Gaulle is rebuffed today at Dakar when he arrives in the expectation that French West Africa will come over to the Free French. Lives are lost on both sides before the Allies withdraw. A British statement issued later explains: '...it had never been the intention of His Majesty's Government to enter into serious warlike operations against those Frenchmen who felt it their duty to obey the commands of the Vichy Government.'

'Out of the Frying-Pan into the Spitfire'

Lord Beaverbrook's 1940 appeal for aluminum to build more Spitfires and Hurricanes met with a magnificent response from the housewives of Britain. But in fact though the scrap metal was gainfully employed in war work, it was never used in the construction of fighter planes.

'Trained for Murder'

The arming of the Home Guard with rifles over the summer of 1940 provoked fury in the Nazi press. On the Berlin radio an announcer bitterly states: 'The British Government is releasing criminals from prison and training them for murder. Every Englishman who agrees to act as a franc-tireur is digging his own grave. Churchill is leading the British civil population on a fatal path.'

Wartime Commute by Water-Bus

On 13 September 1940 a river service on the Thames between Westminster Bridge and Woolwich was inaugurated in a bid to relieve congestion on the land routes to and from the City. The boats hold up to 200 people and the fare for the complete journey is 9d. London bus conductors have been redeployed to collect the fares.

"we're going to the **WAR-TIME NURSERY**" at

"mummy's doing war work, is yours?"

Battle of Britain

The miracle evacuation from Dunkirk meant that Britain still had the core of her army intact along with many thousands of soldiers, sailors and airmen who had escaped from European nations now fallen under the heel of Hitler and his triumphant forces.

All these men now had the chance to fight on another battlefield on another day. But the weapons they needed to fight with were in desperately short supply as they had by necessity quit the mainland without most of their tanks, guns, vehicles and heavy equipment. If German troops, supported by their panzers, successfully crossed the Channel in large numbers there would be little chance of defeating the Blitzkrieg tactics of the all-powerful Wehrmacht.

Very quickly the Germans developed plans for *Operation Sea Lion*, the codename for their projected invasion of Britain. They also began to build up concentrations of barges and transport ships in harbours along the coasts of France, Belgium and Holland. In June 1940 the outlook was bleak but the British did have three vital trump cards to play before the Germans could have things all their own way.

Formidable air obstacle

Firstly, there was the Royal Navy. The fleet was largely intact, had already bested the German navy in a whole series of engagements, and could, with luck, smash any enemy invasion fleet at sea well before any troops could be landed. True, in the narrow confines of the English Channel, the British ships would be vulnerable to air attack. That's where the second trump card would come into play. The RAF had not been defeated in the Battle of France; they had given a splendid account of themselves. Though they had lost a total of 1029 aircraft and over 1500 personnel killed, wounded or captured, thanks to the foresight of Air Chief Marshal Lord Dowding, enough fighter squadrons had been kept in reserve in Britain to pose a formidable obstacle to the Luftwaffe. Thirdly, there was the indomitable figure of Winston Churchill, who was swift emerging as the right man at the right time to inspire the British people and her armed forces and instill the belief that victory was not just possible but was certain.

At this stage of the war, Britain's Hurricanes and Spitfires broadly matched the German single-seater fighter, the Messerschmitt Bf 109,

Above: A swarm of Junkers Ju 87 dive bombers. They were known as Stukas – an abbreviated form of the German word for dive bomber. They were deployed early in the Battle of Britain but were soon found to require constant fighter protection or they became easy prey for the Hurricanes and Spitfires of the RAF.
Right: A Bf 110 fighter on an airfield near Lille in Northern France in August 1940.

in speed and armaments. The Luftwaffe was numerically superior. But the RAF machines would have the advantage of operating over their homeland. In addition, the network of Royal Observer Corps posts, anti aircraft guns and barrage balloons, added to the problems faced by the Germans. Last but not least, Britain had an efficient and effective radar system set up along the coast and also had access to top secret Ultra intelligence intercepts revealing the Luftwaffe's strategies. Even so, the battle must be finally decided by the bravery and skill of the individual pilots on both sides. Fortunately, in 'The Few' the RAF had plenty of magnificent men to pilot their flying machines.

Sinister siren wail

The first phase of the battle opened on 10 July with attacks on south coast ports and Channel shipping. People living near the coast got used to hearing the sinister siren wail of the Ju 87 'Stuka' as they plunged to dive bomb vessels and shore installations. However, the Ju 87 by itself soon proved to be an easy target for the RAF.

The aerial fighting raged all summer and the high altitude vapour trails circled and criss-crossed the skies of southern England. Adler Tag – Eagle Day – was 13 August when no less than 1485 German sorties were mounted in a bid to finally break the heart of Fighter Command. Dogfights erupted right along the coast as far as the south-west where pilots of No 609 Squadron from RAF Warmwell went up against a swarm of Stukas escorted by Me 109s.

Whilst engaged in an inspection of coastal defences, Winston Churchill and Major General Bernard Montgomery became spectators to this particular action. Five Stukas and three Me 109s were shot down into the sea, adding to the tally of 38 other German aircraft destroyed that same day in other sectors. By comparison, just 13 RAF fighters were lost.

On 15 August five major air assaults were mounted. These included targets in the

northeast using 220 aircraft based in Norway and Denmark. The Germans believed that most of the remaining RAF fighter squadrons had been transferred to the southeast where the main Luftwaffe blows had been falling. They were wrong; Dowding had anticipated the move and retained sufficient forces to blunt the enemy attack. More than this, not a single factory was hit and it wasn't until late in the day when just one airfield – Driffield – sustained serious damage.

On 16 August the Germans, with a total of 1720 aircraft, mounted three great air assaults in the southeast aimed firstly at Kent and the Thames Estuary and next Sussex and Hampshire. Finally, in the early evening they crossed the coast almost simultaneously at four points between Harwich and the Isle of Wight. As a measure of how effective the RAF pilots were proving, out of the 1720 aircraft deployed by the Luftwaffe, all but 400 were fighters. It was during the second of the day's operations, when Gosport came under attack, that Flight Lieutenant J B Nicholson of No 249 Squadron won the first Victoria Cross to be awarded to a pilot of Fighter Command. His Hurricane hit and set on fire by cannon fire, Nicholson was about to bale out when he saw a Me 110 in a vulnerable position. He decided to stay in his blazing aircraft and attack the enemy. Not until he saw the German fighter diving down out of control did the RAF man quit his Hurricane. Severely wounded and badly burnt, Nicholson descended by parachute – only to be shot in the buttocks by a trigger-happy Local Defence Volunteer!

Desperate need for pilots

Tactics developed. For example, ideally the faster Spitfires would attack the Me 109 escort fighter leaving the slower but more numerous Hurricanes to take on the bombers. However, pilots also learned to take advantage of the Hurricane's tight turning radius. Squadron Leader Peter Townsend followed the maxim for dealing with 109s: 'Never climb, never dive; just turn.' In a single action he bagged two German fighters. Post-war Townsend would have a romance with Princess Margaret, the Queen's sister.

The relentless German attacks on RAF airfields throughout August and early September took their toll. Fortunately the Luftwaffe did not realise how badly they had hurt Fighter Command and their bases and how desperate was the need for replacement pilots and aircraft; all they knew was that RAF Spitfires and Hurricanes seemed always able to get into the air to

Right: 'Bombers over England' was a film released by the Germans in 1940. Despite what's depicted on the poster the Luftwaffe never sent bi-planes into action over Britain although the Italian air force did. The theme song to the film became a popular hit in Germany. It was written by Norbert Schultze who also penned Lili Marlene. *German children were encouraged to play a board game of the same name as the film!*

An RAF fighter pilot makes good use of the time as he awaits the order to scramble.

confront their bombers and fighters. Then, in one of those unusual twists of fate upon which wars and history so often turn, something happened to change the situation; on 6 September RAF Bomber Command carried out a long-range raid against Berlin.

Hitler and his air chief, Goering, had promised the German people that their capital would never be subject to aerial attack. Infuriated by the British raid, the Nazi pair decided that London must be made to suffer. They called off the Luftwaffe's assaults against airfields and control installations and instead ordered a massive and intensive bombing campaign against London intended to terrorize its citizens and weaken morale.

In fact, the coming Blitz would have the opposite effect; the British public became

even more determined to endure whatever trials and tribulation they had to in order to win the war. The change of German tactics also worked to the benefit of the RAF for they were able to concentrate their efforts in one area and so began to take an increasingly heavy toll of the attackers.

Even though his air force had failed to eliminate the RAF, *Operation Sea Lion* remained on Hitler's agenda. During the night of 13-14 September, RAF bombers and Royal Navy ships jointly attacked ports in France and the Low Countries that were full of invasion barges, destroying almost 200 of them. On 12 October, Hitler postponed the invasion indefinitely. By the end of the month the Battle of Britain was over. From 10 July to 31 October, the Germans had lost 1733 aircraft of all types against the RAF's 915.

Frank Wootton's famous painting 'Looking for Trouble' depicts three Spitfires flying in a typical formation deployed in 1939 and early 1940. By the time of the Battle of Britain it had been found to leave the aircraft vulnerable to attack and was replaced by a 'finger four' formation that was easier for the pilots to maintain and afforded better all-round observation. The painting here (and reproduced in full on page 21) appears with the kind permission of Mrs Virginia Wootton. An account of Frank's own fascinating wartime adventures appears later in this book.

The most decisive battle of all time?

Though fought by relatively few men, the Battle of Britain stands out as one of the most decisive conflicts ever. Had the Luftwaffe won then Britain would most likely have been invaded. This was at a time when neither the USA nor Russia was involved in the war. With Germany the master of all Europe, it would have been incredibly difficult, if not impossible, for the Americans to come to the rescue even if they were willing to do so. Hitler would also have been able to field far bigger forces for the invasion of the Soviet Union and devote much greater resource to the development of technologically advanced weapons such as rockets, jet aircraft and perhaps even the nuclear bomb. We can only speculate by how much, but for certain world history would have been radically different without the victory of 'The Few'.

David Arnold

Free Europe fights on with the RAF

Poland's little Air Force numbered just some 300 aircraft and was swiftly crushed by the Luftwaffe in September 1939. However, because of conscription to her armed forces, there were a large number of Poles who had experience of flying. As Poland's fate became apparent with the Russian intervention from the east, thousands of Polish airmen planned their escape to fight again with the Allies. They came through Romania, through Greece and Yugoslavia, Turkey and Spain to rally in France. Other Poles living in the USA and South America also returned to free Europe. They joined Czechoslovak pilots who had fled the German take-over of their country in 1938 and 1939.

The Few would have been fewer

Poles and Czechs first fought with the French air force. Then when France fell in June 1940 the Poles – almost 5500 of them – joined the Czechs, Norwegians, Danes, Belgians, Dutch and French making their way to Britain, determined to carry on the fight against Germany. Some of the French even managed to hijack aircraft from Vichy airfields and fly them to Gibraltar.

Training requirements and language complications meant that the new arrivals could not all go straight into the Battle of Britain frontline. But without the Europeans it is certain that the Few would have been considerably fewer; 147 Polish pilots fought with the RAF against the German onslaught in the summer of 1940, all of them flying in the sturdy Hurricane. Fifteen of them were recognized as 'aces' for scoring five or more victories. There were also 29 Belgians along with 14 Free French and 87 Czech pilots involved in the Battle. The French air contribution would build up steadily in subsequent years.

In September 1940 the first of the American volunteer Eagle Squadrons went into action. Eventually three squadrons with 244 pilots were formed. Some of the pilots had originally come to Europe to fight with the Finns against Russia in the Winter War; others crossed the US border to join the Canadians.

Princess Elizabeth Goes On Air

On 13 October 1940 Princess Elizabeth made her first-ever radio broadcast, an address to evacuee children at home and in the Empire. Princess Margaret and the King and Queen were with her as she delivered a message that began: 'I am wishing you all "good evening". I feel that I am speaking to friends and companions who have shared with my sister and myself many happy Children's Hours.

'Thousands of you in this country have had to leave your homes and be separated from your fathers and mothers. My sister, Margaret Rose, and I feel so much for you, as we know from experience what it means to be away from those we love most of all... All of us children who are still at home think continually of our friends and relations who have gone overseas – who have travelled thousands of miles to find a wartime home and a kindly welcome in Canada, Australia, New Zealand, South Africa and the United States of America.'

The message concluded: 'I can truthfully say to you all that we children at home are full of cheerfulness and courage. We are trying to do all we can to help our gallant sailors, soldiers and airmen, and we are trying, too, to bear our own share of the danger and sadness of war. We know, every one of us, that in the end all will be well... And when peace comes, remember it will be for us, the children of today, to make the world of tomorrow a better and happier place.'

The German bombing campaign against British cities, particularly London, was gathering momentum even as this historic broadcast was made. A month earlier on 10 September, a Luftwaffe bomb with a timer had exploded on the terrace of Buckingham Palace at 1.30am. Their Majesties were not in the Palace at the time but later, along with Winston Churchill, they went to inspect the damage.

THE BLITZ

BRITAIN MUST TAKE IT

"Let 'em all come"

MEN 41-55

HOME DEFENCE BATTALIONS

Apply at any Army Recruiting Centre Now

16 September: Invasion?

In the weeks and months following 16 September 1940 there was much speculation in the national and international press that a fleet of German barges had embarked on an invasion of England that very night. Circumstantially, it was a perfect night for such an operation. A harvest moon, the brightest of the year, shone full. The sea was calm and the high tide peaked at around dawn. *The New York Sun* carried what it claimed was detailed information; the barges were 'very light, of wood and metal, and obviously intended solely for a one-way trip. Each carried 200 Germans with full equipment. Evidently the Germans had counted on their airmen being able to silence the land batteries before these were able to annihilate the invaders, who were helpless because they did not carry artillery ...they sank under a withering fire as they appeared. Meanwhile detachments of the Royal Navy appeared to the rear cutting off the barges from France.

'The carnage was reported to have been terrific. All available hospital accommodation in and around the Channel ports had to be commandeered for the German wounded. By way of explanation for these American reports and English rumours, responsible quarters in London expressed the opinion that a considerable proportion of the German divisions detailed for the invasion had actually embarked, when the fleet of flat-bottomed barges was caught by the bombers of the RAF. Yet another explanation was that the barges were caught during an invasion rehearsal.'

The mystery of 16 September has never been explained. The day before had seen the RAF bring down nearly 200 enemy aircraft so German bodies in the sea could well have been hapless Luftwaffe airmen. However, three and a half years later as the Allies prepared for D-Day the US army and navy sustained serious losses off the coast of South Devon in the course of an exercise that was intercepted by German E-Boats operating out of Cherbourg. The incident was hushed up for decades after the war.

Britain's cities bombed

London and most major British cities took a massive pounding in the winter of 1940-41. On 15 November it was the turn of Coventry to experience the terrible violence of the Blitz. The heart of this Midland city of 225,000 residents was devastated, its ancient cathedral being reduced to rubble.

German radio claimed the raid was a reprisal for a British attack on Munich. For 10 hours aircraft after aircraft flew over and simply unloaded their bombs with no pretence of selecting military or industrial targets. Hundreds of civilians were killed and many more were seriously injured as residential areas were hit.

Newspapers likened the attack to the one that befell the town of Guernica in Spain when German bombers aiding Franco's rebel army killed thousands of civilians in a similar indiscriminate raid.

CADBURY MEANS QUALITY

DAILY HERALD EXTRA LATE EDITION

SATURDAY, NOVEMBER 16, 1940

ONE PENNY

There's nothing like BIRD'S CUSTARD & JELLIES

Midlands City Is Now Like A Bombarded French Town

COVENTRY HOMELESS SLEPT BY ROADSIDE THIS MORNING

NOT A MORTAL BLOW —WORK WILL RESTART

RAF STRIKES AT BERLIN

21 Down—Three In Last Night's Raid

BRITAIN'S OFFER TO RUSSIA

Dusk To Dawn Raid

NAZIS SAY 30,000 FIRE BOMBS FELL

STOP PRESS BERLIN RAIDED AGAIN

AN ITALIAN LIE

THE SECOND GREAT FIRE OF LONDON

An estimated 10,000 incendiary bombs dropped by 150 bombers rained down on the City of London on Sunday night 29 December 1940 as the Luftwaffe attempted to burn down the 'Square Mile'. The attack began in the early evening and ended just before midnight. Four firemen buried beneath a collapsed wall in City Road were among the many casualties. The Guildhall was left a blackened ruin and nine churches, eight of them built by Sir Christopher Wren, including the lovely St Bride's in Fleet Street, were burnt out or seriously damaged.

'Malicious bloody flame'

Three centuries before Samuel Pepys had wrote of the 1666 Great Fire of London: 'As far as we could see up the hill of the City...there was a most horrid, malicious, bloody flame.' His words describe perfectly this second Great Fire.

Next day Mr and Mrs Churchill toured the City streets to survey the damage. Just a few days before in a speech in Parliament, the Premier had said that every method of dealing with air fighting by night was being studied by 'able and brilliant scientists and officers'. He added: 'So far we have been no more successful in stopping the German night raider than the Germans have been in stopping our aeroplanes that range freely over Germany.'

Top: A barrage balloon manned by women auxiliaries is being inflated.

Above right: A Heinkel bomber is pictured over the Docklands of London.

Right: Churchill seen inspecting bomb damage in the capital.

An American in London

American commentator Ralph Ingersoll came to London to report on how the British capital and its people were coping with the German bombing campaign that will go down in history as the 'Blitz'. Here are his words from a USA radio broacast made on 29 October 1940:

'This city lives two lives, one by day and one by night. By day, life in London is almost normal; there is the cheerful noise of traffic in the street, people come and go from offices and shops, restaurants are crowded at lunchtime. Now and then there is a siren to startle the newcomer, but Londoners pay little attention to daytime raids. There is no rush for shelters, but if the sky is clear people look up to see if they can see the raider.

'It is different at night. The papers publish in a prominent position the exact minute at which the black-out begins. In the half-hour preceding, the entire city of 8,000,000 people shut, curtain, board up and black out every window in their dwellings, offices, hotels - everywhere people live or work. The streets suddenly empty. The only lights that come on are hooded or masked, lights giving directions to shelters, first-aid posts, or showing obstructions in the highways.

Clap of boots on the pavement

'The only noises on the streets are the gears of the buses which run on through the night, the clap of boots on the pavements – usually the service boots of the police, the ARP wardens and the Home Guardsmen, who challenge you in the dark when you cross their beat.

'All but a few of the taxis have disappeared. Within a few minutes after the black-out the city is ready. It is a little after 6.30pm. Within a few minutes it comes; the evening siren.

The Germans are methodical and punctual fellows. They come droning through the black, and some nights the searchlights spout into the air to meet them around the edge of the city. Sometimes the tall fountains of light disappear up into the mist. Sometimes they break against low clouds in a white glow. Sometimes there are no searchlights and you can trace the approach of the planes by the sound and flashes of the anti-aircraft guns. They thud far off over the horizon. Then those near the city bark with a hollow sound; then all of a sudden you jump out of your boots when one goes off a few hundred yards away.

'When they are close you can wait and count to 10 or 11 and then see the little flicks of exploding shells in the sky, and a minute later you hear the thud, thud, thud of the explosions themselves coming down from miles in the sky. Often the German aircraft fly round and round trying to orientate themselves and it is a fine, heartening feeling to think that one of those shells may be knocking the tail off the man who is trying to drop nitro-glycerine on your head.

A carpet of sleeping humanity

'Under the streets there is a whole other life. There is no precise pattern to the London shelter, they are improvised and of all sizes. People bring their own bedding. Most are crowded and people sleep there in rows, shoulder to shoulder. In one of the big underground shelters in which I spent most of one night, 8000 people of all ages slept. Cold and draughty at one end it was thick and uncomfortable at the other. The big shelters in the deep Tubes, 60ft underground, are at once the safest and the most depressing. In one you can walk a full half-mile, stepping over the feet of an absolutely solid carpet of sleeping humanity.

'The wardens and the nurses in the first-aid shelters were to me the most inspiring people I have met in London – calm, courageous, tireless volunteers, interested only in the people they look after. They will one day erect monuments in this city to the unknown shelter warden.

'The bombing of civilians is a brutal and ugly thing, but the heroism with which it is met and endured here restores one's confidence in humanity. Nowhere in nine days of walking and talking did I see the slightest evidence of indecision or faltering. Here Fascism has stubbed its toe on the character of a people who can "take it" and who obviously propose to take it until the last German raider has gone down in smoke or hot-footed it for home with two Spitfires on his tail.'

Kids at War

Affection for flying

As a seven-year-old schoolboy in NW London during the war, one morning playtime an Allied aircraft flew overhead trailing smoke. The crew were bailing out and I believe the pilot died in the crash not far away. After the midday break, on returning to school, a mate told me that one of the crew had landed in a tree and his mother had rescued him and taken him for a 'cuppa'. I was most envious and wished it had been my back garden.

This incident left me with a long affection for flying and development of the jet age. I just managed National Service in the RAF.
John Cameron

Wimbledon Common gun

My mother's family led by my grandmother decided in 1938 to move from the East End of London to Wimbledon for the convenience of my uncle who had a protected trade, I being a mere 18 months old. It was a large house that catered for my mother and father and older brother, my single uncle, another young newly married aunt and uncle and grandmother.

I do not remember the early years of the war but my first vivid memory is of the time when iron was required for making armaments. Lorries were sent down our road collecting any metal objects. My three wheel bike was hidden away but an old tin peddle car was forfeited along with the lovely ornate iron railings in front of the house.

There was a large gun on Wimbledon Common in front of the windmill which proved to be quite noisy when enemy aircraft were spotted. We may have been lucky to have moved out of the East End but our garden at the new house backed on to Wimbledon Station. This became a hazardous location as the armaments going down to Portsmouth by rail proved to be a prime target for the

Hitler will send no warning – so always carry your gas mask

ISSUED BY THE MINISTRY OF HOME SECURITY

Luftwaffe. One night I was awakened in the Morrison Shelter by a loud bang followed by falling glass. This was a result of the side of the station being hit by a bomb. Great excitement the next morning with a WVS canteen wagon serving tea and buns.

One day my friend and I were on our bikes a long way along the road when the sirens sounded and a Doodlebug followed us dead in line with the road. On reaching home we ran into the outside loo and cuddled each other until it went off with a bang. There were many more to follow. My dad and married uncle were away in the army and the single uncle was in Dad's Army like Pike, whilst my mother was on war work building parts for Spitfires.

After the near miss it was decide to move down into the cellar which was carpeted and bedded where it was hoped we would stand more chance of survival. As things got worse

and the V1s were being superseded by V2s it was time to evacuate to the Midlands where some relatives made arrangements for our accommodation. When the bombing stopped we came home and VE Day dawned with family celebrations up in Trafalgar Square. By the time the Japanese surrendered I was in hospital with suspected TB but was carried out by nurses to celebrate world peace. In later years as a boating enthusiast I was pleased to be in attendance with the flotillas of private boats invited to take part in the 50th and 60th Dunkirk Evacuation commemorations.
Bob Wootton

Wartime memories

I was but a child at the time (born in 1937) but have some clear memories of what for us all then were the 'normal' events of the times. For example, I recall emerging from the Anderson

GOOD ADVICE FROM THE MINISTRY

This Ministry of Health poster by Dudley S Cowes dates from late 1940. It reinforces the message that children should be evacuated. The background is a blitzed street with the Union flag flying defiantly from the rubble.

Shelter in our garden in Yeovil to see a massed armada of German bombers filling the skies on their way to blast the hell out of poor Bristol; bombing raids on Westlands Aircraft Company with stray bombs demolishing nearby houses; collecting shrapnel which had broken our conservatory windows and taking some to swap at school; the arrival of US troops in the months before D-Day, including black men (that we had only ever seen before in Hollywood films at the Saturday morning pictures) and their kindnesses to us kids with unaccustomed gifts of chewing gum and other goodies!

It is curious to recollect that although there was a war on we enjoyed far more freedom to roam without supervision than children typically do today. Of course there were no computers or television, there could be no trips to the seaside and for the most part we had to make our own amusement. I have fond memories of cycle rides with friends out to the local airfield for some plane spotting, or down to the railway line for train spotting, or out to the countryside for scrumping, mushrooming or gathering chestnuts. These were common activities for seven and eight-year-olds then.

It is true that there were very few cars on the roads – even the minority who owned a car could not use it for pleasure trips due to the petrol rationing – but parents did not have the same fears for the safety of their children that unfortunately have become so prevalent today. And despite all the privations of total warfare, with food, clothing and much else severely rationed, I think we were generally much healthier than children are today – there was certainly no childhood obesity!

Peter Parker CBE

Witness to tragedy

I was a child evacuee during the war. Contrary to popular belief, most evacuees did not go to wonderful loving homes, but had a wretched time. I suffered along with the majority of evacuees. My story, though, concerns an incident in September 1942 when I was seven years old.

I had been evacuated to Haslemere, Surrey. One evening, at about 6pm we were surprised by a very dark-coloured aeroplane that descended out of the cloud layer with a terrible grinding noise coming from its engines. It flew directly over our house towards the centre of Haslemere. It was gradually losing height and, as we watched, it broke into three pieces and fell to earth.

It fell on and around the Rex Cinema in the town. One part went through the roof, but no civilians were seriously injured as the cinema was almost empty at that time in the evening. As a child I was deeply shocked because I realised that I had witnessed someone dying.

A few years ago I undertook some research on this incident. The aeroplane was a British

Havoc Mark III from Flight 1455 based, I believe, in Lincolnshire. It was a night stalker and was painted black. It had a searchlight in the nose. When it found a German bomber in the dark it would train its searchlight on it so that the night fighters could home in. The crew, who all perished, were Flying Officer W Winter, Pilot Officer J Lindley and Flight Sergeant W Cleall.

The cause of the crash has been ascribed to mechanical failure, but even in those days aeroplanes did not fall out of the sky for no reason, and the noise that it made indicated that the engines were damaged. I believe it had encountered a lone German fighter above the clouds and was badly shot up.

I still get upset when I think about it.

Peter Lane

Seashore memories

At the beginning of the war I lived very near the sea in Wales and enjoyed all that a huge beach provides for children during the summer months. It was idyllic, apart from the chilly sea – but that was accepted in view of the fact that we had no other experience of any warmer waters.

You can imagine the shock then, when going for a stroll to our beach, we found it out of bounds to the public and guarded by troops. It was soon covered by mines and spikes and barbed wire. How sad a sight.

Months later and rationing began to bite seriously (especially for my poor mother trying to make meals). One day I was walking on the promenade overlooking the sea and was horrified to see the incoming tide bringing in broken boxes and hundreds of oranges, swollen in size by the water. I remember I nearly cried because this fruit was what we really needed but these oranges would never be eaten; they would return to the sea on the outgoing tide.

I suddenly felt a shudder when I realised that there must be seamen from sunken ships many miles out to sea, struggling in the icy cold water with little chance of rescue. On telling my father of what I had seen, he said, 'Let's all say a prayer for the poor men who will have given their lives in an effort to keep us fed.'

This is in memory of those who died.

Mrs C Walker

Memories of the Blitz

I was almost seven years old when Hitler enforced my evacuation from London, label and gas-mask round my neck, carrying a little brown case. I spent a couple of months with a large family in Dunmow in amazement at their happy noisiness before the authorities realised that this was exactly below the flight path of German bombers jettisoning their loads when they couldn't get through to London. With a pleasant young couple in Kings Lynn I lived another life, although I was regularly slyly

pinched and kicked by the son of the house who saw me as threatening his domain.

Getting back to my London home was a welcome relief, at a time of low blitzing, and I joined with relish in the occasional night-time adventures of wailing sirens and rushing down to the half-buried Anderson Shelter in our garden, or for a social change to neighbours' shelters, where grown ups played cards as I lay on a bunk listening to the whistle and crump of bombs and noisy machine-gun fire.

Returning home in the dawn, with the soothing steady all-clear, it was always necessary to climb over mounds of broken glass even when there had been no nearby bombs – was it caused by the mobile anti-aircraft batteries?

As the Blitz reached new levels I was off again, this time to a family in a large council house on the edge of Cullompton in Devon. With Mr and Mrs, Grandpa and son Jimmy I settled in to rural life for several years so that when my mother made her occasional visit – travelling in wartime trains was no easy or safe life – she could barely understand my accent.

As things calmed down I joined my family in Caversham, near Reading, where I happily lived with my parents, sister and brother in a single room with a cold water tap and an outside loo. Looking back I am amazed we all coped so well and easily with such conditions. Reading was not immune from Nazi raiders and a single bomb, falling at lunch time on the town's British Restaurant, killed hundreds. My primary school in Hemdean Road was a between-the-wars single storey building with large asphalt playgrounds. It was so obviously a school but a Nazi fighter thought it a good idea to strafe it one Wednesday afternoon – which thankfully was a half day off – certainly lucky for me for when I came in next morning I found a machine-gun bullet had passed through the lid of my desk.

Tony Lake

Dinner with the enemy

I can remember two or three German POWs coming to our house for Christmas dinner. I think it was the year 1945. I have always admired my parents for welcoming the POWs into their home, especially as they were poor even by the standards of those days and it must have stretched the budget. My father fought with the Canadian Expeditionary Force in the Great War and I wonder if it was a result of his experiences then that coloured his actions that Christmas.

From what I remember, the German POWs were billeted at the back of the local steam laundry and worked on concreting a large area. I do recall them teaching me the German numbers, something that came in useful much later when I spent some time in Berlin.

Mrs J Z Chambers

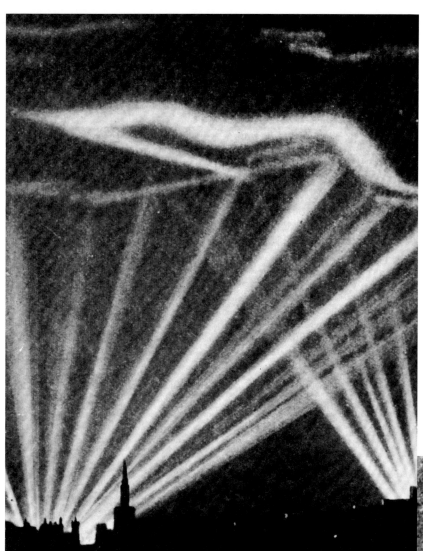

PATTERNS OF WAR

When viewed from afar, war can produce some compelling and often strangely beautiful images. Here are three examples.

On the left we see an array of searchlight beams probing the night sky over London during the Blitz. Below left, a slow exposure camera has captured a curtain of ack ack fire aimed at British bombers over Germany.

The final image shows a flotilla of German mine-sweepers at work in the North Sea. The hulls and trailing paravanes of the ships make intricate wave-patterns on the surface of a calm sea.

The Mediterranean and North Africa

The Italian entry into the war on 10 June 1940 was an opportunist strike by Benito Mussolini. With France already on her knees and about to surrender and with the BEF bundled off the Continent in the face of Hitler's Blitzkrieg 'Lightning War' tactics, the Italian dictator saw the chance to seize British and French overseas dominions and enlarge the Italian empire at a bargain cost.

Mussolini thought there would never be a better time for expansion. Even if Britain did not surrender to Germany the country would clearly need every available soldier, sailor and airmen plus their weapons, ships and aircraft, in order to defend their home island. He expected to make an easy conquest of British and French colonies in Africa, advance into Egypt to take the Suez Canal and turn the entire Mediterranean into an Italian-dominated lake.

But Mussolini seriously miscalculated British resolve. Though the latter were vastly outnumbered in manpower, ships and aircraft, morale was high and there was a confidence that they could beat the Italians in all forms and theatres of warfare.

Britain's advantages included holding Gibraltar, a fortified cork in the neck of the bottle that is the Mediterranean. Then there was the little British-held island of Malta with her Grand Harbour and airfields, just a short flight (60 miles) from Sicily. Much farther away from Italy, Alexandria on the north coast of Egypt was the main home of the Royal Navy's Mediterranean Fleet. The Suez Canal gave another advantage in that reinforcements and supplies from the British Empire in the eastern hemisphere could be easily transported to Egypt and Palestine where the British held sway. Or they could be brought

around the much longer sea route from Britain via South Africa and the Cape.

Faith, Hope and Charity

However, depending on who could wrest command of the air and sea, these advantages could quickly become disadvantages. When the war in the Mediterranean began, Britain had about 400 combat planes in the Middle East, including some on Malta. The Italians lined up 1500 machines that were newer and faster than most of the RAF aircraft.

Immediate air attacks were directed at Malta but the obsolete fighters on the dusty little island proved more than a match. In June 1940, at one point the island had just three Fleet Air Arm Gladiators – dubbed Faith, Hope and Charity – to defend itself from enemy bombers. By July the trio had been augmented by the arrival of four Hurricanes. Then in August 1940, Italian troops in Abyssinia (Ethiopia) invaded British

Right: Italian cruisers in line astern. Their fleet was a powerful one and a big threat to the Royal Navy in the Mediterranean once Italy had entered the war.

Somaliland. The small British garrison withdrew, largely intact, across the Red Sea to Aden. At the same time, other Italian troops began to move westwards from Abyssinia into the Sudan in order to seize the upper Nile Valley. They quickly captured Kassala and Gallabat, while more Italian troops moved south to take Moyale, in the northern part of the British colony of Kenya.

The British did not flee nor surrender and the Italians realized they were in for a hard fight. Accordingly, they changed their plans and decided to postpone their offensives from Abyssinia until they had captured the Suez Canal. This would enable them to move forces by sea to reinforce their East Africa army.

The advance into Egypt from Libya began on 13 September 1940 with an army of some 200,000 men backed by a powerful air fleet all under the command of Field Marshal Rodolfo Graziani. They reached Sidi Barrani, in north-western Egypt, and halted. Wary of the difficult Western Desert terrain, before pushing on, Graziani wanted to build up a massive stockpile of supplies and he even had a pipeline built to bring freshwater to his front-line troops.

Outnumbered five to one

The British Middle East force of just under 30,000 men was commanded by Field Marshal Archibald Wavell. He was outnumbered by nearly five to one. A further headache came in the form of the French garrison of Syria who were under the sway of the Vichy authorities, who were themselves, in turn, puppets of the Germans. The latter were also interfering in politics in Iraq, the main source of Britain's fossil fuel supplies.

More trouble occurred in the north of Greece when Italy launched an invasion of this British ally from across the border with Albania. Wavell was ordered to send aircraft and material support to the Greeks but he clung on to most of his manpower. In the event, the Greeks rebuffed the Italians.

Back in the desert Wavell seemed to face impossible odds on all fronts but it was now that he displayed unique qualities of leadership and military imagination. He decided to keep small forces in Kenya and the Sudan, gambling that the Italians would keep quiet. He did the same for Palestine and Iraq. Then he concentrated every available man, armoured vehicle and gun in Egypt's Western Desert opposite the dug-in Italians at Sidi Barrani. The British commander on the spot was the highly rated soldier, General Richard N O'Connor. By early December 1940, his army comprised about 40,000 men.

O'Connor's spectacular success

Despite being greatly outnumbered, Wavell ordered the attack to start on 9 December. It met with immediate and spectacular success as the British raced through a gap in the Italian line; some units dashed for the coast at Sidi Barrani while others turned left and right to create chaos and confusion behind the Italian defences. Within two days nearly 40,000 Italians surrendered while the rest streamed westwards pursued by the British who later made a bold foray across the bulge of Cyrenaica to overtake the enemy who mainly kept to the single coast road that followed the North African shore.

By 7 February 1941, Wavell and O'Connor's army had advanced 500 miles. In the process they had killed, wounded or captured over 130,000 men together with 1290 artillery pieces, 400 tanks and masses of ammunition and supplies. All this at a cost of 2000 British killed or wounded.

If Wavell had been allowed to maintain his momentum he surely would have gone on to expel Italy completely from North Africa. But now there was more trouble brewing on the other side of the Mediterranean; it appeared

> 'Wavell's victory was spectacular with 130,000 Italians captured together with 400 tanks and masses of war material. British losses were 2000 killed or wounded.'

that Hitler was about to intervene in the Balkans in order to assist Mussolini in his so far unsuccessful attempt to occupy Greece.

Military aid for the Greeks

Wavell was apprehensive about going to the aid of Greece if the Germans really did invade. However, Churchill was determined to demonstrate solidarity with the Greeks in a tangible form; he thought it would send a clear message to the likes of neutral Turkey, Russia and Yugoslavia that Britain was prepared to rally around to help its friends. Thus the victorious Western Desert Force – including many ANZAC troops – found itself crossing the Mediterranean to Greece and a confrontation with a tough and seasoned foe who was bound to prove far more competent than the Italians. Just one infantry division and one untrained armoured brigade were left to defend newly conquered Cyrenaica.

Even before Wavell's North African victory

was complete, the commander began reinforcing his forces in East Africa and put them under the command of Sir Alan Cunningham. His force soon numbered about 70,000 men but was still only a third the size of the Italian army. The British advance into Abyssinia and Italian Somaliland began on 15 January 1941. The Italians offered token resistance but then fell back. By 26 February, the British were in Mogadishu, capital of Italian Somaliland (now Somalia). Abyssinia's capital, Addis Ababa, was taken on 6 April. By May the main Italian army had surrendered and by the end of the year all of Italian East Africa was firmly under British control.

Before this happened, there were developments in North Africa that gave the British an unpleasant surprise. In March 1941 Hitler sent two divisions – one armoured and one infantry – to Tripoli, the Libyan capital. The Afrika Korps had arrived.

In April 1941, Raschid Ali seized power in Baghdad. Backed by German Luftwaffe units he intended to deny British access to the oilfields of Iraq and eventually pave the way for an Axis invasion of Egypt from the Middle East. Raschid Ali's army of some 7000 men laid siege to the RAF base at Habbaniya where the No 4 Flying Training School had some 60 Audaxes. Together with a few advanced pupils, the RAF instructors flew around 1400 sorties against the enemy in May 1941. The siege was broken by the end of the month and Raschid Ali was forced to flee Iraq. No 4 Flying Training School had saved an entire country for the Allied cause and also safeguarded Persia's oilfields as well as those of Iraq. This painting of the Battle of Habbaniya is by Frank Wootton and is reproduced with the kind permission of Mrs Virginia Wootton and the RAF.

'Stringbags' at Taranto

Though it boasted an impressive array of warships, the Italian navy (Regio Marina) was loath to risk its battleships following an inconclusive encounter with the Royal Navy off Punta Stilo in Calabria on 8–9 July 1940. This was, in fact, the largest engagement of the two navies in the entire war and featured battleships, cruisers and destroyers plus, on the British side, the aircraft carrier *HMS Eagle*. The Italians should have had the big advantage of shore-based air cover but their bombers operated from too great a height to have any accuracy and the British ships could take evasive action. Both sides also kept their distance. At one point a duel between the battleships *HMS Warspite* and *Giulio Cesare* was fought at a distance of 15 miles, setting the record for naval gunnery against a moving target that has stood ever since. *Warspite* made one hit on the Italian ship before both sides withdrew, their missions to shield respective convoys heading for Benghazi and Malta fulfilled.

As the year went on, Italian pressure on Malta mounted and the Royal Navy deemed it a top priority to damage the Italian fleet's fighting capacity. On 10 November a British reconnaissance aircraft sighted five battleships, 14 cruisers and 27 destroyers at anchor in the important Italian naval base at Taranto. Another battleship joined the fleet on 11 November. In a daring and well-planned strike that night, 21 Fairey Swordfish torpedo bombers – affectionately known as 'Stringbags' – flew from *HMS Illustrious* to launch a low-level attack. Though obsolete and slow, the *Swordfish* were very robust and the raid was pressed home through a storm of defensive fire. Three battleships were seriously damaged (one being put out of action for the rest of the war) and two cruisers hit for the loss of two aircraft.

Lesson learned by the Japanese

On 13 November Churchill told the House of Commons: 'Taranto was a glorious episode that reflects the greatest honour on the Fleet Air Arm. This result, while it affects decisively the balance of naval power in the Mediterranean, also carries with it reactions upon the naval situation in other quarters of the globe.'

Churchill's observation was extraordinarily prescient. It was not only the first all-aircraft naval attack in history but the raid on Taranto also influenced the course of the coming war with Japan. Tokyo's interest in the operation was intense and a naval delegation was at once sent to Taranto to study the operation and its consequences. A year later their findings were put into devastating practice in the surprise attack on the American Pacific Fleet in Pearl Harbor.

Victory at Cape Matapan

Taranto was not the end of the Regio Marina. On 27 November the two navies clashed off Sardinia at the Battle of Cape Spartivento after the Italians sailed out of Naples to intercept a convoy bound for Malta. The engagement took place at long range and hits were scored by both sides before the Italians withdrew. A few

Above: Taranto, 11 November 1940. Frank Wootton's painting shows Fairey Swordfish from the aircraft carrier Illustrious *delivering a devastating blow against the Italian fleet. Reproduced with the kind permission of Mrs Virginia Wootton and the Fleet Air Arm Museum, Yeovilton.*

days earlier a tragedy occurred when eight Hurricanes and a Skua were lost in the Med after they ran out of fuel. The aircraft had been launched too early from the *Ark Royal* to search out Italian warships.

It was to be March 1941 before the Royal Navy struck the decisive blow to Italian sea power. On 27 – 29 of that month, Ultra intercepted signals that placed a major enemy fleet to the south west of the Peloponnesian Islands of Greece. The existence of the Ultra codebreaker had to be kept top secret. Therefore a reconnaissance aircraft was sent out with orders to make sure it was spotted by the Italians.

The British force sailed out of Alexandria to do battle. The ships included the aircraft carrier *HMS Formidable*. The two opponents met off Cape Matapan and in the resulting engagement three heavy cruisers and two destroyers of the Reggio Marino were sunk and other ships damaged. Total Italian casualties were 2303 dead with many more wounded. The British lost just a single torpedo bomber. In an act of chivalry rare in the war at sea, the British commander, Admiral Andrew Cunningham invited the Italians to send a hospital ship to pick up survivors as it was judged the risk of being attacked from the air made it too dangerous for the Royal Navy to linger in the area.

WAR DIARY 1940

"Two German agents were hanged in Pentonville Prison on 10 December. They were the first spy executions to be announced in Britain during this war."

27 September: Germany, Italy and Japan conclude a military, political and economic Pact in Berlin. In brief, Japan recognizes the leadership of Germany and Italy in the establishment of a new order in Europe while Germany and Italy recognise Japan's desire to establish a new order in East Asia. Japan is now a member of the Axis. Although she is not at war with Britain, Japan will assume the right to a footing in French Indo-China (Vietnam), Siam (Thailand) and the Dutch East Indies.

11 October: British and Commonwealth forces are fighting the Italians in North and East Africa. RAF bombing raids are made today over Benghazi and Tobruk in Libya as well as targets in Asmara, Eritrea, and Gura in Abbysinia.

22 October: There are 25,000 Belgians now living in Britain. Today they're joined by their Prime Minister and Foreign Minister after the pair escaped from detention in Spain and flew to the UK. The Germans are angry that Spain did not hand the politicians over to them.

27 October: Figures released by the Ministry of Shipping show that the week ending 20 October was the blackest week of the war so far for the Mercantile Navy mainly due to U-Boat actions; 47 British, Allied and neutral vessels were sunk sending 154,279 tons to the bottom of the sea. The situation is greatly improved this week with just 16,860 tons lost.

28 October: At around 6am today Italian troops begin an invasion of Greece, crossing the frontier from their bases in Albania in several places. This follows an ultimatum demanding that Greece give up certain strategic points so that the Italians can counter alleged British influence and provocations in the region. General Metaxas, President of the Greek Council, rebuffs the threat. King George of the Hellenes states: 'At this moment I am sure that every Greek man and woman will do their duty to the end and will show themselves worthy of the glorious history of Greece.' Under a guarantee given on 13 April 1939, Britain pledged to come to the aid of Greece if she were attacked. Following a Greek request for aid, within a few hours British air and naval forces prepare to intervene.

1 November: Press coverage is given to the 'Eagle' Squadron of the RAF. Led by Colonel Charles Sweeny and composed exclusively of American volunteer pilots (34 at present), it has taken its place as an operational unit of Fighter Command.

8 November: A tomato-grower, George Turner, along with eight islanders, has escaped from occupied Jersey in a small boat skippered by an Irishman. Quoted in the *News Chronicle*, Mr Turner says: 'The Germans told us that the Channel Islands would be German forever and that we were all Prussians from now on. They also told us that their Foreign Minister, Rippentrop, would be the boss for Germany after they had invaded England.'

9 November: Neville Chamberlain dies. Britain's Prime Minister on the outbreak of war, he will always be remembered for his trip to Munich in 1938 from which he returned with a piece of paper signed by Hitler that Chamberlain believed guaranteed 'Peace in our time.' Ironically, last night saw RAF bombers successfully attack Munich's rail marshalling yards. It is believed that Hitler was in the city at the time to celebrate the anniversary of his 1923 Beer Hall Putsch.

Succeeded by Churchill as Prime Minister on 8 May 1940, it has been said that Chamberlain always had the greatest admiration for the man but harboured ... 'a fear of his restless genius in a peacetime Cabinet.'

12 November: The Italian dictator Mussolini boasted that his forces would be in Athens within 12 days of invading Greece. That deadline has come and gone and instead the Italians are reeling from a series of defeats amidst the rough mountain passes and meagre roads in the border area of Greece and Albania. British troops have been arriving in Crete in a move that threatens the Italian-held Dodecanese Islands of which Rhodes is the largest.

Eighty Italian biplanes on a bombing mission are routed over the Thames Estuary with 13 of them shot down.

14 November: Coventry is hit by a big raid that leaves the Cathedral wrecked and 172 people dead. Nazi propaganda will describe towns and cities subsequently hit by similar indiscriminant attacks as having been 'coventrated'.

20 November: Hungary is the latest country to sign up to the Axis Pact. Officials in Budapest maintain that 'Hungary's position is similar to that of Japan, namely, the closest collaboration in the common aim of the signatories of the tripartite pact, but without belligerency'. Slovakia and Rumania will sign in the next few days and it is no secret that Germany seeks for Spain and Bulgaria to also join.

21 November: London Zoo's celebrated ravens, Jack and Jill, have been bombed out of their home. Jack is safe but Jill has not been seen since the raid.

30 November: On this Saturday night Southampton is the target of a big air raid that leaves the city centre smouldering. Casualties total 370 killed or seriously wounded. Thousands of people lose their homes and the workplaces of many more are destroyed.

5 December: The King visits Southampton to inspect the bomb damage. Reporting on the raid the *New York Times* says: 'The Germans can no more destroy the spirit of this seaport city than King Canute could push back the waves. It will be rebuilt. The deep ship sirens will echo through the streets again. New armies of Americans will visit it with a new reverence as one of the places where ordinary men and women died for freedom.'

10 December: In the first spy execution to be announced in Britain during this war, two German agents are hanged in Pentonville Prison today. The men had been posing as refugees but were found to have a German-manufactured radio set. Their brief had been to pick up as much military information as possible and were promised swift relief when the German invasion of Britain took place.

15 December: The Italian armed forces are being routed by the British Army of the Nile in North and East Africa and by the Greeks who have now advanced well into the south of Albania. Polish, Free French, Indian and South African troops are fighting with the British in North Africa.

19 December: London has its first Air Raid Alert in four days following a nationwide lull in German air raids.

25 December: On Christmas Day 1940 no enemy bombs fall on Britain.

28 December: London's night life underground is becoming highly organized. Food trains carrying hot drinks, meat pies, sausage rolls, sandwiches and so on now regularly draw up at dormitory platforms where thousands of people go to escape the bombs. Statistics show that in one night Tube shelterers consume 30,000 buns, more than 21,000 slices of cake and 13,000 gallons of cocoa.

1941

WAR DIARY 1941

5 January: The pioneer woman aviator Amy Johnson is killed when her aircraft crashes into the Thames estuary. A ferry pilot with the Air Transport Auxiliary, Miss Johnson is thought to have lost her way in bad weather and ran out of fuel. The naval trawler *Haslemere* saw her bale out and went to the rescue. The trawler skipper, Lt-Commander W E Fletcher, dived into the ice-cold water in an heroic attempt to save the pilot. He reached Miss Johnson but himself succumbed to exhaustion and extreme exposure and died on arrival at hospital. In 1930 Amy Johnson became the first pilot to fly solo from England to Australia in an epic 19-day journey.

7 January: The founder of the Boy Scout movement, Lord Baden-Powell, dies in Kenya.

10 January: News is received that the British island of Nauru in the South Pacific has been bombarded by a German surface raider bearing Japanese colours. The island's phosphate industry has been put of action for many months to come.

Press reports allege that there are dozens of German ships sheltering in Japanese harbours ready to make for the open sea when the word is given. *The Daily Telegraph* has highlighted the *Scharnhorst* (not to be confused with the Kriegsmarine warship of the same name). The newspaper says that the 21-knot turbo-electric liner is being fully reconditioned below decks and that armaments have been observed being taken on board, contrary to international law. Recently a captured Norwegian tanker, converted by the Germans into a prison ship, entered Kobe port, discharged her prisoners, took aboard provisions and water and steamed away without interference. British warships used to patrol outside Japanese ports to prevent this practice but the Royal Navy no longer has enough ships for this purpose.

15 January: After five years of exile Haile Selassie, 'Lion of Judah, King of Kings of Ethiopia', has crossed the frontier from the Sudan into his own country.

20 January: The Vichy France Government is having problems coping with the number of Jewish refugees from Germany who have sought sanctuary within its territory. An appeal to the USA to take the refugees has been turned down on several grounds, one being that it would be playing into Hitler's hands to receive Jews whom he is driving out of his country and another that no distinction could be made between refugees on religious and racial considerations. Beside these reasons the US say that immigration quota limits were already filled. Relief

Mystery of Raid on Curacao

In a story attributed to 'sources in New York', the British press has reported that a German raiding party attempted to destroy oil refineries on the island of Curacao in the Dutch West Indies six months earlier on 28 July. Apparently the raiders came ashore from a surface ship but were detected by members of the British garrison who had been on the island since 11 May to prevent the oil falling into enemy hands. In the ensuing fighting involving machine-guns, rifles and hand grenades it is said that 35 of the raiders were killed or wounded. There were no figures given for British casualties. Two tankers were in dock to be loaded with aviation fuel at the time of the attack. Though it is recorded that German U-Boats occasionally lobbed shells at the island's oil refineries, no further information on this apparent commando-style raid has been uncovered.

> **21 March: Oil-rich Iraq in the Middle East is pledged to give Britain the right to maintain air bases in the country. In the event of her being invaded, then the Iraqi armed forces would have the support of Britain. The oil of Iraq and neighbouring Iran is vital to sustaining Britain's war machine.**

supplies of food and clothing are being transported from America to unoccupied France unimpeded by the Royal Navy. This concession follows an appeal by President Roosevelt.

31 January: In response to questions as to why German bombers can range over Britain on nights when the RAF suspends raids on Germany, it is explained that the RAF policy is to attack definite military objectives. On the other hand, the Luftwaffe appears to bomb indiscriminately and have the advantage of operating from much closer air bases in Occupied Europe.

14 February: World famous American aviator Charles Lindbergh – first man to fly across the Atlantic Ocean – has been publicly pessimistic about Britain's chances of defeating Germany. Senior US political and military figures are now contradicting Lindbergh and backing Britain to win the war.

15 February: A small British force has been parachuted into the Calabria region of Italy to damage the regional water-supply system. Today Rome reports that they have been captured and will be 'treated as prisoners of war in the honourable and chivalrous manner which is characteristic of the Italian people'. In London the Ministry of Information announce: 'Soldiers dressed in recognized military uniforms have been dropped in Southern Italy to demolish certain objectives ... some of the men have not returned to their base.' Later it will be learned that one of the raiders was Fortunato Picchi, former assistant banqueting manager of London's Savoy Hotel. Having fought for Italy in the Great War as an ally of Britain, he had been in England for 20 years and was an anti-fascist, despite being interned for a while on the Isle of Man after Italy had entered the conflict. He volunteered to parachute with the British into Calabria to act as a guide. Unfortunately he was captured, charged with sabotage and shot near Rome on Palm Sunday.

21 February: Swansea endures a third consecutive night of fire-bombs that have wrought massive damage and caused considerable casualties. It seems the Germans are targeting British city after city for concentrated bombardment. Swansea joins Liverpool, Manchester, Portsmouth and many others in the air war front line.

Sir Frederick Banting, discoverer of the wonder-drug insulin, dies in an air crash at Trinity Bay, Newfoundland. He was flying to England on a mission of high scientific importance, rumoured to be linked to developing a new method of combating the effects of poison gas on the human body.

1 March: The current conflict is revealed as the costliest war in Britain's history with the average daily expenditure revealed as £10,500,000.

The Greek town of Larissa is badly damaged by an earthquake. RAF personnel in the area turn out to help the residents with medical assistance. Twice in the day Italian aircraft drop bombs on the town; after the last raid all five of the enemy planes are brought down.

WAR DIARY 1941

Bulgaria became a satellite of the Axis today when Premier M Filoff signed up to the Tripartite Pact in Vienna. Simultaneously, German troops crossed the Danube and moved into the country.

4 March: British forces stage a major raid on Norway's Lofoten Islands to destroy fish oil plants. The oil is a major source of glycerine for making explosives and the Nazis lose 50,000 barrels and much vital equipment as a result of the attack. Eleven German ships are sunk while the Allies sustain no fatal casualties. Over 200 Germans are taken prisoner and 300 Norwegians return with the Royal Navy to join fellow patriots in exile.

14 March: The British press is often speculating on the prospects of war with Japan in the Pacific Ocean and Far East. Noting that the Pacific covers a quarter of the surface of the globe, the importance of the American Pacific Fleet base at Pearl Harbour in the Hawaiian Islands is frequently stressed. Some American newspapers are dismissive of the Japanese threat. *The New York Herald Tribune* has asked whether the Japanese dare confront a potential USA, British Commonwealth and Dutch East Indies coalition '... when their army is third-rate and more than waist-deep in the Chinese bog. Their navy's worth is untried and short of fuel. Finally, they are down to living off the population's jewellery. Can they risk it, even if they would?'

18 March: Secret plans have been made for a British invasion of the Canary Islands should Spain enter the war on the side of the Axis.

21 March: Oil-rich Iraq in the Middle East is pledged to give Britain the right to maintain air bases in the country. In the event of her being invaded, then the Iraqi armed forces would have the support of Britain. The oil of Iraq and neighbouring Iran is vital to sustaining Britain's war machine.

27 March: Two days after Yugoslavia's Prime Minister Dragisha Tsvetkovitch signed up to the Tripartite Pact with Germany, Italy and Japan, there is a coup d'etat in Belgrade. Those associated with the effective surrender of the country's independence are arrested and King Peter assumes power. Hitler is furious; Churchill says that the Yugoslav nation has 'found its soul'.

4 April: German soldiers are in North Africa to bolster the faltering Italians. Today it is announced that the Axis forces have captured Benghazi in Cyrenaica. The British have greatly weakened their army in North Africa in order to counter the Nazi threat against Greece and Yugoslavia.

6 April: Preceded by no declaration of war, the Germans invaded Yugoslavia and Greece at dawn today, striking from Austria in the north right round to across the Bulgarian border in the south east. German troops will also go to assist the Italian forces struggling against the Greeks in Albania. The British public is surprised to hear that a British Expeditionary Force drawn from the Army of the Nile was already in Greece.

15 April: The lightning advance of the German 'Afrika Korps' continues and today they claim to have reached Egyptian sand.

17 April: With Belgrade already occupied, Yugoslavia today surrenders in the face of the German onslaught. Fighting continues in Greece.

18 April: German soldiers have advanced past both sides of Mount Olympus as British, Anzac and Greek forces retreat.

19 April: British Imperial forces land in Basra to reinforce the British garrison there and 'safeguard lines of communications' in Iraq. A pro-Axis politician, Rashid Ali, has come to power and believes Britain is going to lose the war. Iraq's oil is vital to the British war effort and it is imperative that the Nazis do not gain control of it.

20 April: Two nights ago and last night, London suffered bombing raids worse than any since 29 December 1940. Both attacks lasted practically from dusk to dawn and casualties were heavy with many civilian and service personnel dead and injured.

22 April: Malta suffers its worst night raid since hostilities began.

26 April: The outnumbered Greek army has been fighting with little pause for six months and the strain shows as they crumble against the onslaught of fresh German formations who enjoy complete air superiority. Local surrenders have been proceeding for some days. A final broadcast is made from Athens tonight: 'Greeks, stand firm. Be each one proud and dignified ... have Greece in your hearts... Greece will live again and will be great because she fought honestly for a just cause and for freedom.' Just a few hours later the Germans march into the Greek capital.

27 April: It is reported that four fifths of the BEF and Dominion troops in Greece have been successfully evacuated though they have lost a lot of transport and heavy equipment.

2 May: Iraqi troops attack the British air base at Habbaniya, south west of Baghdad. The British Middle East Commander responds by ordering forces in India he can ill afford to spare to proceed to Iraq. It is known that German and Italian fighter pilots are preparing for action on an airbase at the oil centre of Mosul, north of the Iraqi capital.

3 May: On the 609th day of the war, it is announced that just two destroyers, *HMS Diamond* and *Wryneck*, have been sunk during the course of the evacuation of British forces from Greece. British forces are preparing defences on the island of Crete.

7 May: Churchill addresses the House of Commons and explains the background to the Allied reverses in North Africa in the face of determined German drives led by the resolute and

Poetry Across The Ocean

Winston Churchill and the American President Roosevelt have struck up a warm and close friendship. Both have characters cast in heroic mould. Churchill recognizes that the USA is the key to democracy winning the battle against totalitarianism. In a personal letter to the British Premier penned in January 1941, Roosevelt concludes with a quotation from the American poet Longfellow:

Sail on, Oh Ship of State!
Sail on, Oh Union strong and great.
Humanity with all its fears,
With all the hope of future years
Is hanging breathless on thy fate.

Churchill, too, recognized the power of poetry. In a broadcast to the nation on the evening of Sunday 27 April 1941, he ended with an extract from a poem by Arthur Hugh Clough, '*Say Not The Struggle Nought Availeth*' with words which could have applied equally to Britain as well as the US:

For while the tired waves, vainly breaking,
Seem here no painful inch to gain,
Far back, through creeks and inlets making,
Comes silent, flooding in, the main

And not by eastern windows only
When daylight comes, comes in the light
In front, the sun climbs slow, how slowly
But westward, look, the land is bright.

WAR DIARY 1941

opportunistic General Erwin Rommel. Acknowledging a swift reversal of fortune in the Western Desert, the Premier says: 'Tactical mistakes were committed, missed chances occurred and our armoured force became disorganized ... when the Germans won their surprising success, they exploited it with that enterprising and organizing audacity which ranks so high in the military sphere. They pushed on into the blue, or might I say the yellow ochre of the desert, profiting by their easy victory ... with little thought of what they should eat or drink. They pushed on until they came up against Tobruk.' Churchill concludes: 'Loss of the Suez Canal, loss of our position in the Mediterranean, loss of Malta would be among the heaviest blows we could sustain ... We intend to defend to the death and without thought of retirement, the valuable and highly defensive outposts of Crete and Tobruk.'

10 May: The world will be astounded when it hears the news that Hitler's Deputy, Rudolf Hess, has tonight parachuted down near Glasgow and jumping out of a Me 110. Hess had convinced himself that he could negotiate a peace with Britain that would allow the Nazis to turn their full military might against Russia. Hess got it badly wrong; he will be imprisoned in the Tower of London and at the end of the war will be tried at Nuremberg with the other Nazi war criminals. Hess will spend the rest of his life in Spandau Prison.

14 May: British dogs can now be registered with the War Office for national service. Only those of certain breeds and with natural qualifications of a high order will be recruited. Airedales, Collies, Cross-breds, Lurchers and Retrievers (Labrador and Golden) are the most suitable kinds, but other breeds will be considered provided that their intelligence and ability are of a high standard. Friendly aliens, such as the Alsatian, will not be turned down through prejudice! Successful dogs will serve in the army for the duration of the war.

16 May: History will consider tonight's attack on Birmingham by over 200 German aircraft to be the end of the full-scale Blitz on Britain. Even so, 90 bombers will strike at Liverpool and Bristol on 31 May. Some stray too far to the west and bomb Dublin where 28 people will die. Most of Germany's air formations are being moved east towards the border with Russia.

19 May: British forces in Iraq capture the town of Fallujah where Rashid Ali's army had moved after their siege of the RAF base at Habbaniyah was broken.

20 May: German parachutists and airborne troops drop in large numbers onto the Greek island of Crete.

27 May: 'I have just received news that the *Bismarck* is sunk'. With these words Churchill informs the House of Commons of the result of the dramatic five-day 1750 mile Atlantic chase between Hitler's most powerful battleship and the Royal Navy.

30 May: After a month of intermittent fighting, Rashid Ali flees Iraq and takes refuge in Iran. In the next few days, the pro-British Iraqi Regent, Emir Abdul Illah, and the young King Feisal will return to Baghdad to take up the reins of power. Around 600 Axis prisoners will be interned and 500 British hostages will be released.

The number of women ferry pilots is being increased in order to release more men pilots for service in the RAF. A lot of the men pilots in the Air Transport Auxiliary (ATA) are airmen debarred from RAF service for reasons of health or age – hence the nickname for the ATA of 'Ancient and Tattered Airmen'. But some of the men are suitable for active flying duties and the recruitment of more women will enable them to be redeployed.

Below: In 1941 before the German invasion of Russia there was much speculation about German intentions towards Turkey and the oil-rich countries of the Middle East, a vital source of supply for the Allied war effort. A continuous rail link between Berlin and Baghdad was completed in July 1940. It passed through neutral Turkey and as can be seen from the map below that country was the only obstacle between German troops in Rumania and Bulgaria and the oilfields of Iraq and Iran. Both the Allies and the Axis courted the Turks. There were an estimated two million soldiers in the Turkish army and they would give a massive advantage to whatever side they might choose to join.

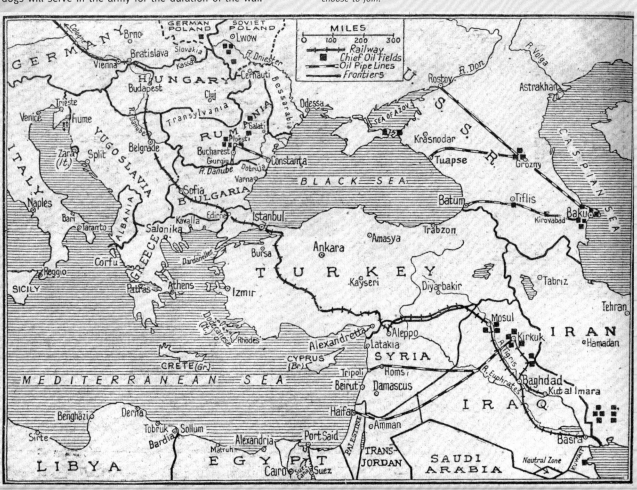

Von Werra: The One That Got Away

German pilots captured after being shot down over Britain proved to be enthusiastic escapers. Franz Von Werra was one persistent example. After several unsuccessful attempts to abscond in this country, he was transported to Canada where he was successful in escaping across the frozen St Lawrence into the then neutral USA. With help from the German consul he got to Mexico then Rio in Brazil from where he got a passage in a neutral ship bound for Barcelona. He arrived back in Germany to a hero's welcome on 28 April 1941. On that same day, back in Canada 28 German prisoners tunneled their way out of a POW camp in Angler, Ontario. All were quickly recaptured.

Back to Germany

Von Werra is believed to be the only German POW to escape from a British or North American camp and get back to the Fatherland. A friend of Von Werra – Lieutenant Walter Manhard – escaped from an Ontario camp and made it to New York where he decided to stay. Manhard gave himself up in 1952 and by then he had married an American woman who was an officer in the US Navy. Another intrepid but ultimately unsuccessful escapee was Karl Robe whose attempts included one using a home-made hot air balloon measuring 24ft by 10ft.

Von Werra flew again with the Luftwaffe. On the Russian Front he raised his tally to 21 'kills'. But back in Western Europe his luck finally ran out when his aircraft disappeared without trace in the course of a flight over the North Sea on 25 October 1941.

Our Superb Women

The Australian Prime Minister, Robert Menzies, visited Britain in **May 1941**. Before leaving for America he broadcast a message to the nation in which he paid particular respect to the women of Britain: 'If anyone were to ask me, "What is your outstanding impression of Britain today?" I can think of many things. I can think of Winston Churchill, the resolute and supremely eloquent embodiment of the British fighting spirit. I should think of the Royal Air Force; the boys in blue uniforms questing among the clouds or groping in the dark empyrean for the invading bomber. I should think of the factories with wounded roofs and walls, with shattered homes about them, roaring out their busy answer to the enemy. I should think of the strange new life in Tube shelters and basements, often grimy and drab and yet a life accepted philosophically as part of the price of a just war. I should think of the men of the Fire Service and Bomb Disposal Squads. I should even think of that frequently forgotten man, the London taxi driver, always, as it seems, old, whiskered, casually humorous, cap on head, battered pipe in mouth, plying his humane trade while bombs fall. I should think of many things, all of them great and moving.

'But my answer to the question would still unhesitatingly be: The courage, the action, the endurance of Britain's women. Wherever I go I see them and I marvel at them. Is it possible to believe that not long ago we called them "the weaker sex"? Women conducting vast organizations; women in the uniforms of the Navy, the Army, the Air Force; women at fire brigade stations in blue overalls, always ready; women driving great vehicles; women digging in the fields; women at their gentle work of nursing the sick soldier; women doing their turn of fire-watching in their own suburban streets as the incendiary bombs rain down. In any war factory you may see hundreds of women not merely doing the fine precision work of testing and gauging but wielding the hammer, operating machines, riveting metal sheets; all in trousers and overalls. And everywhere I heard the same story; the morning after the blitz the women are on time and they are on the job. If they have tears to shed, they shed them privately. They are among the great soldiers of this war.

'The vast movement of women into the service of the nation, doing these things and a hundred others, is spectacular. It marks the beginning of a new era. It will usher in enormous social and other changes about which one can only speculate.'

War at Sea

Hurricanes, Catapults and Condors

range. Most of the modified aircraft were assigned to the Fleet Air Arm, although the RAF retained and operated a few. The aircraft were manned by pilots from the specially formed Merchant Ship Fighter Unit, based at RAF Speke near Liverpool.

The first CAM to deploy was the *SS Michael E* in May 1941. Ironically, she was sunk by a torpedo before having a chance to employ her fighter. By the end of 1941 the CAMs and their Hurricats had drawn first blood, shooting down five Condors. The first victory was achieved by Lt R W H Everett RNVR who was awarded the DSO for the destruction of a Condor on 3 August 1941. After Everett ditched his aircraft it rapidly sank but he managed to exit the cockpit under water and was rescued. Before the war, Everitt rode several times in the Grand National. In a newspaper interview he said that as a water-jump Becher's Brook was not to be compared with the Atlantic!

Three ships sunk under him

In the same period that Everitt won his medal, a young radio officer in Britain's Mercantile Marine was unfortunate, but not unique, in having three ships sunk under him. Ian A Phillips left England in a convoy in early August. Several days later the ships were bombed in the afternoon and attacked by a U-Boat in the evening. Next day at 3am Ian's ship was hit by two torpedoes and went down in 15 seconds. A non-swimmer, he already had his lifejacket on and was picked up by another ship after 150 minutes in the sea. After surviving a further air attack by a Condor, he reached Gibraltar and joined another convoy that set sail in September. They were shadowed by a German aircraft who must have alerted U-Boats to their position. On the second day of their subsequent attack on the convoy, Ian's ship was hit and he again found himself in the water until he was picked up by a ship's lifeboat. At 5am the lifeboat occupants got aboard a ship; at 6.30am this vessel was also torpedoed and Ian had to jump for it yet again. He joined 21 men packed like sardines in a lifeboat with the seas running high in a north-westerly gale. They drifted for 15 days, surviving on rain water and meagre rations, before landing on a small, sandy beach on the coast of Galway, Eire. Three of his companions died in the course of the voyage.

Britain was in a desperate fight for survival. Isolated from Occupied Europe, the country was relying on an ocean lifeline extended from the USA via merchant convoys. Plying the North Atlantic, out of range of land-based air cover, the convoys were subject to attack by German U-Boats and surface raiders and from the air, in the main from the long-range Focke-Wulf Fw 200 Condor. First operating from Norway and later from France, the Condors were able to fly far out to sea, beyond the reach of the RAF, and provide detailed reports on convoy positions to waiting wolf packs or launch their own bombing attacks on under-armed merchant ships. Between June 1940 and February 1941, Condors alone accounted for sinking over 365,000 tons of shipping.

Something had to be done. Sea-based air power was an obvious answer, but it would be some time before escort carriers could be developed.

Once launched, no way back

Meanwhile a stopgap solution was proposed in the shape of a modified Hurricane fighter that could be catapulted from a merchantman. Informally called the 'Hurricat', they were deployed on specially configured merchant ships called CAMs – Catapult Aircraft Merchantmen. The big drawback was that once launched there was no way to recover the Hurricane – the pilot would either have to fly to the nearest land airport or be forced to ditch alongside a merchantman and hope that he would be subsequently picked up. After August of 1941, long-range tanks were added to the Hurricat to expand its

> **Everitt rode several times in the Grand National. But he always said that as a water-jump Becher's Brook was not to be compared with the Atlantic!**

The North Atlantic in 1941 presented a deadly spiderweb of hazards for the myriad merchant ships sailing from America and Canada to the British Isles. Without this lifeline the war effort could not be maintained and Nazi dominance of the air and land would go unchallenged. Who would have thought that a handful of primitive bi-planes, affectionately dubbed 'Stringbags', could have made a major difference to the course of the war at sea?

At first the chief threat to the convoys came from the U-Boats. But then in May of 1941 came a nightmare scenario. The mighty German battleship, *Bismarck*, slipped her Norwegian fjord moorings and sailed out in search of easy targets for her massive long-range guns. *Bismarck's* captain had orders to join battle with the Royal Navy only if he had to. Vulnerable merchant shipping was her priority prey. To broaden the canvas the weather was a common enemy to both sides; high cruel seas crowned with white breakers, low cloud and

Peter Champion recounts an extraordinary tale linking a young air cadet and a veteran Fairey Swordfish pilot who helped sink Germany's mightiest battleship, the *Bismarck*.

rain. The Atlantic took no prisoners!

Here's how the timetable of destiny unfolded in the late spring of 1941.

22 May. 6.30pm. A Martin Maryland twin engine reconnaissance aircraft reports *Bismarck* and the cruiser *Prinz Eugen* departing from Bergen, Norway. They steer into the Atlantic on a north west course that will take them between Iceland and Greenland. The Admiralty in

London is alerted. British capital ships are despatched post haste.

23 May. Cruisers *HMS Norfolk* and *Suffolk* sight and shadow *Bismarck* and *Prince Eugen* in the Denmark Strait.

24 May. 6.30am. The battleship *HMS Hood*, pride of the Royal Navy, engages *Bismarck* and a duel of 15 inch guns ensues. At 6.37am *Hood* takes a shell from *Bismarck* into her main magazine. There is a massive explosion. From a complement of 1441 men just three survive. The Atlantic is in greedy mood with an appetite for more death and destruction.

Frightening weather

HMS Prince of Wales, another British battleship, sustains damage in the duel with *Bismarck*. Winston Churchill issues a signal to the Admiralty: 'Sink the *Bismarck*.'

At this time the aircraft carrier *HMS Ark Royal* is steaming up from Gibraltar. The vessel is part of Force 'H'. Their mission is to traverse the Bay of Biscay and get between *Bismarck* and Brest,

Sink the Bismarck!

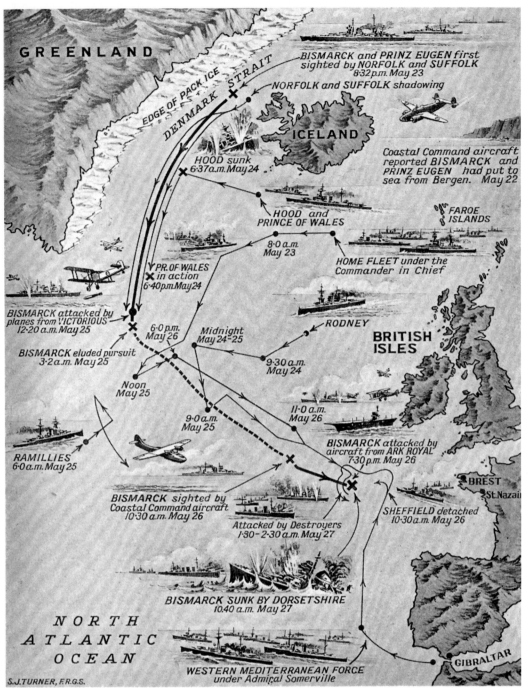

GREENLAND

EDGE OF PACK ICE

DENMARK STRAIT

BISMARCK and PRINZ EUGEN first sighted by NORFOLK and SUFFOLK 8·32 p.m. May 23

NORFOLK and SUFFOLK shadowing

ICELAND

Coastal Command aircraft reported BISMARCK and PRINZ EUGEN had put to sea from Bergen. May 22

HOOD sunk 6·37 a.m. May 24

HOOD and PRINCE OF WALES

FAROE ISLANDS

8·0 a.m. May 23

HOME FLEET under the Commander in Chief

PR. OF WALES in action 6·40 p.m. May 24

BISMARCK attacked by planes from VICTORIOUS 12·20 a.m. May 25

6·0 p.m. May 26

Midnight May 24–25

RODNEY

BRITISH ISLES

BISMARCK eluded pursuit 3·2 a.m. May 25

9·30 a.m. May 24

Noon May 25

9·0 a.m. May 25

11·0 a.m. May 26

RAMILLIES 6·0 a.m. May 25

BISMARCK attacked by aircraft from ARK ROYAL 7·30 p.m. May 26

BISMARCK sighted by Coastal Command aircraft 10·30 a.m. May 26

BREST
St.Nazaire

SHEFFIELD detached 10·30 a.m. May 26

Attacked by Destroyers 1·30–2·30 a.m. May 27

BISMARCK SUNK BY DORSETSHIRE 10.40 a.m. May 27

NORTH ATLANTIC OCEAN

S.J. TURNER, F.R.G.S.

WESTERN MEDITERRANEAN FORCE under Admiral Somerville

GIBRALTAR

The flak from the ship's battery of 4.1in anti-aircraft guns looks impossible to avoid.

Moffat holds the Swordfish steady in the turbulent air and rain, with one hand on the control column and the other on the torpedo release button. His Observer, now unstrapped in the cockpit and literally leaning out of the aircraft peering down at the giant waves, shouts above the roar of the engine and bursting anti-aircraft shells: 'Not yet... not yet... not yet.' He knows that for a successful launch and a true torpedo run they must launch into the crest of one of the waves and not a trough. Suddenly the Observer shouts: 'Now!'

Moffat presses the button. The torpedo drops. Moffat holds his course as the *Bismarck* fills the windscreen, framed in the frightening flak. The Observer shouts: 'Running straight and true.'

Out of harm's way

The pilot banks his aircraft in a tight turn to fly low over the crests of the waves and out of harm's way. Moffat and his Observer do not see their torpedo hit the *Bismarck's* steering gear. They do not know that the mighty battleship has been so badly hurt that she is unable to steam in a straight line and is doomed to sail in a circle. But they do make it back to *Ark Royal*.

The remaining Swordfish score two other hits. Refuge in Brest and the comfort of Luftwaffe fighter cover is now a forlorn hope for Hitler's flagship.

27 May. 11.01am. *Bismarck*, pride of Germany's battle fleet, is sunk by the pursuing British ships. Of her crew, only 112 survived. In a dreadful irony of war, many Kriegsmarine sailors drowned simply because the Royal Navy ships could not hove to and risk attacks from any lurking German U-Boats. The cruel Atlantic had claimed the lives of more than 3000 men in just three days.

Three years later...

Let's now move forward to 13 June 1944. It was the day I met Lt John Moffat. Yours truly was a cadet in the Air Training Corps, having joined despite being under the 14 years of age limit (along with about half our Squadron, No 1933). Some 20 of us were on an ATC summer camp at the satellite airfield of Selham in Hampshire. Selham sported Swordfish and Albacore, the latter boasting the luxury of Perspex covered cockpits.

One day we were visited by a young Fleet Air

a heavily defended deep water port on the Atlantic coast of occupied France. Aboard *Ark Royal* is young Lt John Moffat, a Fairey Swordfish pilot.

In the meantime, Fleet Air Arm Swordfish from the British carrier *Victorious* sight *Bismarck*, on a south east course heading for Brest.

25 May. 12.20am. Swordfish from *Victorious* attack *Bismarck* and make a single torpedo hit amidships. She slightly reduces speed. The valiant Swordfish crews now have to battle frightening weather with high seas, rain squalls and darkness in order to get back to *Victorious*. An Air Staff Officer on the carrier hears the first plaintive call from a returning Swordfish asking for bearings. Searchlights are switched on. By 2.30am all had landed back on *Victorious*; three of the pilots performing their first-ever night deck landing in the process. By 3am *Bismarck* has eluded the searching pack of British warships and disappears into poor visibility where she will stay obscured for nearly 24 hours.

26 May. 10.30am. *Bismarck* is spotted by a

vigilant Coastal Command Catalina flying boat. The signal is relayed to *HMS Ark Royal*, now in the area.

26 May. 11.15am. *Ark Royal's* Swordfish locate and shadow *Bismarck*. Shortly after 8pm 15 Swordfish loaded with torpedoes assemble on the flight deck of the aircraft carrier: *Ark Royal* is pitching 15 to 20ft in the white capped waves and the howling wind. Lt John Moffat is one of the pilots taking off in these testing conditions, not made any easier by the fact that his cockpit is open to the elements. Behind him is strapped his Observer. As the bows of *Ark Royal* rise on yet another wave the aircraft moves forward and suddenly they are airborne.

Through the poor visibility and enveloping clouds, *Bismarck* is located and the 15 Swordfish make their independent attacks. Lt Moffat drops his aircraft down to 50 feet. Torpedo attacks are usually made at a range of 900 yards. The art in aiming is to allow for the ship's movement during the torpedo's running time. Now approaching the *Bismarck*, Lt Moffat sees the target looming larger by the second.

Arm pilot with his 'wings' displayed on the left arm of his tunic. He arranged with the CO at Selham to fly the cadets around for what he called an 'air experience flight.' The only aircraft available was a Percival Proctor, a small single-engined liaison aircraft.

As my turn came to fly a fellow cadet sidled up and said, 'you know who he is don't you?'

'Lt Moffat' I replied.

'Yes', agreed my confidant, before adding, 'he's the guy who tin-fished the *Bismarck*.'

'Bloody hell,' I said and climbed aboard the Proctor.

We did a gentle circling climb to 1500ft and a few more turns and then John Moffat let me try my hand. The results were not good. John Moffat was smiling as he took control: 'We'll go down now,' he said .

Emotion beyond terror

'Going down,' as he put it, consisted of flicking the Proctor on to its back and diving vertically at the ground. The green fields and other aircraft on the field were hurtling up at us at an alarming rate. If there is an emotion beyond terror, I experienced it at that moment.

My fear was not diminished by John Moffat heaving back on the stick as we pulled out of the dive. I looked at the mirror just above the instrument panel and was transfixed by the sight of all the flesh on my face being pulled towards my chin. A first experience of 'G' force! It was to be repeated many times later in my 17 years as a glider pilot, but fortunately you get used to it. I climbed out of the cockpit of the Proctor and the next cadet heaved himself aboard. On the ground another cadet asked, 'What's it like?'

'Piece of cake,' I lied, adding a manufactured grin. I still have my ATC Flying Log. In it an entry reads: 13 June 1944. PROCTOR. Z7248. J. Moffat, Lt. 10 min. turns.

The war trundled on. There were other ATC camps, but they were tame compared to that one. After hostilities ceased I often wondered what became of Lt John Moffat. Then, approaching the age of 40, I suddenly switched from being a sales manager to being a professional aviation artist. At first the quality of my art and consequent sales of my paintings were meagre. My wife returned to work so that we could afford to put some jam on the bread.

Top: Peter Champion's ATC Flying Log that records the flight of an RAF Proctor aircraft on 13 June 1944. The pilot was Lt John Moffat and his passenger was young air cadet Peter Champion enjoying a flight experience.

Peter went on to become an accomplished aviation artist. He depicted Lt Moffat's attack on the Bismarck *in the painting on page 71.*

In 2006 Peter and John renewed contact after an interval of 62 years. Peter was astonished to learn that the former Swordfish pilot still had his own aircraft (right) which he flew as often as possible.

But over the years my painting skills improved and so did sales.

Some 20 years ago I completed what I consider one of my best paintings, the attack by Lt John Moffat and his Swordfish on the *Bismarck*. I also attempted to find out what had happened to him but drew a blank. Time rolled by and it was not until the year 2006 that the veil was lifted.

Discovering the Ark Royal

A BBC TV programme – *Shipwreck Ark Royal* – told the story of the sinking by a U-Boat of *Ark Royal* on 14 November 1941. The precise location of the wreck was pinpointed with ultra-modern search equipment. The *Ark* sat upright on the sea bed, her 20,000 tons of metal quite clear in the radio controlled undersea search vehicle's cameras.

John Moffat (he'd retired from the Fleet Air Arm as a Lt Commander) was given the opportunity of controlling the landing of the submersible on the deck of the sunken ship. He performed a perfect touch down and, well over

six decades after his return to the *Ark* following the attack on the *Bismarck*, he could justly claim to be the last man ever to land on *Ark Royal*.

His address in the programme was given as Dunkeld, Scotland. With this limited address I wrote to him and enclosed a print of my painting. He wrote back including a snap of himself standing by his own Piper Colet (which he still flew at least every week, weather permitting) and a black and white photograph of the wartime Proctor in which I had completed my 10 minute flight with him in 1944.

It was simply an astonishing and humbling experience to be in contact with this man again after over six decades. I learnt that just a month or so before the RAF had flown him down to Yeovilton for the weekend to honour his achievements. Whilst there he flew a dual control Jet Provost for an hour and more – quite an achievement for a man then 86!

To me, though, he will always be that intrepid Fleet Air Arm pilot who 'tin-fished' the *Bismarck*, and introduced a very young air cadet to the forces of 'G'.

Salute the Stringbags

Despite being bi-planes and looking obsolete, Swordfish flew operationally with the Fleet Air Arm right through the Second World War. Probably the aircraft's finest hour came with the attack on the Italian fleet at Taranto. Originally planned for 21 October – Trafalgar Day – 1940, the operation finally took place on 11 November. Torpedoes from the Swordfish sunk or crippled Mussolini's finest fighting ships as they lay at anchor.

A Swordfish operating out of Gibraltar is credited with the first sinking of a German U-Boat by an aircraft at night on 21 December 1941.

The last contact between a Swordfish and a U-Boat was recorded on 20 April 1945 when the aircraft dropped two depth charges on a periscope but failed to destroy the vessel.

A Swordfish is also believed to have made the last attack of the war on enemy shipping when it bombed a midget submarine spotted stranded on a sandbank. This incident took place just three and a half hours before the German surrender came into effect on 4 May 1945.

On 21 May 1945 the last operational squadron to fly Swordfish, No 836, was disbanded.

WAVES OF TIME

EYE WITNESS

HMS Dorsetshire's role

I was fortunate to watch the whole action with long-range binoculars from the exposed position high up on the After Conning Position of *HMS Dorsetshire* with Commander Bias. *Dorsetshire* had left a convoy, SL74, of 43 ships in the sole charge of an armed merchant cruiser in order to race to the action.

At 09.00hrs on 27 May, proudly streaming her battle ensign, *Dorsetshire* arrived unexpected out of the mist, to be greeted with a salvo from one of our own capital ships that screamed over our heads and landed off our port quarter. Not being expected, *Dorsetshire* was mistaken for the German battle cruiser *Prinz Eugen* that had been previously escorting *Bismarck*. Frantic signals soon made our presence known to the rest of the Fleet.

At 09.10hrs with only the destroyer *HMS Zulu* between us and the *Bismarck*, *Dorsetshire* commenced firing, first with salvos and then with full broadsides. Much has been recorded of *Dorsetshire* sinking *Bismarck* with torpedoes without mention of the 254 main armament shells it fired with great accuracy into the battleship. German survivors remarked afterwards on *Dorsetshire*'s rate of fire and its destructive effect, especially when the second salvo put their Fire Control out of action.

At 10.25hrs Admiral Somerville in the battle-cruiser *Repulse*, commanding Force H, unable to arrive in time for the action signalled C in C Admiral Tovey in *HMS King George V*: 'Have you disposed of the enemy?' The reply was: 'Have to discontinue action for fuel.' A short time later she added: 'She is still afloat.' At 10.44hrs the C in C sent a general signal to the Fleet: 'Any ships with torpedoes are to use them on *Bismarck*' and a few minutes later sent a message to Force H to the effect that gunfire would not sink the German vessel.

Captain Martin on *Dorsetshire* had

anticipated the C in C's order and had already started his approach to attack with torpedoes. The Fleet had departed the scene before *Bismarck* finally sank, leaving the destroyer *HMS Maori* and *HMS Dorsetshire* to pick up survivors. Most of the Fleet were running short of fuel and there was the added danger of a Luftwaffe air attack from Brest. Of the estimated 2200 ship's company on board *Bismarck*, 112 were rescued; *Dorsetshire* picked up 82 while *Maori* rescued 25. A further two were found by the German weather ship *Sachsenwald*. Three more (Georg Herzog, Otto Hontzsch and Herbert Manthey) were taken aboard the *U-74*. Her captain had been ordered to rendezvous with *Bismarck* to pick up war diaries.

Midshipman Brooks, later Commander Brooks, jumped into the oily water to tie lines onto Germans unable to climb the ropes. He was later severely reprimanded by Martin for endangering his own life. The Spanish cruiser *Canarias* arrived later to help with the rescue but reported it could only find floating dead bodies. Made aware of the presence of a U-Boat, Captain Martin aborted the rescue and left the scene refusing to endanger his ship and crew, Whilst returning to England one of the survivors, Gerhard Luttich, unfortunately died from his injuries although our surgeons tried hard to save his life. His coffin was brought on to the Quarter Deck and draped with the Imperial German flag because a Nazi flag was not available. With the German survivors lining one side and British sailors the other, a short service was conducted before the ship stopped engines and his canvas-encased body was committed to the deep.

When rescued the German survivors received the best care we could provide and little luxuries that were available such as chocolate bars, cigarettes and playing cards were freely given by our people.

I myself have some experience of the German sailors' feelings of desperation in the water for at 16 years of age I had to jump into the Atlantic in my underpants without a life belt when I survived the sinking of

A computer-generated image of how the Bismarck rests on the seabed of the Atlantic nearly three miles down. The wreck was discovered in 1989. The first manned submersible to visit the site went there in 2001 when a memorial plaque was placed on the ship's hull.

the aircraft carrier *HMS Courageous*, with the loss of 518 souls. At the age of 19 years I jumped, again without a lifebelt, into the Indian Ocean when *Dorsetshire* was sunk by the mass attack of dive-bombers and fighters from the combined Japanese carrier force of Admiral Nagumo. It was nearly 30 hours later, hanging on to a piece of flotsam, before I was eventually found.

JOHN CANNON

Bismarck resurfaced?

A crew member of the Polish destroyer *Priorun*, Richard Polanski, wrote an article for the 1995 *Caithness Field Club Bulletin* describing his destroyer hitting the *Bismarck* with torpedoes and 4.7" gunfire and later seeing the Stringbags attack. Long after the *Bismarck* sank it reappeared upside down and Richard had time to examine the hull, failing to see signs of their torpedo hits, before it sank again.

Presumably the submerged hull was turned over by the great weight of armour and guns, and, when the gun turrets fell free, became buoyant again. The finding of the *Bismarck's* hull on the sea bed, the right way up but missing the gun turrets, would appear to support this account.

Incidentally gun turrets were not normally secured to the deck and on one occasion in World War Two a destroyer in the Pentland Firth pitched violently and tossed out the rear turret.

GEOFF LEET

Ludovic Kennedy's account

The final sinking of the *Bismarck* was witnessed by sailors on the British destroyer *HMS Maori* and the cruiser *HMS Dorsetshire*. Even the British Home Fleet flagship *HMS King George V* and the other battleship present at the final gun battle, *HMS Rodney*, were forced to turn for home before the *Bismarck* sank. Admiral John Tovey RN, C in C Home Fleet onboard *HMS King George V*, only saw *Bismarck's* final moments through his high powered binoculars. A German survivor said she rolled over, the bow pointed into the air and she sank by the stern. Royal Naval accounts confirm this report.

The Polish *Priorun* was part of a group of destroyers under Captain Vian RN who commanded the famous *HMS Cossack*. Another destroyer present was *HMS Tartar*. Onboard *HMS Tartar* was Sub Lt Ludovic Kennedy RNR. He has written probably the most accurate record of *Bismarck's* one and only operational voyage. His book *Pursuit: The Sinking of the Bismarck* is still in print and is a fair and balanced record of those dark days.

While destroyers did fire torpedoes at *Bismarck* none was successful. The Swordfish aircraft of *HMS Ark Royal* did deliver a torpedo hit on the *Bismarck's* rudder which effectively ended the *Bismarck's* dash for the German-held French ports. *HMS Dorsetshire* hit the *Bismarck* with torpedoes after the gun battle had left her a blazing, wrecked hull.

The Polish sailors onboard the destroyer *Priorun* that took part in the sinking were brave men and we all have much to thank them for together with their brave colleagues in the Royal and Commonwealth Navies and the RAF. We should also pay a small tribute to the American airmen who, having delivered Catalina flying boats to the RAF, then, unofficially, went on RAF operational missions to instruct the new owners. In 1973 Ludovic Kennedy tracked down one of these men – Ensign L R Smith USN. It was he who sighted the *Bismarck* making for France after the British had lost contact.

One irony is that Ludovic Kennedy's father, Captain E C Kennedy RN, was lost at sea on the Armed Merchant Cruiser *Rawalpindi* in 1939 when she was sunk by the German battle-cruisers *Scharnhorst* and *Gneisenau*. Commanding the German squadron was Admiral Lutjens. Admiral Lutjens lost his life on the *Bismarck*.

A J SLATTER

Posted from the Bismarck

In early February 1976 while serving on *HMS Ashanti* we visited Hamburg. Part of our duties was to host guests and we entertained the equivalent of the RNA one afternoon. Amongst the guests was a gentleman called Hans Zimmermann and we chatted about many things, two of which were the *Bismarck* and the action in the North Atlantic and stamp collecting.

A few days later I was piped to the gangway, where Hans was waiting for me with an elderly lady. This lady was the widow of an Engine Room Petty Officer who was lost when the *Bismarck* sunk. She had with her a letter from her husband, posted whilst he was on the *Bismarck* and she wanted me to have it. In the end, I persuaded her to keep the letter and just let me have the envelope.

Reading about the *Bismarck* and the Stringbags brought this all back to life for me and made me think of how families on both sides suffer from the terrible effects of war. I believe Hans Zimmermann died a few years ago and no doubt the lady has as well, due to age, but I will be forever grateful for the memories shared.

DAVID THOMPSON

HMS Rodney and the Bismarck

Quite by chance I found myself right in the middle of the final action. I was training to be an observer in the Fleet Air Arm, and the flying school had been moved from Sussex to Trinidad as being a safer place to fly. Our party of 45 formed part of a large draft which embarked in the battleship *HMS Rodney*. We were to be dropped off at Halifax, Nova Scotia, with the ship continuing on to the US for a major refit. Life on the lower deck at sea was something new to us all, not least finding out how to rig a hammock and find our way to the galley!

Two days out we heard of the news of the destruction of *HMS Hood*. Later contact with *Bismarck* was lost, but *Rodney* set off in a SW direction heading towards the Bay of Biscay. On

Right: This envelope was posted home to his wife by a crew member of the battleship. He perished when the *Bismarck was sunk in May 1941.*

the day before the action we were joined by the C in C Home Fleet flying his flag in *HMS King George V*. By this time both ships were flying quite enormous battle ensigns. We were told that unless contact was made early the following morning we would have to go home because of lack of fuel.

I had been roped in to be an extra lookout, stationed at the very top of the bridge superstructure, but was not required when we went to action stations, which we did at 20.00 hours. Our action station was an empty store room down below the armoured deck. I did not fancy being stuck down there for hours, having no idea as to what was going on topside so instead went up to the lookout station and mingled with the standby lookouts. Next day contact was made about 08.00, with *Bismarck* and *Rodney* engaging each other. German gunnery had a high reputation for quickly finding the range, and I just missed seeing the splash from one shell of the third salvo, just 20 yards short. Fortunately their accuracy fell away and the firing became ragged. We were closing the range rapidly and even without binoculars it was possible to see the damage being inflicted. The ship was reduced to a floating wreck, all firing long having ceased. We therefore left the scene, leaving *HMS Dorsetshire* to sink her with torpedos. Expected air attacks on the way home did not materialise, though the destroyer *Mashona* was not so lucky, being sunk the following day.

Some time later, having re-ammunitioned the ship, we had a quiet trip to Halifax where we transferred to the weekly mail boat for a pleasant cruise down the Windward and Leeward islands to Trinidad.

FRANK R BARCLAY

I served on HMS Rodney

At the time of the *Bismarck* engagement I was a Leading Seaman/Leading Torpedo Operator serving in the *Rodney*. My action station was in the torpedo (body) room where we had 16 torpedoes fitted with war heads. At the other side of the forward bulkhead was the torpedo tube room where the settings were put on the torpedoes according to orders from the bridge. Then either one or both torpedoes could be fired from the port or starboard tubes when the

Frank R Barclay pictured 'then and now'. The photograph in uniform was taken at a Naval Air Station in 1944. Three years earlier he had been aboard *HMS Rodney* when she went into battle against the mighty *Bismarck*, a story he recounts on this page. 'One reason for joining the Navy' he says, 'was to travel and I spent over 18 months around West, South and East Africa followed by a spell in Bombay. Then, in the last winter of the war I did four convoys to Russia. My most vivid memory is of a Force 12 storm with gusts of up to 100mph. For a short time the ship rolled 45 degrees each way (I am not exaggerating – it's in the history books). So I think I was lucky to survive in one piece and lived to remember those days.'

rear doors were closed and the front doors were open. The tubes were fitted in the bows below the waterline.

After discharging all the torpedoes two of us were ordered to report to the damage control party situated in the ward room flat. However, we decided to go to the area at the rear of the bridge structure (known as the 'octopedial'), where an officer was stood watching the *Bismarck* which was on our port side about a half mile away. Our main armoury of 16 inch guns were firing salvo after salvo at the battleship and I remember seeing part of the ship's bridge disappear in a large flash. Shortly afterwards a shell from the *Bismarck* landed just short of the *Rodney* and showered us with cold seawater; the officer's cap was blown into the air.

We could see dozens of German sailors in the water as the enemy was still being battered by us and the battleship, *King George V*. I remember feeling sorry for the German sailors in the freezing sea for they were only, like us, following orders.

J E MCLEAN

WAR DIARY 1941

1 June: The War Office tonight announces that British forces on Crete are being withdrawn: 'Some 15,000 of our troops have gone to Egypt but it must be admitted that our losses have been severe.' The German airborne forces have also suffered high casualities. One of the Fallschirmjager killed on Crete is Max Schmeling, former world heavyweight boxing champion.

All clothing and footwear is subject to rationing from today. Each Briton will have 66 clothing coupons to last for 12 months. An overcoat for a man requires 16 coupons; a woollen dress or gown for a lady needs 11 coupons.

3 June: After seeing how effective Germany's airborne troops can be in campaigns even before the latest one in Crete, Britain is rapidly building up a parachute force comprising volunteers from the army.

British troops occupy Mosul, removing the last element of possible resistance in Iraq.

8 June: An Allied army of some 20,000 Free French, British, Imperial and Indian troops is moving into Syria from Palestine, Transjordan and Iraq. The aim is to end Vichy French control of the country and reverse the growing German influence in Damascus.

12 June: Civilian losses due to the German bombing campaign in the period September 1940 to the end of April 1941 amount to 34,284 killed and 46,119 wounded. April was a particularly bad month with 6065 killed and 6926 wounded.

16 June: There is press speculation that Cyprus – Europe's third largest island – may be the next target of a German airborne invasion. A few weeks ago Italian aircraft bombed the island for the first time.

President Roosevelt has ordered the freezing of all German and Italian assets in the USA.

18 June: Lord Beaverbrook broadcasts an appeal for technicians with radio and electrical experience to come forward to aid the war effort. Recently, the existence of Britain's vital radar device has been made public and now many more men and women are required to maintain and develop radar and similar technology.

20 June: Miss Jacqueline Cochran of New York today became the first woman to pilot a bomber across the Atlantic. The experienced pilot hopes to deliver many more bombers to the RAF.

22 June: At dawn today, the Wehrmacht supported by the Luftwaffe and Axis partners attack the Soviet Union along a massive front of over 1100 miles from the Baltic to the Black Sea. *Operation Barbarossa* involves three million soldiers and is the largest invasion in history. Army Group Center, commanded by Fedor von Bock, attacks north of the Pripet Marshes from Brest-Litovsk. Army Group North, commanded by Wilhelm von Leeb, attacks through the Baltic states in the direction of Leningrad. Army Group South, commanded by Gerd von Rundstedt, attacks south of the Pripet Marshes toward Kiev. In the far south, the 11th Army of Romanians and Germans attack into Bessarabia. German planes begin bombing and strafing Soviet airfields. By the end of day, 1200 Russian aircraft are destroyed.

24 June: The Spanish Foreign Minister encourages Spaniards to volunteer to fight with Germany against Russia. Within days, 18,000 openings for a complete division will be filled. The unit will become known as the Blue Division. On this day also a gathering of young Falangists outside the British Embassy in Madrid turns into a riot and stones are thrown at the building.

26 June: It is reported that the 450,000 Jewish inhabitants of Warsaw have been forced into a small area enclosed by high walls. German policemen exercise ruthless control within this ghetto.

Finland declares war on Russia. The Finns hope to recover the territory they were forced to cede to the Kremlin at the end of the Winter War in 1940.

2 July: An Imperial conference is held in Japan. Leaders decide to try to settle the conflict in China and prepare for war with Britain and America, if diplomacy fails. Japan will not enter the German-Russian war now, but if the conflict develops to its advantage, it will use its military strength to secure its northern borders.

12 July: After putting up an unexpected tough resistance to the Allied invasion, Vichy French commander, General Dentz, surrenders to the Allies in Syria. With victories in Iraq and now Syria, General Wavell has successfully

GET THERE ON A .....
GAZELLE

WARNING UNEXPLODED BOMB

DROP IN FOR A CATALOGUE

PRINTED IN ENGLAND

WAR DIARY 1941

removed threats to the rear of the British position in the Middle East and safeguarded vital oil supplies.

19 July: Winston Churchill starts the 'V for Victory' campaign in a BBC Radio broadcast to the world. The first four notes of Ludwig von Beethoven's Fifth Symphony match the Morse code for the letter 'V': dot dot dot dash. Listeners are instructed to tap the code, and to paint the 'V' in occupied territories.

20 July: Before the war, British smokers lit up about 195 million pounds of tobacco each year. The present consumption has increased to around 240 million pounds.

21 July: German bombers raid Moscow for the first time tonight. Britain is buying 150,000,000 tins of sardines from neutral Portugal.

A tablet has been unveiled in St Paul's Cathedral to commemorate Pilot Officer W M L Fiske, first American to die for Britain in this war.

26 July: Berlin has been regularly announcing fast progress in the German invasion of Russia with large numbers of prisoners taken. However, the Germans admit that their advances often leave Russian units at large in the woods and marshes behind their forces.

A raid by Italian E-Boats against Valleta is broken up by the Royal Malta Artillery. Later it is discovered that the E-Boats were a screen for eight small torpedo-carrying 'chariots' trying to access the harbour. All are sunk. Malta continues to suffer from bombing raids.

6 August: P G Wodehouse – creator of Jeeves – is attracting strong criticism in Britain because he is making regular broadcasts to America on Berlin radio. Wodehouse is an internee in Germany but is allowed to stay in the city's fashionable Adlon Hotel rather than an internment camp.

15 August: One year ago the Battle of Britain was fought out in the skies over southern England. Today those same skies are still full of aircraft but they are, in the vast majority, British aircraft going to and fro the Continent by day and night to bomb Axis factories, airfields, ports and rail links. The Russian Front is making tremendous demands on the German military machine; the Luftwaffe cannot sustain the bombing campaign at the same intensity as that of the Blitz on London and other major cities last winter and spring.

The RAF are using US-built Boeing B17 bombers which are designated 'Flying Fortresses'. They participated in a recent daylight raid on the battleship *Gneisenau* berthed at Brest.

19 August: Wing Cmdr Douglas Bader's fighter plane was brought down over France on **14 August** and the pilot captured. It was reported that one his two artificial legs was damaged so today one of his 'spares' was dropped over an enemy airfield. German fighter ace Adolf Galland apparently brokered the arrangement and guaranteed a safe passage to the RAF plane making the drop.

21 August: A test parcel sent to a POW camp holding British prisoners in Germany took five months to arrive, reports the *Daily Telegraph*.

26 August: A German aircraft drops several bombs on the Scilly Isles tonight.

27 August: Dusko Popov, former spy of Germany, now double-agent for Britain, meets with US FBI Bureau Chief J Edgar Hoover in Washington. Popov shows a German spy questionnaire, with a section asking detailed questions about Pearl Harbor, Hawaii, intended for Japanese intelligence use. Hoover will not act on the information.

28 August: In the Western Desert there exists a highly exclusive Allied club known as the 'Late Arrivals'. To be eligible for membership you must be an airman who has been shot down in action and has, on one's own initiative, succeeded in eluding the enemy and making it back to your base.

Spitsbergen: War in the Arctic

Some 360 miles to the north of Norway, on the very edge of Europe's frozen north, lies the archipelago of Spitsbergen. Not a tree grows there, hardly a bush. For four months of the year it sees perpetual daylight and for the other eight months it is plunged in darkness or, at best, half light. Yet even in winter, when Spitsbergen is covered with a thick mantle of snow, the white tracks crossing the wilderness are sooty with coal dust for here are some of the richest coal deposits in the world.

In **mid-1941** the island was home to around 750 Norwegian miners and their families while 25 miles away on the other side of the island there were some 2300 Russian miners. The 600,000 tons of coal produced annually had been going to the Germans, although they did not have a military presence on Spitsbergen. With Russia now counted as an Ally, it was decided that an expedition should be mounted with a view to destroying the mines and denying the Germans their coal supplies.

On **25 August 1941** a Royal Navy flotilla with Fleet Air Arm planes transported a mixed force of Canadian, British and Norwegian troops to the island. The men were well received by both the Norwegians on Spitsbergen and the Russians. Coal stocks were destroyed and machinery put out of action. When the naval force withdrew they took all the Norwegians with them. The Russians were evacuated on Royal Navy ships to Archangel.

Late in September 1941 the Germans moved in and constructed an air base from where they could harass Allied convoys delivering aid to Russia. When free Norwegian and British forces arrived in the following year they found the Germans had gone.

4 September: Finland turns down a German request that it should advance on Leningrad.

6 September: The British press reports that the Germans have taken a census of poultry in Belgium. Only one chicken per inhabitant is to be allowed. It is also reported that meat, bacon and eggs are now practically unobtainable in Norway.

8 September: German forces have surrounded Leningrad. The subsequent siege will last 900 days.

11 September: President Roosevelt broadcasts a warning to Axis ships against entering US water.

14 September: A trusted Soviet spy in Japan, Richard Sorge, informs Moscow that the Japanese do not intend attacking Russia. The disclosure will enable the Red Army to transfer large numbers of fresh troops from the east.

19 September: In the Grand Harbor of Gibraltar, the British naval tanker *Denbydale*, cargo ship *Durham*, and tanker *Fiona Shell* explode from charges attached by midget submarines of the Italian navy.

The Soviet Union's third biggest city, Kiev, falls to German Army Group South; 665,000 men are captured, the greatest number of prisoners ever taken in one battle, and the largest single military success in history. Kiev was defended for 72 days.

20 September: Some 700 British fascists interned in a camp at Peel on the Isle of Man riot in protest at their incarceration and conditions.

22 September: Five French boys aged between 16 and 19 who landed on the beach near Eastbourne five days ago after paddling across the English Channel from Occupied France in canoes were today entertained at Downing Street by Premier Winston Churchill. The boys say they left France in order to join the Free French leader Charles de Gaulle's forces.

BARBAROSSA

Hitler's invasion of the Soviet Union: The most titanic clash of arms and ideology in history.

On 22 June 1941 over four million Axis soldiers backed by masses of panzers and fleets of aircraft invaded Russia along a front of 1800 miles. Complete surprise was achieved and in just a few weeks the Nazi armies were reporting astonishing progress with 300,000 Russians taken prisoner, 4000 tanks and 3000 aircraft destroyed.

Hitler had predicted: 'We only have to kick in the front door and the whole rotten Russian edifice will come tumbling down.' As the summer of 1941 progressed and his armies advanced inexorably towards Leningrad and Moscow and fanned out across the vast open spaces of the Ukraine, capturing countless thousands more Russian soldiers in giant battles of encirclement, it seemed as if Hitler's uncanny instinct for conquest would triumph yet again.

Operation Barbarossa's goal was the rapid conquest of the European part of the Soviet Union west of a line connecting the cities of Archangel in the far north and Astrakhan on the shores of the Caspian Sea. By the autumn the Germans and their Axis partners looked poised for a stunning victory. Leningrad was surrounded, under siege by the Finns to the north as well as by the Germans advancing from the south. The great city of Kiev in the Ukraine was in German hands and the Crimea

was threatened. Most ominously for Stalin, Smolensk had fallen and on 1 September 1941 German Army Group Centre, commanded by panzer wizard General Heinz Guderian, was just 200 miles from Moscow.

Moscow's limitless manpower

Yet even as the Germans seemed unbeatable in battle they had already seriously miscalculated in three key areas. Firstly, how the sheer size of the Soviet Union posed massive transport and logistics problems for an attacker. Secondly, Moscow's manpower resources were limitless compared to those at the disposal of the Nazis. Thirdly, the Russian climate was Stalin's ally but would prove a deadly adversary for the Germans.

As September drew on, autumn rains turned roads to mud and bogged down the German armour and transport. Hitler's armies were still advancing but at nothing like the breathtaking pace of the summer. Then in November something happened to shock the German generals. Despite all their losses of men and territory the Russians mounted a big counter-attack against German forces moving on Rostov. The result was the first German reverse of the war and the realization that the Russians could field twice as many men as Hitler's intelligence services had predicted.

In December the Germans were in front of Moscow, a city Hitler had said he would capture before the end of the year. But winter had arrived with a vengeance and it caught the Wehrmacht totally unprepared for its harshness. There were few winter clothes and hardly any gloves and the German infantry suffered terribly if they fought in the open air. In temperatures that could drop as far as minus 30 degrees centigrade, their machines would not function. On the other hand, the Russians were well prepared and well used to the conditions. They had warm clothes and boots and they knew how to make engines and weapons work in the freezing conditions.

The Russians, led by General Georgi Zhukov, launched a big attack spearheaded by tanks and fresh infantry formations called up from Siberia. The Germans had no choice but to pull back as best they could. Moscow was saved and would never be threatened again.

Hitler's strongest blow is blunted

The aura of German invincibility was tainted by their defeat in the winter of 1941–42. It also greatly cheered Allied morale in the West where encouraging headlines on the course of the war were rare.

By the end of January, the Red Army had repelled Hitler's strongest blow. He had not achieved the expected victory, even though Russia's position remained precarious. Tactically, the Germans had won some resounding victories and would do so again in the spring and summer of 1942. But the winter losses meant that Germany could never again mount an offensive simultaneously along the entire Soviet-German front again.

Operation Barbarossa and the areas that fell under it became the site of some of the largest battles, worst atrocities, highest casualties, and most horrific conditions for Soviets and Germans alike

Barbarossa's failure led to Hitler's demands for further operations inside the USSR, all of which also eventually failed. These included maintaining the siege of Leningrad and initiating the drive on Stalingrad and the oil-rich Caucasus. In the course of the war Russia was the site of the world's biggest battles and some of the worst atrocities. The casualty toll was monumental with over 20,000,000 Russian dead, including countless civilians.

After their shattering defeat at Stalingrad in the winter of 1942–43 the Germans marshaled the strength for one last major effort to turn the military tide. At Kursk in the summer of 1943 occurred the greatest tank battle in history. The Germans lost and with that defeat the last chance for them to win the war, or at least reach a stalemate, was lost. After Kursk it was just a question of time before the Russian colossus would roll into the lands of Germany's allies and the German-occupied territories of Eastern Europe. By then the Nazi war machine would be damaged beyond repair; Stalin's triumphant Red Army could burst into the Fatherland at will.

Why was Stalin caught by surprise?

On 5 May 1941 Stalin gave a speech to graduates of Moscow's military academies in which he declared: 'War with Germany is inevitable. If Comrade Molotov can manage to postpone the war for two or three months that will be our good fortune, but you yourselves must go off and take measures to raise the combat readiness of our forces.'

Given the above statement by the ruthless and politically cunning Russian leader, why was it that some seven weeks later Stalin and the entire Soviet military machine seem to have been taken by total surprise when Hitler invaded? It's a mystery that has never been fully explained.

As early as 1925, Hitler made his intentions clear in his book *Mein Kampf* ('My Struggle'). He wrote that if he became leader – the Fuhrer – of Germany he would invade Russia, on the grounds that the German people needed Lebensraum ('living space') and that

these should be sought in the East. Nazi racial ideology cast the Soviet Union as populated by inferior Slavic people ruled by their Jewish masters. *Mein Kampf* said that the end of Jewish domination in Russia would also be the end of Russia as a State. Victory for the Nazis would lead to German mastery of the world. Pragmatically, Hitler added that Germany would 'walk part of the road with the Russians, if that will help us'.

Russians helped Germany beat British blockade

This explains Hitler's agreement to the Molotov–Rippentrop Pact signed shortly

Opposite page: German infantry backed by a panzer advance towards Moscow as winter draws on in late 1941. ***Above:*** *Britain sent Hurricane squadrons to Northern Russia to aid the Red Air Force. Here a British fighter is depicted in action alongside Russian planes. A Luftwaffe dive bomber is going down in flames beneath them (National Archives).*

before the German and Soviet invasion of Poland. Secret protocols outlined an agreement between the two powers on the division between them of the border states including hapless Poland. The pact surprised the world because of the two parties' mutual hostility and their opposed ideologies. Nazi Germany and the Soviet Union subsequently entered a trade pact in 1940, in which the Soviets received German military and industrial equipment in exchange for raw materials, such as oil, to help Germany circumvent a British blockade.

After Germany entered the Axis Pact with Japan and Italy, the Nazis presented a proposal for Soviet entry into the alliance. Moscow made a written counterproposal in November 1940, to which Germany did not respond. As both sides began colliding with each other in Eastern Europe, conflict appeared more likely, even though they signed a commercial and border agreement addressing several open issues in January 1941.

In preparation for *Barbarosso*, 3.5 million German soldiers and about one million Axis allies massed on the Soviet border along with vast tank and artillery parks. Hundreds of aerial surveillance flights were made over Soviet territory. Stalin certainly received intelligence of the build-up but chose to turn a blind eye. Perhaps he was convinced the Nazis must conclude their war with Britain before opening a new front. He also suspected the British of spreading misinformation intended to spark a war

Main picture: *German soldiers on the march. The swastika on top of the panzer is there so that Luftwaffe aircraft crew can identify it.*

Inset: *Countless thousands of Germans will never return home.*

between Germany and the USSR and therefore took no notice of several direct warnings from London of German intentions.

There must have been high-ups in the Kremlin who watched with horror the unfolding nightmare. Yet such was Stalin's iron grip on the whole apparatus of Soviet Government that the holder of any opinion that dissented from that of their leader risked being dismissed or, worse, sent to the gulags. Stalin's brand of tyranny was not so very different to that of Hitler. Except that in the end Stalin won.

Richard Sorge – Master Spy

Stalin had a master of espionage in Tokyo. Dr Richard Sorge was a tried and tested source of reliable information. He gave Stalin the exact date of the coming German invasion. But Sorge and other informers had previously given different invasion dates that had passed peacefully so, again, clear indications of imminent danger went unheeded.

The spy had earlier provided the Kremlin with information about Germany's position in respect of the Japanese attack on Russia's Manchurian territory in the Far East in 1939 (see page 14). Sorge's finest hour came with a key piece of intelligence about Tokyo's intentions in the early autumn of 1941. With the Germans threatening to occupy Moscow, Sorge confirmed that the Japanese would definitely not attack Russia even if Hitler requested their help. Stalin was able to move fresh Siberian divisions westwards to massively reinforce the exhausted Russians defending Moscow. They were put under the command of General Georgi K Zhukov who had defeated the Japanese. The appearance of the Siberians, well used to the harsh winter

conditions, changed the balance of power on the Eastern Front and saved the Russian capital. The Red Army's ultimate victory over Germany can be traced back to the receipt of Sorge's information.

Frederick Forsyth's verdict

Richard Sorge was born in the Caucasus region of Russia to a German parent and Russian mother. The family moved to Berlin when he was a child. In the Great War he served in the German army. Post-war he became a journalist and earned the respect of the Nazis. However, his secret Communist sympathies led him to offer his espionage services to the Soviet Union. He travelled widely and in 1929 visited England. Later he went to Japan in the role of a German journalist where he became a regular visitor to the German Embassy. Eventually the Japanese became suspicious of Sorge and he was arrested in Tokyo in October 1941. Ironically, at first they thought he was an agent for the Nazis. Though tortured, it is believed he did not admit to being a spy or

divulge the extent of his activities. Sorge was hanged on 7 November 1944.

Thriller writer Frederick Forsyth said of Richard Sorge: 'The spies in history who can say from their graves that the information they supplied to their masters, for better or worse, altered the history of our planet, can be counted on the fingers of one hand. Richard Sorge was in that group.'

WAR DIARY 1941

The substantial ethnic German population living in the area around Russia's River Volga where the main city is Stalingrad has been 'resettled' hundreds of miles to the east in the Novosibirsk and Omsk districts of Siberia and in the Kazakhstan Republic. A Soviet decree announcing the decision includes the statement: 'There are tens of thousands of diversionists and spies among the German population in the Volga region who are prepared to cause explosions... at a signal from Germany.'

A population of 600,000 is affected by the order. The majority are descended from Germans who were invited to settle in the region by Catherine the Great in the 18th century. Moscow maintains that the land in Siberia they have set aside for the exiled Germans is 'rich and fertile'.

2 October: Work continues on a Trans-Sahara railway running from Vichy France controlled North Africa south across the Sahara via Timbuktu to link with an existing line from Segou to Dakar on the West African coast. German engineers are supervising the construction. If the Germans occupied Dakar they would threaten Allied convoys heading for the Middle or Far East via the Cape. Dakar is also just eight hours flying time from Brazil.

12 October: The sound of distant artillery has been heard in Moscow for some days now, proof that the Germans are not far from the Russian capital.

16 October: The black-out has led to a big increase in deaths on the road. For example, in Britain in June 1941 road deaths totalled 618 while air raid fatalities numbered 399.

17 October: The Axis siege of the Black Sea port of Odessa ends with a Russian surrender. The Germans are expected to swiftly increase naval and U-Boat activity in this 700-mile long stretch of water that historically has been referred to as a 'Russian Lake'.

18 October: General Hideki Tojo has become Prime Minister of Japan. Nicknamed 'Lamisori' (the Razor), he is a committed militarist who will not hesitate to resort to force to further Japan's quest for regional domination.

19 October: Afghanistan announces that it is expelling all nationals of all countries that are part of the Axis Pact.

25 October: The first all-Norwegian squadron has been formed and is operational with the RAF. Free Norwegians – being seafaring folk – have, in the main, tended to join the merchant marine.

29 October: Roast cygnet could become a wartime dish if the Ministry of Food gives permission for swans to be killed for food purposes.

1 November: Moscow's population is copying what Londoners did back during the worst of the Blitz – they are sheltering underground in the Russian Metro stations. German raids are made almost nightly now.

2 November: A Reuters correspondent reports on preparations for defending the Khyber Pass in southern Afghanistan: 'Should Hitler, like Alexander, sigh for new worlds to conquer, his mechanised Nazi savages will find this portal to the riches of India heavily barred and locked with every defensive device against their lust for loot.'

4 November: Soviet troops evacuate Hango. Finland was compelled to lease the Baltic port to Russia in 1940.

7 November: Red Square, Moscow: Stalin addresses the Soviet people on the 24th anniversary of the Russian Revolution: 'We celebrate under difficult conditions. The treacherous attack of the German brigands has created a threat to our country. We have temporarily lost a number of regions and the enemy has appeared before the gates of Leningrad and Moscow.'

12 November: Sir John Hammerton, Editor of *The War Illustrated*, has penned the opinion: 'I sometimes speculate on what might have happened had the promoters of the Channel Tunnel scheme between 1918 and 1939 realised their aims. It was intended to unite France and England – a France that 45 years ago might have used it to our hurt, or sabotaged it, a France that 20 years later would have co-operated with Britain in its use against the Hun, and a Britain that in June 1940 would have had to destroy it as a protection against the effete and traitor-led French. So goodbye to all Channel Tunnel schemes "for a thousand years," as Hitler is so fond of saying.'

17 November: Siwa is an isolated oasis in the Great Sand Sea of Egypt's Western Desert that is the base of the British Long Range Desert Group. Now it is regularly visited by the Luftwaffe; the local Berber population seek shelter from the bombing in ancient tombs.

25 November: Certain Allied ships have been fitted with catapult devices that launch planes into the air. Once air-borne the plane can deal with an enemy long-range bomber or U-Boat threatening a convoy. Engagement complete, the aircraft must either fly to a land base or ditch in the sea as close to its mother ship as possible so that the pilot can be recovered.

Figures have been released that show the RNLI saved 136 lives in October 1941 from ships and planes in distress.

29 November: Heightened tension in the Far East leads to all leave for British forces in Singapore being cancelled.

1 December: The Nazis are ruthless in their suppression of any form of resistance in all the territories they control. Fifty hostages are reported executed at Bordeaux in reprisal for the shooting of a German officer. A similar incident a few weeks ago occurred in Nantes where 50 hostages were also shot.

3 December: The Russian winter is taking a heavy toll on the German armies before Moscow and Leningrad. In the south a Red Army counter-attack has led to the recapture of the key city of Rostov-on-Don.

6 December: Today the Russian forces in front of Moscow have changed from the defensive to the offensive and are battering the Germans. In the next five days the Red Army under General Sergei Zhukov will push back the Wehrmacht, destroy masses of tanks and artillery and recover great swathes of territory. Berlin radio will say that the Russian winter has been colder than usual and had come earlier than expected.

7 December: A quiet Sunday at Pearl Harbor on Oahu in the US Hawaiian Islands is shattered by a massive Japanese air assault on the American Pacific Fleet. When the attack began no declaration of war had been received in Washington. An hour after this assault, Japanese aircraft bombed the British colony of Hong Kong, again without warning.

10 December: Two of Britain's most famous ships are sunk by Japanese aircraft off the east coast of Malaya. *HMS Repulse* and *Prince of Wales* were heading a naval force aiming to intercept Japanese transports bringing an invading force to the shores of Malaya.

19 December: A Royal Navy flotilla – Force K – runs into a newly-laid Italian minefield. *HMS Kandahar* and *Neptune* are sunk and the light cruiser *Aurora* is badly damaged but is repairable. Force K was set up to intercept Axis convoys bringing reinforcements and supplies to North Africa. On 9 November the flotilla achieved a major victory in the Battle of the Duisburg Convoy, sinking nine Axis merchant ships and two destroyers to the south of Taranto in the Mediterranean. The British press reports that up to 7000 Italian soldiers have died following troopship sinkings.

25 December: Hong Kong surrenders on Christmas Day.

27 December: Malta has been on the receiving end of 60 air raids during Christmas week.

NIGHTMARE

Ingrid Pitt recalls a fraught wartime childhood spent in part in Stutthof Concentration Camp

Left: *Ingrid Pitt with her father in Bialystok in 1942.* **Below:** *Ingrid pictured recently.*

The day I last saw my grandmother Melanie and grandfather Albert I was being hustled onto a railway truck in the stockyard just outside Bialystok. Baba Melanie was sitting on an old box or something with grandad standing beside her. The scene was reminiscent of a photographer's stock studio pose of the time. But this was no studio pose. Instead of the obligatory aspidistra and idyllic woodland scene background they were surrounded by hundreds of other dejected victims of Nazi tyranny and confronted by an array of cattle trucks and swastikas. It was 1942 and Bialystok, 100 miles north east of the Polish capital, Warsaw, was not a good place to be.

Getting there, finally, had been surprisingly easy. My father had lived in England before the Great War. He was a Prussian and had been to Heidelberg and Oxford Universities. He considered himself British in everything but birth. Born in Potsdam in 1870, he had a British wife and five British children and lived in New Malden. He'd even competed in the London to Brighton Run in 1896 in a battery-driven car. How much more British can you get? By profession he was a successful engineer, but he'd also patented several automobile parts which would have made him a rich man had he been allowed to stay around and reap the rewards. But it was not to be. Archduke Ferdinand inconveniently got himself shot on a friendly visit to Sarajevo and the invitation to the Great War was accepted by the nations of Europe.

My father had the alternative of staying in England and sweating it out in a Detention Centre or returning to Germany. He took the latter course and spent the war on horseback as a cavalry officer. He later said that he wished he had opted for the Detention Centre – at least it would have given him the chance to improve his cricket. An all-round sportsman, he had a natural love of horses. It was at a horse show that he met my mother, Katarina. She was a prize winning dressage champion at the time and he was a widower. She was 30 years younger than Papa, came from Lithuania and was Jewish. Within a year they were married. The Nazi party at this time was little more than a joke. The laughter stopped soon after they were married. Although he'd initially admired the drive and vision of the National Socialist Party he soon began to see it for what it was. He also had a developing interest in 'lighter than air' flying machines and worked as a consultant for the Zeppelin company. His credentials sparked interest within the party and they tried to get him involved. He prevaricated. The mood had turned decidedly nasty in recent months. So far Jews married to Aryans had not been subjected to anything but the mildest inconvenience and Papa thought he could sit it out, falsely secure in the knowledge that he knew a lot of powerful people. Soon the stupid Jewish pogrom would exhaust itself and the leaders of the party begin to see sense. That wait very nearly proved fatal.

> '**In 1937 my father had a visit. Men who were Gestapo in everything but name politely asked him to accompany them to headquarters for a little chat about his future**'

In 1937 my father had a visit. Men who were Gestapo in everything but name politely asked him to accompany them to headquarters for a little chat about his future. They suggested that he should come and work for them. They thought his experience in England as well as his well documented engineering expertise would be complementary to the aims of the Party. They also asked after his Jewish wife. Papa promised to think about it and give them his answer the following week. He had no intention of being there when the time for an answer arrived.

All over Germany people were selling up and moving out. And how many grand pianos or sideboards from your sitting room can you sell for next to nothing? There was another fly in the rapidly deteriorating ointment – me! My mother was a full nine months pregnant. I was due any day. When my father hesitated my mother drove him on. She had friends who had already felt the heavy hand of the Nazis and she was in no mood to taste their venom. I would have to wait until we were out of Germany. And I very nearly made it.

Papa decided to escape through Poland. They got as far as the border town of Czestochowa. That's when I decided to make an appearance. A doctor was sent for and everyone seemed pleased that their little country station had been turned into a maternity ward for the night.

Now it was decided we would go to my mother's family in Grodno. We were there when the war broke out. In time the SSD (State Security Police) got back on Papa's case and it was again time to move on. Papa insisted we head for Bialystok. Probably not his best decision ever. Hitler had just invaded Poland and nobody knew what was going to happen to them. There was plenty of speculation – most of it foretold a fraught future. I was nearly two now with a good pair of lungs which I exercised frequently. We lived like hoboes, going from town to town, staying wherever we could find shelter. Luckily my mother's family was fairly extensive and a lot of them lived in Poland. One distant relative, a farmer, agreed to let us stay for a while.

It is about this time my first memory seems to kick in. I remember playing in the fields. Sometimes we dug into the mole 'castles' to try and catch one of the velvety little beasts. I don't think we ever did. There were butterflies to run after and grasshoppers to make jump. So idyllic I have a hard time believing it happened.

After Hitler invaded Russia, life got even harder for the Poles. The occupying soldiers feared that if they appeared to be too lax in their treatment of the population, they would be drafted to the front. When one of the women workers on the farm was raped by a soldier my father decided it was time to move on again. And that's how we finished up living with Baba Melanie and Grandad Albert just outside Bialystok.

My grandparents had moved from Vilna to Bialystok with the same hope of security as a passenger on the *Titanic* changing deck chairs. They were happy to see us. We spent the summer and autumn with them and began to relax. The surrounding fields were flanked by old irrigation ditches. When the sluices were closed the ditches became a series of small pools. The fish knew about these pools and, as the water level dropped, gathered in them. They probably thought they were safe. But that's life. Just when you think you are safe something ugly falls on you from a great height. In this case it was us kids who fell on the stranded fish. We would harvest enough crayfish and trout to keep the table supplied for days.

I think my parents knew our peaceful existence couldn't last, but they were too exhausted to take to the road again. One day a little convoy of trucks trundled into the yard. The trucks were already heavy with people the Germans had picked up around the neighbourhood. When my father was unable to present correct credentials we joined them.

The journey was torture. I sat and sniffled while my parents tried to calm me down and keep me warm. Baba Melanie and Albert were in even more distress. The hard, jolting wooden floor of the truck brought agony to their arthritic bones. After a long time the truck came to a halt inside a railway depot. We were all ordered out. Soldiers with fierce dogs and heavy rifle butts surrounded us.

A week later my mother and I were in Stutthof Concentration Camp. We didn't know where Papa was. He had been singled out and marched away back at the stock yard. We were shouted into a hut lined with three-tier bunks. Shouting was the constant background noise now and we obeyed the commands automatically, knowing that the slightest tardiness would be rewarded with a beating. It's surprising how quickly one gets used to anything. Only a few days ago we had been living quietly in the country and now we were struggling for existence against a relentless cacophony of noise in hell's kitchen. But at least we were surviving.

The morning kicked in with the door bursting open and Kapos, prisoners who had been put in charge of the other prisoners, rushing around the huts shouting and banging on the wooden bunk frames with sticks. My mother grabbed me and forced me to be quiet. I had learned a lot in the last week. She told me to lie still, nestled in the straw with the blanket over me until she returned. It was weeks before I saw her again.

A few days later, bored with staying under cover all the time, I was playing on the floor when a guard walked in. He grabbed me. I remember screaming and struggling. The guard slapped my face and dragged me out. Suddenly we were in an enclosed patch of grass with huts all around the sides and children playing. I couldn't believe it. I was handed over to a woman in a white

uniform. She seemed friendly and took me towards an elderly woman sitting watching the other children at play. I screamed and clung to the woman in white. Babi Yaga. The witch of the woods. The old lady was right out of a Grimms fairytale. She had a wrinkled, caved-in face with a huge nose. Her body was twisted and there was a hump on her shoulder. And she cackled.

I soon found that her name was actually Frau Gloge and that she was not a witch. She was sweet and caring and, given the circumstances, did everything in her power to make our lives bearable. It was some time before I saw my mother again. The day I did started differently from others. We were washed and dressed in clean clothes. Frau Gloge told us not to be frightened. Nothing bad was about to happen.

A little later a gaggle of women in striped prison clothes entered the compound. We children all huddled together. Sheltered from the life of the main camp we had forgotten what it was like for the less privileged prisoners. I heard my name called and this strange, thin women with a shaven head approached me. Frau Gloge held me close and whispered, 'It's your mama.' I ran forward and was swept up in my mother's bony arms. We sat on the grass and I told my mother about Frau Gloge and what we did all day and what we ate. I was still in full flood when Frau Gloge started rounding us up again. I had the unworthy thought that my mother would snatch me up and take me back to the grim existence outside the childrens' compound. The children were separated from their mothers and lined up. The gate opened and a man in a suit walked in, accompanied by an officer and a couple of nurses. They walked slowly along the line, inspecting the children. One or two were selected and taken to one side.

I later learned that the crèche was a staging post for children who were being vetted to be given to childless German couples. My white blonde hair and fair skin had marked me down as a suitable candidate but I think the fact that my head had been ravaged by lice and was livid with the scars from relentless scratching counted against me. The relatively comfortable lifestyle didn't last long after that. The compound was needed to house an influx of Russian POWs and we kids were sent back to the grim conditions of the main camp.

The war was going badly for the Nazis and morale among the guards was low. They took their fears out on the inmates. Hangings became a daily event. Rape was even more frequent. Earlier the guards had opened up a brothel in one of the huts and had been reasonably civil about the whole idea. Now no one was safe. One of the girls I had teamed up with in the crèche, Rachel, was three or four years older than me, about nine I would think. We were playing with a rag doll that somebody had made for us when a couple of guards came by. One of them picked up the doll and tossed it to the other. It was all in fun to begin with. Then one of the guards grabbed Rachel and tried to kiss her. Inflamed, he started pulling away her rags. The other guard joined in the fun. I realised things were going badly wrong and rolled under the nearest hut. I could hear Rachel screaming but could do nothing to help her. The brutal attack on her emaciated body was too much to bear. She died that night.

But that was the way it always was in the camp. Left alone with a child the guards rarely passed up the opportunity to give vent to their pent up frustrations.

The seasons came and went and not a lot changed. People died or were deemed unfit to work and sentenced to the gas chamber. Every day there were new rumours. Hitler had won the war. The British had won the war. The camps were to be wiped out. New camps were to be built. The Red Cross was sending parcels. To add to my woes I had developed some sort of cyst in my throat. I could hardly breathe. Then Max Stein, someone whom my mother had met at her job in the laundry, appeared one night and cut open the cyst with a pocket knife. Just like that. The wound took a long time to heal but I gradually recovered.

Then one day we heard the rumble of distant artillery. The Russians were coming.

Each day inmates were lined up outside their huts and marched off. The Nazis had given orders to obliterate the camp. Our day was not long in coming. It was snowing hard and we stood shivering outside our hut. Nobody spoke. The guards appeared in their long warm overcoats. On their backs they had large packs. Then an amazing thing happened. We marched off, not down the road leading to the gas chambers but instead towards the gates. The whispering started then. Were the gas chambers overworked and were we going to be shot in the woods instead? We trudged on through the snow. None of us had anything to eat for over 24 hours and soon people were dropping in their tracks. Every time I tried to sit down my mother half pushed, half carried me on.

I remember when the snow stopped and weak sunlight broke through the clouds. It didn't get any warmer but now there was a new menace. Allied fighter planes. From the air, at 300mph, we probably looked like a column of soldiers. The planes dived in and strafed the column. My mother pushed me into a ditch and dived on top of me. When the planes had gone and the guards starting herding everyone back onto the road we stayed where we were. Mercifully, the shouting faded away into the distance. We climbed out of the ditch and hurried into the forest.

I was in a bad state. I was running a temperature and too tired even to grizzle. Exhausted, my mother slumped onto a fallen tree trunk and held me close. At that moment, out of nowhere, two Angels manifested themselves. At least, in our present situation, that is how they appeared. Actually they were an old man and a boy.

Twenty four hours without food and with very

little shelter had pushed me into a state of near coma. My normally indefatigable mother was also sinking fast. After all her battles to stay alive in the hell-hole of Stutthof Concentration Camp, only her determination to save me had kept her going and now she was worn out. It was a gigantic effort for her to call out and attract the attention of the two miraculous passers-by. And it needed all her powers of persuasion to get them to allow us to go in company with them. But the terror did not abate.

As the Russians advanced, the forests all over Poland became hiding places for refugees, deserters and escapees from the berserker Nazis, who were intent on hiding the horror of their crimes. With very few resources, especially at the rag-end of winter, those already in the woods, and mustering themselves as Partisans, were inclined to send newcomers on their way. Just how unwelcome we were was obvious when we arrived at the encampment of rag covered lean-tos huddled around a one-roomed cottage that had been the home of a charcoal burner in happier days. I was in a bad way, drifting in and out of consciousness. After being given a bowl of hot soup my mother was led out the back of the cottage and shown a place under a heap of branches and rags where she could sleep for the night. She was told that in the morning it would be decided whether or not we could stay.

It was the most horrendous night my mother could remember, strangely even worse than the nights back in Stutthof when one never knew what daylight would bring and if you would live to see another moon. By the morning I had developed a full-blooded fever. It was the onset of TB and, ironically, the illness probably saved us. The people in the encampment couldn't bring themselves to push us out. It was all the chance my mother needed. She had a look around the camp and realised that it was little more than a spot in the woods where exhausted travellers flopped down and waited for whatever was going to overtake them. A few of the more enterprising characters had sorted themselves out the best positions and occasionally the more able bodied would wander off in search of food. It meant that the more forceful lived in reasonable comfort, compared to the less fortunate. But my Mother had a mission. She had got me this far and had no intention of losing the battle just when it appeared to be moving into its final stage.

One of the other women, Tchechia, also had a baby, a six month old bundle of giggles and black hair. Tchechia was the woman of one of the strongest men in the camp, Kuragin. He was a big, boisterous Russian fighter pilot who had been shot down and captured by the Germans but managed to escape. Friendship with Tchechia was important and my mother made the most of it. With Tchechia's help she was able to secure a spot abutting the chimney at the back of the house. All of this passed me by. By the time I began to take an interest in what was going on the snow had thawed out and the bitter cold had given way to drizzle, a sea of mud and nowhere to stay dry.

With the coming of warmer weather and my return to something like health my mother turned her attention to improving our lot. She

had already taken over the cooking and had got some of the men to fetch stone and bits and pieces of old iron from a bombed out mansion. She arranged the salvaged material a little way from the cottage and moved the primitive, cut-down oil drum that served as a stove, out from a shed that leaned against the cottage to its new location. Which move left the shed empty – so we moved in. It was wonderful. Even though it was floating in a sea of mud I can still dream about that shed. In my memories of childhood it was my first real home ever.

Next my mother tackled the sanitation situation, which was dire. Bored, with time on their hands, the men tended to lie around in the cottage most of the day, playing cards, chatting or just dozing. My mother's suggestion that they should go and fetch water from the spring and store it in some big, empty oil drums, was not looked upon with favour. Undefeated my mother offered Tchechia a deal. If Tchechia could prevail upon Kuragin to get the men mobilised I would look after the baby on a more or less permanent basis. This was all news to me. I was very fond of little Mila, but I wasn't keen on being saddled with her every day. I was beginning to explore the possibilities my new, free life presented. My mother took me aside, told me what time of day it was and I grudgingly took over my new responsibilities.

> 'Once we discovered half a dozen Nazi deserters in a hide-out. We told the Partisans where they were and they went out and shot them out of hand...'

I had found out that the boy who had rescued us was called Yuri. He was about four or five years older than me and had an appealing arrogance. His clothes were all hand-me-downs and miles too big for him and he insisted on humping around an antique rifle which would have blown his head off had he ever had to use it. To me he was magnificent. I tried trailing around after him for a while. He pretended not to see me most of the time. Then I got burdened with little Mila and that impaired my mobility somewhat. At first I was desperate. I wanted to be Yuri's friend more than anything in the world.

I began to hate the baby – but in the end it was the baby who broke the ice. I guess Yuri missed being the object of desire when it became impossible for me to follow him around. Whatever, one day when I was playing with the baby he came and sat on the ground a little way off. On this occasion I pretended not to notice him. After a while he got up, hesitated for a moment and then bent down and started playing with the baby. A link was forged. Soon we were an item. Yuri striding along in his filthy rags and me stumbling along behind carrying the baby.

The war was getting closer. Aircraft frequently roared low overhead. Suddenly one day a plane

swooped overhead, lower than anything Yuri and I had seen before, and smashed into the trees a couple of hundred yards ahead. We were terrified and the baby started to bawl. Even so, curiosity drew us to the crash site. The plane was huge and had ploughed a wide furrow through the trees before coming to rest. Smoke dribbled from several places and it creaked ominously. Soon we were joined by others from the camp. After a while the stricken aircraft settled down and some of the men climbed onto it. They found only one survivor, Mike. He was the navigator, I believe, and had broken legs and was covered in cuts and bruises. Again my mother came to the fore. She was the only one in the camp who could speak English. She patched Mike up as best she could and probed for information about the war. Some of the men had been stripping out bits from the plane which might be useful. Among all the clutter Yuri found a radio. While Mike was convalescing he tried to fix the radio. Nobody ever believes me but he did get it working for a brief time. And who should be giving a speech? Winston Churchill. I swear!

The atmosphere in the camp had changed now. There was a lot of talk about the end of the war and 'going home'. I can't remember it having much resonance with me. I didn't really want to leave. I had got used to the daily routine, of following Yuri around, of looking after the baby, of the painful job of collecting nettles for the pot and all the other familiar chores. We were told to watch out for deserting Germans and each day we went through the woods to the nearest road and kept a vigil for the arrival of the Allies. There was evidently a lot of hostility between the camp and the people in the local village and we were wary. If we saw anyone suspicious Yuri would run back to the camp to get the men. By now I had managed to shed some of my baby sitting responsibilities and imagined myself a proper little sniper. Once we located half a dozen Nazi deserters in a hide-out. We told the Partisans where they were and they went out and shot them out of hand. After this the people in the camp went very silent and nobody talked about what had been done.

After a time the firing which had been a background constant for many weeks stopped. There was speculation. Had the Nazis beaten off the liberators? Were they even now preparing to wreak revenge on those who opposed them? The thought of the bodies of the deserters in the forest was always with us but never mentioned. Now everything started to speed up. Suddenly big army lorries, cars, motor bikes and marching men appeared on the road. We were all still fearful. The sight of all those uniforms reminded me of all the terrors I was just beginning to put behind me. Yuri tried to reassure me and said he could tell from the uniforms that it was the Red Army we were watching. He wasn't all that reassuring. I had listened to some of the older people talking in the camps and they invariably painted the Russians as monsters.

I told this to Yuri. He put on a brave face but settled a little deeper into the bushes anyway and seemed in no hurry to rush out and confront our liberators. Instead we sneaked away and hurried back to the camp with the news. Kuragin and a couple of the men went with us back to

Ingrid Pitt grew up to be a successful actress after the war. She is pictured above and right with Richard Burton and Clint Eastwood on the set of the blockbuster film Where Eagles Dare.

the road and we were disappointed that there was no sign of any troop movement. The following morning a small squad of soldiers moved in on us. I can still feel the fear. My mother made Yuri take me into one of the out buildings and we covered ourselves in some old, evil smelling tarpaulin. We seemed to lie there for hours before my mother came to get us. The soldiers were Russians. They had taken a note of everyone's name and arrested a couple of their fellow Russians who had recently joined the camp. The Englishman Mike made himself known to them and the man in charge of the party promised to let his boss know his whereabouts. Satisfied there was nothing else to be gained the soldiers moved on.

Kuragin was lucky. He had been out of the camp searching for food when the Russians had arrived. Now he knew the score he wasn't going to hang around and get picked up. He stuffed a few bits and pieces into a bag and left with Tchechia and little Mila. The promise of liberation seemed to knock the kingpins out of everybody. No one was interested in doing anything but sit tight and talk about 'going home' and finding loved ones. I had different emotions. I wanted to stay in the forest – with Yuri.

The sudden release of tension hit my mother hard. She began to feel weak and suddenly unable to cope. No more troops came and the days drifted into weeks. My mother was confined to bed and I heard the word, 'typhoid' muttered from time to time. I was desperate but didn't know what to do. It was all taken out of my hands by the arrival of a group of Red Cross personnel. In a whirl I was paraded before doctors, given injections and clothed in warm new clothes. Next day I was told that I would be

leaving for the hospital immediately with my mother. I was devastated. I went to look for Yuri. I had a vague hope that he might be able to sort it out. Maybe we could run away or something. I couldn't find him. Around mid-day some more men arrived with a stretcher and my mother was carried off. I trailed along behind, on the brink of tears and more miserable than I had been for ages. The stretcher was loaded onto the back of a canvas topped lorry and I was handed up to the nurse sitting in the back. Mike was sitting next to my mother on the stretcher. He was the only one who looked happy. Several of the partisans had come down to the road to see us off. I waved to them but they just stared back.

As the engine revved and the gears crashed into place, Yuri, still in the rags he had worn since I first saw him and carrying his rifle, came out of the trees and stood in the middle of the road. I tried to jump over the tailboard to run to him but the steely hands of the nurse held me back. Yuri hoisted his gun up into the firing position and pretended to shoot at me. I thought it was wonderful. The lorry started to move and gradually Yuri faded into the distance and was lost to view as we rounded a corner.

My mother recovered after several weeks in hospital and we set off on a journey across Europe looking for my father. It would last for over a year before we were reunited. Over six decades later, polished and enhanced by time, I still have a vivid picture in my mind of Yuri standing in the road pointing his gun at me.

Above: Ingrid is pictured with Christopher Lee at a film festival. The two made regular appearances in Hammer Horror films.

They also featured in the original production of The Wicker Man.

Christopher Lee himself had a varied wartime career that began when he volunteered to fight with the Finns against Russia. See page 37.

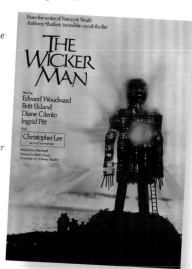

DECEMBER 1941

It's as if everyone is declaring war on everyone else.

The first 11 days of December 1941 saw a bewildering round of declarations of war. In invading Poland in late 1939, Hitler gambled that Britain and France would again follow the path of appeasement. The Fuhrer had called it right many times before and in the case of the Poles he'd cannily reached an accommodation with Stalin, even to the extent of encouraging the Soviets to grab a big slice of hapless Poland for themselves. But it turned out to be one occasion when Hitler got it wrong and in consequence most of Europe was plunged into war. Now, over two years later, a conflict hitherto largely confined to Europe, North Africa and the Atlantic Ocean suddenly envelopes every corner of the globe. It really is a world war. At stake with the Axis is the triumph of fascism and militarism whilst with the Western Allies it is the survival of democracy. For Hitler's former partner in crime in Poland, Stalin, it is the preservation of the communist system.

Looming over all is the Japanese attack on Pearl Harbor on Sunday 7 December and subsequent declarations of war on the United States, Britain and her allies. Next day Britain declared war on Japan while President Roosevelt asked Congress for a similar declaration. Canada, Costa Rica, Dominica, Haiti, Honduras, Nicaragua, Free France and the Netherlands Government-in-Exile all declared war against Japan.

On 9 December the rest of the British Empire declared war against Japan, as did Cuba and Panama. China had never formally been at war with Japan so now took the opportunity to declare that a state of

> " Churchill announced in Parliament that four-fifths of the population of the globe was now in the Allied camp and arrayed against the Axis... "

hostilities exists, adding Germany and all the Axis powers to her list of enemies. British newspapers welcomed 400,000,000 Chinese as our Allies.

Two days later and Hitler declared war on the US. Mussolini's Italy quickly followed suit. America responded in kind.

Britain had already declared war on Axis partners Hungary and Romania on 5 December 1941. When, despite intense diplomatic lobbying, Finland would not desist in her fight against Russia a state of war between the Finns and Britain came into

> " Haiti, Costa Rica, Honduras and Nicaragua join the Allies in the war against Japan. China declares war on Germany and Italy "

being at 1am on 7 December. Finland's reluctant role in the world conflict had begun when the Soviet Union attacked her in November 1939. Despite initial success in the snowy forests, civilian casualties were too high for Finland and a harsh and punitive treaty was signed on 12 March 1940. Fifteen months later Finland joined forces with Nazi Germany to exact revenge on the Soviet Union. From 25 June to 6 July 1941, the Finns fought the largest military battle in Nordic history alongside the Germans, regaining much of the territory they had lost during the earlier Winter War.

Romania and Hungary had joined Germany, Japan and Italy in their Tri-partite Pact in November 1940, even as Hitler honed his plans for invading Russia. The Hungarian leader Admiral Horthy knew the Red Army would be a formidable foe but was forced by geography and regional differences into the Axis camp. Oil-rich Romania played a vital role in supporting the German war effort. By 1941, German-owned companies produced nearly half of Romania's crude oil output.

Though nominally enemies of the Western Allies, Finland, Hungary and Romania would all switch sides before the end of the war. The Romanian ruler Antonescu made contact with the Western Allies and declared war on Germany on 24 August 1944. Hungary began talks with the Allies early that same year but was occupied by German forces in March. Finland defied German demands and made peace with the Soviet Union on 19 September 1944. The Finns lost even more territory than they had under the Winter War treaty.

Total war means total disregard for diplomacy in references to the enemy. Less than a quarter of a century before Pearl Harbor the Japanese had been allies and friends of the USA and Britain in the Great War, but now that they have launched a ruthlessly executed surprise attack on the US and the British Empire they are at once cast beyond the pale. *The War Illustrated* of 20 December 1921 comments: 'This new Japan, with all the accoutrement of scientific destruction in her greedy paws, which she will use with the atrocity of a wild animal gone mad, will eventually find her only honour in self-destruction. Generations of British traders, officials and sojourners in the East have borne testimony to the deceit and trickery of the Japanese... the Chinese are as noted for their peaceful disposition as their envious enemies of the islands for their aggressive spirit. Never has the innate treachery of these swaggering invaders of China been so completely illustrated as in their method of making war on Britain and American under cover of peaceful talks at Washington. They have gone one step beyond Hitler and many steps back to the barbarism of the Mongol Khans.'

Having already established a record for the most terrible and sustained cruelty against civilians in China, there was no empathy for the Japanese plea that their way of life was threatened by western colonial ambitions and US trade embargoes. In their subsequent treatment of Allied prisoners and European internees, the Japanese army unfortunately proved that the militaristic creed of their leaders had unleashed a xenophobia only surpassed by that of the Nazis against the Jews.

WAR with Japan

Trouble between China and Japan had been simmering for many years in the first half of the 20th century. Japan resented that most of China had been unified under the able military and political leadership of Generalissimo Chiang Kai-shek. At the same time, many Chinese decided to boycott trade with Japan. With China her most important market, this angered the Japanese even more.

In September 1931, Japanese agents exploded a small bomb on the railway line near Mukden in Manchuria but declared that this act of sabotage must be the work of bandits. Claiming the Chinese Government could not keep order, a Japanese army marched in and seized control of Manchuria. In February 1932, Japan declared that Manchuria had become the independent empire of Manchukuo – de facto, it was a colony of Japan.

In consequence the boycott of Japanese goods spread even wider. Japan threatened to punish China if the boycott continued. Japanese troops landed to occupy Shanghai but were kept out by a spirited Chinese resistance. Tokyo sent reinforcements and finally took the

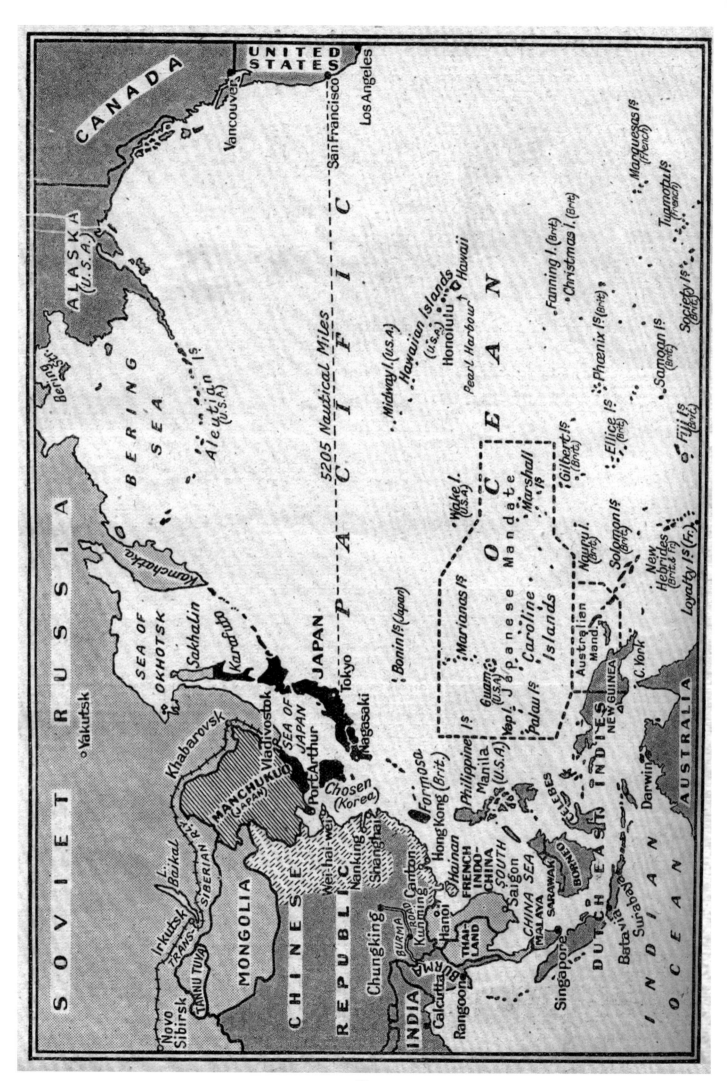

city. Chiang had to make peace. The next year Japanese troops occupied the Chinese province of Jehol.

Despite these setbacks, Japan's aggression actually served to strengthen Chiang Kai-shek's position. He was able to suppress the rebellions of numerous warlords and in early 1937 Chiang reached an agreement with Mao Tse-tung to end the civil war with the Communists.

Alarmed at the revival of Chinese fortunes, the Japanese decided there was nothing for it but an outright war to overthrow Chiang and take over all of China. This would be the first step in establishing what Tokyo termed 'The Greater East Asia Co-prosperity Sphere.' In reality the Japanese wanted an empire.

The 'China Incident'

In July 1937, Japanese troops started a fight with Chinese soldiers guarding the Marco Polo Bridge near Peking (Beijing). Affairs swiftly escalated into full-scale war in all but name. The confident Japanese quickly captured the capital and invaded north China. But they received a bloody nose at Shanghai in August 1937; it took several months of hard fighting to capture the city.

Next the Japanese advanced on China's

capital, Nanking. On 12 December 1937, Japanese aircraft made a surprise attack on British and American gunboats moored in the broad Yangtze River; the USS Panay was sunk. The American people were outraged and their indignation increased during the days following, when the Japanese captured Nanking, then ravaged the city for several days in a horrific orgy of slaughter and wanton destruction. Only a public apology from the Japanese placated the US Government.

The Nationalist forces fell back into the vastness of China. Early in 1938, the Japanese mounted a pincer movement around the rail centre of Suchow. Chiang Kai-shek's counter-attack surrounded 60,000 of the enemy. In their first military defeat in their undeclared war against China, over 20,000 Japanese troops were killed.

However, the heavily reinforced Japanese gradually recovered the initiative. After a five-month battle, Hankow fell on 25 October 1938. During the same month, the Japanese landed on the south China coast, a few miles north-east of the British colony of Hong Kong. In a swift advance, they captured the major prize of Canton, China's main seaport.

In 1939 the Japanese halted their land

offensive and instead sought to choke off all China's remaining seaports. This accomplished, there remained just two routes by which China could receive supplies. One was along the narrow-gauge railway to Kunming from the port of Haiphong in French Indo China. The other was through British Burma, with goods and material being landed at Rangoon, then forwarded by rail to Lashio before being trucked over the famous Burma Road into southern China.

China cut off from the sea

The Burma Road opened to traffic in December 1938. It ran the 720 winding miles from Lashio in north-east Burma to Kunming, capital of the Chinese province of Yunnan. En route there were 300 bridges, 2000 culverts and innumerable twists and turns as the road climbed up and down mountain ranges and crossed two of Asia's greatest rivers, the Salween and Mekong. These rise in the mountain plateau of Tibet and rush south with tremendous force on their way, respectively, to the Bay of Bengal and the South China Sea.

By the middle of 1940 with the Japanese holding most of China's coastline and – after the surrender of France – having access to French Indo-China where they were able to cut the rail link to Kunming, the road had become China's main outlet to the wider world. However, with Britain herself seemingly in imminent danger of a German invasion, Churchill was anxious not to provoke the Japanese into attacking Britain's Far East territories. Accordingly, on 18 July in response to Japanese pressure the Burma Road was closed.

Victory in the Battle of Britain changed the world picture again. Japan had shown her hostility when she signed the Axis pact with Germany and Italy, proving again that appeasing totalitarian regimes was ultimately futile. Churchill grew in confidence and on 8 October 1940 he announced that the Burma Road would be re-opened. In free China the news was received with great joy.

Weeks later, the Japanese extended their occupation of Indo-China and seized airfields from which the Chinese end of the Burma Road could be bombed. A deeply concerned President Roosevelt warned Japan against further military adventurism in Asia. The Japanese did not heed the warning and in July 1941 the Americans invoked a complete trade embargo; US steel and oil no longer flowed across the Pacific to fuel Japan's civilian and military industries.

Previous page: A Japanese light tank negotiates a bridge that was supposed to have been destroyed. The Japanese proved innovative in their approach to warfare in inhospitable terrain. In the early months of fighting the British kept to the few passable roads in Malaya and Burma and allowed the Japanese to outflank them by infiltrating the 'impassable' jungle.

Left: An American battleship ablaze at Pearl Harbor. Fortunately the US carrier fleet was at sea on the day of the attack and escaped destruction.

aircraft carriers were at sea and out of harm's way. The providential escape of these carriers was something that would come back to haunt the Japanese just six months later at the decisive Battle of Midway.

West of the international dateline it was already 8 December; at dawn in Hong Kong, just an hour after they had struck at Pearl Harbour, the Japanese air force bombed the city while at the same time their land forces advanced across the border from China. Within 48 hours the attackers had punched a hole in the main British defensive line and forced them to withdraw from the mainland to Hong Kong island. Despite desperate defending in the face of a hail of artillery and bombs, the British were overwhelmed and forced to surrender on Christmas Day 1941. The Japanese lost 3000 men; the entire 12,000 man British garrison was killed or captured.

Cruel and barbaric acts

In an incident that would demonstrate the war-long capacity of Japanese officers and soldiers to commit the most cruel and barbaric acts on captured soldiers and civilians, wounded British were bayoneted in their beds in St Stephens College, an emergency hospital. Four Chinese and seven British nurses were savagely raped and murdered.

On 10 December the potency of Japanese air power was demonstrated once again when the famous British battleships, *HMS Repulse* and *Prince of Wales*, were sunk off the north east coast of Malaya while leading a fleet against Japanese troop transports. Admiral Tom Phillips (known to his men as 'Tom Thumb' because of his short stature) was one of 840 sailors lost.

A *Daily Express* war reporter, O D Gallagher, on the *Repulse* was one of the few survivors. He later wrote: 'It was a superb air attack by the Japanese. Royal Navy officers had earlier predicted that the greatest danger would be the possibility of them flying their whole aircraft into a ship and declaring hara-kiri. But it was most orthodox: They came at us in formation, flying low and close. The Germans have never done anything like this in the North Sea or Atlantic.'

But the British had against the Italian fleet at Taranto in 1940. The Japanese had learned their lessons well. Now Singapore was left with no capital ships for protection and further Japanese landings down the east and west coast of Malaya were unopposed.

Churchill was shocked at the loss of the ships. Worse was to come. As the Japanese drove into Malaya, they surprised the British by their ability to work their way through the dense, tangled jungle. They simply went round any roadblocks on the main roads and jungle trails and moved rapidly through areas considered impassable.

The two countries were in a diplomatic deadlock; Japan decided that war was the only way out of the impasse.

Pearl Harbor: Day of Infamy

In October 1941 the aggressive Hideki Tojo became Prime Minister of Japan. He saw seizing the oil, rubber and rich mineral deposits of south-east Asia and the East Indies as an ideal step to making Japan independent of external economic resources. With Indo-China already occupied, an invasion of British Malaya and Burma, the Netherlands East Indies and the American administered Philippine Islands seemed a gamble worth taking. If they could achieve surprise and apply overwhelming force, surely Japan could later defeat any British or American attempts to win back their lost possessions.

During the first week of December 1941, the Allied leaders in south-east Asia became aware that Japanese naval forces were on the move in the South China Sea. But nobody knew if it was sabre-rattling sanctioned by Tokyo or a full-scale invasion in the offing.

The answer came at 7.55am on Sunday 7 December. Under the codename 'Tora, Tora, Tora' hundreds of aircraft launched from Japanese aircraft carriers attacked the home of the American Pacific Fleet at Pearl Harbor in the US Hawaiian Islands. Surprise was complete and dreadful damage was inflicted on battleships and cruisers with the loss of thousands of lives. By great good fortune, however, the US Navy's vital

Far East, December 1941. A Royal Navy officer says: 'The greatest danger is of the Japanese flying their whole aircraft into a ship and committing hara-kiri.'

SMASH JAPANESE AGGRESSION !

1942

British retreat to Singapore

By early January 1942, the British were in serious trouble having suffered heavy losses and worsening morale. The British, Americans, Dutch and Australians set up a unified command (ABDA) for south-east Asia and Sir Archibald Wavell was put in command. Wavell saw that the British defences in Malaya were collapsing. He ordered his local commander, General A E Percival, to fall back to Johore in the south of the Malay Peninsular. On 17 January, the Japanese tore into the new line; on 31 January Percival was compelled to withdraw all his remaining troops back to Singapore. A 30-foot section of the causeway connecting the island to Johore was blown up.

Singapore Island had strong fortifications. Unfortunately they had been constructed on the premise that any threat would come from the seaward side. Now the Japanese were on the landward side and the island's big guns were facing the wrong way and impossible to shift from their concrete emplacements. Nevertheless, with the addition of a division newly-arrived from Britain, there seemed to be enough forces in Singapore to resist any assault and buy time for Allied reinforcements to arrive in the region.

The Japanese had other ideas. They began an intensive air and artillery bombardment. After three days of preparation, the Japanese made an audacious amphibious assault across the Straight of Johore under the cover of darkness. They used armoured landing barges and quickly established a grip on the northwest coast of Singapore. Next they drove eastwards to capture the southern end of the causeway and seized three airfields. The causeway was quickly repaired and Japanese tanks rumbled across to spearhead an advance into the centre of the island, defeating a desperate British counter-attack in the process.

After four days of fighting, Percival recognized the British were beaten and was forced into a humiliating surrender. In just over two months, the Japanese had taken Hong Kong, conquered Malaya and captured Singapore, the much-vaunted bastion of British power in the Far East. The Japanese campaign cost them some 10,000 men killed and wounded. British losses amounted to almost 140,000 men, killed or captured.

The war comes to Burma

During December 1941 Japanese troops moved to occupy the neutral country of Siam (Thailand) that bordered British-administered Burma. The latter was part of Wavell's vast area of responsibility, which extended from India to Australia. In the face of simultaneous invasions of Malaya, the Philippines and sprawling islands of the Dutch East Indies, the Japanese threat to Burma was just one more problem amidst a heap of trouble.

In mid-January 1942, Japanese troops supported by several hundred fighter and bomber aircraft, mounted two thrusts into Burma from Thailand. These were seasoned soldiers, well-trained veterans of the war in China. They were up against about a division and a half of British, Indian and Burmese units charged with the defence of the country. The first clash took place at Moulmein in the south of Burma. After two days of hard fighting, the British retreated across the unbridged Salween River. The Japanese momentum took them across this formidable barrier at Paan, prompting a five-day

Above: *A British officer surrenders in Singapore while a Japanese soldier looks on.*

running battle as the British withdrew north-west towards the only bridge across the River Sittang. Suddenly, on 23 February, a second large Japanese force approached the bridge from the north-east, even while two British brigades were still locked in combat several miles to the south. There was no choice but to blow the bridge leaving half the defence force of Burma on the wrong side of the river. Though many of the isolated troops got across the Sittang by any means possible, they had to abandon all their heavy equipment and transport.

Soon the Japanese were across the Sittang and driving towards the city of Pegu and the important seaport of Rangoon. At this time General Harold R L Alexander took command of the Burma theatre. He quickly realized that the incessant fighting and constant retreats had exhausted and seriously demoralized the Allied forces. Total collapse had only been staved off by vital air support from a group of American airmen known as the 'Flying Tigers' and a number of RAF aircraft. Led by retired Captain Claire L Chennault, the Tigers were former US military pilots – now civilians – who had volunteered to fight for China.

Alexander evades capture

On 7 March 1942, with the Japanese closing in from the east and the north, Alexander

Left: *The Japanese attempt to cut off British and Chinese forces in Burma in 1942.*

abandoned Rangoon. The defenders had to fight their way out through the narrowing gap between the converging columns; Alexander himself narrowly escaped capture. They withdrew north-westwards. The loss of Rangoon, and later Akyab, meant that the Allies in Burma were effectively cut off from relief from the sea. Ringed in by virtually road-less mountains, reinforcements and supplies could only come in over the mountains from India or over the Burma Road from China, herself subject to a sea blockade.

Even as the British withdrew from Rangoon, 30,000 Chinese troops of the Fifth and Sixth armies arrived in the country via the Burma Road that ran to Lashio where there was a rail link to the Burmese capital, Mandalay. One army moved to Toungoo, arriving on 19 March, where it was in position to block any Japanese drive on Mandalay. The other army moved south from Lashio to protect the southern end of the Burma Road from attack by the Japanese who were established over the border in north-western Thailand.

This commander of these Chinese units was an American, General Joseph W Stilwell. He had recently arrived in Chungking with an American military mission tasked with assisting the Chinese. Eager to secure US aid, Chiang Kai Shek had appointed Stilwell as his chief of staff and put him in charge of Chinese operations in Burma. Stilwell was a fighting infantryman with a forthright attitude and a sharp tongue; his nickname was 'Vinegar Joe'.

Another new name to the Burma fighting was that of General William Slim, also a fighting infantry soldier, with an excellent war record. Bristol-born Slim was appointed by Alexander to command the British Burma Corps, which then amounted to two small, exhausted divisions.

On 21 March Japanese bombers destroyed the Flying Tiger base at Magwe, forcing Chennault's flyers to retreat into southern China. At the same time, Japanese troops attacked the Chinese near Toungoo. The Chinese 200th Division was cut off but put up fierce resistance. With British help, the unit fought their way out of the trap. Japanese pressure was maintained. The British were forced to withdraw north to positions protecting oil fields near Yenangyaung on the right of the new Allied line. Stilwell's two Chinese armies held the centre and the left.

Infiltration and encirclement

In late March, two more Japanese divisions arrived at Rangoon, still exultant at their victories in Malaya and Singapore. On 10 April they went into action against the British, successfully employing their usual tactics of infiltration and encirclement. Timely Chinese intervention orchestrated by Stilwell allowed the British to withdraw north towards the border with India. Before departing, British engineers blew up the oil wells.

Now the Japanese switched their attention to the left flank and attacked the Chinese Sixth Army. On 19 April they broke through and

Japanese tanks began a charge up the Salween Valley. They captured Lashio on 29 April, cutting the Burma Road. Next they turned south-westwards to advance on Mandalay. At this point, Alexander realized that holding the capital was untenable. He pulled back the British and the Chinese Fifth Army and had them cross the Irrawaddy River on the sole bridge, just south of Mandalay. By 30 April, with most Allied units safely across, the bridge was blown up.

Across the Chindwin

The retreat continued. On 11 May the Allies crossed the next major river barrier – the Chindwin – with the Japanese again in hot pursuit. Slim and his men were following a narrow trail that led from Tiddim in western Burma to Imphal in eastern India. Around 12,000 British, Indian and Burmese survivors would get there, barely one-third of the total that had taken part in the campaign.

Meanwhile, the Chinese armies had been split into several groups after the breakthrough at Lashio. About half of them got across the mountains to the east and back into the province of Yunnan in south-west China. The others went on circuitous but ultimately successful marches into Burma's mountains to either eventually arrive in Yunnan or, in the case of the 38th Division, to reach Imphal. Stilwell himself led his HQ team on an epic 400 mile journey by car, jeep and truck up the Irrawaddy Valley, heading for Imphal. For the last 150 miles the group travelled on foot over the rugged Chin Hills, along trails already slippery from the first monsoon rains. They finally reached Imphal on 20 May. Stilwell's comment on the campaign: 'We got a hell of a

Above: General Bill Slim – he led the 'Forgotten' Fourteenth Army in Burma and was popular with the troops.

beating. We got run out of Burma and it's humiliating. We ought to find out why it happened, go back, and retake it!'

Slim had his own observations to make about the men who fought in the battle for Burma: 'On the last day of that 900-mile retreat I stood on a bank beside the road and watched the rearguard march into India. All of them, British, Indian and Gurkha, were gaunt and ragged as scarecrows. Yet as they trudged behind their surviving officers ... they still carried their arms and kept their ranks, they were still recognizable as fighting units. They might look like scarecrows, but they looked like soldiers too.'

Weather and the War in Burma

The ability to wage war in Burma is governed largely by the monsoon. From about October to May, the prevailing winds in this region blow generally southwards from the high, dry Himalaya Mountains of central Asia. There is almost no rain during this period. But for the remainder of the year the monsoon winds blow back on the continent from the Indian Ocean, bringing with them thick cloud and heavy rain which inundates the coastal lowland regions and the slopes of the southern Himalayas and their spurs in south-east Asia. This heavy summer rainfall nourishes a blanket of dense rain forest throughout most of Burma. However, in the centre of the country, the broad Irrawaddy Valley has only a light monsoon rainfall due to being in the 'rain shadow' of the surrounding mountains. The area is known as the 'dry belt' and has few trees; most of the valley is a flat plain covered with rice fields.

Except in this relatively small dry belt, military movements on a large scale become virtually impossible in the rainy season. Burma in wartime had few hard-surface roads and the dirt tracks would become streams of mud while clearings turned into swamps and rivers swelled into raging torrents. Trenches quickly filled with water. In the highlands of mountainous Burma, the clothes of soldiers would be constantly wet and prey to mildew. Guns and equipment would rust and signal equipment became prone to failure. In the wet, leeches thrived and were everywhere – a constant torment to the troops. There were diseases of all sorts and no one could escape the bites of malaria-bearing mosquitoes.

Cricket and the Japanese

Early in 1942, Winston Churchill felt that he must ask the House of Commons for a vote of confidence, saying 'things have gone badly and there is worse to come'. A three day debate started on 27 January 1942. In the course of it Tory MP for Kidderminster, Sir John Wardlaw-Milne, comments: 'I realise that in Libya the weather has been bad. It is right that we should be told that it is bad. But you would think, to listen to the BBC, that the dust-storms fall only on the British troops and that the Germans never had a dust-storm. Again we hear that it is "not cricket" and that it is "hitting below the belt", for the Japanese to land in sampans and proceed up creeks. Also when the Prime Minister tells us that our production has gone up by four or 10 times, or whatever it was, over that of 1917 he might as well tell us that it is 100 times more than it was in the Boer War or 1000 times more than what it was at Agincourt.'

Plenty of Civil Service overtime

Sir Herbert Williams (Tory, Croydon South) thought that the Prime Minister should not also be Minister of Defence because, 'you have one man dominating the chiefs of staff who are, after all, only employees whom he can sack at any moment'. This view was strongly rebutted by Clement Atlee. Sir Herbert responded, 'I don't want to change the Prime Minister. I want a changed Prime Minister.' The MP then proceeded to lambast the Civil Service machine: 'Whitehall swarms with committees, and they are all reasons for not coming to a decision about something or other... no one in the commercial world would ever take the job of a Parliamentary secretary. There is no zeal in our Government departments, but there is plenty of overtime.'

When it came to the vote, 464 voted for the motion of confidence with just one against.

Channel Dash

The German battleships *Gneisenau* and *Scharnhorst* had been anchored at Brest on the Atlantic coast of France since March 1941. The heavy cruiser *Prinz Eugen* had also been tied to the French port since the *Bismarck* sortie in May 1941, when it and the ill-fated battleship made their own mad dash through the Atlantic and the Denmark Strait to elude Royal Navy gunfire. All three were subject to bombing raids and the constant watch of British submarines and aircraft. Bottled up in Brest, the ships were of no use to the German war effort. Early in 1942 the German Vice Admiral Otto Ciliax initiated a daring plan – *Operation Cerberus* – to lead the ships out of the French port and make a dash through the English Channel and north to German waters.

The Germans chose a date when the weather and visibility were forecast to be

BAD NEWS DAYS

Early 1942

poor. Shortly after a British bombing raid, the *Gneisenau*, *Scharnhorst*, and *Prinz Eugen* departed under a defensive smoke screen. Six German destroyers and 21 torpedo boats accompanied the ships for protection as they moved north late on the night of 11 February.

In the morning, German planes provided air cover as well; ace pilot Adolf Galland led 250 other fighters in an unusually well coordinated joint effort of the German navy and Luftwaffe. It was not until 11am next morning that the RAF spotted the enemy squadron and by then, despite there having been three hours of daylight, the ships were already approaching the Dover Straits with a swarm of protecting fighter aircraft above them. The coastal guns at Dover commenced

firing at 12.19pm. The first RAF action came at around 12.30pm when six Fleet Air Arm Swordfish based at Manston, Kent, attacked. The 'Stringbags' were no match for the fast German fighters and the wall of flak put up by the warships; none returned to base and just five of the 18 crewmen were rescued from the sea. Later the Swordfish leader, Lt Commander E Esmonde, was awarded a posthumous VC.

MTBs from Dover launched torpedoes into the smoke surrounding the ships. Cannon-firing Hurricanes attacked some of the escorting destroyers. No hits were scored. By 13.25pm the German force was beyond the range of British radar. Confusion in the RAF camp meant that it was 3pm before Bomber Command aircraft appeared on the scene. Unfortunately low cloud and poor visibility meant that the 242 bombers involved did not score any hits. Royal Navy destroyers from the Thames estuary pressed home attacks but were also unsuccessful. All three German warships made it safely home on 13 February, although the *Gneisenau* and *Scharnhorst* had been damaged by British mines along the way.

The British lost 40 aircraft and six Navy Swordfish in the confrontation, while the Germans lost a torpedo boat and 17 aircraft. The 'Channel Dash', as it came to be called, was extremely embarrassing to the British. *The Times* thundered: 'Nothing more mortifying to the pride of sea-power in Home Waters has happened since the 17th century.'

There would be revenge of a sort, though. On 23 February *Prinz Eugen* was torpedoed by the submarine *HMS Trident*. On the night of 27–28 February the *Gneisenau*, lying at Kiel, suffered two direct hits and the loss of 90 of her crew in a bombing raid. The Royal Navy would sink the *Scharnhorst* on 26 December 1943 as the vessel attempted to attack a Russian convoy.

U-Boats off US coast

After Pearl Harbor and the American entry into the war, it was not long before German U-Boats moved en masse into the eastern seaboard of the US and the Caribbean. U-123 was commanded by 28-year-old Reinhard Hardegen. He led a group of five submarines to begin their attacks on 13 January 1942. Each U-Boat carried 15 torpedoes and 180 rounds of artillery for their gun mount. When he returned to occupied France he had sunk nine ships. He began another voyage on 10 April 1942 and by the time he returned to France again, he had sunk a total of 19 ships on the two cruises. More than 400 Allied ships were sunk in the first six months of 1942.

Japanese submarines operated off the west coast of America. The first merchantman to be sunk was the *SS Medio* which went down near Eureka, California, on 20 December 1941. On 23 February 1942 a submarine surfaced north of Santa Barbara and fired around 20 rounds at an oil installation. This was the only instance of enemy gunfire striking the soil of the USA.

MIGHTIER YET!

In ships, tonnage and gun-power, the Navies of the British Empire are the most powerful sea force in the world — and another million tons of British warships are building

Though the Royal Navy may still have been the most powerful sea force in the world, in February 1942 it was humiliated when German capital ships daringly sailed through the English Channel and past Dover under the very noses of the Admiralty and RAF.

WAR DIARY 1942

1 January: A 'Declaration by the United Nations' is concluded in Washington today when the representatives of 26 countries sign a solemn declaration of mutual support and resolve to fight the war together to a successful finish. Winston Churchill is present on this historic occasion. Two days before, he had addressed the Canadian Parliament in Ottawa.

2 January: Manila, capital of the Philippines, is occupied by the Japanese.

4 January: The British press reports how the West Coast of America is subject to a black-out each evening as a precaution against a Japanese attack. On the first night in a darkened tinsel town a huge illuminated sign at the airport is left switched on. It reads: 'Welcome to Los Angeles'.

10 January: The last major German air raid on Liverpool destroys the home of William Patrick Hitler, nephew of the Nazi leader, Adolf Hitler. William Hitler is unhurt and subsequently will go to the USA and join the US Navy to fight on the side of the Allies.

11 January: Japanese forces enter Kuala Lumpur. Japanese troops have also landed at four points in the Dutch East Indies.

14 January: News is coming through of a Chinese victory over the Japanese at Changsha. It is reported that Japanese casualties total 21,000.

15 January: 'General Winter' is aiding the Russians and forcing the Germans to retreat or go on the defensive all along the front. Commentators are making comparisons with the fate of Napoleon's Grand Army. However, although they were defeated, Napoleon's surviving men had re-crossed the Russian frontier en route home well before Christmas 1812. It is now the New Year, the Germans are still there and the winter has many more freezing months to run. Ironically, Yasnaya Polyana, birthplace of *War and Peace* author, Tolstoy, has been recaptured by the Russians. The writer is buried there and the Russians say that many dead German soldiers have been interred in the same graveyard.

24 January: It is revealed that the Minister responsible for feeding the nation, Lord Woolton, received 13,000 letters individually addressed to him last year. Most were sent by housewives; all were answered, despite the paper shortage.

30 January: British boys of 17 are requested to register for national service.

2 February: There are regular press reports on the exploits of squadrons of Hurricanes flown by British pilots in support of the Red Army in northern Russia. On the Moscow front, the

> **The birthplace of 'War and Peace' author, Tolstoy, has been recaptured by the Russians. The writer is buried there and now his graveyard is shared with many dead German soldiers.**

Soviets are employing large numbers of paratroops as they push the Germans back. In the biggest operation this month, 10,000 will drop behind the retreating Germans.

14 February: Japanese parachutists land at Palembang on Sumatra in the Dutch East Indies in an attempt to seize oil wells. Some are successfully taken but the majority are set on fire by the well managers while Dutch soldiers hold off the attackers.

15 February: Singapore surrenders to the Japanese.

19 February: Nearly 100 Japanese bombers raid Darwin in Northern Australia for the first time.

20 February: The Japanese landings on New Guinea and the Bismarck Archipelago are bringing Australia alarmingly close to the enemy. An Australian Government Minister has said: 'The rising sun is nearly overhead. If the Battle of the Pacific is lost, the Japanese navy is ready for service in the Atlantic. So the Battle of the Pacific is the Battle of the Atlantic.' A *Melbourne Herald* article carried the opinion that, 'The Pacific struggle is primarily one in which the United States and Australia must have the fullest say in the direction of the fighting plan. Australia looks to America, free from any pangs as to traditional links or kinship with the UK. We know the problem that the UK faces, but we know that Australia can go and Britain still hold on.' There is a considerable force of ANZAC soldiers in the Middle East.

27 February: A major battle takes place in the Java Sea. British, Australian and Dutch ships under the command of Admiral K W F M Doorman are attempting to attack Japanese troop transports. The Japanese navy is highly trained in night fighting; the Allies lose two cruisers and four destroyers. Two

India and Independence

In March 1942 Sir Stafford Cripps went to India on a fact-finding mission. The rapid Japanese conquests in the Far East have put India's position in the spotlight. One million Indians already form a vital part of the Allied war effort with many serving in the British Army in the Middle East. But India's population is 400,000,000, many of whom want independence from Britain. Some of the people Cripps would meet are: Mahatma Ghandi. Immensely popular, Ghandi advocates passive resistance to the British Raj. Though he hates British Imperialism, he has no hate for the British themselves. At this time he holds no official position in the Nationalist movement. Jawaharlal Nehru. A Cambridge graduate who was called to the Bar, Nehru is a socialist who is anti-Nazi and anti-Fascist but is also a bitter opponent of British rule in India. He represents the Congress Party, the largest political organization in the country. Next in size and political importance comes the Moslem League representing India's 90,000,000 Moslems. They demand independence but also seek the establishment of a Moslem state to be called Pakistan that encompasses the province of Sind, the Punjab, Kashmir, the North-West Frontier and possibly Afghanistan. There are many other parties including the National Liberal Federation who are prepared to work in close co-operation with the British and favour Dominion status over complete independence.

WAR DIARY 1942

more Allied cruisers will be sunk in two days time although the ship will first sink six transports.

Following the loss of most of the Far East tin sources to the Japanese, production in Cornish mines is rapidly being increased. Formerly closed mines are being reopened.

3 March: The Red Army has made enormous progress over the winter. A matter of weeks ago the enemy was at the gates of Moscow, Leningrad was besieged, Rostov in the south was in German hands. Now Rostov has been liberated, the Germans pushed 100 miles and more back from Moscow and advances of up to 250 miles have been made at some points. Leningrad is still threatened but the freezing of Lake Ladoga enabled Russian supply convoys to drive across it and bring ammunition and food to the city. But spring is coming and it remains to be seen what strength the Axis forces will muster despite their recent heavy losses.

Japanese aircraft raid the airfield and harbour at Broome, Western Australia.

4 March: All Japanese-Americans, especially on the West Coast, find themselves subject to relocation in special camps.

New conscription laws in the UK will apply to women and men up to the age of 45.

12 March: British and Indian troops have been evacuated from the Andaman Islands in the Bay of Bengal. The islands are considered too close to the Dutch East Indies – now being occupied by the Japanese – to be defended. The Allies also have an acute shortage of warships.

19 March: In the House of Commons, A P Herbert urges

Thirteen Japanese flying-boats were smashed in a heavy Royal Air Force raid on the harbour of Port Blair in the Andaman Islands.

SMASH JAPANESE AGGRESSION!

This poster depicts an RAF raid on a Japanese flying-boat base in the Andaman Islands on 14 April 1942. (National Archives).

Tragedy of Lidice

On 27 May 1942 two British-trained Czechoslovak patriots attempted to assassinate Reinhard Heydrich, Reichsprotektor of the German Protectorate of Bohemia and Moravia, whilst he was being driven to his office in Prague Castle. Heydrich had a reputation for being an exceptionally cruel and ruthless Nazi. He survived the bomb attack but succumbed to blood-poisoning in hospital on 4 June.

Reprisals were swift; it is estimated that the final death toll was in excess of 1300 with scores of Prague residents being summarily executed. Hitler in person ordered that the Czechoslovak village of Lidice which had a reputation for being supportive of partisans, be wiped from the map.

All 192 male villagers were shot. All 184 women of the village were deported to Ravensbruck Concentration Camp. Of the 88 children, seven were selected for 'Germanification' – adoption by a German family. In late May, on the orders of Karl Adolf Eichmann, the rest were sent to the extermination camp at Chelmno. The two assassins were captured and executed.

The Nazis openly and proudly broadcast the events in Lidice and news of the atrocity was quickly spread by the Allied media. In September 1942 coal miners in Stoke-on-Trent founded the movement 'Lidice Shall Live' to raise funds for rebuilding the village post-war. It was also discovered that two men from the village were pilots serving with the RAF at the time of the massacre.

Adolf Eichmann had been charged by Heydrich with managing the logistics of mass deportations of Jews and as such was an architect of the holocaust. He survived the war and escaped to Argentina. He was tracked down there by the Israeli secret service, Mossad, and abducted in 1962. Brought to Israel he was put on trial for genocide, found guilty and hanged on 31 May 1962.

that a message of goodwill, hope, admiration and gratitude should be sent to the 'gallant officers and men of the Mercantile Marine'. The Allied merchant shipping fleet is vital for Britain's survival.

28 March: Bulgaria declares war on the Soviet Union.

5 April: Japanese bombers raid the British naval base at Colombo, Ceylon.

8 April: US troops besieged on the Bataan peninsula in the Philippines surrender. The nearby fortress island of Corregidor in Manila Bay continues to hold out.

28 April: York is bombed tonight as the German 'Baedecker Raids' continue. They are a reprisal for the RAF bombing of German cities such as Rostock where the target was the Heinkel aircraft factory and munition works but where some bombs inevitably go astray. The Germans have said that the Luftwaffe would go all out to destroy every building in Britain that is marked with three stars in Baedeker's guide-books. Bath, Exeter and Norwich are among the towns hit so far.

30 April: The 10,000 ton cruiser *HMS Edinburgh* is torpedoed while on Russian Convoy escort duty. Despite efforts to save her the ship is doomed to sink.

5 May: British troops land on the Indian Ocean Vichy France-controlled island of Madagascar off the east coast of Africa. It is vital that the island does not fall to the Japanese as they would be able to intercept Allied convoys heading for the Middle East via the Cape route.

6 May: General Jonathan Wainwright surrenders the island of Corregidor. He will also order all remaining US forces in the Philippines to surrender in two day's time. The epic siege of Corregidor has caught the imagination of the American public. There is a mood of determination to exact retribution from the Japanese.

7 May: The main French naval base at Diego Suarez on Madagascar surrenders today. The French had put up a largely token resistance. It is believed that British casualties total less than 100 killed and about 350 wounded.

WAR DIARY 1942

8 May: Since 3 May a battle has been raging in the Coral Sea, north of Australia. A US fleet under the command of Admiral Frank Fletcher is turning back a Japanese invasion fleet bound for Port Moresby, New Guinea.

There are signs that the Germans intend resuming their offensive in Russia now that better weather has returned. Today they attack towards Kerch in the Crimea.

9 May: Washington reports the loss of two merchant ships to U-Boat activity in the Gulf of Mexico. A third ship will be sunk near the mouth of the Mississippi in six day's time.

12 May: Three British destroyers – *HMS Lively*, *Jackal* and *Kipling* – are sunk in the Eastern Mediterranean.

21 May: Within the last few months Iran has become a major conduit for Allied supplies going to Russia. A new railway and new roads have been opened that link the Persian Gulf with the Caspian Sea. British soldiers are reminded of home and holidays when they see powerful locomotives, with familiar UK markings, puffing into Teheran, drawing behind them truck after truck full of crates of war materials.

24 May: The Russians say they have evacuated by sea their forces from Kerch. Sevastopol in the south of the Crimea remains under German siege. It appears from Soviet reports that Marshal Timoshenko's offensive before Kharkov is going well.

Three million Chinese civilians have been driven from their homes in Honan Province by floodwater.

28 May: Mexico declares war on the Axis countries after several of her ships have been sunk by U-Boats.

30 May: Cologne is the target as the RAF mount their first-ever '1000 Bomber' raid. The attack is supported by 13,000 RAF combined air and groundcrew.

Japanese submarines are unsuccessful in an attack on Allied shipping in the harbour of Diego Suarez, Madagascar.

31 May: Timoshenko's offensive in the Kharkov region ends today.

Four small Japanese submarines make an abortive attack on Sydney Harbour, Australia. All are sunk; one is later raised from the seabed.

8 June: Sydney and the town of Newcastle, New South Wales, are shelled by a Japanese submarine.

12 June: Anne Frank, a young Jewish girl in hiding in Amsterdam, receives a diary for her 13th birthday.

18 June: A top secret operation called the *Manhattan Project* is started by the Allies. The aim is to develop a nuclear weapon of awesome power. It is known that the Germans are also aware of the potential of the atom bomb.

Winston Churchill arrives in Washington for meetings with President Roosevelt.

21 June: Britain and her allies have held the port of Tobruk in Libya for 517 days. Today the nation is shocked to learn that the Afrika Korps have overwhelmed the fortress in their latest offensive. Tomorrow Hitler will make the German General Rommel a Field Marshal.

1 July: 'No pleasure motoring' rule comes into force. Drivers have up until 30 July to use up whatever fuel is in the tanks of their vehicles. After this time no civilian motor car can be used unless it is for essential purposes.

3 July: Sevastopol has fallen to the Germans after an epic siege lasting nearly eight months. Many of the defenders were evacuated eastwards across the Black Sea. A German summer offensive is underway. Military analysts believe it is aimed at the oil-rich Caucasus in the south of Russia.

4 July: American engineers assisted by 2000 local workers have constructed a huge new naval base at Londonderry in Northern Ireland. Opened last February, today the base celebrates American Independence Day.

6 July: A U-Boat enters the Gulf of St Lawrence on the Canadian East Coast and sinks three merchant ships.

7 July: Two convicted German spies, Jose Key and Alphonse Timmerman, are hanged at Wandsworth prison.

11 July: In the first 11 days of July, 83 enemy aircraft have been destroyed over Malta as the Axis air force continues to bomb the island. In the same period the RAF have lost 21 aircraft with nine pilots saved.

21 July: In the last three weeks there has been a grave deterioration of the situation on the Russian Front. The Germans have crossed the River Don in strength and appear to be driving eastwards towards the city of Stalingrad on the River Volga. Further north the Nazis appear to have been held before the city of Voronezh.

26 July: An air armada of RAF bombers set off to raid Hamburg tonight. They carry 175,000 incendiaries as well as 4000lb bombs.

Rationing of chocolate and sweets begins today; two ounces per head for adults and the same for children.

30 July: The great German drive in the south of Russia continues. Rostov at the mouth of the Don has been captured. The Germans are across the Don in several places and threaten the rail line that runs south from Stalingrad to Novorossisk on the Black Sea. Even though it must be under immense pressure, the Red Air Force has been conducting long-distance raids on East Prussia. The important transit centre of Konigsberg has been hit.

Doolittle did much!

In **April 1942** Major James Doolittle led the famous bombing raid on Tokyo – launched from the aircraft carrier Hornet – that signaled the intention of the US to eventually bring the war to the Japanese homeland. On **19 July 1943** Doolittle, now a major-general commanding the North-West African Strategical Air Force, led a daylight bombing raid on transport targets in Rome, the second Axis capital he had visited in this conflict. Prior to the attack, leaflets were dropped informing the inhabitants that the raid was being made against military targets only. The American bomber crews have been told: 'Bomb accurately or not at all.'

A casualty in one of the aircraft shot down near the city was Gunner Sgt Ed Bain, a veteran of the Tokyo mission. In the 110,000 sorties that comprised the Allied Rome air campaign of 1943-44, 600 aircraft were lost and 3600 aircrew members died.

Doolittle was a remarkable airman. For two decades before the war he was a daring stunt flier and later a test pilot. In 1925 he won the Schneider Trophy for the USA in Chesapeake Bay, beating the British entry, the Supermarine S4 designed by R J Mitchell. The S4 was a forerunner of the Spitfire and held the world air speed record at the time. Doolittle was also the first man to fly across the United States in less than 12 hours.

Ordeal of Convoy PQ17

A convoy carrying aid for Russia assembles off Iceland.

U-Boats and the Luftwaffe exacted a dreadful toll in the merchantmen that made up the aid convoys to Russia. The worse losses of all befell PQ17 in July 1942.

In 1942 Allied losses from the aid convoys to Russia rapidly increased as German aircraft flying from Norway and prowling U-Boats took their toll. In May PQ16 had lost seven ships, but PQ-17 was the largest and most valuable convoy to date. The 35 merchant ships (22 American, eight British, two Russian, two Panamanian and one Dutch) and escorts had assembled off Iceland and were bound for Murmansk, under the command of Commodore John Dowding. Crammed into bulging holds were nearly 300 aircraft, 600 tanks, more than 4000 trucks and trailers, and a general cargo that exceeded 150,000 tons. It was more than enough to completely equip an army of 50,000.

'Convoy is to scatter'

Providing immediate cover was the First Escort Group (EG1) under Commander Jack Broome with four destroyers, 10 corvettes or armed trawlers and two ack-ack auxiliaries. A much larger fleet formed a more distant covering role and included the aircraft carrier *HMS Victorious*. The convoy route took them close to Spitsbergen, north of Bear Island and skirted the edge of the ice pack. Eventually it would enter the Barents Sea and then the White Sea. The convoy was sighted by U-456 shortly after it cleared Iceland. The Luftwaffe began its attacks during the evening of the next day. The *Christopher Newport* and *William Hooper* were the first losses on 4 July. That night the Admiralty learnt that the German capital ships

Tirpitz, *Admiral Scheer* and *Admiral Hipper* had left Trondheim to intercept the convoy.

First Sea Lord Sir Dudley Pound called an emergency meeting of his staff. Vice Admiral Sir Henry Moore recommended that if the convoy was to be dispersed, there was no time to waste. Every other officer wanted the ships to stick together. But Pound himself feared that *Tirpitz* with its high speed and 15-inch guns, would inflict massive losses on the closely bunched merchant ships. At around 9.30pm that night he made a signal: 'Most immediate. Convoy is to scatter.'

The German naval force went to sea the following day but was then ordered to return to port, unknown to the Allies who had no intelligence at all on the enemy fleet location. Meanwhile, the bigger convoy escorts were returning to Scapa Flow. Only the smaller ships were left to attempt to protect the scattered merchantmen, making them easy prey to U-Boats and aircraft. On 5 July the Luftwaffe sank six merchant ships and six more were dispatched by U-Boats.

On 6 July the *Pan Atlantic* was sunk by bombs and the *John Witherspoon* was torpedoed. On 7-8 July five more ships were sunk. The remaining escort vessels withdrew into the Arctic Ocean on 9 July but the merchant ships suffered no more losses that day. The last to be sunk were the *Hoosier* and *El Capitan* on 10 July.

Luftwaffe flew 202 sorties

The Luftwaffe flew 202 sorties and lost only five planes. In all, 24 ships were sunk out of the 33 in the convoy; 153 merchant seamen lost their lives. Of those men only seven had perished before the convoy was scattered. A total of 142,518 tons of shipping was lost along with 3350 motor vehicles, 430 tanks, 210 bombers and 99,316 tons of general cargo.

Additionally the Soviet tanker *Azerbaijan* lost her cargo of linseed oil and much of the cargo of the *Winston-Salem* cargo had been jettisoned in Novaya Zemlya. Two surviving ships made port at Archangel on 10 July. Another nine arrived over the following week, having been rounded up by Commodore Dowding, who, having been rescued from a raft after his ship was torpedoed, immediately set off up the coast of Novaya Zemlya to look for stragglers. Three of the surviving ships were sunk on the return journey.

The Soviet Union did not believe that so many ships could be lost from a single convoy and openly accused the Allies of lying. So, despite the help provided by the material that did arrive, PQ-17 actually worsened Soviet-Allied relations for a time and the Soviets never acknowledged the sacrifice of the Allied seaman.

The heavy losses of PQ-17 compelled the Allies to delay the sailing of the next convoy, PQ-18 until September. Despite having over 40 escorts, 13 ships were sunk from PQ-18, and convoys were then suspended until the darkness of the Polar winter set in.

ORDER of the BLUE NOSE

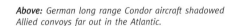

Chief Steward Horace Carswell sailed in Convoy PQ-17 on the *SS Empire Tide*. His previous ship had been the *SS Pampas* that he'd left at Malta 'bombed into scrap iron'. He then went on 'survivor's leave' and stayed with relatives in Reading before volunteering to join the *Empire Tide* on a convoy to Russia.

We first made a curiously peaceful Atlantic crossing to an American port where we took aboard our cargo before proceeding to Reykjavik. From there we set out for Archangel in the White Sea.

'It was midsummer and once over the Arctic Circle daylight had lengthened to about 20 hours. Three days out from Iceland the first German scout came nosing along, a Focke-Wulf 190. Others followed, like birds of ill-omen.

'We managed to keep cheerful. The threat from the Jerries did not prevent some of us from being initiated into the Order of the Blue Nose, the Arctic seas equivalent of the ceremony of greeting King Neptune when crossing the Equator.

'The vicinity of Bear Island offered the greatest danger being within easy range of German airfields in Norway. The enemy's assault was launched on a grand scale. Between 40 and 50 Jerries came racing in from all directions – bombers, fighters and torpedo-carrying planes that filled the Arctic air with the thunder of high-powered engines. It was the Fourth of July. With unconscious irony, the winged squadrons of the Reich began a rip-snorting celebration of Independence Day in the tough Nazi

manner by slamming bombs and cannon-shells at two of our American ships. A ship on the *Empire Tide's* port quarter erupted like a volcano and disappeared into the frigid depths.

'The sea spurted in columns of foam. Fragments of ice from the shattered floes spattered our decks. The guns of warships and merchantmen filled the sky with high-explosives and the rain of steel made you grateful for a tin "battle bowler". The only notes of real music in this devil's concerto were the whine of stricken Jerry planes spiralling into the sea. While the battle was at its height I stood on deck and thought to myself, "This is about as hot as the party we had on the Malta convoy."

'The white route to Russia was certainly no picnic in those days when the Luftwaffe was riding the skies in strength. Things were bad enough in the Med when your ship was scuppered but if you took to the boats or went overboard in these icy seas your ordeal was a sight worse and chance of survival considerably less.

'The going was so tough that our captain decided to make for temporary haven at Novaya Zemlya island. On the way we picked up 148 survivors from drifting lifeboats with men suffering from frostbitten hands and feet. Once we gained shelter, radio signals were made. These brought a plane from Russia with a lady doctor; a few of the severely wounded were flown to Archangel.

U-Boat surfaced close by

'We set off unescorted on the last leg of the voyage. On the way we spotted three lifeboats manned by survivors of a ship slowly sinking beside them. Suddenly the green-grey conning-tower of a U-Boat emerged close by the boats. The neighbourhood was not so healthy! Our captain altered course and ordered full-ahead on the engines and these turn-tail tactics must have been unspeakably galling to him. No one would have taken a crack at that U-

Above: *German long range Condor aircraft shadowed Allied convoys far out in the Atlantic.*

Boat with more zest than Captain Frank Willis Hardy, but all our ammo had been expended in the bitter fighting.

'The submarine hove to and did not appear to take offensive action against the men, though it was difficult to see what was going on. Then we saw the U-Boat make off. Captain Harvey decided to turn around and go back for the survivors, though many an anxious eye on the *Empire Tide* scanned the sea for a periscope or the bubbling wake of steel "fish". The men we picked up said that the Jerries had given them water and biscuits. The U-Boat captain spoke English and asked the men why they were helping the Russians when they were not Bolsheviks themselves. Told that it was because they were our allies in this war that was started by the Germans, the captain had retorted, "Britain and France declared war on the Fatherland."

'Eventually we got to Archangel where our arrival with munitions and supplies was greeted cordially by Russian officials but there were no wild demonstrations of welcome by the people.

*Chief Steward Carswell got back safely to Britain from Russia. For his outstanding conduct aboard the Empire Tide *he was awarded the Lloyds Medal for Bravery at Sea to add to his DSM, MM and BEM. The Empire Tide was a Catapult Armed Merchantman (CAM) though it is not known if it launched its Hurricane fighter when it was part of PQ-17. CAM ships were ordered to be disbanded in June 1943, a fact picked up by German intelligence. As part of a Britain-bound convoy at the time,* Empire Tide *and another ship with her still had their Hurricanes when two Condor long-range bombers attacked on 28 July in the Bay of Biscay. The Condor crews had a nasty shock when the two Hurricanes were launched; both German machines were shot down.*

POSTER ART of the AXIS

War in the Pacific

Following a disastrous opening phase, America took the fight to the Japanese at sea, in the air and on land.

After the attack at Pearl Harbour, the US faced a whole series of further reversals in the opening months of 1942. The Japanese invaded the American-controlled Philippine Islands and rapidly conquered them, having earlier caught a substantial portion of the US bomber force as sitting ducks on the ground at Clark Field. As they had with the British in Malaya, the Japanese tactics caused chaos and confusion, particularly amongst the Filipino troops.

American forces under General Douglas MacArthur were soon forced to retreat into the Bataan Peninsula, across the bay from the capital, Manila, which the Japanese entered on 3 January. A siege resulted and despite high casualties, the Japanese gradually wore down the US-Filipino forces. On 12 March MacArthur, acting on a direct order from President Roosevelt, left the Philippines to go to Darwin in Australia. His parting words were: 'I shall return.' Bataan came under the command of General Jonathan Wainwright.

The Japanese received fresh troops and brought up heavy artillery. They had complete air superiority. Meanwhile the Allied forces were suffering shortages of food and ammunition and were also being decimated by sickness and disease. On 9 April they surrendered, believing further resistance to be futile if not impossible. A number of men escaped to the island fortress of Corregidor out in Manila Bay but 78,000 were captured and forced into a 65-mile 'Death March' in which many thousands perished from thirst, hunger and the cruelty of their captors.

Island fortress surrenders

Corregidor was supposed to be invulnerable. But it could no longer receive supplies, had been savagely bombed and was soon under a rain of shells from Japanese guns on the mainland. The island held out for nearly a month after the fall of Bataan. On 5 May the Japanese landed on the island and established a beach-head; next day the 15,000 man garrison surrendered.

Within days of losing the Philippines, American fortunes at sea received a boost at the Battle of the Coral Sea, north of Australia. A US fleet under the command of Admiral Frank Fletcher sought to turn back a Japanese invasion fleet bound for Port Moresby, New Guinea. At first it seemed the Americans had the advantage when they bombed and sank the carrier *Shoho*. The excited US pilot responsible, Lt Cm Robert Dixon, radioed: 'Scratch one flattop.' In the next engagement the carrier *Shokaku* was damaged. But the Japanese hit back, sinking the US carrier *Lexington* and damaging a second, the *Yorktown*. At this point the Americans withdrew. However, the Japanese called off their attack on Port Moresby. In addition, they lost a lot of aircraft and crews. The threat of a Japanese invasion of Australia also receded.

A month after the inconclusive Battle of the Coral Sea, American and Japanese carrier fleets clashed, this time near the island of Midway in the middle of the Pacific Ocean. As at the Coral Sea, the opposing ships did not sight each other; the battle was decided by air power alone.

Enemy code broken at Midway

The Americans had broken the Japanese code and knew their enemy had a fleet at sea. They suspected Midway was the target but needed to be sure. So they had the garrison on Midway put out a message 'in the clear' to the effect that they were short of fresh water. The Japanese heard this and confirmed it in code to their fleet, using their codename for Midway. The Americans picked this up and then knew for certain where the enemy fleet was bound.

The Japanese had four carriers, the Americans three but they also had aircraft based on Midway itself. As a diversion, on 3 June 1942, the Japanese staged an air attack on Dutch Harbour, a US naval station in the Aleutian Islands. On the same day the

opening action at Midway took place when land-based US Avengers attacked the Japanese fleet. They failed to score a hit and only one Avenger returned home. At 7am on 4 June the carriers *USS Enterprise* and *Hornet* launched their strike groups. The first 15 aircraft were shot down by Zero fighters; only one crew member survived. In fact, of the 41 aircraft deployed just six returned to the US carriers.

But their sacrifice was not in vain. They had absorbed the bulk of the enemy fighter attacks and the deadly Zeros were still scattered when 37 Dauntless dive-bombers from *Enterprise* and 17 from *Yorktown* made their attack, sinking three of the Japanese carriers. The US carrier *Yorktown* was then caught by a Japanese torpedo-bomber attack. Her crew abandoned ship; the carrier's hulk was later sunk by a submarine. The fourth Japanese carrier was crippled and set on fire in an early evening attack.

Four Japanese carriers sunk

It was the turning point in the Pacific war. For the cost of 92 carrier aircraft, 40 shore-based aircraft and the *Yorktown*, the US claimed four fleet carriers, three-quarters of the Japanese navy's carrier strike force. In addition to the carriers the enemy had lost 258 aircraft and a large number of their most experienced pilots. On 6 June they also lost a heavy cruiser and had another severely damaged in an air strike launched from *USS Enterprise*.

Fate favoured the Americans at Midway. The two Japanese carriers that survived the Coral Sea encounter were supposed to form part of the Midway force but were unable to be made ready in time. On the contrary, the *Yorktown* – also damaged at the Coral Sea – was able to get to Pearl Harbor for emergency repairs carried out quickly enough that she was able to join the US fleet at Midway.

Two months later the Americans went on the offensive in the Pacific and seized an airfield on Guadalcanal in the Solomon Islands. It would take a tough seven-month land, sea and air battle before the Japanese admitted defeat and withdrew their few remaining battered ground troops. Guadacanal cost them 24,000 dead against 1600 killed and 4709 wounded on the US side. There were many more islands to be captured in the months and years ahead but after Midway and Guadalcanal the Americans knew that Japan's rising sun was rising no more.

In early 1942 the Japanese advanced to within a few hundred miles of Australia.

Desert Fox and the Afrika Korps

The German forces newly arrived in Libya in March 1941 were called the Afrika Korps and came under the command of General Erwin Rommel, a soldier who had distinguished himself as a master of mobile warfare and audacious manoeuvre in the German blitzkriegs in Flanders and France in May and June 1940. The wide open spaces of the North African desert would soon prove ideally suited to his military skills.

On 24 March 1941, Rommel carried out a raid against the small British force holding advanced positions at El Agheila. Quickly realizing how weak the British were, he continued the attack into Cyrenaica, capturing Benghazi on 3 April. On 6 April, one of Rommel's probing panzer columns captured the British commander, General O'Connor, while he was driving unescorted.

Tobruk stands firm

O'Connor's capture was a major blow to Wavell who could only scrape together the few remaining Allied units in Egypt and rush them to the port of Tobruk where they joined up with the retreating men from El Agheila. Supplied by sea, the garrison just had enough time to construct defences strong enough to stand against repeated attacks by the German and Italian forces. Tobruk stood firm but the rest of Libya was now firmly under Axis control. Rommel also took Bardia and Sollum just inside the Egyptian border but with Tobruk a threat to his long lines of supply, he could go no further.

On 15 June it was Britain's turn to go on the offensive again. Wavell hoped that his army, largely made up of recently arrived reinforcements, would be able to emulate the spectacular successes enjoyed against the Italians six months earlier. Unfortunately, the circumstances had drastically changed; Rommel was an inspirational leader and even the Italians responded to his drive and enthusiasm. As well as reliable tanks and the addition of a newly-arrived panzer division, the Germans also had the light but powerful 88 millimeter gun that had been originally designed as an anti-aircraft weapon but which proved to be devastating when employed against Allied tanks. A direct hit from the 30-

pound projectile fired from an 88 could turn a British tank into an inferno of exploding ammunition and blazing fuel. British tank crews called this 'brewing up'.

The Eighth Army is born

The British attack failed and they were forced back into Egypt. Tobruk still held out. Churchill had been a champion of Wavell but now thought a change of commander might bring a change of fortune. Sir Claude Auchinleck left his command in India and arrived to take over in the Middle East in July; he at once began preparations for another offensive. Troop reinforcements from India and Britain and large numbers of US-built light tanks arrived to replace earlier losses. Auchinleck reorganized the Western Desert Force into the Eighth Army.

'The Auk' ordered the attack (*Operation Crusader*) to start on 18 November. He had seven divisions and some 700 tanks going up against Rommel's army that was probably about equal in manpower but had a third fewer panzers. A two-week seesaw battle ensued south of Sollum and Tobruk. At Sidi Resegh, 20 miles from Tobruk, the Afrika

Korps gave the British armoured corps a bloody nose, knocking out hundreds of tanks.

Auchinleck refused to be panicked. Shored up by air superiority, for the most part the Allies stood their ground. Soon Rommel had to redeploy. On 26 November, the Eighth Army

renewed the attack. New Zealand troops advancing from Sidi Resegh met up with Australians breaking out of Tobruk. Rommel counter-attacked and re-took Sidi Resegh but in an attempt to relieve his frontier garrisons in Bardia, Sollum and Halfaya, cut off by the first British attack, he was defeated with heavy loss. However, the Germans in Bardia and Sollum would hold out until 17 January 1942, pinning down a considerable portion of the Eighth Army.

The Allies resumed the attack and once again linked up with Tobruk. Rommel retired in good order. Short of supplies, Rommel realized his whole army was at risk of encirclement. By 31 December he was back at El Agheila, almost at the same place from which he'd started his first offensive in April.

The Allied troops dubbed these great tank races across the desert, the 'Benghazi Handicaps' and this was the third and, hopefully, the last one. The public at home were cheered by the Eighth Army victory. It was some good news at a time when Hitler's armies – although turned back at the very gates of Moscow – had already occupied half of European Russia and their Japanese partners in aggression were running rampant in the Far East and the Pacific.

The Mediterranean and North Africa

Captured German General bombed by his own side and rescued by the Royal Navy!

Operation Crusader fought between 18 November – 30 December 1941 successfully relieved the 1941 Siege of Tobruk. In the process it was the first big victory over the Germans by British-led forces in the Second World War. It was also the first occasion in which a German General was captured by

the Western Allies; Johann von Ravenstein was on a reconnaissance mission near Tobruk when his lone car crested a ridge and was confronted by a Bren gun carrier manned by New Zealanders.

The general later said: 'I had no choice but to give myself up. It is something that might happen to anyone in this damned desert. It's a perfect ground for armoured forces such as are engaged at present. Rapid manoeuvres make it a game of surprise, a paradise for a tactician but a nightmare for a quartermaster.'

A British general, Richard O'Connor, had been captured in similar circumstances while in his unaccompanied staff car not far from Tobruk in April 1941. O'Connor was held as a POW in Italy until he escaped in December 1943. He returned to command Allied forces in Normandy and Holland and later served in post-war India.

By contrast von Ravenstein saw no more action, at least not on the German side! He

departed Tobruk on *HMS Chakdina* on 5 December but she was sunk that night by Axis aircraft.

Taken by liner to New York

The general was rescued by *HMS Thogrim* and was taken to Mersa Matruh and on to Cairo. He then proceeded to Durban before joining the *Queen Elizabeth* at Simonstown. The liner docked in New York on 22 May 1942 and von Ravenstein was escorted to a POW camp in Canada.

In 1946 he was brought to the UK and housed in the Island Farm Camp at Bridgend in Wales. In November 1947 he was repatriated to Germany. Commenting on his years in captivity, he said he preferred his Canadian incarceration because there were younger officers there who enjoyed learning and the arts whereas at Bridgend there were too many men who had been rapidly promoted simply because of their loyalty to Nazi ideals.

The Afrika Korps in action. The panzer above is seen in typical desert terrain where the heat and dust were the enemies of both sides. However in springtime the desert could burst into colourful bloom as witnessed around the big artillery piece pictured below.

With the impassable Libyan Sand Sea to the south, Rommel's position at El Agheila was a strong one. He was now nearer his own main base at Tripoli and could enjoy better air support while, for the Allies, it was a long way to haul supplies from Egypt. Rommel had no intention of quitting North Africa and persuaded Hitler to give him precious supplies and reinforcements, despite the pressing need for more men and munitions on the Russian Front.

Rommel rebounds at El Agheila

On 21 January 1942 the Germans attacked in force on a narrow front. Caught unprepared, Auchinleck retreated. The Afrika Korps poured forward so fast that they overran large Allied fuel and ammunition dumps. Feeding off these supplies, Rommel's onrushing men captured Benghazi before the end of January. Then they came up against a hastily prepared defensive position at Gazala, about 40 miles west of Tobruk where they paused to reorganize.

Stalemate ensued for the next three months although in this period the RAF took a heavy toll of German and Italian truck convoys. The Luftwaffe, for its part, mounted a terrifying blitz to neutralize Britain's vital island of Malta, a constant thorn in the side of the Axis shipping supply route across the southern Mediterranean to North Africa.

Auchinleck built up a powerful defensive position that stretched 40 miles south of Gazala. Facing it, Rommel realized that the Allies would be gaining strength faster than he was, especially in the all-important tank numbers. On the night of 27 – 28 May, Rommel's Italian troops attacked all along the front from Gazala on the shore of the Med to the Free French-held fort of Bir Hakim, end of the line about 40 miles to the south. At the same time the German leader personally led three divisions of his Afrika Korps panzers on

a wide sweep of the desert south of Bir Hakim. Harassed by the RAF and in the face of stubborn French resistance, Rommel cleverly revised his tactics and attacked two gaps in the British line on either side of the 150th Northumbrian Brigade. Despite a brave resistance, the latter were worn down and ceased to exist as a fighting unit. Bir Hakim fell on 10 June; most of the surviving French defenders got away in good order. Rommel rushed up dozens of 88mm guns and devastated a British counter-attack before going over to the offensive. On the morning of 13 June, the Allies had about 300 tanks in action but by nightfall just 65 were left intact. The Eighth Army had no choice but to stream back in disarray towards Egypt.

Tobruk surrenders

The German storm now burst upon Tobruk. Having withstood one siege, this time Tobruk could not resist the rain of artillery and Luftwaffe bombings that Rommel concentrated upon the port. At dawn on 21 June, Tobruk surrendered. The Afrika Korps inherited a massive haul of supplies and precious petrol.

This latest offensive had cost the Allies 80,000 men, killed, wounded or captured. But the Eighth Army was still receiving reinforcements and had the benefit once more of a shrinking line of supply. On 28 June, the British rearguard fought a skilful delaying action. Pounded from the air, Rommel now pushed forward more cautiously. Auchinleck meanwhile had done a tremendous job in restoring order to his army. He had established a new defensive line extending from the railway halt at El Alamein for 50 miles or so south to the Qattara Depression, desert terrain totally unsuitable for tanks and mechanized forces. When Rommel's leading panzers probed the El Alamein position they were easily turned back.

DESERT DEBATE

The first two days of July 1942 witnessed a debate in the House of Commons concerning the surrender of Tobruk and its garrison of about 25,000 troops on 21 June, an event that shocked Britain and dismayed Churchill. It was utterly unexpected not least by the British commander in North Africa, General Auchinleck. The night before the port fell he had sent a telegram to London stating that Tobruk's defences were in good order with an adequate garrison and supplies good for 90 days.

In the middle of May the Allied and Axis armies both had around 100,000 troops of which on Rommel's side, 50,000 were German. The Allies had more tanks and a third more artillery pieces plus enjoyed superiority in the air and shorter lines of communication. The key date was 13 June when the Allies lost 230 tanks without any corresponding loss to the enemy.

Tank turret too small

The Commons heard that the main Allied battle tank, the Crusader, was unreliable and unsuited to desert conditions. There was something fundamentally wrong with the cooling system. The driver's vision was too limited and the turret was too small for 'a man of ordinary physique'. The Minister of Production promised that new and better guns and tanks were under production. There was also criticism of the organization of the army: 'There are almost two armies in the Middle East, the Army of the Desert and the Army in Cairo.' A favourite wisecrack with the frontline soldiers went like this: 'If Rommel gets to the Pyramids and GHQ turns out in its own defence, for the first time in his career Rommel will be outnumbered.'

Aneurin Bevan summed up the mood of the House: 'This is a proud and brave race and it is feeling humiliated. It cannot stand the holding out of Sevastopol for so many months and the collapse of Tobruk in 26 hours. It wants leadership... It is getting words. This nation can win, but it must be properly led, it must be properly inspired, and it must have confidence in its military leadership. Give us that and we can win the war...'

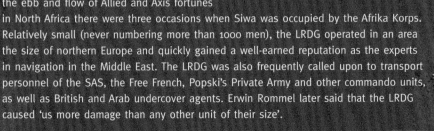

Long Range Desert Group

The LRDG was formed at Siwa Oasis in Egypt's Western Desert on 13 September 1940. Siwa became their base although with the ebb and flow of Allied and Axis fortunes in North Africa there were three occasions when Siwa was occupied by the Afrika Korps. Relatively small (never numbering more than 1000 men), the LRDG operated in an area the size of northern Europe and quickly gained a well-earned reputation as the experts in navigation in the Middle East. The LRDG was also frequently called upon to transport personnel of the SAS, the Free French, Popski's Private Army and other commando units, as well as British and Arab undercover agents. Erwin Rommel later said that the LRDG caused 'us more damage than any other unit of their size'.

PAGES from HISTORY

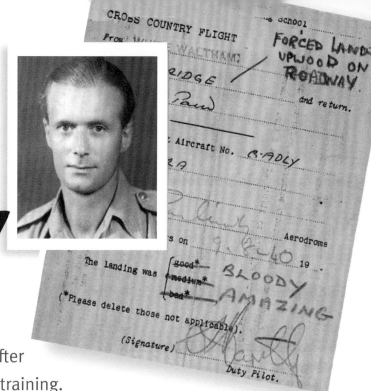

The story of a British Hurricane pilot who fought with the Western Desert Air Force after surviving one 'Bloody Amazing' landing in training.

Top: A Test Certificate for Francis Pain (pictured inset) issued when he was a Pilot Officer. On this occasion it appears he landed on a road rather than a runway!

Main picture: Hurricanes flying over Egypt's Western Desert.
Above: A section of the Logbook. The crosses indicate confirmed kills.
Right: The Logbook's striking cover complete with DIY gazetteer of North Africa and the Middle East circa 1942! As a F/Lt, Francis Pain served there with Nos 213 and 73 Squadrons (Hurricanes).

'**F**urther Activities Classified'. These three words dated 18 April 1943 are the final intriguing entry in the RAF Logbook of F/Lt Francis Pain. Not even his children could say what the rest of the war held in store for their father. That he survived, yes. But what those classified activities were remain a mystery - apart from vaguely remembered table talk of D-Day and Doodlebugs.

I first came across Francis Pain's story back in 1994. His son Ian, a one-time professional Sussex County cricketer, was then the landlord of the Battle of Trafalgar pub near Brighton Station. He learnt of my interest in World War II and produced his father's Logbook and other documentation.

'My father died in 1969' he explained, 'And it wasn't until he had gone that my brother and I realised that there was a big gap in our knowledge of what kind of war he had. On the other hand, we were lucky to have such a priceless souvenir as his Logbook. Whenever I look at it I get this wonderful picture of him and a tremendous feel for the life of an RAF fighter pilot all those years ago.'

And what a life. From the first entry in the Logbook (2 July 1940) which features a training flight in a Tiger Moth at White Waltham, to the very last, a Channel sweep in a rocket-firing Tempest that left an E-Boat destroyed and an Me 109 damaged, history, humour and tragedy of war are combined in fascinating fashion. Rarely can so few words have succeeded in conveying so much meaning.

Here we take a tour through some of the pages starting in 1940 when the risks involved in learning to fly are dramatically highlighted.

1940. TRAINING

30 August: Completed Tiger Moth training. Proficiency as pilot - 'Average'.
12 September: Harvard training at Kiddlington. 'Glenville killed. Spun in minus one wing.'
25 October: 'Townsend killed. Spin in night flying. Flamer. Instructor F/O Cassells saved but badly burnt.'
19 November: Completed Harvard training. Proficiency as pilot - 'Average. Only one solo flight at night.'
20 December: Hurricane Mk 1 training at Aston Down. 'Vernon killed. Spun in from 28,000. Oxygen trouble.'

1941. OVERSEAS

9 January: Hurricane Mk II. 'Formation (Coventry Patrol). Three of us engaged Do 17. Damaged and passed into cloud.'
12 January: Assessment of ability as a pilot: 'Above average.'
In late April Francis was posted to Middle East Command, of which he apparently took a poor view. The logbook reads more like an atlas as he and his Hurricane are transported

Above: The enemy. A cleverly camouflaged ME Bf 109 flying over the Libyan desert.

to Freetown in West Africa and then pair up again to fly from country to country on the back-door route to Egypt. Takoradi on the Gold Coast is succeeded by Lagos (where he reports a dredger torpedoed on 11 June) and then Kano in the interior of Nigeria. Next he goes to Ati in Free French Equatorial Africa (Chad) before flying across the Great Nubian Desert to Khartoum in the Sudan and finally, Egypt. On 15 June he reports: 'P/O Pound shot down. Turned up some days later.'

26 June: 'Germany declared war on Russia. Good show!'
21 August: Limassol and Famagusta in Cyprus. 'Sgt Lock accidentally fired his guns at me as we took off. As usual, he missed.'
20 September: Larnaca, Cyprus. 'Dogfighting with F/O Temlett DFC.'
6 November: Canal Zone. 'Landed down wind and overshot flarepath, aircraft tipped on nose in the sand (exonerated).'
8 December: 'Japan declared war on America. GB declared war on Japan.'
10 December: '*HMS Prince of Wales* and *Repulse* sunk. Everybody has declared war on everybody else.'

1942. COMBAT

In March, Francis transferred to 'B' Flight of 73 Squadron, part of 250 Wing, 202 Group in Egypt's Western Desert. He is a Hurricane fighter pilot but the Logbook also records numerous flights in a variety of other aircraft including a Lockheed Lodestar, Bristol Bombay and Vickers Vincent.

28-29 April. North Africa, Hurricane Mk II: 'Scramble Tobruk. Patrol. Large fire started in harbour. Confirmed as oil tanker.'
26 May: 'Jerry push started. Got caught in Tobruk barrage - terrific flak - shaky do.' On this day Francis was credited with shooting down an enemy aircraft.
29 May. 73 Squadron in retreat: 'Two visuals. Attacked and damaged Ju 88. Two guns on port side jammed. Lost him near Tobruk.'
14 June: 'Sweep over El Adem. Ammo ship on fire on coast north of base.'

At this point in the desert war the Eighth Army was in retreat, a fact reflected in the Logbook. On 17 June, 73 Squadron moved back from Gambut to Sidi Eziz and just 24 hours later they evacuated this place to fall back on LG 115. The LG stands for Landing Ground. A whole series of these desert air strips had been prepared so that the various air units, each split into two parts, could leap-frog back to Egypt whilst still maintaining a minimum 20 mile distance between the advancing Afrika Korps armour and RAF aircraft on the ground. Air Marshal Sir Arthur Coningham described the technique thus: 'Being able to see from the LG the bursting of our own bombs on the approaching enemy is

'Famagusta. Sgt Lock accidentally fired his guns at me as we took off. As usual, he missed..'

our deadline to depart. Our airmen are fearful of being taken too far from the enemy as they like the present form of warfare.'

The system worked remarkably well. During the whole of the retreat just five serviceable aircraft were left behind. Tobruk was the exception. On 18 June Pain wrote: 'Tobruk surrendered. The CO, seven pilots and 27 aircrew now behind the wire.'

10 July: 'Sweep over enemy lines. Tank battle going on south west of Alamein.'
19 July: 'Sweep over enemy lines. Jumped by 109s and 202s. Hell of a party.'
22 July: 'Move to Ballah. Three weeks rest. Good show!'
29 August: 'Freelance strafing. Patrol over base. One visual of He III but last saw him when searchlights picked me up (damn them). Posted UK. Wizard!'

1943. TANGMERE

Francis returned to Britain in September 1942 taking in reverse almost the same circuitous route home as that of his outward-bound journey but this time stopping in neutral Lisbon and Foynes in Eire where the Allies had a flying agreement with the Dublin Government. His transport included a place in a Lockheed Electra. Once home he undertook a variety of flying roles and by the spring of 1943 he was an instructor at RAF Tangmere where he went up in Hurricanes, Spitfire Mk IXs and Tempests. On 27 March he recorded a strafing trip to Abbeville in a Typhoon: 'Lovely party - 43 holes in tail.' Two days later, again in a Typhoon, he carried out a rocket-strafing sortie on the Paris - Lille railway.

The pilot's RAF service commenced at Uxbridge on 3 September 1939, the day

Britain went to war. Up until that mysterious 18 April 1943 final Logbook entry, Francis Pain was credited with six enemy aircraft plus one probable. Five others were marked down as damaged. In addition he went 50/50 on shooting down an Italian Cat 1007 with P/O Westlake and was also awarded the tanker and an E-Boat.

Ian Pain definitely inherited his father's sardonic way with words. In 1994 he told me: 'I find my father's wartime exploits amazing but I'm sure they were not at all unusual for those times.

'The most terrifying things I've faced up to so far in my life have been cricket balls delivered by the odd demon bowler and the occasional visit by the VAT inspector - pretty small beer compared to a dogfight with a pack of Me 109s!'
David Arnold

Bravo! Merci pour la RAF!

Between 6-11 June 1942 it is clear from the Logbook that Francis Pain and his fellow pilots of 'B' Flight, 73 Squadron, played a vital role in the famous action at Bir Hakim in Cyrenaica. The latter was a desert outpost at the southern end of General Auchinleck's Gazala line and was manned by a Free French brigade. It had come under renewed attack by Rommel's Axis forces on 2 June. The RAF History records: 'At Bir Hakim the military glory of France, so sadly tarnished in 1940, shone out again with undiminished splendour. It was an episode in which the RAF played no small part. Owing to its isolated position, our ground forces could give Bir Hakim little support. Air Vice Marshal Coningham's fighters therefore decided to adopt the Free French and their Fortress.'

Pain's Logbook records 'Sweeps over Gazala and Bir Hakim' around this time. The entry for 6 June is detailed: 'Patrol forward area over Bir Hakim. Big tank battle still going on. First Tank Gun on aircraft.'

This last is a reference to the new Hurricane IID 'tank-busters' which initially comprised the aircraft of No 6 Squadron equipped with 40mm cannons. The next day Pain was flying one of 36 planes engaged in a dogfight with FW 109s over Bir Hakim which finished with 'four planes missing - three pilots safe'.

Desperate struggle at Bir Hakim

The RAF History describes the desperate struggle: 'On 8 June it became evident that Rommel had decided to reduce Bir Hakim at all costs ... his 90th Light Division had joined in the siege and the fortress was being subjected to ceaseless attack by infantry, tanks, artillery and an ever-growing number of enemy aircraft. Despite continuous shooting-up by our fighters the enemy pressure increased. On 9 June an overwhelming mass of artillery was trained on the fort. That day two Hurricanes under protection from 14 others dropped supply canisters within 100 yards of the isolated defenders.

'On 10 June Hurricanes and the first squadron of Spitfires to appear in the desert (one is pictured here) saved the garrison from a heavy raid by 50 bombers. Shells from the enemy guns were also now pouring in without respite.'

That same night the fort's survivors were ordered to retire and 2000

A Spitfire in action in North Africa in 1942.

men made their escape, completing their withdrawal the next day under cover from RAF fighters. Pain's Logbook entry for 10 June tells of a sweep over Bir Hakim as top cover to 213 Squadron that resulted in a dogfight with a rival top cover of 109s to a Stuka party. Pain needed to make a forced landing to refuel at a desert airstrip.

Defeat brought victory

At the time Bir Hakim seemed like a defeat. Later it became clear that the garrison's stand had bought time for the Eighth Army to retire back to El Alamein. The Afrika Korps had just one month's supply of fuel to feed their offensive. Bir Hakim was supposed to fall no later than 1 June. As the Luftwaffe's own history puts it: 'The delay meant nine days' gain for the enemy and for our army and air force, nine days of losses in material, personnel, armour, aircraft and petrol. Those nine days were irrecoverable.'

The reckoning came, of course, at El Alamein in October. By then, Francis Pain was back in the UK. But he must have been aware of the salutation offered up by the French at Bir Hakim. They had been grateful observers of much of the battle in the clear blue skies overhead and passed on a message to the men of the Western Desert Air Force: 'Bravo! Merci pour la RAF.'

In best Service style and admirable command of the Gallic idiom, a reply was promptly despatched: 'Bravo a vous! Merci pour le sport!'

ALAMEIN

Soldiers, sailors and airmen from the Dominions and Empire fought alongside British and Free French forces throughout the North African Campaign. Here an Australian sums up how he feels following the decisive victory at El Alamein that turned the tide of the war in the Mediterranean.

Inset: A New Zealand recruitment poster alongside the badge of the famous British 7th Armoured Division who fought at El Alamein. This unit were the true 'Desert Rats' and the emblem on the badge represents the jerboa, a desert rodent.

NEW ZEALAND

FIGHTS

Desert Victory

By October 1942 General Montgomery felt sure that his reinforced and rejuvenated Eighth Army was ready for the decisive showdown with Rommel's Afrika Korps. The Battle of El Alamein would begin before the month was out.

Summer 1942 saw Rommel's German and Italian forces advance into Egypt only to be checked at the little railway halt of El Alamein. Now the German leader needed to reorganize, refit and reinforce. Given sufficient resource, Rommel's men felt confident they could win again; this time they would make it all the way to the Royal Navy's bastion at Alexandria and on to the Suez Canal. Their opponents had other ideas. The British and US governments were rushing masses of fresh equipment, tanks, aircraft and men to the Middle East. Churchill himself went there to encourage his generals and troops.

The British leader urged an early Allied attack but Auchinleck wanted more time. Frustrated, early in August 1942, Churchill decided to bring in a new commander for the Middle East; Harold Alexander, head of British forces in Burma early in 1942. As his second-in-command, Alexander had Bernard Law Montgomery, who was appointed head of the Eighth Army.

Ironically, Montgomery and Alexander both agreed with Auchinleck that their forces were not yet ready to attack. But they did embark on sweeping changes to the Eighth Army organization. As more men, tanks, artillery and aircraft arrived in Egypt, Monty set out to inspire the belief in his men that when the time was right, the Eighth Army would take on the Afrika Korps and beat Rommel.

For his part Rommel knew that the Allied army was growing steadily stronger while his own forces grew short of armour, aircraft and fuel. Typically, the 'Desert Fox' decided to go for a last throw of the dice. On 31 August he mounted an outflanking attack in the south of the British line at El Alamein. After hard fighting the Germans thought they had made a breakthrough but their advance foundered when they came up against Montgomery's powerful reserve position based on the southward-facing Alam Halfa Ridge. Now in ill-health, Rommel realized he could not win, broke off the attack and began a retreat into Libya.

Montgomery amasses his forces

At this stage Hitler intervened and ordered Rommel to hold firm. The Field Marshal obeyed and began to dig in even deeper in the hope that his fortifications would prove as tough a nut for the Allies to crack as he had faced at Alam Halfa.

Montgomery continued to mass troops, equipment and supplies. At the same time he worked out a detailed battle plan and made sure his officers knew exactly what their role would be in ensuring the defeat of the Afrika Korps.

In September the Long Range Desert Group

Desert war scenes: In the background an Eighth Army infantryman is seen charging forward. An explosion can be discerned in the bottom right of the picture.
Above: Australian troops aiding a wounded German. On the opposite page (**inset**): A crew member of an immobilized German tank surrenders at bayonet point.

and other special forces mounted three audacious raids far to the rear of the German front line. One was a combined sea, land and air assault on Tobruk. It failed and cost the Royal Navy two destroyers and other warships while around 1000 Allied soldiers were killed, wounded or captured. Attacks made on airfields at Barce and Gialo met with some success. Of the series of operations, General Alexander said: 'From a material point of view the raids were a failure and our losses were heavy but it is possible that they had had the psychological effects we'd hoped for. They probably assisted in diverting Rommel's attention to the possibility of seaborne raids on his long open flank.' Montgomery made no public comment on the operations, but his Chief of Staff, de Guingand, says he viewed them with disfavour.

When battle commenced during the evening of 23 October 1942, the Eighth Army went on the offensive with a two to one advantage in troops over the Germans and Italians. Montgomery had been painstaking in his preparations and battle plan. His soldiers rehearsed the plan time and again. The attack began with a massive artillery and air bombardment, the heaviest ever seen so far in the North African campaign.

Eighth Army breaks through

For 10 days the fighting raged; true to type,

Rommel counter-attacked as often as he could. But the Eighth Army was strong; its ranks were filled with determined soldiers – British, ANZAC, Indian, South African, Free French, Greek and even Jewish volunteers from Palestine. In the air the RAF ruled the skies, taking out panzers and transport and rupturing the Axis supply lines.

On 2 November the Australians pushed north in a move that caught Rommel unprepared. In the chaos the Eighth Army was able to break through the final Axis defensive line. Despite Hitler urging him to hold on, Rommel knew he had to retreat or risk losing the entire Afrika Korps. On 4 November he began to withdraw. Monty and his men had won the Battle of El Alamein.

Though decisively defeated, Rommel's men were far from routed. They were forced to leave a large force of Italian infantry divisions to their fate but the majority of the Afrika Korps with some mobile Italian units retreated in reasonably good order albeit much harassed by the RAF. They lost a lot of panzers and heavy weapons. On 23 November he halted at El Agheila in Libya where a batch of reinforcements and fresh supplies had arrived. On 11 December Montgomery's men attacked and, after a two-day battle, Rommel again had to pull back. The Desert Fox showed his mettle though with skillful delaying actions over the next two weeks or so. It was also a time when the Eighth Army had paused to draw breath after its astonishing drive along the North African shore.

March across the Sahara

On 23 January 1943 the British advanced and this time they took Tripoli, capital of Libya. Here they rendezvoused with a large force of Free French soldiers led by General Philippe Leclerc. Long-based at Fort Lamy near Lake Chad, the French had been raiding Italian outposts in southern Libya when they got news of the Eighth Army breakthrough. They immediately set out on an epic 1600-mile march across the Sahara to reach Tripoli just as Monty's men arrived.

Continuing the chase, the Eighth Army pushed on into southern Tunisia. But here, early in February, they were forced to halt. Rommel had finally gathered enough troops and artillery to make a stand behind a strong defensive position called the Mareth Line. The leading troops of the Eighth Army came up against this formidable barrier on 15 February and halted. They had covered some 1500 miles since the battle at El Alamein – one of the longest continuous military pursuits in history.

TORCH

Just as Rommel was retreating from El Alamein westwards along the coast road, British and American forces landed at three places in French Morocco and Algeria and began moving east towards Tunisia. *Operation Torch* began on 8 November 1942. It immediately posed Hitler a stark choice; rapidly reinforce his forces in Tunisia to confront the Allies or evacuate what men and material he could and abandon an Axis presence on the south shore of the Mediterranean.

Ever since the desert campaign began in 1940 the Axis had been able to fight the British without worrying about what was happening behind them in north-west Africa. Morocco, Algeria and Tunis were all under the administration of Vichy France, the puppet government controlled by the Germans. With the Allied landings, at once the Nazi grip on the French colonies and Vichy France itself began to weaken.

Afrika Korps reinforced

Faced with fighting the Allies on two fronts, logic suggested a withdrawal to Europe was the sensible recourse, especially as Hitler's armies in Russia needed all the help they could get if they were to triumph at Stalingrad and win the Caucasus oilfields. But Hitler realized that quitting North Africa would put Sicily and mainland Italy firmly in the sights of the Allies. Or the latter could choose to invade the South of France or Greece or even Yugoslavia where the partisan armies were growing stronger and stronger. So within 24 hours of the Allied landings the Germans began rushing troops by sea and air across the 90-mile stretch of the Mediterranean that separates Tunisia from Sicily. In the days that followed masses of aircraft, tanks and guns would arrive in Tunis. In this race against time it was the shorter supply lines of the Axis that would prove crucial.

On 6 November, an American lieutenant-general flew from London to Gibraltar to establish a new Anglo-American headquarters. His name was Dwight D Eisenhower and his mission was to lead the Allied forces in Operation Torch. Three great convoys of transports, escorted by powerful US and Royal Navy units, were headed for Casablanca, Algiers and Oran. Two had come from Britain and one direct from the USA.

At Algiers there was little resistance.

Late 1942. A US medic tends a wounded German airman.

Admiral Darlan, nominal commander of all the Vichy armed forces, was in Algiers at the time. As Allied forces closed in on the city soon after dark on 8 November, Darlan ordered his troops to surrender. The fighting lasted longer at Oran; it was noon on 10 November before the French surrendered having inflicted a number of Allied casualties. At Casablanca and Lyautey (where a smaller landing took place), the Americans ran into fierce resistance and French destroyers even put to sea to attack the Allied fleet. It wasn't until the morning of 11 November that French troops in Morocco finally gave up.

Advance on Tunis and Bizerta

The First British Army under General Anderson was at Algiers and being the closest to Tunisia, Eisenhower ordered them to capture the key cities of Tunis and Bizerta as swiftly as possible. The American II Corps was to advance on Anderson's right. Meanwhile the troops in Morocco and western Algeria, up to 600 miles from Algiers, were organized into the American Fifth Army under the overall command of General Mark Clark. They were prepared to march north into Spanish Morocco should the Spanish dictator, General Franco, intervene or if German forces were able to move south through Spain. In the event, Franco prudently maintained his country's neutrality.

Hard fighting between isolated German and Allied columns began in north-central Tunisia as early as 17 November. The enemy was able to make good use of the rugged, easily defended mountains in the region. Hitler had placed General Jurgen von Arnim in command of his Fifth Panzer Army in Tunisia and this energetic officer counter-attacked effectively against the weaker Allied columns. Eisenhower rushed reinforcements to the front as soon as they arrived, however, and by 28 November the Allies were within 20 miles of Tunis. Here they were again attacked by von Arnim and pushed back. Lack of suitable airfields meant that the Allies could not rely on air superiority whereas the Germans could operate from established bases. A stalemate ensued. In December both sides remained on the defensive.

Scourge of the Desert Flies

Flies were as much of a nuisance in the North African conflict as the enemy. Traps would be baited with meat, left for days to attract hundreds of thousands of flies and then collected for the catch to be destroyed. Refuse also had to be buried deep in the ground as research proved that a determined fly can work its way down through up to eight feet of sand in pursuit of food.

The Germans and Italians suffered as much. A captured German officer's 1941 diary that found its way to Sir Claude Auchinleck includes the entry: 'At last the oppressive heat abates. We now get some respite from the flies, which nearly eat us alive here. It is hopeless arguing with these unwelcome guests. We sent about 100 into the hereafter in our tent alone – and then we gave up.' On 16 June: 'No sleep all night. Fiendish heat. The Tommies seem to have encircled our position. Our supply column has not arrived today, or have the British nabbed it?' Another entry: 'Everything fine. I am fit and well and I am glad I was there when the British were given the thrashing they deserve at Sollum.' The officer mentions a message from HQ saying, 'Hold on.' He comments: 'We promise old Rommel we will do that all right. We would have held on, even without the message, to the last man. Even if the British took the position (but it is not theirs yet) they would not take a single German soldier alive.'

Ironically, in the last 10 days of fighting in Tunisia in May 1943 no less than 275,000 Germans and Italians surrendered.

WAR DIARY 1942

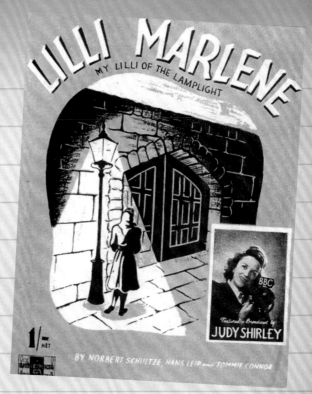

12 August: Winston Churchill arrives in Moscow for a conference called by Stalin. US President Roosevelt is not attending but has said he will support any decisions made by Mr Churchill. The latter pledges to 'struggle hand in hand with our comrades and brothers until the last remnants of the Hitler regime have turned to dust and remain in our memories as a warning and example for the future'. Mr Churchill will return via the Middle East where he will visit the front line at El Alamein.

17 August: As well as threatening Stalingrad the Germans have wheeled south into the Caucasus. Berlin reports that the Russians have abandoned Maikop after destroying oil wells around the city.

Tonight the first all-American bombing raid in the European war takes place when the US Army Air Force (USAAF) delivers a high-level attack on marshalling yards at Rouen.

19 August: A large force of Canadians supported by British Commandos land in and around the port of Dieppe in Normandy at dawn. There are some minor successes on the flanks but the frontal assault on the seaside town's steep shingle beach by troops and tanks is a bloody failure. Of 6086 troops landed, 3623 will be killed, wounded or captured. The Royal Navy loses 555 men. The RAF sustain bigger losses than the Luftwaffe.

21 August: US Marines landed at three places in the Solomon Islands in early August in the first Allied ground advance of the war against Japan. Today they have occupied an important airfield on the island of Guadacanal.

22 August: Brazil today declared war on Germany and Italy and joined the Allies. This huge country is ruled by President Vargas, a benevolent dictator. Brazilian ships have been regularly sunk by U-Boats. Nevertheless, the declaration is a bold move, for Brazil is home to at least 800,000 German and 300,000 Italian immigrants. Brazil is not yet at war with Japan; it is reckoned there are around 200,000 ethnic Japanese also in the country.

23 August: There is a lull in the fighting on the ground in Egypt though there's no let-up in the air as Allied fighters and bombers constantly harass enemy positions and supply lines. The British are building up their strength along the line that hinges on the railway halt of El Alamein. A convoy with precious supplies recently reached Malta but suffered heavy casualties en route. Losses included the aircraft carrier *HMS Eagle* sunk by a U-Boat on 11 August – 930 of her crew were rescued.

25 August: HRH the Duke of Kent – brother of King George VI – is killed today when the Sunderland flying boat he is flying to Iceland in crashes into a hillside near Dunbeath, Caithness. There is one survivor. Later the official cause of the crash will go down as 'pilot error'.

26 August: A Japanese attempt to land troops at Milne Bay on the eastern tip of New Guinea has been decisively defeated.

'Lilli Marlene' is said to be this war's most popular song because it is a favourite with both the Germans as well as the British and their Allies. Sung respectively in German or English, it is often played on the radio stations broadcasting to the troops of the two sides ranged against each other in North Africa.

The French territory of Chad in West Africa declares for the Free French.

27 August: Official figures say that during July the Axis lost a total of 424 aircraft over Britain, Western Europe and the Middle East. The figure includes aircraft shot down by Allied navy ships. In the same period the RAF lost 432 aircraft.

1 September: The German Sixth Army under General von Paulus is reported to be the spearhead of one million men charged with conquering the city of Stalingrad, one of Soviet Union's largest industrial centres. Tanks built in the city's Tractor Factory are being driven straight off the assembly line to the front line that is coming closer by the day.

Jungle fighting is going on in the Kokoda area of New Guinea as the Japanese attempt to cross the rugged Owen Stanley mountain chain that is the spine of the eastern end of the island. The Japanese want to capture Port Moresby on the southern side.

4 September: Members of the IRA make several bomb and rifle attacks on police stations in Northern Ireland.

9 September: A lone Japanese bomber drops incendiaries on Oregon, USA, but with little effect.

10 September: The Vichy French authorities on Madagascar have been reluctant to co-operate with the Allies despite the occupation of Diego Suarez in the north of the island. Allied forces have now landed at several ports on the west coast and have met with sharp resistance in places.

13 September: The battered, bruised but unbowed island of Malta today received the George Cross awarded to it on 17 April 1942. At that time Malta had been on the end of 2000 air raids and alerts. There have been many hundreds more since then.

15 September: News is released of a U-Boat attack on Bridgetown, Barbados. The vessel approached Carlisle Bay and fired at least five torpedoes into the port. No serious damage resulted. A few months ago a U-Boat torpedoed a merchant ship tied up in the port of Limon, Costa Rica.

Left: Men of No 3 Commando pictured at Newhaven, East Sussex, on the afternoon of 19 August. They were lucky to get away from the French coast after the main landing on the beach at Dieppe went disastrously wrong resulting in the death or capture of thousands of Canadian troops.

WAR DIARY 1942

23 September: Madagascar's capital, Antananarivo, is now in the hands of British troops. Vichy authorities on the island accept further resistance is futile. The defenders were, in the main, French colonial troops.

25 September: The Gestapo HQ in Oslo is the target of a precision raid by four of the RAF's new Mosquito twin-engined light bomber. The low level attack involved a round flight of about 1000 miles and interrupted a speech being made by the Norwegian puppet leader, Quisling. One Mosquito is shot down.

1 October: The Germans are in the suburbs of Stalingrad but their attack has stalled. House to house fighting is required if the Sixth Army is to move forward to the banks of the Volga. Already the British press is saying that the Reds and the Nazis are now engaged in the world's greatest battle.

3 October: The funeral takes place today of 25 children killed when a German bomb struck their school in Petworth, West Sussex, on 29 September. The schoolchildren were buried in a single grave along with their headmaster, Charles Stephenson. In all 32 died.

British Commandos carry out a raid on the tiny Channel Island of Sark.

3 October: Today sees the first successful launch of the experimental A4-rocket at Peenemunde in northern Germany. The rocket flies a distance of 147 kilometers and reaches a height of 84.5 kilometers thereby becoming the first man-made object to reach space.

8 October: Technical developments in the performance of fighting aircraft are constantly being introduced by all sides as they seek to attain superiority in performance and armaments. The introduction of turbo-superchargers to US Flying Fortresses has enabled them to operate above the most efficient operating height of German fighters and bomb with impunity in daylight. In response the Germans are producing a new version of the Me 109G that can fly up to 41,000 feet and a twin-engined Ju 86 bomber capable of climbing to nearly 50,000 feet.

The RAF currently lead the world in payloads with their 8000lb bombs but the Luftwaffe's latest He 177 are being converted to take similar-size bombs.

14 October: The Italian press is predicting an Allied offensive in Egypt is imminent. Axis air raids continue on Malta. Rommel is away in Germany apparently on health grounds.

18 October: The Japanese have pulled back from the Owen Stanley Range in New Guinea. The Australians are cautiously moving north up the Kokoda Trail and are in contact with the enemy.

21 October: Winter has arrived in and around Stalingrad. Heavy rain turns the ground to mud, bogging down troop movements and hampering transport. The German push inside besieged Stalingrad loses all momentum.

23 October: The Eighth Army begin their long-anticipated offensive at El Alamein in Egypt. It opens tonight with a massive artillery and air bombardment of the Axis positions.

2 November: For 10 days the Eighth Army have battered the Afrika Korps and their Italian partners. Today a decisive breakthrough is made. Allied air superiority means it will be a hazardous retreat for Rommel and his men.

Allied forces recapture Kokoda in New Guinea. In the Solomon Islands, Japanese attempts to recapture the airfield on Guadalcanal have failed.

8 November: *Operation Torch* begins with British and American troops landing at three places in French Morocco and Algeria. With the Afrika Korps pursued westwards by Montgomery's Eighth Army and this new force pushing eastwards, the entire Axis position in North Africa is threatened.

10 November: Oran in Algeria is captured by US forces but in Casablanca, Vichy loyalists still resist. Their main base, the battleship *Jean Bart*, has been shelled by the US Navy and set ablaze.

11 November: The Germans move fast to occupy Vichy France, fearful that the Allies might invade.

13 November: This Friday sees the Union Jack flying once more over Tobruk. South African troops are the first to enter the port which has been left undefended by the Germans.

15 November: It is Civil Defence Day in Britain and there is a parade at St Paul's, London, in front of the King and Queen. Victory bells also ring out from cathedrals and churches in thanksgiving for the Allied successes in North Africa.

16 November: There has been a relative lull in the fighting at Stalingrad. The Russians have been reinforcing their positions on the west side of the Volga.

19 November: Russia launches an offensive in the Caucasus where Hitler had hoped to seize and hold the chief source of oil for the Soviet war machine.

22 November: The BBC announces news of a massive Red Army offensive to the north and south of Stalingrad. It has been masterminded by Marshal Georgi Zhukov who is already credited with saving Moscow last winter.

24 November: The Red Army assault continues apace, advancing scores of miles each day. A further 12,000 prisoners are captured to add to the many thousands of Axis troops who have already surrendered.

25 November: Thirty two US bombers with fighter escorts make a surprise strike at a Japanese base on the island of Formosa. They destroy 42 aircraft on the ground.

27 November: As German soldiers enter Toulon, the French navy scuttle their fleet in the South of France port.

28 November: Yet another Russian move forward – this time it is on the front in the Moscow region.

29 November: Winston Churchill makes a broadcast aimed at the Italian nation, who are known to be wavering in their support of the war: 'If the enemy should be blasted from the tip of Tunisia – which is our aim – the whole of Italy, all the naval bases and all the munition establishments and other military objectives will be brought under a prolonged and shattering air attack. It is for the Italian people, 40 million of them, to say whether they want this terrible thing to happen to their country or not.' In a few days time, Churchill will make a speech to the British public telling them that driving the Axis out of Tunisia will be no easy task.

2 December: A team of scientists led by Enrico Fermi initiate the world's first nuclear chain reaction in secret laboratories at

WAR DIARY 1942

the University of Chicago. A coded message, 'The Italian navigator has landed in the New World' is sent to President Roosevelt.

6 December: In a daylight raid 100 RAF Bostons, without fighter escort, attacked the Philips radio works at Eindhoven in Nazi-occupied Holland. Twelve of the bombers failed to return.

7 December: War has brought social changes to the British way of life. Pubs have quietly but successfully been invaded by women. They have become the gossip-shop of both sexes, with darts and other diversions jointly shared. Women everywhere are working side by side with men so naturally they come to sit by their side and drink by their side in times of leisure in the 'local'.

The film Casablanca *had its world premier in New York on 26 November 1942. Ironically, the city – formerly under the control of Vichy France – is now in the hands of the Allies following the recent US and British invasion of North West Africa. The film's release was brought forward to take advantage of the invasion publicity.*

On the first anniversary of the attack on Pearl Harbour the world's biggest battleship is launched. The *USS New Jersey* is one of 10 ships launched today in American east coast yards.

20 December: Japanese aircraft have made their first-ever raid on Calcutta in India. Nearly 150 bombers and fighters attack the city. Ten British fighters are downed for the loss just two enemy aircraft. They will return on the next four nights, including Christmas Eve. British aircraft operating from a carrier in the Bay of Bengal tonight carry out a heavy raid on the port of Sabang, at the northern end of Sumatra.

24 December: Admiral Francois Darlan is shot and fatally wounded at Algiers by a French assassin described as a 'monarchist'. General Henri Giraud will succeed him as High Commissioner in French North Africa. Darlan was once a senior Vichy Government figure but he did not enjoy the confidence of the Germans and lost a lot of his powers. He was in Algiers in November when *Operation Torch* took place against some serious Vichy French resistance. Darlan was held by pro-de Gaulle activists and eventually had to negotiate with General Eisenhower. In return for surrendering French forces, Darlan was allowed to act as High Commissioner.

25 December: On Christmas Day the Eighth Army occupy the town of Sirte about halfway along Libya's Mediterranean coast.

27 December: Since 8 November until today the Allies claim to have destroyed 277 enemy aircraft for a loss of 114 in the North African theatre.

30 December: German aircraft bomb Casablanca.

31 December: On New Year's Eve 1942, the 1217th day of the war, RAF bombers and fighters are active over the west of Germany, targets in Tunisia and Japanese-held Akyab and Shwebo in Burma.

Mums and their children spent three days in a U-Boat

In late 1942, the *Daily Mail* carried the story of how British families from a torpedoed ship were taken aboard a U-Boat. Mrs Blanche Allen told correspondent Geoffrey Simpson how they had been sailing home from Durban in South Africa when their ship was struck by a torpedo and everyone took to the lifeboats. Mrs Allen was with her husband and six-year-old son Michael and they drifted for three days in the open boat:

'Then suddenly six German U-Boats and an Italian submarine surfaced around us. A U-Boat captain ordered us alongside. He was a tall, fair, good-looking man of about 35. He ordered the distribution of hot coffee, cigarettes, food and water to the men in the boats. He spoke excellent English and told us he would take the women and children aboard, but he regretted that he must leave the men. I was terrified but my husband insisted that I should go. I kissed him goodbye and entered the conning tower.

Captain said sorry

'It was stifling inside in the long oven-like corridor of winding pipes, wheels and dials. The captain went out of his way to reassure us: "I am deeply sorry you have been torpedoed, ladies. Please make yourselves comfortable and be sure I will see you to safety."

'We were fed well and sailors gave up their bunks for us although it was hard to sleep because of the noise and heat. The crew played a radiogram for most of the day. At one time the captain came to see us and asked if we would like to listen to the BBC. We said we would and he switched on Bruce Belfrage reading the nine o'clock news.

'One of the crew – they called him Hans – played a lot with Michael. He produced a photograph of his own little boy. Others in the crew showed us pictures of their wives and families.

Spotted by a US bomber

'The last day was dramatic. The crew suddenly became tense and strained. We were diving. They said a US bomber had spotted us. Everything went very quiet but then there came two distant crumps of falling bombs or depth charges. It shook all of us and I was glad Michael was sound asleep. We remained submerged for two of the most anxious hours I have ever spent.

'In the afternoon we cruised up to a Vichy destroyer and were transferred to her. The U-Boat captain, still a model of courtesy, again apologized for the inconvenience and wished us a safe return. Later we were put aboard a Vichy France cruiser that eventually took us to Casablanca. There we were transferred to an internment camp under Vichy guards. By comparison with our treatment in the U-Boat we were badly dealt with by those people. For two months we were on semi-starvation rations.

'How glad we were when the Americans landed in North Africa. The guards came and told us. They had the impudence to say, "Tell the Americans when they arrive that we looked after you properly."

'Our group came home via Gibraltar. I was overjoyed to be eventually reunited with my husband. He had been picked up by a French warship and taken to Morocco.'

MAGIC MAN

Jasper Maskelyne – Master Magician at El Alamein.

Jasper Maskelyne was a famous star magician in Britain in the Thirties. Upon the outbreak of war he enlisted in the Royal Engineers, convinced his professional skills in concealment and deception could be employed on the battlefield. Initially his offers to help were met with scepticism. Sent to North Africa he found himself more in demand as an entertainer for the troops than as a master of illusion on a grand scale.

Then in January 1941, General Wavell, commander of British forces in the region, created a unit called A Force, which was dedicated to counter-intelligence and deception. Maskelyne was posted to A Force, where he was able to apply his skills to the task of concealing British forces from German aerial reconnaissance. He led a 14-strong group, known as the Magic Gang, whose members had had careers in analytical chemistry, electrical engineering and stage set construction. Maskelyne was said to be a hard taskmaster with a sizeable ego.

Dummy tanks, fake harbour

Applying Maskelyne's professional knowledge of cheap and lightweight construction techniques, the group produced dummy tanks made of plywood and painted canvas; Maskelyne even devised a means of faking tank tracks after the dummies had been moved into position. In 1941, Maskelyne was involved in an elaborate operation to divert German bombers from the port of Alexandria by setting up a fake harbour in a nearby bay. This involved constructing dummy buildings, a dummy lighthouse and even dummy anti-aircraft batteries that fired thunderflashes. He also tried to make it difficult for German bombers to locate parts of the Suez Canal by fitting searchlights with a revolving cone of mirrors, producing a dazzling wheel of spinning light beams nine miles across. It is impossible to measure what success, if any, the latter achieved but Maskelyne went into war lore as the 'man who made the Suez Canal disappear'.

Maskelyne's crowning achievement came in late 1942 with his involvement in Operation Bertram, prior to the Battle of El Alamein. Rommel's Afrika Korps knew that a British attack was inevitable; the trick was to mislead them as to where and when it would take place. In Maskelyne's own words, his Magic Gang must undertake 'the mass production of tricks, swindles and devices.'

The attack was to take place near the coast, at the northern end of the German line. Accordingly, in the north 1000 tanks were camouflaged as lorries, while 30 miles south 2000 fake tanks were assembled, complete with explosive special effects. To support the illusion, a dummy railway line was built; there were even fake radio broadcasts and sound effects to mimic the noise of construction. Crucially, a fake water pipeline was built to supply the simulated armies. It's progress could easily be tracked from the air by German planes; the key was to convince the enemy that it was not be ready, and that no attack could begin until November at the earliest.

The actual offensive began on the night of 23 October, catching the German forces unprepared. After 10 days of bloody attrition, the British forced the Germans into a retreat that would continue all the way to Tunisia. The role played by the element of surprise in weakening the enemy defences was recognised by Churchill, who paid public tribute to the 'marvellous system of camouflage' which had contributed to the victory.

From victory to obscurity

After El Alamein, the Magic Gang disbanded. There were no further wartime coups for Maskelyne although he has been linked by some sources to the fake damage constructed around the de Havilland aircraft factory in Hertfordshire in late January 1943. However, it seems improbable that he would have returned from Egypt to England at a time when the Eighth Army was on the advance.

Either way, he received no decoration or honour; official accounts of the war in North Africa make little or no mention of him. After the war, Maskelyne resumed his stage career, but found that work as a magician was now becoming scarce. Embittered at the lack of official recognition, widowed and estranged from his children, Maskelyne emigrated to Kenya where he ran a driving school. He died in obscurity, aged 70.

Return to El Alamein

Eighth Army veteran Peter Theobald lives in Lewes and is an old friend of mine. I was at school with his daughter, Pauline, writes David Arnold.

Through a keen shared interest in our local non-league football club, Lewes FC, I see Peter regularly and inevitably we often talk about his wartime service in North Africa and, later, Palestine. Five years ago, in 2005, my wife Barbara and myself were able to take Peter back to the battlefield of El Alamein in Egypt's Western Desert. The trip was made under the generous Heroes Return scheme funded with Lottery money.

We were able to visit the cemetery at El Alamein and the battlefield museum. In addition we went to Cairo and in a Coptic church in the city Peter lit a candle of remembrance in the very spot where he remembered lighting a candle over six decades before.

Peter made the rank of Sergeant in the Royal Army Medical Corps, having gone to the Middle East in mid-1941 aboard the troopship *Strathnaver*. Though he remembered Luftwaffe air raids and occasional artillery bombardments Peter was lucky; the worst that befell him was a very

Cold Beer at Ye Olde ME 110

RAF groundcrew in Egypt's Western Desert have turned the wreckage of a shot-down German fighter into a reminder of pubs back home. Shades of 'Ice Cold in Alex'!

painful injection following contact with a suspected rabid dog.

Not so lucky was Norman Gordon, a Flight Sergeant in RAF 205 Squadron. We heard Norman's sad story from his brother, Arthur, who happened to be visiting El Alamein on a mission of remembrance at the same time as we were there. On 15 April 1942 Norman's aircraft was reported missing over the Mediterranean. Though no body was ever found Norman's name appears on the El Alamein Memorial alongside many others having no known grave.

Arthur's own war began in 1943 when he joined the Fleet Air Arm. He went on to serve on the MV *Alexia*, a Merchant Aircraft Carrier (MAC) that he described as an 'oil tanker with a lid on top'. It carried four Swordfish. On his very first flight, his Swordfish had to ditch in the sea some 15 miles ahead of the convoy

after suffering engine problems. Arthur and his two crew companions scrambled into a dinghy and were eventually picked up by HMCS *New Glasgow*. For ditching in the sea, Arthur qualified as a member of the 'Goldfish Club' (airmen who successfully baled out of their aircraft were admitted to the 'Caterpillar Club', so-named because of the silk that made up their parachutes).

Apart from a month's leave around about the time of VJ Day, Peter didn't see England again until January 1946. Soon after arriving home he married his girlfriend Ethel. Arthur wasn't demobbed until October 1946. He had earlier met his wife-to-be, Irene, in Londonderry where she served in the WRNS.

Opposite page: *Eighth Army veteran Peter Theobald pictured in the El Alamein Museum in 2005.*
Right: *Arthur Gordon in the same Museum that same year.*

The ship that won the war?

Eric Sellars served aboard *HMS Petard*, a destroyer that sank submarines from the German, Italian and Japanese navies. But the greatest achievement of the ship's crew was the recovery of a top secret Enigma machine and codes from a sinking U-Boat.

On 12 February 1944 the Royal Navy Fleet Destroyer *HMS Petard* completed an astonishing hat trick of submarine sinkings when it fired a final torpedo to send the Japanese vessel *I-27* to the bottom of the Indian Ocean, 60 miles north west of Addu Atoll near the Maldives.

Just a short time earlier, *I-27* had fired a torpedo of her own at the troopship *Khedive Ismael*, part of British convoy KR 8 bound for Colombo, Ceylon. The troopship broke in half and went down in just 36 seconds with the loss of over 1200 men and women.

HMS Paladin went to rescue survivors. Meanwhile, *HMS Petard* detected the submarine's location and dropped Mark 7 depth charges. While the blasts succeeded in bringing the *I-27* to the surface, they also caused a number of casualties among the troopship survivors stranded in the water.

As Japanese sailors rushed to man their deck gun, machine-gun fire from *Petard* cut them down. *HMS Paladin* then rammed the enemy vessel's port hydroplane but itself sustained a serious gash in the side. It was left to *HMS Petard* to administer the knock-out blow to *I-27* but stubbornly the submarine was still afloat even after six torpedoes had struck it. A seventh finally sank *I-27*; just one crewman out of 100 on the big submarine was picked up alive.

Some 15 months prior to the Indian Ocean action, *HMS Petard*, in the space of some six weeks, had managed to sink the German U-Boat *559* (30 October 1942) and capture an Italian submarine, *Uarsciek*, (15 December 1942). Further, crewmen from *HMS Petard* were able to board both these vessels and capture codebooks and maps of incalculable value to the Allies.

From the German craft came elusive codebooks and an actual 4-Rotor Enigma machine. It was Eric who carried the Enigma machine to a place of safety on the *Petard*. With these prizes the codebreakers in Hut No 8 at Bletchley Park could decipher Kriegsmarine radio signals, pinpoint the positions of U-Boats and sink them. It was the turning point in the Battle of the Atlantic.

From the Italian submarine came maps detailing the locations of minefields in North Africa and in and around the Italian coast and islands. Mine-free channels into Italian harbours were also indicated, along with current codes for the German and Italian navies. This haul was invaluable to the planners of *Operation Husky*, the invasion of Sicily that was to take place in the spring of 1943. For this action alone, *HMS Petard* earned a personal 'thank you' visit from General Dwight D Eisenhower.

Eric Sellars was serving aboard *HMS Petard* in the course of all three submarine sinkings. He was part of the ship's Submarine Warfare Team and he personally pursued and eventually made possible the capture of the *U-559*. Here he recounts the story of the capture of *U-559* and tells why the incident remained a secret for many decades after the end of the war.

Left: Eric Sellars aboard his ship in the Tropics and pictured in recent years at Bletchley Park.

Above: The HMS Petard Association commissioned this painting of the Enigma incident by military artist Michael Roffe a few years ago. Eric says that in fact the night was a very dark one and the sea wasn't nearly so rough as depicted here. Painting reproduced courtesy of the Cambridge Stamp Centre Ltd.

On 1 February 1942 the German Navy introduced M4, a new version of their Enigma code machine. The effect of M4 was to immediately lock the British codebreakers at Bletchley Park out of SHARK, the Atlantic and Mediterranean U-Boat communications traffic. The Allied navies were no longer able to intercept the deadly U-Boat packs that were strangling Britain's maritime lifelines.

Later that year, on 30 October off the coast of Egypt, four Royal Navy destroyers, including *HMS Petard*, obtained ASDIC contact with a U-Boat. After a sustained depth charge attack lasting 10 hours the submarine was finally forced to the surface at about 22.40. *Petard's* searchlights stabbed through the night and picked out the U-Boat's conning tower which had a white donkey emblem and the numerals U-559 painted on it. The conning tower was soon struck by a shell from one of *Petard's* four-inch guns causing the U-Boat's crew to abandon ship. *Petard's* first officer, Lieutenant Anthony Fasson, dived into the sea followed by Able Seaman Colin Grazier and Tommy Brown, a 16-year-old civilian canteen assistant who had lied about his age to get the job. They swam to the stricken U-Boat and climbed down inside the conning tower to find the lights still on.

In the submarine, Fasson found some documents printed in water-soluble ink. Despite the water pouring through the shell hole, Brown succeeded in keeping them dry as he clambered up the ladder in the conning tower and passed them to others waiting in *Petard's* whaler made fast alongside. Brown twice re-entered the U-Boat, each time returning with more items.

Fasson returned to the control room to wrench a radio or radar set from its fixings, but

by this time the water inside the U-Boat was knee-deep and rising. Brown, now on top of the conning tower, shouted for them to come up as the U-Boat's afterdeck was well underwater. As Grazier and Fasson started up the ladder, the U-Boat suddenly sank. Brown jumped clear, but U-559 made her last dive taking Fasson and Grazier with her.

Shipping losses halved

The material retrieved from U-559 reached Bletchley Park on 24 November. By 13 December 1942, after a blackout of 10 months, Bletchley Park called the Admiralty's Operational Intelligence Centre to report a break into SHARK. Within the next hour the first intercept chattered off the teleprinter indicating the position of more than a dozen U-Boats. A stream of intercepts followed allowing the rerouting of convoys around the waiting wolfpacks. Allied shipping losses in the Atlantic were consequently halved in January and February 1943 and, perhaps even more vitally, procedures were developed which facilitated the breaking of SHARK for much of the remainder of the war. Fasson, Grazier and Brown's action consequently saved millions of tons of Allied shipping and thousands of Allied lives.

Tony Fasson and Colin Grazier were to

This statue in Tamworth commemorates the bravery of Tony Fasson, Colin Grazier and Tommy Brown in recovering the Enigma machine and codes from the U-Boat.

be awarded the highest possible medals for bravery. Tommy Brown would get the George Medal. As Head of the ship's Submarine Warfare Team who had pursued and eventually made possible the capture of the U-559, I was to receive the Distinguished Service Medal.

Churchill now intervened. No medals to be awarded at that time. No written records to be made and submitted to higher authority. Any reference to the success of the *Petard* was to be deleted lest German Intelligence became aware of the coup. The crew were told that everything was now secret and would remain so for at least 40 years.

In 1980 the records became available. Lt Tony Fasson was to be honoured with a plaque on the wall of his village church telling his story. The George Cross was presented to his family. Able Seaman Colin Grazier's family also received the George Cross. Tommy Brown was awarded the George Medal. Ironically, his medal was also posthumous as he died two years after the U-559 sinking while trying to save his sister in a house fire.

Colin Grazier came from Tamworth and when the local paper's Deputy Editor, Phil Shanahan, discovered the story he decided to honour the World War Two hero. A fund eventually raised around £20,000 and an impressive sculpture was commissioned.

It was dedicated in St Editha's Square, Tamworth, on Sunday 27 October 2002.

For the same day, the *HMS Petard* Association had hoped that the Admiralty could arrange for a wreath to be put in the sea near the spot where the U-559 went down. It wasn't possible. However, on 9 November 2002, a Type 23 Frigate, *HMS Argyll,* did visit the location. The ship's crew put on a full Guard of Honour and laid a wreath. Honour was paid.

ERIC'S NAVY DAYS

Eric Sellars joined the Royal Navy in 1938 when he served on the ill-fated battleship, HMS *Royal Oak*. Luckily for him he had been transferred by the time the ship was sunk in Scapa Flow just five weeks after the outbreak of war. But then his very next sea-going posting found him aboard HMS *Khartoum*, a ship that soon sailed into the torpedo sights of an Italian submarine in the Red Sea. Eric's wartime story is an astonishing account of one man's epic seafaring adventures.

'In 1938 I was serving aboard a battleship, *HMS Royal Oak*, flagship of the Second Battle Squadron, Home Fleet. The ship was destined to be one of the early British naval losses of the war, being sunk at Scapa Flow in the Orkneys by the German submarine U-47 on Friday 13 October 1939 in an action that cost the lives of 833 seamen.

Fortunately for me, I was no longer with the ship at the time she was sunk. At Christmas 1938-39 I had been sent on two weeks leave with instructions not to return to the *Royal Oak* but to instead report to *HMS Osprey*, a 'stone frigate' (Navy slang for a barracks). Situated on the very tip of Portland Bill in Dorset, it turned out to be a top secret establishment, devoted to anti-submarine warfare. The ASDIC system was born there. ASDIC stands for Anti Submarine Detection Investigative Committee.

I was placed on a special course and by July 1939 was considered fully qualified in all aspects of anti-submarine warfare. So secret was it all that we were not allowed to wear any badges of recognition and totally forbidden to discuss anything to do with ASDIC outside the barracks.

War was declared on 3 September 1939 and by the evening of the following day I found myself stepping aboard one of the most modern fleet destroyers ever built in the dockyard at Wallsend-on-Tyne. With the exception of a single period of three months, from this day forward right through to the end of World War Two, I was at sea. If there was fighting to be done, it seemed we were always there.

The Fighting Fifth

The destroyer was *HMS Khartoum*, one of eight identical vessels, all with names that began with the letter 'K'. The others were called *Kipling, Kelvin, Kandahar, Kashmir, Kimberley, Kingston* and *Kelly*. The latter's captain was Louis Mountbatten. Known as Captain 'D', he commanded this 5th Destroyer Flotilla which became known as the 'The Fighting Fifth'.

With the Admiralty rightly worried that the Germans would make every effort to get their capital warships out into the Atlantic, our 'working up' period of three weeks was cut to seven days and we were rushed out into the cold Arctic seas without delay. Each ship was given an overlapping patrol area. Within a week of commencing our patrol, the ASDIC system proved its worth. Despite rough seas and atrocious weather we were able to detect a submarine on the surface, charging its batteries.

After closing to the point where the U-Boat could be seen through binoculars, our Captain decided that the best course was to close quickly with the U-Boat and ram it. The destroyer was aimed, bows on, at the enemy vessel. They didn't see us coming until it was too late; we struck the sub just below the conning tower. It split wide open and sank like a stone.

With the bow of our ship left twisted and mangled we were ordered back to Newcastle. There were no enemy survivors and nor did we pick up any wreckage. In the absence of any other ships to witness the sinking the Navy refused to give *HMS Khartoum* official credit for destroying the U-Boat. Even so, we of the anti-submarine team were much congratulated.

The ship was given temporary repairs and within 48 hours was back at sea with flat plate for a bow, rendering the ASDIC useless. A proper bow was fitted later. For the next six months we were guarding Atlantic convoys and participating in the ill-fated Norway campaign (in which *HMS Kelly* was almost lost).

Then one day all eight ships were ordered into port. Their boilers were cleaned, the ammunition was stocked up, stores of all kinds – including tropical gear – came aboard and the fuel tanks were topped up to the very limit. The 'buzz men' worked overtime speculating on where we were going.

Eventually, all eight ships sailed south. To our surprise, off Land's End, four of the flotilla turned east into the English Channel, leaving *Khartoum, Kelvin, Kashmir* and *Kandahar* still heading south. The Fighting Fifth never worked together again.

Exquisite haberdashery

We sailed through the Bay of Biscay and on to Gibraltar. Compared with the furious North Atlantic and Arctic seas, the Mediterranean was paradise. The street lights were on in Gib, all the bars were open and people strolled around in summer gear.

Two days later we were on our way again, this time to Grand Harbour, Malta. Here the war did not yet exist and the Maltese poured aboard, laden with lace tablecloths, beautiful bedspreads and handmade scarves. They didn't want money for their goods, preferring to trade them for our northern clothing – long underpants and vests etc. Very soon the lockers were full of exquisite haberdashery.

Our next destination was Port Said where the statue of de Lesseps invited us to enter his creation, the Suez Canal. After traversing this we sailed down the Red Sea and into the port of Aden. It seemed to me that we'd gone from the bitter cold of the northern seas to the balmy warmth of the tropics in just a few days.

So what was our mission? The Captain explained that there were four Italian destroyers and a submarine in an Eritrean port and with Italy now in the war these warships were a threat to our command of the Suez Canal and the Red Sea. Our spies on the African coast were keeping a close eye on the Italians and one day word came that the enemy was preparing to put to sea.

We set off to meet them, lying in wait just out of their sight. As soon as they came into view we attacked them and sank all four destroyers without receiving even one hit in return. It has to be said that the Italian ships had been lying idle for a long time and their crews clearly lacked practice.

There had been no sign of the Italian submarine and consequently *HMS Khartoum* was ordered to patrol the deep water channel and watch out for it. Sure enough, next morning we made ASDIC contact with the submerged vessel as it travelled south. A full load of depth charges blew the sub to the surface and the shocked crew abandoned ship a short time before it sank.

'Abandon ship'

With the five Italian warships accounted for, our Captain stopped *HMS Khartoum* and ordered all boats away to pick up survivors. Soon our ship was host to scores of prisoners. It was a bright and sunny afternoon when, at just about lunchtime, a torpedo came out of nowhere and hit the *Khartoum* just above the keel, blowing out the bottom of the ship. Ten of our crew were either killed or seriously wounded. The Captain ordered us to abandon ship.

Unfortunately, at this time our own lifeboats were full of Italian seamen making their way to the small island of Perim. hTis meant most of us had to make do with Carley Floats or swim for it. I found myself in the sea alongside my mate. We kicked off our shoes and set off in the warm sea. I consoled myself with the thought that any sharks would have been driven away by the many explosions. It must have been about four miles to Perim and we made it there ahead of the Carley Floats. A platoon of Indian soldiers commanded by a British officer were stationed on the island and they took charge of the Italians.

There had been enough time before *Khartoum* sank to radio Aden and the other ships about our plight and *HMS Kelvin* and *HMS Kashmir* set off at full speed to rescue us. Myself and the rest of the crew were spread around the other ships on a temporary basis and I was allocated to *HMS Kelvin*. We learnt that the source of the torpedo that sunk us was a second submarine in Eritrea whose presence had not been reported. It had been following the first submarine but had been some distance behind it.

Back in Aden the expected position of the second submarine was worked out by the Navigator of *HMS Kelvin*. He was Second Lt David Dunbar-Nasmith, a relation of Mountbatten and the Royal Family. He explained that if our destroyers steamed at full speed to the south of the sub's location and then reversed course, there would be a good chance of finding it using ASDIC. Dunbar-Nasmith later became an admiral.

In those days a submerged sub could only travel at between five and eight knots. To our absolute amazement we found it and *Kelvin* began her depth charge attacks which very soon blew the Italian vessel to the surface. To the credit of the enemy, they managed to reach their deck guns and open fire. But they stood no chance against our four-inch guns and after a few shells had hit their conning tower they gave up and struck their colours. After removing the crew we towed the submarine intact into Aden.

My own part in the war at sea now took me to *HMS Petard*. The ship started naval life as *HMS Persistant*, a name so unpopular that it was changed to *Petard*. Her first Captain was

Lt Cdr Sam Beattie. Before he could even take the vessel to sea he was recalled to the Admiralty for special duty. He was the man who would ram the *Campbeltown* into the dock gates at St Nazaire, winning the Victoria Cross in the process.

HMS Petard was one of only three 'P' Class destroyers to survive the war (*Paladin* and *Penn* being the other two) and was the last 'P' to be broken up in 1967. In 1942 the shortage of guns for new destroyers was so acute that *HMS Petard* was fitted with single four-inch weapons that dated back to 1916. We were the laughing stock of the Flotilla but would come to bless the day they were fitted because while the twin turrets of other destroyers could elevate to only 60 degrees, our single weapons could elevate to 89 degrees, as the German dive bombers soon discovered. All four guns firing together could deliver 22 shells per minute.

When the ship was fully commissioned, Lt Cdr Mark Thornton was Captain. He ordered 'Clear Lower Deck' which meant that everyone who could should 'fall in' on the Upper Deck. He wanted to say a few words that went much as follows: 'I am fully aware of the humorous remarks regarding our First World War single guns fitted to this ship and would refer you to

The Italian submarine that sank the Khartoum *was captured a short time later by* HMS Kelvin. *Here it flies the White Ensign as it is taken into Aden.*

a speech made by Lord Nelson.

'Now it's generally known that Nelson was often quite ill and always seasick when he first set off on a voyage. One of his fellow Captains remarked to Nelson how sorry he was about this situation. Nelson's response was: "Pity Sir? Pity? By God you will live to envy me!"'

Thornton went on, 'so it will be with this ship'. How right he was for *HMS Petard* was to play a key role in winning the war.

Some six weeks after the sinking of U-559, *Petard* captured the Italian submarine Uarsciek after its crew had abandoned it. The vessel was taken in tow with the intention of taking it as a prize to Malta. Unfortunately, the submarine sank en route. With two destroyers sent out to assist, we formed up in line ahead on our way into Grand Harbour Malta, with *HMS Petard* leading. As we entered the harbour we suddenly became aware that the walls and battlements were packed with Maltese people. Word had somehow got around the island that *HMS Petard* was towing in a sub belonging to the hated enemy who had been bombing them for so long.

The silence was so profound that it literally could be felt. Then the Captain had a brilliant idea. He ordered one of the signalmen to climb upon the forward bridge superstructure and unfurl the Italian Royal Standard, which we had removed from the sub. The crowd went mad, shouting and cheering until we thought they would never stop. That Royal Standard is now in the Imperial War Museum.

HMS Khartoum resting on the sea bed after being torpedoed off Perim near Aden in 1940.

Early in 1943 the Germans in North Africa were on the back foot in Tunisia although still capable of landing hard blows against the Allies. However, the savage air attacks on Malta had ceased and the Royal Navy wasted no time in returning to their old anchorage. Soon Grand Harbour was full of battleships, heavy and light cruisers and a whole mass of Fleet Destroyers.

Though they had an air bridge from Sicily to Tunis, the only way the Germans could seriously supply the Afrika Korps with men, fuel and ammunition was by sea around Sicily sailing to the west of the fortified island of Pantelleria and heading for Tunis or Bizerta. About noon every day at least three destroyers left Malta intent on intercepting German convoys in operations that were dubbed 'Club Runs'. One day *HMS Petard* was one of three destroyers on just such a mission. A night flying reconnaissance aircraft sent a signal indicating they had sighted a small enemy convoy on its way to North Africa. Two Italian destroyers were escorting three large merchant ships. The spotter aircraft had a clear view of the ships and said they would drop flares when the British destroyers were in position to open fire.

German paratroopers on board

We approached in line abreast and upon a signal from the senior ship turned into line astern. Down came the flares and all three destroyers opened fire on the lead Italian destroyer. In a few minutes it had become scrap metal heading for the bottom of the sea. Next we fired on a very large merchant ship. It exploded with a mighty blast, the loudest explosion I heard in the entire war. The other two merchant ships were also disposed of, leaving just the second destroyer afloat although it was rapidly dropping astern and not firing at us. Our Captain, Mark Thornton, took us alongside and to our amazement we could see the ship was deserted; the entire crew had taken to the sea in small boats. We could easily have boarded their ship and taken it as a prize but were instructed to sink it.

The Captain then invited any of our ship's company who were normally down below when at 'Action Stations' to come up on deck and open fire on the enemy vessel. Firing continued until the ship sunk. Watching from a safe distance was the Italian crew. We took aboard the most senior officers and the rest were left to row or sail to Africa, or so we thought.

Our three ships continued the patrol as ordered and then turned back for Malta, expecting to arrive there in daylight. In the early morning light we saw an ambulance ship fully lit up and obviously sailing from Africa to Sicily. We ordered her to stop. A fully armed boarding party left the *Petard* and went aboard the ship to search it from stem to stern. All was well and after our crew returned to the *Petard* the ambulance ship was led to the area where the Italian survivors were gathered together in their lifeboats.

Several days later it was our turn again. To our surprise we again sighted an ambulance ship. Our suspicions were aroused when it made every effort to avoid us. We went alongside and ordered the ship to put down a landing ladder. They refused and only changed their minds when the guns of three Royal Navy destroyers were trained on the ship at close range. There was quite a panic; the ship stopped and a ladder came down. Our boarding party went across. No sooner had our men set foot on deck when a stream of German paratroopers in full uniforms and carrying their arms appeared from down below. They laid their weapons at their feet and fell at full attention.

All their weapons were thrown overboard and the ship was searched but nothing else was found. When the boarding party returned they had with them a Nazi ensign (it can be seen today at Bletchley Park). We had the impression the Germans were, in the end, glad to be made POWs. The ambulance ship was escorted into Malta.

As time went by an entire battle fleet of Allied ships arrived in Malta; two aircraft carriers, four battleships, heavy and light cruisers and no less than 23 destroyers. We had no idea why we were all together until word came that the Allies were invading the Italian mainland at Salerno.

Our massive fleet moved into the Ionian Sea to protect the two invasion forces; the Eighth Army in the Gulf of Taranto and Fifth Army in the Gulf of Salerno (*Operation Avalanche*). What we didn't understand at the time was that by now we had nothing to fear from the Italian fleet because Italy was about to come over to the Allied side. It wasn't long before much of their fleet ended up in Malta.

Battle for Salerno

The Americans and British forces at Salerno were in serious trouble once ashore. Major German forces with panzers brought south to attack the Eighth Army (who'd landed first) were in position on high ground from where they could menace the beach-head. The invaders had not managed to get more than six miles inland before being driven back towards the beaches. The Germans also deployed a new weapon – radio-controlled glide bombs (the Henschel 293 and Fritz-X) that were released from aircraft – and they were taking a toll of our ships.

A German attack was made with paratroopers supported by powerful Tiger tanks. They nearly split our forces and almost reached the coast. The American admiral in charge of the landings sent a signal to the British Admiral Cunningham asking for help. The response was immediate. Three British cruisers were loaded with as many troops as they could carry and set off at full speed for Salerno. The battleships *HMS Warspite* and *Valiant* escorted by the 14th Destroyer Flotilla also made for Salerno; *Petard* was one of the destroyers. We tore through the Straits of Messina at full speed and arrived offshore the next morning. The battleships moved into their bombarding positions. We were now in range of German guns on land.

Forward observation gunnery officers went ashore and were soon directing the fire of the battleships. A full broadside of eight 15-inch guns created a dreadful roar that drowned out all other noises of battle. British cruisers and destroyers joined in for there was a constant call by the army for fire to be directed on German positions. At times the firing was over open sights at targets that were sometimes just hundreds of yards inland.

The six-inch shell

My ship had come in as close as possible to the landing beaches and had joined in the bombardment of the advancing Germans. Suddenly there was an almighty crash aboard our destroyer. After a while we learnt that a six-inch shell had penetrated the ship's side and exploded in the forward messdeck reducing it to a bloody shambles. This did not impair

Petard's fighting effectiveness that also had to be turned to warding off succeeding waves of incoming enemy torpedo bombers.

The ship's Doctor and a first aid party entered the dark and wrecked messdeck to salvage and save the wounded survivors. Two Able Seamen had been killed instantly. There were six wounded with three of them badly hurt. Among the wounded was a member of my ASDIC team, Able Seaman Jack 'Nobby' Hall, who was on 'other duties' that day.

Jack later wrote a report of the action for me: 'I was in the forward Messdeck passing shells from the top of the magazine hoist up the shute to 'A' Gun on the fo'csle deck. Suddenly there was an explosion, a terrific flash, a shower of sparks and then complete darkness. I knew that we had been hit, of course, but had no idea by what nor what the extent of the damage was. I heard moaning and wondered if we were about to sink and whether we'd be caught like rats in a trap before we had a chance to get out.

'I darted into the port passage and saw it still had an emergency light burning at the far end. I was also blowing air into my lifebelt. Imagine my horror when I became aware of blood bubbling from a hole in my chest. I made my way into the sickbay to have my shrapnel wounds treated.

'I felt no pain at the time because I was given morphine. We were most likely the victims of 'friendly fire' from one of our ships who got the range and elevation wrong. Later I learned that two of my shipmates had been blown to pieces. Volunteers were asked to collect their remains to be placed in their hammocks for burial. No-one stepped forward for the awful task so two men were detailed and given a double tot of rum.'

The action at Salerno on the west coast of Italy was a prelude to the Dodecanese Campaign for *HMS Petard*. Once the landing forces were safe on shore and the Germans were pulling back we withdrew from the beach area to form part of the escort for *HMS Warspite* which had been badly damaged by glide bombs.

Soon after setting off, *Petard* hauled out to sea away from the other ships to carry out a traditional burial at sea of our two crew members who'd been killed by the shell.

In early October 1943 we were assigned to the Levant Command of the Eastern Mediterranean along with five other Fleet destroyers plus a number of smaller Hunt Class destroyers. With Greece, Crete and Rhodes firmly in German hands, the British had moved into only a few of the smaller Dodecanese islands and there were also some with Italian garrisons.

'Thorn in the enemy's side'

The Germans also gradually moved into the smaller islands, constructing airfields wherever they could. In the end only Leros and Samos were occupied by our troops and we had a lot of men and equipment on both islands. The obvious course of action would have been to have learnt a severe lesson from the 1941 battle for Crete and withdraw the lot. But no – some bright spark had the idea that our troops should remain in place 'as a thorn in the side of the Germans'. The Royal Navy's task was to keep our forces fully supplied, ferry in reinforcements and bring out any wounded.

A certain senior RN officer stated that our Fleet and Hunt Class destroyers – supported by cruisers – would have no trouble with the job. His idea was that our destroyers would speed between the islands at dusk and be out again before dawn. Because we were warships all the men and materials had to be packed on board wherever we could fit them.

The obvious big problem was that the Germans had large numbers of Ju 87 'Stuka' dive bombers and Ju 88 high level bombers. For our part, we had no really effective air cover at all because of the distance involved! When *HMS Petard* arrived in Alexandria to join this group of suicide ships we learnt that *HMS Intrepid* and the Greek destroyer, *Queen Olga*, had already been sunk on 26 September by a swarm of Ju 87s off Leros, with a great loss of life. The situation was desperate; the Germans had gained the initiative and effectively already won the battle for the Dodecanese. Yet we were to persist with the fight.

Having repaired damage to our ship and completed oiling, *Petard* sailed with another of our 'P- Class' Flotilla, *HMS Panther*, together with *HMS Carlisle*, an old light cruiser now converted to an anti-aircraft ship. There were also two Hunt Class destroyers – the Royal Hellenic Navy's *Thermistoklis* and *HMS Aldenham*. Our orders were to sail north through the Scarpento Channel to look for German forces attempting an invasion of Leros. A thorough search yielded no sightings so we turned southwards and entered the Channel again where we remained. The two Hunt Class destroyers were sent back to Alexandria and replaced with two more, *HMS Rockwood* and another Greek ship, the *Mialaulis*.

Our group was to receive air cover from American long range Lightnings flying from Gambut (near Tobruk in Libya – over 300 miles away). Every half hour the US planes would depart as a new squadron arrived. While this was going on, an enemy Ju 88 was watching every move, from a safe distance and height. Late in the afternoon the sky became very cloudy and as the Lightnings departed we could see no sign of their replacements. After a while a report from the radar cabin informed us that the aircraft were closing in now. We sent the usual recognition signal but received no reply. This was put down to bad weather interference. The warships were sailing in a V formation with *Petard* on the port wing. Suddenly, through the clouds and without any of us having fired a single shot, a horde of Stukas with sirens screaming plunged down at us.

Ship split in two and sank

HMS Panther was hit amidships with two more bombs close alongside. The ship split in two and sank in three minutes. *HMS Carlisle* was hit by a bomb on the after gun turrets and a second bomb destroyed the starboard propeller and shaft. By this time *HMS Petard* and the other two ships had swung into action and had already knocked four German Ju 87s out of the sky when the US aircraft arrived. The dive bombers fled for their lives but were too late and I believe every single one was shot down. The Americans were full of remorse at their late appearance but explained that due to the heavy cloud they had been unable to find our ships until spotting the smoke from the burning cruiser.

HMS Carlisle was able to steam along for some time until the boiler rooms were flooded and she came to a standstill. *HMS Rockwood* took the cruiser in tow while we and the Greek destroyer provided the guard. German bombers attacked us repeatedly as we set off for Alexandria but eventually they gave up. We met a tug sent out to help and the *Carlisle* was taken into port destined never to go to sea again. She was patched up and used as a base ship.

Why I went to Liverpool alone

Many years after the war ended I had an official letter from the Admiralty inviting me to Liverpool to represent *HMS Petard* at a function dedicated to the Royal Navy's role in the Battle of the Atlantic. The day would conclude with a dinner in St Georges Hall.

I was able to take a shipmate of my choice with me. Jack Hall was my first choice because he'd been badly wounded and was one of my team. With all expenses paid he was thrilled at the idea and readily agreed to join me. Bookings were made, seats in Liverpool Cathedral reserved and we learnt we would even have places at the dinner next to the First Sea Lord.

I was looking forward to this occasion and a reunion with Jack. Then the telephone rang: 'This is Rita Hall speaking. I am the wife of Jack. I am sorry to tell you Jack is dead.'

It appears that Jack and Rita had decided to visit their daughter at Romsey in Hampshire. Jack was driving and emerged out of a side road straight into the path of a fast-moving car on the main road. Jack was killed and Rita injured and put in hospital.

I went to Liverpool alone.

British garrisons in peril

The action had cost us a destroyer sunk, one light cruiser wrecked and many lives lost. Leros and Samos are just north of Kos and a lot further north of Rhodes. With German airfields on both of the latter islands, it made it very dangerous to get to the British garrisons on Leros and Samos. Our attempts to sustain the islands now developed into a pattern of nightly infiltration by destroyers. The troops carried on these trips usually numbered around 60 per ship. Torpedo tubes were trained outboard so that jeeps could be accommodated and motor vehicles were even slung from lifeboat davits to increase the payload.

Apart from a few Beaufighters based on Cyprus there was now no air cover at all. On the other hand, there were so many German aircraft around that nothing larger than a destroyer could risk sailing north of Rhodes. The burden fell on the smaller ships.

The Germans took to dropping flares by the dozen, turning night into day and illuminating the ships on the dark sea. To counter the flares the ships made black smoke until it was impossible to distinguish them from the air and the German aircrew had to bomb 'blind'.

As dawn approached our ships were able to slip into previously selected Turkish harbours where they spent the day under way at slow speed to prevent the Turkish authorities from boarding. German bombers would skim down over the ships almost at mast height, tempting us to open fire – something that would give them the right to use their bombs in neutral territory. When darkness returned the ships resumed their perilous passage to deliver their precious cargoes.

On one visit to a Turkish port it became necessary to carry out some serious repairs to *Petard*; at the same time the crew could get some much-needed sleep. We dropped anchor and invited the Turks to come aboard. They demanded to know why we had anchored up. Of course, we really wanted the protection of the Turkish flag. We didn't want them to know the nature of the repairs that were required so they were shown a perfectly sound electric motor that was being stripped down for their benefit. Our guests were then invited into the Wardroom and plied with copious food and drink. When the time came for them to leave the ship they were almost out on their feet and did not want to go but we packed them off with a bottle of spirits each!

Mine traps in the channels

It became clear that the Germans must eventually invade Leros and Samos. They had also laid mine traps in all the narrow channels between the islands and had even placed some in Turkish waters; the Turks simply looked the other way. This was a time when the ASDIC system came to the fore. Since I already had three year's experience of sea warfare I was able to demonstrate to the Captain that if we entered a narrow stretch of water at slow speed the anti-submarine equipment would also detect mines; not perhaps a single mine but certainly a mine trap. It worked. I often wonder how many of ship's crew know they owe their lives to ASDIC. *Petard* lived to fight another day.

Disturbed by reports from ships' captains returning to Alexandria to the effect that the missions were futile and becoming more and more costly, a top Commodore decided he needed to see the situation for himself. He embarked aboard *HMS Eclipse* and led a convoy that included *HMS Petard* and four Hunt Class destroyers. In spite of repeated warnings about mine traps, the Commodore steered the ships to pass to the east of Kalymnos Island and off the coast of Turkey. We proceeded in total darkness with only a faint green light on the stern of each ship, *Petard* in second place, at a speed dictated by others and unable to use the ASDIC. Suddenly there was a gigantic explosion ahead and *Eclipse* sank in seconds.

Petard's Captain gave the order 'Hard a Port' with the engines thrown into full emergency astern. We came to a dead stop and an awful silence followed. In complete darkness all boats were lowered to search for survivors. They came back time and again with men plucked from the sea, covered in oil, wounded and in a state of despair. After four hours, signs of daybreak brought the search to an end. We later learnt that some of the crew had swum to the Turkish mainland and safety. *Petard* and the other two destroyers moved into a Turkish harbour to lie up. Some MTBs arrived to collect the survivors. The Captain of *HMS Eclipse* and the Colonel in charge of the troops were rescued but of the Commodore there was not a sign.

Invasion craft illuminated

The ships carried on with the transport of men and material even though it was obvious to us that the soldiers would be killed or captured when the Germans invaded. Much effort was made by the British ships to intercept German vessels. Came the time (10-11 November) when *HMS Petard* led two Hunt Class destroyers, *HMS Rockwood* and the Polish *Krakowiak* into the islands to watch for invasion forces. A group of vessels were detected just 3000 yards away. We closed on them in line ahead and switched on our searchlights. Two caiques and a landing craft absolutely packed with German soldiers were caught in the beams. All three destroyers opened fire at once and wiped out the three craft. There were no survivors. Later a German merchant ship was found trying to hide behind a harbour breakwater; it was hammered into a blazing, broken wreck.

When our ships sailed out into open water they were attacked by growing numbers of German aircraft. Eventually *HMS Rockwood* was hit by one of the glide bombs. It did not explode but went straight through the ship and out the side. *Petard* and *Krakowiak* then accompanied *Rockwood* as she was towed back to Alexandria.

Once in the Egyptian port, *HMS Petard* tied up alongside Depot Repair ship *HMS Woolwich* to have her gun linings replaced for the second time in four weeks. She had three times fired her entire 800 round stock of four-inch ammunition plus all her semi-armour piercing and direct impact ammunition.

While this work was being undertaken word came that the Germans had captured Leros and Samos. Most of those men we had fought so hard to land on the islands plus all the supplies and weapons were little more than gifts for our enemies.

I believe the Dodecanese Campaign was the most hazardous period of the war for the Royal Navy in the Mediterranean. In the course of the battle we lost six destroyers sunk and three damaged; three cruisers damaged, one beyond repair plus two submarines and eight smaller vessels sunk. But somehow *HMS Petard* and her great crew managed to survive.

*Eric Sellars passed away on 17 November 2009.

HMS Petard's Fighting Record

Stephen Harper served aboard *HMS Petard* as a coder on her second commission at the end of the war. He went on to become Chief Foreign Correspondent of *The Daily Express* and wrote the following in respect of the ship:

'The fighting record of the Royal Navy Fleet destroyer *HMS Petard* was unique in the Second World War. She was the only Allied warship to sink submarines of all three enemy navies. She was also a survivor of the Malta convoys and of the disastrous Aegean campaign that became known as the "Destroyer's Graveyard".

'The enormous consequences of *HMS Petard's* action against U-559 in the Eastern Mediterranean on 30 October 1942 may well have put the ship almost on a par with Nelson's *Victory*, had it been possible to release the facts at the time.

'The capture of the secret German Enigma coding material and a Four-Rotor Enigma Machine cost the lives of two of the *Petard's* crew. But Bletchley Park's success in using the captured items to break the U-Boat signals traffic was the crucial factor in defeating the U-Boat Wolf Packs when they were on the brink of triumph in the winter of 1942/43.'

1943

WAR DIARY 1943

1 January: Big bombing raids are mounted against German bases on Crete and Italian warships in Palermo.

3 January: A rare Luftwaffe raid on the Isle of Wight causes civilian casualties.

5 January: Eighth Army advances to Buerat, 60 miles west of Sirte in North Africa.

8 January: General von Paulus, commander of the German Sixth Army trapped in Stalingrad, rejects a Russian demand that he surrender. The situation faced by the Germans is grim as the Luftwaffe can only deliver supplies at a fraction of the quantity promised by German air force chief, Herman Goering.

10 January: The Red Air Force is exacting a heavy toll on the Luftwaffe resupply mission at Stalingrad. Today MiG-3 fighters intercept a formation of 16 Ju 52 transports heading for Pitomnik and shoot down 15 of them.

16 January: Soviet troops have captured the airfield at Pitomnik, cutting off this key re-supply route for the remnants of the trapped Sixth Army in Stalingrad. In the Middle Caucasus the Germans are in full retreat, all their hopes of exploiting the Russian oil reserves in the region are dashed.

21 January: The final mission by 25 aircraft to the last viable airfield serving the rapidly shrinking Stalingrad enclave lands at Gumrak tonight. Gumrak will be over-run by the triumphant Red Army tomorrow.

23 January: The Eighth Army enters Tripoli, Libya's capital and the 'jewel city' of Mussolini.

31 January: Sixth Army chief Field-Marshal von Paulus and 15 generals surrender at Stalingrad.

3 February: The Luftwaffe has flown its last supply-dropping mission over Stalingrad; crews reported no sign of Wehrmacht recognition signals on the ground. Yesterday the Russians said they had captured eight more generals.

10 February: Remaining Japanese forces are being withdrawn from Guadalcanal. During the fighting for the island over the last six months it is estimated that the Japanese lost 50,000 men, many of them in destroyed troop transports. Some 800 enemy aircraft have also been lost.

14 February: Rostov-on-Don, capital of the North Caucasus, is liberated by the Red Army. The Germans had held the city since last July.

17 February: An attack by Rommel's Afrika Korps aimed at US troops in Tunisia is meeting with alarming success in the Kasserine Pass area.

18 February: Public complaints that many air raid shelters

Bethnal Green Tube Tragedy

On **3 March 1943** Bethnal Green tube station was the scene of the largest loss of civilian life in the UK in World War II and the largest loss of life in a single incident on the London Underground network. By that time of the war, the numbers using the station as a shelter had dwindled, only rising when retaliatory bombing in response to RAF raids was expected. This was the case on **3 March**, as the British press had reported a heavy RAF raid on Berlin two nights before. The air raid siren sounded at 8.17 pm and people began filing down the short flight of steps into the underground booking office area. Ten minutes later a battery in nearby Victoria Park loudly launched a salvo of anti aircraft rockets. The weapon was new and the unexpected and unfamiliar sound caused a panic. As the crowd surged forward, a woman, possibly carrying a baby, tripped on the stairs, causing many others to fall. Within a few seconds 300 people were crushed into the tiny stairwell; 172 people were dead at the scene, with one more dying in hospital later. Sixty two of the dead were children.

A secret enquiry concluded that the principal cause was the irrational behaviour of the crowd and there would have been a loss of life even if precautions had been taken. It was not until 50 years after the disaster that a discreet commemorative plaque was erected at the site.

have remained locked during recent Luftwaffe attacks on London have been answered by the authorities who explain that a number of shelters have been raided by thieves and also deliberately damaged when left unattended.

24 February: The old port in Marseilles on the Mediterranean is being blown up by the Germans. They suspect that many of the 40,000 inhabitants are working against them. A U-Boat base is planned for part of the cleared area.

26 February: The 155th Battery of the Royal Artillery supported by a battalion of the Hampshires make a gallant stand in the Tunisian hills. Attacked by a large number of German tanks, infantry and aircraft, the British hold out for the whole day until their guns are destroyed and they are overwhelmed. At around 5.30pm a final message is received from the 155th: 'Tanks are on us' followed by the single 'V' tapped out in morse. Their stand will not be in vain for they have bought time for reinforcements to deploy and stem the German advance.

27 February: US troops have moved back into the Kasserine area of Tunisia as the Germans fall back in good order.

3 March: Daylight raid by Mosquitoes on molybdenum mines at Knaben in Norway.

In the Far East an entire Japanese convoy of 11 transports and 10 warships is sunk by Allied bombers in the Bismarck Sea.

5 March: Rommel's panzer force make a violent attack on the Eighth Army who face them across the Mareth defence line in Tunisia; 52 German tanks are knocked out and the attack fails.

6 March: Soviet Marshal Timoshenko has led a Red Army offensive in the Lake Ilmen area. Demyansk has been liberated and today the important German base at Gzhatsk is captured. Moscow is now 140 miles behind the Russians who are advancing swiftly along Napoleon's road of retreat in 1812.

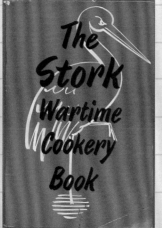

WAR DIARY 1943

12 March: German fighter-bombers make a low-level day raid on the Greater London area; five out of 24 FW 190s are shot down by fighters of 331 Norwegian Squadron who operate out of North Weald. This squadron will go on to be the highest scoring in the whole of Fighter Command in 1943.

14 March: Royal Norwegian Navy forces penetrate a fjord and torpedo two German vessels in Floroe Harbour, north of Bergen, Norway.

Despite their huge losses at Stalingrad the Germans have managed to mount a serious counter-attack in the Kharkov area. Today they capture the city.

18 March: French Guiana breaks off allegiance to Vichy France.

19 March: The Eighth Army go on the offensive against the Mareth Line.

25 March: Malta-based British bombers attack the Rome-Naples railway.

27 March: A curfew has been imposed and hundreds of civilians are being arrested in Aarhus, Denmark, following some sabotage incidents.

7 April: After weeks of bitter fighting, the US II Corps link up with the Eighth Army to isolate the Axis forces in Tunisia.

18 April: An intercepted message decoded by the Americans reveals the coordinates of a flight to be made by Admiral Isoroku Yamamoto to inspect Japanese bases in the Bougainville area of the Solomon Islands. His Betty aircraft is shot down by a Lockheed P-38 Lightning and all on board are killed. The loss of Yamamoto is a major blow to the Japanese military machine.

The Luftwaffe's resupply flights for their besieged forces in Tunisia are being seriously disrupted by the Allies. Today 90 Ju 52s escorted by 50 German and Italian fighters are attacked by US P-40 fighters and RAF Spitfires who destroy 77 enemy aircraft for the loss of just seven of their own.

29 April: An enemy bomber is shot down over Cyprus. The island is an infrequent Axis target – this is only the fifth bomber to be downed in this area of the Mediterranean.

7 May: The war in North Africa is over with the surrender of over 275,000 Axis prisoners in Tunisia – three times the number

Famine Stalks Bengal

A famine of Biblical proportions struck the Bengal area of India in 1943. The final death toll was officially 1.5 million but the real figure was as high as 3,000,000, making it the world's worst-ever food disaster. Famine was not new to India but this one was made far worse because of the war against the Japanese on the Burma–India border. Problems began on 16 October 1942 when a huge cyclone inundated the whole coast of Bengal and Orrisa, destroying rice fields up to 40 miles inland. Farmers lost their autumn crop and were forced to eat the seeds intended for the next planting season. In addition, the 15% of India's rice that normally came from Burma was cut off because of the fighting. The situation was compounded by an outbreak of the rice disease, Brown Spot, in areas unaffected by the cyclone. Rice was also bought up by the military to feed the Allied forces (who included hundreds of thousands of Indian troops) on the Burma front and in the Middle East. Finally, fear of future shortages caused widespread hoarding of rice and a consequent sharp rise in prices. The result was hunger on an unprecedented scale, only alleviated when the British authorities arranged for a million tons of grain to be imported into Bengal causing food prices to rapidly fall.

Laurence Binyon's Legacy

"They shall not grow old, as we that are left grow old,
Age shall not weary them, nor the years condemn.
At the going down of the sun and in the morning
We will remember them."

Laurence Binyon, author of the above stanza, died on 10 March 1943 at the age of 74. The words form part of his poem, *For the Fallen*, which was first published in September 1914 at a time when the first British casualty lists of the Great War were being distributed. The stanza is engraved at the doorway to the British Museum where Dr Binyon worked for nearly 40 years.

Son of Quakers, Binyon was too old to enlist but went to the Western Front in 1916 to work for the Red Cross as a medical orderly in an ambulance unit. In 1940 he was appointed Byron Professor of English Literature at Athens University. He was forced to leave when the Germans invaded Greece in 1941.

On 11 November 1985 Binyon was among 16 Great War poets commemorated on a slate stone unveiled at Poet's Corner in Westminster Abbey. The inscription was written by fellow Great War poet, Wilfrid Owen. It reads: 'My subject is War, and the pity of War. The Poetry is in the pity.'

captured by the Russians at Stalingrad.

31 May: From January 1943 to date, 96 U-Boats have been sunk – 52 by Allied aircraft. This month has seen the greatest toll with 41 enemy submarines destroyed.

20 June: Tokyo Radio has said that a film is being made called the Siege of Singapore about the Japanese conquest of the island city early last year. Thousands of British POWs are participating as enforced 'extras'.

29 June: A French fighter squadron formed at the initiative of General de Gaulle has been flying Yak 1 aircraft with the Red Air Force since last December. A pilot with the Normandie Squadron, Major Jean Louis Tulan, has just been awarded a Soviet medal for bravery.

4 July: 'Farm Sunday' is celebrated throughout Britain. There is a call for half a million additional workers to come forward to assist with this year's predicted record harvest. Total food production in the UK has increased by 70% since the war began.

7 July: China today entered its seventh year of war with Japan. Around 5,000,000 Chinese soldiers hold a battle-line 1500 miles long. It's estimated there are still 50,000,000 able-bodied men of military age who could be called up.

17 July: Transport targets in Amsterdam, Holland, bombed by US Flying Fortresses.

21 July: Around one half of Sicily is now in Allied hands.

The Ministry of Home Security issues a warning about needless fires caused by the careless disposal of cigarette ends and used matches. It is estimated that 2,000,000 cigarette ends are thrown away every day in Britain.

22 July: For the first time since the Japanese arrived there, Surabaya on the island of Java is bombed by Liberators flying from Australia.

31 July: Berlin claims that a U-Boat has sunk a 7000-ton Russian tanker in the Black Sea.

1 August: Ploesti, Rumania's oil centre, is raided in daylight by 177 US Liberators flying from the Middle East. Allied long-distance bombing raids are increasing in range. It is not uncommon for aircraft taking off from Britain to bomb their far-away targets and continue on to land somewhere along the southern Mediterranean shore rather than return to their home base and risk being caught in daylight over German-occupied Europe.

ENDGAME in North Africa

Early 1943. Rommel feels confident a panzer attack can hurt the Americans in Tunisia.

The Germans had won the race for Tunis. Determined to capitalize on this success, Hitler continued to pour men and material into the country on a scale that he had never done before, even when the Afrika Korps had been at the high tide of their advance into Egypt. For his part, Rommel was comfortable with his position at Mareth. So much so that he took time to make a thorough survey of the Allied situation in the west of Tunisia. He concluded that his enemies were poorly organized and that the command structure between the Allies was a confused one. Rommel next proposed to Hitler an immediate joint attack by his own panzer and motorized divisions and von Arnim's Fifth Army. Leaving a few Italian and German infantry units to hold the line at Mareth, Rommel began preparations for the attack.

Germans attack at Kasserine

Now Hitler introduced his own element of command confusion. Instead of making von Arnim subordinate to the master tactician Rommel, he kept the two German armies independent of each other. Von Arnim agreed to participate in an attack on the American II Corps, but he did not co-ordinate his plans closely with those of Rommel and nor did he put as large a force into the attack as Rommel wanted.

On St Valentine's Day, 14 February 1943, Rommel struck. He mounted the kind of surprise attack that had so tormented the British in the desert before El Alamein. The Americans were shocked as panzers raced into the mountain passes and smashed into their lines in a brilliantly executed offensive that swept forwards to Sbeitla and Kasserine in the broad valley beyond. Despite confusion and heavy losses, the Allies fought well but lacked the combat experience of the crack German forces facing them. On 18 February, Rommel seized Kasserine and continued on to the Kasserine Pass. Here he was held up for a time by desperate American defenders before resuming his advance towards Tebessa, the main supply point and communications centre for the Allied forces in the region. Fortunately, the Americans mustered enough men, guns and tanks to block Rommel short of Tebessa.

A young German soldier surrenders in Tunisia.

He switched his main attack to Thala from where he could menace the whole Allied force in Tunisia. He almost grasped the prize but was beaten back after a furious fight against British tanks and British and American infantry.

Rommel had severely shaken the Americans and bought precious time to continue the military build-up in Tunisia. But he had not achieved the decisive victory that he might have done if von Arnim had committed his whole army to the attack. The Allies had also learned valuable lessons about German tactics. Plus Eisenhower would reorganize and improve the Allied command system. Finally, the British and Americans had worked out an effective formula for using air power in support of ground troops, a method that would be used successfully by the Allies throughout the rest of the war.

Desert Fox falls ill

Belatedly, Hitler now put Rommel in command of all German forces in Tunisia in anticipation of a renewed attack by the Eighth Army and the US II Corps in southern Tunisia. On 20 March a frontal assault on the Mareth Line was repulsed. Montgomery next decided to send tanks supported by New Zealanders on an outflanking movement into the desert and around the end of the Mareth Line. At the same time, the II Corps – now commanded by General George S Patton – attacked southeast from Gafsa against the right rear of the German positions.

This powerful joint attack threatened to cut off the Germans in the south of Tunisia compelling Rommel to abandon the Mareth Line and withdraw northwards to link with von Arnim's army. At this point, the Desert Fox succumbed to serious illness. He was ordered back to Germany. Von Arnim was made commander in Tunisia.

Eisenhower prepared for the endgame. On 3 May British and American forces attacked towards both Bizerta and Tunis. The Germans resisted but harried from the air and pounded by artillery and tank fire, were slowly worn down. On 7 May British tanks entered the city of Tunis while American troops fought their way into Bizerta. Von Arnim's men now had no ports from which they could escape to Sicily but they fought on for some days to come, despite being surrounded.

On 13 May, the last Axis fighting men in North Africa surrendered. About 275,000 Germans and Italians had been captured during the last 10 days of the battle. That was more than the number that surrendered to the Red Army at Stalingrad.

STALINGRAD OF THE MED

John Gunther was an American writer and radio journalist who had a roving brief in the European sphere of operations. In the summer of 1943 he visited Malta.

The shrewd and courtly Field-Marshal Lord Gort VC, Governor and Commander-in-Chief of Malta has, indeed, every reason to speak with pride of Malta's struggle and the role he has played in it since he became Governor in its grimmest days. Now the secret is out and the world knows how Malta revenged itself for its bitter months of embattled siege, how it became transformed from what seemed a hopelessly isolated island into an essential springboard for the invasion of Europe through Sicily we have been witnessing.

A couple of nights ago from the balcony of Verdala Palace I watched Malta's 3322nd raid. The overwhelming impression I got was of how something so terrible could be also so very beautiful. The alarm came at about 11pm. We were several miles from the harbour; we could only hear the sirens faintly. Then the shafts of searchlights began to move slowly through the sky, until a dozen converged to the same point of focus; then solidly, smoothly – almost tenderly, if that doesn't seem too strange a word – they probed through the velvet darkness. The lights continued to finger their way sideways – so smoothly, so silently, so very slowly – until there came sharp pin-pricks of yellow light, the bursts of ack-ack. The sound reached us in a steady succession of neat cracks. Then the real barrage went up. It was coloured red, the colour of rubies. Slowly, very slowly, with extreme slowness, so that you could see each individual light, the ruby-coloured tracers expanded into successive rows and lines of jewels. Chains of these rubies spread evenly in the sky, so slowly, so confidently, and then met in sparkling criss-crosses – like bunches of ruby necklaces suddenly intertwined and torn apart. Then came pulsating flares, reflections

Gort took me into a sunny garden outside Verdala Palace and said with a good-humoured, grim irony, 'You know, Napoleon once remarked he'd rather have the British in Montmartre than in Malta. Interesting statement, what? Ha, ha!..'

of the Bofors guns firing. And finally every kind of noise barked out savagely, and one by one the rubies separated, faded, and disappeared.

Only German grand master

Malta is a curious little place, with much to show. Its people are of mixed stock, who claim descent from the ancient Phoenicians; they are partly Arab, and they speak a language quite unique. Most Maltese are small shopkeepers, fishermen and cultivators of olives and grain; above all, they are islanders. No Maltese has ever seen a railway,

a tramcar, a river or a wood – except in the movies, or unless he has left the island.

The history of Malta, which ramifies back to the most remote antiquity, is remarkable. This island has successively been ruled by Romans, Carthaginians, Visigoths, Saracens, Normans, Spaniards, French and British. For many centuries it was the home of the Knights of Malta and of St John of Jerusalem, the grand master of which was its ruler. The last grand master – and the only grand master ever to be a German – was Ferdinand von Hompesch; he held power from 1797 to 1799, when he traitorously turned the island over to Napoleon. As Lord Gort put it, he was the first great Quisling in Mediterranean history. Malta has been besieged twice. The first siege, the Great Siege, came in 1565; it was made by the Turks, who were repulsed after four months of bitter struggle and blockade. Deriving a lesson from this, the Maltese knights set out to build the vast series of complex battlements that still engird parts of the island. The work took 14 years. The knights, using slave labour from the Levant, erected walls 10 to 20 feet thick; they

This cartoon of 1803 depicts Napoleon confronting a British seadog who is determined to keep a firm foothold on Malta. The island was described as a 'Bone of Contention'. The Maltese people had invited the protection of the British in 1798.

set up formidable bastions and watch-towers; they tunneled deep into solid rock and made a city inside a city. And it is a striking example of continuity of history that these identical battlements withstood another enemy in the second great siege, in 1942, when German bombs blasted them in vain. Eisenhower, Cunningham, Alexander and Montgomery, as we know, established their headquarters in the same caverns, tunnels and underground passages which the knights built four centuries ago. The knights built well. No modern engineer could have constructed a more secret, a more ingenious or a safer shelter for the base of a great military operation.

Intensive and merciless attacks

Malta today looks like what it is – a community subjected to one of the most intensive and merciless attacks ever made anywhere. Down the narrow streets of the towns are ruins where whole blocks have disappeared. A few broken pillars stand out of the white rubble, nothing more. Then you get near the harbour and gasp at the fury that once eviscerated it. Even now, months after the worst of the blitz, there is a harbour district known as Three Cities, once the bustling centre of the maritime community, where exactly one street has been scraped clear. But to an amazing degree life goes on almost in a normal manner.

The story of the Malta siege is one of

indomitable resistance against the most strenuous odds. The Axis air forces opened up on the islands on 11 June 1940, and have been at it ever since. There were 3322 raids up to the date I left, and more than 16,000 tons of bombs were dropped. Some 6000 tons descended in one month, April 1942 – much more than were ever dropped on the whole of England in any single month. Yet the total area of Malta is only 98 square miles, its total population only a quarter of a million. On a per capita basis the Malta death toll – about 1500 – would thus represent almost 200,000 dead in Great Britain. The toll would have been much worse if Malta did not have a perfect natural shelter system and stone buildings that did not burn.

One thing the Maltese are intensely proud of, I learned, is that the island caused more casualties to Axis airmen than it suffered itself. More than a thousand enemy aircraft have been shot down over Malta, which means at least 1500 Nazis dead or prisoners. Most of the people will concede, though somewhat grudgingly, that the Germans and Italians did their best to avoid non-military objectives. About 30,000 houses were destroyed and famous historical monuments were damaged, but even though the island is cramped, with everything close to everything else, the enemy never hit the big hospital that dominates the entrance to Valetta. 'Maybe they spared it deliberately in order to

use it as a landmark,' I heard it said. A queer item is that the only chapels destroyed in the great cathedral were the German and Italian chapels while the only one damaged belonged to Vichy France.

Spitfires filling the whole sky

The worst period of the blitz began in December 1941 and lasted until the middle of May 1942; the raids these months were incessant, day and night, and some of the longer ones lasted 12 hours without interruption. If, at this time, the Germans had been able to locate and destroy the hidden bakeries that were feeding great masses of refugees in the villages, they might have forced the island to capitulate. As it was – a curious detail – underground grain stores built by the Knights in 1565 helped save Malta in 1942. You can still see them, their covers set in flagstones, before Floriana Church.

The turning-point came explosively in May 1942, when some newly arrived Spitfires destroyed 102 German raiders. One officer told me, 'My God, what a day that was! I was in the hospital, ill and shaken from the unbelievable raiding all day and night. One afternoon I heard a dog-fight and I looked out of the window and I saw 10 Spits. Then I saw 20 Spits. I couldn't believe my eyes. I saw 30 Spits, then 40 Spits. My God, it was wonderful. Those Spits of ours were filling the whole bloody sky!'

I asked another soldier what the bombing was like, whether the enemy came in high or dive-bombed. He replied, 'Both, sir. Sometimes the Messerschmitts came in much lower than the dive-bombers and tossed grenades at us out of their windows. That is something, sir, to have grenades tossed at you out of an aeroplane window. Being grenaded from an aeroplane is quite something, sir.'

Then began the siege. It lasted from June 1942 until December 1942, and tapered off in February 1943. During all this time Malta submitted to what was nothing more nor less than slow starvation. There was hardly a ship in the harbour when Gort arrived, and for month after month none got through. Then came the November convoy, which – British air superiority having become more marked – reached Malta without too serious loss. During the siege people were tried to their utmost; almost everybody lost between 15 and 30 pounds. There was no fresh meat, no soap and little bread. The total ration for one person was one tin of bully beef, one small tin of sardines, and one and a half ounces of tea every 16 days. Petrol had to be guarded drop by drop and since power was so limited, there were no lights at night. It wasn't a mere matter of a black-out for month after month; no lighting existed at all.

Probably it was the air factor that was decisive once the danger of starvation passed,

but other elements contributed to victory. I asked Gort one morning what he thought were the main things responsible, and he answered three: First the Church, second Maltese nationalism, third Maltese loyalty to Britain. The people here are extremely religious and the clergy has been outspokenly anti-Axis. As to Maltese nationalism, the islanders like to say that they have never been 'conquered' and that they are the only people who have ever 'volunteered' to join the British Empire. Any former leaning they may have had towards Italy was blasted away by the first Italian bomb and the knowledge that the Italian consul-general, long a resident of Valetta, had probably told the fascists where to aim. In the dark days of the Battle of Britain in 1940 the Maltese sent a message to England that no matter what happened they would continue to consider themselves as 'Britain's ally'.

No more crosses. Give us bread!

The George Cross, as everybody knows, was awarded the island as a whole in April 1942; but I found that many Maltese were somewhat indifferent to this honour. They said, 'We have had enough crosses. Let us have more bread.'

Why is Malta so important to Britain. Why did the Germans so badly want to knock it out? The answer is, of course, obvious; the island is the central crux of Mediterranean communications. If the Nazis could have reduced it they might have been able to maintain Rommel in North Africa indefinitely. Had the enemy rubbed Malta out, the only

Allied link between Gibraltar and Alexandria would have disappeared. Why then did the Germans not attack Malta even more fiercely, why didn't they attempt an actual invasion at the peak of the blitz or during the siege? The answer seems to be that Rommel, too, confident, thought he could reach Cairo anyway. Marshal Kesselring, the German Commander-in-Chief in the Mediterranean, was not so confident. He wanted to assault Malta and try to finish it off. Rommel's point of view prevailed. This, I heard it said, was because Rommel could get the ear of Hitler himself, whereas Kesselring only had direct access to Goering.

A couple of months ago a Russian journalist visited Malta. He prodded through the smashed streets; he looked at the pulverized harbour and the terrible devastation in the town. He exclaimed, 'This is war, all right. This is the real thing. This is Stalingrad.'

Below: Malta today is a popular holiday destination for British tourists. But occasionally warships still call in at Grand Harbour, Valleta. This is the USS aircraft carrier JFK, big enough to make the mighty ramparts of Malta's capital look puny.

Sicily

Operation Husky: July 1943

The Italian Campaign

Even before the final Allied assault in Tunisia, the Combined Chiefs of Staff had ordered Eisenhower to prepare for an invasion of Sicily. The island's location made it very important to Allied strategy being just 90 miles off the coast of North Africa. All the time that Axis air and naval forces, especially submarines, could be based in Sicily and southern Italy, Allied shipping would be in peril if it sailed through the Mediterranean to or from the Suez Canal. The latter was the shortest route to the war theatre in Asia and the Far East.

The invasion – *Operation Husky* – began just before dawn on 10 July 1943. The Eighth Army struck the south-east corner of the island, just below the city of Syracuse, while the US Seventh Army landed a few miles further west, along the south coast, on both sides of the town of Gela. The Italians were taken by surprise.

Patton manned an anti-tank gun

However, things didn't go so well for the British and American paratroops and glider-borne infantry. The Dakota transport aircraft were flown by inexperienced pilots and were blown off course by a storm during the night. The paratroops were scattered all over southern Sicily. Tragically, of 137 gliders released, 69 fell into the sea. Only 12 gliders reached their assigned landing zone. Then

Below: Sicily is beautiful but in wartime it did not necessarily appear so to Allied troops locked in deadly combat. Mount Etna can be seen in the background to this recent photograph.

when later waves of Allied planes came in with reinforcements, Allied warships and ground units mistook them for German planes and shot many of them down. Those airborne soldiers who did land safely fought well.

From the outset success everywhere crowned the early efforts of the seaborne invaders. The Italian defenders had no heart for the fight. But then the Germans got involved with a counter-attack by tanks and infantry of the Herman Goering Division against the Americans. The attack was blunted with the invaluable assistance of naval gunfire. The American General Patton personally manned an anti-tank gun in this action.

By 15 July the Allies had control of southeastern Sicily and seven days later captured Palermo, Sicily's capital. Allied airfields were established and Spitfires flew in from Malta. The day before a second airborne operation had been launched with the object of capturing the important bridge of Primo Sole, south of Catania on the east coast. The 1st Parachute Brigade of the 1st Airborne Division, together with a number of glider-borne anti-tank units, made the attack. They were unfortunate to arrive in the midst of a German air raid and the ack-ack fire in progress caused casualties and a scattering of the force. Some 60 aircraft failed to find the landing zone (14 were shot down); just 13 gliders made the rendezvous. By dawn 200 paratroops had seized the bridge and removed the German demolition charges. Driven off in the evening, the British returned next morning and retook the bridge.

Not for the first time in the war, this was an airborne operation that was successful despite mistakes which, added to the inevitable hazards of war, had caused just a fifth of the allocated force to arrive at the right place at the right time.

John Frost captures a bridge

Ironically, one of the victorious participants in the battle for the Primo Sole Bridge was Colonel John Frost – in September 1944 he would jump into Holland with the 1st Airborne Division. His mission: To capture the Rhine crossing in the town of Arnhem. As history has recorded, this time it would indeed be a 'Bridge Too Far'.

German reinforcements arrived and the experienced General Hans Hube took charge. Making skilful use of the rugged mountains, Hube anchored his left flank on the slopes of Mount Etna and organized a defensive line to hold the north-eastern part of the island. In July and August Montgomery and his Eighth Army were unable to break through. Further north and west, however, the Americans inched forward and General Patton forced the German right flank back by making several small amphibious landings on the north coast.

By mid-August Hube realized it was time to quit the island or risk losing all of his men. The Germans began a skillfully conducted evacuation across the narrow Straits of Messina. Despite the overwhelming Allied superiority in warships and aircraft just about the entire German force escaped, although the majority of Italian troops chose to surrender.

Cocky British Cruiser

After leaving Malta, John Gunther went to Sicily in the wake of the Allied invasion. Here are some extracts from his news reports:

Sunday 25 July. Went for a quick swim and for the third time saw a battle from our beach at Agnone. Really this is remarkable. And this time it was a naval battle. Directly before us, not more than half a mile offshore, a workmanlike-looking British cruiser appeared steaming calmly for Catania. It got closer and closer to the German defences. We saw white water-spouts splash up near the ship as the Germans went after it with artillery; we heard the sharp, crashing bark of enemy guns. Imperturbably, the cruiser continued across the brilliant blue water; imperturbably, arrogantly, disdaining any note of apprehension, it kept pushing its nose farther in. Then, very close in to the harbour, it opened up with its own guns. We watched the shore and the ship exchange salvos, and for a second I could not believe that this scene could possibly be real. Warily, cockily, the cruiser heeled about and began to withdraw. Almost at the same instant, a big flight of our bombers flashed north very high. This was all so exhilarating that it was a welcome anti-climax when someone said, 'Bloody silly, those naval chaps! They'll knock the place apart! Won't be anything for us to see!'

Mussolini resigns

Saturday 26 July. At briefing we learned that Mussolini had resigned. Apparently the news was out last night – one wonderful rumour is that an 11-year-old houseboy at AMG heard it on a clandestine radio and was the first to tell our commanding general – but we, who represent the entire press of the Anglo-Saxon world, didn't catch on until this morning.

We came across some wounded sitting under the wings of Red Cross planes. An Irish doctor explained his work; up to 50% of all wounded on this front are now moved by air; what this saves in human suffering can only be understood by those who have been over these unimaginable roads, which shake the stretcher cases to a jelly. Also the doctor told us of some tremendous air battles going on here. One wing of 60 Spits got 25 German planes in one operation; 21 were Ju 52s carrying two and half tons of petrol each. One German baled out and landed plunk in the middle of the raging fire set by his own crashed plane. 'Poor chap,' said the doctor.

Too 'Scotch' to speak English

Today we perched on a hill-top about a thousand yards from enemy lines. The Germans up here are aggressive and full of fight. They rake the valley with shellfire by day and send out infiltration parties at night, crossing no man's land in small groups and seeking to get behind British units. Sometimes a German will call out in excellent English, 'Halt! Who goes there!' thus trying to entrap a British patrol. But this stratagem doesn't work well in these parts, because, as I heard it said, 'Jerry is up against the Argylls here, and they're too Scotch to speak English.'

We met an officer who told us, 'My men are tired. They're shag tired. The Germans are thickening up around here, mark ye. There was a bit of a shambles last night. One of our battalions was isolated up there for 23 hours; nobody could get any food or water to them and they could not get the wounded out; the shelling was too heavy. It was a hellish business, mark ye. A man is useless after eight to 10 days on this front. He needs a chance to recuperate. My men get no sleep. The artillery and infiltration parties keep them busy at night and, by God, there is no shade by day.'

On our way back we saw fantastic big fires on the slope of Mount Etna; there were huge purple and orange explosions. We thought the Germans might be burning their stores of magnesium flares, Very lights, and the like. If he can help it, Jerry never gives anything away.'

Above: A section from Frank Mason's depiction of a British fleet in the Mediterranean.

EIGHTH ARMY ESPRIT

While in Sicily, John Gunther filed this story about Monty's legendary fighting force.

For a good many reasons the British Eighth Army, that unique organism, is unlike any other army in the world; it has an individual character, an esprit, quite its own. What is it that makes an army elite? For one thing consider its worship of its leader, General Montgomery, which is little short of idolatrous. And Montgomery has imparted to his men something of his distinctive personality; Monty, his officers say, gave the Eighth 'its soul'. Another point is that, above all, the Eighth is an informed army. It carries its own printing press everywhere, and publishes a small but fairly substantial daily newspaper. Montgomery briefs his own officers, and the officers in turn tell the men the essentials of every forthcoming operation. This is valuable in case an officer or man gets into difficulties. First, he knows without having to await orders how to put himself right again; second, if he is taken prisoner his knowledge of the operation as a whole makes for more rather than less security, since he knows just what he should keep his mouth shut about.

Another point about the Eighth is its self-sufficiency; it is one of the most self-contained of all modern armies. Discipline is strict, but the camaraderie between officers and men is remarkable; probably this is a result of long experience of hardships in the desert. A great institution was, and is, the 'brew-up,' the afternoon cup of tea which is invariable no matter where the men happen to be. In the desert, officers and men, working in small armoured car or tank units, always had tea together; there was little distinction in rank, and each unit maintained its solidarity not only out of necessity but as a matter of principle; in the desert, no visitor was ever refused anything. And the 'brew-up' led to 'vehicle feeding,' whereby clusters of tanks would meet towards sundown and have tea together.

Magnificent disdain

One peculiar instance of the superb morale of the Eighth is the fine contempt most of its units have for every other unit. Divisions get shuffled and reshuffled, but every division in the Eighth likes to think of itself as something special. But let any rash and unwary outsider say anything critical about a division and all will band together to hurl fury on the interloper. The Eighth as a whole has an utterly magnificent disdain for any other army. Its men call outsiders 'palefaces' and

An Eighth Army tank in a wrecked Sicilian town. Imperial War Museum.

they say sardonically, 'Wait till their knees get brown.' What they despise most in the world is any creature so witless as to be seen wearing a sun helmet. The Eighth itself fights in the fiercest of all possible suns, but any trooper would be seen dead rather than in such headgear. This is odd because for many years the sun helmet was practically a trademark of the British in the East.

Of course the desert, next to the personality of Monty, has been the greatest single factor that has shaped and moulded the Eighth. It is desert-bred and desert-trained. Its men are proud of the appellation 'Desert Rats,' and many are what the officers call 'sand-happy; this is a phrase almost equivalent to punch-drunk, except that it does not mean lack of fighting instinct. The Eighth has, of course, its own insignia: A white Crusader's shield on a black background, with yellow crossbars. And the atmosphere of the desert, its vast and starry emptiness, its windswept loneliness, has given many Eighth Army men something of a crusading spirit. The exigencies of desert warfare have also contributed to the way the Eighth Army looks. The men wear, it seems, any kind of old uniform; many are naked to the waist, with ragged shorts and every variety of headgear; they look like pirates,

ragamuffins. But they're tremendously clean. The life of the desert enforces an extreme and drastic simplicity. There are no women; there is very little alcohol. The health rate of the Eighth is always astonishingly high, and it is characteristic that before any engagement the rate of illness goes sharply down; the men want to be fit to fight.

Bugs and choking dust

Consideration of the desert leads to another point: The Eighth Army doesn't like Sicily very much. Partly this is because no army enjoys terrain in which it is stalled, held up, no matter how temporarily. And here in this convoluted and corrugated battlefield, it cannot easily use its favourite weapon, the tank. But above and beyond this there is something else. The desert did something to these warriors; they cannot get over it and they miss it; they are unhappy to have conquered and thus lost it. The desert was hot, yes; but not so hot as Sicily. The desert lacked water, yes; but water is very short here too. Above all, the desert was clean, and the Eighth Army veterans despise Italy – full of bugs and choking dust – as 'a filthy place'.

When the Eighth Army was advancing in Tripoli the troops dreamed of grass, of fresh fruit; they prayed for the sight of green, for trees, for vineyards. And when they arrived in Tunisia they were delirious with excitement. Every man picked flowers; on every tank, every jeep, there was a bouquet. Now a certain amount of green does exist in Sicily. But even so this isn't quite the place they thought it would be. This is not the 'sunny Italy' of picture postcards. In Africa the Eighth Army had a kind of good-natured contempt for the Italians. But here even the attitude of the Italians seems changed. The troops simply cannot understand the crowds of young men, civilians, squatting along the streets. Of course the Eighth, used so long to working in small detachments and alone, does not like crowds in any case. Many of the men have not been in a foreign city before. And they find the complexities of a town like Syracuse or Augusta bewildering.

I asked one officer why the Eighth Army was originally called the 'Eighth' army. He replied, 'Oh, that's easy. So the enemy would think we really had seven others.'

> " I asked one officer why the Eighth Army was originally called the 'Eighth' Army. He replied, 'Oh, that's easy. So the enemy would think we really had seven others. "

YANKS at the Court of King George

More and more American soldiers, sailors and airmen were arriving in the British Isles throughout 1943. Before they crossed the Atlantic they were given a booklet, *A Short Guide to Great Britain*. Here are some extracts:

'England is still one of the great Democracies and cradle of many American liberties. Today the King reigns but does not govern. British people have a great affection for their monarch, but they stripped him of practically all political power. Be careful not to criticize the King. The British feel about that the way you would feel if anybody spoke against our country or our flag. Their King and Queen stuck with the people through blitzes, and had their home bombed just like anyone else. So their people are proud of them.

'The British don't know how to make a good cup of coffee. You don't know how to make a good cup of tea. It is an even swap.

'Keep out of arguments. You can rub the Briton the wrong way by telling him, "We came over and won the last one." Each nation did its share, but Britain remembers that nearly one million of her best manhood died in the last war. America lost 60,000 in action.

'The British will welcome you as friends and allies, but remember that crossing an ocean does not automatically make you a hero. There are housewives in aprons and youngsters in knee pants in Britain who have lived through more high-explosives in air raids than many soldiers saw in first-class barrages in the last war.

'If you are invited to eat with a family, do not eat too much, otherwise you may eat up

> '..two actions will annoy the British Tommy. Swiping his girl and then rubbing it in that you are better paid.'

their weekly ration. Don't criticize food, beer or cigarettes to the British. Remember they've been at war since 1939.

'You will be welcome in British pubs (what we call a bar or tavern) as long as you remember one thing – the pub is the poor man's club or gathering-place where men have come to see their friends, not strangers.

'The British are tough. Don't be misled by their tendency to be soft-spoken and polite. If they need to be they can be plenty tough. The English language did not spread across oceans and over the mountains and jungles and swamps of the world because these people were pantywaists. Sixty thousand British civilians – men, women and children – have died under bombs and yet the morale of the British is unbreakable and high. A nation does not come through that if it does not have plain, common guts.'

Mapping Out The Allied Future

With Sicily in the hands of the Allies it was time to consider where next to strike. This map shows some of the options. If it had been published six months later it would have caused a real security flap because it shows an arrow pointing into the heart of Normandy – exactly where the Allies were planning to land on D-Day!

Possible Allied attacks
Allies & occupied areas
Axis, occupied areas & Finland
Nonbelligerents

WAR DIARY 1943

6 August: Munda in the Central Solomons falls to General MacArthur's troops after a one-month campaign.

10 August: Winston Churchill is in Quebec where he will meet with President Roosevelt.

14 August: American B-24 bombers attack Haiphong in Japanese-occupied French Indo-China; two are shot down and 10 badly damaged. It is an irony of history that 24 years later on 11 August 1967 US B-52 bombers will return to the skies above the same city to bomb it in an escalation of the Vietnam War.

The new Italian Government leader, Marshal Badoglio, declares Rome an open city.

16 August: A Me 109G on a photo-reconnaissance mission seven miles high over Portsmouth is shot down by a 4.5 inch anti-aircraft gun. The German plane was moving at over 400mph and the gunners aimed their shot at a spot five miles ahead of the unarmed fighter. It took 40 seconds from leaving the barrel for the shell to reach the proximity of the target.

17 August: For the first time the RAF bomb a top secret German military establishment on the Baltic island of Peenemunde. It is believed research into new weapons of mass destruction is taking place there.

The volcanic Aeolian Islands of Lipari and Stromboli, north of Sicily, surrender to US warships. Sicily itself is now completely in Allied hands and an artillery duel has begun across the narrow Messina straits.

23 August: The important city of Kharkov is captured by the Red Army.

US troops land on Segula in the Aleutians. Two days earlier the Japanese withdrew from their last important base on Kiska.

24 August: The heaviest raid to date on Berlin took place last night; 58 of the 700 RAF bombers failed to return.

The Quebec Conference concludes today.

25 August: Lord Louis Mountbatten is appointed Supreme Allied Commander of the newly-formed SE Asia Command. SEAC leads operations against Japan from India and Ceylon. Recapturing Burma is a key objective. Mountbatten was recently in Quebec for the Anglo-American summit.

Four RAF Coastal Command Beaufighters from RAF St Eval in Cornwall are shot down when they tangle with FW 190s over the Western Approaches.

28 August: King Boris of Bulgaria dies. He was a vassal of Hitler although most of his fellow countrymen are pro-Russia.

29 August: The Germans have cracked down in Denmark where waves of strikes, riots and acts of sabotage have been steadily growing. Up to now Denmark was portrayed as a 'Model Protectorate', a perfect example of willing cooperation in the Nazi New Order. The Danish Navy scuttles 20 warships in Copenhagen harbour before the 50,000 Germans now in the city can seize them. There has been shooting and explosions and reports of cannon pounding the Royal Barracks. King Christian has been interned by the Nazis.

A SHORT GUIDE TO

GREAT BRITAIN

WAR AND NAVY DEPARTMENTS
Washington, D. C.

THE WARSAW GHETTO

The Germans created the Warsaw Ghetto on 16 October 1940. At this time, the Ghetto contained around 400,000 people, about a third of Warsaw's population. However, the Ghetto occupied just a tiny fraction of the city space.

It was split into two areas, the 'small ghetto', generally inhabited by richer Jews and the 'large ghetto', where conditions were very difficult. A single footbridge linked the two. The Nazis sealed the Warsaw Ghetto from the outside world on 16 November 1940, building a wall patrolled by armed guards.

During the next year and a half, thousands of Polish Jews as well as some Romany people were brought into the Ghetto where disease and starvation kept the population at about the same level. Average food rations in 1941 for Jews in Warsaw were limited to a maximum 1200 calories per day, compared to 1600 for ordinary Poles and 2600 for Germans.

Despite the wall and guards, people could get in and out of the Ghetto. Illegal workshops were created to manufacture goods to be sold on the outside and raw goods were smuggled in – often by children. Smuggling was often the only source of subsistence for Ghetto inhabitants. Despite grave hardships, the inmates attempted to live as normal a life as possible; clandestine hospitals, public soup kitchens, orphanages, refugee centres and recreation facilities were established. There were libraries, classes for children and even a symphony orchestra.

West learns of Genocide

Over 100,000 of the Ghetto's residents died due to rampant disease or starvation, as well as random killings, even before the Nazis began massive deportations of Jews to Treblinka. Between July and September 1942 over 250,000 Ghetto inmates were murdered in the extermination camp. In 1942 Polish Resistance officer Jan Karski informed the West about what was happening to the Jews of Warsaw. By the end of the year, it was clear to the Ghetto leaders that genocide was underway; many of the remaining Jews prepared to fight.

On **18 January 1943** came the first instance of armed resistance using smuggled or stolen weapons. The Jewish fighters had some success; the expulsions were halted and the resistance organizations took control of the Ghetto, building shelters and barricades. During the next three months, the Jews in the Ghetto prepared for the final struggle.

On the eve of Passover, 18 April, a large Nazi force entered the Ghetto. After initial setbacks, the Germans systematically burned and blew up the Ghetto buildings, block by block, rounding up or murdering thousands of Jews. Significant resistance ended on 23 April and the Nazis declared the operation officially ended in mid-May. On the same day they demolished the Great Synagogue of Warsaw. Nazi reports claimed that at least 56,000 people were killed in the Ghetto or deported to the death camps, most to Treblinka.

Left: Indian troops with a Canadian armoured regiment of Sherman tanks at San Donato in southern Italy.

Close call at Salerno

The invasion of Sicily was the last straw for the many Italians who viewed Mussolini's reign as an unmitigated disaster for their country. Hundreds of thousands of Italian soldiers, sailors and airmen had died or were in POW camps as far away as Canada and Siberia. Now it looked inevitable that the Allies were coming to the mainland with the promise of only more death and destruction.

For their part, the Allies had long agreed that invading the Italian mainland as soon as possible was a necessary step. For one, it would almost certainly knock Italy out of the war and Germany would have to take on sole responsibility for defending the peninsular. To do so would require more German soldiers and aircraft and these could only be found by transferring experienced units from the Russian Front. This by itself would partly answer Stalin's insistent demands for a Second Front in Europe to relieve pressure on the Red Army.

Advance on Naples and Foggia

The Allies planned a two-pronged invasion. The Eighth Army (now half of Alexander's 15th Army Group – the other half being General Clark's Fifth Army) would cross the Strait of Messina, the shortest route. They expected the Germans to rush south to the toe of the Italian boot to confront Montgomery. A few days later, Clark's army was to land further up Italy's west coast at Salerno, near Naples, from where it could strike the German flank. When the two Allied armies joined together they would advance to take the great port of Naples and the east coast town of Foggia.

Monty's Eighth Army veterans invaded on 3 September 1943. The Italians didn't resist and the British made rapid progress until they ran into the first German troops and were slowed down.

On 8 September Italy surrendered. The Italian fleet sailed out to join the Allies at Malta and the Italian army prepared to help the Allies drive the Germans from Italy. Allied POWs in Italian camps suddenly found themselves with the chance of early freedom.

Unfortunately, Hitler had acted on his suspicions concerning the Italians. With lightning speed, German troops occupied Rome and in southern Italy they captured and disarmed all the Italian servicemen they could find. The Luftwaffe pursued the Italian fleet and launched a devastating attack on it using new glide bombs, sinking the battleship *Roma* with the loss of 1255 lives. Though some POWs did escape, most the camps were quickly taken over and thousands of men simply saw their Italian guards swopped for German guards.

Early on 9 September, British and American troops of the Fifth Army came ashore on the beaches of the Gulf of Salerno, about 30 miles south of Naples. The Germans had a panzer division in the vicinity and the fighting along the beaches was bitter and desperate. On 13-14 September the Germans came very near to driving the Allies back into the sea; they were saved by the big guns of the British and US navies.

Daunting heights near Cassino

By 15 September the Allied build-up made them strong enough to advance intent on joining up with Montgomery's men. The German General Kesselring began withdrawing northwards. The invasion was now certain of success, but the Allies knew they were in for a tough fight in Italy.

The Eighth Army advanced on the right between the Apennine Mountains and the Adriatic Sea, moving towards Foggia. The Fifth Army stayed on the west coast and on 1 October entered Naples. A few days later, however, the advances were stopped by strong German defensive positions along a line from the Volturno River in the west to the Trigno River on the east coast. Beyond this line Kesselring was preparing an even stronger position in the Gustav Line that broadly followed the line of the Rapido River in the west and the Sangro River in the east. The part of the line between the sea and the daunting heights behind the town of Cassino was particularly strong and Kesselring believed he could hold the Allies here right through the coming winter.

By 15 November the Allies had almost closed up on the Gustav Line.

This Daily Telegraph map depicted the Allied landings on the Italian mainland in the autumn of 1943.

The Italian Campaign

Rescue of Mussolini

With Italy facing defeat and dishonour, the country's leader, Benito Mussolini, was forced to resign on 25 July 1943. Forty-three days later, Italy signed an armistice with the Allies and effectively changed sides in the war. Hitler was enraged; he poured troops into Italy and Greece and disarmed all 'disloyal' Italian forces they could find. Thousands of soldiers were murdered after surrendering. Meanwhile Mussolini – who was being held in custody in a hotel atop the Gran Sasso mountains in central Italy – was rescued on 12 September by German commandos in a daring glider-borne coup led by Colonel Otto 'Scarface' Skorzeny. On 18 September Mussolini declared a new Italian Socialist Republic but it had little support within Italy.

Main picture: *A German commando in front of a glider atop Gran Sasso.*

Above: *Colonel Otto Skorzeny. Note the dueling scar across the side of his face.*

Austrian-born Skorzeny's dramatic rescue of Mussolini earned him the admiration of Hitler. Skorzeny went on to become involved in an aborted plot to kill 'The Big Three' – Stalin, Churchill and Roosevelt – at the Tehran Conference late in 1943 and an attempt to assassinate the head of Yugoslavia's partisans, General Tito.

In late 1944, Skorzeny and his men were responsible for ensuring the continued support for the Axis of a wavering Hungary, known to be negotiating with the advancing Red Army. They achieved this by seizing control of the buildings on Castle Hill in Budapest where the senior Hungarian politicians were based and kidnapping the son of the Hungarian Regent, Admiral Horthy.

Skorzeny also led the German forces involved in *Operation Greif* during the Ardennes Offensive in December 1944. Using captured jeeps and disguised as US Army troops, Skorzeny's men drove ahead of the advancing Wehrmacht with orders to sow chaos and confusion behind the lines of the retreating Allies. The plan met with some success in the early days but ultimately failed to affect the course of the battle.

Skorzeny survived the war and was never convicted of any war crimes. He died of cancer in Madrid in 1975.

AEGEAN DEBACLE

The Dodecanese Campaign of late 1943

The Dodecanese in the south east of the Aegean Sea are part of Greece today but at the beginning of World War II they were under Italian control and had been since the end of the Italo-Turkish War of 1910-11. The islands had become a focus of Mussolini's colonial ambitions in the Eastern Mediterranean. Rhodes, the largest of the islands, along with Leros were major military and aerial bases.

After the fall of Greece in April 1941 and the German air assault on Crete a few weeks later, the country and its many islands was occupied by German and Italian forces. The tide of war slowly turned and with the final defeat of the Afrika Korps in Tunisia in spring 1943, Winston Churchill's attention turned to the Aegean, a region he deemed to be part of the 'underbelly' of the Axis. His planners envisaged an operation to capture the Dodecanese and the big island of Crete. Through this display of Allied power, it was hoped that nearby neutral Turkey would feel compelled to join in the war against Hitler.

Codenamed *Operation Accolade*, the original plans called for a direct assault on Rhodes and Karpathos; Crete was considered too well fortified to attack. A major problem would be countering the large German Luftwaffe presence in the region; US and British aircraft were based far away in Cyprus and the Middle East. From the outset the US questioned the need for the operation, maintaining that the utmost priority in fighting men, ships and aircraft must be given to the invasion of Italy itself. In the event, they refused to support *Accolade*, warning the British that they would have to go it alone.

In August 1943, with an Italian surrender becoming more and more likely, the British moved to take advantage of a possible Italian-German split. A scaled-down version of *Accolade* was proposed.

Germans capture Rhodes

The Italians surrendered to the Allies on 8 September. With Italy out of the Axis,

> Germany's last big victory of the war was due to air superiority which caused great naval losses to the Allies and allowed the enemy to support their forces effectively.

most of their Dodecanese garrisons either wanted to change sides and fight with the Allies or simply go home as quickly as possible. But the Germans acted swiftly, rushing troops from mainland Greece to take control of key islands.

Of the forces already in the Dodecanese the largest was the 7500-strong Assault Division stationed on Rhodes. The latter had three airfields for the Luftwaffe. Occupying Rhodes was therefore absolutely vital for the British.

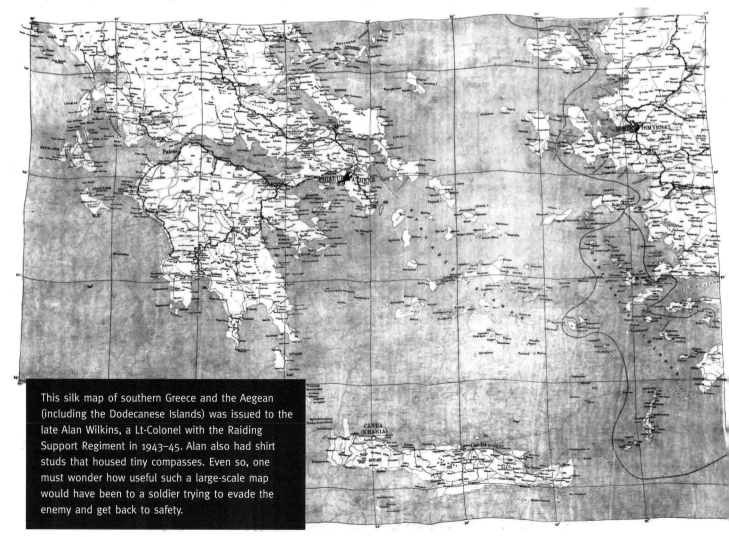

This silk map of southern Greece and the Aegean (including the Dodecanese Islands) was issued to the late Alan Wilkins, a Lt-Colonel with the Raiding Support Regiment in 1943–45. Alan also had shirt studs that housed tiny compasses. Even so, one must wonder how useful such a large-scale map would have been to a soldier trying to evade the enemy and get back to safety.

On 9 September, a British delegation, under Lord Jellicoe, parachuted on to Rhodes, with the aim of persuading the Italian troops there to join the Allies. The day before, the Italian garrison on the little island of Casterosso (Megisti) near the coast of Turkey had surrendered to a British detachment and Allied naval forces moved into the area. Already suspicious, the Germans on Rhodes did not wait for the Italians to declare their intentions, but instead attacked the island's 40,000-strong garrison, forcing it to surrender by 11 September.

Despite this critical setback, the British pressed ahead with the occupation of the other islands, including the three larger ones of Kos, Samos and Leros. They were counting on Allied superiority at sea making the difference. But the British commanders had underestimated the German determination to hold the Dodecanese. By 19 September, Karpathos, Kasos and the Italian-occupied islands of the Sporades and the Cyclades were in German hands and orders had been issued for the capture of Kos and Leros.

Battles for Kos and Leros

With the only Allied airfield being on Kos, bombers of X Fliegerkorps commenced raids from 17 September. A South African Spitfire squadron fought hard but was quickly reduced in numbers. Luftwaffe reinforcements were arriving from all theatres of war. By 1 October the Germans had 362 operational aircraft in the Aegean compared to just 400 left to defend the whole of Italy and France.

There were about 1500 British servicemen on Kos, 880 of them infantrymen. There were also 3500 Italian troops. Brave Dakota crews carried out a hazardous resupply mission on 2 October. Next day the Germans invaded by sea and air and reached the outskirts of the island's capital by dusk. The British withdrew under cover of night only to surrender the next day; 1388 British and 3145 Italian servicemen were captured. The fall of Kos also deprived the Allies of vital air cover.

Then the Italian garrison of Kalymnos (Calino) surrendered, providing the Germans with an island 'stepping stone' in the direction of their next target, Leros. On 7 October, the Royal Navy intercepted and destroyed a German convoy headed for Kos. The Germans were forced to bring in new transport vessels by rail, and it was not until 5 November that they had assembled a fleet of 24 light infantry landing craft that were camouflaged and dispersed around several islands. Despite Allied efforts to locate and sink the invasion fleet, as well as repeated shelling of the ports on enemy-held islands, the Germans were able to muster an impressive assault force that included veterans from the 22nd Infantry Division and a Fallschirmjäger (paratrooper) Battalion.

The failed campaign in the Dodecanese, and in particular the Battle of Leros, is said to have inspired the 1957 Alistair MacLean novel *The Guns of Navarone* and the massively successful 1961 movie of the same name that featured a galaxy of big movie stars including Gregory Peck and David Niven. Another actor was Anthony Quayle. In the war he actually served for a time north of Greece in Albania helping organize guerilla forces.

Alistair McClean himself joined the Royal Navy in 1941, serving throughout the war with the ranks of Ordinary Seaman, Able Seaman, and Leading Torpedo Operator. He was first assigned to *PS Bournemouth Queen*, a converted excursion ship fitting for anti-aircraft guns, on duty off the coasts of England and Scotland. From 1943, he served on *HMS Royalist*, a Dido-class light cruiser. On *Royalist* he saw action in 1943 in the Atlantic theatre, on two Arctic Convoys and escorting carrier groups in operations against *Tirpitz* and other targets off the Norwegian coast. In 1944 his ship went to the Mediterranean theatre, supporting the invasion of Southern France. Later *HMS Royalist* helped sink German blockade runners off Crete and bombarded Milos in the Aegean Sea so it must be highly likely that this experience stayed with him and later gave birth to his famous high adventure novel.

In 1945, in the Far East theatre, his ship escorted carrier groups in operations against Japanese targets in Burma, Malaya, and Sumatra. After the Japanese surrender, *Royalist* helped evacuate liberated POWs from Changi Prison in Singapore.

Germans establish a bridgehead

The British on Leros numbered over 3000 men. There was also a big contingent of Italians. The island had been regularly bombed since 26 September causing much damage. In the early hours of 12 November, the German invasion force approached Leros from east and west in two groups. Despite resistance, the Germans established a bridgehead, while airborne forces secured Mount Rachi, in the middle of the island. Allied counterattacks were repulsed and after being reinforced the following night, the Germans cut the island in two. The Allies surrendered on 16 November. The Germans suffered 520 casualties but captured 3200 British and 5350 Italian soldiers.

After the fall of Leros, the Germans bombed Samos with Stukas, prompting the 2500-strong Italian garrison to surrender on 22 November. By then the Germans had completed their conquest of the Dodecanese in a campaign that represents one of the last big defeats of the British Army in World War II, and the last complete German victory. Their triumph was predominantly due to air superiority.

Tragic fate for Italian POWs

The hapless Italian forces caught up in the Dodecanese conflict suffered cruelly. Following the capture of Kos, a war crime was committed when the Germans obeyed a direct order from Adolf Hitler and executed the Italian commander Colonel Felice Leggio and 101 of his officers as punishment for

supporting the Allies.

Tragedy awaited the Italians at sea as well. The Germans used their naval forces for reinforcing and supplying the isolated German garrisons as well as in operations against Allied-held islands. But these same ships also transported thousands of POWs to the mainland. On 23 September, *HMS Eclipse* sunk the torpedo-boat TA 10 and the steamer *Donizetti*, which had 1576 Italian captives on board. A month later, USAAF B-25s and RAF Beaufighters sunk the cargo ship *Sinfra*; of the 2389 Italian POWs she carried just 539 survived.

Winston Churchill to blame?

Critics at the time and since have blamed Winston Churchill for the ill-fated foray. A great wartime leader, Churchill had a penchant for colourful military adventures; in his youth he had participated in the charge of the 21st Lancers at Omdurman and later was hotly pursued as an escaped prisoner during the Boer War. In the Great War he had been the champion of the disastrous Gallipoli operation and later would strongly advocate the costly Allied landings made at Anzio in January 1944. But the British Premier was never going to be the operational leader of the forces tasked with undertaking his audacious military visions. In the Dodecanese the Allies had little air support; Churchill had argued for the attack to be made on the islands long before the operation was actually mounted and he would have assumed that Allied dominance of the air was a given.

WAR DIARY 1943

30 August: It has been a quiet month for U-Boat sightings. The Battle of the Atlantic is by no means over but it seems the U-Boat offensive has been decisively defeated.

5 September: Yesterday Australian forces came ashore on the coast of Huon Gulf, east of Lae on New Guinea. Today US paratroopers drop in Markham Valley to complete the encirclement of 20,000 Japanese.

6 September: The battleships *Tirpitz* and *Scharnhorst* sail from Norway to shell an Allied weather station and installations on Spitsbergen.

8 September: The German HQ in Italy at Frascati, near Rome, is heavily bombed.

9 September: A battalion of German troops leaves the island of Spitsbergen today. They were landed three days ago to destroy Allied meteorological installations. The battleships *Tirpitz* and *Scharnhorst* were part of the naval force that bombarded the island; the mission is the first (and only) time that the *Tirpitz* sails on active duty.

17 September: Yugoslav partisans led by General Tito announce the capture of Split on the Adriatic coast.

Three days delay and the bloody fighting at Cassino and Anzio may never have happened

The Germans always thought that Salerno was a likely landing place for an Allied invasion of mainland Italy and had stationed a division of troops nearby. However, if the landings had taken place three days or so later than they did there is reason to believe that the Germans would have been gone, possibly as far to the north as Rome. This is because the Germans had no reliable intelligence as to what the Italians and the Allies were going to do. Hitler thought an assault on Yugoslavia where the partisans were growing steadily stronger was likely. Field Marshal Albert Kesselring expected the decisive battle would be fought near Rome and heralded by landings from the sea and air. So when pilots reported the *Avalanche* convoy was at sea, destination unknown, Hitler issued an ultimatum to Italy demanding clarification of their intentions. If the Italian reply proved unsatisfactory, Hitler would withdraw his troops from southern Italy immediately. The ultimatum was ready to be sent on 8 September, just when the Italian surrender was announced. Had the invasion of Salerno happened two or three days later, and the Italian surrender been delayed the Germans might well have been in the process of moving to the Rome area. If this had been the case, there would have been no desperate fight at Salerno, awful winter and spring facing the Germans at Monte Cassino and no costly Anzio landings. As it was, the Germans moved to man the coastal defences vacated by the Italians at Salerno and elsewhere and a collision with the Allies in the south of Italy became inevitable.

18 September: Work continues in London to dismantle a temporary bridge over the Thames at Waterloo. Some 3000 tons of steel will be released for the war effort.

22 September: *Tirpitz* is attacked and badly damaged in Altenfjord, Northern Norway, by British midget submarines. Three fail to return.

23 September: 'Monty's Highway' along which the Eighth Army is now advancing in Italy has reached Foggia. The Highway started on 27 September 1942 in Egypt and has traversed the whole North African shore to Tunis, then Sicily and now Italy.

24 September: Over the last two days 28 troop-filled Ju-88 transport aircraft have been shot down as the Germans evacuate Sardinia.

25 September: Smolensk – once the site of Hitler's Russian Front HQ – is liberated by the Red Army.

29 September: Major-General H B Klopper, Commander of the South African 2nd Division at the time of the surrender of Tobruk in June 1942, reaches British lines near Foggia after a three week trek through Italy's mountains. When Italy surrendered he was able to walk out of his POW camp before the Germans arrived to take control.

2 October: Finschafen Airfield north of Huon Gulf in New Guinea is captured after fierce fighting.

9 October: Moscow's victory guns salute the Red Army which has now cleared the Germans completely out of the North Caucasus. Many of the enemy escaped by sea to the Crimea.

12 October: Neutral Portugal is granting Britain naval and air facilities in the Azores to afford better protection for merchant shipping in the Atlantic.

13 October: The Germans have expelled partisans from Dubrovnik and now hold all the main ports and airfields of Dalmatia. Partisans still hold all the islands and the rest of the Adriatic coastline.

15 October: Fifth Army troops are across the River Volturno. Rome is just 80 miles to the north.

19 October: Some 50 German divisions are at risk of being trapped in the huge bend of the Dnieper River to the north of the Crimea.

27 October: An exchange of invalid Allied and German POWs takes place today in Barcelona.

1 November: US troops land on Bougainville in the Solomons.

6 November: The Kremlin complains that the German and Finnish guns are shelling non-military targets in the besieged city of Leningrad.

3 November: In the early morning darkness a number of E-Boats attempt to intercept a convoy in the Channel between Dungeness and Beachy Head. The escort destroyer *HMS Whitshed* damages three of the enemy craft and drives them off. Germany's light naval forces have lately increased their activity. On 23 October around 30 E-Boats concentrated off Lowestoft apparently intent on ambushing a coastal convoy. Royal Navy destroyers and MTBs were on the alert and engaged the enemy, sinking four E-Boats and damaging others at no cost to themselves.

5 November: A single German aircraft drops four bombs on the Vatican in Rome. There are no fatalities but the windows of the high cupola of St Peter's are broken and the Vatican Radio studios are damaged. The Vatican will be hit once more on 1 March 1944 when the Luftwaffe drop six bombs, littering the Court of Saint Damaso with debris.

6 November: The Red Army liberates Kiev, third largest city in Russia and capital of the Ukraine. The Soviet air force is now within 40 flying miles of Rumania's important Black Sea port of Odessa.

8 November: Adolf Hitler addresses a Nazi Party rally in Munich and says that Germany would never give in. He adds, ominously, that the 'hour of retaliation' will come.

10 November: Britain's civilian prison and borstal population is about 13,000. Inmates now have some 5000 acres under cultivation and producing vegetables and fruit. They also build roads and work in factories. Prisoners have also produced thousands of degaussing coils. Attached to ships, these anti-

WAR DIARY 1943

magnetic cables render magnetic mines harmless.

In the six months from May to October last, 150 enemy submarines were sunk.

11 November: The Allied advance reaches Cassino, some 70 miles from Rome. It is the first time the town has been mentioned in frontline reports from Italy.

18 November: Allied bombers are ranging over Germany tonight in the largest numbers ever.

20 November: US Marines land on Makin and Tarawa islands in the Pacific.

25 November: The British press carry a picture of the car once used by the British ambassador to Germany. The former British Embassy in Berlin was damaged by RAF bombs and when German firemen went in to put out the blaze they found the car intact and still flying the Union flag.

30 November: In a rare reverse on the Eastern Front the Russians announce their withdrawal from Korosten, liberated by them 13 days previously. The Germans are mounting a counter-offensive.

2 December: The Luftwaffe demonstrates that is not yet a spent force when 40 bombers raid crowded Bari harbour in southern Italy and sink 17 Allied ships.

8 December: Oslo students are being deported to Germany. Mass arrests began on **30 November** after students protested against the arrest of eight professors and students accused of being anti-German and anti-Quisling.

13 December: President Roosevelt is on his way back to the USA after attending a conference in Tehran with Churchill and Stalin. En route he has visited Malta and Sicily.

15 December: Allied progress in Italy has slowed. Since liberating Naples at the beginning of October, Mark Clark's Fifth Army has advanced just 30 miles. In the same period the Eighth Army has covered 60 miles. The terrain favours the resolute and determined German defenders and the weather has been poor.

19 December: Long-distance Allied bombers hit targets in Bangkok.

28 December: The Eighth Army finally triumphs in the bitter battle for Ortona, a town considered key to the German defence line on the Adriatic coast.

A two-day battle in the Bay of Biscay has ended in the destruction of a 5000-ton German blockade runner and the sinking of three enemy destroyers. Royal Navy cruisers *Glasgow* and *Enterprise* took a leading role in the running fight while the RAF provided air cover.

29 December: It is revealed that Ascension Island in the South Atlantic has been a vital staging post in the passage of 5000 warplanes flying from the USA to Africa from where they have flown on to war theatres in the Mediterranean, Middle East, Ceylon and India.

Moscow's take on Mussolini in late 1943 as he contemplates his fate on the torn and tattered boot of Italy.

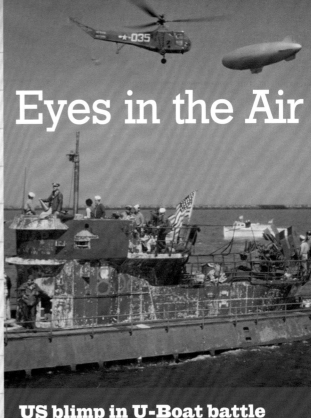

Eyes in the Air

US blimp in U-Boat battle

The US Navy already had a fleet of non-rigid airships or blimps but in **June 1942** in response to the growing threat to shipping, Congress authorized the construction of a further 200 airships. During the war, the Navy airships patrolled an area of over 3,000,000 square miles over the Atlantic and Pacific Oceans (they were also deployed in the Mediterranean). By the end of hostilities, 532 Allied ships had been sunk off the coast of the United States. But of the 89,000 ships escorted by airships, none were lost to enemy action. In addition to convoy protection, the airships conducted search and rescue, photographic, and mine clearing missions.

Just one US airship was lost to enemy action. K-74 was on patrol off Florida on the night of **18 July 1943** when in the bright moonlight they spotted the surfaced U-134. The airship captain decided to attack and a 17-minute battle ensued between the airship's .50 calibre machinegun and the submarine's 20mm ack ack guns. The airship was shot down and settled on the water, allowing the crew of 10 to escape. Nine were rescued by US Navy ships but one man is believed to have died following a shark attack.

Meanwhile, U-134 had also sustained damage and found itself unable to submerge. It headed home to Germany for repairs but was spotted and sunk by British bombers in the North Sea.

Helicopters in World War II

On 22-23 April 1944, US Army Lieutenant Carter Harman conducted the first combat rescue by helicopter using a Sikorsky R-4 in the Burma - China theatre. Despite the high altitude, humidity, and official capacity for only a single passenger, Harman rescued two at a time a downed liaison aircraft pilot and his three British soldier passengers. That month six ships set sail with two R-4s on board each vessel. The ships had been configured as floating repair depots for damaged Army Air Force airplanes in the South Pacific. When the helicopters were not being used to fly the parts from one location to another, they were enlisted for casualty evacuation and other mercy missions.

In RAF service, the R-4 was called the Hoverfly. The Helicopter Training School, formed January 1945, at RAF Andover, was the first British military unit to be equipped with the helicopter.

How did companies and institutions not engaged in essential war work cope with the many problems imposed on them in the years 1939 to 1945? Ian Saddler recounts the experiences of the mighty Liverpool Victoria Friendly Society that had its Head Office in the City of London.

Company Policy

The precarious nature of peace in the Thirties was becoming apparent when, on 20 September 1938, the Board of 'The Vic' resolved: '...that the Holborn Borough Council be granted the use of the South Hall, Victoria House, for the distribution of gas masks during an emergency.' Not long after this a request was made to the company architect, Mr C W Long, asking him to report upon what measures should be taken to best ensure the protection of Victoria House against enemy aircraft.

In the spring of 1939 preparations for war began in earnest and £25,000 was released to pay for precautionary measures against air raids. One such measure was the securing of an option to take over a hotel in Wales where vital sections of the business could be moved out of harm's way in the event of war. That year the Society employed 12,387 staff in the Head Office and across the nation, servicing nearly 14,000,000 policies that covered the entire fabric of domestic and financial life in this country.

Hitler aside, it seemed at the time that Britons were quite competent at killing each other when it was announced that in the year from March 1938 to March 1939, 656 Liverpool Victoria members had met their death in road accidents.

In July 15,000 sandbags were supplied to Head Office. These could be used to protect the building against bomb and fire damage. Work also accelerated in the provision of shelters and training began to ensure staff were ready to deal with all conceivable emergencies.

Records evacuated to Wales

On 24 August, when, apparently, only Neville Chamberlain still believed that war could be avoided, the Vic's Board reported that in their opinion: '...a state of hostilities between Great Britain and a Foreign Power is to be immediately anticipated involving a reasonable apprehension that London may

Volunteers of the Liverpool Victoria Fire Brigade fight a blaze at Sentinel House opposite their Head Office in Southampton Row, London, in 1940.

Inset: *A unique view of Victoria House, courtesy of Adolf Hitler.*

become subject to a severe attack by hostile aircraft or other destructive methods.' Consequently they ordered the immediate evacuation of all valuation and accounting machinery to Wales.

On 3 September war was declared. In consultation with the staff organisations, emergency measures and regulations were implemented. The basements of Victoria House were designated as air raid shelters with first-aid and gas-decontamination stations. Space was allocated for Police and Fire Brigade sub-stations and a Warden's Post was established. The South Hall of Victoria House would become a huge air-raid shelter.

Fortunately, Hitler was not ready to attack these islands immediately or otherwise the course of history may well have been different. The period known as the Phoney War gave not only the Government time to prepare its own war-machine, it also gave the likes of Liverpool Victoria time to take more calculated measures that would enable them to carry on with business as usual so far as was possible.

By May 1939 the war was going badly for Britain. In consequence the 1222 Head Office staff were polled as to whether they should be evacuated to Wales or work on in London. At home that evening they must have pondered the question for many hours. All had read of the merciless bombing of other cities in Europe and yet none could have wanted to leave their homes. They had safety offered to them but it did not extend to their families, a fact which made their choice far easier. Few would countenance leaving their loved ones to face the nightmare whilst they headed for the hills.

BEF cornered at Dunkirk
Even as King Leopold surrendered the Belgian Army to Hitler and it became apparent that the BEF was cornered with its back to the sea at Dunkirk, the vote was counted. The offer of evacuation was overwhelmingly rejected and staff gave an assurance to do everything in their power to stick at their jobs in London. In the meantime microscopic records of all the Society's business were taken to be stored in a bank several hundred miles away.

With the threat of invasion, large areas of vulnerable coastline had been evacuated, which left local Agents with very few Members on whom to call. The Society's own newsletter carried this story by D J Rowlands in September 1940: 'As I put pen to paper to try and describe the difficulties of our Agents in this area, I can hear the bombs exploding in the distant town, nine miles away. The air-raid sirens have been wailing continually all day, following the all-clear at 3am this morning after last night's raids.

'But with all our worries there is a humorous side; it is laughable to see our

Agents dodging from one dug-out to another in pursuit of the premiums, at the same time keeping a wary eye out for the Police and ARP Wardens who are determined to keep the streets clear during air raids.'

The passage of the war alleviated the financial hardships of the Agents. The call to arms had reduced the number of Clerks and Collectors and many of the Agents whose Members had been evacuated were given clerical jobs for the duration of the emergency. The 1941 AGM was held in Cardiff in March, to the sound of heavy gunfire from the anti-aircraft batteries.

Hit by incendiary bombs
Liverpool Victoria's HQ in London had its own Fire Brigade manned by volunteer staff. Twice Victoria House was hit by incendiary bombs and on one occasion a high-explosive bomb smashed through the roof, failing to explode but lodging in a fourth floor office. It was quickly located and an Army Bomb Disposal Team came to disarm it and take it away for detonation on Hackney Marshes.

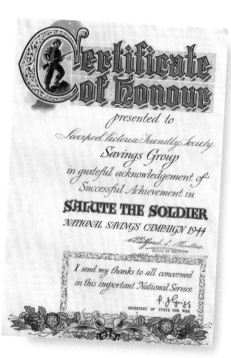

Above: *A Certificate of Honour awarded to the Society in 1944 for its support of the war effort.*

Victoria House survived but Sentinel House opposite was not so lucky. The fire was enormous and was fought for 14 hours solely by the gallant men of the Liverpool Victoria Fire Brigade with water from Victoria House reserves, as the total resources of the regular fire service were fully occupied by the great City conflagration.

By the end of 1941, over 4000 members of staff were absent on active service, nearly £8,000,000 had been invested in National War Bonds and Savings Bonds and the Society had paid claims on nearly one in four of the civilians who had lost their lives by enemy action. The work of Liverpool Victoria carried

> **"Despite all our worries it is still amusing to see our Agents dodging from one dug-out to another in pursuit of the premiums, at the same time keeping a wary eye out for the Police and ARP Wardens who are determined to keep the streets clear during air raids."**

on despite the shortage of staff and the severe physical and mental strain on all grades as they strived under harrowing conditions. Older staff shouldered an ever-increasing workload as their younger counterparts were called up. At one time there were nearly 3000 temporary lady Collectors, many of whom were the wives of those who had joined the Forces.

Slave labourer in Germany
There was full recognition of the loyal and invaluable services rendered by the men and women, permanent and temporary, who stuck to their jobs despite all the odds stacked against them. Nowhere was this more true than in the Channel Islands, the only part of Britain to fall under the Nazi jackboot. The Vic's manager, a Mr Hammond, was deported to Germany as a slave labourer.

In March 1943 the Society at its AGM agreed to present £1,000,000 to the Mayor of Holborn to inaugurate the 'Wings for Victory' campaign that would fund the building of new aircraft. It was reported: 'As the Members left the hall, although the red glow of many fires was still to be observed, the "All Clear" sirens were sounding – an omen that the Nation and Society would win through.'

So it was. There were still many individual acts of bravery and tales of suffering during the final two years of the War, but by then the question of victory was never in doubt and when it came, in 1945, the men and women of the Society threw themselves into the celebrations as did their counterparts throughout the world. Liverpool Victoria Friendly Society got on with the business of peace.

Ian Saddler worked for Liverpool Victoria from the age of 16. He is the author of the history of the Society called A Mission In Life *published in 1997. Liverpool Victoria (LV=) continues in business as Britain's biggest Friendly Society and a major player in the insurance world. The company's Head Office is now in Bournemouth.*

Save waste fats for explosives

TAKE THEM TO YOUR MEAT DEALER

We Can Do It!

POSTER ART of NORTH AMERICA

IT CAN HAPPEN HERE!

—UNLESS WE KEEP 'EM FIRING!

When you ride ALONE you ride with Hitler!

Join a Car-Sharing Club TODAY!

YOUR SCRAP ...brought it down

KEEP SCRAPPING
Rubber · Metal · Rags

GIVE TO A COLLECTOR,
SALVAGE DEPOT OR SELL TO A DEALER

KEEP THESE HANDS OFF!

BUY the New VICTORY BONDS

To Have and to Hold!

WAR BONDS

We Are Ready · What About You?

Join the SCHOOLS AT WAR Program

SPONSORED BY — THE WAR SAVINGS STAFF OF THE U. S. TREASURY
DEPARTMENT, THE U. S. OFFICE OF EDUCATION AND ITS WARTIME COMMISSION

Wacker's War

A daughter remembers her Dad's tales of wartime life as a Fitter working on Beaufighters in the RAF.

Sidney Wickens (Sid, nicknamed 'Wacker') joined the RAF on 10 October 1938 aged 21. After failing an eye test to train as a pilot he turned his attention to a 'trade' and became a fitter, joining 272 Squadron in November 1940. He sailed from Liverpool in a convoy escorted by *HMS Rodney* bound for Freetown, Sierra Leone. The convoy then continued on around the Cape to Durban. The usual 'Dipping and Ducking' ceremony was performed for the lads crossing the Equator for the first time.

The squadron flew Bristol Beaufighters and missions included convoy escort duties, fighter patrols and recces over a wide area of the Mediterranean and the North African shore. Sid was based for a while at Edku in Egypt. It was a critical period of the desert war and Sid remembered experiencing hard times when they were regularly losing aircraft and crews. Even so, there were a few light hearted moments and like just about every serviceman posted to Egypt he visited Cairo to view King Farouk's Palace and the Blue Mosque. But, unlike most, he never got to see the pyramids

Life on a desert airfield was very basic with baking heat in the day, especially in the long summer months, and extreme cold at night. Sand and engines don't mix and it was a constant battle to keep the aircraft in tip top flying condition. Crews worked on the aircraft in

the very early mornings, rested during the hottest part of the day, and worked again in the late afternoon and on into the evening. No doubt the RAF ground crews in Afghanistan today will be experiencing similar conditions.

For the ground crew, teamwork, getting the job done and surviving was paramount. They were adept at improvising, striving to make their living conditions as comfortable as possible. On one occasion Sid and some pals found a burnt out lorry in the desert, hauled it back to camp and spent many hours of their spare time kitting it out for living quarters. The Medical Officer waited until they had finished the job and then commandeered it for use as a sick bay! Though the MO had

Above: A Beaufighter has just landed at Tal Qali airfield on Malta in June 1943.

Left: Sid Wickens (on the right) in best uniform with a couple of pals.

pulled rank on that occasion, Sid always said that the desert was a great leveller and the divide between the ranks became blurred and far less fussy than it was in Britain.

Extra cleaning duties

Ever resourceful, Sid once set up a contraption for heating one of the water tanks so that the lads would always have hot water for washing. One day the device backfired on him and Sid received burns to his face, lost his eyebrows and the front of his hair. He was put on a charge and punished with extra cleaning duties in the officers' mess.

Fitters frequently went on test flights with pilots following major repairs to check that all was well. During one such flight Sid found that the original problem had been fixed only for another snag to arise when the undercarriage refused to engage. After trying every trick he could think of to lower the wheels to no avail, the pilot was forced to make a crash landing.

Below: This is one of Sid's own photographs. On the back of it he's written: 'The First Prang.'

As Sid was in the well of the plane the pilot advised him to take his weight upon his forearms and elbows and elevate his legs or they might be broken on impact. Glad to survive the landing, Sid left the plane as quickly as possible knowing that it could burst into flames at any moment. For this he was put on another charge (more cleaning) for leaving the aircraft before the pilot!

The desert wasn't always dry. On one occasion Sid's unit pitched their tents in a wadi; unluckily for them it rained for the first time in three years and the flash flood swept away all their tents and equipment. It was some time before new tents arrived from Britain and when they did they were khaki and green not cream-coloured to blend in with the desert.

Brother's out of date telegram

Whilst Sid was in North Africa he received a telegram saying that his brother, Stanley, had been injured and was in hospital many miles away. The CO granted him two days leave. Sid cadged a lift part of the way in an aircraft going to pick up supplies. When they landed the pilot advised Sid to put the pilot's flying jacket over his corporal's uniform so that he could take him into the officer's mess to ensure he had a good meal before sending him on. Sid sweated buckets in the mess as the airman's fleece certainly did its job in keeping him cosy in addition to the already sweltering heat! He thumbed lifts and walked the last six miles to the hospital arriving early in the morning only to be informed that his brother was now fit and had been back at the front for a month! The telegram had been hopelessly out of date. The next time he was to see Stanley was in Italy after his brother had survived the fierce fighting around Monte Cassino.

A more successful meeting was made one evening when Sid met Jack Downs who lived in the same village as Sid back in England. Jack was in a different RAF unit and the pair

> **Happy and Glorious, One between four of us, Thank God there's no more of us, Hallelujah, Amen!**

shared a few beers – 'Ice Cold in Alex.'

Following a brief spell in Cyprus, Sid flew to Malta where, from November 1942, his squadron was based at the Tal Qali airfield in the centre of the island (today it's the site of the Malta Aviation Museum). Sid was billeted in the old Crown Hotel in Sliema Creek. On 17 March 1943 a Beaufighter encountered engine trouble and had to ditch in the sea off Dragonara Point, Sliema – the crew survived. The wreckage is a popular dive site today.

During his time off he liked swimming off the rocks along the coast and he tried roller skating at the Rocky Vale rink. He was always hungry as food was in short supply. At meal

times he and his pals used to sing their own version of the National Anthem: 'Happy and Glorious, one between four of us, thank God there's no more of us, Hallelujah, Amen!'

As the war moved up the leg of Italy, in February 1944 Sid was flown to Alghero in Sardinia where his Squadron's task was to provide anti-flak escorts for strikes on shipping carried out by by 39 Squadron. Sid always wanted to go back to Sardinia for a holiday telling his wife Daphne it was a beautiful island. Though the couple never went together, Daphne did stay in Alghero with her daughter, Rosemary, in June 2009.

With the war over in Italy, 272 Squadron disbanded on 30 April 1945. They were credited with having destroyed 185 enemy aircraft, damaged 177 more, sunk 12 ships of over 1000 tons, sunk 56 smaller vessels, damaged 318 others, destroyed 12 trains and 832 transport vehicles.

Just before sailing home in August 1945 Sid was able to visit Rome. Then it was time for a reunion with the parents he hadn't seen for four years. Subsequently, he met and married Daphne and had two daughters, Christine and Rosemary. After the war Sid worked for many years on the country estate of Lord Rupert Neville at Little Horsted, near Uckfield in East Sussex. The Queen and Royal Family were frequent visitors.

Sid passed away in 1991. His story was recounted to David Arnold by his daughter Rosemary. David writes: I knew Sid for many years. Rosemary is my sister-in-law. Sid was a good judge of race horses. One Boxing Day morning he gave me a tip for the King George being run that afternoon. Foolishly, I didn't take his advice and missed out on Desert Orchid's first big win at 16-1. I always enjoy a happy coincidence bet, but at the time I didn't know Sid had served in the desert, otherwise I would have definitely backed it! By the way, I first met my wife Barbara at Little Horsted.

The Beaufighter Story

In May 1941 the Middle East RAF received its first Bristol Beaufighter Squadrons, numbers 252 and 272. By early June Beaufighters of 272 Squadron had begun offensive operations from Egypt, being based at Edku, some 25 miles east of Alexandria. From then until the end of the Mediterranean war, Beaufighters were to wreak havoc and destruction among the enemy land, sea, and air forces. With its four 20mm Hispano cannon in the belly and up to six 0.303-inch calibre Browning machine-guns in the wings, the Beau was the RAF's heaviest-armed fighter of the war. The aircraft's rugged construction could absorb astonishing amounts of damage and still deliver a live crew from any potentially disastrous crash-landing.

For a while in 1942 the CO was Wing Commander Micky Ogden. On 11 July, the Squadron intercepted a large formation of German Ju 52s off the North African coast. The enemy transports were heavily escorted, and in the ensuing scrap Ogden and his crews accounted for at least 12 aircraft destroyed or badly damaged; Ogden himself shot down one Ju 52. He recalled later: 'We were on patrol when we caught up with the Junkers. We followed in line astern, diving on them to attack. They were about 50 feet above the surface. My victim went into the sea with a terrific splash, an engine on fire and the fuselage burning.'

Top: Sid with the banana finds something to sing about.

Above: Sid and Daphne on their wedding day at Eridge Church, 28 August 1948.

Right: Another photo from Sid's collection. This is the Marlas Cinema in Alexandria.

Pyramid selling

This is John Cooper's photograph of his late father, George Moore Cooper, on the camel in the centre in front of the Great Pyramid and Sphinx in 1944.

The name Sphinx means 'strangler' and was first given by the Ancient Greeks to a fabulous creature that had the head of a woman, the body of a lion and wings of a bird. The Sphinx has survived because it was buried under sand for several thousand years. Napoleon's army once used it for target practice for their cannons.

For most of us, the war years were not doom and gloom all the time, and we took whatever pleasures came our way. Once North Africa had been cleared by mid-1943, Cairo became even more the leave honeypot for Service personnel in the Middle East. I had the luck of being stationed there for nine months at Kasr-el-Nil barracks in the city centre. As such, I was able to find my own way around the fascinating ancient sites, away from the standard tourist-like groups of servicemen with all the guides, camels and traders. When time allowed, I could hop on a tram to Giza and relish pottering around the awesome Pyramid plateau far from the madding crowd.

During the war many hundreds of servicemen took up the challenge of clambering up the Great Pyramid, Cheops, 449ft high. It was no mean feat. There was no recognised route to the top and the ascent took about half an hour.

Many centuries ago, builders constructing the growing city of Cairo had torn down the limestone cap which originally adorned the top, leaving a flat uneven stone platform about eight yards square (as far as I can recollect), bare except for a pole in the middle, supported by a tripod, which soared 30ft up to mark the original top of Cheops.

I climbed Cheops on 1 January 1944. The view from the top was magnificent with Cairo and the sandstone cliffs beyond bathed in the gold of evening sunshine. There was also a unique view of the second Pyramid, Chephren. Nowadays, visitors are forbidden to climb Cheops on the grounds that it's dangerous. No doubt the ruling is also aimed at saving the great monument from gradual erosion. Anyone who has gazed upon the glory of this 4500-year-old edifice would want it to be still unharmed 4500 years hence. Nevertheless, the climb is certainly not without danger – the sides and top platform have no guard rails.

At the end of 1943, Churchill and Roosevelt were at the foot of Cheops in the Mena Palace Hotel conferring on war strategy after their meeting with Stalin in Tehran. By then the secret that the two war leaders were in the area had leaked out and to improve surveillance in case of an enemy air assault we in RAF AHQ Adem sited a light Type 6 GCI radar unit on Cheops' top platform for the duration of the talks.

In those days, when workhorse helicopters did not exist, the radar unit airmen had to hump all their equipment to the summit, set it up and then climb up and down to go on and off duty. With no guard rails anywhere, it was no place for anyone afflicted with vertigo, especially during the pitch blackness of night watches. In the event, no enemy aircraft came within hundreds of miles of the venue.

The ancient Egyptians built into their Pyramids a complex network of concealed channels so that the spirits of the deceased Pharoahs buried within could make their way to the distant stars. We therefore had the bizarre situation in 1943 where airmen were stationed on top of the world's greatest mausoleum sending out streams of radar pulses far into Outer Space – I hope they did not interfere with Cheops' lines of communication.

Ron Purser

CAMOUFLAGE NETS
Baffle the Hun

nearly all of his nine decades plus he had the distinction of having played for the Army on grounds in Yorkshire, Cairo and Italy!

Under the Military Training Act 1939, Bernard was called up to the First Militia in June of that year along with 700 other London lads aged 20 who had been required to register for military training. He spent his first three weeks confined to barracks in Blandford, Dorset; not because he'd done anything wrong but because the Army were embarrassed that the only uniforms they could issue were of Great War vintage. It was feared that our troops being seen in them would damage public morale by showing that Britain was not prepared for the threatened war.

In theory, the First Militia lads were supposed to serve for six months but by August 1939 the looming war caused them to be absorbed into the regular forces. Now properly kitted out, Bernard joined the Royal Artillery and was sent to France with the BEF in March 1940. He was part of a unit that operated a pair of huge railway mounted guns but never got the opportunity to fire them in anger; just as the German Blitzkrieg was about to burst upon Holland, Belgium and France, Bernard went down with appendicitis and was rushed to hospital. Appendix removed, by 12 May he found himself in Blackburn, Lancashire, after a most uncomfortable and painful evacuation out of Dunkirk. Bernard was never reunited with his fellow soldiers from the railway guns and to this day does not know what became of them.

To Egypt via Cape Town

Instead he was redeployed to an artillery unit. He sailed to join the Eighth Army in Egypt on 23 May 1942, leaving from Liverpool aboard the troopship *Mexico City*. They first called at Greenock in Scotland before heading south into the Atlantic. Next port of call was Freetown in Sierra Leone, West Africa, where they arrived on 13 June. Six days later the ship set off for Cape Town which they reached on 1 July. By 4 July they were anchored off Aden on the south west tip of the Arabian Peninsular. From there the ship headed up the Red Sea to Port Suez in Egypt where he and his fellow soldiers disembarked and were driven to Camp Khatatha, an Eighth Army base.

All these dates and details are contained in a little diary that Bernard kept (most likely against regulations); he still has the notebook

Bernard Brind served in the Eighth Army with the Royal Artillery. First going into action at El Alamein, he says his 25-pounder guns never retreated but were always advancing right up to the end of the war in Italy.

Bernard Herbert Brind was born in South East London in 1918. My wife Barbara and I met him for the first time in 2008 when we discovered he was celebrating his 90th birthday at a football match at Lewes FC.

We got chatting - initially about football but then about anything and everything and very quickly it was clear that Bernard had led a very interesting life, not least when serving with the Eighth Army in North Africa and Italy. It was also fascinating to note that football had been a constant thread throughout

today. It records that on 13 August he went on a day's leave to Cairo. The next entry reads: 'Went into action 16 August.' There's a big gap then until 4 October when Bernard notes that he went to Almaya Camp, Cairo, on a Survey Course.

He rejoined his unit, the 65th Field Regiment (the Black Cats), on 29 October where his notes observe: 'Big battle on. Came out of action 10 November. Still in desert. Moved westwards on 4 December and I crossed into Libya, arriving at El Adem 20 miles south of Tobruk on 9 December.'

Just a pair of shorts!

The 'big battle' was, of course El Alamein. Bernard told me the scariest moment for him during that fight came when four Stuka dive bombers plastered his unit and destroyed all his personal kit leaving him with just a pair of shorts to his name. Luckily his diary and remittance book were in the back pocket of the shorts!

Bernard served as a Gunner/Surveyor (a position that earned him extra pay). His task was to recce new locations for his Regiment's 25-pounder guns. This meant going forward of the guns and Bernard says it was sometimes a bit hairy having 'friendly' shells whizzing over en route to the enemy. He proudly told me that joining the unit at the time he did meant that he never took part in a retreat but participated in the Eighth Army's advance right across North Africa and later in the hard but ultimately successful slog up the boot of Italy.

By 28 February 1943 Bernard had travelled nearly 1000 miles across Libya and entered Tunisia where his unit went into action against the German-held Mareth Line on 13 March. It was a tough fight; the diary notes that the line did not fall until well into April after which he writes: 'Mareth taken and we are following Jerry northwards through Gabes, Sfax and Sousse. Jerry has dug in in the hills 60 miles from Tunis. Big battle started 18 April. Still fighting in Enfidaville area. Germans pack in on 12 May. War in North Africa over.'

Bernard vividly remembers the sight of countless thousands of surrendered Germans and Italians and the masses of captured transport. He told me how the rumour went around that the Jerries were about to pack it

in. The night before it happened Bernard saw the sky over Tunis turn red from numerous fires and heard explosions galore as the Germans blew up their remaining ammo and destroyed their armoured vehicles. But they kept their transport intact. The next day he saw an endless convoy of lorries packed with German soldiers streaming past on their way to captivity. He noticed that the Italians in the main had to walk. Bernard says that lots of the POWs waved cheerfully and looked pleased that their war was over. He believes that the majority of the Afrika Korps wanted to surrender to their old adversaries, the Eighth Army, rather than give in to the Americans who were relative newcomers to the North African campaign.

Heavy fighting at Salerno

Bernard then spent some months in various North Africa locations before embarking for Italy: 'Arrived on Italian soil 17 September. Heavy fighting in Salerno area. Advancing slowly

Above: Bernard Brind (on the right) pictured with two chums from the Eighth Army.
Below: A battery of 25-pounder field guns ready for action in Sicily.

northwards. Come out of action 18 November and go to Caserta for a rest. Had four days leave in Naples. Went back into action on 29 November.'

Bernard witnessed the bombing of the abbey at Monte Cassino in February 1944. He told me how the German anti-aircraft guns couldn't fire high enough to hit the Allied aircraft but their shell bursts nevertheless showered shrapnel down on him and his comrades, adding: 'I can't tell you how much we appreciated our steel helmets.'

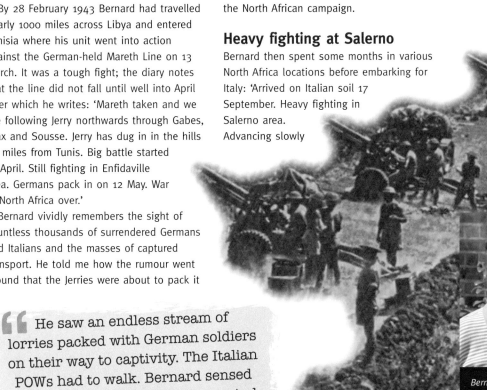

Bernard Brind (right) with his friend Ron Thomas pictured in June 2010 just a couple of months away from Bernard's 92nd birthday. The pair are near neighbours in their Lewes homes. Ron himself served in the Middle East from 1942 to 1945 and was a radar mechanic in a mobile ack-ack unit. He was stationed in various places between Tobruk in Libya and Aleppo in Syria.

> **❝** He saw an endless stream of lorries packed with German soldiers on their way to captivity. The Italian POWs had to walk. Bernard sensed that the proud Afrika Korps wanted to surrender to their old adversaries, the Eighth Army, rather than the Americans... **❞**

Above: A 25-pounder gun being made ready for action.

Next his unit was brought out of the Cassino front and embarked from near Naples to sail to reinforce the Allied troops who were stalled in the beach-head at Anzio, south of Rome. The diary records: 'Very heavy fighting. Air activity terrific on both sides.'

Bernard told me that the Black Cats lost a lot of men and guns at Anzio. They were pulled out in order to rest and refit and the gunner left Anzio on 16 March. They were under German fire but he remembers the most terrifying minutes came when he had to climb the rope ladder on the side of their US transport vessel: 'I had a full pack and rifle and the ship was pitching in the slight swell when suddenly the chap above me froze. The two of us behind him were left swinging on the ropes until he was finally coaxed into moving up.'

Bernard eventually arrived at Altamura near the Adriatic Coast of Italy. By the end of the month he was back in Port Said and was able to take a day's leave in Cairo on 10 April. Unfortunately, while in Egypt he sustained a severely injured right elbow while participating in a football game organised by the Regimental Sports Officer. Though he was patched up and soon returned to active duties (which included a sojourn in a training camp in Palestine), the accident left him with a lifelong problem with the elbow. Indeed, the problem was only finally acknowledged by a medical tribunal a decade or so ago and Bernard now receives a war disability allowance.

Christmas bombardment

On 11 July he embarked on a ship that took him from Alexandria across the Med to Taranto. The diary notes that on 3 August 1944 Bernard enjoyed a day's leave in liberated Rome. But now it was time to return to front line duties: '21 August. Advancing on Gothic Line. Very good situation so far. 2 September. Hard fighting. 28 September. Bitter fighting continues. Progress very slow due to heavy rain. Came out of action on 19 November and went on leave to Florence. Go back into action on 2 December. Christmas spent in Faenza under shellfire.'

On one occasion the gunner was driving an officer down a rough track when they found themselves confronting a party of British soldiers coming the other way, engaged in sweeping for mines. Bernard was horrified at the implications but also mightily relieved as one of the mine sweepers piped up: 'No need to worry now. We've just swept the road behind us.'

Bernard was in and out of action until 31 March 1945 when he was hospitalised after sustaining a shrapnel wound in the hand, an event noted in the diary. But what the latter doesn't reveal is that the incident took place in a farmhouse by the River Po. Bernard says it was a warm and sunny afternoon although there was plenty of incoming enemy shellfire. One round scored a direct hit on the farmhouse killing three signallers who were in a different room to him. A jeep took a fourth casualty off to an advance dressing station but Bernard later learnt that the man died on the way to Rimini. He told me: 'It was such tough luck on those men what with the war being nearly over. As for me, I just knew I had been incredibly lucky.'

On 7 April Bernard returned to HQRA to participate in a big attack that took him across the River Po and eventually on to Venice where the diary notes he had a half day's leave. The war in Italy ended on 2 May 1945. The diary reads: '4 May. Go to Trieste area where there is trouble between Italy and Yugoslavia about who will have the city.' Bernard told me that at one point he encountered six girl Yugoslav soldiers who were festooned with hand grenades that they wore like necklaces: 'It was a bit of a worry but, fortunately, they were not interested in fighting the British.'

David Arnold

Batting left-handed led to romance!

Bernard got home in July 1945. There was a special someone he dearly wanted to meet. Early on in the war he had received a 'Dear John' letter in which his sweetheart had told him that their relationship was ended. Later he received a Valentine's Card that was passed on to him via his sister. Bernard was suspicious that it was just a ploy by his sister who was most likely simply trying to cheer him up. So he asked her to send him a picture of the girl. Mollie turned out to be real and the pair exchanged regular letters of friendship. Finally the pair met with Bernard's homecoming: 'Mollie invited me to play in a cricket match at the Royal Arsenal sports field. Because I was in the girl's team I was made to bat left-handed.'

The pair eventually married and raised two sons. Today there are also four grandchildren plus four great grandchildren. Bernard joined Longleys, the builders as an estimator / surveyor. He rose to become a director in 1968 and for 10 years in his leisure time managed the company's football team before retirement in1978. Mollie sadly passed away in 2005 but Bernard remains spritely and active. As well as keenly following the local football in Lewes, he still goes swimming every Monday.

Bernard and his late wife, Mollie, pictured post-war on a beach holiday.

JANUARY

The Italian Campaign

As 1943 grew to a close, the British and Americans had many of their best divisions withdrawn from the line and sent to Britain in preparation for the invasion of France planned for the spring of 1944. One of those who would go was the Eighth Army commander himself for Field Marshal Montgomery had been selected to direct the Allied ground forces making the assault. Ironically, his opposite number across the Channel would be none other than Erwin Rommel, his old adversary from North Africa.

Reinforcements did arrive in Italy but these included many new troops lacking in battle experience. It took time to get them ready to take the offensive. The Eighth Army attacked on 20 November while the Fifth Army got started on 1 December. Both advances stalled in the face of determined German resistance anchored on well-constructed bunkers. The enemy also had the advantage of excellent observation points on the mountain heights above the valley roads. The Eighth Army called off its attack on 30 December and the Fifth Army followed suit in the first few days of 1944. Kesselring's Gustav Line was holding.

Setbacks at Cassino

Winter in Italy, even south of Rome, can be a wet, miserable time, especially in the mountains. As 1944 dawned with the Allies facing the Gustav Line running across the Italian peninsula from the Adriatic to the Tyrrhenian Sea, the poor weather favoured the defenders rather than the attackers.

Montgomery succinctly summed up the situation before he left for the UK: 'Caesar used to go into winter quarters about this time, when he commanded an army in these parts. And very wise too..' But politics and ambition would not permit such a course in 1944. Churchill, for one, sought decisive action in what he termed 'the soft

British infantry cross a pontoon bridge over the Garigliano river on 19 January 1944. Jim Pybus from Yorkshire says that he had an uncle killed in action in the vicinity of the bridge on that same day. Trooper Seymour Fletcher, 10601829 46th Regiment Recce Corps, RAC, is buried in the Minturno Commonwealth War Graves Cemetery. Jim writes: 'Clearly I never knew him but remember my Grandmother talking about him when I was a child after I had found a cap badge in a button box at Grandma's house. For me it drives home the sacrifices made by so many in order to ensure our freedom.'

underbelly of Europe' whilst US General Mark Clark vowed he would soon head '..the first conquering army to enter Rome from the south in 2000 years'.

With the Eighth Army stalled on the River Sangro in the east, the attention of the planners shifted west. The Liri Valley, dominated by the mountains around the town of Cassino, was the key to any advance on Rome. The mouth of the valley was bisected by the connecting rivers Garigliano and Rapido which in turn are joined by the Liri as it flows south down the valley.

Clark wanted the British 10th Corps to undertake three diversionary assault crossings of the Garigliano near where it met the sea. Then the US 36th Division was to attack across the Rapido and erupt into the Liri Valley, forcing the Germans to abandon the line at Cassino or risk being outflanked and surrounded.

The British 'sideshow' began on 17 January and met with encouraging success. Indeed, if the success had been reinforced without delay it may well have forced a full German retreat all by itself. But time was wasted and the chance was lost. Later some blamed Clark for dallying, claiming he did not want to see the British taking the lead over the Americans.

On the night of 20 January the US 36th Division attempted to cross the Rapido. The river alone was a formidable obstacle, 12ft deep, 50ft wide, fast-running and freezing. Add the seasoned German Panzer Grenadiers manning strong defensive positions on the north bank and able to pour a withering fire on the attackers and the result was disaster. The Americans suffered 1681 casualties and over 500 men were captured.

After the war the Veterans Association of the 36th Division pressured the US Congress into an inquiry about 'the fiasco of the Rapido'. Congress concluded that General Clark's order to make the attack was a necessary one.

The reversal on the Rapido led to a lull in the Gustav Line fighting as both sides drew breath. Allied soldiers around Cassino found their attention drawn more and more to the historic Benedictine monastery set high above the town at the top of Monte Cassino. Senior commanders became convinced that here was the key to the German defensive system that wound its way along the heights. Soldiers and ordnance were surely sheltered within those massive walls; artillery spotters must be following the every movement of Allied troops and vehicles on the valley floor far below.

Something would have to be done. Unless, that is, the Allies could successfully land an amphibious force far to the rear of the German lines and close enough to Rome to liberate the Eternal City in a single bold stroke...

Anzio

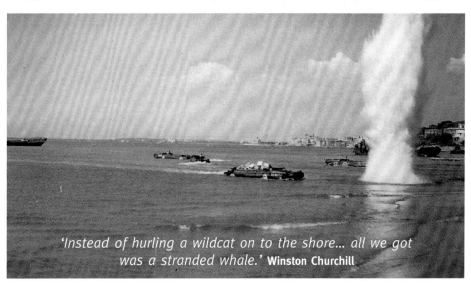

'Instead of hurling a wildcat on to the shore... all we got was a stranded whale.' **Winston Churchill**

The British Premier's bitter words are in dramatic contrast to the high hopes he held for the success of this audacious plan where a powerful Anglo-American task force was to storm ashore at Anzio and Nettuno and at once drive on Rome, just 40 miles away. 'Operation Shingle should decide the Battle of Rome', said Churchill, as the landing got underway: '...Anzio will astonish the world.'

What turned into a 125-day siege and one of the bloodiest European campaigns of the Second World War opened on 22 January 1944 when 36,000 Allied troops and 3000 vehicles disembarked in the face of minor resistance. The Anzio beach-head was some 80 miles north of the stalemated frontline at Cassino. Just 13 dead and 97 wounded were reported on the first day.

Perhaps the landings went too well. Instead of pushing out to find an enemy to fight, all the Allied efforts went into creating a defensible area. Yet it was nearly six hours after the landings began before the Germans in Rome were alerted. In this time armoured columns could have made it to Rome and, crucially, occupied the high ground of the Alban Hills south of the city.

By midnight, however, the initiative was already shifting in favour of the Germans as Field Marshal Kesselring could now call on some 20,000 fighting men to block any break out. Within a day the Germans had makeshift lines of defence in place just five miles from the Allied perimeter. Major General John P Lucas remained loathe to go on the offensive; he felt that his three divisions were a force insufficient to risk against a proven campaigner like Kesselring who always reacted to threats with skill and vigour. Lucas also knew that staying put allowed his men the continued protection of the navy's big guns, while riding shotgun over the beach-head skies were the numerically far superior Allied air forces.

Commonwealth soldiers prepare to embark from the southern Italian port of Castellaware bound for the landing beaches at Anzio-Nettuno. F E Weeks from Wiltshire spent almost three and a half years of the war on this landing ship – LST 368 – and made a number of trips to and from Anzio as well as participating in the earlier Salerno invasion. Mr Weeks points out that the Fifth Army under US General Mark Clark also included a substantial British force. He commented, 'I know we couldn't have won the war without America, but don't let them take all the glory.'

British forces were tasked with holding the left flank of the beach-head on a five-mile front. Troops and fighting vehicles from many units had landed; Royal Tank Regiment, Grenadiers and Sherwood Foresters among them. The Irish Guards recorded: '...a sickening feeling of anti-climax. There were no Germans so what was stopping us? The 23rd was a completely wasted day.' On 25 January came

Main image: German artillery zeros in on the Nettuno beaches as amphibious DUKWs land supplies. This is a rare colour action photograph.

Above: The Anzio-Nettuno coastline as it is today.

CAMPO DI CARNE

ON THIS SITE THOUSANDS OF MEN
FOUGHT AND DIED

AN DIESEM ORT TAUSENDE VON MENSCHEN
KÄMPFTEN UND FIELEN

IN QUESTO LUOGO MIGLIAIA DI UOMINI
COMBATTERONO E MORIRONO

"BATTAGLIA DI ANZIO—APRILIA—CISTERNA 1944" 1979

Anzio

Nettuno

This astonishing aerial composite photograph of the Anzio –
Nettuno beach-head was taken early in 1944. The invasion
fleet and landing craft can clearly be seen below Nettuno
where the Americans came ashore. The British beaches
were to the north of the port of Anzio.

A view of Anzio today is inset along with a sign
commemorating the fierce fighting that took place at
Campo di Carne in the vicinity of 'The Flyover'.

Anzio

movement at last. Two RTR troops of Sherman tanks began moving up the Via Anziate, spearheading an advance of the 24th Guards Brigade. Italian farmers waved them on as they lumbered under an overpass, known as The Flyover. By mid-morning the fighting started in earnest around a tower in Aprilia that earnt the town the nickname of The Factory. Ominously, one of the 100 or so German prisoners taken early on remarked casually upon seeing a Sherman tank: 'If we were you and we had those, we'd have been in Rome by now.'

At dawn next day the Germans counter-attacked with the support of Tiger tanks, infiltrating the numerous creek beds, or *fossos*, that dotted the Anzio plain.

At 0800 hours the British front line was engulfed in a massive artillery barrage fired off from the Alban Hills where the Germans were gathering an arsenal of guns which included captured pieces from France, Yugoslavia, Russia and Czechoslovakia. As the history of the Guards puts it: 'The heavens opened and the air was full of iron dug from every mine in Europe; the shell fragments were marked in every known language west of the Urals.'

The Factory was to change hands many times in the coming months of deadly struggle. The last day of January saw the Americans suffer a major blow. Two Ranger battalions under Colonel William Darby advanced on Cisterna by way of a half-dry irrigation channel. Slowed by enemy strongpoints, the men found themselves caught on open ground half a mile from their objective as dawn broke. In the ensuing fierce close quarter battle, despite knocking out 15 assorted enemy vehicles, the Rangers were overwhelmed. Of 767 men who set out, just six returned to the US lines.

I saw Anzio from the air

I was stationed at Foggia aerodrome in early 1944 and was the bomb aimer in a crew of five flying a Wellington bomber. Our boys had landed at Anzio but had not advanced because of German pressure.

In mid-February we were briefed to cross the coast and fly over the beach-head dead on midnight – no stragglers as the Navy were lying off the coast and would open up on any aircraft in the vicinity. We had to fly in to a lit-up 'T', then do an 11 second timed run before letting our bombs go (18 x 250lb) in a cluster.

Suddenly in the run-up to the 'T' another 'T' appeared. German Intelligence had gained news of our 'T' and put one of their own up to confuse. Pathfinder Force called up and told us to bomb the 'T' which was being illuminated by the Army boys with various coloured verey lights but by this time we had all gone too far!

We turned to do another run and came in to line up on the correct 'T' whereupon the Royal Navy opened up, making it quite hectic up there. I heard later that several of our aircraft were hit by what we nowadays call 'friendly fire'. We returned to base, had a snack, 'bombed up' again and then set off back to Anzio.

I was very pleased to receive a very nice 60th anniversary citation from the 'Municipal de Anzio' thanking all those who were involved on land, sea and air in the 1944 operation. I have had it framed as a piece of history!

Fred Clarke

..and on the ground

My husband was in the thick of the Anzio fighting and got a bullet wound to the head. Although he didn't much like to talk about it, I can remember tales of The Factory and how he was caught out on open ground and bullets rained down on him and the lads so that they didn't stand much of a chance. Once he was out of the army in 1946 he used to have mood swings which you can understand, given what he'd gone through.

Malcolm Philip Williams was a young farm worker before he joined the London Irish Rifles in 1943. He was one of a family of six boys and two girls born and bred in the village of Loppington, Wem, Shropshire. They spent many happy days at Yew Tree Cottage, Brown Heath, near Ellesmere. Sadly now passed on, Malcolm was a wonderful husband and good father to our three children.

Mrs Winifred Williams

Gunner was an early casualty

I was a gunner in the Royal Artillery in 10 Corps at Anzio. I paid a visit to the town and the area in April 2002. The British Forces Cemetery is in immaculate condition. There is a register at the entrance which gives details of all the personnel interred there and the grave numbers. I also visited the Beach-Head Museum. Upon learning of my participation in 1944, the Museum President gave me a scroll depicting the landings. The Italian people are still very appreciative of what we did to rid them of the Nazis.

I did not progress very far on the beach-head as I was wounded and returned to Britain via Naples, Tunis and Algiers.

N Hamilton

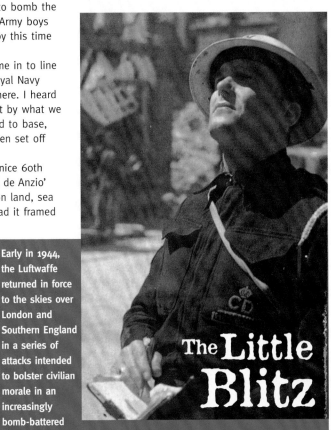

The Little Blitz

Early in 1944, the Luftwaffe returned in force to the skies over London and Southern England in a series of attacks intended to bolster civilian morale in an increasingly bomb-battered Germany and at the same time demonstrate to the British populace that Hitler's air power remained a potent threat. *Operation Steinbock* began on 21 January with 447 sorties by various aircraft including Heinkel 177 heavy bombers. The resulting damage was slight compared to that of the 1940 –41 Blitz. Civilians were inclined to shrug off the air raid warnings and go about their business unperturbed. Because of this, deaths and injuries from 'friendly fire' greatly increased. In the course of an air raid many thousands of anti-aircraft rounds would be fired skywards only to fall back to earth in a deadly rain of shrapnel spread out for many miles around the anti-aircraft batteries. Quite a number of shells would fail to explode in the air but would detonate – effectively like a bomb – when they hit the ground. British fuses for AA shells were notoriously quirky; prior to the war efficient clockwork fuses had been imported from Switzerland, a source cut off once France fell in June 1940.

Ocean Odyssey

Jack Cooper was presumed dead after his ship was sunk by a German surface raider in the South Atlantic. In fact he ended up as a slave labourer in Yokohama, Japan. Bev Cooper recounts his father's amazing wartime experience.

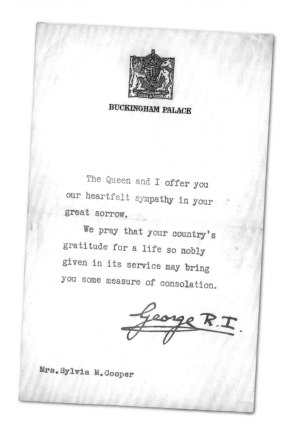

The letter of sympathy Mrs Sylvia Cooper received from King George when it was believed her husband Jack has perished at sea.

On 3 January 1944 my mother receives a postcard from my father, just as many thousands of other wives have from their husbands who are overseas. But there's something very different about this communication. Firstly, the postcard was dated 4 June 1943 and had taken a long time to arrive. Secondly, on 30 April 1942 my mother had received a letter from Royal Naval Barracks Portsmouth informing her that her husband's ship was overdue and presumed lost with all hands. By 7 July 1942 this was confirmed and my mum received a letter from King George and Queen Elizabeth offering their sympathy in mum's great sorrow.

Clearly my dad was alive. What had happened to him makes for a very unusual story of wartime loss and eventual happiness. He first told his tale publicly in a Radio Norfolk interview a couple of decades ago. What follows is a synopsis of that recording.

Let me take you back to 1917 when a boy is born in Tottenham, North London. He often visits relatives in Caston and Great Ellingham, Norfolk, and grows to love the county, spending as much time there with his cousins as he can. Schooldays over, he moves to Norfolk on a permanent basis, finding whatever work he can – it is all rural jobs or forestry pit propping. One day his landlady's niece has a wedding to which this now tall and handsome young man is invited. The bride's sister is unattached but she sure is soon enough and that leads to another wedding between my mum and dad.

Bound for Middle East

The war comes along and dad is called up. His father had been a seaman in the Merchant Navy so dad goes for the Royal Navy. He went to *HMS Collinwood* for his basic training and then was sent to *HMS Nelson*, followed by three weeks Gunnery School. After this it was onto the DEMS (Defensively Equipped Merchant Ships). All merchant ships were equipped with guns manned by navy personnel. My dad ended up in Middlesborough where he was posted to *SS Wellpark*, a Scottish-owned ship. He was on the Atlantic run and made two successful trips, one to Norfolk, Virginia, and the other to Canada even though this was during the height of U-Boat activity.

The third trip (early 1942) was again to America but this time to pick up cargo for the Middle East. The voyage took him to the South Atlantic to round the Cape, as the Mediterranean was too dangerous. Whilst on board they heard that Singapore had fallen (15 February). When they sailed from New York they'd been warned that German surface raiders were in the Atlantic but due to the shortage of ships they could not go in a convoy but had to risk it and go on their own.

'Abandon ship'

The journey was uneventful until they were three days out of Cape Town. Dad was on watch at the time and looking forward to some time off in South Africa when the alarm bell went off. The Chief Officer ordered the A gun to be manned. Dad was more than perplexed at this as they were way out in mid-ocean. They had seen a smoke haze on the horizon but it was dismissed as a friendly ship. Suddenly dad saw an aircraft diving down out of the sky straight at him. He saw a splash and thought the 'b****r' had launched an aerial torpedo. He braced himself waiting for the bang but all he heard was a loud 'ping'. The aircraft had dropped a hook and as it flew over the ship it lifted the hook and pulled away the aerials leaving the ship without any means of communication to the outside world.

The aircraft returned and this time dropped a bomb that caused some damage. The next thing was the arrival of the German raider equipped wi

The illustration below is derived from a poor quality photograph of the British ship Kirkpool, *sinking after being attacked by the German surface raider* Thor. *This incident occurred during the same operation that saw the sinking of* SS Wellpark *and the capture of Jack Cooper.*

6-inch guns. The 4-inch guns on *SS Wellpark* were not much use against such an adversary. The German shells straddled the merchant ship whilst the replies from dad's ship were falling far short of their target. At this point the captain ordered 'abandon ship'. The two remaining lifeboats were launched and all 50 crew were safely evacuated. They expected to be left to their fate but the German vessel came round and picked them all up. The next round it fired sunk dad's ship. He always believed that the Germans could have sunk their ship with all hands lost, but they did not and he was treated very well all the time he was in German hands.

The German ship was the *Thor*. It had been made to look like a merchant ship but as it went into action the sides fell away to reveal the guns. It had two aeroplanes – the one that attacked dad had USA markings on it. Dad spent three weeks on board the German raider during which time it sank another four ships. When it went into action all the prisoners were locked in the hold below the water line so if anything had happened they had no chance of escape.

Across the Pacific

From the German raider he was transferred to the German prison ship *Regensburg* whilst still in the Atlantic. This ship took them round the Cape of Good Hope (not much Good Hope for those on board) across the Pacific to end up at Yokohama in Japan in August. They had to stay on a ship – the *Ramses* - as no prison camps had yet been built. It's ironic that dad can boast that he and his comrades were the first British prisoners in Japan. Not only that, he had the 'pleasure' of watching a Red Cross ship sail full of departing British and German diplomats.

The POW camp was in Kawasaki where dad remained for some considerable time. After about six weeks there was a further influx of prisoners. These were Middlesex Regiment and Royal Scots men plus some engineers and medics, all captured in Hong Kong. The prisoners found Japanese food unpalatable but after a short time every scrap was eaten. Work commenced on unloading railway trucks, hard and unrelenting toil seven days a week.

Life in the POW camp is a story in its own right, perhaps one day I will put that part of dad's story into print. Suffice to say here that dad survived the harsh conditions and came home alive and well. There is another story – that of my mother and how she coped in such dreadful circumstances before learning of my dad's survival but unfortunately she is no longer here to tell me.

THE THOR STORY

SS Wellpark was one of 10 ships sunk by *Thor* in the course the German surface raider's second South Atlantic sortie. *Thor* sailed from Kiel in January 1942. It's interesting that Jack Cooper says the ship had two aircraft; official records show it carried one Arado 196 but perhaps they didn't want to let the world know they had a second aircraft with US insignia. A favoured aerial attack technique was to dive down out of the sun with the engine switched off. This tactic made a surprise approach possible. At the last minute the pilot would switch the engine on, deploy the hook and skilfully whisk away the victim's radio mast.

Ironically, *Thor* met her own end in Yokohama harbour on 30 November 1942. She was tied alongside a German tanker called the *Uckermark*. This vessel was previously named the *Altmark*, the same ship that was stormed by sailors from *HMS Cossack* in February 1940. With the famous cry 'The Navy's here' they released 299 prisoners who had been transferred aboard the *Altmark* from the pocket battleship *Graf Spee*. A cleaning operation in the *Uckermark*'s hold resulted in a huge explosion that sank four ships in total. *Thor* was one of them; 13 of her crew were lost.

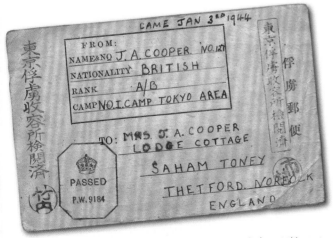

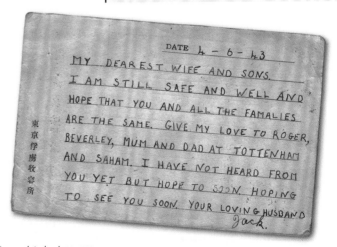

Jack sent this postcard from Japan dated 4 June 1943. It was delivered to Sylvia in England on 3 January 1944.

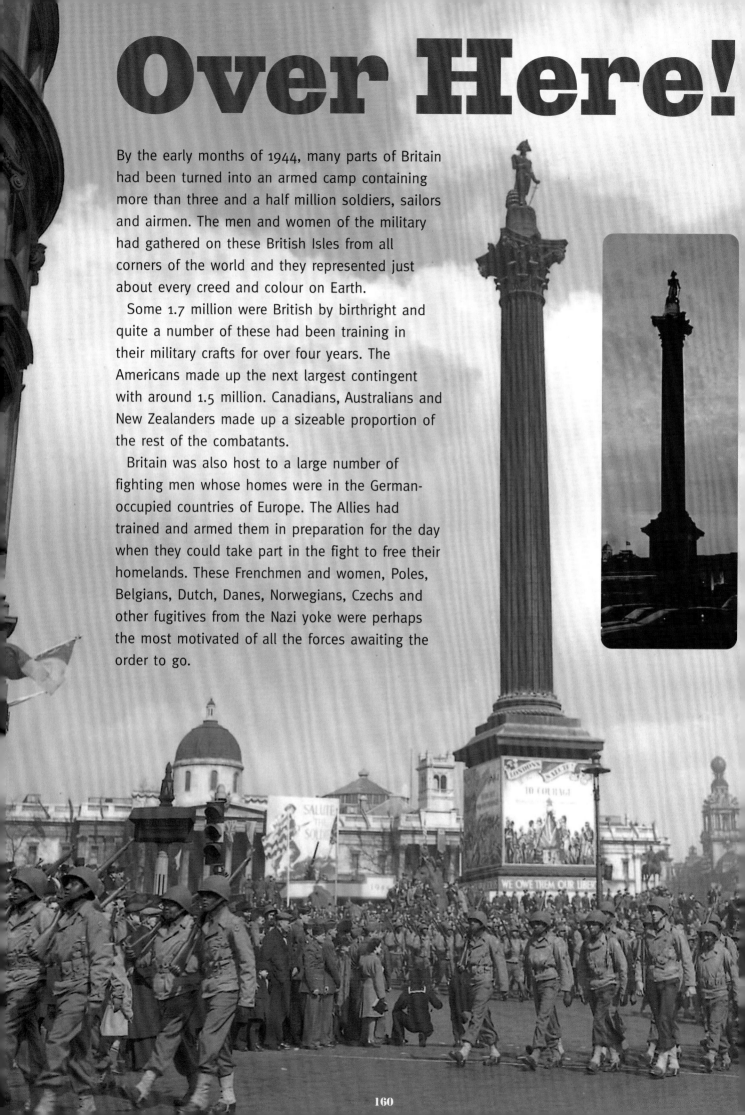

Over Here!

By the early months of 1944, many parts of Britain had been turned into an armed camp containing more than three and a half million soldiers, sailors and airmen. The men and women of the military had gathered on these British Isles from all corners of the world and they represented just about every creed and colour on Earth.

Some 1.7 million were British by birthright and quite a number of these had been training in their military crafts for over four years. The Americans made up the next largest contingent with around 1.5 million. Canadians, Australians and New Zealanders made up a sizeable proportion of the rest of the combatants.

Britain was also host to a large number of fighting men whose homes were in the German-occupied countries of Europe. The Allies had trained and armed them in preparation for the day when they could take part in the fight to free their homelands. These Frenchmen and women, Poles, Belgians, Dutch, Danes, Norwegians, Czechs and other fugitives from the Nazi yoke were perhaps the most motivated of all the forces awaiting the order to go.

WAR DIARY
January 1944

1 January: The year opens with Australian and US troops gaining the upper hand as they fought the Japanese on New Guinea. General MacArthur says that the capture of the whole island is likely 'within months'. It is less than 24 hours since General Montgomery had his first sight of the master plan for the Allied invasion of North West Europe, codename *Overlord*. The famous former commander of the Eighth Army has been appointed commander of ground forces for the invasion which is provisionally scheduled for May 1944. Monty's superior is the Supreme Allied Commander, US General Dwight D Eisenhower.

On **2 January** it is reported that Australian and US troops are gaining the upper hand in fighting against the Japanese on New Guinea.

On **3 January** a big RAF raid on Berlin sees some 1000 tons of bombs dropped on the German capital. The RAF lose 27 Lancasters out of the 383-strong bomber force.

The next night *Operation Carpetbagger* begins setting in motion regular supply drops to resistance forces in France, Belgium, the Netherlands and Italy. In the months ahead, fast Mosquito light bombers sometimes fulfil 'special delivery' requests within an hour or so after a coded radio message is received.

On **6 January** Berlin Radio broadcasts a statement from the German High Command: 'We will make no effort to hold Russian territory purely for reasons of prestige.' That same day General Vatutin's First Ukrainian Front army crossed the pre-war border and entered Poland.

Next day Hollywood film star James Stewart finds himself in a real-life wartime starring role. Stewart – a major in the USAAF – led a daylight mission to bomb Ludwigshaven. On the return flight, Stewart noticed that a number of the 420 aircraft on the mission had taken a wrong bearing and were heading in the direction of German fighter stations in France. With radio contact lost, Stewart decided to follow them and lend fire support. Although eight of the strayed Liberators were shot down, Stewart's action was credited with helping prevent the destruction of many more.

In Italy Allied talk of 'swanning up to Rome' evaporates in the face of strong German defensive positions around the Liri Valley in the mountains overlooking Cassino. American General Mark Clark pins his hopes on an audacious seaborne invasion at Anzio, far north of the front line, just 40 miles from Rome.

On **8 January** the RAF announced the development of a jet propelled fighter, the Gloster, to counter the threat from German inventors to produce aircraft capable of flying at 500mph. In a radio broadcast, Britain's jet propulsion pioneer, Group Captain Frank Whittle, says he finds the sudden publicity very embarrassing as a great many people besides himself had contributed to the work.

Polish leaders based in London received a message **(11 January)** from Moscow stating that the Curzon Line, the frontier proposed by the Allies in 1919, should be the basis of a post-war settlement between Poland and the USSR. Effectively it will mean the annexation of large areas of eastern Poland by the Russians.

On the same day in Verona, Count Galeazzo Ciano, Mussolini's son-in-law and former Italian Foreign Minister is executed by firing squad. The previous July, Ciano had helped oust the dictator from office. Now the resurgent German-backed fascists exact revenge.

On **12 January** Free-French leader General de Gaulle meets with the Prime Minister Winston Churchill in Marrakech to discuss

WAR DIARY
January 1944

THEY'RE USING Osram LAMPS ON BOARD

Your favourite lamps are helping to bring Victory

Franco-British co-operation. Convoy JW-56 loaded with vital supplies to support Russia's war effort sets sail for Murmansk from Liverpool.

On **14 January** the Russians attacked the rear of the German forces ranged around Leningrad. Two days later the Soviets announce the capture of 37 long range guns which have been pounding the city since it was first besieged in 1941.

In Britain (**18 January**) the first 600 'Bevin Boys' begin training for work in the coalmines. The youngsters have been conscripted by ballot to replace adult miners called up by the armed forces.

On **20 January,** coastal guns at Dover engage and sink the German blockade runner *Munsterland*. On the same day in the Far East, Lt A G Harwood of the Northants Regiment becomes the first British officer to be awarded the VC in the Burma Campaign. Harwood's posthumous citation says he had displayed 'calm, resolute bravery' in several actions in the preceding days. Thirty-year-old Harwood had been taken prisoner by the Germans in France in 1940 but escaped and reached Dunkirk in time to be evacuated.

On **22 January** 50,000 British and American troops plus 3000 vehicles land unopposed on the beaches near Anzio and Nettuno, less than 40 miles from Rome. Four days later the Germans declare martial law in the Eternal City as the populace grow restless in anticipation of the imminent arrival of the Allies. US General Lucas makes no move to liberate the Italian capital but concentrates instead on building up his forces.

Relations between the London Poles and the Kremlin deteriorate. The former believe that Stalin had ordered the murder of thousands of Polish officers at Katyn Wood on Soviet territory even though the Russians blamed the Germans for the massacre. History will eventually record that it was indeed Stalin who had ordered the liquidation of the officers in a bid to wipe out this important section of the Polish middle class who would be likely to resist an imposed communist regime controlled by Russia.

23 January: More success for the Red Army is reported as another offensive tears into depleted German lines in the Ukraine. Two Wehrmacht Corps are threatened with encirclement as Field Marshal von Manstein seeks Hitler's permission to withdraw.

24 January: The hospital ship *St David* is sunk by German aircraft off Anzio. Still in Italy, to the south, the French Expeditionary Force launches an attack across the River Rapido. After initial success, German reinforcements stop them just short of Monte Cassino.

In London on **26 January** the trial by jury of 58-year-old Oswald Job, finds him guilty of spying. He is sentenced to death. British-born Job had German parents; following internment in Germany upon the outbreak of war, Job was persuaded to return to England posing as an escapee. He then sent intelligence reports back to the Reich using invisible ink to write between the lines of letters written to British POWs in German camps. It is believed that Job's activites were uncovered by a double agent.

27 January: The Argentine severs diplomatic relations with Berlin becoming the 27th republic in the Continent of North and South America to do so. President Ramirez says that German spying activity in his homeland have provoked the action. Foreign observers in neighbouring Chile believe that Ramirez is merely backing the winning side and avoiding a confrontation with the USA.

On the same day in London, D-Day planners veto any further commando raids on Occupied France or the Channel Islands. They say that to continue them will only spur the Germans to speed up work on the so-called Atlantic Wall. German engineers, soldiers and Todt Organisation slave workers are building coastal fortifications from Norway and Denmark all the way to the Bay of Biscay. Complete sections are still few and far between, one exception being the coast around the port of Dieppe, scene of an unsuccessful 'reconnaissance in force' by a mainly Canadian force on 19 August 1942. After the raid Hitler demanded that the port be made impregnable.

28 January: The people of the battered but unbowed city of Leningrad are celebrating the best they can the official end of the 900-day German siege. The event was marked last evening when 24 salvoes were fired by 324 guns and massive firework displays went off. The securing of the Leningrad - Moscow rail link marked the end of the German investment. At one time nearly three million people were trapped in Leningrad but by the end there was just under half the original population, with the rest killed by German bombs and shells or by their allies, 'Generals Hunger, Cold and Terror'.

On **29 January** the first serious attempts by the Allies to enlarge the Anzio beach-head are rebuffed in the face of tough German resistance. A deadly glider bomb sinks the cruiser *HMS Spartan* off the invasion coast.

30 January: Brunswick and Hanover are raided by day by USAAF Flying Fortresses and Liberators. That night Berlin is raided; over 5000 tons of bombs have now been dropped on German targets over the space of three days and nights.

On the last day of the month, American Marines continue an offensive on Kwajalein in the Marshall Islands. It will take another four days of fierce fighting to win the battle. US dead total 372; only 130 Japanese out of an initial garrison of 8000 survive.

Night raids by up to 200 Luftwaffe aircraft continue on London and the South East. The RAF say that the enemy never succeeds in dropping more than 32 tons of ordnance in any single night. By contrast a single 'Tallboy' bomb used to blast recently identified V-weapon sites in France weighs a whopping 12,000lbs – nearly six tons.

The
Bombing of
Monte
Cassino

FEBRUARY 1944

Bombed in error?

On 15 February 1944 Allied bombers obliterated the historic monastery at Monte Cassino, Italy, a sanctuary founded by St Benedict himself 14 centuries before.

The resulting shattered ruin made a perfect defensive position for the German paratroops who were holding off an entire Allied army. The rights and wrongs of the decision to bomb have been shrouded in controversy ever since.

Today the monastery has been completely restored to its former glory. Only the cemeteries bear silent witness to the battles.

A Flying Fortress pictured in the course of bombing Monte Cassino.

ITALY: CASSINO IMPASSE

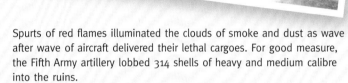

The Abbot of the Benedictine monastery pictured with German officers assisting him into a staff car shortly before the bombing.

Early in February almost all the Allied activity on the front facing the German Gustav Line hinged around bombed and battered Cassino. The first battle for the town and surrounding heights had ended in a stalemate. In the town itself and up on the mountain peaks and ridges, the Germans took full advantage of their good fortune in facing piece-meal rather than co-ordinated assaults. The flat plains on the valley floor were easily observed from the heights and areas had also been deliberately flooded.

XIV Panzer Corps commander, Lt-General Fridolin von Senger, headed the German defence of the Liri Valley, up which ran Route 6 to Rome and the besieged Allied beach-head at Anzio. He had converted the ground around the historic monastery into a strong defensive position manned by tough paratroops. However, Senger – by coincidence a lay member of the Benedictine Order and a devout Catholic – forbade occupation of the actual building, an edifice founded in person by Saint Benedict in 529AD. But Senger sensibly recognised the danger that fighting posed to the structure and he went to great lengths in first persuading and later assisting the Abbot to evacuate the monastery's priceless artifacts to the Vatican.

Senger's fears were well-founded. After an attack by the US 34th Division failed to make progress despite the soldiers battling bravely for days on the cold, rugged and very steep terrain, the eyes of the Allied commanders could not help but be drawn to the fortress-like white walls on the mountain top.

It was Lt General Bernard Freyberg VC of the New Zealand Corps who first requested that the monastery be destroyed. His men had replaced the Americans in the line at Cassino and they quickly formed the opinion that the building must be a key part of the German defences blocking access to the Liri Valley. The American General Mark Clark and British General Sir Harold Alexander were not convinced that bombing would achieve anything of real value but at the same time they could hardly refuse a measure which Freyberg was convinced would save the lives of his men.

Leaflets warning of the impending destruction were dropped in the vicinity of the monastery on 13 February. When the Germans told the occupants that the threat was an Allied bluff the monks decided to stay and took shelter in the deep cellars along with a large number of refugees, several hundred of whom were about to lose their lives.

It was a clear, bright morning on 15 February 1944 when over 200 USAAF Flying Fortresses, Mitchell bombers and Marauder aircraft flew over the Abbey. The resulting bombing was spectacular to behold. Allied troops in the valley below had a grandstand view as massive explosions rocked the hilltop.

German paratroopers assist a wounded British soldier in Italy early in 1944.

Spurts of red flames illuminated the clouds of smoke and dust as wave after wave of aircraft delivered their lethal cargoes. For good measure, the Fifth Army artillery lobbed 314 shells of heavy and medium calibre into the ruins.

Cheering it may have been to the watching Allies and certainly deadly to any enemy soldiers in the immediate Abbey vicinity. But in terms of gaining any tactical advantage, the raid was a failure. When it was over, the Germans simply moved into the rubble to enjoy the vantage point they'd denied themselves before. Von Senger was incensed. He is recorded as saying: 'The idiots! They've done it after all. Our efforts were in vain.'

Worse followed. An attack on Monte Cassino by the 4th Indian Division on 17 February was flung back at a cost of 600 casualties. So ended the Second Battle of Cassino.

PHOENIX FROM THE RUBBLE

The 1944 air raid was not the first time that the Abbey of St Benedict had been destroyed. Down the centuries since 529AD, invading barbarians, Saracens and an earthquake (1349) have periodically brought down the mighty walls of this enduring emblem of faith. Each time the monastery has reappeared atop its mountain peak, assuming once again its role as a centre of religious, spiritual and artistic life. So it was post-war when work began on clearing the rubble and painstakingly restoring the building's glories. It was a mammoth task. American money helped fund the work. Even so, the monks refused to include any English language tourist signs. As late as 1948, an unexploded bomb was still lodged in the flooring in front of St Benedict's tomb.

Today the quiet and tranquil environs of the Abbey make it difficult to imagine the chaos, cruelty and desolation wrought by war. But in the vicinity are the cemeteries filled with the fallen of both sides. Italian writer G Spadolini penned of the Cassino dead: 'In these places the holocaust of youth coming from all over the world was consumed and the losers and the winners joined together under the sign of a common grief and heroism.'

Most visitors first sight the Abbey from their car or coach on the A2, the modern Autostrada that lances down the Liri Valley to link Rome with Naples. Follow the signs for Abbazia di Montecassino on a road which winds laboriously up the mountainside. A panoramic view unfolds, one that makes it easy to understand why it took so long for the Allies to prise open the Gustav Line.

THE PAPER WAR

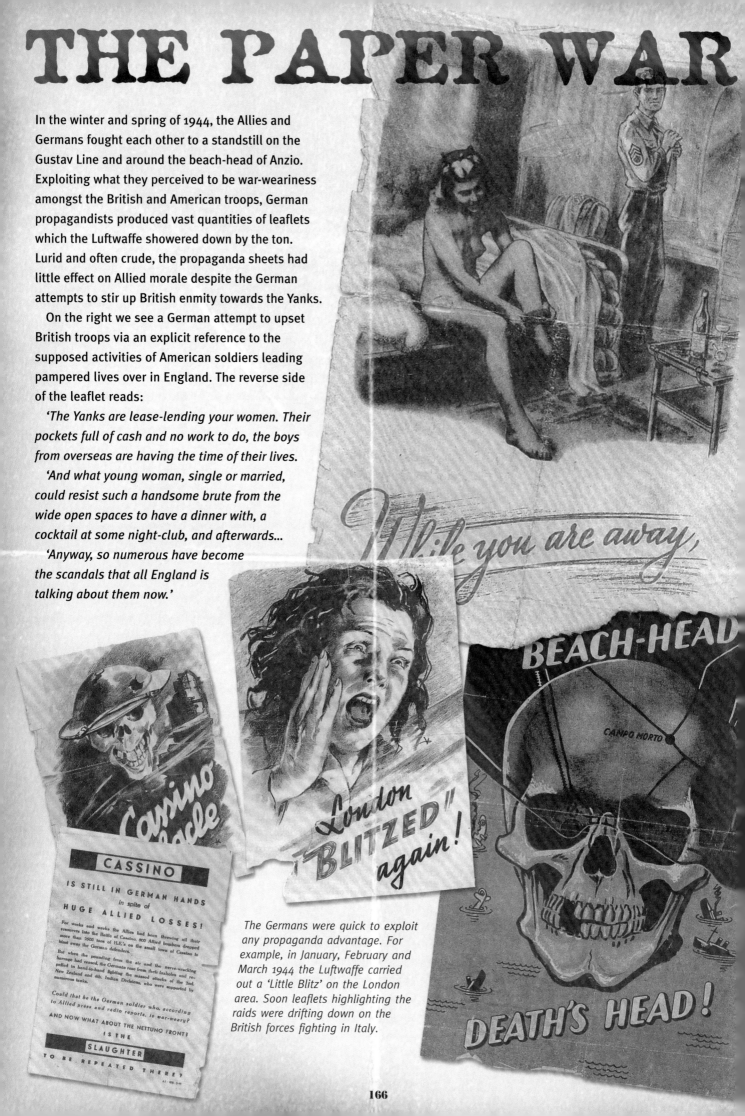

In the winter and spring of 1944, the Allies and Germans fought each other to a standstill on the Gustav Line and around the beach-head of Anzio. Exploiting what they perceived to be war-weariness amongst the British and American troops, German propagandists produced vast quantities of leaflets which the Luftwaffe showered down by the ton. Lurid and often crude, the propaganda sheets had little effect on Allied morale despite the German attempts to stir up British enmity towards the Yanks.

On the right we see a German attempt to upset British troops via an explicit reference to the supposed activities of American soldiers leading pampered lives over in England. The reverse side of the leaflet reads:

'The Yanks are lease-lending your women. Their pockets full of cash and no work to do, the boys from overseas are having the time of their lives.

'And what young woman, single or married, could resist such a handsome brute from the wide open spaces to have a dinner with, a cocktail at some night-club, and afterwards...

'Anyway, so numerous have become the scandals that all England is talking about them now.'

The Germans were quick to exploit any propaganda advantage. For example, in January, February and March 1944 the Luftwaffe carried out a 'Little Blitz' on the London area. Soon leaflets highlighting the raids were drifting down on the British forces fighting in Italy.

Anzio: a fire-raked cockpit

February 1944 in and around Anzio-Nettuno was a wretched time for the Allied troops as they struggled to consolidate their precarious beach-head. It was no better for the Germans as they attempted to drive the British and Americans back into the sea in the face of overwhelming air power and the big guns of the invasion fleet lying a short distance offshore. Spare a thought too for the hapless Italian civilians caught up in the vicious struggle and subjected to the grapeshot spray of deadly ordnance fired off from land, sea and air, not to mention the privations imposed by lack of provisions and access to medical help.

The War Illustrated of the time reported, '...this is the fire-raked cockpit of Anzio. The whole compact and ferocious bag of tricks is contained in an area less than that bounded by Battersea, Marble Arch, Holborn and Southwark. Every acre can be swept by enemy fire. The Fuhrer sees an immense political prize in throwing the attack back into the sea.'

Axis Sally broadcasts:

'Anzio has become the largest self-supporting prisoner-of-war camp in the world'

On 3 February the Germans mounted an attack on the Campoleone sector as they attempted to cut off an Allied salient known as 'The Thumb' along the line of Carroceto and The Factory. Supported by heavy artillery, they made slow but steady progress but sustained heavy losses in the process. Tiger tanks entered the fray and ground down entire companies of the Gordon Highlanders in the gullies and ridges around Campoleone.

At one point some Guardsmen were marching a group of captured Germans towards the unhappily-named Dung Farm when they in turn were surrounded by some 30 more Germans. Erstwhile POWs, they were being prodded towards the German lines when Captain Simon Lane led a revolt in which the captives turned the tables and overpowered their captors. The British then made it back to Carroceto with their wounded and nine prisoners.

On the night of 7 February, war correspondent Wynford Vaughan-Thomas recounted: '... one of those rare incidents where the fighting seemed for a few brief minutes to

HMS 'PEPPERPOT' IS SUNK

There were serious Naval casualties in the course of the Anzio operation. On 18 February *HMS Penelope* was torpedoed by U-Boat 410 off Nettuno and sunk with the loss of 417 of her crew including Captain D G Belben. *HMS Penelope* had already earned fame for her Malta role when she was nicknamed *HMS Pepperpot* due to the extensive damage she sustained whilst protecting the vital convoys to the island. Today 'The Penelope Association' is made up of survivors and friends and family of former crew members. The Association also encompasses the crew of the frigate *HMS Penelope* (F127) which was commissioned in 1963.

concentrate on one place and one man. That man was Major W P Sidney of the Grenadier Guards, defending a crucial point on the Via Anziate. If the Germans were to cut the road then the defenders of Carroceto and The Factory would be surrounded. In the action that night, Sidney and his men held fast, earning him a Victoria Cross in the process.'

But German confidence was growing. One cocky captive asked his British guard in which direction the sea was. When told he responded, 'Thank you very much. I needed to know, for very soon you will be in it.' In mid-February, Kesselring ordered *Operation Fischfang* to begin and his troops attempted to smash their way down the Via Anziate towards The Flyover.

The battle swayed back and forth, with thousands killed or wounded on both sides. By the end of it, the future for the beach-head was clear. To quote author Carlo D'Este in his enthralling account of the whole Anzio operation, *Fatal Decision*, '... what had started out a month earlier with lofty intentions ... had now turned into the bloodiest stalemate on the Western Front in the whole of World War II.'

Major General John P Lucas was replaced as Allied commander at Anzio on 23 February 1944. His successor was Major General Lucian King Truscott.

By 29 February the German counter-offensive was running out of steam as casualties steadily mounted. But would the Allies have the strength to break out? Propaganda radio commentator 'Axis Sally' didn't think so. Nightly on air she was boasting to her listeners: '...Anzio has become the largest self-supporting prisoner-of-war camp in the world.'

Despite the danger and hardships in the Anzio beach-head, soldiers kept a sense of humour. Note the Sea View Hotel sign! We also picture a 5.5 inch gun of the Royal Artillery in action.

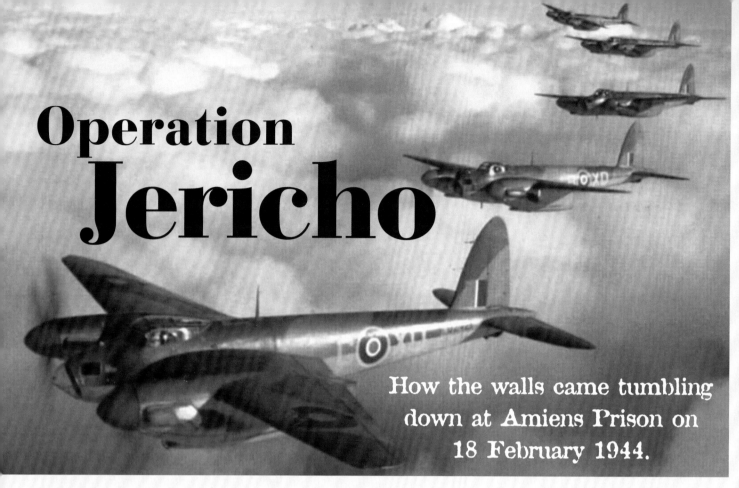

Operation Jericho

How the walls came tumbling down at Amiens Prison on 18 February 1944.

The Mosquito Mark VI was particularly suitable for low-level precision attacks where accuracy was all-important. Built of plywood, the light aircraft was powered by two Merlin engines. On 18 February 1944 the opportunity came to demonstrate the Mosquito's prowess in the most dramatic fashion.

Nineteen Mosquitos – six each from No 487 Squadron RNZAF, No 464 Squadron RAAF and No 21 Squadron, plus one Photographic Reconnaissance aircraft – all under the leadership of Group Captain Charles Pickard, attacked the jail at Amiens on 18 February 1944. The object was to release some 700 prisoners, many of whom faced execution as members of the French Resistance. They included a Monsieur Vivant, a key member of

the Resistance Movement in Abbeville. The prison, built in the form of a cross, was surrounded by a wall 20 feet high and three feet thick.

A model of the target constructed in Plaster of Paris (wedding cake decorators were found to be particularly skilful at this form of work!) was used for the briefing. It was designed to show the objective as it would appear four miles away to a pilot flying at 1500 feet.

The weather on 18 February was bad but it was the pilots themselves who insisted the mission went ahead. They took off from RAF Hunsdon an hour before mid-day, flying through storm and snow at close to sea level. Two waves of the attack approached the prison using the straight Amiens-Albert road as their guide.

Their bombs were so accurately placed in the prison walls and buildings that Pickard

called off a third follow-up wave. A few moments later his aircraft was shot down by two Focke-Wulf 190 fighters, crashing just a few miles from the prison. Pickard and his navigator, Flight Lieutenant J A Broadley, were both killed.

The daring raid resulted in the escape of 258 prisoners including Monsieur Vivant but the bombs killed 102 others.

The German FW 190s were out of the Luftwaffe's Abbeville fighter base and sported the bright yellow nose of German air ace Adolf Galland's squadrons.

The Amiens area on a Michelin map of 1947. The road network was the same in 1944. Note the straight stretch between Amiens and Albert which the Mosquito pilots followed on their bombing approach to the prison. Abbeville – where German fighters were based – can also be seen.

Le vrai visage de la "France libre!"

GRAND RABBIN DR WISE · NEW YORK
JE PRENDS L'ENGAGEMENT DE RÉINSTALLER APRÈS LA GUERRE LES
ISRAÉLITES DANS TOUS LEURS DROITS ET SITUATIONS EN FRANCE
DE GAULLE

LE GÉNÉRAL MICRO,
FOURRIER DES JUIFS!

Édité par L'INSTITUT D'ÉTUDES DES QUESTIONS JUIVES

SECOURS NATIONAL

ILS ONT FROID
ILS ONT FAIM
Aidez-moi
A LES SECOURIR

POSTER
ART of
Occupied
EUROPE

La fine del Sabotatore!

PROFIJT VAN
EIGEN
VERBOUW

GEMEENTE STELT GROND
TER BESCHIKKING

VOORLICHTING IN DEZE GEMEENTE
WORDT VERSTREKT DOOR:

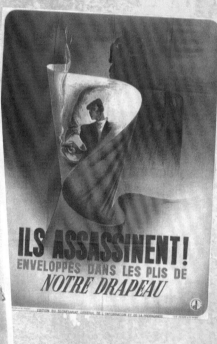

ILS ASSASSINENT!
ENVELOPPÉS DANS LES PLIS DE
NOTRE DRAPEAU

LA GERMANIA E VERAMENTE
VOSTRA AMICA

EN TRAVAILLANT EN ALLEMAGNE
tu seras l'Ambassadeur de la
QUALITÉ FRANÇAISE

February 1944

WAR DIARY

The second month of 1944 opens with the repeal of a wartime austerity measure. Men can once again buy suits with as many pockets as they wish and the trousers can also sport turn-ups. Similar restrictions are lifted on pleats and buttons for women's clothing.

On **2 February** 300 Polish civilians are executed in Warsaw in reprisal for the assassination of SS Major-General Franz Kutschera the day before by resistance fighters.

In Moscow the Soviet leader Joseph Stalin finally agrees to the use of Russian air bases by American bomber planes. Aircraft hitting targets in German-occupied eastern Europe can now fly on to the nearer Soviet bases and re-fuel and re-arm for another mission before flying back to Britain. This 'Shuttle Bombing' allows for more missions and shorter flying times.

The head of Vichy France, Pierre Laval, accedes to Nazi demands for more Frenchmen to be made available for forced labour in Germany. The plan is to have 1,000,000 more men in service by June.

Red Army troops cross the border into the German-occupied Baltic republic of Estonia, capture the city of Vanakula and push back General Walther Model's Army Group North.

On **3 February** New Zealand and Indian divisions join the US Fifth Army in front of the Gustav Line in the Cassino area. Meanwhile, at Anzio the Germans begin a major offensive to reduce the beach-head. At one point along the front line a herd of 1000 or more sheep rush through the sector defended by the Irish Guards; it is thought the Germans purposely stampeded the herd in order to detonate as many mines as possible.

On the same day the Russians report the entrapment of 10 German divisions in the Dnieper River Bend, south of the Ukrainian capital, Kiev. Artillery salutes are fired in Moscow to celebrate the biggest such encirclement since Stalingrad in 1942.

On **4 February** the Japanese launch their 'Ha-Go' (operation Z) counter-offensive in Burma's Arakan region and bring the British forward movement to a standstill.

Meanwhile, a brigade of Major-General Orde Wingate's famous Chindits prepare to depart Ledo in Assam on a march that will take them far behind enemy lines. The troops will be resupplied by air.

In the North Pacific, US Navy surface warships sail the closest so far to the Japanese mainland when they bombard Paramushiro, one of the Kurile Islands. Down in the South Pacific, mopping-up ends on Kwajalein atoll as the Americans close in on their next Marshall Islands objective, Eniwetok.

British Intelligence receive news from Paris of the arrest of Michel Hollard **(5 February)**. Hollard is an agent who has been feeding back valuable information about the progress of Germany's secret V-weapons programme.

Newspapers report the recent sinking of three German blockade runners in the Atlantic by the US cruiser *Omaha* and two destroyers.

On the night of **6 February** a big German shell crashes through the roof of Major-General John P Lucas's command post at Anzio but fails to explode. Artillery fire is the major cause of casualties on both sides. For the Allies one statistic makes particularly ominous reading; on average 900 men are killed or wounded every day while just 500 reinforcements arrive.

Next day sees a Red air force raid on the Finnish capital Helsinki apply more pressure on the Finns to make peace now that the German armies have been forced away from Leningrad. Finland only entered the war against Russia in order to regain the territory ceded to the Soviets at the end of the 1939 'Winter War'. In that conflict Stalin was the aggressor; the Red Army initially received a bloody nose from the tiny Finnish forces but eventually their overwhelming superiority in numbers forced the Finns into a humiliating peace agreement.

On **8 February** the Japanese continue their attack in the Arakan, infiltrating the British and Indian troops of XV Corps and attempting to encircle them. The subsequent fighting mainly centres on the Corps forward administration area in the village of Sinzweya, an area that will go down in military history as 'The Admin Box'.

Next night a dozen Lancasters of 617 'Dambusters' Squadron led by Wing Commander Leonard Cheshire make a night raid on an important aero-engine factory at Limoges, dropping 12,000lb 'Tallboy' bombs to devastating effect. In the House of Lords earlier that day, the Bishop of Chichester, Dr George Bell, questioned the morality of the RAF area bombing of cities and civilians. He quoted a figure of 74,000 persons killed in Berlin alone where 'our policy appears to be one of obliteration'. In reply, a Government

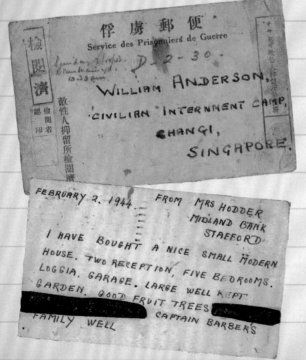

INTERNMENT

Postcards were the only means of communication between Prisoners of War and internees and their folks back home. Martin Barton-Smith of Haywards Heath, Sussex, had an uncle, William Anderson, held in Singapore's Changi Camp. The postcard on the top left was sent to him by his wife who was in the Women's Internment Camp at Palembang. On the reverse side (not reproduced) she wrote reassuring words about being well treated. Mrs Anderson subsequently died in Japanese custody. The second postcard was sent by Mr Anderson's mother-in-law to him in February 1944. The card was censored by the British authorities before being forwarded on. Martin does not know what information on such an innocent document was considered of potential value to the enemy.

WAR DIARY
February 1944

This example of Soviet poster art graphically depicts the Nazi beast being put to the bayonet. In the early spring of 1944, the Germans were in retreat all along the Russian Front.

spokesman denies that the RAF actions amount to terror raids, adding that the British will continue bombing 'with ever more crushing effect until final victory is ours'. Ironically, despite the weight of explosives falling on the Fatherland, production of tanks and aircraft within the borders of the Reich is rising at this time.

On **10 February** the Japanese decide to abandon the Pacific island of Truk. Holding it is untenable in the face of increasing US navy and air action following their invasion of the Marshall Islands to the east. On New Guinea, Australian forces link up with the Americans to further strengthen their grip on this immense island.

With a world war raging, Parliament still finds time for political conflict. Anthony Eden, Foreign Secretary, denies allegations by Welsh Labour MP Aneurin Bevan that the Government has been illegally putting many MPs on the State payroll with jobs outside the House of Commons (11 February). Under wartime legislation the Prime Minister can exempt MPs from having to give up their seats in the House if they accept 'offices of profit under the Crown'. Bevan says such jobs have been given out 'like confetti' to ensure Parliamentary support. The appointments are alleged to range from ambassadorships to seats on various tribunals.

12 February: Channel Islands. In the only part of the British Isles under the Nazi heel, Gestapo agents capture the author of Guernsey's clandestine newsheet (G.U.N.S.) and the duplicating machine that prints it in St Peter Port. Charles Machon and four accomplices face trial and likely death sentences. Other Channel Islanders have already suffered harsh retribution for 'crimes' such as the possession of radio sets or painting anti-German slogans on walls. One offender, cinema projectionist Stanley Green, has ended up in Buchenwald Concentration Camp. The Germans have heavily fortified the Channel Islands through the efforts of slave labour; all sorts of nationalities including Poles, Russians and even Mongolians, now live in appalling conditions in various camps.

This day also saw the sinking of the British troopship *Khedive* and the loss of 2000 lives when the ship is torpedoed by a Japanese submarine in the Indian Ocean. British destroyers later sink the submarine.

In Berlin suspicions of a plot against Hitler lead to the merging of the Abwehr military intelligence organisation with the Gestapo and Himmler's own SD security service.

On **14 February** the Germans inform the Vichy Government that they are taking direct control of the entire Mediterranean coast of France from the Spanish border all the way to Monte Carlo. Martial law will be imposed in the area, reflecting German fears of an Allied invasion and the prospect that Vichy might emulate Italy and change sides overnight.

In the Malacca Straits near Malaysia, the British submarine *HMS Tally Ho* sinks an enemy sub. Subsequently the crew is found to be German whilst the vessel itself was formerly in the Italian navy.

Pro-Nazi Argentinian army officers attempted a coup against the South American country's government on **15 February.** This is the same day that the Polish Government-in-Exile in London rejects Soviet proposals to make the Curzon Line the eastern border for a post-war Poland.

On **16 February** the German III Panzer Corps leads the Korsun Pocket break-out west of Cherkassy. Soviet claims of some 52,000 Wehrmacht troops killed or captured are denied by the German High Command who say that over 30,000 men have already made their way back. Nevertheless, German losses in tanks and aircraft are severe; 45 Ju52 transport planes are known to be destroyed.

In neutral Stockholm a meeting is brokered between Finnish and Soviet representatives to discuss armistice terms. The Russian delegation hold all the aces and the Finns know they must make painful territorial and political concessions to win peace.

The night sky over Berlin is filled with 891 British bombers returning to batter the city for the first time in a fortnight. Losses total 43 aircraft and it is apparent that the city's defences have been considerably stiffened with additional anti-aircraft guns and night-fighters.

On **17 February** American marines storm ashore on Eniwetok atoll, last bastion of the Japanese in the Marshall Islands. Fierce fighting lies ahead. Though the Japanese have already decided not to defend Truk in the Caroline Islands, they fail to evacuate their air and naval forces in time. In an intensive attack from the air, American fliers destroy 275 Japanese warplanes and sink around 40 ships gathered in and around the coral island's lagoon.

In London, plans for post-war Britain are revealed which include the introduction of a free health service for all citizens.

Off Anzio on **18 February,** the light cruiser *HMS Penelope* – a ship already nicknamed *HMS Pepperpot* on account of the number of hits it has sustained in various actions - is torpedoed and sunk by the German submarine U410 after it manages to penetrate the defensive naval screen. The Luftwaffe find success when they sink the cruiser *HMS Spartan* not far off the port. Losses of ships and landing craft are rising.

This night also sees the biggest German raid on London since the time of the 1940-41 Blitz. News is received next day of a vicious battle around the 'Admin Box' in the Arakan. Dependent on supplies brought in by air, the fighting saw rear echelon clerks, cooks and pay staff drafted into the front line in a successful bid to blunt the Japanese 'Ha-Go' offensive.

Even though the war had long since moved to the Italian mainland, Egypt remained an important staging post for the British not least because the Suez Canal was a vital link to the Indian Ocean and Far East. Here a Hudson bomber of RAF Coastal Command is shown flying over the pyramids.

WAR DIARY
February 1944

On **20 February** there is action in Norway where British Special Operations Executive (SOE) agents, aided by the Norwegian Resistance, sink a ferry taking a consignment of heavy water across Lake Tinnsjo en route to Germany. Heavy water is needed for the embryonic Nazi nuclear weapons research programme. (This incident formed the basis for the 60's Hollywood film, *The Heroes of Telemark*, starring Kirk Douglas.)

The Caribbean island of Trinidad is recognised as the British Empire's biggest source of oil with nearly 2500 wells yielding 20 million gallons a year.

American officials in Dublin pressure the Irish Government to expel German, Japanese and 'puppet' Italian diplomats. Whilst many Irishmen serve in the Allied armed forces, Dublin, as an 'anti-British' statement, continues to maintain full diplomatic relations with all the Axis powers.

On **22 February** Greek partisans blow up a German troop train on the main Athens – Salonika railway line. Over 400 soldiers die when the crowded carriages plunge into a flooded river. British SOE agents are believed to be to be assisting the Greek 'Andarte' partisan movement.

'Big Week' is well underway by 23 February. It's the codename for a joint RAF – USAAF campaign to blitz Germany's vital fighter and ball-bearing production centres. A secondary purpose of the concentrated air offensive is to draw out the enemy's fighter strength and destroy it in the air. Bomber formations pack an increasingly heavy defensive punch with machine guns covering approaches from all directions. In addition, long range Mustang fighter aircraft can now accompany the bombers all the way to their target and all the way back home.

Meanwhile London continues to receive the attention of the Luftwaffe as German planes bomb the capital for the fourth night in a row. The city's anti-aircraft defences take a heavy toll of the attackers. Press commentator Captain Norman MacMillan says that the raids are happening because the Germans are bringing aircraft to Western Europe in anticipation of the Allied invasion: 'The attacks are a combination of reprisal, exercise and employment of waiting forces... it is one of the penalties that Britain has to pay for being an advanced base.'

In the South Pacific aircraft from US carriers mount raids on the islands of Saipan, Tinian and Guam. At Anzio the besieged beachhead commander General Lucas is replaced by Major-General Lucien Trustcott.

On **24 February** the situation swings in favour of General Slim's 'Forgotten' Fourteenth Army in Burma as they eject the Japanese from the Ngakyedauk Pass in the Arakan. American-built Grant tanks of the 25th Dragoons blast the enemy positions in advance of the infantry going in.

In Helsinki the Finnish Prime Minister publicly announces a willingness to sign an immediate peace agreement with the Russians but subject to certain conditions. Moscow's angry response the next night comes in the form of a massive 600 bomber air attack on the Finnish capital.

That same night there's a huge 'Big Week' RAF raid by 594 bombers directed at the Augsburg aircraft plant. Success is limited as only 22 RAF planes find the target; 33 others were shot down. Nevertheless, 'Big Week' overall achieved its aims; immense damage was inflicted on Germany's industrial capabilities and 517 enemy fighters were destroyed. In pilot attrition, Germany will not be able to long stand losses of this magnitude.

On **26 February** the Japanese Premier, General Hideki Tojo, fires a number of top-ranking officers in a search for scapegoats to blame for his country's continuing reverses in the Pacific. Tojo appoints himself Chief of the Army General Staff, adding this title to his other ones of Premier, Minister for War, Controller of Munitions, Minister of Commerce and Industry and Minister of Education.

INSIGNIA OF VARIOUS ANTI-AIRCRAFT UNITS

6TH ANTI-AIRCRAFT DIVISION	8TH ANTI-AIRCRAFT DIVISION	H.Q. ANTI-AIRCRAFT COMMAND

News is released this day that Captain Randolph Churchill, the Premier's son, has parachuted into partisan-controlled Yugoslavia. A day later the BBC report German pressure on Tito's Yugoslav partisan forces south of Mostar. However, this is a minor offensive and it is becoming clear that the Germans will settle for containing the partisans rather than risking a large-scale engagement that would stretch their troop resources.

On **28 February** a big Allied convoy comprising 42 ships and a tanker arrive safely at the Russian port of Murmansk. Two U-boats were detected and sunk in the course of the voyage for the loss of the Royal Navy destroyer *HMS Mahratta*.

This being a leap year, on **29 February** the 1st US Cavalry Division lands on Los Negros in the Admiralty Islands and seizes the airfield at Momote. Debate now centres on where the US force will strike next. General Douglas McArthur says he is morally obliged to liberate the Philippines rather than by-pass the huge island chain and threaten an assault on Formosa and then Japan itself. In 1942 he had famously vowed, 'I shall return' when forced to quit the doomed fortress of Correggidor in Manila Bay.

On this day also the Finnish Parliament (The Diet) is urgently discussing the peace terms with the threat of more Russian bombing hanging over them. The bitterest pill for the Finns to swallow is the Russian insistence on occupying the Finnish naval base of Hango, key to control of the Gulf of Finland.

SHINE YOUR TORCH DOWNWARDS WHEN CROSSING THE ROAD

Government advice on how to cross the road during the black-out.

Desperate days in Italy

MARCH 1944

Anzio under siege

As March 1944 approached it was clear to the soldiers on the ground on both sides of the Anzio beach-head that neither adversary had the strength to defeat or dislodge the other. The most recent German offensive, *Fischfang*, had come close to a decisive breakthrough. But desperate Allied resistance, especially in an area known as 'The Caves' where men of the Queen's Royal Regiment at one stage found themselves holding off an estimated five enemy battalions, blunted the onslaught.

Yet still Hitler demanded one more effort from his men. On 29 February three German divisions of the LXXVI Panzer Corps attacked the American-held perimeter in the south of the beach-head, between Cisterna and Nettuno. But by 6.30pm on 1 March Field Marshal Kesselring had abandoned the attack. German losses included hundreds killed and more than 30 tanks, some of them flame-throwing types, destroyed. With some six weeks having elapsed since *Operation Shingle* began, the Germans admitted to casualties numbering 16,000 dead, wounded and missing, though the true figure was believed to be much higher. The Allies had sustained nearly 21,000 casualties, including many crew members of ships sunk or damaged.

Clear blue skies on 2 March invited Allied air action. Nearly 600 aircraft flew over the beach-head and dropped 350 tons of bombs on the surrounding German positions and troop assembly areas. BBC correspondent Wynford Vaughan-Thomas described the great flight of aircraft as '…looking strangely beautiful, remote and efficient as they came in from the south in an endless stream, jettisoned their load of death with a clinical detachment and swung back for more'.

Also watching was the beach-head's new commander, Major General Lucian Truscott. At one point an aide turned to him to exclaim, 'Christ General, that's hitting a guy when he's down!' But his mood quickly changed when he observed a B-26 bomber in flames following a direct hit by the German ack-ack.

A German gun on tracks prepares to fire on the beach-head.

174

THE FORTRESS

On the British side of the beach-head, fierce fighting continued well into March. Northwest of The Flyover and the main Via Anziate (the road to Rome) were a number of positions with names like 'The Boot' and 'Lobster Claws'. These were part of an area of deep gullies or wadis and large tracts of dense vegetation. For the infantry, fighting in this terrain was particularly difficult with visibility being restricted and infiltration after dark a constant threat. Close-quarter combat was common.

On 4 March the Sherwood Foresters in The Boot were relieved by the arrival of 660 men of the Royal Marine Commandos. The Foresters had suffered severe losses from nightly incursions by the men of the German Fourth Parachute Division who would lob grenades from the edges of the gullies into the British trenches – by day mortar 'stonks' and artillery barrages were plentiful. Following an ambush near a location called Pantoni, several hundred yards west of The Boot, there were only around 100 Foresters remaining who were able to stagger back to relative safety.

The fresh Commandos however, soon established their own regime of harassment and raids, giving back to the Germans more than a little of what they'd been dishing out for several weeks.

W J Campbell of Heswall, Wirral, was a Lieutenant and Intelligence Officer with the 2nd Battalion Cameronians (Scottish Rifles), part of the 5th British Division in Italy in 1944. After the fall of Rome he returned to Anzio and took the photographs reproduced above which depict the landscape of The Fortress, the most advanced and dangerous area in the British sector of the beach-head.

Anzio Annie opens fire

Raleigh Trevelyan came ashore with the Green Howards on 2 March. He remembers how, '...within 10 minutes I was almost killed by a shell from Anzio Annie, the railway gun. Within three days I was at a spot in the gullies called The Fortress... upon my arrival in the dark I was greeted with the warning, "Quiet, yer bloody fool – Jerry's only 70 yards away!"

'By day around our position it could be fairly quiet. But at night shells whirred and sighed continually overhead and there were airbursts. Machine-guns spattered, Jerry mortars coughed, ack-ack crackled and bombs crumped.

'Often we heard German voices. At one time we spotted a spandau post on a ridge too far away to snipe at the men walking so obviously on the skyline but too near for our mortars and anyway we

didn't want to attract fire on our own positions. On another occasion two Germans, who turned out to be Danes, wandered into our lines carrying a dixie of greasy stew.'

Trevelyan also remembers the frogs in the springtime at Anzio. When they stopped croaking it was a sure sign of the approach of possibly unfriendly humans. 'On a number of occasions they warned us of the approach of Jerry marauders,' he recalls.

The young Green Howard officer had his diaries published in 1956 in a book called *The Fortress*. Following this he established contact with a number of Germans who had fought opposite him at Anzio a dozen years earlier. Trevelyan went on to write another excellent book about the Italian Campaign. *Rome '44 – The Battle for the Eternal City* was first published by Secker and Warburg in 1981.

The Goliath effect

On the ground in front of the Allied lines, a small remote-controlled tracked vehicle made its appearance. Trundling into minefields and against fortified positions its toy-like appearance belied a sinister intent. The Gerat 67 – 'Goliath' – was attached to a 2000 metre cable fed from a drum at the rear of the vehicle. Powered by petrol or batteries, Goliaths were used to move explosive charges as close to the Allies as possible before they were detonated. Over 5000 had been built before the Germans halted manufacture in late 1944. It seemed a good idea, but in practice the Goliath was slow and cumbersome and made an easy target.

*An American swings a baseball bat for the camera
in front of an anti-aircraft gun.*

*A convoy at sea laden with trucks and supplies heads
for the Anzio beach-head.*

Inside the beach-head a network of new roads were constructed under the most testing conditions. Any movement in the rear areas in daylight was likely to be spotted by German observers up in the Alban Hills and a rain of artillery shells could be expected. Fortunately, in the early months of 1944 the wet weather kept tell-tale dustclouds to a minimum. The US 36th Engineer Combat Regiment were especially accomplished road-builders. They also laid out the surfaces and storage facilities required for the many ammunition dumps. And when necessary these men took their place in the front line.

One unit that won itself a legendary name at Anzio was Brigadier General Robert T Frederick's colourful Canadian American First Special Service Force which has gone into the military history books under the name of 'The Devil's Brigade'. With 2500 men, one third of them Canadians, this elite force was created to 'perform impossible missions no other unit was trained to carry out.'

Frederick said that he only needed men who were 'rough, tough and unafraid of anybody or anything' and whilst the Brigade's ranks held a fair share of misfits and even criminals, the vast majority were volunteers. They wore red berets and carried razor-sharp sheathknives. When Anzio settled down into a stalemate Frederick's 'Forcemen' continued to carry the fight to the enemy in sorties out of their positions on the extreme right flank of the beach-head. Just how effective these men were in unnerving their opponents can be gauged from a diary entry of a dead German officer: 'These devils are all around us every time we come into the line and we never hear them approach.'

The little village of Borgo Sabotini, around a quarter mile outside the 'official' beach-head front line, was taken over by the Forcemen and re-named 'Gusville' after a favourite Special Service Force Officer. They also gave new names to the village roads. The main thoroughfare became 'Tank Street', for the many German Panzer rounds that whizzed down its length. Another became 'Prostitute Avenue' after a war correspondent wrote that 'A man walking down it a little ways will soon find himself without visible means of support'. Gusville's 'mayor', Lieutenant Gus Heilman, proclaimed that his town had 'no strikes, unemployment or black market'. It also ran a well-stocked bar!

Audie Murphy's War

Audie Murphy was already a soldier with experience of fighting in North Africa and Sicily before coming ashore at Anzio on 22 January 1944 as a Staff Sergeant in the US 3rd Division. It was in the cauldron of the beach-head that this small in stature, baby-faced 19-year-old displayed the kind of coolness and courage under fire that marked him out to become one of America's most decorated war heroes.

Murphy's 'first blood' came at Cisterna. Following the disaster that befell the American Rangers on 30 January, his unit was sent in to reinforce the line. Later he was involved in dangerous night patrols, probing for German weak spots and hoping to pick up prisoners. A report from a Lt-Colonel said of Murphy, 'He could not stay out of a scrap at a Peace Convention!'. On one occasion he was awarded a Bronze Star for destroying an enemy tank with molotov cocktails and rifle grenades whilst under fire.

Audie Murphy went on to become a Hollywood film star, his biggest movie being the *The Red Badge of Courage*, in which he played a rookie Union soldier in the Civil War. In 1957 Murphy went to Rome to film scenes for *The Quiet American*. Whilst there he paid a return visit to Anzio and recorded his impressions: 'To look around it didn't seem like there had ever been a war there. But there was one thing that

makes you stop and remember ... the cemetery. Seeing those rows and rows of white crosses and knowing what they stand for surely takes away the holiday spirit.'

Audie Murphy died in a plane crash in 1970.

CASSINO –
Heights of despair

One month after the formidable walls of the monastery atop Monte Cassino had been blasted into rubble by Allied bombs and shell-fire, it was the turn of Cassino town below to feel the full terrible force of Allied airpower.

'Between breakfast and lunch today', reported Christopher Buckley, Special Correspondent of Britain's *Daily Telegraph* on 15 March 1944, 'in brilliant weather, I saw Cassino flattened from the air by persistent almost ceaseless bombing over a space of four hours. The bombing, intended to reduce the German strongpoints to rubble, was followed by a terrific artillery barrage from massed Allied guns, after which the infantry went forward to the assault.'

There can have been but few occasions before or since - atomic devices apart – when a bigger load of bombs had been dropped on to so small a target. To observers watching from a hillside some two miles away, nearly all the bombing seemed to be remarkably accurate. Yet later it was discovered that less than half of the ordnance had fallen within the target area – and this in bright sunshine with practically no opposition – and the artillery bombardment also proved ineffective in crushing German resistance. As soon as the guns ceased and the troops moved forward, 'From the rubble,' reported Buckley, 'machine-gunners sprang to life. From caves and tunnels on the hillside, many of them prepared or enlarged during the previous week's lull caused by the weather preventing air operations, the enemy emerged.

Storm of explosions

'They came from the cellars of houses in front of and behind our advancing infantry. Three-quarters of Cassino was cleared and then, with the impetus of our attack partly lost, the enemy began to counter attack.'

Once more the Allies were thwarted. The combined explosive loads of 500 bomber aircraft and countless shells from 748 guns failed to subdue the tenacious German Third Parachute Regiment. Their losses had been severe: half of one battalion alone had been killed, wounded or simply buried alive in the storm of explosions. But in and around

In this propaganda leaflet the Germans cleverly illustrate the problem facing the Allies on the Gustav Line – whoever controls the mountain tops also has control of the roads in the valleys below. In March 1944 the German grip on the top of Monte Cassino and in the ruins of the town below seemed as strong as it had ever been.

some hotel ruins in the heart of town, Major General Richard Heidrich had set up a strong central position surrounded by pockets of his men able to give mutually supportive fire in the face of assault from any direction. Many German snipers as well as some heavy weapons survived the air and artillery bombardment and these were soon back in action and taking a toll of the advance.

The biggest problem for the Allies though, was one they had created for themselves. The craters and vast heaps of rubble resulting from the

The ruins of the town of Cassino photographed after the massive Allied aerial bombing assault of 15 March 1944. The Germans retreated to the cellars during the attack and many later emerged unscathed to pour a withering fire on advancing New Zealand troops.

German observers survey the countryside from their vantage point on the heights at Cassino. It's easy to see what a tough task the Allies faced in trying to scale the mountains in the face of determined opposition from highly experienced paratroops.

bombs and shell-fire proved a major handicap for the attacking Second New Zealand Division. Their tanks were unable to negotiate a way through the sea of wreckage.

The Allied assault's ultimate goal was the bombed and blasted monastery at the top of Monte Cassino. But first a number of key points needed to be captured on the way up. Castle Hill was one that the New Zealanders secured by nightfall on 15 March. A prominent height nicknamed Hangman's Hill because of a gibbet-like structure visible on it from the plain below, was then the target of Gurkha soldiers of the Fifth Indian Brigade.

A company-strong group fought their way up to their objective but then found themselves cut off when the Germans counter-attacked furiously. Throughout the first night, mortar bombs, shells and small arms fire rained down on the Gurkhas. The Germans were so close at times that hand-grenades were lobbed by both sides. When daylight came the Gurkhas were forced to dig in as deep as the rocky mountainside would allow and keep their heads down. Many found themselves in hopelessly exposed positions and were picked off one by one.

For the next week these men endured a siege of their precarious mountainside position which turned into one of the most epic sagas of the whole Italian Campaign. Raleigh Trevelyan in his book *Rome '44* paid tribute thus: 'It seemed impossible that these small brave brown men, from a remote land thousands of miles from Europe, could exist up there, without enough cover from enemy fire, let alone the weather, and without enough to eat or drink.'

Gurkhas and Maoris

Soon the only means of supply for the isolated men was by air. Inevitably, most of the parachutes fell out of reach or straight into German hands. Wounded Gurkha Bihm Bahadur, a section leader, recalled after the battle: 'I can hardly remember the first supplies dropped by planes – just the sight of coloured parachutes fluttering to earth. I saw one of the cases land a few yards away, but I couldn't leave my trench because I would have been a "sitter" for the ever-alert Jerry snipers.'

Men of the Essex Regiment made a brave attempt to reinforce the Gurkhas but only 70 soldiers got through. Meanwhile, around Castle Hill and down in the town, the Allies had other problems. On the hill, other Essex soldiers, along with men of the Rajputana Rifles, found themselves under ferocious attacks by German parachutists reinforced by a Pioneer battalion. In the town, Maori troops took over 100 prisoners but were hard hit by rifle, machine-gun and mortar fire. A panzer half buried in the lobby of the Continental Hotel sprayed deadly rounds at the Maori positions.

New Zealand General Freyberg next pinned hopes on a surprise attack into the German rear via a mountain track known as the Cavendish Road. Sappers had worked on this trail in secret to make it negotiable for tanks. In Fred Majdalany's definitive account *The Battle of Cassino* the author

says: 'The effect of the attack was likely to create similar consternation amongst the Germans as that experienced by the Romans when greeting Hannibal's elephants after their Alpine crossing.'

Twenty two tanks destroyed

Unfortunately, things didn't work out according to plan. German surprise at the sudden appearance of American and Indian-crewed Sherman and Stuart tanks was short-lived. Panzerfaust – German bazookas – blew up the lead tanks and proceeded to decimate the rest of the column: 22 tanks were destroyed.

General Sir Harold Alexander, Commander of the British Forces.

Within days the Third Battle of Cassino was effectively over when General Sir Harold Alexander called a halt to further offensive operations. By then Freyberg had already called off the frontal assault on the Monastery and had recalled the valiant Gurkha and Essex soldiers from Hangman's Hill.

On the night of 25 March the difficult withdrawal by 257 men began. The Monastery was bombed again to provide a diversion and fighting patrols of the Royal West Kents – who'd earlier relieved the New Zealanders in The Castle – went out to engage German attention. A heavy fall of snow settled on the mountain. Eventually all the men got safely down with the exception of several severely wounded soldiers who had to be left for the Germans to tend to. Despite the ferocity of the fighting, the Cassino battles were notable for various acts of chivalry. Red Cross flags and truces to enable the wounded to be evacuated or treated were usually respected by the fighting men on both sides.

The Colonel of the Gurkhas reported that when told they were leaving their desperate and untenable position, his men were only concerned as to which unit would they be handing the safekeeping of Hangman's Hill. Imagine their sorrow when – next morning – the German flag once more flew over their former position, so hard won.

The surviving Germans on the Gustav Line at Cassino counted the Third Battle as a victory. But the Allies hadn't so much been driven back as denied an advance. Time could only favour one side and the certainty of better weather and better visibility gave an impetus to Allied preparations for re-newed attacks with fresh forces in the springtime.

Roman relics

In one of the strange ironies of war, even as the Allies and Germans battered the town of Cassino into a vast heap of rubble, there were parts of the place that had already lain in ruins for some 1500 years past. 'Casinum' had been an important town in Roman times, famous for the thermal properties of its waters. Visitors today can view the amphitheatre (pictured right) and other examples of Roman architecture whilst in the town's National Archaelogical Museum there is a fascinating collection of exhibits ranging from the prehistoric period through to the age of Rome.

NORTH SEA RENDEZVOUS

Bernard Hagger remembers cold nights and deadly fast boat encounters.

Early in 1944 I returned to MTB 241 at Felixstowe after three weeks in an RAF hospital with pneumonia. Not surprising really – the North Sea gets extremely cold in winter and being soaked with it nightly is not to be recommended.

MTB 241 was part of the 21st MTB Flotilla. The late Peter Dickens (great grandson of the author, Charles) had departed a few months previously and his role of Senior Officer had been taken over by our skipper Jim McDonald, the youngest ever at 21.

I had done my Light Coastal Forces training at Fort William in the summer of '43 where we were told that crews were in the main aged under 25. Imagine my surprise on joining 241 to find Ginger Harry, a 47-year-old 'three badge' gunner – and what a character. He was much liked and knew all the wrinkles – how to get in and out of the base without going through the regulating office and how to get rabbits ashore without troubling Customs etc.

Our tasks were mainly to attack German convoys off the Dutch coast but also on moonless nights to lay mines in and around their harbours. Also there was the much detested Z patrol which entailed laying silent in the water about 40 miles off the East Coast waiting for the return of E-Boats which had attacked our coastal convoys. Their convoys were almost the exact opposite of ours in that while we generally had 20 or 30 merchantmen protected by two or three destroyers, they would have two or three merchantmen protected by 30 or more armed vessels of varying types. We would quit the enemy coast an hour before dawn.

RAF Beaufighters attacked us

On 19 February 1944 whilst on night patrol we encountered a convoy and after spending some 90 minutes making unsuccessful attempts to infiltrate we broke off with dawn about to break. Mac called for air cover and very soon two Beaufighters appeared and exchanged signals, circling us several times before disappearing. Ginger Harry manned the twin Vickers .5 gun turret just aft of the bridge and I was his re-loader. Sudden gunfire alerted us. One of the two Beaufighters had returned but peeled off and was strafing MTB 223 on our starboard quarter. Then he started to dive on us; Ginger didn't wait for any order from the bridge – he opened up. The plane pulled out of its dive and flew off.

All five boats stopped. Half the crew of 223 were dead or dying. Two of the badly wounded were transferred to the fastest boat with instructions to proceed full speed to Felixstowe, but they died before arrival – six of the 12 crew were lost.

We received an apology next day. With most so-called 'friendly fire' incidents some reasonable excuse can be found but try as I might I can make none for this. Visibility at the time was 12 miles with no other surface craft to be seen and our five boats were in an area the size of a football pitch, flying white ensigns and heading towards our East Coast.

A couple of weeks later we had just begun a patrol between the Hook of Holland and Ijmuiden when we sighted a large convoy protecting two big merchant ships. Torpedoes were primed and we went to infiltrate. Maybe our concentration was too much on the target as suddenly an E-Boat appeared about 100 yards off our port bow and a shower of tracer crossed our bridge. We accelerated to our maximum speed of about 38 knots and by this time were being attacked from several directions. The tracer seemed mostly aimed at the following four boats but suddenly there was a load crack and our speed dropped dramatically. The ERA emerged

Anti-Aircraft gunner on alert aboard a British Motor-Torpedo-Boat (MTB) in the North Sea.

from the engine room to report that there was three feet of water down there resulting from a below water line explosion, probably an 88mm shell.

At this point one boat came alongside to take us in tow and Mac left with the remaining three boats to continue the fruitless attack. In the meantime while ropes were being passed we came under attack again apparently from some straggling defenders of the convoy. Fortunately for us they did not press home their advantage. We were towed for 10 hours by which time the after third of 241 was completely submerged. The crew dismantled guns and took all useful items (including the rum jar!) on to the towing boat. 241 was then sunk by gunfire. On return to base Mac was very upset that we'd lost the boat.

We were sent on seven days survivors' leave and were due to return to pick up MTB 234. At 1200 a week later there was one absentee – Ginger Harry. Mac came aboard mid afternoon and noticed his absence. He did eventually arrive at 1630 and the following day he was up before the skipper to receive two days stoppage of pay and leave. I had never seen Ginger so upset; all day he kept chuntering on that he wasn't working two days for nothing, but by evening he had found his solution. 'I've had this hernia for years – it doesn't trouble me but tomorrow I shall be at the Sick Bay'. And sure enough he was – but we never saw him again. Apparently it was decided that he needed an operation but he did not survive the anaesthetic.

Enemy coaster set ablaze

About mid-March again on patrol we encountered another German convoy about an hour before dawn. It was decided that two of our five boats should separate and create a diversion from the inshore side while we attacked from the seaward side. A rendezvous was pre-arranged. Once again our clever ploy was doomed to failure and we had to break off.

We'd been proceeding to the rendezvous for about 20 minutes when six ships were spotted on the horizon. We simply continued on our course and as the gap closed we came under some fairly inaccurate fire. At about 1500 yards we turned hard to port and then hard to starboard so that we had the targets – 2000-ton coasters – broadside on. Our three boats each sank one ship with one torpedo and then a coaster was selected for a concentrated gun attack. Within 10 minutes the coaster was well ablaze and the other two enemy vessels disappeared in seconds. No survivors could be observed. Our other two boats had also encountered two armed minesweepers apparently intended as escorts for the six coasters, and sank one of them.

Years later it did occur to me that Mac's determination not to ask for air cover again was a good move. If our arrival near the enemy coasters had coincided with that of the Beaufighters we would probably have been taken to be their escorts and suffered the same fate.

TUNNEL VISION

The Mirisch COMPANY Presents

Steve McQUEEN · James GARNER · Richard ATTENBOROUGH

A GLORIOUS SAGA OF THE R.A.F

JOHN STURGES'

THE GREAT ESCAPE

JAMES DONALD · CHARLES BRONSON · DONALD PLEASENCE · JAMES COBURN · JOHN LEYTON · Produced and Directed by JOHN STURGES · Screenplay by JAMES CLAVELL & W.R. BURNETT · Based on the book by PAUL BRICKHILL · Music by ELMER BERNSTEIN A MIRISCH-ALPHA PICTURE

COLOUR BY DE LUXE PANAVISION®

Today the place is called Zagan and is part of Poland. But in 1944 it was known as Sagan and was in the German territory of Upper Silesia, around 100 miles south east of Berlin. Two years earlier, the Luftwaffe had chosen the area's bleak and wooded terrain as the site for a new POW camp when it became evident that extra accommodation would be needed for captured Allied aircrew officers. An isolated clearing in a pine forest with a harsh and cold climate through the long months of winter became Stalag Luft III, ideally suited in the eyes of the Luftwaffe planners for discouraging escapes.

Persistent escapees purged from other camps found on arrival six bare barrack huts ringed by a nine-foot double barbed wire fence. Just outside, 100 yards apart, on 15-ft stilts, stood sentry towers or 'goon-boxes', equipped with searchlights and machine guns. Ten yards inside the fence ran a warning wire; any POW seen crossing the wire risked being shot without warning by the guards.

In spring 1943 the inhabitants moved to a new, larger, compound containing 15 huts. Eventually it grew to hold 10,000 prisoners contained in 59 acres encircled by five miles of perimeter fencing. By that time Stalag Luft III, under the leadership of Squadron Leader Roger Bushell, a South African-born London barrister, had become one large escape factory divided into a variety of 'trades'. There were specialists in the forgery of documents, passes and tickets, map copying, metal work, carpentry, rail and air pump manufacture, compass making, tailoring, German language tuition and counter-spying on the camp's 'ferrets' who were on constant look-out for tell-tale signs of unusual activity by the prisoners.

Tom, Dick and Harry

While individual escape attempts continued, work began on three major projects – the digging of tunnels code-named 'Tom', 'Dick' and 'Harry'. Each tunnel was to be around 30-feet deep to thwart the German sound detectors. To preserve secrecy only a few dozen men knew the whereabouts of the tunnels and most inmates were even unaware of what huts the trap doors were in. Elaborate effort went into diverting the attentions of prowling 'ferrets'.

In the summer when 'Tom' was well advanced there was a slip up. One of the 'penguins' – the sand disposal team – was spotted emptying the contents of his trouser bag. A prolonged German search led to the discovery of the tunnel's trap door in one of the huts.

For a while tunnelling was suspended. Then tunnel 'Dick' was abandoned when it was seen that the area where it was due to surface had been cleared of covering vegetation. But 'Dick' did prove useful for storing much of the sand extracted from the third tunnel, 'Harry'. Another useful depository for the tons of yellow sand was under the stage of the camp theatre.

On the night of the 24-25 March 1944 the chosen 220 assumed their varied 'civilian' clothing (although one man was dressed in a 'home-made' German army uniform), checked counterfeit papers and tickets, pocketed food rations and made their way to the escape hut, which rapidly became very crowded..

Complications set in. Men lying horizontal on trolleys became wedged. Wheels came off the wooden rails. Digging up to the surface took much longer than planned. Then, horror of horrors, it was found that the exit had emerged in the open, 10 foot short of the line of trees. Nevertheless, over a period of seven hours, 76 men had scrambled up through the hole in the ground at the end of 'Harry' and made off into the darkness.

At this point, by sheer bad luck, an armed guard wandered within a few feet of the tunnel and spotted an emerging escapee. He raised the alarm and captured a couple of men on the spot. Many others in the tunnel had to wriggle around and crawl back to the hut where they were soon discovered by the alerted Germans.

The break-out sparked a nationwide hue and cry. In his Berchtesgarden mountain retreat, an enraged Hitler ordered that all recaptured escapees be shot. He later amended this instruction, demanding instead the execution of at least half of those rounded up.

Most of the escapees were quickly caught. In fact just three eventually reached safe havens. Per Bergsland and Jens Muller (Norwegians serving in the RAF) made it to neutral Sweden while another foreign volunteer pilot, Bran 'Bob' van der Stok, finally reached Gibraltar via Holland, Belgium, France and Spain.

'Great Escape' organiser Roger Bushell and companion Bernard Scheidhauer caught a train from Sagan Station and made it as far as Saarbrucken before being caught. Fifty recaptured escapees were executed. Bushell and his companion were amongst the victims.

Bushell had always known that few escapees would get home to freedom. He was more interested in creating maximum chaos and confusion inside the Reich and forcing the Germans to divert precious troop resources in time-consuming manhunts. But he couldn't have expected such vicious retaliation that totally contravened the Geneva Convention. The Germans themselves issued identity discs to Allied POWs with which they could prove they were not spies should they effect an escape in civilian clothes and later be recaptured.

At the war's end, teams of Allied investigators launched intensive searches for the guilty Gestapo men; in the resulting trials many received the death sentence or lengthy imprisonment. Roger Bushell's killer Leopold Spann died in an air raid on Linz in the closing days of the war. His accomplice Emil Schulz was hunted down, tried and found guilty of murder. He was hanged at Hamelin on 27 February 1948.

Carry On Escaping!

The popular comedy actor Peter Butterworth was an inmate of Stalag Luft III. He was captured in Holland in 1940 while serving in the Royal Navy and went on to make three escape attempts and helped organize attempts by other prisoners. In Stalag Luft III he became close friends with Talbot Rothwell (later a writer on the 'Carry On' series, on which Butterworth often worked) and the two began writing and performing sketches for camp shows to entertain the prisoners (and to cover up the noise of other prisoners digging escape tunnels). After the war Butterworth decided to continue his acting career, and soon regularly featured in films and TV. He specialized in playing gentle, well-meaning but somewhat eccentric characters. He was married to impressionist Janet Brown. Butterworth died suddenly in 1979, as he was waiting in the wings to go onstage in a pantomime.

While being held as a POW, Peter played a part in the escape later filmed as The Wooden Horse (1950). He actually auditioned for a part in the film without disclosing his part in the real incident. He failed the audition as the producers felt he did not look heroic or dashing enough!

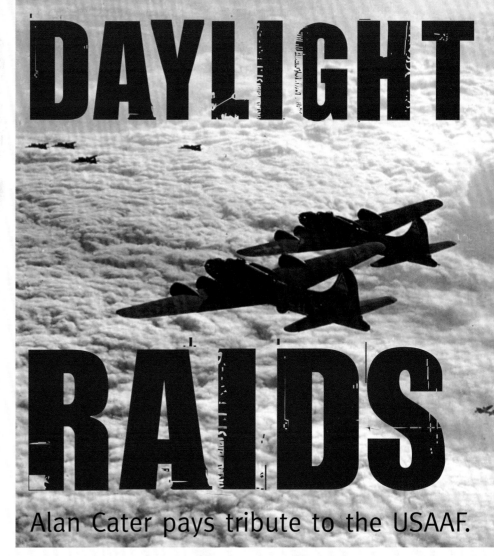

DAYLIGHT RAIDS

Alan Cater pays tribute to the USAAF.

I started work for the BBC in October 1944 and my title was 'Boy'. I was just that – an errand boy. On one occasion I was walking along Portland Place when there was an explosion in the sky which caused a violent concussion wave. There was a huge cloud of smoke but what caused the blast I know not, most likely a V1 or V2 rocket.

When I got back to the office for my next errand my boss asked me if I was OK. 'Yes', I replied. 'Right.' he said, 'It's now time to get the evening papers'. No post-traumatic stress or counselling in those days! Getting the evening papers involved a scrum which usually took place on the steps of the church opposite Broadcasting House. I had to get the right number of copies of *The Star, Evening News* and *Evening Standard* (the latter being the only survivor today). I recall one occasion near Christmas 1944 when the headlines read, 'Germans break through in Ardennes, Allies fall back, heavy fighting', etc etc. How could this be, wasn't the war nearly won?

Another of my routine tasks was to file the previous day's news bulletins. Here's a typical example: 'This is the nine-o-clock news read by (Alvar Liddell / Bruce Belfrage / Stuart Hibberd). Last night a strong force of RAF Lancaster and Halifax bombers attacked targets in Germany, 42 of our aircraft are missing.'

First US daylight raid

Several decades later my interest in those times resurfaced. One day I was tramping around the remains of an old wartime American airbase at Horham in Suffolk. This was the home of the 95th Bomb Group of the Eighth USAAF. There also happened to be some former veterans visiting and we got talking. One story they related concerned 4 March 1944 when the 95th was part of an 800-strong force of B17s and B24s which took off to make the first American daylight raid on Berlin. On the way a recall signal was received and most of the aircraft did a 180 degree turn for home. All that is, except the 95th and 100th BGs. The 95th was led by one 'Lootenant' Alvin Brown with Lt/Col 'Grif' Mumford as his co-pilot (it was Brown's aircraft so he was the boss). For the sake of brevity it is only necessary to say that Brown and Mumford ordered the rest of the group to press on to Berlin. They got there and bombed and were about to face the wrath of the Luftwaffe when P51 Mustang fighters appeared. As one aircrew member remembered: 'It was just like the movies.' Four aircraft were shot down. Brown and his crew returned safely.

Two days later on 6 March it was the 'Big B' again. This time it was different. No recall. So all 800 set off on a mission that saw the Americans suffer their biggest loss in a single day of the air war; 69 aircraft were shot down along with 11 fighters. This was 69 times 10 plus 11 fighter pilots. Many of the aircraft carried back dead and wounded aircrew. There is a book, *B17's Over Berlin*, by Ian Hawkins which I recommend to anyone wishing to find out more about this period of history.

Moving on – in later years I have attended several Eighth Air Force reunions as a 'Friend of the Eighth'. One in particular stands out. It was in St Louis, Missouri, where I met for the first time 'Lootenant Al Brown', a very fit 80-something. I asked him about that 'recall signal' (it had always been a bit of a mystery).

To use his words, 'We were suckered.' Apparently the Germans had been able to crack the code of the day and it was they who had sent the recall signal. They too must have had a Bletchley Park and a Hut 3.

To this day many friendships still exist between the folk of East Anglia and the American veterans with reciprocal visits taking place. The USA's involvement made it possible for the Allies to win the war. At their peak they were producing 400 aircraft a day. Their resources were such that when there were parties for the children living around the UK air bases they would think nothing of making an ice cream mix and sending up a B17 to 30,000 feet to freeze it!

All of the above is certainly not meant to diminish what the Royal Air Force achieved. Up until early 1944 they had carried out the brunt of the bombing campaign. It was in that year that the Americans overtook the British in numbers of aircraft but never the tonnage carried. One other tragic reminder; on 30/31 March the RAF attacked Nuremburg and lost 100 aircraft.

Above: A formation of Boeing B-17 Flying Fortresses on a bombing mission early in 1944. The US Eighth Air Force made daylight precision attacks on factories engaged in war work and on military targets.

Left: Alan Cater with Jane and Bob Lash in Tucson, USA, in 1998. Bob was a pilot with the 95th Bomber Group in Suffolk in 1944. Bob passed away shortly after this reunion.

Spring 1944 in Italy. Around Monte Cassino and the beleaguered beach-head at Anzio, the Allies and Germans remain locked in deadly struggle. Rome is the prize.

Naples to the south is a popular rest and recreation centre for the men of the Fifth and Eighth Armies. Then on 18 March, ancient Vesuvius awakes. The volcano's spectacular eruption threatens to bury Pompeii once again just as it did nearly 2000 years before.

The enormous plume of smoke can be seen by the fighting men at Cassino and by Allied sailors far out at sea. Aircraft make wide detours while hundreds of others are destroyed by a rain of ash on their airfields. Mother Nature puts war into perspective.

In the next 10 days Vesuvius will unleash explosive power equivalent and more to that contained in all the bombs, shells and mines in all the arsenals of Europe, those of friend and foe alike.

Having vented her anger, Vesuvius returns to the sleep of ages. She still slumbers today. But for how long?

Photo: *Vesuvius erupting, March 1944 as pictured by William J Skinner of the USAAF 31st Fighter Group.*

VESUVIUS ERUPTS

March 1944. War Correspondent William Connor files a report from Naples.

" This country has got everything. Within an area less than that of an average English county, you can be bombed, shelled, machine-gunned, mortared and volcanoed.

And it's free.

Best, safest and most spectacular is being volcanoed.

I took time off, to see Vesuvius proving the truth of that hoary old gag about the unwisdom of living on the side of a volcano. Since a real volcanic eruption is far more rare than war, I think I should describe to you just what happens.

Away on the top all hell is a-blowing. From out of the crater comes smoke, steam, ashes and a vast, red-hot primeval sludge called lava. This stuff, billions of tons of it, is oozing down the sides of the volcano. It is a vast, crawling slag-heap about 40 foot high. It is the original black guts of the earth. Time has slipped a million years and here, slithering across a Naples vineyard in the bright sunlight, is the stuff this globe was made of when it was just a pup of a world. When it cools you have the stuff the moon is made of – black, cold clinker.

I watched it digest an Italian village for tea. The dark, smoking cliff pushed a wall down and edged into a fresh dewy garden where broad beans were in flower. The heat withered the plants within about 10 feet. On it came.

The tide crept forward and tumbled round a tree that suddenly burst into flame. Then on to the front of a house. Up the walls and round the side. The house caught fire inside and half an hour later vanished without a trace. Nearby a church was being engulfed. The sea of molten clinker came up to the roof. The old building stood it well. All around, houses had fallen, but the church held out. It collapsed suddenly with a roar and a last wild despairing jangle from the bell in the tower.

There is something rather fearsome about a town being destroyed by lava. War leaves some trace – gutted houses, bomb-pitted streets. Vesuvius leaves none.

You can go into a room and see the last few pitiful possessions that the owner could not take away – an old cot, an iron ladle, a faded photograph. Within an hour or so, all will be vanished – a handful of ashes entombed 40 foot below the sunlight. No stone will mark the place where there was once a town. Only a memory.

Vesuvius has 40 winks, and a century is gone. When he awakes he yawns, stretches his arms, and a hundred thousand people start looking for new homes. The big boy seems to be half out of his bed now and looking for a fight. "

Top: A 17th century painting depicting Pompeii during the 79AD eruption.
Below: A revealing fresco discovered in the excavation of the buried city.

The dark cone of Vesuvius silhouetted against a bright blue Mediterranean sky is the most striking sight in the Gulf of Naples, perhaps even the whole of Southern Italy. Over 4000 feet high, the volcano is composed of lava spit forth in the course of eruptions of various intensity (some 70 since the most famous one which buried Pompeii and Herculaneum). The most recent began on 18 March 1944 and continued till the end of the month. For a while the fury and fireworks of Vesuvius convinced many Neapolitans and Allied troops that another cataclysm of the kind that swallowed Pompeii and Herculaneum was imminent. It wasn't to be. Even so the energy released by the volcano in those couple of weeks was reckoned by vulcanologists to have added up to more explosive power than all the conventional bombs and shells used up in the entire Italian Campaign. It was as if Mother Nature herself was demonstrating the futility of man waging war.

A few years ago the editor of *Sixty Years On* walked to the summit of Vesuvius and enjoyed a splendid panorama of the Bay of Naples whilst observing ominous fumirole smoke wisps still emerging from within the cone. Visitors can drive quite a way up the volcano's side but the last half mile must be hiked. A funicular used to run up one side of the mountain but it's been out of action in recent years – this is still Italy, after all!

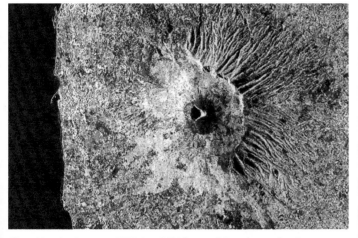

Above: *Vesuvius from space! This is a NASA image of the volcano taken from a satellite. The cone of Vesuvius can clearly be seen in the centre.*

LOST
ON AN AFRICAN SHORE

The poignant story of an astonishing air and sea coincidence in the midst of war, remembered by Ron Holton.

The Wellington bomber 'K for King' photographed in the position where Ron crash-landed it on the Atlantic coast of North Africa in 1942. Notice the kit of the crew in front. The photo alongside shows the aircraft going up in smoke to prevent it falling into enemy hands.

In 1942 I found myself as second pilot of a Wellington bomber and ordered to fly to India. Because Germany at that time occupied most of North Africa, and Vichy-France had gone over to the enemy, fighters operating out of Casablanca were a threat to our aircraft. Furthermore, Franco's Spain was hostile to our cause. Accordingly, it was decided that the safest route for our aircraft bound for Egypt and points east was to travel far down the Atlantic before turning left and flying across Africa. The route comprised: Gibraltar – Bathurst – Kano – Khartoum – Wadi Halfa – Cairo.

Our troubles began when we were about half-way down the long leg between Gibraltar and Bathurst and flying at about 4000 feet when, on switching over to our over-load tank, both engines stopped dead. Rapidly switching back to main tanks got both engines re-started but they ran intermittently and were clearly losing power. At about the same time we noticed that fabric was peeling off the port wing – later we discovered that some corrosive acid had been sprayed on it. Our wireless operator immediately began sending out SOS calls but was getting no replies.

It soon became evident that we must ditch. Being flanked by the hostile Canary Islands to our right and Spanish Rio-de-Oro (territory since annexed by Morocco) to our left on the African mainland, capture or death seemed inevitable. We decided that if only we could reach Africa our chances of escape might be better. Accordingly I turned sharp left and I was faced with the prospect of a dicey forced landing. We just managed to clear the top of the cliffs before I thumped her down causing severe damage to the tail of the aircraft but fortunately no injuries to the crew.

The next three days were spent in clearing the fuel systems of the contaminated fuel and making emergency repairs to the wing. In the meantime the wireless operator kept sending distress signals with a rigged up extended aerial until the batteries were exhausted – no replies were forthcoming. We cleared a strip of stones and rocks heading towards the cliffs which were about a hundred feet high and nurtured the rather suicidal hope of being able to get airborne and not simply plunge into the sea. Our plan was to fly south in the hope of finding a friendly ship near which we could ditch before we ran out of fuel.

Back to Gibraltar

On the very morning selected for making our get-away, the attempt had to be postponed because a heavy sea-fret or haar had crept in adding to our hazards. As the mist cleared, to our astonishment we saw a British warship, *HMS Laforey*, a Lightning Class destroyer, inching her way straight towards our position. At first I thought that the sun had affected me and that it was all an illusion. But it was real enough. Cutting the story short, after destroying our aircraft we spent two days on board the *Laforey* as she sailed back to Gibraltar. Everyone on board treated us as honoured guests – even the main-brace was spliced!

At the inevitable court of enquiry we discovered that the only vessel to pick up our faint distress calls was the battleship *HMS Nelson*, then operating in the South Atlantic. She had relayed our message to the naval base of Simonstown in South Africa, which, in turn, had relayed it to the ship nearest to our position, the *Laforey*, with instructions to search the coastline for a downed Wellington.

Subsequently we were sent back to the UK on board the small troopship *Leinster* and who should escort us on our lonely way? Yes, the *Laforey*. She was going home to be refitted while our future was to pick up another aircraft and fly out east for a tour of operations in Burma.

We now move on to a date in 1944. I was in the middle of another tour but this time in the Mediterranean. My detachment of No 36 Squadron was temporarily based at a small airfield named

Lost, found and lost again! Ron Holton and the crew of his RAF Wellington bomber were miraculously rescued by the Royal Navy destroyer HMS Laforey (pictured here) in 1942. By an incredible coincidence, two years later in 1944 Ron was to witness from the air the destruction of the very same ship, sunk in the Mediterranean by a U-boat that was itself doomed to destruction.

Montecorvino near Naples and close to Mount Vesuvius, which had just started to erupt. A hail of ash and pumice put our airfield out of action and for a time day turned into night. When at last the eruption died down and the wind changed, Herculean efforts soon had a runway cleared and our aircraft serviceable again.

Stromboli erupts

The first task allotted to my crew was to act as cover over a joint flotilla of 11 British and American destroyers and frigates in the area north of Stromboli. It was at night, Stromboli, like

The crew of the Wellington – Mike, Jimmy, Del (left to right, back row) with Tommy, Frenchie and Ron Holton himself in front.

Vesuvius, was in full eruption and made an awesome sight. We used it as a navigational fix. Apparently a U-Boat had made a sinking in the area, and nemesis awaited the submarine as soon as it surfaced, as inevitably it had to. We were there as an insurance policy should the U-boat break through the cordon and head for its base at Marseilles in which event we would pursue it using our radar and Leigh light and sink it with depth charges.

It was a beautifully calm and peaceful night until all hell broke out around us. There came a series of large explosions, tracer fire and more explosions, and then powerful searchlights began sweeping the water, obviously looking for survivors. Soon after this we received a signal recalling us back to base. There we learnt that the U-boat had indeed surfaced but in doing so had discharged its full complement of remaining torpedoes into the hull of the nearest ship. The vessel had immediately exploded and sank within minutes, taking almost all of the crew with it. The U-Boat, whose captain was obviously a very brave man, was also sunk. Several hundred men had died within minutes that night.

Some days later we heard that the ship that had taken the full force of the torpedoes was none other than our beloved *HMS Laforey* which had saved our lives some two years before.

We felt stunned when we heard the news. This beautiful ship and her fine crew had literally saved our lives. They had taken us to their hearts, had shared their rum and meals with us, had entertained us in Gibraltar as only the Navy can, and finally had escorted our transport all the way back to the UK.

THE HOT BREATH OF VESUVIUS

EYE WITNESS

The anniversary of the eruption of Mount Vesuvius in Italy brought back memories of 1944. I was flying from Foggia aerodrome in Wellington bombers with 104 Squadron, 205 Group. We had a rest camp at Sorrento called the Hotel Minerva, financed by Lord Nuffield (of Morris Motors). It was situated on the cliff in full view of Vesuvius, across the Bay of Naples.

We were on leave at the Minerva in March 1944 and whilst sipping our vino on our hotel balcony there was a sudden rumbling and there across the bay was Vesuvius erupting – a quite fantastic sight.

After returning to Foggia our next operation took us to a turning point off the island of Ischia and whilst heading west we experienced a terrific surge of air which pushed us up a thousand feet or more, almost to the point of stalling. No fun with nine 500lb bombs on board! Everybody talked about it at debriefing, at which point we all realised we'd flown close to Vesuvius where the heat from the angry volcano was creating powerful thermal currents. It was these superheated thermals that carried us up.

I did 39 night bombing operations in all. On one occasion at Sorrento when we arrived for a rest period, the Bay of Naples was packed with every type of naval vessel you could think of – landing craft, torpedo boats, destroyers and much more. When we awoke the following morning there wasn't even a rowing boat to be seen.

Upon our return to Foggia we were assigned the target of the port of Genoa. On our way there we witnessed an amazing sight – it was the armada of vessels which had departed the Bay of Naples. They were supporting *Operation Anvil*, the South of France landings, which began on 15 August 1944.

My wife and I have been back to Sorrento. The Hotel Minerva is still there and the staff made us very welcome when we paid a visit. After a tour of Pompeii we went up to Vesuvius to look at the crater created in the eruption I witnessed over 60 years ago. I have a beautiful framed picture looking down into the crater – a little bit of history.

Fred Clarke

*The eruption of Vesuvius in late March 1944 caused havoc on many Allied airfields in the Naples area. Some 90 US bombers were engulfed in ash and destroyed at a single location (see picture below) a loss very much higher than that sustained by enemy action over the same period in the Italian theatre of operations.

Destroyer Laforey is sunk

Captain missing

THE Admiralty announced last night that the destroyer Laforey, commanded by Captain H. T. Armstrong, D.S.O., D.S.C., has been lost.

Captain Armstrong, who is among the missing, was a former officer in the royal yacht. He was 39.

The Laforey was a destroyer of 1,935 tons, laid down in 1938. Her full complement would be over 200.

She was in the Anzio landings and took part in the operations on the east coast of Sicily, covered the attacks at Salerno and helped in the Volturno fighting.

In less than two years she steamed well over 100,000 miles.

It was difficult to believe that now probably all those friendly faces were lying in many fathoms of water. And for us, who owed them so much, it seemed incredible that we alone of all crews should have witnessed their deaths. Since our last meeting the *Laforey* had sailed over 100,000 miles, and we had flown about an equivalent amount in the Far East and the Med, only to come together at the last tragic moment.

The sinking of HMS Laforey as reported in the Forces newspaper, The Union Jack. The ship sank on the night of 30 March 1944.

UXB?

'Did the Luftwaffe plant something highly dangerous in my garden?' asks Bomber Command Memorial champion, David Shepherd CBE.

The book *Seventy Years On* contains a host of extraordinary stories of coincidences that often beggar belief. Here's one that has revealed itself to me over the past year.

My good friend Ron McGill called me in the early summer of 2009 to say he was coming to stay in Seaford in Sussex with a group of pals from his golf club. Now Ron always likes to 'gen up' on any wartime activities pertinent to the locations where he plays golf and given that I live just a few miles from Seaford he wondered if I had could help with any information.

I duly lent Ron some books that included *Bombers Over Sussex* (Pat Burgess and Andy Saunders, Middleton Press, 1995), an exhaustive record of when and where German bombers were brought down in the county. A day later a clearly excited Ron rang again. Had I seen the photograph on page 88? It showed the tailfin of a Heinkel 177 and two policemen beside it at Hammerwood on 2 March 1944.

The significance of Ron's observation took a few seconds to sink in. Hammerwood? Wasn't that where our mutual friend, the artist David Shepherd CBE, lived up on the edge of the Ashdown Forest? It certainly

Police officers pose with the swastika bedecked tailfin of the Heinkel 177 at Hammerwood on 2 March 1944.

was – and Ron wasted no time in letting David know of his find.

Mosquito night fighter

It transpired that David – who moved to Hammerwood many years after the war – knew nothing of the crashed aircraft. His own local enquiries failed to turn up any further information or eye witness accounts. Meanwhile I delved into the website www.aircrewremembrancesociety and discovered the whole fascinating story.

Heinkel He177A-3 had been flying on a mission towards London in the early hours of 2 March 1944 in the course of *Operation Steinbock*, the Luftwaffe's last conventional bombing campaign against Britain. At approximately 03.15am the Heinkel was engaged by a Mosquito night fighter. Hit in the rear fuselage by 20mm cannon rounds, the German aircraft came down in the area of Hammerwood. Though both engines and the main frame fell together, the rest of the aircraft

was scattered over a wide area of woodland.

Two of the Luftwaffe crew were killed in the crash but four somehow survived and were taken prisoner. The Observer, Unteroffizier Friedrich Emmerich, was injured while Unteroffizier Heinz Pohl and Gunner Ferdinand Klari were largely unscathed. Gunner Willi Fischer was seriously hurt and subsequently had both legs amputated.

Two bombs missing

Two unexploded 1000 kg bombs were recovered from the crash area but under interrogation the crew maintained they were definitely carrying four bombs. So that left two unexploded German bombs unaccounted for and presumably buried in the Hammerwood soil for the past seven decades!

David Shepherd is fascinated by this tale and would obviously like to know where the missing bombs are located. Having said that, he says he is not about to go digging up his land willy nilly. He certainly doesn't want the story to have an explosive ending!

DAVID ARNOLD

'Winter of '43 – Somewhere in England' by David Shepherd. The painting depicts a Lancaster being made ready for a mission. Another David Shepherd painting appears on page 292.

Bomber Command Memorial

Photo: Becky Thomas

David Shepherd CBE is renowned for his wildlife paintings and is passionate in the cause of wildlife conservation. But he also has a superb portfolio of aviation and steam train works. In the former capacity his interest is far wider than painting aircraft. In recent years in respect of Bomber Command's role in World War II he has put his considerable influence and energies into supporting the campaign to erect a permanent monument honouring the 55,573 British and Commonwealth aircrew, with an average age of 22, who died in the course of the conflict. In the spring of 2010, Westminster Council finally gave permission for the proposed £3.5m open style pavilion to be built at the Piccadilly entrance to London's Green Park.

The roof of the 8.5m-tall pavilion, made from Portland Stone, will be open to the sky and the open entrance will be made from melted down aluminium sections of a Halifax bomber shot down during the war and in which all seven of the crew were killed.

The memorial should be completed by 2012 and will contain inscriptions, carvings, and a dedication. There will also be inscriptions from Winston Churchill, who said in a speech to Parliament in 1940: 'The gratitude of every home in our island ... and indeed throughout the world except in the abodes of the guilty goes out to the British airmen who undaunted by odds, un-weakened by their constant challenge and mortal danger, are turning the tide of world war by their prowess and their devotion.'

The monument has been promoted by the Bomber Command Association with assistance from the RAF and the Heritage Foundation.

A Boy Scout in Wartime

Ron McGill recalls an incident in the Little Blitz of March 1944.

My family were bombed out in May 1941 and were evacuated from South London to the Berkshire countryside near Reading where we shared a house with a local family. We spent two happy years there until being offered a new home by the London County Council (LCC) at Roehampton in late 1943.

We quickly accepted this chance to have our own home once more and said a fond farewell to Berkshire. Once back into the London area and now 13, I asked my parents if I could join the Scouts.

This was agreed and I was enrolled into the St Margaret's Troop in Putney and allocated to the Owl Patrol. Wartime scouting had a major problem – it was a job to obtain all the pieces of the uniform at a time of severe clothing shortages. For my first active meeting I had a scout's shirt, shorts and a black and white toggle scarf. My friend Peter had a scout's hat – but no shorts – and so it went around the Troop!

Hear the sirens – run home

The meetings once a week were grand and all was going well until the early months of 1944 arrived. At this very time the Luftwaffe decided to start another aerial assault on Britain – it became known as 'The Little Blitz'.

Londoners in particular were the target of these nightly nuisance raids using, in the main, the new Heinkel 177 bomber.

Our parents were unhappy for us to be away from home in the course of these air raids. We all reached an agreement that allowed us to attend Scouts' evenings on the condition that we ran home (in my case about half a mile) if the sirens sounded.

Though untroubled at first, there was one night when things went wrong. The meeting began as usual but then the warning wail sounded and we all scattered homewards. My friend Peter and I were jogging homewards and had reached the main Doverhouse Road when the fireworks started. There above our heads a group of searchlights had 'coned' a German bomber. We stopped to watch, quite fascinated as the enemy aircraft swirled, dived and climbed in a desperate attempt to evade the glare. By now our heavy ack-ack guns in nearby Richmond Park were firing and we could see the sparks of bursting shells near the aircraft. Somehow, it survived the barrage.

I felt a strange emotion, almost pity, as we watched, transfixed, the enemy pilot's efforts to evade the lights and deadly gunfire. It seemed the bomber must be hit at any moment and then we were suddenly aware of the falling shell splinters clattering down on nearby roofs.

Searchlights frantically probing

Then the lights lost the bomber but swung around frantically trying to catch it again. Somehow that pilot had dived his aircraft and zoomed into a very lucky escape. In my heart I do recall feeling that the pilot had deserved his escape and that I was not sorry to see him get away.

It was a different story in the morning when a fireman neighbour told my father that the German bomber had jettisoned his bomb load over Putney and made his escape at a low level. One of his bombs had hit a small dance hall at the corner of Putney Bridge Road and Putney High Street. This was completely wrecked and many people were buried in the rubble. The death toll was around 60 dead and many were injured – amongst the latter was a then teenage female neighbour who was badly crippled for life.

I thought again about my reaction of the night before and how I was somehow relieved that the enemy aircraft had escaped but upon learning of the casualties my mood changed completely. All those young folks enjoying themselves and having their lives snuffed out so brutally.

Scout nights were never quite the same after that tragic night. Mind you, we broke countless speed records getting home whenever the sirens sounded again!

MIXED EMOTIONS

Every schoolboy loves a hero, and one particular wartime pilot delighted Peter Champion with his death-defying swoop over Brighton Station. Trouble was, the aircraft had a swastika on its fin...

The schoolboy of 1944 was the same as the present day version: a mixture of Just William and the Artful Dodger. Brought up in wartime England, he was a scavenger of all wartime relics, from anti-aircraft shrapnel to cartridge cases and pieces of liberated enemy aircraft, and would volunteer for any activity that kept him out of school.

It was with these principles in mind that I volunteered as an ARP (Air Raid Precautions) messenger boy. The only requirement was a bicycle and a willingness to be on duty at an ARP post from 10pm until 4am. The reward? The following day off school.

Our 'post' was the basement of a government-commandeered house near Brighton Station. Most nights (once a week) were spent playing snooker on a well-worn table and making tea for the adult wardens who manned telephones which, in the event of the phone lines being clobbered by bombing raids, would have brought us into being as messenger boys carrying rescue information from one ARP Post to wherever it was needed. Such an incident never occurred!

One cold crisp night in March 1944 air raids were in progress over London and down into Surrey. The reverberating throb of the synchronised German bomber engines meant that you knew when the enemy were overhead, even on a pitch black night, and it was a relief when the noise trailed off.

Dull red glow

This was such a night, attended by the rumble of heavy anti-aircraft fire and distant bomb bursts. At about 2am things were getting extremely busy and four of us left our basement shelter of the ARP Post to cross the road which was on higher ground and looked down at a slight angle over the whole of Brighton Railway Station. This gave us a good view to the north where we saw a continual dull red glow as the raid – presumably on London – progressed.

Stabbing the sky from a dozen different points and locations were the pencil beams of searchlights, criss-crossing the sky in an effort to illuminate the enemy so that the anti-aircraft batteries could get an accurate fix. When caught in the searchlight beams by probably three beams at once, the aircraft would appear as a shiny silver dot. We always hoped to see it erupt in a ball of flame, although invariably it would manoeuvre wildly and escape the lights.

As we craned our necks over the long wall, the anti-aircraft fire increased in volume and the predatory searchlights became closer; they were at a very low angle in the sky, the German was flying very low – and south, towards us!

Explosions and flashes

The excitement mounted. Fear? No, all schoolboys knew they were bullet-proof, and that nasty things always happened to other people. The noise of the German aircraft was becoming more audible now as the twin 1750V horsepower engines bit into the night sky, lending more urgency to the German's flight.

Hearts racing, we suddenly saw the streamlined aircraft almost on the deck flying just above the London to Brighton railway line. The anti-aircraft fire was now ear-splitting – he was so low that small arms fire and machine guns were opening up. There were explosions and flashes all around us. We watched, mesmerised, as it seemed certain that the German aircraft was about to fly straight into Brighton Station. He flashed past us. The aircraft was a German Messerschmitt 410 twin engine machine with a crew of pilot and navigator. It a had a mottled camouflage finish, a large black cross outlined in white on the fuselage and a similarly marked swastika on the fin – all this noted in a fraction of a second.

We astounded ourselves as we heard our own voices shouting, 'go on, go, go, faster, faster!' We were willing the Germans, our bitter foe for years, to escape. The pilot obliged us by lifting his nose just slightly over the station roof to be swallowed by the night sky and the coast. Did he make it, was he injured or is he now resting his weary bones in retirement in some home for ex-Luftwaffe aircrew?

We returned to our ARP Post puzzled by our own reactions to the incident. Was it that every schoolboy is a sucker for any Superman, or that perhaps, just perhaps, we stopped being schoolboys for a moment in time and grew up a little that night? I like to think so.

Peter Champion is a professional artist who still lives in Brighton, some 60 years on from his wartime schooldays. His painting on this page is an impression of how he remembers the incident would have looked from the air.

WAR DIARY
March 1944

March begins with the arrival in France of Field Marshal Erwin Rommel – the legendary Desert Fox. Rommel's Afrika Corps had almost pushed the British out of North Africa before the Eighth Army under Montgomery inflicted a decisive blow at El Alamein in November 1942. Now Rommel has the job of bolstering the German forces in Northern France in preparation for the expected Allied invasion. Fate decrees that Rommel's adversary will again be Montgomery.

Figures released in Berlin on **1 March** reveal that some five million 'guest' workers are now employed in keeping the Nazi war machine functioning. In reality the workers are slaves.

German Navy chief Admiral Donitz requests priority be given to production of the 'Schnorkel' device. This enables U-Boats to stay under the surface for long periods and evade the Allied warships and aircraft. Since 1 January, 34 U-Boats have been sunk.

On **2 March** tragedy befalls a train carrying hundreds of Italian civilians crammed into freight cars near Salerno. Over 400 die from carbon monoxide poisoning after being stuck for several hours deep inside a tunnel.

On the same day in Buenos Aires a coup led by army officers sympathetic to the Nazi cause fizzles out after 48 hours of confusion. Extreme right-wingers in the Argentine armed forces are angry at the government's decision to sever relations with Germany and Japan. The Minister for War, Colonel Peron, is seen as the 'strong man' influential in resisting the rebellion.

The Argentine decision to back the Allies is in contrast to Turkey's neutral stance. Access to Turkish bases would greatly aid bombing campaigns against targets in the Balkans. However, Ankara does turn a blind eye to incursions into Turkish waters by British SBS (Special Boat Squadron) forces as they make hit and run attacks on German garrisons in the Greek islands.

In London, Sir James Grigg introduced the Army Estimates to the House of Commons and reported that the British fighting forces were '...the best we've ever had. Far too little has been said in praise of the British soldier.' Grigg added, 'Sooner or later the enemy must crack. However, Germany is fighting with the utmost resolution and, except possibly where Hitler's intuition has been at work, with consummate skill.'

By **3 March** some six million Italian workers are on strike in protest at the forced deportations of Italian menfolk to Germany where they are made to work in arms factories.

This Vichy poster depicts the alleged toll of French civilians killed as a result of the spring 1944 Allied bombing of strategic targets.

For two days now no trains have left Milan.

In the South Pacific desperate attacks by the Japanese on Los Negros are beaten off by the US forces.

Next day (**4 March**) the Kremlin announces that the Red Army have advanced to the River Bug in the Ukraine and have trapped a large German force in and around the town of Uman.

On **5 March** Paris radio announces the execution of 26 men convicted of resisting the German and Vichy authorities. The victims include four in Clermont-Ferrand who are described as '..members of a gang which had murdered a militiaman and a gendarme and committed many acts of sabotage.'

In Burma three brigades of Chindits begin their airlift to a position 200 miles behind the Japanese lines at Indaw. Chinese forces in the region advance on the town of Maingkwan.

Next day a daylight raid on Berlin by 658 US aircraft results in the loss of 70 bombers and 11 escort fighters, the largest number shot down in a single day so far in the war. The Americans dropped 2000 tons of bombs in and around the city and claim to have destroyed at least 123 enemy aircraft. The RAF are in action over France with a big raid on the important railway marshalling yards at Trappes, south west of Paris.

On **7 March** *The Times* reports the appointment of three additional High Court judges to help relieve congestion in the divorce courts. One of the new judges is Alfred Thompson Denning KC.

8 March: Japan hits back in Burma with a surprise offensive in the south. *Operation U-Go* is a major attack aimed at the key communications and supply centre at Imphal, in the Indian border state of Assam.

On the home front the Government announces plans for 200,000 new houses per year after the war. Meanwhile miners at pits in Wales and around Durham have gone on strike for higher wages.

On **9 March** the Americans begin air operations out of Momote in the South Pacific Admiralty Islands.

In Belfast a hunger strike by 22 jailed IRA men enters a second week. The men seek recognition that they are political prisoners and should not be made to wear prison clothes. In Dublin, the Eire Government turn down renewed US demands that German and puppet Italian diplomats be expelled. The Americans fear that the Germans are spying on the large numbers of US troops in transit through Northern Ireland as they prepare for the invasion of Europe. However, the Irish will claim they have shut down a powerful radio transmitter inside the German legation.

On **10 March** Convoy RA-57 returns to Loch Ewe in Scotland from Northern Russia. Just one vessel was lost on the way, further proof that the U-Boat threat is greatly diminishing. On the Russian Front, the Soviets say they have captured the German airbase in the Uman pocket, east of the River Bug.

In Hungary, Nazi leader Adolf Eichmann is formulating plans for the deportation of the country's Jewish population.

Berlin: **11 March.** The Germans call for more women to come forward for community service and take over jobs vacated by men called up for military service. In Russia, German Army Group South is in retreat across a 500-mile front. Some 200 Tiger and Panther tanks are abandoned for lack of fuel.

Next day in Algiers the Free French authorities sentence Pierre Pucheu, former Vichy France Minister of the Interior, to death for treason. Members of the Vichy-backed 'African Phalange' are also on trial for treason.

Casualty figures for troops from the British Empire reveal that in four years of war it is the New Zealanders who have suffered the most in relation to their home population. Some 7100 have been

WAR DIARY
March 1944

Lancasters, workhorses of the British Bomber Command. Statistically, in Spring 1944 bomber crews had just a 50% chance of safely completing their tour of 30 operations.

killed, 7300 wounded and 801 are missing. Australian casualties number 16,600 killed, 18,000 wounded and 7000 listed as missing. Aussies known to be POWs number 30,000.

13 March: The UK has acted to isolate Eire following Dublin's refusal to cut Axis ties. Around 250,000 Irish citizens working in the UK are refused permission to go home for fear of intelligence leaks to the Germans. The same measure applies to 164,000 Irish serving in the British armed forces.

On **14 March** three German rocket scientists at Peenemunde on the Baltic coast are put under temporary arrest by the Nazis. The trio includes Werhner von Braun and they are accused of failing to give enough attention to the military applications of new rocket devices dubbed 'V for Vengeance' weapons.

15 March: Reports of German forces gathering on the border of Hungary. Hitler fears Hungarian regent Admiral Horthy will defect to the allies. Tonight 863 RAF bombers target Stuttgart.

16 March: South Pacific: A US task force bombards Manus in the Admiralty Islands as marines prepare to storm ashore.

Next day in the Mediterranean the troopship *Dempo* is torpedoed and sunk by a U-Boat – 498 US soldiers are lost.

In Finland, the future of 100,000 German troops in the country is undecided. Moscow wants them to be interned whilst the Finns insist that their former allies be repatriated to Germany.

Allied aircraft attack industrial targets around Vienna. Britain and the US are undecided how to treat a post-war Austria. Germany had annexed Austria into the Reich via the 1938 *Anschluss;* even the hardline Soviets describe Austria as '...the first country to fall victim to the Nazi aggression.'

On **18 March** the Nazis arrest Admiral Horthy in Salzburg whilst German army units move to occupy key locations in Hungary. This is also the 100th day of Russia's increasingly successful Great Patriotic War against Germany. Artillery salvoes are fired off in Moscow to celebrate new victories. The Russians are nearing the border with Rumania; Dubno, an ancient fortress known to the cossack warriors of Taras Bulba, has been captured.

Next day there are reports of German troops moving into Hungary from the Yugoslavian province of Slovenia despite the fact that Tito's partisans are operating as close as 10 miles from the Austrian border.

20 March: British newspapers fill with stories of the Russian advances all along the Eastern Front. The BBC discuss the proper pronunciation of 'Bug', a river on the Russian – Polish border. The Poles say it as 'Boch' as in 'Loch'; the Russian pronounce it 'Book' whilst most Britons call it 'Bug' to rhyme with 'Rug'.

21 – 22 March: Japanese units cross the border from Burma and enter India, establishing a foothold in Manipur.

In Budapest, the Germans have installed Dome Sjotay as a replacement for deposed Admiral Horthy. Around 50,000 German troops have also moved into Rumania to protect vital oilfields.

23 March: War Office statistics state that more than four tons of bombs fell on Germany during every single minute of the 24 hours ended at noon today. A big RAF raid on Frankfurt leaves 120,000 civilians homeless and claims nearly 1000 lives, according to German sources. Meanwhile, in Athens, trains full of Greek Jewish families are leaving the city bound for Auschwitz in Poland.

24 March: Rome. A partisan bombing of a parade of German SS soldiers is avenged in savage fashion with the execution of 336 civilians – 10 for each soldier killed - in the city's Ardeantine Caves. Many of the victims are Jews.

Maj-Gen Orde Wingate – charismatic leader of the legendary Chindits – dies in a plane crash on the India – Burma border.

In Britain the unrest in the coalfields is settled by a four-year deal guaranteeing jobs and wage levels from now until 1948. Some 60,000 South Yorkshire miners will now return to work.

A bomb explosion at the British CID Headquarters in Haifa, Palestine, last night killed three policemen. Other bombs go off in Jaffa and Jerusalem. Zionist groups demanding a Jewish homeland state are the prime suspects.

25 March: Two Mosquito aircraft of 248 Squadron armed with six-pounder guns sink a U-Boat close to the Bay of Biscay shore of France.

Next day sees 350 US Marauder aircraft drop 600 tons of high explosive on E-Boat bases at Ijmuiden in Holland. Germany's fast motor-torpedo boats pose a threat to the Allied invasion fleet.

Turkey suspends the despatch of goods to Hungary in protest at the German take-over. The Hungarian Prime Minister, Kallay, has taken refuge in the Turkish Legation in Budapest.

27 March: Vichy authorities exhort Frenchmen to enlist in the German SS, to fight against communism. But the SS also play a major role in the genocide directed at the Jews. Today in Kovno, Lithuania, SS men round up all Jewish children under the age of 13.

29 March: The growing problem of refugees in Europe is addressed by a US Congress decision to grant $1350 million to found the United Nations Relief and Rehabilitation Agency.

In the Pacific, US carrier-borne aircraft bomb Japanese ships at anchor in the Palau Islands.

Next night sees 795 RAF bombers in a major raid on Nuremberg. RAF losses are heavy with 95 aircraft lost and 12 making crash landings back in Britain at the end of the 1500-mile round trip.

Meanwhile Arctic Convoy JW-58 has arrived wholly intact in Murmansk, Northern Russia, despite sustained Luftwaffe and submarine attacks. Four U-Boats were sunk and six aircraft shot down by the powerful escort force.

On **31 March** an invasion exercise at Slapton Sands in South Devon ends in chaos. Men of the US VII Corps use live ammunition to give realism but the results are 'unimpressive' to observers.

The Luftwaffe's 'Little Blitz' of the opening months of 1944 has faded away in past weeks; figures released by the War Office show that 279 civilians died and 633 were injured by enemy air action during the month of March.

You forget — but she REMEMBERS

CARELESS TALK COSTS LIVES

APRIL 1944

The Italian Campaign

'Italy is like a boot. You must, like Hannibal, enter it from the top…'

Napoleon's words from nearly a century and a half before would have rung true with any students of history caught up in the Italian Campaign of 1944.

The Allies in April were still stalled in front of the Gustav Line, unable to find a way past the resolute German defenders who held the high ground. Monte Cassino's position at the mouth of the Liri Valley – the route to Rome – was a textbook 'impregnable' natural fortress as taught in Italian military staff colleges for years past.

Winston Churchill posed the question to General Alexander, '..I wish you would explain to me why this passage by Cassino, Monastery Hill etc, all on a front of two or three miles, is the only place which you must keep butting at. About four or five divisions have been worn out going through these jaws… looking at it from afar, it is puzzling. Please explain why no flanking movements can be made.'

Alexander responded patiently, blaming a combination of the country's geography, bad weather and the extraordinary tenacity of the German paratroopers. He might also have pointed to the German containment of the Anzio beach-head, the ambitious 'wildcat' landing far behind the Gustav Line that had become, in Churchill's words, 'a stranded whale'.

German propaganda found innumerable ways to exploit the slow advance of the Allies in Italy. This leaflet points out that by 1 April 1944 their progress towards Rome since the invasion of the Italian mainland on 6 September of the previous year amounted to 0.80 metres a minute. A snail's pace. The geographical shape and topography of the country counted against the Allies.

British troops on the Cassino front firing a captured German 75mm Pak Gun.

Anzio Annie

The men on both sides at Cassino saw the eruption of Mount Vesuvius which had begun towards the end of March. Writing 10 years ago, J A Baynes of Knutsford, Cheshire, a Royal Signals wireless operator attached to an Royal Artillery Field Regiment equipped with 25 Pounders, recalled, '..a distinct memory of the time was the eruption. The huge black clouds of ash belched out by the volcano could be seen from Cassino and earth tremors felt'.

Up at Anzio, constant bombing and shelling were the main hazards in the bridge-head with the railway gun, Anzio Annie, a particularly deadly nuisance. But the mined waters off the Anzio-Nettuno coastline could be just as dangerous as the land. Ships and landing craft were shuttling non-stop backwards and forwards bringing men and supplies and taking off casualties and units going on leave. Some 20,000 Italian refugees were evacuated to Naples.

Minesweeping was an endless task. Lt Commander G H Dormer was in charge of a British minesweeper. His diary for 13 April records: 'We started sweeping again at 0800. A few minutes later ... BANG ... the sweep just ahead of us is blown up. As we alter course sharply to stay in swept water, someone looks over the side amidships ... there is a mine just under the water, about six feet away ... phew! We had to go back again to find it to sink.'

Newsman Colin Wilson filed a beach-head report on 16 April highlighting the exploits of the 18th Light Anti-Aircraft Regiment who had set up a 'world record' by shooting down 31 German planes and 10 more 'probables' during a single week: 'Here these crack Ack-Ack marksmen have to be on the alert 24 hours a day for the chance of a few seconds' snap shooting and into the bargain are watching and waiting under almost continual shellfire.

'They sleep fully dressed, ready to man the guns against night raiders or infiltration by German infantrymen.'

Wild flowers bloom

The weather improved and wild flowers bloomed all around the Anzio beach-head. Honeysuckle, narcissi and cyclamen appeared, swiftly colonising even the most recent shell and bomb craters. Apart from the ever-present sound of artillery, naval gunfire and aircraft overhead, the days saw little front line activity. At night patrols went out to recce enemy positions and hopefully capture an unwary sentry or two.

But the warmer weather brought a new hazard as mosquitoes put in an ever more frequent appearance. Lice had never gone away and were as persistent and unwelcome a guest to the Tommies in Italy as they had been to the British soldiers in the trenches on the Western Front during the Great War.

In the town of Anzio an underground cinema had been constructed, seating 35 people at any one time. Not that the troops anywhere in Italy were particularly impressed with the films on offer. A columnist in the Eighth Army's *Crusader* newspaper of 16 April 1944 complained that the 'newsreels we see out here are so old they're already history. We like to see what's happening in England. Bring our homes a little bit closer to us. That's the greatest service they can provide.

'And why aren't there any cartoons available other than Pop-Eye? Even his staunchest fans are beginning to get tired of seeing him every time they go to a show.'

By now the port of Anzio-Nettuno was said to have become the seventh busiest in the world with up to 8000 tons of supplies landed on a single day. There were setbacks; on 3 April 150,000 gallons of petrol ignited in a spectacular explosion that claimed several lives.

This early spring period seems, with the value of hindsight, to have been one where the Allies were marking time. The destiny of the beach-head was going to be decided by events elsewhere. Senior officers realised this. Indeed, neither General Sir Harold Alexander, Allied forces supremo in Italy, nor Fifth Army commander General Mark Clark, visited the beach-head at any time during the month of April.

Relentless air attack

On Easter Sunday British troops at Anzio had powdered eggs for breakfast. Their enemies fared a little better; German front line soldiers also had eggs but theirs came hard-boiled but at least were fresh.

The Germans knew they had done a good job in containing the invading forces within the confines of the beach-head for so long but

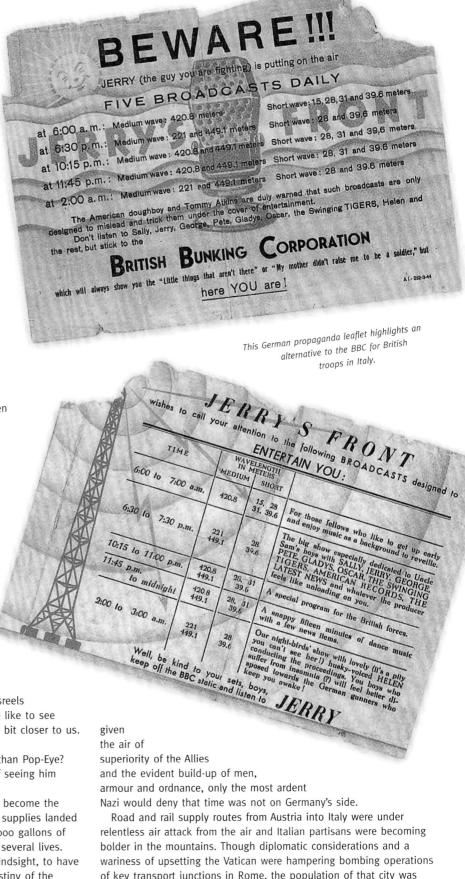

This German propaganda leaflet highlights an alternative to the BBC for British troops in Italy.

given the air of superiority of the Allies and the evident build-up of men, armour and ordnance, only the most ardent Nazi would deny that time was not on Germany's side.

Road and rail supply routes from Austria into Italy were under relentless air attack from the air and Italian partisans were becoming bolder in the mountains. Though diplomatic considerations and a wariness of upsetting the Vatican were hampering bombing operations of key transport junctions in Rome, the population of that city was severely repressed by the Germans and their Italian fascist supporters but could rise up in open revolt at any time.

Down south on the Gustav Line, the Allied commanders had been mesmerised by the heights of Cassino and Liri Valley for many months. Their hammering on this door - behind which lay the road to Rome - had been immensely costly in the lives of soldiers of both sides and the hapless Italian civilian populace. But by the end of April there were signs that the military hinges of the door were weakening. Would one final push at Cassino provide the impetus for an Allied advance here and a break-out at Anzio?

The Eternal City, Rome, is the glittering prize.

Echoes from Anzio

We reproduce below extracts from a letter sent out of the Anzio beach-head early in 1944 by Sergeant Henry Patrick King to his brother Chris who was also serving in Italy.

Mike King's father is in this picture taken by an official Allied photographer visiting the Anzio beach-head. Sergeant Henry Patrick King is the one with the woolly hat, bending over a machine gun. He is binding asbestos tape on the barrel to reduce the effects of heat. The weapon is a .303 medium machine gun weighing about 56lbs and water cooled. The rounds came in boxes of 1000 and the gun could fire 500 rounds per minute but was usually fired in five second bursts. Mike believes that his father was killed within a few hours of the photograph being taken.

Dear Christy

What ho, here I am deep down in the bowels of the earth, doing my best to rattle off a couple of letters. I've just managed to write one home to Joan letting her know I'm OK. We are living like snakes out here, as soon as a Jerry plane comes over there's not a soul to be seen, everyone goes to ground a bit lively.

The lads here are still in action but will be out in a day or so for a rest, so we were lucky not to be sent up the line right away. It may be a week or so before I go up I hope. At present I've got the job of teaching them a few things they have probably forgotten about the gun. Perkins and all the others are OK. He's on guard tonight by the way. You might tell Dick Bellinger and Tom Sanders that I am OK and will do my best to win this ******* war for them. Also tell them that Mr Wallwork has gone like a lot more. Dead. I don't know how he got it.

Captain Weatherhead and Mr Smythe got here today. Weatherhead is here in MGs and Smythe in mortars. Tell Dick Bellinger to give my regards to all the sergeants, hoping to see them all soon. Also give my best to George Turner. All his old crew up here seem to be alright, though I have only seen George Blacknell so far. Jimmy Moy is alright, tell him.

Well, Chris, I think that is about all the news I can give you at present. I'll write home as often as I can, but once I do get into action I don't suppose I shall feel much like writing. Jerry planes came over last night... he doesn't dare show himself during daylight because the sky is alive with Spitfires. Our bombers give him hell during the day too. There are tons of ack-ack guns here so tell the experts that oerlikons are a thing of the past. There's a lot of stuff flying around now, ack-ack and bombs, so it's flat on my belly, safest place.

All the best Chris, don't forget to write home now and again.

Henry

PS. Any of these lads would willingly go back and do an RSM's parade every day. They're sick of it!

Mike King of Lowestoft, Suffolk, writes:

I know all about the Anzio campaign as my father was killed in action there when I was three months old. He knew of my existence but never saw me.

I have a letter my dad wrote from Anzio to his brother Chris who was elsewhere in Italy. Dad was not with the assault troops when they first landed but was transferred there a few days later. His name was Sergeant Henry Patrick King of the Middlesex Regiment. Nine days after writing the letter, he died. A shell burst close to him, knocking him into a ditch and causing wounds that were fatal.

During the Anzio fighting, the whole of the beach-head area was the frontline. Nowhere was safe, not even the field hospital. It was only a few years ago that I found out exactly what happened when I was fortunate to speak to a fellow soldier who was injured in the same mortar blast. My dad was between the shell and his colleague and took the brunt of it.

I learnt that the colleague in question, Frank Ashton, once fired 28,000 machine gun rounds in a single engagement with the enemy. When he ran out of ammo he then engaged the enemy with his rifle! As a result a very important attack was repelled and Frank Ashton was awarded the Military Medal.

My father was killed near The Flyover when he was going (in a bren-gun carrier) to relieve another unit. This was at a time when the Jerries had pushed the Allied forces back beyond the Lateral Road and were lobbing mortar shells over. Apparently there was a German tank situated by The Flyover and nobody dared poke their heads up. What our chaps did was dig holes through the embankment and crawl through so they could 'spot' for the artillery. The Lateral Road was the last line of defence before Anzio itself. Luckily it held!

Ten years ago when we were on holiday in Sorrento, I hired a car and took my wife and youngest daughter to the war cemetery at Anzio, the first (and probably the last) family visit. This was a long drive and was quite an experience in itself. We also drove around Naples; I'm afraid I wouldn't have the nerve for it now!

Left: *Sergeant King never saw his son, Michael.*
Above: *Mike King at his father's last resting place in Anzio.*
Right: *The Flyover pictured after the break-out.*

BAMBINI & BOMBS

The astonishing story of two little girls who left England to escape the war and ended up in the midst of the fierce battles for Monte Cassino.

EYE WITNESS

A British soldier befriends a little girl refugee in Southern Italy 1944.

Escaped prisoners-of-war

During this time our grandfather helped many escaped prisoners of war. As the Germans were getting ready to retreat they evacuated the village starting at the bottom and as we lived at the very top together with two other families we were the last to be moved.

By now it was dark and we were escorted to the bottom of the village and locked in a new stable. In the middle of the night we escaped to a higher mountain and all of us hid in woodland with a small dugout where we could sleep.

The first Allied soldiers to arrive in the village were Moroccans; they were on the front line in the mountains. After some time word reached us that it was safe to go back home. Our house had been hit and left with a big hole in the side so we stayed with friends. Women and children were not allowed out and were never left alone.

Whilst the battle for Cassino was still going on there was bombing all around us. The soldiers evacuated us in the middle of the night down the mountainside to Sant Elia in the valley where open backed lorries were waiting for us. Being inquisitive children, we did wander off to look in nearby empty houses and in one there was a German soldier, tied up. I can still see the image of him even today.

We were then loaded on the lorries and set off over the mountains in the dark to Venafro. Fortunately for us, the flats we should have stayed in were full so we were moved to an old sanitorium in Aversa. There the British soldiers (who were always lovely to the children) gave us two tins of food, one was mixed vegetables, the other sweets and biscuits. We spent the night in tents.

Deserted village, ransacked homes

In the morning after being processed we were put into rail carriages and sent to Reggio Calabria. It was very crowded in the carriages and there were no windows but luckily my grandfather managed to sit near the sliding doors and wedged something in it so we were able to get some light and fresh air.

In Reggio Calabria we were put in a school prior to being moved to surrounding towns. The men checked out the availability of accommodation and work and one night with two other families we left via the windows, leaving the others behind.

We don't recall how and when we went back home, only that it was hot and that we walked from wrecked Cassino to Valvori. The village seemed deserted and homes had been ransacked. We later learned that the flats in Venafro had been bombed, killing our Aunt, Cousin and many villagers.

Seven years in all passed before we got back to England where we found we could no longer speak or even understand English. This is our experience of the Second World War, which is still very vivid in both our minds.

**Mrs Silvia Ferrari and
Mrs Julia DiMascio**

It was an irony of war that the home of these two children in Ottaviano near Naples should have survived the fighting only to be destroyed in the eruption of Mount Vesuvius in the spring of 1944.

In August 1939 with the threat of war with Germany my parents decided it would be better for my sister Julia and myself to leave England and go to Italy to be with our grandparents.

Their home was in Valvori, a village that looks across to Monte Cassino. Life was quiet and we lived a normal country life. Italy entered the war and it became impossible for us to go back to England. As the years went by, the war came closer. We knew the Germans had occupied the mountains around Monte Cassino but it was not until the Allies arrived in the area that the conflict had any impact on us.

Bombing raids became frequent all around and one stray bomb did actually land in the village but did not explode. We used to watch the four engined planes dropping bombs on Cassino. The noise of the aircraft was frightening but the shelling was more dangerous and most of the houses in the town were hit.

Skull and crossbones insignia

On the day the Monastery on Monte Cassino was destroyed (15 February 1944) we all left our houses to watch the repeated bombing and the clouds of dust and debris thrown up. It was after this that the German soldiers came to our village regularly to patrol it and check every house for able-bodied men. They never found any. I remember the German uniforms were black and had skull and crossbones insignia on the collars.

One day we heard they were on their way to the top of the village where we lived. My aunt took me down to the cellar (where we had our beds as it was safer). She painted both our faces with lipstick to look like spots. There was only a small window and it was very dim. The soldiers put their heads round the door but would not come in as they thought we had measles – which was just as well as we were hiding an English Captain under the bed!

After that near miss my grandfather hid the Captain in the mountains on land he owned. They made him a shelter by bending down the branches of a tree.

My sister took food to him daily but never saw him; she often passed German soldiers who believed she was taking food to workers. One day he just left. We later found out that he sent messages back to his headquarters.

DEADLY REHEARSAL

On 28 April 1944 a flotilla of German E-boats surprised a convoy of Allied transports carrying thousands of US troops and their equipment on an invasion exercise off the coast of South Devon. British sailor Derek Wellman was a witness to the tragic aftermath of the incident.

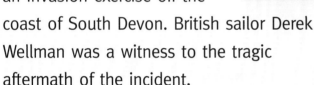

I served for three and a half years aboard *HMS Onslow,* leader of the 17th Destroyer Flotilla, and known to the Home Fleet as 'the VC Ship' after her Captain had been awarded the Victoria Cross for his part in the Battle of the Barents Sea. Almost exactly a year later she took part in the same waters in the sinking of the German battleship *Scharnhorst.*

In April 1944, however, she came south to prepare for D-Day. General Eisenhower was greatly concerned by the fact that most of the million US soldiers on British soil were young men with no previous experience of action. His staff therefore sought to ensure that they participated in the most realistic of exercises beforehand. Many of these took place on a single stretch of coast in Devon known as The South Hams.

On 28 April 1944, *Operation Tiger* – the second of three so-called 'dummy runs' – began. Three LSTs (Landing Ship Tanks) each carrying around 250 men, were escorted by a trawler and a corvette, all the

Royal Navy could spare. Unhappily, on leaving harbour, the corvette was fouled by one of the LSTs. Though it was still seaworthy it was ordered to return to harbour and, as a fact, was not replaced. Nine German E-boats came across from Cherbourg on a routine night patrol and, crossing Lyme Bay, were astonished to find three large targets apparently unprotected from the rear. Like jackals round an elderly prey they circled and fired their torpedoes, hitting all three ships. Two sank quickly leaving a heavy slick of diesel oil. Many men leapt overboard with their lifejackets inflated but were wearing them in the wrong position. They were the first to drown.

HMS Onslow and two of her sister ships were summoned to the spot. I had been on watch below and was only aware that after dashing at full speed we had for some hours been bumping along and then stopping, an unusual experience with E-Boats in the vicinity. After being relieved I needed a wash but found the sliding doors to the bathroom secured by a rope. Suspecting a practical joke by some prankster I forced them open. The sight was unforgettable. On the deck, gleaming like freshly caught mackerel, lay the bodies of a dozen or more American soldiers, all covered by the slime of black fuel oil. Before I slammed the doors closed again I took in the fact that some had limbs missing, presumably from when the torpedoes had struck their ship.

Events took a somewhat bizarre turn. Once the bodies, each wrapped in the US flag, had been taken ashore at Portland, the Captain cleared lower deck and told us we were never to speak of this event, not just for the war's duration, but for the rest of our lives.

The reasons for silence were obvious. One was to prevent panic among those due to land at Utah Beach six weeks later. The other was to conceal what General Bradley called a 'colossal blunder leading to a major tragedy', probably the worst in scale of dead – more than 750 – that ever occurred in sight of our own coast. A secret US naval enquiry was hindered by the fact that the Commodore in charge, Admiral Moon, shot himself just after D-Day and before the enquiry was due to take place.

The next of kin of those who died were not told of their deaths until after D-Day but the inference was that they had met their deaths at that time, not weeks earlier.

With Dieppe, the *Operation Tiger* incident remains one of the greatest blunders of the war in Europe. Some say we learned from these experiences. The evidence is pretty thin. I believe they demonstrate clearly the remorseless pity of war.

Kriegsmarine torpedo boats were called E-boats by the Allies (the 'E' stood for Enemy) and S-bootes by the Germans themselves (the 'S' stood for Schnell – fast). They had two 21 inch torpedo tubes and could carry up to eight mines. They were capable of up to 40 knots and displaced around 100 tons which made them larger than the British Motor Torpedo Boats and Motor Gun Boats (MTBs and MGBs).

ENFORCED EXILE

The civilian population was evacuated from many parts of Britain's coast to make way for the military. South Devon was particularly affected as the Allies prepared for the much anticipated invasion of occupied Europe.

One reason that news of the *Operation Tiger* disaster did not spread was the lack of a civilian population on the stretch of coast closest to the scene of the naval action. The South Hams in South Devon, a 100 square mile area lying between Kingsbridge and Dartmouth, had been completely taken over and sealed off by American forces.

The South Hams is best known for the beach at Slapton Sands (nearby Blackpool Sands too). The location had a similarity to the coastline of Normandy, especially the beach code-named Utah, which made it an ideal training ground for the US forces involved with the invasion.

On 12 November 1943, the bemused residents of the South Hams were informed that the area was to be immediately and totally vacated. They were given just 32 days – until 20 December – to get out. The operation involved six parishes, 180 farms, 750 families and 3000 people. Everything and everyone had to go: the young, the old, the sick, livestock, pets, agricultural machinery, the contents of every single church, shop and home, all household goods, furniture and personal possessions, even crops still in the ground if they could be saved.

Some people, the very sick, had to be carried off on stretchers. One committed suicide rather than leave. A few of the most elderly died within days of the move, victims of the stress and strain.

Six months was set as the period of American occupation, after which the residents would be able to return – once repairs and refurbishment had taken place. In the event, because of the damage and disruption, some of the locals were not able to come back for nearly a year. A few

Above: Ken Small pictured in 2004 beside the Sherman tank he was instrumental in retrieving from the sea. *Below right:* A postcard of the beach at Slapton Sands in the South Hams. *Below left:* The inscription on the memorial presented by the US Army to honour the sacrifices made by the people of South Devon evacuated in late 1943 to make way for the military.

never returned, having made new lives for themselves elsewhere. Decades later, bomb disposal units were still dealing with cases of unexploded mines and shells in the area, left over from the 'friendly invasion'.

A Sherman tank from one of the LSTs involved in *Operation Tiger* has been recovered from under the sea and today is on display at Slapton Sands as a reminder of what happened. It stands just above the beach, not far from an American memorial to the men who died in *Operation Tiger*.

Ken Small was the local resident responsible for the recovery of the tank. He devoted most of his adult life to uncovering the truth behind the tragedy. For many, many years he has kept an almost daily vigil at this site. His autobiographical *The Forgotten Dead*, tells the story of his struggle to discover the facts and provide a fitting memorial to the casualties.

Ken died in the spring of 2004, almost on the 60th anniversary of the tragedy.

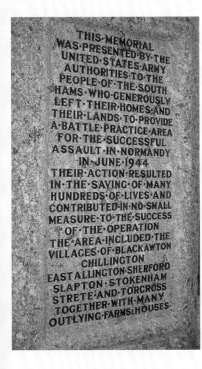

THIS MEMORIAL WAS PRESENTED BY THE UNITED STATES ARMY AUTHORITIES TO THE PEOPLE OF THE SOUTH HAMS WHO GENEROUSLY LEFT THEIR HOMES AND THEIR LANDS TO PROVIDE A BATTLE PRACTICE AREA FOR THE SUCCESSFUL ASSAULT IN NORMANDY IN JUNE 1944 THEIR ACTION RESULTED IN THE SAVING OF MANY HUNDREDS OF LIVES AND CONTRIBUTED IN NO SMALL MEASURE TO THE SUCCESS OF THE OPERATION THE AREA INCLUDED THE VILLAGES OF BLACKAWTON CHILLINGTON EAST ALLINGTON SHERFORD SLAPTON STOKENHAM STRETE AND TORCROSS TOGETHER WITH MANY OUTLYING FARMS HOUSES

Torcross and Slapton Sands

COUNTDOWN TO D-DAY

'Over-paid, over-fed, over-sexed and over here!' This famous description of the American 'friendly invasion' of the British Isles has become a legend in its own right. Yet it is in large part a true reflection of the way it was in spring 1944. There was a degree of resentment that the Yanks seemed to have so many more material benefits than the British had in their own land. Added to this were pay packets that afforded a buying power three times that of their British military counterparts. Coupled with the glamour and attractiveness of being an American in a country where much of the home-grown manpower was itself abroad, at sea or even locked up in POW camps in Europe and the Far East, it was small wonder so many young British women formed relationships. Over 60,000 would become GI brides by the end of the war.

It was not only the girls who took to the Yanks. Their mums and dads found canned fruit, chocolate bars, cigarettes, nylon stockings, scented soap and other prized items coming their way, not to mention chewing gum and candy for the kids. Other compensations included razor blades and the music of Glenn Miller. To help smooth their path, the Americans were educated as to the eccentricities of the British and each serviceman was issued with a booklet to help him avoid any social transgressions that might upset this island race.

One area of surprise came with the black Americans. The US forces were still almost entirely segregated, with Negro troops mainly deployed in non-combat roles, prior to D-Day, at least. Most people in Britain had never seen black soldiers before but accepted the American practice as normal - after all, the British themselves had hundreds of thousands of men from India, Africa and the Caribbean serving in what were for all intents and purposes 'segregated' units with a white officer hierarchy; the famous Gurkhas, for example. But what the majority of the British public found hard to understand was the overt racist attitude displayed by many white Americans against their fellow black countrymen, even when they were outside the confines of the camps.

British and Canadians

The plan drawn up for the invasion of occupied Europe, *Operation Overlord*, entailed approximately 1,500,000 troops being assembled along the south coast of England. *Overlord* divided the Normandy beach-head into two sectors. British and Canadian forces were to land in the eastern sector – beaches code-named *Gold*, *Juno* and *Sword*. American troops would spearhead the invasion to the west on the beaches known as *Utah* and *Omaha*.

Reflecting that east-west Normandy split, Allied troops were assembled along the south coast with the dividing line roughly along the Dorset/Hampshire border. British and Canadian forces were grouped to the east, American troops to the west.

The whole of Dorset had a pre-war population of just 240,000. But the county played host to considerably more than half a million GI's who famously came 'Over Here'. No fewer than 518,000 embarked for France from Weymouth and Portland.

All of the principal Dorset towns as well as many smaller centres of population were involved in preparations for D-Day. For example, Blandford Forum was the site of the US Army 22nd General Hospital which opened for business in April 1944. In Bournemouth, the Ambassador Hotel became the US Officers' Club while the Marsham Court Hotel and the Miramar Hotel were turned into Red Cross Clubs. The Carlton hosted Eisenhower and Montgomery in February 1944 on a visit to observe a practice beach landing in Poole Bay.

Lovely Lulworth was a US tank gunnery practice area while Lyme Regis housed units of the 1st (US) Infantry Division – the famous 'Big Red One' – who had already been bloodied in action against a desperate German counter-attack led by Tiger tanks in the Kasserine Pass, Tunisia, at the end of the North African campaign.

Above: The quiet little village of Burton Bradstock is located on the Dorset coast overlooking Lyme Bay and lies between Bridport and Weymouth, close to Chesil Beach. American Rangers practised beach landings and cliff climbing there. A popular meeting place for GI's and local people at the time was the village pub, The Dove. A photograph from the period shows Americans enjoying a drink with some of the locals. The building is still there but it is no longer a pub.

D-Day landing ships in England.

Portland was the hub of the county's invasion activity. 'The biggest little port in the world', as the US Navy dubbed it, Portland was the major loading point for the majority of GI's involved in the D-Day assault.

On 26 April, the Allied invasion forces were sealed into their various embarkation areas whilst airmen and sailors were confined to their bases or ships. Thousands of security men watched over the Americans in the south and south-west whilst others maintained a vigil around the British and Canadians and other nationalities crowded in their own perimeters further east.

War Baby

Baby Anna entered a world at war on 19 April 1944. As time went by she learnt about how her parents coped on the Home Front in the midst of the momentous events unfolding.

My story begins some years before I was born. Actually it is more the story of my parents, Win and Robert Bunning, an ordinary couple who had met, fallen in love and married during extraordinary times in England.

Win and Bob met through their work at the Northmet Power Company. Win's job was cookery and appliance demonstrating in people's homes. Bob was an electrical engineer. He was blind in one eye, and that, coupled with his job, meant that Dad's war years were spent at home. Home was Harpenden, Hertfordshire, close to de Havilland's airfield and the Vauxhall plant at Luton, both tempting bombing targets. As Harpenden was only 20 or so miles from London it was also a victim of

'London – miss' bombs. Mum says that when they said goodbye each morning they were all too well aware that that was exactly what it might be. Many was the time she had to dive for cover in the nearest ditch.

Their first home was in digs, though they were lucky enough to have their own sitting room. They lived on Win's salary (under £2 a week) and saved Bob's income for a deposit for a house. Bob was on call 24 hours a day and everywhere they went contact phone numbers had to be left in case a power line went down and a crew had to be called out.

Night on the tiles

Mum spent many a night out on the tiles. Quite literally. Both she and Dad were fire watchers on the rooftops of St Albans. Whilst Dad did spend a fair amount of time on the roof (and on account of his one good eye probably needed to look around twice as often as the other fire watchers!) he was more frequently manning the phones and co-ordinating operations. Meals were taken care of by the St Albans food kitchens and very good they were too, according to Mum.

Their first home came about thanks to Danny Howe, a local builder. Houses in Harpenden were in short supply but he heard that two old ladies were fed up with the bombing and moving away. The house was in bad condition and the window frames looked as if they had been devoured by a thousand woodworms where the old ladies had tried to pin up the black-out paper at the windows. From their front doorstep Mum and Dad watched the sky turn red as London burnt and, much later, the sky turn black when gliders filled with troops were towed towards the Channel and France.

Born after bombing raid

My own arrival on the scene was two to three weeks sooner than predicted. There had been a bombing raid on de Havillands and the leap out of bed resulted in my early birth at the Red House Hospital in Harpenden, Herts. Conditions were good there, much better than in London hospitals.

Like all other babies of those days I had my own special cardboard box in case of gassing. Mum never had to put me in it, but much of my first few months were spent under a table or in the tiny understairs cupboard crammed in with Mum and Gran. They dreaded most of all the silent V-weapons, first praying that the flying bombs would continue on their deadly journey and then praying for those further down their paths. We had an Italian POW to help with the garden who evidently did all he could to spoil me. With my black hair I reminded him of his own tiny daughter back home.

My own memories begin when I was three. I can remember being pushed to the shops, children playing in the nearby playground and the treat of a banana, but by then we were at peace.

Out of curiosity Anna Hyman has looked up one or two happenings that occurred on the day of her birth. The Times of 19 April 1944 reported that a horse called Happy Landing was just beaten by Borealis at Newmarket. A four-bedroom house near Guildford was on the market for £3500. It was estimated that UK householders kept 12 million hens and 'pig clubs' had been formed where individuals bought shares in a beast and saved scraps to help feed and fatten it up. In 1939 two-thirds of the food consumed in Britain came from overseas but by 1944 only one-third was imported. All available land was turned over to food production or livestock grazing. The Royal Family's Great Park at Windsor was turned into the largest wheat field in the country. By 1944 there were over 1,400,000 allotments, growing an estimated one million tons of vegetables. In the same year the Women's Land Army numbered 80,000. 'Dig for Victory' was the Home Front battle cry and potatoes and onions were said to be munitions of war as surely as bombs and bullets.

DIG FOR VICTORY

PRINTED FOR H.M STATIONERY OFFICE BY H MANLY & SON LTD. 51-9421.   ADAPTED FROM THE PRIZE-WINNING DESIGN BY MARY TUNBRIDGE.   37

Whale meat again!

I was 17 in 1944, ready to leave school and begin a catering course at the College of Domestic Science in Sheffield. The city suffered many air raids because of the steelworks and I often watched the factories burning in the distance after a raid before scouring the garden for scraps of shrapnel to take to school for the daily competition to see who had the largest piece.

As a child, the war had an indirect effect on me naturally, but mostly I hated having to carry my gasmask everywhere, the dreary blackout and dearth of sweets. Food rationing was strict, but enough, with imagination, for survival. Indeed, we now know that we were much healthier on the wartime diet than with the present-day surfeit of sugar and fat.

Cholesterol? Unheard of! But, as a child, health was not my first priority – I missed my chocolates and sweets!

Posters demanded 'Dig for Victory', so we buckled to after school and dug, sowed and planted, replacing garden flowers with regimented rows of vegetables. Chickens ruled the roost in the yard and I enjoyed collecting the eggs to supplement our one-per-week ration.

We registered our ration books with a grocer and collected the same rations each week, so shopping offered little interest or challenge. Every Saturday I took our meat coupons to the same butcher who then handed me whatever meat he had that week. My Aunt did the cooking and my sister and I

ate what was put before us. On one occasion I was told we'd just eaten whale meat!

Lord Woolton broadcast regular tips and recipes on the radio – one of his most famous was for 'Woolton Pie', a concoction of potatoes, carrots, cauliflower and swedes, topped with either pastry or mashed potatoes and a sprinkling of cheese. Rabbit – unrationed – became a favourite. Spam was delicious in fritters.

Vegetables were fairly plentiful as were carrots. Sweet carrot cake, carrot fudge and even carrot drink became firm favourites. The sweet ration was 12 oz (350 gms) per month, but occasionally the lady in the shop gave me a few extra crumbs of chocolate from the bottom of the jar. We may have had a far less varied diet than nowadays, but I do not remember ever being hungry.

Teenage ingenuity

As a teenager, I wanted to look smart, and this, in a way, was more difficult. By 1944, we were allowed 20 clothing coupons a year, so, as a skirt cost six and a dress eight, I knew I would have to make my own clothes, probably out of old ones, if I wanted a change or grew out of something. Luckily, I always enjoyed sewing and women's magazines were full of helpful hints on 'Make Do and Mend'. With my Aunt's old Singer sewing machine, I tackled old curtains, bedspreads, sheets and even a blanket once to produce some different and surprising outfits. I scrounged any old woollens I could, unravelled them and re-knitted 'new' socks and jumpers. On one occasion I remember getting a length of parachute silk, a rare treasure indeed. I happily listened to the radio whilst sewing industriously away.

Stockings cost coupons, so we girls painted our legs with tea or gravy browning sometimes getting a friend to draw the 'seam' down the back with a dark pencil.

Once at college, we learned at first hand how our mothers had coped with the difficulties of keeping families healthily fed and clothed. As children we had, of course, taken everything for granted. I still have the recipe book that was our Bible from all those years ago, with a complete 'Supplement of Economical Recipes'. It was well used and is splashed with drops of this and that as we assiduously learnt how to create masterpieces from very little.

Recipes featured dried egg, Marmite (which gave both flavour and colour to otherwise insipid looking dishes), dripping (delicious on hot toast) instead of butter; oatmeal for thickening; and so much more. Saving fuel we learnt an intriguing one-pot cooking method where vegetables boiled and meat and pudding steamed using just one pan.

Our tutors emphasised economy above all else, proving an excellent training for the future – meanwhile, most importantly, we survived and we thrived.

Audrey French

The delightful poster above was adapted from a prize-winning design by the artist Mary Tunbridge. (National Archives).

Patten of Life!

The wartime dietary work of Marguerite Patten OBE had a major impact on keeping the nation well fed and healthy. Anna Hyman met this remarkable lady to talk about food and trends in the kitchen over the last seven decades.

The words 'formidable', 'indomitable', 'feisty' come to mind when describing Marguerite Patten. She is also 'kind', 'courageous', 'entertaining' and a talented cook, very firmly rejecting the title celebrity chef. 'I am not a celebrity chef', she tells us. 'I am a home economist, a cook'. She may not be a celebrity chef, but for anybody interested in food and cooking Marguerite Patten is certainly a celebrity cook.

Born in November 1915 Marguerite Brown started cooking when she was 13 following her father's death in 1928 and her mother's return to teaching. As the eldest daughter it fell to her to help her mother in the kitchen. She obviously enjoyed it as when she left school she trained as a home economist before joining the Eastern Electricity Board. But she had another interest besides cooking – acting – and for a season took to the boards in repertory. The season ended, and Marguerite, in need of an income, joined Frigidaire promoting the benefits of refrigerators.

The War Years

World War II and the skills she had learnt when acting were to change her life. Rationing had been imposed on Britain in 1940 and in 1942 Marguerite, instead of joining the RAF, was hired by the Ministry of Food to help people eat healthily and make the most of the limited choice of food available. In 1943 Marguerite Brown married 'Bob' Patten and after the birth of their daughter was appointed by the Ministry to run their food advice bureau located in Harrods giving advice and regular cookery demonstrations.

'Were we really more healthy in the war years?' I wanted to know. After all with the restricted diet there was not the 'five-a-day' opportunity that we have today. Yes, she thought, we were. We ate less meat and fat and more importantly the fruit and vegetables, thanks partly to people turning

Marguerite Patten OBE receiving a Lifetime Achievement recognition from Angela Rippon at the Good Food Awards 1998. Marguerite was still going strong in 2010 making regular public appearances.

their gardens over to growing food, were much fresher and therefore full of essential minerals and nutrients. The problem with the diet was its dreariness and part of Marguerite's work involved how to make the ingredients in plentiful supply more

GROW FOOD
IN YOUR GARDEN
OR GET AN ALLOTMENT

The illustration above is original 1944 poster artwork by Le Bon featuring a box of winter vegetables (National Archives – Art of War).

interesting and go further.

They were dreadful years of fear and uncertainty for everybody. Marguerite made every effort to get back home to her mother and baby daughter in north London each evening (her husband Bob was away flying Lancasters with the RAF). But the war, she said, brought people together; there was a strong sense of community and pulling together, sadly missing today.

Peacetime

The end of the war had not mean the end of rationing and Marguerite recalled those extra years of hardship and then the joy when, overnight in 1954, the butchers' shops were full and there was a choice for housewives.

In spite of the continuation of rationing the Ministry of Food closed their advisory bureau in 1947. However, this was taken over by Harrods as their own Home Service Bureau with Marguerite in charge of both the cooking and household appliances demonstration kitchens. She was to remain at Harrods until 1951 when she left to become a freelance presenter and cookery writer.

It was in 1947 that Marguerite Patten wrote the first of the 170 cookery books that she has produced. This was also the year that Marguerite made her television debut on a programme called *Designed for Women* – making her one of the first TV cooks in Britain. She remained with the programme until it ended in the early 1960s.

The thought of those early days in television led her to today's TV celebrity chefs and Jamie Oliver in particular. She admires his efforts to introduce more healthy school dinners for children. And, what a shame, she continued, that home economics is no longer taught at schools.

She has not stopped working, though sadly, she has now been slowed down badly by the crippling arthritis that she held at bay by diet for over 13 years. (*Eat to Beat Arthritis*, Marguerite Patten and Dr Jeannette Ewin.) Marguerite still acts as a adviser to various bodies, appears on radio and television, writes books, gives cookery demonstrations and tests recipes – though she confesses, with considerable annoyance, that these days somebody else has to stand and cook whilst she sits and does the commentary.

Over tea I asked her what was her favourite meal. It all depended, she said, on the season and time of day. But, added the indomitable Mrs Patten, what she really loved and often craved was a perfect, ripe tomato!

SURPRISE ATTACK FROM THE AIR

A British Hurricane fighter attacks a Japanese troop convoy in Burma in this painting by Roy Nockolds. The date of the work is unknown but it reflects the fact that air superiority was a key element in ensuring an Allied victory in the Far East (National Archives - The Art of War).

Forgotten Front?

British troops check out their location in the Burmese jungle. The key to Allied success in 1944 was air supremacy that enabled Dakota aircraft to transport enough supplies and ammunition to keep isolated and surrounded garrisons or advancing troops well fed and able to fight on.

In the early months of 1944, news from Burma was constant but rarely prominent.

A war was being waged in the jungles, mountains and plains of Burma and Assam but it was of a nature perhaps too alien and too far away to really hold the interest of most folks on the Home Front. Unless, of course, they knew of someone serving there or who had, perhaps, been made a prisoner of war of the Japanese in the opening period of the war.

British civilians still faced the occasional air raid but what the war meant to most was the sight of the vast military build-up of men and equipment in preparation for the Allied invasion of mainland Europe. The British Fourteenth Army on the Burmese – Indian border under its commander, General William Slim, even at the time considered themselves 'forgotten', a feeling which still persists amongst surviving veterans nearly 70 years later.

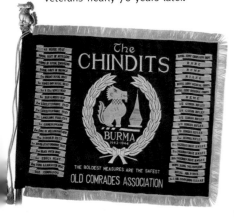

The colours of the Old Comrades Association of the famous Chindits who fought in Burma 1942 - 1944. The name 'Chindits' was derived from 'Chinthe', a mythical dragon that guards Burmese temples and which is depicted in the centre of the colours.

British, American and Chinese actions in south and north Burma in the opening months of 1944 met with considerable success. In what was called the Second Arakan Campaign, the Fourteenth Army had relieved the Seventh Indian Division and gone on to all but annihilate the Japanese forces who had encircled them. A slow advance on Akyab on Burma's Bay of Bengal coast was resumed.

Then in late February, the first American ground combat unit arrived with General 'Vinegar Joe' Stilwell in the north of Burma. This was an infantry regiment destined to go down in history as Merrill's Marauders, from the name of its commander, Frank D Merrill. His 3000 men were to be used in an encircling role, whilst their Chinese allies battered the Japanese in frontal assaults.

During March and into April the strategy worked well. Japanese General Sinichi Tanaka was forced into a series of rapid withdrawals. The American and Chinese efforts were sustained by air by US transports flying from bases in north eastern India.

Then, unexpectedly, both Stilwell's forces in the north and the Fourteenth Army in south and central Burma, found their own sources of supply – and indeed their own existence – under threat when a 100,000-strong Japanese army crossed the Chindwin River on an 80-mile front in central Burma. The Japanese goal was nothing less than the invasion of India where they hoped to find a population ready to rise up against their British rulers.

The speed of the advance surprised the British. They retreated in some disorder into the Indian state of Assam. By early April resistance was centred around Imphal – where three divisions of the British IV Corps were surrounded – and Kohima.

Up till then an unimportant little hill town, Kohima became a key position in the defence of India. Its capture would open the way to Dimapour and the cutting of the Assam railway, supply lifeline for the Allies on the Burma front. On 5 April 1944 the Japanese besieged Kohima and a bloody, close quarter, battle ensued.

In the course of April, the fight swung this way and that. Allied air power hit the Japanese supply lines and the enemy commander, over-confident of being able to capture supplies, realised he did not have sufficient material to sustain his assault. On 20 April Kohima was relieved.

But the Japanese didn't retreat. Instead it was now the turn of the British to try and dislodge their enemy from strong positions on the surrounding hilltops.

The Burma - India frontier, scene of a major Japanese offensive in March - April 1944. Kohima (not shown) is about 70 miles north of Imphal.

Men of the three-inch mortar platoon of 1st Battalion The Gambia Regiment pictured at Karvetnagar in Madras province, India, at the end of the war. They had just been provided with new uniforms and kit. Despite some of the men being away from home for more than five years, they faced a long wait for ships to take them back to West Africa.

WEST AFRICANS GO EAST

In 1944, Dr Ian Morris was a soldier fighting the Japanese on the India-Burma border. This is the story of his unit, the 81st (West African) Division.

Winston Churchill decided that West Africans should be used in the war against Japan and expressed the wish that they 'make a name for themselves'. Thus began the difficult logistical task of bringing men from Gambia, Sierra Leone, Gold Coast and Nigeria to a holding area around Ibadan in Nigeria via poor roads and one railway line, before shipping them out of Lagos and on to Bombay.

At Capetown the Africans learned that not everyone saw them as potential heroes as they stretched their legs in short marches around the town. The gibe of 'White Officers with Black Privates' was heard.

From Bombay they were taken by road and rail to camps at Nasik, a Holy City that's less famous than its neighbour Doolali, the town associated from the days of Kipling with 'Doolali tap' or mental illness. There was some perfunctory training and then a journey for five days by rail to Calcutta. At the many stops bedraggled Indian men, women and children walked along the track begging. The Africans concluded that Indians were a lesser race than they were. Bengal was in the grip of a severe famine and the Australian Governor, R G Casey, used the services of pagan Africans to collect the dead bodies in trucks and transport them to the lime pits at DumDum.

The journey continued by ship to Chittagong then to railheads, road ends and on foot in the Arakan until the 81st (WA) Division could head east for the Pi Chaung and Kaladan Valley protecting the eastern flank of those in 15 Corps who had the objective of capturing Akyab. It was the first Empire Division to make contact with the Japanese. Elements of it were seen by General Christison of 15 Corps and General William Slim, later of Fourteenth Army. Christison

considered them to be ill-disciplined carriers and Slim stated that the ratio of whites to Africans was too high at 72 to 1200, thus preventing African NCOs from taking initiatives. An Indian division had a higher ratio. Just as the Africans drew conclusions about Indians from an unrepresentative sample so Christison and Slim did the same with the Africans.

Harsh country

Enter Orde Wingate. He wished to have European and Gurkha troops but not Indian soldiers with his Chindits. The shortfall had to be made up with Africans and 3 Brigade from 81st Division was given to Wingate. Although it was the most experienced formation of the division with troops well able to live and move in harsh country, Wingate deployed the men as garrison troops. Wingate had charisma in spades and an unshakeable belief that he was always right. The troops under him were favoured in obtaining supplies and dedicated aircraft. They were brave men who in dark days gave people at home something to be proud of. However, Wingate was a master of PR; in time the historian revisionist will catch up with him.

The badge of the 81st (West African) Division features a spider. It was worn face down on the sleeve so that when the soldier holds a rifle to his shoulder the spider is facing the enemy. The spider is not a tarantula but represents Ananse who in Ashanti mythology can change into many guises to perform impossible feats, relying on guile rather than brute force.

Back in the Kaladan the truncated 81st Division fought their way south. They were totally dependent on supplies from the air for much longer than the Chindits. There were no battles greater than company strength but it was endless patrols and skirmishes that wore everyone down. At Kyaukta/Pagoda Hill the 1st Gambia Battalion and the East African Scouts were driven back. The division retreated to Frontier Hill, the boundary of India and Burma – a distance of about 66 crow/fly miles and 200 PBI (Poor Bloody Infantry) miles. Here a battalion of 81st Division, the 7/16 Punjabis and a State Force battalion of Tripura Rifles provided determined opposition until the Monsoon ended all movements. In fact, the entry of Japanese forces into India mattered psychologically but not at all tactically.

The respite ended when 81st Division fought its way south again eventually occupying Myohaung, which had been an objective of the first campaign. It was relieved by the 82nd (WA) Division.

Pack bullocks

Maj Gen C S Woolner, the 81st Divisional commander, had been a contemporary of Christison as young officers. He was an engineer, Christison a cavalryman. Only the engineer could have found a way into the Kaladan over hostile terrain. The cavalryman was asked for a company of medium machine gunners by the engineer; it was turned down for lack of space and 74 pack bullocks were provided instead! Now it is a court martial offence to kill a pack animal while on active service. Sadly all of them broke legs early on and the Africans being compassionate put them out of their misery. The fresh meat was welcome.

1944 was a grim year. Fast forward to 1984. I visited the Imperial War Museum. There was one postcard representing the contribution of Africans in Burma, wrongly captioned. Of the two books formally commissioned to cover the war in Burma, one, approved by Christison, was scathing about Woolner and the 81st Division. The other with about 700 pages managed a mainly inaccurate single paragraph on Africans. I attended our Divisional Reunion lunch and suggested that we should put the record straight. The result was the book *War Bush* by John Hamilton, published by Michael Russell in 2001. It took 14 years of effort. Three of us financed it and after some three years were fully reimbursed. Descendants of Slim and Woolner have copies of the book and it graces the UN library in New York. All the West African states bought copies.

If numbers matter there were 300,000 Indian, 98,000 European, 36,000 Gurkha and 82,000 African troops in Burma. Oh, by the way, survivors of the Japanese 28th Army, formed in 1944 to defend the Arakan and the Irrawaddy delta, said that Africans were the best jungle fighters the Allies had.

Ian Morris pictured in 1995 following a parade at Edinburgh Castle marking the 50th anniversary of the end of World War II. He had served as a mortar officer and later as a patrol leader. He says, 'Our job in the second Burma campaign was to maintain contact with the Japanese which made us a sort of permanent recce force. I was a lieutenant for most of the campaigns, then captain and for a short time before demob, a major. It was said to help with the final pay-off! In best Raj tradition Europeans were considered to be attached to West African forces. In the main cemetery in Rangoon all casualties are listed with their original British units. I fear racism has long roots.'

DAKOTA LIFELINE

The official history of the Royal Air Force* contains the following account of the exploits of the 81st (West African) Division in the Kaladan at the beginning of 1944. Lt Gen Sir Philip Christison's XV Corps was pressing over the Nyakyedauk Pass (called the 'Okey Doke' by the British) and to guard against any Japanese outflanking move he ordered the West Africans forward to the distant Kaladan Valley beyond the next range of hills.

'In the early stages of its march the 81st was supplied by a jeep track 73 miles long. After this, however, the Dakotas of Troop Carrier Command were to be entirely responsible for bringing the formation all it needed.

'The jungle in the Kaladan is the thickest in Burma and the flight over the hills was notable for its turbulence and the presence of the dreaded cumulo-nimbus cloud formations. Aircraft usually needed to go round about eight times to push out the entire load of supplies and the gorges made it difficult. Pilots had to get low down for the dropping and then if there was a hill in front of them it meant pretty well tearing the guts out of the engines to climb over it.

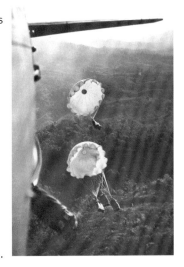

'The West Africans and the RAF were soon on terms of mutual friendship and, indeed, affection. On occasions when it was possible for a Dakota to land on a hastily devised air strip, the West Africans would flock around the aircrew with the liveliest expressions of regard.

'Admin Box' siege

'When landing was impossible and the supplies were dropped by parachute, they took the greatest care of what they received. One of them, indeed, in his zeal went so far as to try to catch one of the hundredweight bags of rice as it descended, for he had noted with regret that since these were dropped 'free', many of them burst and scattered their contents far and wide. Unfortunately, he was successful, and at once became one of the more severely injured passengers in the Dakotas detailed to fly out the sick and wounded. 'Thrice daily did the Dakotas of No 62 Squadron bring in supplies. Fortunately, the Spitfire squadrons kept any Japanese fighters well away; without the air supply the West Africans would have had to surrender within a week.

'In February a final Japanese attack of the war in the Arakan region of Burma led to our forces being besieged in what became known as the 'Admin Box' at Sinzweya, where the HQ of the administrative troops of the Seventh Indian Division was situated. The 81st (WA) Division participated in this battle and achieved success with the capture of Kyaukkwaw and Apaukwa, although a Japanese counter-attack later drove them out.

'By the beginning of April 1944 the Arakan battle was over and the Allies were the victors, having vanquished more than 5000 of the best troops the Japanese had in Burma.'

Volume III – The Fight is Won by Hilary St George Saunders, published in 1954 by HMSO.

KILLED IN ACTION

Sgt Mervyn Hicks wrote a number of letters to his sister Doris while serving as an Air Gunner with a Canadian Squadron in RAF Bomber Command. Peter Champion has compiled the following extracts.

In January 1944 he writes: 'Many thanks for your letter and good wishes for 1944. Yes dear I had a nice Christmas and it was good to be home for three weeks, but my how the time flew. I took the family to Wales for a week... I intended coming down to Brighton to see you but alas the RAF had other plans for us...'

In a reference to Doris taking on another evacuee, he says: 'You certainly keep yourself busy, fancy you taking on another boy. It is kind of you but I feel there were others who should be doing this. However, as you say, there are many heartless people about.'

In another letter he writes: 'Well dear on Saturday morning my name went down for Op's, gave my old tummy a turn but glad to say the flak was not too hot and all turned out OK. However, the next morning I had a shock to see my name down again and for a bigger one when we knew we were off to Essen, one of the most defended targets in Germany. Glad to say when take off came along I felt quite cool, but on the way out thought of all you dear ones and just wondered if I would see you all again. Glad to say we had cloud cover and got back safe and sound. On returning to base had an issue of rum and coffee followed by eggs and bacon, we certainly needed it. Got to bed at 4am but did not get up until 11.30 the next morning.

'The take-off was most impressive and everybody turned out to bid us bon voyage and thumbs up. I felt quite cheered. My old tummy was not too good but I did not tell the skipper as I hope to beat it and see this job through to the bitter end..

'It was an experience and sight not be forgotten in a hurry. One reads of these raids in the paper but one needs to be there to know the real thing.'

Sgt Hicks ended the last letter with a plea not to let any of this news get to '...Vic's paper or I should get into trouble'.

A snippet from another other letter reads: 'Please give Peter 3/6 out of the enclosed 10/-.

Hope you can both get a little something with it. I'm afraid it is not much but now your brother is a poorly paid air gunner.'

In one letter there is a reference to the tummy problems he suffered from: 'I have been in hospital with my tummy. They would not ground me but said I could ground myself but should get LMF (Lack of Moral Fibre). So I refused and shall try and go flying with my crew.'

In a letter from the spring of 1944, he writes of a visit to the cinema: 'This week I saw Anna Neagle in "Yellow Canary", a very good Picture.' In the same letter he confides, '..Have been on six trips now, the one yesterday, we went to Paris. It was the roughest journey we have had so far and once or twice I wondered if I should ever place my feet on ground again and was damn pleased to get back to my coffee and rum. We got back at 5am this morning and am feeling very tired. Guess you heard us return as we passed over Brighton. I thought of you below and wished I could have been with you instead of flying above.

'We then saw the London raid from above; it was hot with plenty of flak coming up... I suppose it will be as bad when we get detailed for Berlin. I have got over my attack of nerves but the old tummy turns over when I see the old name goes down for Op's.

'Well darling guess this is about all my news. Let me know if you can get to London when I get my leave. Tons of love, Mervyn.'

Earlier in this last letter the airman remarks that he has not had leave since he came to the Squadron and that leave he was due to start on 20 April had been cancelled.

Sgt Mervyn J Hicks was killed in action on 25 April 1944 when his bomber encountered severe weather and heavy icing over Karlsruhe. With the aircraft out of control, the captain ordered the crew to bale out but for some unknown reason Mervyn and another member of the crew failed to do so.

Doris was Peter Champion's mum. Peter's father was Victor Champion who worked on the Brighton Evening Argus *newspaper throughout the war. Peter remembers him as having to do everything from reporting on the war through to being the sports correspondent writing under the pen name 'Crusader'. Victor and Doris both died within a month of each other in 1977.*

WAR DIARY

April 1944

April 1944 begins with the British authorities declaring a 10-mile deep strip of land from Land's End to The Wash closed to the public as a security precaution in preparation for the invasion of Northern Europe.

On **1 April** a navigational error sees 26 US aircraft drop their bombs on Schaffhausen in neutral Switzerland. First reports indicate 35 dead.

The British Red Cross are now sending 97,000 parcels each week to British prisoners of war. There are seven different kinds of parcel and 41 varieties of food which can be included in them.

Next day near Ascq in Belgium, Resistance fighters derail a German troop transport train carrying men of the 12th SS Panzer Division Hitler Jugend. In reprisal the SS murder 86 civilians.

SIGNAL · NUMMER 16 · 1944

BILDTIDNINGEN
Signal

Signal was a military magazine produced by the Germans in many different languages (including English). It gave the Nazi slant on the progress of the war. This is the cover of a mid-1944 edition and shows German troops on the Eastern Front.

In the Ukraine, the Russians have surrounded 40,000 Germans in and around the town of Skala. To the south, the Red Army crosses the River Prut and enters Rumania.

US aircraft bomb a ball-bearing factory at Steyr, 90 miles from Vienna in Austria, sparking a major air battle. Over 300 Luftwaffe planes attack the bomber formations; there are reports of the enemy dropping their own bombs from above the US aircraft in the hope of knocking them out of the sky. Long-range Lightning and Thunderbolt fighters shoot down at least 100 enemy aircraft.

Soviet Foreign Minister Molotov demands £150,000,000 in war reparations from Finland. The Russians do not ask for Finnish labour to carry out reconstruction work in the USSR, as Helsinki feared, but are insisting that the 1940 border imposed by Moscow at the end of the 'Winter War' be re-established. In that conflict the Finns had invented a simple explosive device that proved effective against Russian armoured vehicles; bottles filled with petrol and capped by a flammable rag were dubbed 'Molotov Cocktails'.

> **The British Red Cross are now sending 97,000 parcels each week to British prisoners of war. There are seven different kinds of parcel and 41 varieties of food which may be in them.**

3 April – Naples. Against a clear blue sky the snow-capped peak of Mount Vesuvius continues to erupt in spectacular fashion.

Royal Navy Barracuda bombers from the carriers *HMS Victorious* and *HMS Furious* strike at Germany's only remaining battleship, *Tirpitz*, at Altenfjord, Norway. The vessel is damaged but not sunk.

Next day an RAF reconnaissance flight takes the first photographs of a large camp in Poland. It is identified as Auschwitz.

From Egypt come reports of a mutiny in the Greek Army Brigade. There is a crisis brewing within the free Greek forces as communists and royalists stake their claims for power in post-war Greece.

Algiers: The Head of the Committee of National Liberation, General de Gaulle, takes full control of all Free French armed forces.

In Burma around 12,000 Japanese soldiers are reported to be closing in on a mixed British – Indian force of just 1500 at Kohima.

5 April: In Britain, all military leave has been cancelled and postal and telephone services now operate under strict supervision. Even so, there are security scares. In one incident a packet sent from London to Chicago bursts open in transit to reveal secret invasion plans. An American officer had posted them to his sister by mistake. In another instance, US General George Patton is given a stern dressing-down over his loose talk of the invasion that was overheard at a party.

6 April: The UK sees the introduction of a new personal taxation system. Tax will be easier to collect and harder to dodge with the pay-as-you-earn (PAYE) system. Newspapers also report that a wartime research and development programme has led to a useful invention for the home; wallpaper which can be washed clean with soap and water thanks to a thin film of transparent plastic coating. The new product will not be available until after the war.

Up to 10% of the Allied troops in embattled Anzio are allowed leave at any one time. Four-day R&R (rest and recreation) breaks usually centre on Naples where there are ample quantities of wine, women and song. The Neapolitans much prefer their Allied customers to the Germans who occupied the city last year.

On the night of **8 April** the Volkswagen plant at Fallersleben near Hanover is bombed. Source of Hitler's famous 'Peoples Car' (better known as the Beetle), the VW factory's priority has been the manufacture of vehicles for the military.

In Moscow, Molotov announces that the USSR has no territorial designs on Rumania or the country's existing social order. They simply require the restoration of the 1940 border. A 324-gun salute in the city celebrates the First Ukrainian Front army's recent advances to the Rumanian and Czech borders. In the Crimea, only evacuation across the Black Sea can save the trapped German forces.

9 April: The Vichy authorities ban dancing in public in France. The measure is the latest in a series that keeps large groups of civilians from assembling and becoming 'politically irresponsible'.

10 April: Royal Navy midget submarines – X-Craft – are in action in Bergen harbour, Norway. X-24, commanded by Lt M H Shean, evaded German defences and placed explosives beneath the 7500 ton merchantman, *Barenfels*. X-24 escaped undetected, leaving the Germans suspecting the sinking to be the work of land-based saboteurs.

WAR DIARY
April 1944

Next day sees a daring but highly successful low-level precision bombing attack by RAF Mosquito aircraft of 613 Squadron on a building close to the Peace Palace in The Hague. The five-storey Kleizkamp Art Gallery holds detailed records relating to Dutch citizens. These records are invaluable to the Gestapo.

12 April: King Victor Emmanuel says he will give up the throne of Italy when the Allies enter Rome. This seems a distant prospect with the Allies still contained within the Anzio beach-head and unable to break through at Cassino.

On **13 April** Britain and America issue a joint demand that Sweden halt the export of ball-bearings to Germany. On the other side of the world in New Guinea, Australian troops have pushed the Japanese out of the town of Bogodjim.

Russian General Nikolai Vatutin dies today **(14 April)** in a Kiev hospital from wounds sustained in February when he was ambushed by a band of anti-Soviet Ukrainian nationalists.

A terrible accident in Bombay leaves 740 people dead when the ammunition freighter *Fort Stikine* explodes. The blast severely damages 27 other vessels and destroys 40,000 tons of food.

15 April: Flying from Foggia in the south of Italy, 448 US Flying Fortresses and Liberators escorted by 150 long-range Mustang fighters, bomb the Ploesti oilfields in Rumania. It's Germany's only substantial source of oil and is also threatened by the advancing Red Army who are only 140 miles away. RAF Wellingtons joined in to bomb key rail targets in the country.

16 April: Yalta in the Crimea recaptured. Sevastopol is now the only major port from the Germans can evacuate their trapped forces. The city's airport is already in Soviet hands and fighting ranges over the old battlefield of Balaclava where the famous Charge of the Light Brigade took place nearly a century earlier.

Next day liberated Italy finds itself without a government as Marshal Badoglio in Naples announces the resignation of his entire cabinet. He is asked to form a new government that must include communist leader Palmiro Togliatti.

The Japanese launch *Operation Ichi-Go* in China with the aim of crushing the forces of Generalissimo Chiang Kai-shek between the Yellow and Yangtze rivers and neutralising US air bases in Honan and Kwangsi provinces. The Japanese also want to open an overland supply route to their Southern Army in Thailand and Malaya. Following a personal request from President Roosevelt, Chiang Kai-shek has ordered Chinese troops to enter Burma in support of the hard-pressed Allies; now he finds his own country under renewed savage attack.

In London, the privileges of diplomats are restricted. All foreign embassies are put under surveillance in the run-up to the invasion. The only protest comes, ironically, from representatives of the Free French. Tomorrow, a new Defence Regulation - supported by the TUC - confers drastic powers for dealing with persons responsible for inciting strikes or lock-outs which interfere with essential services.

18 April: The Swiss give refuge to Giuseppe Bastianini, former Italian ambassador in pre-war London and Warsaw. The diplomat has been sentenced to death in absentia by a fascist tribunal in Verona for his role in the overthrow of Mussolini last year.

19 April: Allied raids on key transport links in France are incessant; in the last 36 hours over 7000 tons of bombs have been delivered. Unfortunately, French civilian casualties are mounting. Overnight 14 Allied aircraft were lost.

In a joint Anglo-American operation, planes from the carriers *HMS Illustrious* and *USS Saratoga* combine to bomb the important harbour of Sabang on the island of Sumatra.

On **20 April** the discovery of a set of orders on a dead Japanese NCO alerts the British to plans for enveloping the Imphal area of Assam. General Slim is able to put pressure on the Japanese who have almost encircled the hilltown of Kohima. The enemy intention to secretly divert part of their force for a march on Imphal is

abandoned. Slim's 'Forgotten Fourteenth' Army includes West African troops from the Gambia and the Gold Coast.

21 April: German-controlled Paris radio claims that 641 French civilians died in an Allied air raid on Lille earlier in the month.

In England, Princess Elizabeth celebrates her 18th birthday and attends a Changing of the Guard ceremony. The popular royal is Colonel of the Grenadier Guards.

Next day a massive US Task Force under General Douglas MacArthur begins landing a 52,000 strong invasion force on Dutch New Guinea. They seize the administrative capital, Hollandia. An equally large force of Japanese are positioned elsewhere on the island at Wewak, due to faulty intelligence.

The Japanese are faring better in China where they capture Chengchow in Honan Province and rout 300,000 Nationalist troops.

23 April: Blood is shed for the first time in the Greek forces crisis. The crews of five warships at Alexandria, Egypt, have been refusing to obey orders. Unrest has spread to shore-based personnel and army units. Root cause of the trouble is dissatisfaction with the Allied-recognised Greek Government-in-Exile. Today 50 men die as Greek officers storm three of the vessels. Next day the crews of the other two ships and the First Brigade of the Greek Army end their mutiny.

24 April: Allied intelligence believes that German aircraft production for the whole of 1944 will be around the 20,000 figure. For the same period, the combined USA - British Empire output will be around 140,000 aircraft.

> ❝ **Actor Ivor Novello is sentenced to eight weeks in gaol for the illegal use of a motor vehicle.** ❞

By **25 April,** Hollandia is well on the way to becoming the biggest military base ever seen in the South West Pacific. US Construction Battalions (The Fighting Seebees) are working at a frenzied pace to build docks, airfields and housing for the 140,000 men who will augment McArthur's steady advance on the Philippines, the islands where he famously vowed, 'I will return' early in 1942.

Actor Ivor Novello is sentenced to eight weeks imprisonment for conspiring to commit an offence against the war-time restrictions on the use of motor vehicles.

Also in London, the outspoken General Patton causes controversy with congressmen back home when he tells an English audience that it is the destiny of Britain and the US to rule the world once the war is won. A later version of the speech reported in a newspaper has Patton including the USSR as a third party governing the globe.

26 April: Off the Brittany coast of France a British naval force engages a flotilla of E-Boats, sinking one. D-Day planners give attention to the potential U-Boat threat posed to the Allied invasion fleet when it finally sets sail across the English Channel. A marked reduction in recent U-Boat activity is interpreted as evidence that Admiral Donitz is preserving his strength for an all-out attack. U-Boats would have difficulty operating undetected in the shallow Channel waters but the big ships of the Allies will be tempting targets.

From midnight on **27 April** all civilian travel abroad from Britain is banned and exit visas already issued become invalid. German intelligence sources on the UK mainland are virtually non-existent but the Allies know they must be prudent and assume the worse. The Germans have imposed their own 'no go' zone for civilians along the coast of Occupied Europe from the border with Spain in the south to beyond the Arctic Circle in Norway.

28 April: US aircraft are bombing bridges on the Yellow River in China to hold up the Japanese advance.

29 April: A night-time training exercise goes wrong off South Devon, when German E-Boats out of Cherbourg intercept transports loaded with troops. In the resulting chaos hundreds of US servicemen drown or die from 'friendly fire'. Bodies will be washed up on beaches in the area for many days to come.

The last day of April sees a further increase in bombing raids over France. Trains, road and rail bridges, radar and radio installations, power stations; the entire infrastructure of France within 150 miles of the planned invasion zone is being relentlessly pummelled.

HITLER'S FORTRESS EUROPE

MAY 1944

OCCUPIED PARIS

Paris came under German control in June 1940 with the fall of France. In that month Hitler himself paid his only visit to the French capital to inspect his greatest conquest to date. The Eiffel Tower was on his tourist intinerary.

The familiar faces of Maurice Chevalier and Edith 'Little Sparrow' Piaf can be seen in two of the photographs above. Both of these celebrated singers stayed in Paris for the whole of the Occupation along with literary luminaries such as Jean Paul Sartre. Chevalier was later much criticised for entertaining audiences that included German soldiers and known collaborators.

The famous girlie shows didn't stop either and fraternisation between French women and German soldiers, sailors and airmen was not uncommon. Three photographs above show the Moulin Rouge 'Then & Now'. The famous church of Notre Dame also features in a wartime photograph here.

HITLER'S ATLANTIC WALL

'I am the greatest fortress builder of all time..'

Hitler was boasting of his vaunted Atlantic Wall. Yet the Führer's Atlantic Wall at the beginning of 1944 was largely a figment of his imagination. Certain locations – the ports such as Cherbourg, Le Havre and Dieppe and the Pas de Calais and Belgian coast – were heavily fortified. Much of the Channel Islands too – conquests highly prized by the Nazis – had been turned into concrete fastnesses bristling with guns. On Jersey they built a massive bomb-proof underground hospital. But these were the exceptions. From Denmark down to the border of France with Spain, most of the coastline was protected by a few minefields, some strands of barbed wire and poor calibre troops. Many of the latter originated from the conquered territories of Eastern Europe, men who preferred to don a German army uniform rather than endure the terrible conditions in the PoW camps. They would be unlikely to put up a fight in the event of the invasion.

Even so, by the late spring of 1944, feverish work was underway to make the Atlantic Wall a reality. The driving force was Field Marshal Erwin Rommel, the legendary 'Desert Fox' of Afrika Korps fame. He believed that the best place to stop an Allied invasion was on the beaches before armoured units could gain any substantial foothold.

Rommel shared an intuition with Hitler that the Allies would mount their main assault in Normandy, a view not shared by the Commander-in-Chief West, Field Marshal Gerd von Rundstedt, who thought the short sea crossing to the Pas-de-Calais the most likely Allied invasion route. The Todt Organisation comprising thousands of virtual slave labourers hurriedly constructed strongpoints, laid millions of mines and began covering potential landing beaches with a vast and ingenious array of obstacles – many designed by Rommel himself.

It was a race against time. A 'Second Front' to liberate Western Europe and crush the German armies between the Allies and the Russians was long overdue. But could the Germans build defences strong enough to resist the Allied invasion that must surely come in the early summer of 1944?

Top: A German sentry stands guard at Etretat near Le Havre, Normandy. The distinctive chalk arch also features in the recent colour photograph.
Centre left: Rommel pictured beside an artillery bunker.
Centre right: Another bunker designed to look like a typical Normandy house.
Bottom: A poster with a message for French civilians is seen alongside two Germans on a sand dune.

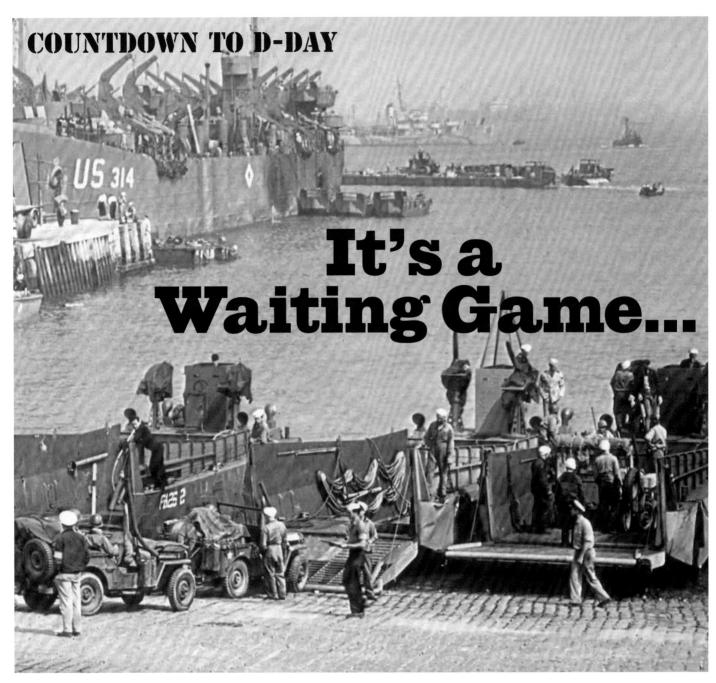

It's a Waiting Game...

With the advent of May 1944 and the promise of good weather, everybody in Southern England knew that the invasion of France was imminent. In ports and sheltered waters all along the coast, there was a massive assemblage of warships, transports and landing craft. Inland, fields and forests and country lanes were jammed with military vehicles of all shapes and sizes together with thousands of tanks and guns. On hundreds of airfields, fighters, bombers, gliders and transport planes were lined up waiting for the order to go into action.

Civilians were not encouraged to travel and so would miss much of the spectacle of these mighty forces, pent up in so many locations. But the thousands of vehicle convoys on the roads passed through cities, towns and villages and were there for all to see. Indeed, casualties - both civilian and military - from traffic accidents reached appalling levels due to the sheer volume on the highways and byways, coupled with the fact that so many of the drivers were unused to driving on the left and also had minimal lighting at night.

A further clue to the approach of D-Day came with the 'disappearance' of many servicemen from everyday life as most became confined to their camps and barracks. Pubs and cinemas lost lots of their best customers and public transport in London suddenly seemed empty. The final military exercises took place; after *Operation Fabius* in May was deemed a success, US commanders declared that their men were as ready as they ever would be.

Incredibly, the Germans were still guessing as to where the big assault would take place and had to maintain armies in all the likely landing areas such as the Pas de Calais; even an Allied invasion of Norway was not ruled out; a massive garrison remained stationed there until the end of the war. No reliable information filtered out from their spies and sympathisers in Southern Ireland and other neutral countries. The Luftwaffe in France was a shadow of its former self and with Allied superiority in the air total, they could mount few, if any, successful reconnaissance missions. In case they did, the Allies even had a phantom army of dummy tanks and guns

camped conspicuously in Kentish fields under the 'command' of the flamboyant General George Patton.

Of course, the Allies had to assume that their *Operation Overlord* plans were compromised, in part at least. There was the famous Daily Telegraph crossword coincidence when in the period between 2 May and 1 June no less than five key D-Day codenames appeared as the answers to clues on various days. And who had tipped off the German E-Boats from Cherbourg who raided Allied troop transports on exercise off South Devon earlier in the spring? This was the tragedy, veiled in secrecy for years afterwards, in which over 700 US soldiers and sailors lost their lives. It was indeed difficult for either side to discern fact from fiction when peering into the fog of war and deceit.

But as the decisive day loomed nearer, plans compromised or not and with the exception of the relentless bombing campaign against Europe's road and rail network, the gargantuan Allied war machine paused, almost as a living thing might pause to draw breath, before embarking on its mighty and long-awaited endeavour.

The Italian Campaign

May 1944. The Allied superiority in fighting men, machines, aircraft and warships must surely prevail at Cassino and Anzio.

Fifth Army General, the American Mark Clark met with the Commander-in-Chief of Allied land forces in Italy, General Sir Harold Alexander, on 1 May 1944. It was for a final briefing between the two and their senior officers and planners concerning *Operation Diadem*, a major offensive to at last crack the Gustav Line and precipitate a break-out by the Allied soldiers still penned into the Anzio beach-head.

The meeting was not a smooth one, being marked by bickering and dissent. Whilst all agreed that the trapping and destruction of the German forces south of Rome must be a primary objective of any offensive, it seemed to the British that Clark was also giving priority to ensuring that American soldiers would be the first into the Italian capital.

To overcome the Gustav Line more than 1500 artillery pieces were assembled and two million rounds stockpiled. The American Fifth and British Eighth Armies underwent a complicated switch of roles with the Fifth taking over the left flank, north of the Garigliano, and the Eighth shaping up for the major push up the Liri Valley. Infantry assaults were to breach the German defences and powerful armoured formations would exploit the breakthrough.

German intelligence of the Allied plans was meagre. Fearing another amphibious landing north of Rome, they left sorely needed reserves around Civitavecchia. The Germans also believed that their enemies had already received enough bloody noses from battering against the mountain fastnesses around Cassino that they were likely now to favour a coastal advance and accordingly reinforced

that area. To cap it all, two senior German commanders both agreed on 10 May that the Allies would not attack in the immediate future. On the very next day dawn was heralded with a thunderous artillery barrage. *Operation Diadem* had begun.

In the next six days some half a million rounds were fired off by guns supporting the British 13th Corps. One witness reported: 'In those few miles between the hills (on either side of the Liri Valley), a thousand guns let go as one and then kept on firing. We'd never seen or heard anything quite like this and could only imagine what sort of hell was falling on the German lines. It damn near deafened us.'

Yet *Diadem* failed to yield swift success and 13th Corps - comprising men from the Hampshire Regiment alongside Indians and even an Italian Motorised Group - struggled to create a decisive bridge-head. They sustained nearly 4000 casualties in driving a salient three miles deep into the German lines, a figure that would most certainly have been higher had the British artillery not smothered with smoke the German observation posts on the heights. On 17 May, Eighth Army Commander Lt-Gen Oliver Leese decided the time was right to commit the Canadian 1st Corps; they were to be the spearhead of the push up the valley.

Poles and Goums

Meanwhile there was action elsewhere on the Gustav Line. General Wladislaw Anders commanded a Polish Corps, a unit eager to do battle with the Germans and avenge the brutal invasion of their homeland in September 1939, the act that triggered World War II. The Poles were in position on the Cassino frontline. Now they were ready to assault the heights and capture the ruins of the monastery.

Their first attack went in at the beginning of *Diadem* but the paratroopers facing them seemed as implacable a foe as ever. The Germans knew the ground and had sown minefields and set up deadly cross-fires. By 13 May even the determined Anders realised the task was impossible and reluctantly pulled his men back.

Other Allies now took on a key role. General Alphonse Juin, a soldier noted for his left-handed salute (his right arm having been maimed during the Great War), commanded the French Expeditionary Corps which included three North African Divisions. Among them

Right: A British armoured car in the streets of Cassino after the Germans had retreated.
Left: Two prisoners being brought in under guard amidst the ruins of the town.

were Goums, men from the Atlas Mountains who were used to fighting in rugged terrain. They wore burnooses and carried large knives. Montgomery said of them: 'Dark men, dark night. Very hard to see coming.'

Juin's men faced the steep slopes of Monte Maio, some 15 miles south of Monte Cassino. Only light German forces defended the position for both they and the Allies had hitherto believed the area to be to be impassable by an army in strength. But Juin's Goums proved up to the task and ghosted through the mountains, ruthlessly despatching the opposition.

Too late Kesselring realised that his stubbornly-defended Gustav Line had been compromised. More bad news followed for the Germans when the US II Corps, supported by naval gunfire, made progress in the coastal

region around Minturno. British units such as the Black Watch and Royal West Kents in the Liri Valley were also fighting hard – two VCs were won in this arena. On the late afternoon of 15 May, Kesselring learnt that 100 Allied tanks, crewed in the main by Canadians, had broken through in the valley. Cassino was about to be outflanked. Orders were issued for the paratroopers to pull back from the Monastery and retreat north.

Monte Cassino captured

The Poles didn't know of the German decision. That night they attacked again and fierce fighting erupted at outlying positions such as Albaneto Farm. Mine explosions and mortar barrages, rifle and Spandau machine-gun fire ripped through the darkness. Allied tanks added the blast of their own guns. By 17 May the Poles were at last close to their objective.

Next morning Lt Casimir Gurbiel and a party of Uhlans of the Poldoski Lancers cautiously entered the ruins of the Benedictine Monastery to find only badly wounded Germans remaining in the vaults. Overnight the Germans had gone. Soon the red and white flag of Poland fluttered over the scene of devastation. The sounds of war were distant now and a kind of peace descended on the holy place. Shredded tree stumps, scattered masonry and overlapping bomb and shell craters were everywhere. Yet present also were wild flowers. Lots of them, and in a riot of colours dominated by the red of poppies. Their example would not be lost on the monks of St Benedict. Just a few years later, a new Monastery would rise from the ruins of the old.

Over 850 Poles died and 3000 were wounded in the final seven days of fighting at Cassino. The inscription at the Polish cemetery which faces the rebuilt Monastery across a valley reads: 'We Polish soldiers, for our freedom and yours, have given our souls to God, our bodies to the soil of Italy and our hearts to Poland.'

The war moved on up the 'leg' of Italy. But

not very far. The Germans had another defensive position, the Adolf Hitler Line, already marked out. For a while it stalled the Eighth Army. Then the French Goums, continuing their advance on the heights to the west of the Liri Valley, forced a breach. Excellent fighters, unfortunately the North Africans were earning a reputation for rape and robbery off the battlefield. One Italian report lamented, 'The Germans took away our goats, sheep and food, but they at least respected our women.'

The Canadian 1st Corps went into the attack again on 21 – 22 May and three days later the Hitler Line caved in. On the same day the Luftwaffe put in a major effort for the first time in many weeks but to no avail; they lost 32 precious fighters. Then Formia and Gaeta on the coast were captured by the Americans while the advancing Poles took Piedimonte.

Alexander was pleased to inform Churchill that 500 square miles of Italy had been liberated in just two weeks and over 10,000 Germans taken prisoner. The Allies had developed a powerful forward momentum. Now was the time for the forces cooped up in the Anzio beach-head to burst out and cut off the enemy's line of retreat to Rome and beyond.

Breakout at Anzio

The night of 22 – 23 May was a clear, starlit night over Rome, the Alban Hills and the Latium Coast. In the blacked-out Anzio – Nettuno beach-head, 150,000 men gazed upwards at the panoply of constellations. Operation Buffalo – the long-awaited breakout – was imminent. Would dawn see an end to the terrors and tedium of the months of virtual trench warfare?

Not immediately. Following a massive artillery barrage that started at 05.45 hours, the massed Shermans of Maj-Gen Ernie Harmon's First Armoured Division rolled forward on a mere 2000 yard front, heading for Cisterna. By nightfall, 86 US tanks and armoured vehicles had been destroyed. The stubborn German defenders in Cisterna held out for three days; seven Congressional Medals of Honour were won by US soldiers fighting for the ruined town.

The British at Anzio had a diversionary attack role at the beginning of the breakout. The night before Buffalo, Raleigh Trevelyan, a young officer in the Green Howards, led a recce patrol out to scout around the mouth of the shallow Moletta River, across which the British attack would go. He and his troops walked into a minefield, where two of his men were blown up. Trevelyan reckoned he must have stepped over the very mine that killed them.

In the diversionary attack itself he wasn't so lucky. Wounds from grenades hospitalised him from where he wrote to his brother, 'Of course our barrage was quite fantastic..when I led a section round some bushes, a Spandau opened up only 10 yards away, killing the section leader behind me and badly wounding four others. I chucked a grenade and tore off, only to discover another Jerry trench just below me. The Jerry threw an egg grenade, which hit me on the nose and then bounced back on to him and exploded. The next few hours were a haze of grenade throwing and tommy-gunning, sand and bits of scrub flying everywhere. My platoon took 15 prisoners and we must have killed half a dozen others.'

Some diversion! Trevelyan went on to record his experiences in Italy in two books, *The Fortress* and *Rome '44 – The Battle for the Eternal City*.

After the fall of Cisterna, German prisoners were gathered in ever-larger numbers. Allied air power crippled their ability to move and in one aerial onslaught 15 Tiger tanks were destroyed on a short stretch of road near the town of Cori. Attention turned to Valmontone on Route Six between Rome and Naples. This town was in the heart of a now rapidly diminishing gap between the Allied soldiers advancing from Anzio and the Allies coming up from the south. Closing the gap would seal the fate of a large part of the German army in Italy, leaving but a few effective enemy forces between this place and the Alps.

It was not to be. On the seeming verge of a stunning victory, General Mark Clark changed the momentum of the attack. Instead of reinforcing the advance on Valmontone he instructed Maj-Gen Lucian Truscott – commander of the pent-up Anzio forces, most of whom had not yet been committed to battle – to march his men north. In the direction of Rome.

Controversy about Clark's decision continues to this day. It is said he suspected there was an Eighth Army plot to steal ahead and enter the Eternal City as liberators ahead of his Fifth Army. Was it vanity that made him go for Rome, to be hailed as the first warrior to enter the city from the south in 2000 years? When Churchill learnt of Clark's order he signalled Alexander, 'The glory of this battle, already

Above: Monte Cassino in May 1944. Polish dead are being removed from the battlefield. The Poles suffered many casualties in the final assault on the heights.
Right: British troops of the Fifth Army pictured in the same month. They are taking cover in a German trench whilst waiting for reinforcements before advancing.

great, will be measured not by the capture of Rome or juncture with the (forces from Anzio) but by the number of German divisions cut off.'

The French General Juin made his own comment: 'Questions of prestige are shaping events, with each one wanting to make entry into Rome. History will not fail to pass severe sentence.'

NEWS FROM ITALY

British newspapers carried no news of the D-Day build-up in May 1944. However, events in Italy were reported in detail. The map reproduced here is from the Daily Herald *of 25 May 1944. It shows the Allied advance north from Cassino and the break-out from Anzio. In fact by this date, the two forces had actually linked up.*

Stop Press

Moscow announced late last night that in Tarnopol area, Russian troops have advanced 40-50 miles in four days and captured more than 400 places.

Churchill Tells U.S. Troops

"The Allies Will Strike Soon"

THE Allies will strike "soon," the British Prime Minister, Mr. Winston Churchill, told American airborne troops in Britain yesterday. He added that the blow they would help in striking would be decisive in winning victory, and making the world a better and broader place for all.

"Soon," Mr. Churchill told the troops, "you will have opportunity of testifying your faith in all...

Brenner 'Gateway'

Cassino, Yard By Yard

BRIG.-GENERAL WILLIAM H. WILBUR at a Press conference at Washington said that after the German mountain stronghold of Cassino is taken there will still be hurdles to surmount before the Allies capture Rome.

General Wilbur, second in command of the 36th Division now fighting at Cassino, said that Cassino could not be by-passed because of the mountainous terrain.

Meanwhile, fierce fighting is continuing in Cassino, where

And He Have Mu

A Family at War

William 'Tony' Hathaway served with the Eighth Army in North Africa and Italy. He collected a large number of newspapers relating to the Allied war effort progress during the early desert days right through to VE Day in May 1945. Two examples of publications from March and April 1944 are reproduced above and below.

On the right we also reproduce a cutting from a Lewes, East Sussex, local newspaper of September 1942 which featured a chance meeting of Tony and his younger brother, Raymond. The pair were fortunate to survive the war – two cousins bearing the Hathaway name did not. Their names are recorded on the war memorial at the top of School Hill, Lewes.

Tony passed away in October 1989. His widow Daphne, son David and daughters Susan and Sally all still live in East Sussex though no member of the family now lives in the 'Jolly Anglers'.

A fascinating footnote to the tale comes in the fact that Tony's son David is married to Sonia, a daughter of an English father who married an Austrian girl he met when soldiering in that country at the end of World War II.

A postcard home from Eighth Army veteran, Tony Hathaway. The reverse side included the brief message 'I am quite well.' with a reassuring signature only.

Lewes Brothers Meet in the Middle East

By airgraph letter a few days ago, Mrs. W. Hathaway, of the Jolly Anglers, Station-street, Lewes, received news of the meeting of her two sons who are serving their country in the Middle East. They spent a few days leave together in Cairo.

William   **Raymond**

They are Sapper William Anthony Hathaway, R.E., aged 26, and A.C.1 Raymond Frederick Hathaway, aged 20. The former has been serving his country 2½ years, and he was at Dunkirk before he went to the Middle East. Previously he was an employee of the Ringmer Building Works. His younger brother worked as an electrician in Lewes before he joined the Royal Air Force. Both are old boys of Lewes Central School.

(Army Form A. 2042.)
(R.A.F. Form No. 1929)

FIELD SERVICE POST CARD

OFFICIAL PAID

The address only to be written on this side. If anything else is added the post card will be destroyed.

Mrs Hathaway
"Jolly Anglers"
Station St.
Lewes
Sussex

[Crown Copyright Reserved.]

CRUSADER

FOUNDED BY EIGHTH ARMY

BRITISH FORCES' WEEKLY

No. 98, Vol. 10.   Two Lire
Sunday, April 16, 1944

The Girl who "Stole" the Picture

● The scene is a factory "somewhere in Blighty."

According to the script there should be one "star" in the picture—and a lot of "extra" players.

There was no trouble about finding . . . There never is when

Troops Walk Out On Rooney

MEMBERS of a R.A.S.C. unit in Italy this week stood up for the rights of troops to be shown suitable films.

They were seeing Mickey Rooney in "The Human Comedy." The audience began to walk out before the picture was half-way through. The O.C. protested that this was not the sort of entertainment for

ITALIAN PILGRIMAGE

War documentaries and analyses we get on TV are interesting and well done but cannot portray the reality. War on TV is safe whereas the real thing is very dangerous and frightening: indeed it is largely to do with killing people. Even at the 'effects' level, the sheer noise of battle can never be recreated (it would burst the equipment). Above all, the difference between now and then is that we now know the outcome. At the time there were those who would not live to know it.

This was the sort of reason why I (no doubt like others) was slightly uneasy about the prospect of going back in time (in my case to Salerno, Anzio and Cassino), though I very much wanted and needed to. However, in revisiting the first half of the long Italian campaign, it was for me hugely important to share the experience with my wife Janet, not to mention our elder son Giles. He was splendidly interested as well as being an attentive help to us old folk. He now understands more of what I have been unable to describe properly, and so will his three sons by degrees.

Italy is unbelievably beautiful as well as providing virtually impossible terrain for an army on the attack. To have seen again the southern battlefields (and now also the cemeteries) is to confirm one's sheer luck in coming out of it all unhurt at least in body. I knew that many friends would now be cemetery crosses, with their dates of death clustered around the dates of our battles. But there were new things still to find out or to retrieve memories long overlaid by the rapid movement of war.

For example I took on board for the first time the full story of the London Scottish private who won a VC in my 56th Division – that he was shot by a German soldier who had already surrendered to him. I heard much more from our guide than I had ever known about the shape of the battles and the part played by formations other than my own.

To see the mountains near Cassino brought back the foreboding we gunners felt as our infantry were sent in to capture heavily defended targets in full view of the enemy. There had been pride but also dread as we watched the Scots Guards setting out in single file up the slopes of Monte Camino to the sound of bagpipes.

Nothing on this visit could recreate the sound of the dive bombers as we came in to disembark at Salerno and later at Anzio. Not only did they come with shocking surprise, invisible out of the setting sun, but they were equipped with sirens that shrieked ever louder as they dived. And of course the bombs were visible, seeming to

Above: 'Anzio Annie' captured. This was a massive rail-mounted gun that was housed in a tunnel and brought out to bombard the Allied beach-head in the spring of 1944. Roy Patten has identified the two men in the picture as his friend Staff Sergeant Reggie Wise of 72 LAA Regiment RA ('trying to push the thing off the rails') and (on the barrel), Roy's driver, Lindsay. The photographer was Corporal Stagg and the whole group were heading for Rome. Roy recorded that Reggie Wise died in 2004 and remembered him '...as the strongest man I ever knew – the only man in the Regiment who could lift a spare barrel for the Bofors gun all by himself, always active and good-natured.'
Roy believed there were two 'Anzio Annies' that the Germans called Blucher and Esmerelda. At least two of this type of big gun survive. One is in a museum near Cap Gris Nez, not far from Calais. Another (pictured here) is on display at the Aberdeen Proving Grounds Museum in Maryland, USA.

fall no faster than large tennis balls: where would the next one land?

I served mainly as Assistant Adjutant of my regiment (the 64th Field) with periods back at the guns to keep in practice – and my job included manning the CO's forward command post. I suspect it was unusual (at any rate in my war) for someone in this situation to have lost, as I did, two colonels out of three, killed by shellfire just after they left me to confer with the infantry brigadier. I myself had only a lot of disturbing near misses.

My first colonel, as we approached the Garigliano river, was Angus McCracken, a 48 year old territorial, typical of the citizen soldiery in our territorial regiment – a city accountant, who had told me modestly only a week or two before he died that a field telephone call just received had been to tell him about the award of his DSO. (His wife was Esther McCracken, whose popular stage plays were filling West End theatres at the time he was with the regiment). He was an old fashioned gentleman, who used a cut-throat razor that I kept and threw away only

recently. The manner of his death would have seemed inconceivable in his City office a few years before. Such City links permeated this TA set-up, and one imagines pre-war evening drills for stock jobbers, jaded after days at desks, now suddenly transformed into blood and guts for real. They were splendid people.

The second colonel I lost in a similar way in the Gothic Line, a few months later, was Col Zambra, who from his name must have died in the country of his ancestors. Only 34, he was a Regular, and this was his first command.

In all it was a nostalgic experience rather than a holiday. We all found it worthwhile, though for me it was discouraging to walk uncertainly across beaches where 21 year old limbs had once been so agile.

Geoffrey Cockerill

PS. I saw Alan Whicker's very lively and riveting programme on the Italian campaign, including his account of filming at Salerno and Anzio. Out of curiosity I checked Who's Who *for detail and found that he was born only in August 1925. Hence he must have been an officer aged just one month over 18 and Salerno. To be a director of the film unit in Eighth and Fifth Armies at this age is an astonishing thing.*

WAR DIARY

May 1944

On **1 May** Truk in the South Pacific is again the target of a US carrier task force; over 120 Japanese aircraft are destroyed, over half of them on the ground, in two days of raids.

On **2 May** a crossword puzzle in the *Daily Telegraph* contains a clue at 17 across: 'One of the US'. The answer is revealed as UTAH, an American state but also the code for one of the US D-Day landing beaches in Normandy.

BBC's Voice of Britain is widely listened to throughout Occupied Europe, despite harsh penalties for people caught tuning in. It carries a story concerning two U-Boats attempting to fight back against an air attack that sunk the pair whilst a third U-Boat took the opportunity to submerge and escape. When German monitors pick up the story it leads to the court-martial of the U-Boat's Captain. On his return to port he had claimed that his two companion vessels had declined to open fire but had been destroyed in the act of submerging, leaving his vessel on the surface to fight off the aircraft alone!

3 May: Spanish dictator Franco's refusal to join the Axis Alliance even when a fascist victory in the war seemed assured in 1940 is reaping dividends. He is courted by the Allies who turn a blind eye to Dictator's harsh repression of Spanish communists and suspected republicans. Spain now agrees to cut tungsten ore exports to Germany by one sixth in exchange for US oil. Hitler is incensed. Franco's steady concessions to the Allies have included the release of Italian ships interned in Spanish ports and the recall of Spanish volunteer forces aiding Germany against Russia.

4 May: British civilians used to seeing well-fed Americans 'over here' may not have believed that meat rationing had been enforced in the USA since Pearl Harbour. But from today meat

A massive bunker on the Atlantic Wall built by the slave labourers of the Todt Organisation

goes back on the menu right across the States, thanks to the success of beef farmers in increasing production.

On **5 May** Hitler is able to read the transcript of a conversation between Roosevelt and Churchill thanks to a rare coup by the German intelligence service. No secrets are exchanged.

6 May: That ancient city of the Tartars, Sebastopol, comes under furious attack; the Russians face desperate German defenders.

Mahatma Ghandi is released from prison in India because of ill-health. He has been held since 1942 on fears that he might, even unwittingly, encourage Indians to take a pro-Japanese stance. Despite the current Japanese threat to Assam, there has been no sign of popular support for the invaders.

Below: This painting by Walter Gotscke depicts a German assault gun and crew on the Russian Front. It appeared in the German magazine Signal *in 1944.*

WAR DIARY
May 1944

In France 1800 men are deported to Dora Concentration Camp in Germany to work on the production of Nazi secret weapons. Few will survive.

A five day exercise - *Operation Fabius* - has been taking place at coastal locations in Southern England, from Littlehampton in West Sussex all the way to Slapton Sands in Devon. Allied commanders are putting their men through the final phases of training for D-Day. A second exercise, *Operation Splint*, provides experience in handling the evacuation of casualties via landing craft.

7 May: At Imphal the fighting settles into a stalemate, although it is clear the initiative lies with General Slim. Exploiting the Allied air superiority is the key to future success. In China the Japanese are still making gains; today they captured Suiping and cut the Peking – Hankow railway.

8 May: General Eisenhower sets the date for the invasion of Northern Europe: D-Day will be 5 June 1944. In Berlin tomorrow, Admiral Donitz will tell the German High Command that he doesn't believe the Allies plan a landing in the near future.

In Budapest, a cruel barter is proposed by Adolf Eichmann, Head of the Jewish Office of the Gestapo. Deportations of Jews from Hungary will be slowed, or even halted, if the Allies provide Germany with 10,000 vehicles to be used in the war against the communist Red Army. Joel Brand of the Hungarian Jewish Assistance and Rescue Committee is on his way to Turkey seeking Allied agreement to the plan.

Next day (**9 May**) the Germans declare a 10-mile exclusion zone out to sea along the entire coastline of Denmark. A similar restriction already applies to the Dutch coast. Fish to supplement the rations of the Dutch and Danes will all but disappear from sale.

It's the end for Hitler's 'Aircraft Carrier in the Black Sea' as Sebastopol surrenders to the Red Army. Around 20,000 German and Rumanian soldiers have died in the siege and nearly 25,000 are taken prisoner. Almost all of the Crimea has been freed.

10 May: It's revealed that the Americans have stockpiled vast quantities of food in England to feed the half-starved peoples of Europe in the wake of the invasion. Cereals, dried milk, powdered eggs, canned meats and dehydrated vegetables form the bulk of the growing food mountain.

11 May: *The Marx Brothers Go West* is the film most requested for screening by soldiers of the Eighth Army in Italy.

In Burma, 40,000 Chinese cross the River Salween in an offensive aimed at ejecting the Japanese from the north of the country. If successful then the Japanese on the Burma – India border will be isolated.

Next day London broadcasts messages to the leaders of Hungary, Rumania and Bulgaria urging them to quit the Axis alliance and give up fighting the Allies. Overnight six German plants manufacturing synthetic oil have been hit by a total of 900 Flying Fortresses and Liberators of the Eighth USAAF. Allied losses number 58 while 50 German aircraft are shot down.

13 May: The fourth major Allied assault of the year is underway against Cassino and the Gothic Line. *Operation Diadem* is accompanied by a gigantic artillery bombardment. Over the next six days half a million shells will be hurled at the Germans.

The only Germans now remaining in the Crimea are either killed or captured as the Russians take Cape Kherson. Even for those soldiers who escaped by sea, the ordeal was not ended; Russian submarines, torpedo boats and aircraft have sunk 190 fleeing vessels drowning around 8000 German troops. Hitler had hoped the Crimea would be a fortress where his garrison would hold out until the tide of war turned again. Instead it became a huge trap costing him 110,000 irreplaceable men and vast quantities of arms.

The last resting place for many of the German defenders at Cassino.

In the English Channel, E-boat S147 is sunk in an action with the frigate *HMS Stayning* and Free French destroyer *La Combattante*. S147's captain is Klaus Donitz, son of the German Admiral Karl Donitz, mastermind of the Nazi U-boat campaign. Klaus is the Admiral's second son to die on active service.

14 May: Britain's code-crackers have uncovered a German ploy to trick the Allies into bombing inactive Luftwaffe airfields. Details of the plan were contained in an intercepted message from Luftwaffe boss Herman Goêring. The Allies have their own elaborate deceptions underway. General George S Patton's First Army Group is massing in Kent preparing to invade France in the Pas de Calais area. At least that's what the Germans believe. In fact, Patton's army doesn't exist; fake tanks, sprawling encampments empty of men and busy radio traffic are all keeping the enemy guessing as to what Allied armies are coming and where.

15 May: Civilian travel on the rail network in France has been banned. In Algiers, the French Committee of National Liberation decides on changing its name to the Provisional Government of the French Republic with effect from 2 June. In Italy, Free French forces under General Alphonse Juin consolidate their capture of San Giorgio and Ausonia; the Gustav Line is finally beginning to crack. Juin's men include tough African Goumiers from the Atlas Mountains who are feared as much by the Italian civilian population as by the Germans.

London: The King, Prime Minister Churchill, South African Premier Jan Smuts and other Allied leaders are at St Paul's School in Kensington for a briefing on the impending invasion. In the school hall, General Eisenhower and Field Marshal Montgomery unveil a huge coloured map depicting the Normandy beaches on which the Allies will land in the next few weeks. Monty had attended St Paul's as pupil.

16 May: In Berlin orders are issued for the deployment of the secret V1 rocket-propelled 'Flying Bombs' to their launch sites that stretch from Normandy to the Dutch coast.

Next day the British Far Eastern Fleet sails close to Java and launches an air attack on oil facilities at Surabaya.

In London a conference of Prime Ministers of Britain, Canada, Australia, New Zealand and South Africa ends with the unanimous endorsement of plans for winning the war and a blueprint for post-war relations which includes the foundation of a world organisation empowered to preserve peace.

18 May: At last the Gustav Line is broken. After a six day struggle up the mountain by soldiers of the Polish II Corps, the Eagle flag of Poland flutters over the ruined monastery at Monte Cassino.

In the Turkish capital, Ankara, martial law has been declared following pro-German riots. The unrest demonstrates why the government has been cautious of openly supporting the Allies.

U-241 has been sunk off the coast of Norway by a Catalina flying boat. Two days earlier, sister submarine U-240 suffered the same fate.

In Palestine three truckloads of members of the Jewish nationalist group, *Irgun*, storm a radio station. Their plans to broadcast messages to the Jewish population of Palestine are

WAR DIARY May 1944

thwarted by the arrival of police reinforcements in armoured cars. After a brief gun battle the Irgun men escape.

19 May: The Allied breakthrough in Italy gains momentum as the US II Corp push up the coastal Highway 7 to occupy Gaeta and Monte Grande. The Germans are putting together a new defensive position at the top end of the Liri Valley but this so-called 'Adolf Hitler Line' is unlikely to hold up the Allies for long.

In London the Government confirms that British POWs can have monetary credit balances built up in Germany made available for their families in this country. German prisoners have reciprocal rights. The rate of exchange is 15 Reichsmarks to the £.

On **20 May** the Americans initiate a two-day air blitz on Marcus Island in the South Pacific. Japanese resistance on Wakde Island near New Guinea has ended.

21 May: *Operation Chattanooga* is underway as the Allied air forces systematically bomb rail targets in France and Belgium. On one recent evening residents of an English South Coast town observed a vast formation of RAF bombers heading for the Continent; it took 35 minutes for the full stream to pass overhead.

Unknown to the general public, an embarrassing problem has occurred with some component parts to the top secret artificial harbours codenamed *Mulberry*. Massive floating concrete caissons are to be towed across the Channel and sunk off the Normandy coast to form breakwaters. Unfortunately, a number of the big caissons have stuck firmly in the mud of the Thames estuary and are proving impossible to budge.

22 May: General Mark Clark arrives at Anzio on the eve of *Operation Buffalo*, the long-awaited breakout from the beach-head. As evening comes the guns are strangely quiet as 150,000 Allied soldiers ponder what dawn will bring.

23 May: Anzio. 05.45 hours. Over 1000 guns, tanks and mortars open fire on German positions, mainly in the Cisterna area where the principal Allied thrust will begin.

In London the Ministry of Pensions is considering improving the allowances made for separated or divorced wives of men serving in the Forces. This follows representations from the Soldiers, Sailors and Airmens Association and the Officers Families Association.

The Anzio breakout **(24 May)** is being stubbornly contested at Cisterna by the LXXVI Panzer Corps. So far 86 Allied tanks and armoured vehicles have been lost to mines and artillery fire.

On this same day in Rio, President Vargas reviews men of the Brazilian Expeditionary Force who are embarking for Europe as part of a promised army that will eventually number 60,000. Brazil declared war on the Axis powers in August 1942 following the sinking of several of her ships by U-Boats in the Atlantic.

A small ship carrying 54 Germans and seven Rumanians who escaped from the Crimea has docked in Zonguldak, Northern Turkey, where the men are interned.

25 May: Over 138,000 Hungarian Jews have so far been deported to concentration camps. The Allies refused Adolf Eichmann's 'Jewish lives for Allied trucks' offer made in the spring. Retribution will befall Eichmann some 18 years later when he is kidnapped from his Argentinian hiding place and taken to Israel for trial and execution.

The siege of Anzio officially ended this morning when US troops from the beach-head linked up with the Fifth Army advancing north from Terracina. Later in the day Cisterna is captured after three days of fierce fighting.

26 May: Marshal Petain reiterates his call for prefects and civil servants in Occupied France to give 'complete and loyal help' to the German Army, citing the Armistice Convention and The Hague Convention as the corroborative authority. Allied aircraft today hit military and transport targets in Nice, Marseille, Lyons and St Etienne but there are inevitably civilian casualties.

27 May: A coded signal for the Italian partisans in the hills and towns around Rome is transmitted on London Radio. *Anna Maria e Promossa* – 'Anna Maria is Promoted' - is the signal telling the partisans that the time is right to rise up against the Germans. In Rome itself, the inhabitants are asked to be patient rather than risk the destruction of the city.

28 May: Oil facilities in Germany are the target of big American air raids. However, the enemy are showing great skill in minimising the effects of the bombing. The able and efficient Albert Speer has been in charge of armaments production since February. Production of German fighters is actually rising at present. One of Speer's innovations are the *Jagestabs* – special flying squads of skilled operatives charged with supervising the repair of factories.

In Britain the D-Day security clampdown is absolute. Everyone concerned with the invasion has been sealed within the confines of their camp. No mail is allowed in or out.

29 May: The 11,000 Japanese defenders of Biak have pinned down three US infantry regiments who had landed unopposed 18 hours earlier on this small island off the coast of New Guinea.

30 May: Berlin: A shadowy Nazi boss - Martin Bormann - believed to have considerable influence over Hitler issues a chilling directive telling local Nazi leaders that shot-down Allied aircrew can no longer consider themselves protected under the Geneva Convention due to the 'criminal combat methods' employed in bombing German cities.

Fierce fighting continues in front of the German Caesar Line at Campoleone near Anzio where the Americans have sustained 5116 casualties since 23 May.

The last day of May 1944 sees air attacks on bridges over the River Seine in Normandy but also increased bombing around Calais and Boulogne. The Luftwaffe is largely absent in France although five Focke-Wulf 190s are shot down by Allied fighter-bombers over western Germany.

Monte Artemisio in the Alban Hills to the south of Rome has been seized by the Americans and threatens the flank of the Germans holding out in their Caesar Line. The Eighth Army is coming up Route 6 and approaching Valmontone. The Germans must surely retreat. The question is, will Hitler order the destruction of Rome? The American General Mark Clark has his own vision; he seeks to lead the first army to conquer Rome from the south in nearly 2000 years.

Right: Waiting for the invasion: a German gun position on the coast of France in spring 1944.

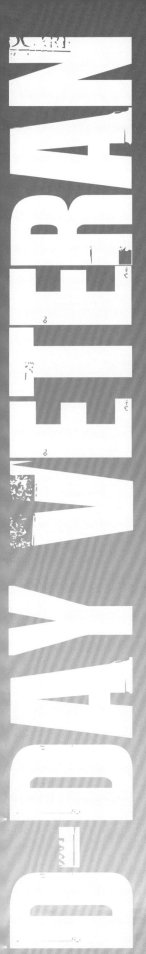

D-DAY VETERAN

The famous Spitfire ML 407 was originally built at Castle Bromwich in early 1944 as a single seat fighter, and served in the front line of battle throughout the last 12 months of World War II, all in all flying 176 operational combat sorties.

It was delivered to 485 New Zealand Squadron on 29 April 1944 by Jackie Moggridge, one of the top lady pilots of the ATA, where it became the 'mount' of Flying Officer Johnnie Houlton DFC who was accredited, whilst flying ML407, with the first enemy aircraft shot down over the Normandy beach-head on D-Day, 6 June.

In December of 1944, ML 407 was transferred to 341 Free French Squadron, becoming the aircraft of Sergeant Jean Dabos. She also flew in Polish, Belgian and Norwegian Squadrons. In 1950 it was converted to a two-seat configuration by Supermarine at Southampton for use as an advanced trainer. ML 407 made an appearance in the film *The Battle of Britain*. In 1979 the aircraft was acquired by engineer Nick Grace.

Today ML407 is popularly known as the Grace Spitfire and is flown by Nick's widow, Carolyn Grace, at air shows and outdoor events all over this country. The aircraft is pictured here in the D-Day livery of black and white stripes.

JUNE 1944

Ted's Pin-ups!

I've often wondered what happened to Old Ted. We called him 'Old Ted' not so much because he was older that the rest of us, but because he had certain fussy little habits of tidiness. Ted may have been a bit of an old woman in the way he carried on if someone used his comb without asking first, but he certainly was a lad for the girls.

Around his bed he had a dozen pictures. Girls in ATS and WRNS uniform. Girls in civvies. Girls with beaming dentrifice faces. Girls with that wistful look which always suggests that they have stomach-ache.

Now and again he added to his collection. But he never tore any up in anger. He never replaced yesterday's favourite with today's dazzler. He never sighed or moaned over them. Ted used to regard his collection with a smug grin and whenever the battalion moved he would wrap up the lot in brown paper and swathe the parcel in his two spare shirts before putting it in his kit bag.

One day Ted was sent to the depot and passed out of my life. Ever since I've been overseas I've kept a look-out for him because I'm hoping that he has kept his art gallery up to date. And what a time he has had if he took part in the Eighth Army's Cook's tour from Egypt to Italy!

'The nice girls of Algiers had caught the secret of Parisian chic. Feminine, charming and a welcome relief from the winning ways of the sergeant-major...'

I suppose he would have had at least two pictures of the sultry brunettes who are such an ornament of the Nile Delta. I don't mean the ones who used to hang about outside Abbassia Barracks – because Ted was rather fastidious – but perhaps one of the girls who used to eat ice-cream in Groppi's every afternoon. And were almost always collected by husband or fiancée just as you had paid the bill and the conversation was getting interesting.

Perhaps he would have shown much better taste by getting to know one of those astonishingly lovely girls of the Women's Auxiliary Forces of South Africa. With their good looks and bright conversation, they cheered up many a man browned off with the Blue.

Certainly he would not have collected any pin-up girls in the desert. The beauteous daughters of the desert mostly ran to blue tattoo marks and cross eyes.

Nor did Tripoli – first stop after the dust bowl – yield anything in the way of feminine charm. Most of the girls were locked up until the Italians decided British troops weren't necessarily sex-maddened apes.

Algiers was a different cup of tea. I think Ted would have collected at least a couple of snapshots because the nice

girls of Algiers had caught the secret of Parisian chic. A little heartless, maybe, but feminine, charming and a welcome relief from the winning ways of the sergeant-major.

Tunis, too, might have given Ted another pin-up girl. She would be, I imagine, rather more sultry than the Algiers girl. Just the faintest hint, maybe, of the Kasbah. But unmistakably there.

Sicily would have disappointed Ted. Hard, grim poverty had left its mark too clearly on the faces of the peasants. Naples was a bit of a mixed bag, too. I should say that Neapolitan girls used more rouge, lipstick and eye-shade than the feminine population of the three equivalent British cities. The results didn't always justify the hard work.

But in Rome Ted would have been in his Italian heaven! He would have seen elegant women who were apparently untouched by and disinterested in a war that has convulsed the world. Women in smart and coupon-free costumes. Women wearing silk stockings that are legend back home. Well-groomed, comfortably-off, superbly poised women. And the art gallery might easily have doubled its size.

Unless Ted – and I think this likely – had stopped to do a bit of thinking. Had torn up his pictures of the whole gang of foreign beauties. Keeping just the picture of a British girl. A girl in dungarees, cleaning a machine with a piece of cotton waste. A girl with oil smudges on her nose. A girl whose face shows the strain of five years on the Home Front.

Not as exotic as the Cairo cutie. Not as chic as the lovelies of Algiers. Not as well dressed as the women of Rome. But a daughter of a nation that has dared and suffered much in the hard march to victory. And still the finest girl in this strange old world!

Reproduced from the Crusader *of 27 August 1944. Words by Cyril James. Drawing by the artist Robb.*

ROME - OPEN CITY

In the very first days of June 1944 nobody on the Allied side knew for certain the German intentions regarding the Italian capital, Rome. Would they defend the city or destroy it in a fit of rage at being forced to retreat? The people of Rome had most to worry about. Already on the verge of starvation, what further horrors now awaited them?

In the notorious city gaol, Regina Coeli, captured British agents could hear the guns of the approaching Allies, But the Germans were still in control. As late as the afternoon of 3 June, 14 men were taken outside the city by lorry and shot. Their number included Captain John Armstrong.

For several days previously, the Allies had been fighting their way towards Rome from the Anzio beach-head in the face of desperate German resistance. With Route Six still open, the Germans facing the Eighth and Fifth Armies and the Anzio forces had taken heart and renewed the fight with grim determination. Field Marshal Kesselring regained his masterly poise in adversity. Though his men had been badly hurt they conducted an orderly retreat in early June – it was certainly no rout.

Unbeknown to the Allies, Hitler then confirmed his decision to spare Rome from destruction, declaring it a 'place of culture' and not fitting for combat operations. The Italian dictator Mussolini was not so charitable. He demanded the defence of the city street by street, railing, 'Why should the citizens of Rome have a better life than those of Cassino?'

The Eighth Army's advance was more or less along the central mountainous spine of Italy leaving the approach to Rome to the American Fifth Army. There was mounting excitement in the latter as units neared the Eternal City. Traffic jams became almost as irritating as the enemy rearguards. On the Appian Way, a German paratrooper corporal and a handful of men with a heavy machine-gun, cut down an advance party of Americans who were unwise enough to stroll down the centre of the road.

Later captured and transported to Anzio, the same corporal realised that Germany had lost the war: 'I saw vehicles, tanks, jeeps, guns and lorries in long columns for as long as the road stretched and as far as the eye could see. Never had I seen such an array. There were even water-trucks sprinkling the ground to damp down the dust. And this was just a supply route. I was used to our lorries sprinting along under shellfire, in ones or twos or threes.'

On the night of 4 June the Americans entered Rome in force. The tanks of Maj-Gen Ernie Harmon's First Armoured Division were in the vanguard. A senior officer recalls, 'There were no Italian policemen, no directional signs, no street lights and no lights in any of the buildings... as we moved along the dark streets we could hear people clapping their hands behind the windows of their homes but we could not see them. Later, when it became evident that the Germans had abandoned the city, men, women and children, in night dress and slippers came down into the still-dark streets to welcome the Americans.

The Italian Campaign

'Some ran up and down the columns offering wine to the soldiers. After daylight the population appeared on the streets dressed for a holiday. Women and children threw flowers at passing troops.'

Vera Cacciatore was the Director of Rome's Keats-Shelley museum. She later remarked, 'How extraordinary it was to see two Armies crossing a city. Very young, worn-out and hungry German soldiers ran through Rome on foot and the people drew aside so not to trouble them in their progress.'

'This is a great day for the Fifth Army.'

Just hours later she was caught by surprise when American troops came to keep watch over the museum and guard against looters: 'One of them asked to visit the rooms where Keats lived and died in 1821 and where 10,000 volumes by poets such as Shelley, Hunt and Lord Byron are kept.'

By the time the people of Roman flocked onto the streets in large numbers in daylight to wildly celebrate their deliverance on the morning of 5 June, most of the front line soldiers had already passed through on the heels of the retreating Germans. Rear echelon troops got the glory. Just a small number of British units came through the city in the first day of liberation.

US General Mark Clark arrived on that first morning, soon making his way to the Piazzo del Campidoglio. To the press of the free world he announced, 'This is a great day for the Fifth Army.'

It was a statement which upset many, including the war correspondent Eric Sevareid. In his memoirs he wrote: 'That was the immortal remark of Rome's modern-day conqueror. It was not, apparently, a great day for the world, for the Allies, for all the suffering people who had desperately looked towards the time of peace. It was instead a great day for the Fifth Army.'

Sevareid continued, 'The men of the Eighth Army, whose sector did not happen to include Rome but without whose efforts this day could not have occurred, did not soon forget the remark.'

Commander of the mainly American Fifth Army, General Mark Clark, pictured (back centre) in a jeep in Rome on 5 June 1944. His overriding ambition to be the first into the Eternal City caused resentment amongst the other Allies.

D-DAY

Ernest 'Geoff' Huxley was a typical 'D-Day Dodger' who served with the Eighth Army first in North Africa and then Italy and who was away from home for years.

Simply getting to North Africa was an ordeal - his troopship *Strathallen* was torpedoed and sunk on the way and he, along with most of the men on board, was fortunate to survive. In Italy, Geoff went from Sicily to the Po Valley and in the course of the campaign the exploits of the 'D-Day Dodgers' were immortalised in the lyrics of a song. This was sung to the tune of *Lili Marlene*, a favourite with the German Afrika Korps that was 'borrowed' by the British. The song expresses the disappointment of the men of the Eighth and Fifth Armies at what they saw as a lack of public recognition of their

WE ARE THE D-DAY DODGERS, OUT IN ITALY
ALWAYS DRINKING VINO, ALWAYS ON THE SPREE
EIGHTH ARMY SHIRKERS AND THE REST
WE LIVE IN ROME AND EAT THE BEST
WE ARE THE D-DAY DODGERS, OUT IN ITALY

WE LANDED AT SALERNO, A HOLIDAY WITH PAY
JERRY SENT THE BAND OUT TO CHEER US ON OUR WAY
HE SHOWED US THE SIGHTS AND GAVE US TEA
WE ALL SANG SONGS AND THE BEER WAS FREE
FOR THE D-DAY DODGERS, OUT IN ITALY

NAPLES AND CASSINO WERE TAKEN IN OUR STRIDE
WE DIDN'T GO TO FIGHT THERE WE JUST WENT FOR A RIDE
ANZIO AND SANGRO WERE JUST A PLEASANT GAME
AND SENIO WAS REALLY JUST AS TAME
FOR WE ARE THE D-DAY DODGERS, OUT IN ITALY

DEAR LADY ASTOR, PLEASE TAKE A NOTE
DON'T STAND ON THE PLATFORM BLEATING LIKE A GOAT
YOU'RE SUCH A SWEETHEART - THE NATION'S PRIDE
BUT YOUR MOUTH IS OPEN FAR TOO WIDE
THAT'S FROM THE D-DAY DODGERS, OUT IN ITALY

IF YOU ARE IN THE MOUNTAINS IN THE MUD AND RAIN
YOU'LL SEE LOTS OF CROSSES
SOME THAT BEAR NO NAME
HEARTBREAK, TOIL AND SUFFERING
THE BOYS BENEATH SHALL NEVER SING
THAT THEY ARE THE D-DAY DODGERS, OUT IN ITALY

DODGERS!

contribution to the war effort compared to the huge publicity given to D-Day and the subsequent battles in Northern Europe.

Geoff took the opportunity to write down the words of the 'D-Day Dodgers' and eventually sent them home to his wife Betty back to Britain. The references to Bologna and the Po indicate that the songsheet was copied some time after D-Day. It's also the 'unabridged' version complete with advice for 'Dear Lady Astor' who was accused of coining the description 'D-Day Dodgers' in a less than kindly reference to the Allied forces out in Italy.

Geoff never spoke very much about the war although he did freely volunteer the information that his driving duties with the RASC (325 General Transport Company) had at one time involved him in ferrying the band leader Mantovani on a troop concert tour.

Even after the end of the war, lots of 'Dodgers' were kept overseas for many more months. It was January 1946 before Geoff got home to Betty and his four-year old son 'Geoffy'. Geoff resumed his pre-war profession of builder – and not just of houses for he and Betty made up for lost time and produced a brood of no less than nine children in their High Hurstwood, East Sussex, home. One of them – Barbara – became my wonderful wife.

Geoff died in 1985 and Betty too passed away four years later. The Huxley family are happy for me to publish Geoff's D-Day Dodger letter here together with the postcard reproduced below.

David Arnold,
Editor, *Seventy Years On*

Postcard to Italy

Betty Huxley sent this postcard to her husband, Driver Huxley, E G, on 14 May 1944. Her message aside, it's interesting to note the quote from Churchill printed on the card: 'We shall never stop, never weary and never give in.' It's unlikely Betty knew for certain that Geoff was in Italy. In a letter to her dated 9 June, he talks of getting a set of postcards to show her what '... some

of the places out here look like.' But he doesn't say where these places are. When she posted the card Betty was in Ayr, Scotland, with her family and in mourning at the news of the death at Anzio of her brother George Kane of the Royal Scots Fusiliers on 18 April 1944. He is buried in the Beach-head Cemetery alongside so many of his comrades who also lost their lives.

George 'Geordie' Kane.

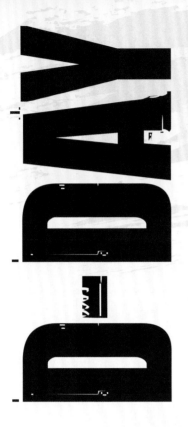

D-DAY

The Invasion of France unfolded on a vast scale. The landing beaches in Normandy were spread along some 60 miles of coast, almost from the mouth of the Seine in the east to the Cotentin Peninsula in the west.

Preceding the sea landings came two vast air armadas with thousands of paratroopers in transport aircraft and gliders. Bombers and fighter planes crowded the skies. The Americans came down in the area behind their two designated beaches of Omaha and Utah. The men of the 101st 'Screaming Eagles' and 82nd 'All American' Airborne Divisions suffered terribly from poor navigation and approach work by their Dakota crews. The Germans had also flooded large areas in recent days to introduce an unforeseen hazard.

The main objective of the US airborne assault was to secure the roads, bridges and causeways leading inland from the invasion beaches, particularly those of Utah, the most westerly. Despite initial confusion and heavy losses, the Americans did well with small groups who joined together to form ad hoc fighting units. A key achievement was the capture of the town of St Mere-Eglise at around 5am; this blocked the route of any German counter-attack in the first vulnerable hours of the sea landings.

How the British air landings fared are covered in more detail on the following pages.

Few of the men who took part in the events of D-Day could have seen the 'big picture'. Only those in the air could get close to gauging the enormity of it all. As dawn broke and an initially uncertain light visited the Normandy beaches, Flight Lt R H G Weighill of RAF No 2 Squadron, 35 Wing, flying a Mustang to spot the fall of shot for *HMS Glasgow*, was privileged to witness a scene without precedent in the history of war.

'The sea was littered with ships of all descriptions, ploughing doggedly towards the enemy's coast, looking very grim and determined. The bombardment was terrific and one could actually see the shells in the form of red and white lights as they left the ships and flew towards the shore. I stayed at 1000 feet and watched five of the naval vessels, about a mile offshore and turned broadside on, proceeding to belch flame and destruction.

'It was a most terrifying sight, for as they fired what I now know to be rockets, a sheet of flame 50 yards long enveloped the ship. By this time the first boat was almost ashore, and as I watched it, the front came down and the men inside jumped into the water and ran towards the beach. It was a wonderful moment when I reported that the first men had actually landed.'

Ashore in force

The RAF's Official History credits Weighill as being most probably the first aerial eye-witness of the landings. By 10.15am the Allies were ashore in force in most places. At this time, Air Commodore Geddes, also in a Mustang, traversed the beaches from one end to the other at a height of some 1000 feet. His flight caught perfectly how the fight was progressing.

In the British and Canadian sector all the beaches (Sword, Juno and Gold) seemed secured. In the centre the village of Le Hamel was shrouded in smoke and dust from which emerged vehicles and the purposeful figures of the invaders. At some places they were already three miles inland; at others half that distance.

As the massive naval force closes in on the Normandy coastline, a vast air armada of aircraft towing gliders flies overhead.

Inset: How the British and US public were informed of where the Allied landings took place.

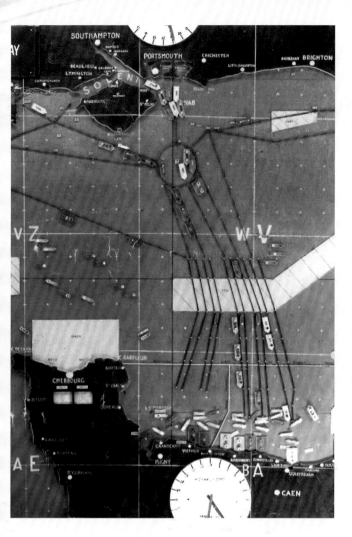

Above: The famous wall map in Southwick House near Portsmouth is preserved in its original position with the clock set for H-Hour on D-Day.

Below: Front page of the Liberation Edition of Yank magazine dated 11 June 1944.

As Geddes approached the Cherbourg (Cotentin) Peninsula, he perceived a place where the 'shore seemed to be congested with vehicles, craft and men with no sign of penetration beyond the sea wall'. This was 'Bloody Omaha' where the Americans were meeting ferocious fire from the Germans atop the steep bluffs rising up from the beach.

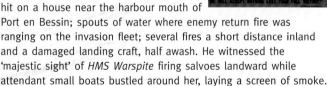

Geddes made another pass, this time in the opposite direction. He noticed a direct hit on a house near the harbour mouth of Port en Bessin; spouts of water where enemy return fire was ranging on the invasion fleet; several fires a short distance inland and a damaged landing craft, half awash. He witnessed the 'majestic sight' of *HMS Warspite* firing salvoes landward while attendant small boats bustled around her, laying a screen of smoke.

By nightfall on D-Day 6 June, the British and Canadians in the east had established a beach-head nearly 20 miles long and some five miles deep. They had secured their flank on the River Orne and were close to the outskirts of the city of Caen.

On the west, around Utah Beach, the Americans held an area nearly 10 miles wide and had spearheads more than four miles inland and in contact with the scattered paratroop units. Only in the centre at Omaha, had there been really serious trouble. But as the light faded in the late evening, even here the US troops were at last making progress and reinforcements were rapidly making good the losses of the day.

The month of June would see gains and setbacks; the German garrison in Cherbourg surrendered on 27 June, though the port was pretty much destroyed. In the east though, the British and Canadians found the going hard against strong German resistance in a countryside and terrain that very much favoured the defenders.

J D Todd landed on Sword Beach:

I was serving on a British Merchant Navy ship carrying ammunition between East Ham and the beaches. We arrived at Sword Beach a few days after the initial assault, by which time we had control of the beaches, although there was considerable activity and much metal flying about. Some days later the ships became the target of long-range shells which we were informed came from a large gun, on rails, sited on the hills above Le Havre.

Under darkness of night, apparently mines were being laid, probably by miniature submarines. I do not know how many ships were lost this way, but recall one morning just as we were approaching the shore the ship ahead was blown up, her back broken, and she went down rapidly. Word later went round that she had been carrying troops for landing and there was much loss of life. Sadly, we could do nothing to help.

Prior to this, there had been a Polish destroyer attempting to shell the long-range gun, but to no avail. We understood that the gun, after a brief spell of shelling, would retract into a cave or bunker. Then, much to our joy, the battleship *HMS Warspite* appeared and stopped not far from our ship, positioned herself, and then proceeded to pound the long-range site. She soon hoisted the 'Target Destroyed' flag and, almost as quickly as she arrived, she vanished. With our ship's telescope we could just make out a large black area where the big gun had been and there was no more shelling from that quarter.

There were many brave men on those beaches, but one group are not often mentioned - the pilots who flew Dakotas loaded with urgently needed cased fuel. Landing these planes on suitable sites was not always possible; apparently any pilot who lost his plane due to these hard landings was required to make his way back to the UK by any possible means. On several of our trips back to East Ham we were able to help. Ironically, by this time the beaches were safer than the Thames due to the daily arrival of the Doodlebugs.

G Hooper was on HMS Ramillies:

I can explain exactly why *HMS Ramillies* was the first ship to open fire on D-Day. She was sailing towards Normandy, some three or four miles distant, when at about 04.30am on 6 June 1944 a shell splashed down scarcely a cable's length dead ahead.

Jerry wasn't playing by the rules. As is now well known, the show wasn't due to start until 05.00. Now, while our Captain Middleton was a gent of the old school, he did have a short fuse, especially when it came to correct procedures not being followed. At this stage I should inform readers, that in action the captain of *HMS Ramillies* wore a grass skirt, a gift from a Maori chief which was guaranteed to keep the ship from harm. (It seemed to work, too, because two years earlier he had taken it off and we were badly hit.) Captain Middleton also wore a monocle. Jerry continued to lob more shells while we could do nothing about it but sail straight on towards our tormentor. Captain Middleton's grass skirt was now rustling noisily, and his face was getting more and more like a monocled turkey cock. At last his short fuse patience snapped and, turning to the gunnery officer, he barked 'Give him one back Guns'. I felt sorry for Guns who was a decent sort (forgotten his name). He hadn't really got a target, but he loosed one off just the same.

And that was why *HMS Ramillies* (pictured above in action on D-Day) became the first of the invasion naval force to open fire.

Gale Force

Cyril Tasker flew in a glider into Normandy in the late afternoon of D-Day.

On 16 April 1942 I was called up for military service. I was 18 then but turned 19 nine days later. I joined the Royal Army Service Corps at Bulford Barracks on Salisbury Plain and underwent five weeks of hard training commencing at the beginning of June.

Next stop for my Company was Hadrians Camp, Carlisle, where driver training and mechanical repairs and maintenance were on the agenda. Along with two others I had already passed my driving test in Civvy Street; after just one Army test we were told we were excused day time training and only had to train at night. Our Instructor Sergeants told us that if we were not doing maintenance or attending repair lectures etc we could 'lose ourselves'. This proved easier said than done with so many permanent camp staff about; in the four weeks we spent at Hadrians Camp we were caught three times and finished up in the cookhouse scrubbing floors and pots and pans etc. We did not actually get charged because it was common knowledge with the camp staff what the Driving Instructors told soldiers like us who were already qualified drivers.

Now came the time when we were ready to be sent to different units stationed oin various parts of the world. They took men in alphabetical order of their surnames. The first batch of 100 or so were destined for the Middle East. They got their required quota just as they got to the letter 'T'. There were only three of us left so it meant we had lost all the mates we'd spent the previous nine weeks or so with. In mid-July we were sent to

a RASC Company stationed by the side of Belfast Lough in Northern Ireland. Our base was a massive house, more of a mansion really, with around 30 large rooms. The grounds were extensive and there was plenty of room to park our three-ton trucks, one of which was put in my care. We were responsible for supplying all the rations, water, arms and ammunition to all the other British Army units stationed in the Six Counties. These units included Royal Artillery, infantry, Military Police, and even the Army prison staff. The most numerous were the anti-aircraft sites.

Sixth Airborne Division

I remained in Northern Ireland until December 1943 when myself and one other chap were posted to the 716 Coy (Airborne Light), Sixth Airborne Division, at a camp on Salisbury Plain a few miles from Salisbury itself. Then it was non-stop training, training, training. We had no idea when the long awaited D-Day would take place. Finally we were moved on to a transit camp. The move took place at night in three-ton trucks that had the sides all shut up and everything was hush hush so we had no idea of where we were.

The transit camp was our home for about a week. Then on the evening of 5 June 1944 we learnt that D-Day was imminent. Next morning, 6 June, we noticed that a unit of paratroopers who had been in an adjoining camp had gone, along with their fold-up push-bikes. Around about midday we moved out, once more travelling in sealed trucks. We did not know we were about to go into action until we found ourselves walking across a small airfield to an array of waiting gliders. Here we again waited for hours. Then we were allocated our individual gliders and

Above: General Richard Gale was in command of the Sixth Airborne Division on D-Day.

inside were the jeeps and trailers we'd trained with at the Salisbury camp; two jeeps and two trailers per glider. It was an absolute marvel how everything had been organised.

Eventually our air armada took off. My own glider landed safely in a field in Normandy on the evening of 6 June. Aircraft were scattered all over the place; some gliders had crashed or smashed into poles that had been dug into the field to form obstructions against just such an attack. There was a lot of noise with mortar fire, shelling, rifle fire and the rattle of machine-guns. Men were getting hurt and men were being killed. I was certainly scared and I'm sure everyone else was as well. We were told to dig in for the night but to stay alert. The shelling eased off. As it got lighter things hotted up again. Later, as the paratroopers (some of whom had push-bikes) advanced to enlarge the perimeters the firing quietened down. The battle had a rhythm – vicious storms of fire were followed by deceptive lulls.

Our two jeeps and trailers were ordered to head for a location close to what was to become known as Pegasus Bridge. I drove the lead jeep and I noticed that though we were less than a mile from our destination we seemed to be going in the wrong direction – not really surprising given all that was happening. Hiding in hedgerows and holes in the ground were hundreds of troops bristling with weapons. German counter-attacks were expected.

General with revolver on hip

I spotted a couple of jeeps parked outside a large house and drove just beyond the gates that opened on to a longish drive. I thought I'd better check on where we were. As I started to walk up the drive I noticed a big burly soldier walking towards me. As we got closer I thought he looked somewhat familiar and then it dawned on me that it was General

Left: British airborne troops drive away from the Horsa glider that took them to Normandy.

Richard Gale, top man of the Sixth Airborne. He had a revolver on his hip. As we met I came to attention, smartly saluted him and said, 'Good morning Sir.' He responded, 'I think you've lost your way soldier.' With that he gave me a hefty push in the chest, strong enough to propel me into a ditch that ran alongside the drive. General Gale dived on top of me. A second later there was a great explosion very close to where we'd just been standing.

As we extricated ourselves from the ditch, General Gale asked, 'Have you been in action before?' I told him this was my first battle. 'You will soon get used to it' he said, 'You will be able to tell by the whine of the shell how close to you it's going to land.' He was right. I did learn to gauge the fall of a shell – although when there was a whole salvo coming down and lots of general noise into the bargain, I didn't always get it right.

General Gale directed us to the area we needed to go to. It was a collection of farm buildings and small fields about 600 yards from Pegasus Bridge. The farmhouse was still occupied by the farmer and his family. The bodies of German and British soldiers could be seen in the fields along with a number of dead cows. Live cows grazed nonchalantly amidst the carnage.

I didn't guess it at the time but we were destined to stay in that same area for the next three and a half months. Our task was to assist in the build up of ammo supplies and fuel dumps. Because we were so near to Pegasus Bridge the Germans kept up persistent shelling and the odd German fighter plane would appear and spray us with machine-gun fire. It took a few weeks but eventually one of the supply dumps took some direct shellfire and the result was absolute hell.

Rendezvous with the Russians

We didn't take part in the great advance through France and Belgium in the late summer but came home and re-grouped. On Christmas Day 1944 we travelled by road and sea and road again to take part in the Battle of the Bulge down in the Ardennes. Two months later we were home again to once more re-group. In March 1945 we went over the Rhine and advanced into Germany to finally meet up with the Russians at Vismar on the Baltic. After 8 May we came home again to be informed we would be going to the Far East to join in the war against Japan. The dropping of the atomic bomb changed those plans and saw us diverted to Palestine in August 1945 where we were stationed for 16 months.

Way back in June 1954 I attended the 10th anniversary commemoration of D-Day in Normandy. There was a rail strike in England around that time and quite a number of next of kin couldn't get across the Channel. I made my travel arrangements through the Airborne Association who booked me on a ferry departing from Newhaven in East Sussex. I travelled in company with photographers and newspaper correspondents. I was asked if I'd be happy to convey a casket of ashes – the remains of poppy wreaths laid at the Cenotaph in London – and present them to Field Marshal Montgomery who would scatter them around the Memorial in Ranville Cemetery. Around 2500 Airborne troops are buried there.

> With that he gave me a hefty push in the chest, strong enough to propel me into a ditch that ran alongside the drive. General Gale dived on top of me. A second later there was a great explosion very close to where we'd just been standing.

As people gathered around the Memorial, Monty asked me various questions concerning where I lived, where I served in Normandy and that sort of thing. I also spoke with General Gale and he remembered the incident when he pushed me into the ditch – and most likely saved my life.

I had another mission to perform for the Airborne Association. They gave me the names and addresses of a number of next of kin who couldn't be there but who wanted me to take photographs of the graves of their loved ones. I had nine graves to find and I took two photographs of each one. This task was the hardest part of my return to Normandy. But it was a great honour.
Cyril Tasker lives in Lewes, East Sussex.

Below: Aerial view of Pegasus Bridge, the area where Cyril Tasker made for on D-Day. Note the three gliders on the ground. These brought in men of the Ox & Bucks led by Major John Howard to seize the bridge in the very early hours of D-Day.
Cyril returned once more to Normandy in June 2010. He visited Pegasus Bridge and the cemetery at Ranville and brought home the commemoration service booklet from which the cover is inset below.

REMEMBRANCE SERVICE
for
THE MEN AND WOMEN OF THE ALLIED FORCES
WHO GAVE THEIR LIVES IN NORMANDY IN 1944
at
RANVILLE CEMETERY
WHERE LIE
Men of the British 6th Airborne Division,
1st and 4th Commando Brigades,
Royal Air Force and other Allied Forces
6 June 2010

JUNO

EYE WITNESS

I was too young to serve in the Forces in 1944 but have been privileged to know many people who did, writes Ron McGill. Sometimes it can be difficult to visualise that these quiet, mild-mannered and elderly men are the survivors of the brave youngsters who, over nearly seven decades ago, fought so valiantly for the precious freedom we enjoy to this day.

One such man is Peter Glanville, now in his Eighties and disabled/wheelchair bound who lives at Hindhead in Surrey with Chris, his wartime WAAF sweetheart who became his wife and is now his constant care and attention officer!

Many Guildford folks will know Chris and Peter from their period in the 1970s/80s when they ran the sub-post office in the Pilgrim's Bookshop in Upper High Street, Guildford, until Peter's retirement in 1985.

Peter joined the Royal Navy in 1940. He later volunteered for Combined Operations in 1943 and was trained as a Yeoman Signaller at Plymouth prior to posting to a new craft LCT.2428 – a Landing Craft Tank that was part of the LCT 105 Flotilla. After a hazardous journey down from Scotland they eventually tied up safely at the Hamble River near Southampton to begin intensive training into the Channel – somehow surviving an attack from German E-Boats that blasted bullets through the sides of his LCT.

Pleasant surprise

Shortly before D-Day, Peter's commander called him in and proudly informed him he was regarded as the most expert wireless/signaller in the group. This was a pleasant surprise for Peter until he was told he would be staying with the Commander in his role as Flotilla Leader on the first craft of the first wave of assault craft to land at Juno Beach on 6 June. At this stage I think it more interesting to hand over to the actual wording of Peter's personal 'Overlord Diary' that he has kept to this day:

'We weighed anchor at 0600 on 5 June 1944 and proceeded down river to the Solent, all the time gradually forming into 'cruising order'. The sight was wonderful to behold...thousands of ships, all shapes and sizes, packed with tanks, guns, men and material setting off on a journey across the English Channel to invade Hitler's European Fortress – commonly known as France.

We had been finally briefed some 24 hours beforehand so all knew what we were sailing into and of course, all wondering if we would ever see the shores of our homeland again – or the ones we loved.

The weather was not ideal for the job, in fact for the small craft it was rough going. How some of them managed to stay afloat under the circumstances was a miracle – due to superb seamanship and our ship-building people. We in LCT 2428 were not having too bad a time as the ship was one of the bigger types of 'Tank Landing Craft'

weighing 120 tons with an additional 100 tons of Army Tanks and Bulldozers aboard.

Hit by a mine

At 0500 hours on 6 June we were a few miles off our objective – Juno Beach – and we then formed into battle stations and went in at the coast – full speed ahead! The beach itself was a mass of obstacles and mines. One type was a huge steel gate arrangement on rollers which allowed a craft to get so far over it then the craft would stick – and they also had mines on them! Although a lot of the craft hit these things and received holes in their ballast tanks they were so constructed that it did not effect them so much.

Our ship's objective was very slightly to the right of the village of Courselles and it was known to be heavily defended. The Army lads were informed we were near and told to stand by to land. On the way over most of them had been very seasick but now they forgot all that!

We went in at the beach in a long formidable line with reinforcement craft in our wake. It must have been a sickening sight for the German defenders behind their guns on the beach. The craft I was in was hit by a mine as we went up onto the beach, a large hole was blown in our starboard side but luckily, nobody was hurt that much and we got our Army gear and infantry off safely.

The Bulldozers cleared away many of the tank traps while our guns blasted away at the enemy pillboxes. At the same time we were receiving covering fire from Landing Craft fitted with 4-inch guns – these were known as LCGs whose job it was to stay off shore and lob shells over our heads into the enemy lines. They and the rocket firing ships gave us good cover but unfortunately some fell short causing us a few casualties.

Good fighting men

It was truly hell let loose – our guns firing over our heads and the Germans firing at us. Somehow we managed it and the landing was eventually 'made'. Our men got to the barbed wire in front of the pill-boxes and then received very heavy machine-gun fire... a lot fell dead or wounded but the rest ran on through the wire and into some trenches, having no mercy and killing as they went. It was a case of get your man or be killed yourself.

We had landed 'Marines – Kent Regiment' and 'Royal Canadian Winnipeg Rifles' – all good fighting men and the Canadians especially so. They ran at the wire, some laid flat on it while others walked over them – a sure way of getting through but not one of my choosing! Once through they slipped off their heavy packs and carried on to charge with fixed bayonets and long thin bladed knives.

'Get out and push it!'

We managed to get back to our craft and cleared the beach although she had been mined – the main thing was to get all craft clear in order that the supplies in our wake could keep coming in to land. Our poor old ship, LCT 2428, made a gallant effort to keep afloat but by midnight we realised she was doomed. It was just a matter of how long she would stay up; unfortunately, not very long! I was busy 'flashing' as many ships as I could asking them to pick us up – but they were all heading for the beaches and could not stop. Their replies included, 'Sorry Chum, cannot stop' and 'Never mind Mate, better luck next time' and even, 'Get out and push it!' One ship was a bit more polite – he flashed back 'Regret unable to help, have a date with Hitler'.

She began turning over on us and it was a scramble to the ship's side. I was still on the Bridge then but it was only a matter of seconds before I had slipped off my oilskins and joined the rest of the crew in the water. I was just thinking that 15 miles to the shore was a long way to swim when a large Tug came by and picked us up. The most welcome sight I had seen for many a day and we could relax a bit as the Tug brought us back to England and landed us at Portsmouth on the morning of 7 June. We were given hot drinks, food and clothing, then asked all sorts of questions as we were the first survivors to come back.

'What was it like?' 'What had we seen?' 'Were our lads ashore and holding?' and a 1001 other questions. We were then issued with a mattress and blanket (on loan) and slept a peaceful night's sleep... the end of a hectic 24 hours indeed!'

TUESDAY, JUNE 6, 1944

FINAL NIGHT EXTRA

Evening Standard

37,357   BLACK-OUT 10 57 pm to 5.0 am.   MOON Rises 9.50 pm; Sets 6.29 am.   ONE PENNY

Churchill Announces Successful Massed Air Landings Behind Enemy in France

4000 SHIPS, THOUSANDS OF SMALLER VESSELS

"So Far All Goes to Plan"— 11,000 First Line Airplanes

SHELLED BY 640 GUNS

An immense armada of more than 4000 ships, with several thousand smaller craft, has crossed the Channel, said Mr. Churchill to-day, announcing the invasion.

"MASSED AIRBORNE LANDINGS HAVE BEEN SUCCESSFULLY EFFECTED BEHIND THE ENEMY'S LINES," HE SAID.

MR. CHURCHILL DESCRIBED THE LANDINGS AS THE "FIRST OF A SERIES IN FORCE ON THE EUROPEAN CONTINENT."

"The landings on the beaches are proceeding at various points at the present time. The fire of the shore batteries has been largely quelled, said Mr. Churchill.

"The obstacles which were constructed in the sea have not proved so difficult as was apprehended.

"The Anglo-American Allies are sustained by about 11,000 first line aircraft, which can be drawn upon as may be needed for the purposes of the battle.

No. 1

At 9.30 a.m. to-day the following communiqué was issued from General Eisenhower's Supreme Headquarters:

"Under the command of General Eisenhower, Allied naval forces, supported by strong air forces, began landing Allied armies this morning on the Northern coast of France."

The statement was marked "Communiqué No. 1." At the same time it was revealed that General Montgomery is in command of the Army Group carrying out the assault. This Army Group includes British, Canadian and U.S. forces.

The King on the Radio To-night

It was officially announced from Buckingham Palace to-day that the King will broadcast at 9 o'clock to-night.

HITLER IN COMMAND

Hitler is taking personal command of all the anti-invasion operations, according to news reaching London from underground sources.

His four marshals are Rundstedt, titular commander-in-chief; Rommel, Inspector-General; Sperrle, in charge of air forces; and Blaskowitz, acting deputy to Rommel.

'LANDINGS ON JERSEY, GUERNSEY'

German Overseas News Agency said this afternoon that landings have been made on the Channel Islands —Jersey and Guernsey—by Allied parachute troops.

Quoting the German High Command spokesman, the agency said: "Early to-day Allied airborne formations landed on Guernsey and Jersey.

"They were at once engaged in extremely costly battles."

"I cannot, of course, commit myself to any particular details, as reports are coming in in rapid succession. So far, the commanders who are engaged report that everything is proceeding according to plan—and what a plan!

"This vast operation is undoubtedly the most complicated and difficult that has ever occurred.

SURPRISE

"There are already hopes that actual tactical surprise has been attained," said the Premier, "and we hope to furnish the enemy with a succession of surprises during the course of the fighting.

"The battle which is now beginning will grow constantly in scale and in intensity for many weeks to come, and I shall not attempt to speculate upon its course.

"Complete unity prevails throughout the Allied Armies." (Cheers.)

"There is a brotherhood in arms between us and our friends in the United States.

"There is complete confidence in the Supreme Commander, General Eisenhower, and in his lieutenants, and also in the Commander of the Expeditionary Force, General Montgomery.

"The ardour and spirit of the troops as I saw them myself embarking in these last few days was splendid.

"Nothing that equipment, science and forethought can do has been neglected, and the whole process of opening this great new front will be pursued with the utmost resolution both by the commanders and by the U.S. and British Governments whom they serve.

WHAT A PLAN !

Replying to Mr. Greenwood, Mr. Churchill said that certainly in the early part of the battle he
(Continued on Back Page, Col. Four)

Thousands Of Fighters Strafe The Nazi Guns

Since the invasion began, Allied fighter-bombers have been dive-bombing, glide-bombing and strafing German defences and communications.

They fly literally into the mouths of guns and dive within feet of the roads which hold bridges together.

A gun is silenced, a truck carrying ammunition for a company of German soldiers is blown up, a bridge is shattered, making German supply convoys detour 20 or 30 miles, a gun crew is wiped out—multiplied by thousands, the fighter-bomber attacks will help the surface forces in 1000 ways, and will have an enormous effect on the battles below.

Bomber Command last night made their heaviest attack to date on the German batteries along the French coast.

In all, Bomber Command despatched more than 1300 aircraft.

The Supreme Headquarters of the Allied Expeditionary Force state that over 640 naval guns, from 16in. to 4in., are bombarding the beaches and enemy strong points in support of the armies.

About 200 Allied minesweepers, with 10,000 officers and men, are engaged in the operations.

The weight of minesweeping material used amounts to 2800 tons, and the amount of sweep wire in use would reach almost exactly from London to the Isle of Wight.

The Press Association learns that enemy destroyers and E-boats are reported coming into the operational area,

'Tanks Ashore on Normandy Coast'
—SAYS BERLIN

The Allies have established beach-heads in Northern France and are driving inland, according to pilots who have flown over the battle.

This afternoon the Germans announced that landings were continuing in the Seine Bay—the stretch of the Normandy coast between the two ports of Cherbourg and Le Havre.

They reported parachute landings on Guernsey and Jersey, the two principal Channel Islands, and said that Allied troops were ashore at these points on the coast of Normandy:

ST. VAAST LE HOUGE (on the Cherbourg Peninsula): "Mass landing" supported by considerable naval forces, while strong American airborne forces jumped near Barfleur, a few miles to the north.

OUISTREHAM (at the mouth of the River Orne): "Landing barges under strong air umbrella are making landings," said the Germans.

Earlier the Germans had mentioned that Caen, a few miles inland up the Orne, was "the first local point," where sharp fighting was taking place. The Germans also reported fighting 10 miles inland.

ARROMANCHES (in the middle of the Seine Bay): Tanks have been landed there, says Berlin.

ST. MARCOUF ISLANDS (just off the coast south of Cherbourg): "New landings made before noon particularly in this area."

VIRE ESTUARY

Another focal point mentioned by the Germans was the estuary of the Vire, another river running north into the Seine Bay.

Parachute landings were reported in several areas besides Barfleur—
(Continued on Back Page, Col. Two)

Stories of The Men Who Watched

Here are the stories told by men who watched the landings.

Fighter pilots returning from over the landing areas report that Allied infantry scrambled ashore at 7 a.m. in two areas of the French coast, apparently without heavy opposition, says Robert Richards, British United Press war correspondent at a U.S. Fighter Base.

One of the pilots, an American Colonel, William Curry, told me:

"I saw the first troops wading ashore about 7 a.m. from light landing craft. From the height at which I was flying they did not appear to be meeting heavy opposition and were covered by extensive and heavy naval bombardment from our warships.

"Flying Fortresses were also bombing the beach which appeared to be marshy instead of sandy.

Major John Locke, of Texas, who led a squadron of Thunderbolts, said:

"I have never seen so many ships in all my life. Flying over the harbour at one port I counted great numbers of cruisers, destroyers, corvettes and other craft. The constant flashes from their guns indicated that the beach was getting a heavy pounding.

"Behind this advance brigade, stretching in a never-ending stream across the Channel, came line after line of L.C.T.s (landing craft, tanks) escorted by corvettes and P.T. boats.

"We were never attacked by enemy airplanes although the flak was terrific."

Second Lieut. Benson, from Iowa, said: "The Channel waters were fairly calm and the boats bounced along smoothly. They were constantly patrolled by warships and many were towing barrage balloons.

Colonel William Schwartz added: "When I arrived over the beach our battleships brought all their fire to bear on the shore."

MULBERRY

Kenneth Bungard went to France aboard various parts of the Royal Navy's famous prefabricated harbours.

My D-Day experience actually began on 24 April 1944, after returning to Chatham Barracks from service with the Fleet Air Arm in Trinidad. Whilst awaiting a ship I went home to see my girl. Being a few hours adrift from my overnight pass, I was consequently put on Captain's Report. Being in the rattle and a 'black list' man, when the tannoy called for volunteers for some mysterious operations called *Party Fun* and *Party Game*, I was first in the queue, with no idea what I was letting myself in for.

'Rig of the day' was overalls, sea boots and lifebelts and it was disconcerting to be issued with red lights and batteries for our lifebelts. When asked for my Station Card, I owned up that it was in the possession of the Master at Arms. They were anxious to get us off, so I was grudgingly told to be certain to report back to the Master at Arms office as soon as the job was over. Naturally, I never did go back and ask for punishment.

Blocks of flats

We were taken to Sheerness where we were confronted by what looked like windowless blocks of flats alongside a quay. We climbed the ladder and found ourselves on top of a huge concrete egg-box type thing with no top but a bit of concrete at one end on which to stand. We were towed at night past Dover to Dungeness Bay, where we opened

the sluices and part submerged the strange object. The Germans used to shell 'Hell Fire Corner', of course, and we felt very vulnerable crawling along behind a tug. Our base at this time was the dear old paddle-steamer *Queen of Thanet*, where our kit was stowed and in theory we slept.

We settled into a routine of bringing these great caissons called Phoenixes round to Dungeness and Selsey Bill. They were about 60ft high, 60ft wide, 200ft long and weighed in at around 7000 tons. When we tried to pump them out to refloat them, our pumps were useless, so civilian contractors were brought in with bigger ones, and, to our great disgust, they were paid danger money just for setting foot on the things. Some stuck firmly to the bottom, despite all our efforts, some broke in half, but most were refloated to be towed across to Normandy.

Lord Haw Haw

Naturally we were not told the purpose of these monsters, which were sunk randomly in Dungeness Bay, where they must have been visible to any German reconnaissance aircraft. Lord Haw Haw remarked that the Germans would sink them for us. Secrecy was vital, of course, and though we could receive mail, we could not send any out, and there was absolutely no leave. Some of the caissons were left sunk around Dover as part of the deception plan. I have a film which shows caissons assembled in Dungeness Bay and I can see the *Queen of Thanet* tied up to one of the pier head parts. I see that I also have the *Queen of Kent* on my naval record for that time. I believe that she was later sunk in a Belgian port by a V2.

Owing to the hard conditions under which we were living, things began to get a bit fraught, with much discontent amongst some of the men who missed their beer and women; the Captain, in his wisdom, decided to give a few hours shore leave. Visions of some of the men disappearing 'up the Smoke' etc, were soon dispelled when we were landed at Ryde on the Isle of Wight, for a single evening's fun. Unfortunately, a long pent-up thirst, plus many Americans also on a run ashore, culminated in a complete mix-up of men who found themselves on all the wrong ships for the night, something which had to be sorted out next morning. A good time was reckoned to have been had by all, even though no one could remember a thing about it.

100 miles to Arromanches

For D-Day we started off across the Channel at about four knots, towed by a tug. The 100 mile trip to Arromanches was very long, very cold and, I suppose, very dangerous. We were issued with duffel coats, but it was still freezing cold up there. The self-heating tins of soup, and I think cocoa, were very welcome. There was nowhere to sit down and in any case we had to walk round all the time to check on whether the thing had sprung a leak. There was an Able Seaman (my rank) in charge of each Phoenix, one Naval Signaller and two Ordinary Seamen.

In the middle there was an AA gun, with two soldiers to man it. It could not be fired at sea. The soldiers were lucky as they could get into a bit of shelter under the gun, but we were exposed to the freezing cold all the way.

Our caisson sprang a leak and I signalled to the tug that I had to let one of the side weights go as we were listing badly. Of course, it then rolled over the other way with the weight of the water sloshing about inside it. So I asked the tug to go as fast as possible as we were sinking and our pump was useless. We got to Arromanches in the nick of time and sank it into position. It was quite a hairy situation. I had to get down onto the narrow ledge which ran round the caisson's base. In calm weather this would have been about four or five feet about the water, but owing to the list it was well awash and the massive side of the caisson looked to me like the Leaning Tower of Pisa overhead. Two of the Phoenixes were torpedoed by E-Boats from Cherbourg or Le Havre, some broke up, some were cut adrift, some went down in the gale that hit us some days after D-Day. As the flat front of the caisson hit the waves, it echoed like a huge drum, with a constant deep booming sound.

On arrival at Arromanches I had to give a paper to a RN Officer, as evidence of safe delivery. He could not have cared less and I wish now that I had just put it in my pocket, as it would be an interesting souvenir today. As far as I recall, it had the codename Phoenix and the number of the caisson at the top. He didn't give me a receipt. We were put on to the first available vessel back to Selsey, to bring another caisson across.

Sodden clothes

It was a really grim time. We could not wash, shave, change our sodden clothes and had just two gallons of fresh water between us per trip. All our kit was on the *Queen of Thanet*

so there was no hope of dry clothes. We had a box of rations containing self-heating cans of soup and cocoa, boiled sweets, a few cigarettes, toilet paper, bacon wrapped in foil (though we had no means of cooking!). We were also issued with 'Wakey-Wakey' tablets.

We received no news whatsoever and had no idea even what day of the week it was. After one of these delivery trips we landed back at Portsmouth Barracks, thinking we would get a shower and a meal, but instead we were put on a train with a warrant for Dungeness via London. That did it. I realised that the train would go through Woking and was determined to alight if it stopped. We all agreed that we deserved a bath and a change of underwear and agreed to meet at Victoria very early next morning.

So, I got off at Woking, filthy, smelly, unshaven; the Redcaps made a beeline for me. A little porter boy saw me and I asked him if he could get me off the station quickly as I had no ticket. He asked if I was a survivor, and when I said yes, he quickly let me out of a side gate, where I fortunately got straight on a bus for Chertsey. An army officer also got on and regarded me with increasing suspicion. I was wearing overalls and had tucked my cap inside, but suddenly realised that my lifebelt was sticking out of my pocket. I hastily alighted at St Peter's Hospital (then Botleys Park War Hospital) and hurried up to Ferndale Avenue to my fiancée's home. Her mother ran me a bath while she cycled off to my home to collect some clean underwear from my mother. I was so exhausted I kept falling asleep in the bath. When they asked what on earth I had been doing, she said I muttered something about sailing a bloody great block of flats - before falling asleep with my face in a plate of dinner. I got the first train next morning, met the others safely at Victoria in spite of the numerous Redcaps, and, clean and fragrant again, we got safely back to Dungeness, where we resumed our shuttle service. We usually came back on a tug, trying to snatch some sleep on open decks in lousy weather. One bright spot was returning on an American

ocean-going tug, where we were able to go below and could help ourselves to some marvellous food, coffee and even ice-cream.

Gliders overhead

I remember seeing gliders going overhead and one coming down in the sea. Star shells were being fired at odd intervals, in the hope of illuminating any prowling E-Boats. Two caissons were sunk by German torpedoes; the crews did not stand a chance of being rescued, as the blocks would have gone down like stones. There were buoyed swept channels going across to the landing beaches, and the E-Boats would tie up to these buoys and lie in wait. These great lumbering slow monsters were sitting ducks.

Once there was no navy vessel to bring us back, so we were sent to a merchant ship rigged out with hammocks to sleep on, as if that was possible with all the shelling going on and general racket. Early next morning we sailed back on a Norwegian merchant ship which, to our great surprise, had some females in the crew.

The saddest memory is of seeing all the bodies floating about in the water off the Normandy coast. Men with boat hooks were fishing the dead out of the water and piling the bodies up on the deck of a big launch. I realised then how lucky those of us were who came through it all unharmed.

On looking back, it was quite something to have had a part in the greatest amphibious operation of all time, though I must admit that I did not appreciate the historical importance of it in 1944. My next posting was to a new destroyer, *HMS Zenith*, on escort duty with convoys to Russia.

Below: The Arromanches Mulberry pictured from high altitude. There was a second artificial harbour at St Laurent that was crippled in a three day storm that struck Normandy on 19 June 1944. Parts of it were salvaged and moved to the more sheltered waters at Arromanches. The harbour then stayed operational until 19 November 1944 by which time over 250,000 men and 40,000 vehicles had been landed there as well as up to 11,000 tons of stores a day.

Around the Orne!

Captain Robert Worth of the Royal Engineers landed on Sword Beach on D+3. During the battle for Caen he believes he witnessed an incident of 'friendly fire' that had a profound effect on the course of the war.

We were transported across from the port of Newhaven by an American LSI. The senior crew kindly invited the Officers into the ward room for dinner and served us with the fattest pork chops I ever saw; being subject to sea-sickness this was a good start! I took pills to stop me being sick, but oh how I wanted to be. The one good result was that the next morning as we sailed into Sword Beach, I didn't care a hoot about the shelling on the shore, all I wanted was to get my feet on dry land.

We sailed in past the bows of battle-cruiser Renown. Her big guns were firing, an ear-splitting experience. The American LSI crew wanted rid of us as soon as possible so they could pull off away from the shelling and in consequence we were landed in quite deep water. I took my platoon in advance to take up our positions around the sea-locks at the entrance to the Ouistreham-Caen Canal. We had been told that the front line would be some two miles up the coast at Cabourg, so I was somewhat surprised to be told by the Ox and Bucks Light Infantry that our position was the frontline and the Germans were some 400 yards away on the east bank of

the mouth of the River Orne. The Ox and Bucks added nonchalantly that they were pulling out under orders and it was all ours! The Sixth Airborne were also on the east bank of the Orne, but at least half a mile inland.

My platoon - men of the 937 Port Construction and Repair Company, Royal Engineers, took up the advanced position on the east side of the lock with a minefield in front of us, but with a dirt track running through towards the Germans. I felt fairly safe as the Orne was between us; that was until a local Frenchman told me that you could drive a car across at low tide, so tanks could certainly traverse it. I often wondered if Monty knew that only a mere Port Construction Company was holding the extreme left of the line. An armoured attack could have overwhelmed us and have enjoyed an open

coast road to roll up the beaches all the way to Arromanches and the Mulberry Harbour.

Dazzling gold braid

This doubt was reinforced after a few days when a number of staff cars drove to the west of the locks and out got A V Alexander, the War Minister, and a dazzling array of gold braid, red tape and all and proceeded to walk across the damaged bridges over the locks and climb onto the top of the heavy coastal gun emplacements in full view of the Germans. I remonstrated with an ADC who said they knew what they were doing. So I got all my men off work and into their slit trenches, expecting a violent German reaction, but nothing happened; perhaps they were so amazed they thought it was a trap.

When the locks and their machinery had been got into working order, the next priority was to ensure that all the lift bridges over the canal were also in working order after being inoperative for some time. We managed all successfully except the famous Pegasus Bridge which was the main access and supply route to the Sixth Airborne Division and by then also to the 51st Highland Division. It also carried festoons of signal cables which precluded lifting the bridge without breaking them. Not being able to agree a possession

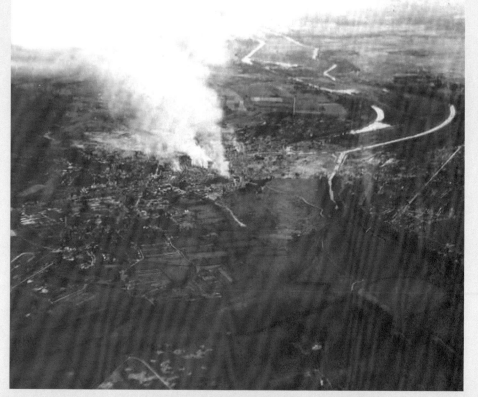

Above: A German armoured vehicle passes a wrecked British glider in the Ranville area near the River Orne on 7 June 1944.

Left: A dramatic photograph of the results of Allied bombing of Caen. The city was largely destroyed after D-Day as the Allies attempted to overcome the stubborn German resistance that centred around this part of Normandy. The Caen Canal and River Orne are the two waterways running down to the coast. Pegasus Bridge at Benouville is in the centre top area of the photograph but the bridge is too distant to be made out. This is the area where Robert Worth and his Royal Engineers platoon operated from 9 June 1944. Although obscured by smoke, Ouistreham and Sword Beach are to the left of the photograph and Cabourg is off to the top right.

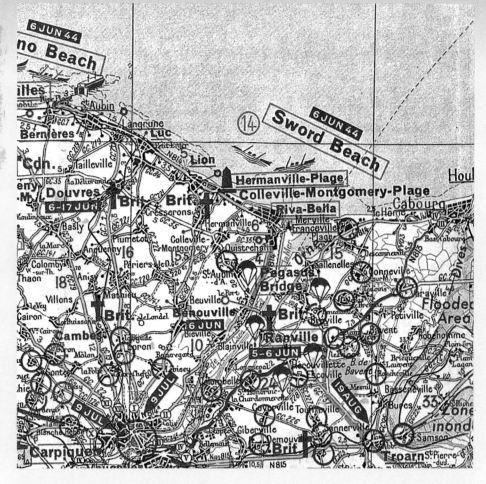

of the bridge at local level we sent a request all the way up to Army Group level and down came permission for a one hour occupation.

A bridge too stuck

These bridges are hand-operated rolling bascule constructions and at the appointed time I was in the winding chamber in one of the abutments having posted sentries to stop any traffic. We wound the bridge up successfully, but when winding it down it stuck with the bridge at two feet above its closed position. Whilst I was in the winding chamber I heard the roar of an engine and the squeal of brakes and looking out saw a jeep had drawn up on the bridge carrying a very irate Airborne Officer who jumped out and – from his elevated height above the road – started to tongue-lash the little Welsh sentry below. When he finally paused for breath this little chap standing as stiff as a ram-rod, looked up at the Officer's red beret and said 'Well sir, you are Airborne aren't you?'.

When the break-out approached, we had moved up to the outskirts of Caen to build additional jetties in Caen docks. We were stationed just to the north west of Caen and all available heavy and medium guns had been drawn up in an arc to be ready for the advance over the open and higher country to the south east of the city. The guns had ample dumps of ammunition behind them. At mid-day, with a clear blue sky, we heard bombs start to come down and saw three Flying Fortresses start to plaster our own ammo dumps – we heard later from the RAF

that a Mosquito was up there too and tried to signal the Fortresses that they were bombing way off target, but with no effect. He shot one down, but by then the damage had been done. The dumps continued to explode for at least 24 hours. Therefore the break-out was delayed to allow for the dumps to be built up again.

The result was that the closure of the trap at Falaise was not total and a number of German divisions escaped though badly mauled. All this I can vouch for, but later I learned that one of the divisions which happened to be re-equipping in Arnhem at the time of the Market Garden attack in September was one of those which had escaped. It thus seems to me that

but for the Flying Fortresses and their 'friendly fire', Arnhem might have been a success and we would have been through to Berlin before Christmas, long before the Russians, with a resulting profound effect on post-war state of affairs in Europe. Perhaps for the want of a horse-shoe the battle was lost.

Above: A section of a 1947 Michelin Map showing the Normandy battlefield.

Below left and right: Two photographs taken just days before the invasion by a reconnaissance Spitfire of No 430 Squadron RAF. Both show the Dives estuary with Cabourg and Houlgate on either side. Robert Worth believed Cabourg would be the frontline on D+3 but it wasn't! Note the extensive beach obstacles – 'Rommel's asparagus' – in the photograph below.

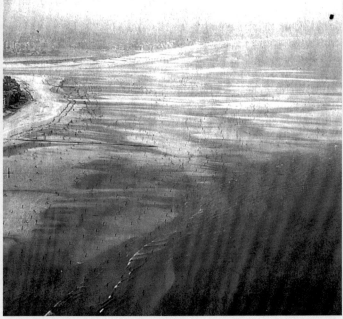

Above: Barbed wire remains on the cliff top at Pointe du Hoc which US Rangers stormed on D-Day. Bunkers thought to contain heavy guns were found to be empty.

Above: Gold and Juno Beaches as they appear today can be seen in this Calvados view. British and Canadian troops came ashore on this coast on D-Day.

Above: Arromanches where the remains of the gigantic Mulberry Harbour can still be seen embedded in the sand. All pictures by John Lloyd

D-DAY TO *Tin Pan Alley*

After Royal Navy service, opportunity came knocking for singing sensation David Whitfield.

The lumpy, windswept English Channel at dawn on 6 June 1944 hampered the vulnerable landing craft, but offshore lay the massive force waiting to provide naval artillery cover. Part of this group was the veteran 29,000 ton battleship *HMS Ramillies*.

Although 28 years old, her 8 x 15 inch guns were still capable of hurling massive shells far inland. She was the first ship to open fire off Sword Beach, and her particular targets included the fortified gun emplacements at Mont Canasy and the German garrison at Vierville - the shell craters are still visible today in the hills behind the beaches. At his duty station serving one of *Ramillies'* gun turrets, was a young seaman who had served a mere seven months in the Royal Navy - JX63035 Whitfield D.

After his demob in 1950, David Whitfield went on to achieve fame and fortune as one of the biggest singing stars this country has ever produced. He was the first British male singer ever to be awarded a Gold Disc. This was for *Cara Mia*, which stayed at the top of the charts for 10 consecutive weeks – a remarkable achievement in its day.

David Whitfield aboard HMS Belfast in the Far East. The ship - herself a veteran of D-Day - is now berthed in the Pool of London and is a popular tourist attraction.

Singapore posting

David Whitfield was born in Hull in the Drypool area on 2 February 1926 and began his love affair with singing as a choirboy at St Peter's Church. During his early years in the Royal Navy, wartime commitments allowed little leisure time to pursue his hobby and it was not until he received a coveted posting to Singapore in 1947 that more opportunities arose. Travelling out to join *HMS Belfast*, David was a passenger on the troopship *Empress of Scotland*. The long voyage provided many chances to entertain the other passengers at concert parties and the talent of the young seaman was noticed.

His time on *Belfast* was short, as the cruiser was returning home. David was posted to the frigate *HMS Black Swan*, one of the first ships to venture up the Yangtze River, scene of the dramatic escape of *HMS Amethyst* in 1949. Visits to Shanghai, Amoy and Hong Kong provided increasing opportunities for David to spend his shore leave singing in hotels, clubs and bars, and to supplement his basic naval pay. A regular 15 minute slot on Radio Hong Kong (ZBW) paid £8 – almost two weeks pay for an able seaman at that time.

Ed Sullivan Show

David returned to the UK and was de-mobbed in 1950. He was establishing a reputation as a promising tenor, but initially found it difficult to repeat the success he'd enjoyed in the Far East. His big showbiz break came when he was admitted as a last-minute replacement to one of Hughie Green's *Opportunity Knocks* heats. Performing *Goodbye from White Horse Inn*, he won the grand final and the 'singing sailor' was finally on his way. Hughie invited him to tour with the Radio

Luxembourg *Opportunity Knocks* show for eight months.

David went on to become one of the biggest and brightest international stars this country has produced. He was the first British recording star to break into the American Top 10 and the first to achieve a US million seller. He appeared no less than eight times on the Ed Sullivan Show, and hosted his own TV shows in this country. He appeared in three Royal Command Performances, featured in the stage version of *The Desert Song*, and his recording of *I'll Find You* was the backing track for the Richard Burton and Joan Collins film *Sea Wife*. Other massive hits included *Marta, I Believe, Answer Me* and *Bridge of Sighs*.

David continued to sing for his myriad fans worldwide for many years after the halcyon days of his singing career. Indeed, he was on a tour of Australia when he died suddenly in January 1980 of a cerebral haemorrhage. His ashes were brought home to England, and were carried out into the North Sea on the frigate *HMS Sirius* – thus maintaining his link with the Royal Navy to the final chapter.

Martin Barton Smith

*The memory of David's remarkable career in entertainment lives on via The David Whitfield International Appreciation Society whose Patron is Dame Vera Lynn DBE. More information and details of how to obtain recordings of David's hits may be obtained from the secretary, Bill Wilkins on 01482 831570. Bill is curator of The David Whitfield Museum & Archives in Kingston upon Hull. Admission is free but by appointment only. Information is also available at: **www.davidwhitfield.com**

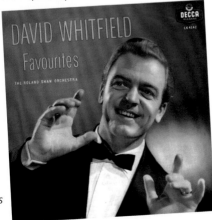

An album of David Whitfield's favourites performed with backing from the Roland Shaw Orchestra.

BAND OF BROTHERS

Frank Bennett in army uniform.

David Arnold recounts how some spilt red wine revealed a fascinating tale concerning seven brothers from a South London family who all went off to war and later returned home safely.

I have made many friends through my abiding interest in the experiences of people in wartime. Perhaps the most unusual circumstance in which I made a new acquaintance came after the publication of the earlier edition of this work that was titled *Sixty Years On*. I took a telephone call just before Christmas 2007 from a Mrs Maureen Bennett. She was enquiring whether there were any copies of the book still available. She explained that she and her husband Frank had borrowed a copy from a friend but unfortunately had spilt some red wine on it and would be very embarrassed to return it in a stained condition.

Highly amused, I introduced myself as the Editor of the book and told Maureen that she was in luck – we did indeed still have a small number of copies available. We went on to have a very pleasant chat in the course of which Maureen told me a little about Frank's wartime experiences as one of no less than seven brothers from South East London who saw service in the British armed forces. It was a fascinating story.

Frank was the youngest of the seven brothers and at the beginning of the war was evacuated to Devon. Upon his return to London he served in the ARP before, at the age of 17, volunteering for the infantry in the Buffs. He spent time at the Black Watch barracks in Scotland and also in Canterbury before being sent to Holland in September 1944, around the time of the ill-fated *Operation Market Garden*.

Base outside Brussels

Later he was sent to a base just outside Brussels. One night he was woken up and told that his brother Fred was in the 21 Club in the city. 'This was cheering news,' said Frank, 'But I was dog tired and it wasn't so cheering to be woken up about 10 times through the night to be told the same story.

'Anyway in the morning I was able to get special leave from my CO to go into Brussels. When I got there I discovered that Fred had been called back. We had a good laugh about the incident for years afterwards.'

Frank continued, 'Later I was in the Bad Harzburg area of Germany attached to a special force tasked with rounding up SS and Gestapo officers. One time we met with some awful bad luck, one of our platoon banged on a door with the butt of his sten gun which fired and killed a colleague behind him.

'Whilst on these duties I came into possession of a dagger type dress sword which I still have. After VE Day I went back to Blighty for a while expecting to be sent to the Far East. In the event I was sent over to Germany again and spent some time on guard

After the end of the war in Europe, six of the seven brothers were reunited for the first time since the outbreak of hostilities. The meeting was reported in the local paper and Frank still has the newspaper cutting which we've reproduced here. It reads: 'Six brothers who have been

Charlton Brothers First Re-Union Since War Began.

James   Charles   Frederick   Harry   Frank   Sidney

separated by their duties with the armed forces since 1939, held a grand re-union party at their parents' home, 9 Pound Park Road, Charlton, last Saturday. The only regret was that a seventh brother, Sidney, is still in the Far East and could not join them.'

The paper went on to briefly describe the military service undertaken by George, James, Charles, Frederick, Harry, Frank and Sidney. Frederick was in the army for six years, serving in France in 1940 with the Dorset Regiment, and was evacuated from Dunkirk. Harry served for four years in North Africa and later in Italy. Sidney was in the Royal Marines and landed in France on D-Day.

At the time of the re-union, Frank had recently returned from Germany and was expecting to be posted to the Far East, where he might have caught up with Sidney. In the event the war with Japan was ended by the atomic bombs dropped on Hiroshima and Nagasaki and he never needed to go.

Surviving Bennett Brother Frank lives with his wife Maureen near Eastbourne in East Sussex.

duties at Spandau Prison in Berlin where most of the Nazi leaders, including Rudolf Hess, were incarcerated awaiting trial at Nuremburg.

Lyons Corner House

'When the prisoners were allowed out to exercise (about eight or nine at a time) they always walked in a very orderly fashion. If they saw us staring at them they would stop and stare back. At my age at the time I thought that this was good fun!'

Maureen and Frank met after the war. She told me that the local dance hall was the place to hang out although the pair liked to go up to the West End for a meal in a Lyons Corner House before taking in a film starring the likes of John Mills, John Wayne or James Stewart. They were married in March 1952 in Camberwell Green and after the wedding went off to her mum and dad's local, The White Horse in Rye Lane. Maureen says that she has sisters who still live in Oglander Road and when she visits them they always go out for a bite to eat in that same pub.

By coincidence, in wartime and for years after my own mother lived with her family in the flats on Dog Kennel Hill, Dulwich, not far from where Maureen and her family lived. Maureen was very pleased for her and Frank's story to be told and wrote to me to say, 'This is all very exciting and it has all come about because we spilt red wine on the lovely book Frank had borrowed!'

Above: *Examples of wartime and post-war memorabilia in the possession of Frank Bennett. The letter from the Commander-in-Chief concerning non-fraternisation with the Germans was signed by Field-Marshal Montgomery. The postcard depicts the cablecar in the town of Bad Harzburg.*

Right: *Nazi leaders on trial at Nuremberg after the war. They include Hermann Goring, Hitler's one-time Deputy, Rudolf Hess, and his Foreign Minister, Ribbentrop. Frank Bennett guarded the captured Nazi leaders while they were held in Spandau Prison.*

The five Sullivan Brothers

All seven Bennett brothers survived the war. Not so fortunate were the five Sullivan brothers from the town of Waterloo, Iowa, who all served in the US Navy aboard the light cruiser *Juneau* in the Pacific Ocean.

The ship was engaged in battle with the Japanese around the Solomon Islands in November 1942. In a 30-minute night engagement off Guadalcanal, the Japanese lost a battleship and two destroyers whilst five out of 13 US vessels were sunk or badly damaged. The latter included the *Juneau* which received a torpedo hit.

During the morning of 13 November, whilst limping back to its base on New Caledonia, *Juneau* received another hit from a torpedo fired by a Japanese submarine. The device struck the ammunition storage area and the whole ship disappeared in a huge cloud of smoke. Witnesses to the huge explosion reported that there could have been no survivors and in consequence no US ships went to the rescue.

In fact around 80 men did survive the sinking, including George Sullivan, the oldest brother who found refuge on a raft. However, in the course of the next 10 days, one by one the men succumbed to their wounds or the combination of intense tropical heat, hunger and thirst. Just 10 men were eventually saved; one of these recalled how George Sullivan had slipped into the water one night to cool off only to be taken by a shark.

News of the loss of five members of a single family prompted an outpouring of sympathy and the 'Fighting Sullivan Brothers' became national heroes. President Roosevelt sent a letter of condolence to their parents and Pope Pius XII sent a silver religious medal and rosary with his message of regret.

In April 1943 Mrs Alleta Sullivan christened a new destroyer, *USS The Sullivans*, in memory of her sons. Meanwhile Congress passed legislation to prevent brothers from serving on the same ship in the future.

Mentioned in Despatches

A mystery concerning his father that John Roy wants to solve.

I have known John Roy for nearly 30 years, originally as someone who undertook work for my company but these days as a friend. He took enormous interest in my book *Sixty Years On* and, indeed, along with his colleague Simon Jones, helped print it.

At that time he didn't mention to me about his own family's wartime connections but this time around, for *Seventy Years On*, he has spoken up. As with so many of us with parents or relations who lived through World

War II, John found himself at an age when his curiosity caused him to research his family's past.

John's father was William (Bill) Roy who was born in Northampton on 5 February 1914. He was the son of Arthur Henry Roy of 1st Northants Regiment who served in the Boer War and in the trenches in the Great War. Continuing the military tradition, William joined the Royal Marines in 1931 and served in various RM establishments. He went on to train as a Commando and reached the rank of Colour Sergeant-Major.

John told me: 'William married my Mum when I was two after my first Dad – a Royal Marine Volunteer Reserve – was killed in a training exercise on the Thames.

'I do have all William's campaign medals: 1939-1945 Star/Atlantic Star/Africa Star/Italy Star/1939-1945 Medal with Oakleaf/Palestine 1945-1948 Medal and Long Service Good Conduct Medal. I also know he served on or at *Resolution/ St Angelo/Revenge/Odyssey* and with 3-42-46 Commando.'

Though he has the information recounted above, John says his father never spoke to him about his wartime experiences so they have been, and remain, largely a mystery. John now says: 'I really would like to know more, especially why he was "Mentioned in Despatches".'

DAVID ARNOLD

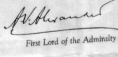

By the KING'S Order the name of
A/Ty. Company Serjeant Major William Roy,
Royal Marines,
was published in the London Gazette on
13 March, 1945,
as mentioned in a Despatch for distinguished service.
I am charged to record
His Majesty's high appreciation.

First Lord of the Admiralty

Top: Sergeant William Roy is seen on the left in this photograph that simply has 'D-Day' written on the back. Above: The official document recognising Bill's distinguished service.

A FAR

John Roy's interest in his family's wartime history has been inherited by his son, Ben. On a Far East trip in 2009 he took the opportunity to visit Singapore to remember a Great Uncle's tragic demise just weeks away from an end to hostilities.

In the course of my Dad's research into his family tree, he discovered that his Dad's brother, Robert Roy, had been held in a Japanese POW Camp in the war and had actually died there. So when I knew I was going to Singapore in 2009 I decided I must go and find the Grave or Memorial for my Great Uncle.

In advance of my arrival in Singapore, I went online and found the Kranji Commonwealth War Cemetery and Memorial. I did a search for Robert Roy, died 30/8/1945 aged 24. The following information that came back told me Robert had held the rank of Signalman (Royal Corps of Signals) and his Service number was 2596603. The Grave Reference was: Column 45 – Singapore Memorial.

I knew now that I had to find the Memorial and Column 45 to find Robert Roy. I arrived in Singapore at 8am on Saturday 13 June 2009. From the airport information desk I learnt that it would take about an hour to the Cemetery using the MRT (train) system. Sure enough, getting there proved pretty straight-forward. From the station, it was a slow 20-minute walk in the heat but early on I could see the Memorial on the skyline.

A piece of family history

I was strangely excited as I walked into the Cemetery; I was going to find a piece of our family history. I hoped that there might be someone there who could tell me a bit more about the war, about the POW camps, maybe even about some of the people who had died there. But when I eventually arrived there was no one about. The place was immaculate with beautiful lawns, plants and trees. I walked through the graves and then up to the Memorial.

I arrived at the Memorial on the right-hand side, where the numbers were well into the hundreds, so I slowly walked along looking for Column 45. Then on the second pillar from the left, facing towards me, I saw Column numbers 41... 42... 43... 44... and

EAST VIGIL

A lot of unanswered questions

It was strange to see my family name inscribed on this wall. It made me want to know more about Robert, about the war, about how he was captured, what it was like in the POW camp, what conditions did he and his fellow prisoners have to endure and how did he die? A lot of questions that may go unanswered? However, for now I am happy that I made the journey and thought maybe I was the first Roy to do so. I sat and looked and pondered and wrote about the experience in my diary. It was nice and tranquil and so I just sat for a while...

I finally left the wall, looking back several times to remember and then removed my shoes and walked barefoot across the lawns. The view of Singapore in the background was breathtaking. It had been a very good day.

then 45. It sat in the middle of the wall. At the top of the wall was the heading 'Royal Corps of Signal' and beneath that it read 'Signalman' and below that were names in alphabetical order and the 17th name down, on the left hand side of the column was ROY R. I had found him!

Ben Roy at the Memorial in Kranji Cemetery.

A Soldier's Resting Place

Alan Clarke recalls a trip to Malaysia and a special mission of remembrance.

The dedication and lasting work of the Commonwealth War Graves Commission is well known in many countries, especially those places where conflict has brought about many thousands of deaths of British and Commonwealth service personnel.

When I think of the well-kept cemeteries my thoughts always turn to the memory of a special visit to one in Taiping in Malaysia made in company with my dear friend and colleague, Lord Evans of Watford. The cemetery was created following the defeat of Japan. Bodies of the fallen were brought from battlefields, temporary burial grounds and from villages and civilian cemeteries where permanent maintenance would not be possible. The Taiping cemetery contains the graves of 867 servicemen; 425 of them are of British soldiers, 31 Australian, 392 from India while the remainder include servicemen from New Zealand, Malaya, the Netherlands and 34 who are Unknown.

East Surrey Regiment

We made our enjoyable, but sad, visit in 1998. It came about due to the fact that I was going to Kuala Lumpur in connection with my work with the Post Office and Telegraph and Telephones International (PTTI). Before I set off, my then Secretary, Mrs Dorothy Lovett, told me that her Mother's brother (her uncle William), was buried in Malaysia. This chance comment led to David and I seeking ways by which we could travel to Taiping and visit the grave of Private William George Dougherty, a soldier in the East Surrey Regiment. We quickly learned from William's sister, Mrs Lillian Grainger, the reference number of her brother's grave. Lillian had never had the opportunity of making the long journey to the cemetery herself and she was pleased that we would try to make the visit on her behalf.

As we travelled towards Taiping, David and I wondered if we would be able to buy some flowers to place on Private Dougherty's grave on behalf of his sister Lillian. Our driver did not think it would be possible, as he did not know of any place where we were likely to get flowers. Undeterred, as we approached Taiping we asked our friend if he could stop and ask the question of someone local. We pulled up in a village and our driver spoke to a lady who was pushing a bicycle along the road. To our astonishment it transpired that the lady was in fact the village florist! We all followed her into a

shed at the side of her home and watched as members of her family produced a truly beautiful floral tribute.

Pristine headstones

We arrived at the cemetery and were immediately struck by the tranquillity of the scene. We knew that it would be a well-kept place and it certainly was. We soon found Private Dougherty's headstone, the regimental badge of the East Surrey Regiment proclaiming the part his unit had played in the war against Japan. We placed Lillian's flowers on the grave and both of us had tears in our eyes as we thought of a young man from Wandsworth lying buried in a grave so far from his home.

As we journeyed back to Kuala Lumpur both of us were sad and at the same time very proud that our fallen soldiers were resting in a place that was both peaceful and immaculately maintained. Once back home we presented the photographs we had taken to Lillian Grainger; as she looked at them the tears welled up. Her advanced years meant she would never be able to visit her dear brother's grave so she thanked us and said how pleased she was that we had laid the flowers on William's grave on her behalf.

Alan Clarke is a member of the House of Lords.

Home & Away

Two scenes from the
early summer of 1944. At the top
we see General Sir Bernard Montgomery
being driven inland from the Normandy beach-
head in a jeep. Note the surprised look on the face of
the German prisoners who have evidently just recognised
Monty. The Allied 21st Army Group Commander had bested Rommel
in North Africa and now faced his old adversary again in France.
The second photograph was taken on the South Coast of England
and shows a heavy anti-aircraft barrage being directed at a V1 flying
bomb. The doodlebug has, in fact, just been hit and has exploded
over the sea in a bright flash of light.

Phantom Memories

'I joined the Army in September 1943 and after 10 week's combat training at Maryhill Barracks, Glasgow, and five months training as an OWL at Slaithewaite near Huddersfield, I found myself posted to Richmond in Surrey and the GHQ Liaison Regiment Royal Signals, RASC, REME.

We became better known as 'Phantom' and had black berets sporting the regimental badge of our originating regiments. In all cases, the shoulder badge was a white 'P' on a black square. The main function of Phantom was the gathering of operational information from local commanders and for eaves-dropping frontline radio links and passing any information we gleaned directly to Army Command.

My activities in Normandy were confined to 'A' Squadron. Having arrived on what I believe was Juno Beach we set up our HQ, erected our tents, had our first taste of Compo rations and settled in as best we could. My first job was to be in the Combined Ops room taking down messages received by the radio networks. I soon became a member of a team who worked the network day and night for many weeks. Then came the Normandy breakout and we eventually arrived at Waterloo in Belgium following closely behind the Guards Armoured Brigade who had liberated Brussels. This was at the time of *Operation Market-Garden* when, it was said, we Phantoms were the only link with our paratroops at Arnhem for the first day and a half of the fighting.

My next move was to our No 8 Patrol based with the 53 Welsh Division. When the Division fought for s'Hertogenbosch we were disturbed by a few 88mm shells falling in our patch. Our Sergeant was carried off in an ambulance with lacerations to his back. Next day we moved back to HQ for repairs and replacements only to experience an attack from the air. Then with repairs completed and new equipment installed we were off again – this time over the Rhine to Hamburg and the end of the war in Europe.

IFOR (TAFFY) DAVIES

∎

My father was in the Phantoms. He joined up in 1939 into the Bedfordshire Regiment. Following several disagreements between the two, he ended up being given the opportunity to join what was to become the Phantoms, a group of which he became very proud.

Much of his time was spent in this country escorting convoys and taking messages

between Richmond Park in London and Bletchley Park. Sometimes he frequented Achnacharry in Scotland where, I believe, he trained alongside the Commandos and SAS. There is a memorial at Speen Bridge that we took Dad to visit.

He also undertook parachute training near Manchester, jumping from a platform, balloons and lorries that were moving at 30mph to simulate landings. Unfortunately, Dad was injured in training and didn't get to join the parachute group.

Dad was proud to participate in the D-Day landings even though he and his companions were dropped off into about six feet of water. He was lucky to receive a helping hand as he couldn't swim. I remember he told me he was at Caen and, later, Paris. I believe they were with 30 Corp as far as Brussels where they spent quite some time liaising with the Resistance. He also had some involvement with the Welsh Guards Armoured Brigade. At the time of my birth in December 1944, I understand that my father was somewhere behind enemy lines.

Dad was a radio operator and I still have one of his note books about how to operate and fault-find on the different radio sets of the time. Whilst staying with civilians in Brussels he picked up a good command of colloquial French and made friends with a Resistance couple called Gaston and Claudette. I think she was quite a crack shot with a .25 pistol. After the war the pair apparently came over for my christening – bringing champagne with them.

I don't know by what date my Dad was in Germany but he did get to see Belsen soon after it was liberated by the Americans. He told me some horrific stories about the surviving prisoners.

There is a memorial to Phantom in the National Arboretum near Lichfield and I went

Above: *Famous actor David Niven saw wartime service with the Phantom Regiment. Here he's seen with Peter Sellers in a scene from* The Pink Panther *where he played the notorious jewel thief, Sir Charles Lytton – better known as 'The Phantom'! After transferring from the Rifle Brigade, Niven commanded A Squadron, Phantom Regiment. Later he took up a liaison post with US forces.*

Niven gave a few details of his war experience in his autobiography, The Moon's A Balloon *including his private conversations with Winston Churchill. Niven first met Churchill at a dinner party in February 1940. Churchill singled him out from the crowd and stated, 'Young man, you did a fine thing to give up your film career (in Hollywood) to return and fight for your country. Mark you, had you not done so – it would have been despicable.'*

A few stories have surfaced. About to lead his men into action, Niven eased their nervousness by telling them, 'Look, you chaps only have to do this once. But I'll have to do it all over again in Hollywood with Errol Flynn!'

Niven ended the war as a Lieutenant-Colonel. Back in Hollywood after the war, he received the Legion of Merit, the highest American order that can be earned by a foreigner. The jockey Sir Gordon Richards also served with Phantom. Peter Sellers saw wartime service in the RAF, spending time in India and Burma.

The Phantom Reconnaissance Unit was created in 1939 and men of the unit served in Greece, Palestine, Iraq, Syria and North Africa before going moving into Europe with the advancing Allies. By 1944 Phantom's reputation for intelligence-gathering was so great that the SAS, North American, Free French and Polish forces all wanted detachments working them.

along to the unveiling. I met Len (Joe) Owen, the man who was instrumental in creating the memorial. My sister still has Dad's badge. My Mum would say that when she asked Dad about his war work he answer 'P for comfort' being forbidden to discuss what he did.

Sadly both my Mum and Dad have died in recent years and I find myself unable to check up any of the things I've written about. The Phantoms must be a rare group now.'

TONY MASON

Christopher Portway was a D-Day veteran who came ashore in Normandy on 6 June 1944 as a 21-year-old soldier in the British Army. Down the years he returned to France many times to revisit the beaches and battlefields and pay his respects at the cemeteries. His last visit took place in June 2004 on the 60th anniversary of the invasion. He subsequently wrote this story in which he explained why it is so important to remember what happened all those years ago and also recalled some of his own experiences at the time.

Past Reunion. Christopher Portway is in the picture between the French and British flags at this reunion at Tilly sur Seulles, Normandy, in 1984.

It was nearly 930 years ago that the conquest of England was launched by Duke William of Normandy from the small seaport of Dives. It was some 880 years later on 6 June 1944 that the greatest armada of ships ever assembled converged upon the yellow-sanded Norman beaches within a very few miles of that same little port. The two events, unconnected but strangely similar in method if not intention, offer those of our citizens who visit Normandy a uniquely close relationship to France.

The year 2004, the 60th Anniversary of D-Day and the Battle of Normandy, was a special occasion, when a diminishing band of men of many nationalities congregated upon Norman shores to relive each his private memories and remember those comrades left behind. There was pomp and ceremony. But for those who came ashore or landed by parachute or glider 60 years before, the most poignant moments will have been the personal pilgrimage to a fragment

GOING BACK

The remains of part of an artificial Mulberry harbour on a Normandy beach.

> We are balding, aged veterans of a war fought seven decades past, but in our ears rise the sound of churning tank tracks in the night and Spandau bullets swishing through the corn.

Left: Ben Evans pictured in Normandy on the 65th anniversary of D-Day in June 2009. Ben's father is Lord Evans of Watford, a Trustee of the Royal Air Force Museum at Hendon. Lord Evans has a keen interest in military history, particularly relating to aviation.

of a field, a corner of a village, farmhouse, hedgerow or orchard that once exuded a terror never completely erased by the years.

There is a tiny cemetery some 10 kilometres east of Bayeux that is, perhaps, the most meaningful place in the world for some. It holds a sadness that screws you up inside. Just a few dozen graves marked by Portland stone comprises the military cemetery of Little Jerusalem where a Pole and a Dorset lie side by side among a sprinkling of names from British tank and infantry units. At intervals down the years I have returned here with the surviving colleagues of my regimental association and are invariably asked to attend the simple act of remembrance by the villagers of nearby Chousain who, through the decades, have looked upon the tiny graveyard as their own.

The village band exhausts itself with spirited trumpetings. Our president, bare-headed, reads aloud his oration in stumbling French, and a line of school children with reproachful faces lay their bunches of wild flowers as if in admonishment to an earlier generation for its glory and its shame. We, who have been spared to grow old, see the flowers, the silent stones, the names, the regiments, the youthful ages preserved in a kind of waterglass. Externally we are balding, aged veterans of a war seven decades past, but in our ears rise the sound of churning tank tracks in the night and Spandau bullets swishing through the corn.

What infantry soldier can forget that sickening pre-dawn hour of 'stand to', when, aroused from fitful slumber on the damp earth of a slit trench, he stands, bleary-eyed, staring into the dying night, tensed for the counter-attack the dregs of darkness so often brought. Or those silent incursions into enemy lines, devoid of anything that might rattle, with the intention of capturing a prisoner for interrogation. And, perhaps worse, those bouts of street fighting amongst the rubble of broken houses and the personal belongings of absent householders, their best china and family photographs trampled underfoot in an orgy of savagery.

Taken prisoner myself and transported to Poland, I was to witness unspeakable horrors and a cruelty so hideous that, in comparison, it made military combat positively saintly. But the threat of death or mutilation spares neither the soldier in the front line, the citizen under aerial bombardment or the captive in the charnel houses and camps of the remote hinterland.

Yet not all my memories of that time are tinged with fear. There was pathos too. Watching crew members eject from stricken Allied bombers, counting them one by one as the parachutes blossomed, our eyes streaming with tears for men we'd never met; for the inevitable few that failed to bale out.

And there was humour too. How can I forget the night while on picket duty behind the front line when two smartly-uniformed German officers emerged and asked to surrender. Nonplussed, I adopted an aggressive stance, covering them with my sten gun, whereupon one of the officers looked at me reproachfully and, in perfect English said, 'Excuse me Corporal, but you've no magazine on that gun.'

Today the memories are fading. Young families holidaying on the sandy coast of Calvados and La Manche are not concerned with the horror that swept across these pleasantly rural departments of North West France and why should they be? The museum of the landings at Arromanches, the concrete bunkers and the occasional rusting tank on its plinth are things to play over and explore in happy laughing groups. The gigantic operation that was the key to the liberation of France and Europe is but a slice of history that happened long ago. Like earlier events it was something that happened in times past; it's something to be learnt in lessons at school together with 1066 and all that.

Yet there are still a large number of us who remain and have our recollections of something real and awesome in scale. We might be the veterans of either side, or could be French civilians, perhaps in childhood at the time of the invasion.

Yes, the anniversary will still be very much an authentic event for a lot of people for some considerable time to come.

Christopher Portway died on 30 July 2009 in the Royal Hospital where he was a Chelsea Pensioner.

The Legion of St George

With so many prisoners of war gathered in the opening years of conflict, it was inevitable that the Nazi war machine would seek 'volunteers' from their captives to form military formations that could fight alongside the Wehrmacht. Once Germany had invaded Russia, the call to arms took on the guise of a crusade against Bolshevism.

The German efforts met with some success in respect of Soviet prisoners and the natives of many Eastern European states that had suffered under the virtual occupation of their country by the Red Army in the years since the Russian Revolution.

But the Germans were far less successful in persuading western European prisoners to go over to the Nazi cause. Perhaps the most outstanding rejection of the Nazi propaganda machine came with the attempt to form a *Britisches Freikorps* – the Legion of St George.

Though they held hundreds of thousands of and Commonwealth POWs, they never succeeded in 'recruiting' more than 60 men who made just two platoons. Even so, the Germans produced Waffen-SS heraldry reflecting the British connection; a collar patch portraying the three lions of England with a cuff-band reading *Britisches Freikorps*.

Those few that joined were told they would bear arms only against the Red Army. Mystery surrounds the tiny Legion's role in the latter stages of the war. It's known they were part of the SS Panzergrenadier Division *Nordland* on the Oder Front in early 1945. The last record of them is dated 15 April 1945 when the 20 surviving men and their sergeant were ordered to Templin, west of Berlin.

The posters reproduced on this page were aimed at British POWs and the populations of Norway and Denmark where the Germans hoped to recruit men with Nazi sympathies. The booklet 'Every Soldier's Problem' was another German attempt to persuade British soldiers to surrender in order to survive the war. As the war was coming to a close, there were a number of Allied deserters determined to hide out until hostilities ceased but it is believed that nobody surrendered to the Germans as a result of this kind of propaganda.

On the first day of June 1944, Resistance men and women all over France hear the BBC transmit two quotations from the poetry of Verlaine. The words signify that the invasion is imminent.

Eamon de Valera's Fianna Fail party in Eire is given a vote of confidence by the Irish people today when they return it to power with an increased representation. De Valera's strict neutrality policy, maintained in the face of British and US efforts to have him expel Axis diplomats in Eire, is believed a main reason for his party's popularity. The cost of his obstinate even-handedness has been economic isolation.

On **2 June** the Royal Navy confirm that it can have the first Mulberry harbour units moving according to schedule. The huge concrete caissons had become stuck in the Thames mud but have finally been floated free. Today also sees warships sailing from Scapa Flow, Belfast, The Clyde and other northern ports and anchorages, heading south towards the English Channel to join the invasion fleet.

Next night 99 RAF bombers drop 509 tons of bombs on the wireless intercept station at Urville Hague near Cherbourg, headquarters of the German Signals Intelligence Service in North Western France. Its loss could have a powerful influence on the course of the imminent invasion.

By **4 June** major sections of the invasion fleet are already at sea believing that D-Day is dawn on 5 June. At 04:30 hours on this Sunday morning the *Overlord* supremos of SHAEF meet to learn of a weather forecast that promises rain, high winds and fog. Eisenhower postpones the invasion for 24 hours. The ships at sea are recalled.

5 June: The Italian capital has been declared an 'Open City' and evacuated by the Germans. Today the soldiers of Mark Clark's Fifth Army enter Rome to a jubilant reception from cheering civilians thronging the streets.

At the end of this victorious day, just one hour and four minutes before midnight, the first aircraft take off and set course for Normandy. They are towing three Horsa gliders carrying Major John Howard and the men of the Ox and Bucks Light Infantry on a daring mission that will open the assault on Hitler's Occupied Europe.

Normandy, **6 June:** 00.16 hours. In what Air Vice Marshall Leigh-Mallory will describe as 'the greatest feat of flying in World War II', Major Howard's three gliders come down precisely as planned alongside the Benouville Bridge over the Canal de Caen. Within less than a minute, the men are emerging from the gliders to execute a classic *coup de main* and seize the bridge. A sentry fires a flare and is promptly cut down, the first German to die on D-Day.

A short time later large forces of British and American paratroopers drop at both ends of the invasion area during the hours of darkness. Many are scattered far away from their dropzones. Some are dropped over the sea.

At 05.30 hours the naval bombardment of the beaches begins. Just over one hour later, US infantry begin landing on Omaha and Utah beaches. A further hour after the first Americans are ashore, British and Canadian tanks and infantry begin landing on Sword, Gold and Juno beaches. Good progress is soon reported everywhere except for Omaha, where German resistance from the bluffs above the beach is fierce for many hours.

In the course of the morning of 6 June, 75,215 British and Canadian and 57,000 American troops will have landed by sea and linked up with the survivors of the 23,400 men who arrived by parachute or glider in the night. Total Allied killed, wounded or

CAUGHT LIKE FOXES IN A TRAP

English and American soldiers !

Why has Jerry waited ten days after the landings to use his so called secret weapon behind your back ? Doesn't that strike you as queer ?

It looks very much as though after waiting for you to cross the Channel, he had set a TRAP for you.

You're fighting at present on a very narrow strip of coast, the extent of which has been so far regulated by the Germans.

You are using up an enormous number of men and huge quantities of material.

Meanwhile the Robot-planes, flying low, scatter over London and Southern England explosives, the power and incendiary efficiency of which are without precedent. They spread death and destruction in the towns and harbours, which should be sending you much needed supplies.

A German propaganda leaflet dropped on the Allies in Normandy soon after the landings.

missing on D-Day number some 10,500; 114 aircraft have been lost. On the German side, casualties total 6500.

By 21.00 hours the fighting dies down along the entire Normandy front of some 60 miles. The Allies have firm footholds in many places and are hanging on determinedly in areas where German resistance has been strongest. Now the Allies must race to build up their strength before the enemy counterattacks.

Normandy **7 June:** More men and supplies pour ashore. British commandos attack Port-en-Bessin, seeking a link-up between the American and British beaches.

Next day **8 June** a set of invasion plans falls into German hands revealing that Normandy is the main thrust and not a feint. Even so, some high-ranking officers remain convinced that a further landing will be made in the Pas de Calais area.

In Italy on **9 June** the German retreat continues. Marshall Badoglio resigns and is succeeded as premier by a civilian, Ivanoe Bonomi.

10 June: The first deployment of Allied fighter aircraft to temporary airstrips in Normandy takes places as Spitfires of No 144 (RCAF) Wing fly in at Ste Crois-sur-Mer.

On **11 June** in the South Pacific Marianas islands, US naval and air forces attack Guam, Saipan and Tinian. Around 200 Japanese aircraft are destroyed.

12 June: Six days after D-Day, Montgomery informs reporters that the Allies 'have won the battle of the beaches'. Winston Churchill and South African Premier Smuts have visited the British beach-head.

On **13 June** six people are killed and nine seriously injured by an explosion caused by a strange new German 'flying bomb' which demolished a railway bridge at Grove Road, Bethnal Green.

In Sweden the authorities have impounded the wreckage of a German experimental rocket that went off course. The A4 - which will become known as the V2 - is more advanced than the V1.

14 June: General de Gaulle makes his first visit to liberated France. He tells his fellow countrymen in Bayeux: 'What the country expects of you is to keep up the fight.' A Vichy France broadcast from Paris urges civilians to shun the Allies. Radio

WAR DIARY
June 1944

announcer Herold Paquis declares: 'If France is to live, England, like Carthage, must be destroyed.'

On **15 June** Tokyo radio claims six US planes shot down in the course of a raid. US sources confirm that 47 Superfortresses of their 20th Air Force based in China hit iron and steel works in Japan.

16 June: Canadian prisoners massacred by the SS on 7 June in Normandy are partly avenged today when a 16 inch shell from *HMS Rodney* lands 20 miles inland and kills the commander of the 12th SS Hitler Jugend Panzer Division.

By **17 June** Hitler's flying bombs are arriving over England in increasing numbers by night and day bringing with them the spectre of a new Blitz. People refer to these new weapons as 'doodlebugs' or 'buzz bombs' because of the drone of their engines. The authorities discourage the term 'V1' because it suggests that even more deadly weapons will follow.

Napoleon's island of exile, Elba, near Corsica, is liberated today.

18 June: In the South Pacific US marines capture Aslito on Saipan. Three days ago the Americans stormed ashore on this Marianas island in a four-mile wave of 600 amphibious craft.

German forces carry out intensive anti-partisan operations in the Lublin region of Poland.

On **19 June** a powerful storm strikes the English Channel. One casualty is the Mulberry artificial harbour off Omaha beach. Heavy seas, the worst in 40 years, decimate it.

20 June: The Battle of the Philippine Sea has been fought over the last two days and resulted in a stunning victory for the Americans. In the greatest carrier battle of the war, the Japanese have lost so many aircraft - 480 in total - that US pilots are calling the action 'The Great Marianas Turkey Shoot'. Japanese plans to destroy the American invasion fleet are in tatters and they've lost three more irreplaceable aircraft carriers plus many other ships.

The air offensive against Germany continues on **21 June** when a massive force of 1234 heavy bombers attack Berlin, Potsdam, Stendal and other targets.

22 June: Belorussia. A Russian army numbering 1.2 million men, 5200 tanks and assault guns supported by 6000 aircraft is today attacking a German force numbering just 400,000 men, 900 tanks

and heavy guns and 1300 aircraft. Great gaps are torn in the German lines as the Red Army armour races towards Minsk.

23 June: There's more savage fighting on Saipan today when US and Japanese forces clash at a place dubbed 'Death Valley' near Mount Tapotchau.

On the India-Burma border, supply convoys are moving again on the Imphal to Kohima road following the lifting of the three month siege of the area. Around 30,000 Japanese have died since the start of their planned invasion of India against Allied losses of 2700 killed and 10,000 wounded. A key turning point came on 17 June when the exhausted Japanese abandoned the Mao Songsan ridges, the first time they have given up a position without a fight in the entire campaign.

Germany still has forces beyond the Arctic Circle in Norway. Desperate to keep the Finland in the war, Germany's Foreign Minister, von Ribbentrop, is in Helsinki with promises of arms and troops.

24 June: North Atlantic. Flt Lt D E Hornell will be awarded the posthumous Victoria Cross for bravery in tackling a U-Boat sighted in far northern waters today. Canadian Hornell's Catalina flying boat spotted U-1225 on the surface and dived to attack. The U-Boat fought back and severely damaged the aircraft before sinking. The burning Catalina lost its starboard engine and had to land on the water. With just one serviceable dinghy, the crew took turns to sit in it or cling to the sides; two died of exhaustion in the freezing sea during the 21 hours they waited for rescue. Hornell died of exposure soon afterwards.

On **25 June**, the British Government begins free distribution to next-of-kin, of a 16-page handbook giving information about prisoners-of-war in the Far East.

26 June: Germany. Hitler emerges from seclusion to address a group of leading industrialists in Obersalzberg. Later he is described as sounding forgetful and looking ill.

Good news from Burma on **27 June** as the Chindit 77th Special Force Brigade together with two battalions of the Chinese 114th Regiment, take Mogaung. Battle and ill-health have taken their toll on the Chindits who have fewer than 600 men on their feet and able to fight. In China, however, the nationalist 10th Army retreats in disarray as the Japanese attack. An airfield used by US bombers to hit Japan has been captured.

On **28 June** there's a general strike in the Danish capital Copenhagen in protest at the German Occupation.

Today the USA cuts diplomatic ties with Finland. Most Finns want an end to the war with Russia but President Rysto Ryti, backed by a pro-German lobby, seeks to fight on.

Next day **29 June** the US Eighth Air Force Flying Fortresses are out in force raiding a score of industrial targets including the Volkswagen factory at Fallersleben, near Brunswick, where V1 flying bombs are constructed.

London: **30 June.** A V1 comes down on Bush House in the Aldwych, killing 198 people. Civilian casualties from the flying bomb offensive total 1935 dead and 5906 injured. Since D-Day, 4868 Americans, 2443 British and 393 Canadians have been killed, a total of 7704 dead. Battle fatigue takes an increasing toll - one fifth of all American casualties are attributed to exhaustion and shellshock.

Jews deported from the Greek island of Corfu arrive at Auschwitz-Birkenau after a 27-day journey in sealed boxcars. Many of the 1795 who set off have died in transit. The survivors are herded straight into the gas chambers.

Left: British airborne troops looking happy with their D-Day mission accomplished.

Wootton's War

Frank Wootton became an Official War Artist to the RAF in France in June 1944 at the invitation of the Commander-in-Chief Allied Air Forces, Sir Trafford Leigh-Mallory. Soon after D-Day he flew to Normandy. Later he would go to Burma. Here are some of his wartime recollections, some sad, some wryly humourous, together with examples of his work.

'Sunday 3 September 1939 was a brilliant sunny day. I had just finished mowing the lawn when Mr Chamberlain's fateful broadcast announced that we were at war. Next morning I reported to the RAF Recruitment Centre in Brighton. It was not long before I received a buff envelope from the Air Ministry. To my surprise, it contained not an invitation to join the service, but one requesting I visit various RAF stations to record the work of the Royal Canadian Air Force. They had two squadrons already in Britain.

'I started work immediately with No 400 RCAF, based at Odiham, and No 401, at Digby and was greatly impressed by the high-spirited enthusiasm I met on my reception. The Canadians of all ranks were congenial and relaxed and very understanding of the work I had come to do. Without any formalities, they flew me wherever I wished. Their aircraft were Hurricanes.'

His Canadian assignment complete, Frank Wootton joined

the RAF in December 1940. At RAF Melksham he was employed in the production of technical illustrations. In 1941 *The Studio* magazine published the first edition of his book *How to Draw Planes*. It was enormously successful but he was not considered for service as an Official War Artist apparently because of his commercial background. It was not until 1944 that things suddenly changed. Wootton wrote:

'On a summer afternoon in June Sir Trafford

Top: *This is Frank Wootton's design for a huge banner to be displayed outside of the Mansion House, London, during a 'Wings for Victory' Week of fundraising activities in 1943.*

Right: *Another 'Wings for Victory' painting dating from around 1942. Every town or village held an annual fundraising day or even a whole week. In big cities like London whole aircraft would be displayed.*

Leigh-Mallory asked me if I would like to paint the work of the RAF in France. Two days later there was an Avro Anson at Northolt ready to fly me to Normandy. From afar we saw the French coast while beneath us the sea was full as far as the eye could see with a fantastic mass of ships.

'We landed at the strip that was my destination and I was escorted to a caravan. It belonged to Colonel Preston, whom I had met when he was Secretary of the Royal Aero Club. One of the strip's mobile Bofors gun, manned by the RAF Regiment, had bagged the first Me 109 to be shot down by Allied ground forces during the landings.

'The bridge-head was small and the beaches congested with everyone busily engaged in their own sections. Leigh-Mallory had granted me complete freedom of movement and I had an authorization letter signed by him. I could request the use of any form of transport wherever I wanted to go. I took up with No 35 (Recce) Wing at Beny-sur-Mer. Squadron Leader Laurence Irving, who by a happy coincidence knew my work, immediately made me feel at home. My attention was drawn to the airstrip that was crowded with airmen anxiously awaiting an incoming aircraft. It was one of No 4 Squadron's Spitfires carrying a 45-gallon drop

Left: NORTH SEA ATTACK, JUNE 1944.   By kind permission of John S Grace

Below: HQ NORMANDY, 1944.   By kind permission of The Society of British Aerospace Companies

tank. An irregular "regular" run had been arranged from England to France. Apparently somebody had some influence with a brewing firm who were able to fill the drop tank!

'My first night in France was a memorable one. We were strafed by low-flying aircraft and shelled by a long-range gun. Aircraft went out the next day to locate the source of this nuisance. They were unsuccessful and nightly the gun bombarded our vicinity. Then someone suggested a night search when the flash of the gun would reveal its position. It turned out to be near Pont l'Eveque in a disused railway tunnel, into which it retreated in daytime. The next day we buried it, for two Typhoons were sent out and closed both ends of the tunnel.

'Some weeks later I drove down to Ranville to see the glider landing fields. East of the River Orne were 246 Horsa gliders of the Sixth Airborne Division. I was impressed at the landings, seeing no evidence of collisions. It was a scene that would have delighted any surrealist painter, an incredible disarray of grounded aircraft, wing tips on the scored grass and others slanting to the sky, tails blown off by charges for easy exit of the troops. I sat on a discarded tail and started work. Later I visited the first house in France to be liberated, a French café beside the intact Pegasus Bridge run by Monsieur and Madame Gondrée, who very kindly offered me a refreshing glass of wine, whilst recounting the stories of their ordeal under German occupation.'

Frank was still in Normandy when the Allied breakout began. The Germans were caught in a bottleneck at Falaise in August. He says the Luftwaffe showed no appetite for combat and the RAF rocket-firing Typhoons queued up to take their turn to help complete the destruction. Frank thought the saddest sight was that of the thousands of dead transport horses caught up in the ruthless onslaught.

As the army advanced, Frank was able to see the ruins of Caen before crossing the Seine. Later he observed a V1 launch site. At St Omer airfield he found evidence of the hurried flight of the enemy in the form of half-eaten meals and personal possessions left behind.

St Omer was the base for Adolf Galland's Me 109s. It was to the local hospital that Group Captain Douglas Bader was taken after he'd been shot down in August 1941.

On 2 October Frank stayed overnight in one of the best hotels in Brussels. Soon afterwards he was recalled to Supreme HQ, Bentley Priory. Whilst flying there his Avro communications aircraft developed a fault and the pilot was forced to ditch in the sea. Air Sea Rescue picked up the plane's occupants and even Frank's paintings (stored in three buoyant waterproof containers) were saved.

Leigh-Mallory had summoned Frank in order to offer him another assignment: 'He said the war in Europe would be over by Christmas. As he had just been appointed to command our air force in South East Asia, he wanted me to go with him to "paint the jungle". He had acquired a new private aircraft, a York, and was flying out with a picked crew. His wife was to accompany him, also his batman, and a ton of personal luggage, but there would be room for me.

'I had to turn down the offer as I had left all my painting equipment in Belgium unaware of the reason for my sudden return to England. He told me to go back and get my gear and join him on the other side of the world as soon as I was ready.

'Leigh-Mallory never reached his new Command. His aircraft took off on 14 November; a few hours later a faint signal reported that it was flying low, circling in a snowstorm. It crashed into a mountain south of Grenoble and all on board were killed. The death of the former leader of Fighter Command was a great loss to the RAF.

'I was still set to go to the Far East.

'On my first night in France we were shelled by a long-range gun. The gun turned out to be concealed in the daytime in a tunnel near Pont l'Eveque. The next day we buried it, for two Typhoons were sent out and closed both ends of the tunnel..'

'I visited the first house in France to be liberated, a French café beside the Pegasus Bridge run by Monsieur and Madame Gondrée, who very kindly offered me a refreshing glass of wine, whilst recounting stories of their ordeal under German occupation..'

I thought it would be better if I could go straight to a squadron engaged in operations rather than call on the HQ of SEAC in Kandy, Ceylon. I wondered about the availability of painting supplies out there. Then I remembered that we had Hurricanes in Burma and if there was a shortage of canvas I might be able to prevail on Stores to let me have some off-cuts. The thought of a painting made on doped aircraft fabric certainly had a ring of authenticity about it.

'The bomber station at Salbani in India seemed very remote after the closer tactics in Normandy, so I asked the station commander to arrange transport to an airfield in Rangoon where fighters were deployed. He agreed and introduced me to a tall Air Force officer wearing a Victoria Cross ribbon. He was James Nicholson who asked me to look after his dog while he flew on a watching brief with the squadron bombing the Japanese-held harbour at Rangoon. Nicholson was killed on 2 May 1945 when an RAF Liberator from 355 Squadron, in which he was flying as an observer, caught fire and crashed into the Bay of Bengal.

'We landed just outside the city at Mingladon, flooded after the monsoon rain, where I joined No 607 Squadron, equipped with Spitfires. A flooded airfield could cause

fighter aircraft to tip over on their nose, bend propellors, and sometimes damage the reduction gear. Whatever your job, it was not easy to work in the conditions. Hot and humid, leather turned green overnight, blankets and sheets were constantly damp, amenities were few, food monotonous and housing uncomfortable. However, the promise of victory with the advent of Spitfire squadrons steadily improved morale.

'I flew to Mandalay to paint the destruction of Fort Dufferin, ancient home of Burmese kings. Thunderbolts, Hurricanes and Mitchells, carrying 500lb bombs, three on each aircraft, breached the 45ft walls of the fort. It was while I was painting these aircraft taking off laden with 1500lb of bombs that one detached itself from its holding just as the aircraft lifted off the rough track. It skipped over my head and finally came to rest in some soft earth a few yards away. Fortunately it didn't explode.

'About 35 years later, by a happy

Above: TYPHOONS TAKING OFF FROM A NORMANDY AIRSTRIP, 1944.

Below: ENGINE CHANGE ON A LIBERATOR OF NO 355 SQUADRON, SALBANI, INDIA, 1945.
By kind permission of RAF Museum, Hendon

coincidence, I was at the Guild of Aviation Artists' Exhibition in London when a man introduced himself. He explained his name was Wallace and that he was flying the Thunderbolt that dropped the bomb that so narrowly missed me in Burma that day.

'After Mandalay fell, IV Corps advanced 85 miles to Meiktila. The capture of Meiktila was a great victory for General Bill Slim and his men. It was the nodal point of the battle for Burma. Some 400 men of the RAF Regiment shared the defence of the airfield. We lost a great many Dakotas as they flew in tons of food and ammunition. I went to Meiktila in an Auster, dropping mail at small airstrips en route. At Mingladon I had been off-loaded from a Dakota which had started moving along the runway to take off when it was stopped. The aircraft was full and a brigadier on an important mission had requested a seat. As I was the only single passenger on

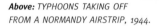

'Arriving at Meiktila, I explained I had been taken off the Dakota and come by mail plane. The sergeant-in-charge looked at me with an amused expression: "You're effing lucky, mate. That Dakota is five hours overdue." In fact, it never did arrive.'

Left: MEIKTILA, BURMA, 1945. Frank Wootton spent some time this air base that was key to the final Allied victory.

'The lake was filled with Japanese corpses.
I noticed an RAF bowser at the edge pumping up water into its tank.
I asked the driver what it was to be used for.
He replied I would be drinking it that night.
Most of us in the mess that evening chose gin and tonic..'

board, I got out and was offered a seat in the Auster. Flying quite low from one grass strip to another was much more fun, even though at the end of most of them were usually a few hideous-looking vultures. Arriving at Meiktila, I explained I had been taken off the Dakota and come by mail plane. The sergeant-in-charge looked at me with an amused expression: "You're effing lucky, mate. That Dakota is five hours overdue." In fact, it never did arrive.

'The clear blue skies, sun and cooling breeze at Meiktila contrasted sharply with the mud of Mingladon. I painted scenes observed from the balcony of the wooden control tower perched high up on teak logs. Nearby was a large lake dotted with islands, on which were some small pagodas looking most attractive in the tropical sun. A few of us were tempted to swim. Fortunately we discovered just in time that under the surface the lake was filled with Japanese corpses. While dressing, I noticed an RAF bowser at the edge of the lake pumping up water into its tank. I asked the driver what it was to be used for. He replied I would be

drinking it that night. Most of us in the mess that evening chose gin and tonic.

'On 6 August 1945, while still at Meiktila, the first atomic bomb was dropped on Hiroshima. On 9 August the second fell on Nagasaki. On 14 August Japan surrendered. This remarkable and awe-inspiring achievement was met at first with composure, almost disbelief. Then we celebrated that night with a whole roast ox and free rum. What little was left of the beast in the morning was finished off by the vultures.

'Shortly after VJ Day, I received a signal requesting my return to SEAC HQ at Kandy. I regretted having to leave and mentioned the fact to the CO, who gently reminded me that these signals sometimes took weeks to arrive in the jungle. I thanked him and stayed a little longer completing some unfinished work.

'Eventually I went to Ceylon via an

overnight stop in Calcutta. In that latter city while waiting in the early hours for a Service bus to take me to Dum Dum Airport, I spotted a notice in my hotel: 'The Grand Hotel is out of bounds to all Service personnel owing to an outbreak of cholera.' I had wondered why it was so unusually empty. Kandy had a relaxed atmosphere now that the war was over. One of the most urgent requirements was to fly former POWs home. A further consideration was to keep the men occupied until their transport could be organized. I was asked to put on an impromptu exhibition of my work. Great interest was shown. The Commander-in-Chief, Sir Keith Park, arrived and we went round the exhibition together. There were a few portraits and I was delighted when Sir Keith named some of them he had known from the Battle of Britain.

'Although I would have liked to stay longer it was felt best that I return to Britain as soon as possible as the facilities at Kandy were already very strained. Soon I was aboard a Dakota bound for Karachi, where there was a Sunderland flying-boat due to leave for the UK. As I went through Immigration, a doctor, looking at my 1250 (RAF identity card), recognized my name. He showed me two consecutive copies of *The Calcutta Statesman*. The entire back pages were filled with reproductions of my paintings.'

* The above is an abridged version of Frank Wootton's own story that appeared in the David & Charles book, The Aviation Art of Frank Wootton, put together by Richard Taylor and first published in the UK in 1992. Copyright rested with the late Mrs Virginia Wootton who had kindly agreed to publication in Seventy Years On.

Frank Wootton looks on as fighter pilot legends Douglas Bader and Bob Stanford Tuck sign prints at the RAF Museum, Hendon. Frank Wootton's favourite charity was the RAF Benevolent Fund.

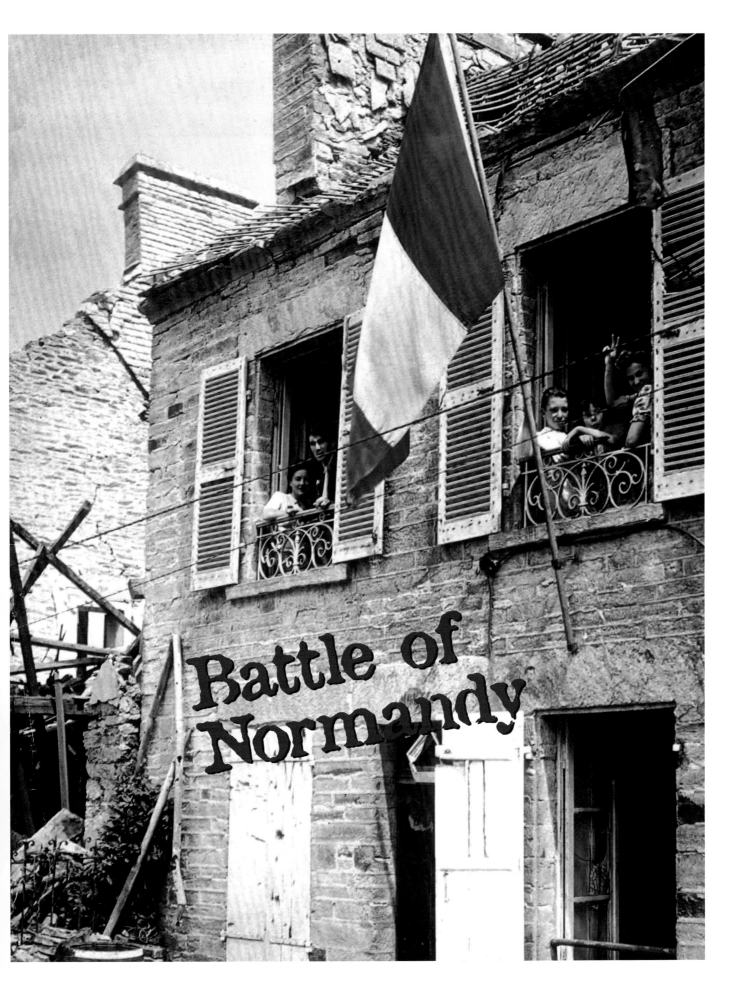

Battle of Normandy

JULY 1944

BATTLE

By July 1944 the Allies were firmly established in Normandy. But battling past the tenacious German defenders of the Norman landscape of dense hedgerows, sunken lanes and meandering streams would prove a costly and protracted struggle.

By daybreak on 1 July all German resistance in the northern part of the Contentin Peninsula had come to an end. Over 10,000 prisoners had been captured in Cherbourg and another 6000 surrendered in and around La Hague in the last days of June.

By this time the Germans had lost all hope of driving the Allies back into the sea. On the other hand, the fighting power of the *Wehrmacht* remained potent and it was now up to the British, American and Canadian forces to challenge that power and break it. Only once this was achieved could the Allies venture forth in confidence to liberate the rest of France and Occupied Europe.

Attention shifted to the eastern end of the bridgehead. The town of Caen, straddling the River Orne, was the key to victory. Attacks preceded by heavy bombing raids in June had come to nought. On 4 July the British General Miles Dempsey put in another assault which gained him only the part of the town on the north bank of the Orne. Then as the Allies drew breath it was noticed that the Germans were switching their reserve divisions to the west where General Omar Bradley's Americans were preparing to break out.

Operation Goodwood

To stop this German movement, the British launched another fierce armoured attack east of Caen on 18 July. This was *Operation Goodwood*. 'My whole eastern flank will burst into flames..' Montgomery told Eisenhower. The latter, haunted by the prospect of the invasion turning into a stalemate like that at Anzio near Rome earlier in the year, felt encouraged. *Goodwood* would be preceded by saturation bombing that would herald an attack by 750 tanks.

Unfortunately, the plan had some serious drawbacks. There was a reluctance to send infantry in with the tank spearheads. The British Army faced a serious manpower shortage. *Operation Epsom* at the end of June had cost some 4000 casualties in five days and the War Office warned that it could not guarantee to make good the losses for much longer. The situation caused General Miles Dempsey to later observe: 'I was prepared to lose a couple of hundred tanks. So long as I didn't lose men.'

The Germans had also prepared for defence in depth with minefields and strongpoints stretching back for 15 kilometres. The Allied bombers pummelled a depth of around eight kilometres. Even so, good initial progress was made. Until the tanks approached Cagny. Here a Luftwaffe flak battery with 88mm guns devastated the onrushing British armour. A German officer described the scene: 'One could see the shots flying through the corn like torpedoes. In the extensive fields to the north (of Cagny) stood at least 40 enemy tanks, on fire or shot up.'

Montgomery called off the attack on 20 July. Dempsey had lost over 400 tanks and sustained 5000 casualties.

For the British and American troops in and around the front line, these summer days of 1944 were a time of terror, maiming and sudden death. The Germans proved skilful and resolute in defence and made good use of the Norman Bocage country. Their weapons were very efficient and more than a match for the Allied equivalents. The range of mortars coupled with the ultra-fast firing Spandau machine-gun afforded valuable back-up for the speedy local counter-attacks in which the Germans excelled. One fearsome weapon was the *Nebelwerfer* - nicknamed 'Moaning Minnie' by the Allies - which had up to eight barrels that could be fired simultaneously accompanied by a screeching roar.

Tiger and Panthers

Their panzers too were in the main superior to those of the Allies. The latter's main battle tanks were Shermans, nicknamed 'Ronsons' by their hapless crews and 'Tommy-cookers' by the enemy. Outgunned by the mighty Tigers and Panthers of the Germans, the Allies most often relied on sheer weight of numbers to force the issue.

In the 88mm gun, an anti-aircraft weapon which the Afrika Korps had found even more deadly when utilised in an anti-tank role, the Germans had a powerful, high velocity killing machine. With the benefit of hindsight, one wonders why the Allies didn't simply produce copies of 88mm and thus even up the odds on the battlefield. The Bren Gun, after all, wasn't a British design; it was named after the Czech town of Brno where it was conceived and the British town of Enfield where it was later manufactured. Besides, in wartime, enemy patents don't count for much!

In the air, it was a totally different story. The Allies had total supremacy of the skies over Normandy, an advantage only annulled when rain and low clouds grounded aircraft. Rocket-firing Typhoons and all kinds of fighters roamed behind enemy lines or waited in 'cab ranks' to be called down on targets picked out by spotter aircraft or observers on the ground.

Eisenhower said of the Allied air efforts, 'The spectacle of our mighty air fleets roaring in over their heads had a most heartening effect upon our men.' Rommel himself fell victim of RAF Squadron-Leader J J Le Roux on 17 July when his staff car was shot up near Bernay. The wounded Field Marshal was succeeded by von Kluge,

IN THE BOCAGE

"FOR THE FIRST TIME IN THE HISTORY OF WAR, AN ARMY IS ATTACKING IN ALL FOUR DIRECTIONS AT ONCE!"

who quickly reported to Hitler that, 'There is no way by which, in the face of the enemy air forces' complete command of the air, we can discover a form of strategy to counter-balance its annihilating effect.'

Ring of Destruction

Before July was out, heavy and medium bombers had traced a ring of destruction around the battle area. It ran along the Seine and the Loire; bridges were blown up and rail links interdicted on a massive scale. The Germans were forced to detrain reinforcements, taken from the Russian Front, as far east as Nancy and Mulhouse. From here the troops marched or wobbled on bicycles towards the battle, hoping their heavy equipment would somehow find a passage behind them. Ironically, Hitler had a formidable reserve force much closer to Normandy. Fortunately for the Allies, he kept the well-armed 15th Army intact and in place around the Pas de Calais, awaiting a further seaborne assault which would never come.

American attention became focused on Saint-Lô on the River Vire, almost in the centre of the bridgehead perimeter. Perceived to be the gateway to the interior of France and already badly smashed up in the opening days of the invasion, the town and locale - stoutly defended by German paratroops - came in for further intense pounding from bombers and artillery. Such was the ferocity of the fighting that Saint-Lô was dubbed 'the Cassino of the north'. Indeed, the lessons of Cassino were having to be learnt the hard way all over again at many places in Normandy. Devastating bombing raids on towns all too often simply made the streets impassable to armoured vehicles and prevented the Allies pressing home their advantage of weight of numbers.

Colourful reputation

By 18 July they had achieved their goal and captured Saint-Lô. The scene was set for *Operation Cobra*, a large-scale south and eastward dash spilling armoured forces out of the Contentin Peninsula and onto a broader landscape more suited to a mobile war. Another huge air assault preceded the advance. Unfortunately it was marred by several instances of bomb 'carpets' falling short amidst the forward American units. Nevertheless, the crust of German resistance was broken and by 30 July Avranches had fallen.

Within days US columns were racing at high speed into Brittany. Rennes was liberated on 4 August, Lorient and Brest on the Bay of Biscay were reached on 7 August. The nightmare of the close quarter fighting in the Bocage seemed over as distant objectives, such as Orleans and St Nazaire, became suddenly attainable. Now a new name sporting a colourful reputation, hard-earned in North Africa and Sicily, appeared on the scene: General George S Patton soon found a phrase to describe the lightning manoeuvres of the armoured Third Army as it undertook a colossal turning movement in the direction of Le Mans: '...For the first time in the history of war, an army is attacking in all four directions at once!'

Left: A young German soldier looking out for Allied aircraft in Normandy.
Above: Two children survey the wreckage of St-Lô while US transport trundles through.
***Below:** A German despatch rider checks his map. Note the bomb damage in the background.*

255

BRITISH AEROPLANES

GUARD AFRICAN SKIES

National Archives - The Art of War

GOLD COAST TO NORMANDY

Renee Pay's life in the Army took her to the Gold Coast of West Africa and later to the killing fields of Normandy in the summer of 1944.

Renee Pay (nee Morris and known as Katherine to some) was born in 1912, the first and eldest child of what would become a large Herefordshire farming family of eight girls and two boys. She was educated at Hereford High School for Girls, and then trained as a nurse, subsequently joining the Army as a Queen Alexandra nurse in 1940. During the next tumultuous years of a world at war, Renee's life was colourful, adventurous and often dangerous, serving as she did in West Africa from 1941-1943 before returning to England to prepare for and take part, as a nurse in the June 1944 Normandy landings.

Through these extracts from her memoirs we can glimpse a woman of courage, determination and lively personality. She seems to embody all that we owe to that special wartime generation. We begin with the story of a perilous 1941 sea voyage from Glasgow to West Africa, sailing in a convoy into the North Atlantic and subsequently zig-zagging southwards to escape the attentions of prowling U-Boats:

'Luxury was now the order of the day. I shared a two-berth cabin, own bathroom, and the food was absolutely super – at least it seemed so to us. We found we were part of a very large convoy with three large liners crammed with troops and of course many merchant ships. *HMS Ark Royal, Hood* and *Warspite*, I remember as being part of our escort, together with destroyers and corvettes. The war at sea was going very badly at this

time. Our losses were enormous. There was no question of going straight down south – we found ourselves getting colder and colder and it was obvious ships were missing from the convoy. To my cost, I found I was the most terrible sailor. One morning, very early, there was a terrific bang followed by a shudder. Alarm bells went off, the engines stopped and the ship seemed to tilt. I was so incapacitated by sea-sickness I couldn't stand. I remember the steward rushed in, pushed me into my greatcoat and life jacket and propelled me towards the deck. Here we confronted nothing but mountainous seas with no convoy on the horizon – nothing but one little corvette. We had been bombed by a solitary plane. We huddled on deck for about 24 hours, feeling like a target for any submarine or for the returning hostile aircraft. Word came through that the German battleship *Bismarck* had been sunk by some of our escort. Later we learnt that *HMS Hood* had been lost earlier in the action.'

Renee provides an amusing description of the final lap of her voyage and her arrival in Ghana, then called the Gold Coast and described, encouragingly, as 'The White Man's Grave'!

'We were escorted down the coast of Africa by a destroyer and a little corvette. Upon arrival offshore, we were put into bark-like canoes rowed by nearly-nude Africans. This really was like something from a film with the Natives singing in time to their rowing against the surf. As our canoes rushed towards the beach, I thought we were in for a soaking. But no. Suddenly I was lifted in the arms of an African, rushed to the beach and plonked down safe and dry!'

Strict security

Renee's memoirs later provide a vivid glimpse of her experiences preparing for and participating in the Normandy landings:

'As a British General Hospital, we mobilised at an unused orphanage in Watford in December 1943. Doctors, RAMC Orderlies and Sisters; some of us knew the ropes, military hospital-wise, and the Orderlies were partly trained. These were the days before plastics so every dish, bowl, syringe, instrument and each piece of equipment had to be greased and wrapped in oiled paper, then packed in chests.

Mattresses and bedding etc, were rolled in oiled paper and stitched into hessian. I remember this as being very hard work.

'About the end of February 1944 we went up to Peebles for physical training. It was realised that we would have to be at a peak of physical fitness. We soon got the message that assembling for anything as an unruly gaggle of girls, was definitely out. We were also, by now, wearing scratchy AV (anti-vermin) battledress, boots and gaiters. Daily drill and route marches together with lectures on possible dangers, were our routine. Here we saw the last of tin trunks and grey and scarlet uniforms for a long time. I don't think they caught up with us again until we were in Eindhoven, Holland, in September.

'I've been back to Peebles to find the hill our drill sergeant used to make us walk up, wearing gas masks, and the streams he made us long jump over. Towards the end of April, we went as a unit to the village of Peasonhall in a quiet part of Suffolk. Security was strict. We took over three empty houses. Here camp beds and everything except the barest necessities were sent away. Now we were really getting down to basics, using the same mess tins, plus tin mugs, as the men and what we learned to call eating irons. Heaven help anyone who lost these essentials. Two blankets only. No camp bed!

'Fortunately it was a lovely spring in 1944, I remember, but the whole area was one armed camp. The villagers of Peasonhall were especially good to us. The WI gave us a party in the tiny village hall. During May, the unit had a Drum Head service in the middle of a forest. Monty came and gave a 'pep talk' at the end. On 12 June we entrained for our embarkation area. Here again, the organisation was meticulous. Now we spent a night in an American assembly area. Then to Southampton – by now everything neatly packed on back or front, leaving both hands free.

A cheer for the Sisters

'When we got out of the buses at the assembly sheds, had fallen in, and started to march towards the ship's gangway, we saw that hundreds of troops were drawn up, waiting to embark. As we marched towards the gangway, we could hear the murmur "They are Sisters". Cheering started and only finished when we

were on board. It was then that we truly realised we were privileged to be part of the much-heralded invasion. Across the Channel and the landing craft were quickly alongside. Scramble nets went over the side and then laden with all the gear, we went down to the very unsteady boat.

'It was just a short distance to the beach. Nearly dark by now, we had to leap up on to the tail-board of a Utility truck that whisked us quickly away to an orchard. "What a day" said our escort, "Winston this morning and Sisters this evening!".

'Early next morning, we boarded a truck for the journey to our hospital site. There were mounds of earth alongside the road, topped with tin hats on top of wooden crosses with identity discs hanging there. Burnt-out tanks and equipment along a recently-made track running parallel with the road. Cows with legs

chained. Dereliction and damage. Then we went down a lane leading to a largish house. This was it. Here our advance party were putting up marquees. From now on, it was a matter of getting ready to admit casualties in the next 36 or at most 48 hours.

'The organisation and back-up were excellent. Equipment we had packed back in January was there and even our own camp beds and the kit bags. It all seemed unreal what with troops glimpsed through the hedges around us and the continuous noise of vehicles. We began admitting casualties at the end of the second day, but nothing had prepared us for the scale of events. We got used to the grind of ambulances coming up the track, the walking wounded being helped along. On bad days, we would admit 600 and evacuate probably 500. On one especially awful day, the number of admissions reached

1000. I remember Dillon, our Batman, coming round that night with the rum ration in cocoa. It had been raining most of the day and we certainly needed it.

'The routine was to get everybody to the beach-head as soon as possible. We kept only casualties with severe abdominal wounds. In theatre we simply didn't know who was going to be on the table next. There was no water coming out of the taps, no automatic turning on of a switch for electricity. I well remember the day our water tanker was hit. Imagine a theatre with three tables working and only four Jerricans of water. I thought, thank heavens for Penicillin powder, as I washed instruments again and again in the same water. Our sterilisation was done by boiling on Primus stoves.

'About this time, which was probably late June, Monty came to the theatre. He told us which road we were on and also said that they'd thought they would have to evacuate us the previous night because just four kilometres down the road was the German Seventh Panzer Division. Only later do these things register – we were much too busy at the time. Meanwhile, wards and the reception area had their own problems. The three Padres attached to us worked in the reception area and also as stretcher bearers when the need arose. The spirit and camaraderie were superb. We became used to the sound of gunfire, but nights were hideous. The Navy were shelling targets beyond us and the return fire was continuous. Shrapnel fell everywhere at night. It was decided we should sleep in the deepened ditch running around the field – I don't know which was worse, and can only say that any degree of personal comfort was not a feature of our lives.

'Towards the end of June, three other hospitals began taking casualties. Things didn't get much better, though, until Caen had been taken in late July. I was grateful for having been part of it all and for coming through unscathed.'

Renee (nee Morris and also known to some as Katherine) died in April 2004. The story here was provided by her niece Mrs Christina Backholer of Haywards Heath, West Sussex. It is based on notes Renee had written for various talks about her experiences.

Left: A convoy of ambulances approaches a hospital ship anchored at the Mulberry Harbour at Arromanches. Allied soldiers knew that if they survived the initial impact of a bullet or shrapnel wound then the casualty evacuation system gave them a good chance of survival.

FROM ROME to *Florence*

Above: *A German propaganda leaflet from the summer of 1944. It invites the Allies to partake of the pleasures of the Po Valley. On the reverse side, however, the scene is one of death and destruction and depicts the real welcome the Germans were preparing for the men of the Eighth and Fifth Armies.*

For the first three weeks of June 1944 the German forces in Italy were in retreat. But by the time Rome was some 130 miles in the rear, the Allied armies faced stiffening resistance.

By 20 June crack Panzergreadier and Parachute units were drawn up close by Lake Trasimeno in the centre of a line which ran from the River Chienti in the east and across the Apennines before taking advantage of other river barriers in the west.

The battle of Lake Trasimeno lasted some 10 days. The Eighth Army found itself fighting on ground which had witnessed the rout of Flaminus and his Roman legions by Hannibal over 2000 years earlier. As July dawned,

General Oliver Leese reported that the Germans had been driven north. They didn't retreat very far. Kesselring had marked a series of phase lines in front of the Arno river and Florence where rearguard actions could be mounted. Each line was known by a girl's name such as Karin, Olga and Paula and the Germans did just enough at each one to hold up the advance of the Allies by a day or two. On 16 July Arezzo fell and on the next day the Arno, south of Pisa, was reached. On 18 July the Poles liberated Ancona and next day US troops entered Leghorn.

The Allies were still around 20 miles south of Kesselring's main defensive position. Called the Gothic Line, it ran along the last barrier of mountains before the terrain opened out into the wide plains of the Po Valley. The wily German commander – master of the spoiling flight – had been

using the time bought by the stubborn resistance of his troops in the face of the Allied advance to strengthen and reinforce the position. At the same time the Allies were diverting considerable land, sea and air forces away from the fighting in Italy in preparation for an invasion of the South of France.

The Po bridges had up to now been immune to Allied bombing in anticipation of needing them intact for the advance of the Eighth and Fifth Armies. But in late July they began to destroy the bridges, hoping to trap German forces to the south of the river. Implicit in this change of strategy was an admission that further rapid victories in Italy were unlikely before the autumn.

On 4 August elements of the Fifth Army entered Florence. The Germans had abandoned the city but before departing had blown up all the bridges apart from the most famous one, Ponte Vecchio. But at least the Allies were now in striking distance of the Gothic Line.

The Italian Campaign

Guns, Mules & Mountains

Gunner Jack Perris served in Italy as a member of a Mountain Artillery Regiment. This is his story.

'I think our unit was unique in this theatre of war. Our guns broke down into a number of component parts and were carried on the backs of mules along with the ammunition. The mules were driven by Basuto tribesmen who had been recruited in Africa.

The weapons were known as 'screw guns' by the gunners and our job was to work in the mountains of Italy in areas not normally accessible to guns towed by vehicles. The gunners walked with the mules. Sometimes we would traverse metalled roads but more usually would traverse the valleys and hills and cross streams and rivers, wading along with the mules, often hanging on to the mule's tail for safety. We covered quite long distances, often 20 or 30 miles, marching by night to avoid German aircraft. Since we had to carry all our equipment, blankets were not included and many nights were spent sleeping in snow and ice with twigs and bracken instead of blankets for comfort.

I was known as a Specialist, a technical assistant to aid the officers in siting the guns and to control their firing from observation points, using trigonometry to transfer information from maps and relay that information to the men manning the guns.

We did not engage in any 'big' battles such as those at Cassino and Anzio but instead acted more like guerrillas, harassing the enemy from unexpected quarters. There were many hair-raising and dangerous incidents, of course, as the Regimental Roll of Honour and list of Citations in the diary proves. For example, Gunner Sydney Roden was awarded the MM on 26 December 1944. The Citation reads: 'During the Monte Cavallo operations, line signaller Gnr Roden was sent back to guide the ration party up to the OP. While crossing a spur, he came under artillery fire and ran towards a house to take cover. When he was close to it he suddenly noticed two Spandau (machine guns) at the ground-floor windows and, a moment later, saw a German cross the open doorway.

'He at once drew his revolver and charged the house, calling loudly to non-existent men behind him to come on. A German promptly came out and surrendered. Gnr Roden drove him into the house at the point of his revolver and there found another 12 armed Germans with an NCO, eating around a table. He called on them to surrender which they did and then he forced the NCO to disarm them all. Subsequently he made them march off, carrying their Spandaus, and handed the whole party over to the nearest Battalion HQ.'

When the fighting ended I was posted to GHQ in Naples and lived in well ordered barracks. Obviously the soft living after the snow and ice of the mountains did not agree with me and I spent three weeks in hospital with pneumonia.'

> **Gunner Roden at once charged to the house calling loudly to non-existent men behind him to come on...**

This is the frontispiece for a diary containing an account of 461 Battery's war service from its official formation on 15 January 1941 through to disbandment in 1945. Below we highlight a number of entries.

The unit sailed from Belfast in October 1942, first stopping at Freetown, Sierra Leone – 'Green, damp and strange. Natives diving for coins' – before passing Capetown and Table Mountain on the way to Durban and some time ashore. The book then records, 'Leave Durban. Rough for four days. Rumours of submarines.'

The unit landed in Egypt and in a series of hops made its way across the Middle East to a camp near Baghdad: 'Visit Babylon. Good food – more smells. Cold nights and sandstorms. Flies – and more flies. Dates, locusts, melons, scorpions, spiders.'

By August 1943 the men were in camp near Tripoli in Syria and a few months later the mules and their Basuto drivers arrived. In February 1944 the Advance Party sailed from Beirut to Bari in Italy and by 7 March they were at Naples. The Mule Party meanwhile sailed from Tripoli to Bari via Port Said in Egypt. The Main Party also went first to Egypt and Tahag Camp where the book records: 'Arrive on same plot of sand we left over a year before in January 1943!'

10 March: 'Embark on *Franconia* and travel with ENSA company and Poles, male and female, and also 600 Basutos – nearly all sick but cheerfully so.' Six days later they arrived at Taranto: 'Cold and rain, chaos unloading stores.'

On 11 May 1944, the entry reads: 'Hear Cassino offensive starts at 23.00 hours tonight! Guns moved forward, just get in by daylight. First casualties by enemy action.'

11 June: 'Battery move up Fara Gorge. Climb 5000 feet in two and a half hours. OP moves up another 1000 feet after an hour's rest.'

29 June: 'Visit Cassino. Description of battle given by Second-in-Command.'

In the summer of 1944 the unit played a role in breaking through the German defenses known as the Gothic Line. 24 August: 'Cagli bridge (blown) had proclamation on it dated June saying hostages would be shot if Partisans continued to interfere with mining of bridge.'

26 August: '338 Battery OP shelled and three signallers killed. Pink airburst fired by enemy over road demolitions.'

The Basuto mule drivers were an invaluable component to the artillery unit. Several of them feature in the Citations in the War History of 461 Battery RA. Gunner (L/Bdr) Mobuoa Mahase was awarded an MM (Military Medal) on 29 December 1944 for managing to get across the seemingly impassable swollen rivers Ronco and Voltre, with his mule, to re-establish communications with two forward Companies of infantry. The entry concludes: 'L/Bdr Mahase's successful crossing of both rivers, alone and after being separated from the British signallers with whom he normally works, showed an exceptional degree of initiative and determination which are worthy of the highest praise. His conduct on this occasion went far beyond his ordinary duty and forms an outstanding example of the soldierly qualities which have distinguished the Basutos since they became mule drivers in the Mountain Artillery.'

3–4 September: 'Warning from Adjutant not to eat grapes because of arsenic insecticide. Allied medium bomber comes down in flames, most spectacularly.'

22 September: 'Officers went up to San Marino, saw girl wearing silk stockings. San Marino a quite astonishing place and like all good Italian towns had no sewage system.'

30 September: 'Move to Secchiano – more river crossings. Popski's Private Army there. Captain N Barras came out to see us. And then we went into action again.'

1 October: 'Fairish bit of shooting at San Donato and other features. 1/2 Punjabs of 10 Indian Division came up and we had to wear tin hats, as they mistook us for Huns in our mountain caps. Went on to attack San Donato.' 29 October: 'OP moved up to house, later found to be within 350 yards of enemy. Considerable firing.'

28 March 1945: 'OP shelled with heavy stuff. After first round, Lt Lowry orders evacuation of OP room. Two minutes later, direct hit completely demolishes room.'

16 April: 'Two platoon attack on Monte Castellaro supported. Counter-attacked on objective, withdrew with 21 casualties.'

8 May: 'VE Day. Bonfires and barrels. Plenty of fireworks.'

The final entry for 1945 reads: 'The Regiment summered in pleasant parts, mainly at Pesaro on the Adriatic Coast south of Rimini. Disbandment started. The aged returned home for release to civilian life, the younger ones were posted to other units and the Basutos started on their way back to Basutoland. A time of parties and partings of old friends and the end of a great comradeship.'

> **Near Baghdad and visit Babylon. Flies and more flies. Dates, locusts, melons, scorpions and spiders.**

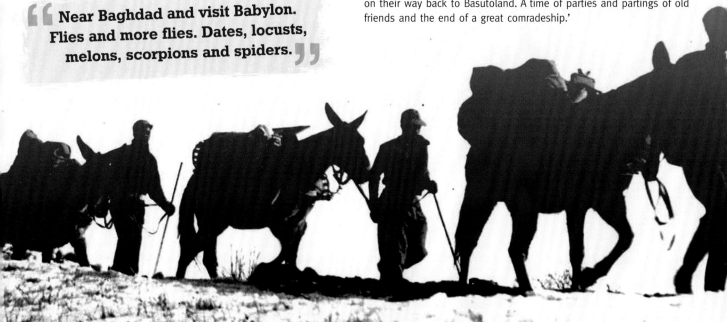

DOODLEBUG
SUMMER

A deadly hail of Hitler's secret 'V for Vengeance' weapons falls on England in the weeks following D-Day. Martin Barton-Smith, a London schoolboy at the time, recalls his own experiences and records the memories of others who found themselves in harm's way on the Home Front.

The summer of 1944 was an exciting time for an eight-year-old schoolboy. Nearly five years of war had accustomed our family to the ever-present threat of German bombers, but to me the 'threat' always seemed slightly unreal - after all, bombs usually fell on other people.

The Surrey Hounds pub at Clapham Junction 'caught it' on 17 June 1944. This photograph was taken just three minutes after the V1 struck and shows the firemen setting up their hoses.

My school friends and I had become expert in the identification of aircraft and other military equipment. There was always something going on, raids at night, huddling in the Morrison shelter, and then the excitement of going out next morning to pick up shiny pieces of shrapnel, still hot to the touch. Best of all, school was often disrupted. On reflection, it seems curious that eight-year-old boys were allowed to go out unaccompanied to examine craters containing unexploded bombs and gawp at houses ripped in two, but we did. The bomb damage in north London was less than further south in the capital, but there were still plenty of incidents to examine at close quarters until we were chased away by zealous ARP wardens (Mr Hodges really did exist!).

In the spring vast quantities of American lorries began to appear in our road, huge tractor units pulling low loader trailers with brand new tanks. Best of all, these units were manned by the fascinating mix of humanity which made up the US army - accents from all parts of North America, soldiers of all types and sizes. We were in seventh heaven, and the legendary generosity of American servicemen towards small children is not exaggerated. At night mobile ack-ack guns would open up and rattle the windows and doors. In the morning more booty, until I was forbidden to bring any more metal into the house!

With the advent of D-Day, our friends moved on to be replaced by a whole mixture of other units. Most of these only stayed overnight en route to the channel ports, and there was a noticeable stiffening of military discipline, particularly when it came to denying access to small boys climbing on lorries. A week after the excitement of the invasion, another event came along which occupied our attention and which, ultimately, changed the direction of many lives. The 'Doodlebugs' started to appear. Quite how they came to be called as such is unclear; maybe the larva of a tropical insect, the antlion (doodlebug), resembled the German flying bomb? The Germans had a rather more prosaic name, calling it V1 (V for *Vergeltungswaffe* or 'Reprisal Weapon').

To we amateur 'spotters' of North London, these were a revelation. The noise of their approach was unmistakable, a sort of stuttering staccato popping noise that led to another nickname - 'Buzz Bomb'. It wasn't long before we realised that when the engine noise stopped it was time to take cover! Because of their primitive guidance system, the bombs were inaccurate and were aimed at London indiscriminately in an effort to undermine civilian morale. They crossed the coast of Sussex and Kent and winged their way to the capital up 'Doodlebug Alley' where most of the damage was done and where most of the defences against them were mounted.

My memories are but a tiny glimpse of that fateful summer. They are a schoolboy's memories, and not tainted by the close reality of death and injury which afflicted so many. Others were not so lucky. Marlene Heselden of Walmer writes in her autobiography how she was visiting her married sister in Lewisham one Saturday in June: 'There had been an unusually large number of air raid warnings that morning. We heard a flying bomb approaching sounding quite close. The engine cut out and at that moment the door bell rang - 'Go and answer the door, Albert must have forgotten his key'. Those were the last words my sister Doris spoke to me. There was a rush of warm air, then black, hot, suffocation, the smell of burnt dust and the taste of it choking me. I was aware of an ambulance bell ringing, and then, thankfully, passed out.'.

New wonder drug

Marlene was the only survivor from the six people in the flat. She spent over a year in hospitals and convalescent homes being treated for severe wounds. She attributes her survival to the new 'wonder' drug, penicillin.

Frank Busby of Knaresborough was also an eight-year-old in 1944, living near Croydon Airport. He recalls: 'These rockets seemed to come over continuously, houses all round were blown apart. Our house was not hit, although windows were out, ceilings were down and there was a lot of other damage. One day I was in the garden when a Doodlebug came over. The engine cut out and I started to run indoors but tripped and fell. I lay on the ground watching the bomb, and I swear to this day if the wind had not blown it off course it would have landed right on top of me. In fact, it landed in the local cemetery!'

Two near misses were reported by Roy Lawrance of Whitstable, this time in the

Harringay area of London: 'I was cycling home from school at about 4.30pm when something caught my eye and I looked up. To my astonishment there was a V1 floating through the air immediately above me, moving like a falling leaf and slowly dipping from side to side. It was heading directly for the shopping centre in Green Lanes, but at the last minute side-slipped into the American Gardens in Finsbury Park where it demolished some houses. I wonder how many of the shoppers that day realised how close they had been to disaster?' On another occasion, Roy was again on his bicycle, this time in thick mist which made the unseen approach of a bomb doubly unnerving: 'I did not know what to do for the best. I remember riding round in circles not knowing which way to go to avoid it. I had just decided to lie down next to a hospital wall when the thing went off with a bang in the distance. I got back on my bike and continued to school'.

The reporting of the first wave of bombs in June was heavily censored. The authorities did not wish to give the Germans the slightest opportunity to plot the detonations and thus assess their accuracy. The guidance system was primitive, being based on a gyro compass and the amount of fuel fed to the engine. However, since these were essentially 'terror weapons', the uncertainty which surrounded their arrival contributed to the nervousness of the civilian population. The first recorded bomb struck a railway bridge in Bow in London and the second fell near Cuckfield in Sussex, some 50 miles away.

No trace of damage

Others recall the widespread sightings of these devices. Gil Graves of Wellington, Somerset writes: 'We arrived for work one morning and one of our colleagues who lived in Newbury said something had exploded near the A4 London Road. It appears it was a V1, but there was no mention in the papers or on the radio about it. Hitler's mob were obviously still testing them for range and direction. A few days later another device landed at Harwell airfield and destroyed a Stirling bomber and left a large crater. By dawn all traces of the damage had been removed and Harwell denied all knowledge of it.'...obviously government `spin doctoring` is not a new science.

Charmaine Burgess' parents had a smallholding on the Essex marshes: 'There was a very dear neighbour who was very nervous about everything at this time, and came running to be with my mother whenever there was a raid. One day, Mum had cooked a huge boiler full of potatoes and put them outside the door to cool. A Flying Bomb passed overhead and the neighbour came screaming up the road, and then screamed even louder,"I've been shot, oh help, I've been shot". Mother ran to get the first aid kit, but neighbour Nell had stepped in the boiling potatoes and only needed cooling down!'

While London and the Home Counties suffered under the V1 rocket onslaught, Occupied Paris was relatively quiet in July 1944 with the Allies reluctant to bomb the city even though it was a very important transit point for German reinforcements headed for Normandy.

Some of those Frenchmen and women who had thrown in their lot with the Nazis still remained stubbornly convinced of an ultimate victory for Hitler. The Collaborationist press highlighted with great gusto the advent of the secret weapons of which the V1 was just the first. Berlin was already announcing the coming of the V2, faster and even more destructive. One broadsheet printed: 'They used to write Vs on the walls. Now write V1, V2 and V3...'

The July weather was superb. Resistance and Collaborators seemed to agree on one thing: the wonderful legs of Parisian girls. Gilles Perrault was 13 years old at the time and remembers the pretty women with skirts billowing in the updraft of passing German trucks: 'I felt life held great promise', he wrote later.

On 20 July, roadblocks went up all over the city and German tanks took up positions outside key buildings. It was the day of the failed bomb plot against Hitler and some senior Wehrmacht officers had showed their hands too early. When it was clear that Hitler had survived, the soldiers hastily assured the Fuhrer of their continued loyalty. Not all of them were convincing enough in their reasons for confining the SS to barracks and were summarily executed. Even the legendary Field Marshal Erwin Rommel, he who had predicted that the success or failure of the Allied invasion would be decided on the landing beaches in the first 24 hours - The Longest Day, was implicated. He later took poison on the understanding that his family would be spared retribution.

In the days following 25 July news reached Paris that the American General Patton had broken through at Avranches and was surging into Brittany. A Collaborator reporter in the city wrote the comforting words: 'This is because it is the only way open to them.'

Very few inhabitants of Paris believed him. But they did wonder just how long it would be before their liberators would arrive.

News Chronicle · No. 30,635 · FRIDAY, JULY 21, 1944 · ONE PENNY · balito STOCKINGS

HITLER: ASSASSINATION ATTEMPTED AT HIS HEADQUARTERS

The Fuehrer escaped with slight burns and concussion, says Berlin

"AIDE-DE-CAMP WAS HURT"

13 HIGH-RANKING OFFICERS INJURED IN EXPLOSION

Himmler is now the Dictator in Germany

Allies storm through 9 Normandy villages

A group of dedicated German anti-Nazis attempted to dispose of Adolf Hitler on 20 July 1944. The desolating story of the failed attempt has been told many times, but what is not universally known is the fact that the attempt was the third that same month, all involving the staunch and courageous Count Claus von Stauffenberg. The first was planned for 11 July at Berchtesgaden when both Himmler and Goring were to join Hitler at a conference. About this time, 'Stauffenberg' had been promoted to be Chief of Staff and deputy to fellow-conspirator Colonel General Fredrich Fromm. This gave him access to certain conferences attended by Fuhrer. In the event, neither Himmler nor Goering attended, so Stauffenbery took it upon himself to delay setting off the bomb he carried in his briefcase; a perfectionist impulse that, in retrospect, proved a fatal error.

BOMB PLOT

WOLF'S LAIR

The second attempt was arranged for a conference to be held at the *Wolfsschanze* – Wolf's Lair – in East Prussia four days later, but again Stauffenberg failed to ignite the bomb in his briefcase. This was because at the last moment he was called upon to address the gathering which threw out his plans for seeing off the explosive; a fiddly task that had always presented difficulties to him resulting from the loss of one hand and injury to the other sustained whilst serving on the Eastern Front.

At the 20 July meeting, all went well initially and the loaded and primed briefcase was placed on the floor on the inner side of the leg of the big oak table close to Hitler. Stauffenberg then left the room on the pretext of making a telephone call. A few moments later Colonel Brandt, General Heusinger's Chief-of-Staff, found the briefcase in his way and moved it a few inches to the far side of the table leg from Hitler. At 12.45 the bomb exploded killing, amongst others, the unfortunate Colonel Brandt, another of the anti-Nazi plotters who, a year before, had attempted to carry aboard Hitler's aeroplane a

couple of brandy bottles primed with explosive. Thus Hitler escaped death on that fateful July day through the inadvertent action of one of the very men wanting him dead.

Conflicting reports emerged from the Wolf's Lair concerning the fate of Hitler resulted in some of the plotters revealing themselves prematurely. One who was more cautious was General Fromm and, upon learning of the failure of the plot, reneged on his fellow-plotters, seeing to it that as many as possible were instantly shot. Then the Gestapo intervened, wanting interrogations before execution. Thus Fromm's efforts to remove all those who were aware of his earlier flirtations with the enemies of the Fuhrer, whose favour he now sought at the last minute, were unsuccessful. The wretched man was finally arrested and executed eight months later, having experienced in the meantime the worst cruelties of which the system which he had helped to create, was capable.

INNOCENT VICTIMS

The effect of the attempt on Hitler was like that of a wound inflicted upon some savage creature at bay. He gave orders for a policy of *sippenhaft* or 'kindred seizure' which entailed all near-relatives of the conspirators being arrested and executed as a sacrifice to the wrath of the insulted divinity of the *Wolfsschanze*. Their number is not known though many wholly innocent victims died in the ensuing massacre.

We should remember Stauffenberg in a good light. He was a professional soldier of fine physique, striking good looks and an infectious laugh. He and his fellow conspirators belonged to an exclusive clique of brave men whose love of their country transcended the evil of Nazism. Their hanging, on Hitler's orders, were performed in the most brutal and agonising fashion, intended to obliterate the memory of those who dared to oppose him. Instead it lit a beacon in the satanic darkness of unspeakable barbarity.

Christopher Portway

DEATH OF A PANZER ACE

On 25 July, three days after the attempt on his life, Hitler met with SS Obersturmfuhrer Michael Wittmann, to personally confer on him the Swords to accompany the Knights Cross with Oak Leaves he already possessed.

This new honour recognised Wittman's outstanding conduct in the course of the Battle of Normandy where, with just five Tiger tanks, in the course of a single day he oversaw the destruction of 30 British tanks and scores of vehicles.

With the Fatherland being battered by Allied bombs, to boost morale, the Nazis needed heroes and they didn't come much larger than life than Wittmann. Yet within a fortnight of the meeting with Hitler, the panzer ace would be dead, a victim of Allied air power. Indeed, Wittmann's life and death in Normandy, mirrors the fate that befell much of the German Army west of the Seine in the summer of 1944.

VASTLY OUTNUMBERED

Wittmann's tally of 'kills' since 1939 amounted to 138 enemy tanks and assault guns together with 132 anti-tank guns before his transfer to the newly formed Waffen-SS 101st Heavy Tank Battalion, stationed in France in anticipation of an Allied invasion.

After D-Day Wittmann's unit was soon in the thick of the fighting. On 13 June his small command found themselves vastly outnumbered at the key junction town of Villers-Bocage. Fortunately for Wittmann, his presence went unobserved and when the British column halted and the crews vacated their vehicles, he at once raced his 60-ton Tiger down the column, wrecking tanks and trucks with shell after shell fired at point-blank range.

Wittmann's force was eventually overwhelmed and he and his crew had to abandon their tank and escape on foot. But they'd succeeded in blunting the British attack; Villers-Bocage would not be liberated until 4 August.

TYPHOON NEMESIS

By this time the Allied breakout was in full swing. Four days later on 8 August Wittmann was in one of a trio of Tigers keeping open an escape route for the *Wehrmacht* forces facing encirclement around Falaise. His tank was hit and set on fire; Wittmann died in the explosion.

For years it was claimed that Sherman Firefly tanks had destroyed Wittman's Tiger. Then some two decades ago, a French farmer, Serge Varin, said he had actually examined Wittmann's Tiger (No 007) after the action. He'd seen no shell damage but noted a big hole in the rear of the tank caused by a rocket fired from the air.

Rocket-firing Typhoons were the nemesis of thousands of German soldiers and vehicles in Normandy in 1944. It seems as though Germany's greatest panzer ace shared that same fate.

War Correspondence

High drama over Essex

19 June 1944 was a fine summer's day over Southern England but the war was about to come home to the people of Canvey Island, Essex. Above the Thames estuary the 379th Bomb Group of the 8th USAAF was returning to Kimbolton after a raid on V1 launch sites near Calais. At the age of only 19, Lt Lloyd Burns, piloting a B17 Flying Fortress, was flying his 24th mission; one more and he could go home. Over the Channel, Lloyd had swapped seats with his co-pilot, Lt Fred Kauffman, so that Fred could gain some 'First Pilot' experience.

Above and behind them another B17 pilot, Lt Ramacitti, fought for control of his aircraft. Having taken enemy fire over the target, one of his engines was giving trouble and the plane was seen weaving about. Suddenly Ramacitti's B17 slammed into the top of Burns' aircraft, killing Fred Kauffman instantly. Lloyd tried the controls, which were useless and ordered the crew to bale out. He tried to rouse Fred, but he was obviously dead.

The radio room, behind the cockpit, was also squashed down but with enough room for the radio operator, Leroy Monk, to squeeze out and put his parachute on before he jumped. In the nose, bombardier Jack Gray was shocked to see the Plexiglas nosecone popped clean off the plane by the impact and found himself staring into space and without a parachute. He managed to scramble back for his 'chute, put it on and jumped.

Underneath the B17 was a gun turret shaped like a ball. The gunner, Bill Farmer, saw that his plane was falling to pieces and baled out. Richard Andrews, normally the waist gunner, was one of the tail guns that day and baled out of the escape hatch. The usual tail gunner, Louis Schulte, also jumped but sadly he drowned in the water.

Moments before the collision, Len Gibbs, the flight engineer/top turret gunner, had climbed down from his turret suffering from an earache and when he picked himself up from the floor he too jumped, to be followed by the last man out, pilot Burns.

Onlookers saw the doomed B17 turn away from the island before crashing into the marshy area known locally as 'The Point'. Many believed that a body recovered from the wreck was that of the pilot who had stayed at the controls to avoid the houses. In fact it was the forces of aerodynamics that steered the aircraft away from Canvey and the body was that of the navigator, Ed Sadler, who never made it out.

Sadly there was only one survivor from the other B17, bombardier Theo Chronopolos. Theo was thrown out when the plane broke in half as it spun down to crash on the Kent side of the river. He landed safely by parachute.

Lloyd Burns flew his 25th mission three days later, but stayed in the air force and went to the Pacific to fly the mighty B29 Superfortress in the war against Japan.

As a boy in the 1970s I dug up some parts of this B17 bomber from the mud of the Thames and was nearly drowned in the process. I knew nothing about the crash until 2004 when I came across research carried out by an eye-witness called Stan Pierce who was himself just a small boy when he saw the incident take place.

Mark Etheridge

Left: A Fieseler Storch of the kind encountered by Philip Mead in the sky over Normandy in the summer of 1944.

Pistols at 2000 feet!

It was March 1944 when I finished my training as a Navigator in the Royal Air Force. After 200 hours of night flying from RAF Mona Anglesey we expected to be posted to Bomber Command but it was not to be. The whole course of Navigators was sent to an airfield near Cardiff and put in a hanger with a similar number of pilots and ordered to 'pair off'. Then each pair as a crew was allotted an Avro Anson. The Anson was a low wing twin engine aeroplane with a wing span of almost 60 feet used by Coastal Command with a crew of perhaps six but we were to fly as transport aircraft with just pilot and navigator.

As D-Day approached we were told our planes were part of 1311 T Flight Transport Command but this was later changed to 84 Group Support Unit 2nd Tactical Air Force and our job was to keep the British and Canadian forces supplied after they landed in Normandy. Unarmed and heavily loaded we took off from bases near the South Coast and flew across the Channel at 2000 feet looking for temporary airfields just our side of the front line (which was of course advancing all the time).

One day in the summer of 1944 when the Allied troops had advanced east of Caen we had taken off and flown towards the French coast. I had given a course to fly to an airfield captured by the Canadians and at 2000 feet was map reading. Suddenly I observed a small black spot moving below us. Gradually it got bigger until I could identify a Fieseler Storch German reconnaissance aircraft coming up from below. It was a sinister looking high wing monoplane painted all in black with white swastikas and formatted a few feet from our right wing tip. The pilot was wearing a black flying helmet and goggles. He looked across at us and stared and then took out and waved his service revolver at us!

We had also been issued with revolvers for protection if we crashed in enemy territory so we both drew out revolvers and shook them back at him! The German then waggled his wings and slowly descended until he was finally lost above the trees below us.

Our Anson slowly plodded its way on at 140 knots until we spotted the Allied airfield where we landed safely.

Philip Mead

Mr Mead was WO Navigator 1805100 in the RAF 1942-1946.

WAR DIARY
July 1944

The beginning of July sees a surge of recruits to the Italian partisan movements. Since the liberation of Rome early last month thousands of men have taken to the mountains and hills to join bands of guerrillas - mainly communist-led - who are carrying out sabotage operations and hit-and-run raids on the German lines of communication.

On **2 July** 5000 men of the Brazilian Expeditionary Force are at sea. This first contingent is bound for Naples where it will join Allied forces fighting north of Rome. Brazil declared war on the Axis in August 1942 but the country's role in the conflict to date has been confined to assisting the battle against the U-Boat menace in the Southern Atlantic.

The following day in Normandy, two squadrons of Northrop P-61 Black Widow nightfighters begin operations over the Allied bridgehead. The Allied air forces have complete command of the air by day and the arrival of significant numbers of nightfighters will reduce the Luftwaffe's ability to mount raids after darkness.

4 July: US aircraft from Task Force 58 raid Japanese bases on the islands of Guam, Iwo Jima and Chichi Jima.

In London the flying bomb offensive has led to a new evacuation of the capital. Mothers of children under five and expectant mothers as well as schoolchildren are to be moved to the country.

5 July: British soldiers in the invasion forces have been allowed to take no more than 10 bob with them to France. This low sum has been fixed to prevent a 'run' on commodities in the newly liberated territory.

By **6 July** the island of Saipan in the Marianas is close to being secured by the Americans. The Japanese commanders Admiral Nagumo and General Saito, both commit ritual suicide rather than surrender. Some 8000 Japanese - soldiers and civilians - follow their example.

7 July: The Red Army enters Vilnius in Lithuania after overcoming fanatical resistance by SS men and paratroops on a 'stand or die' mission. Whilst the Lithuanians and citizens of the other Baltic states of Estonia and Latvia have been treated badly by their Nazi occupiers, many of them do not wish to be 'liberated' by the Russians and are deeply wary of Stalin's intentions.

The following day in Burma, Ukhrul falls to the Allies; the Japanese are still in retreat following the repulse of their invasion of India.

On **9 July** bandleader Glenn Miller - already a showbiz legend - gives the first concert of his British tour.

10 July: The British newspapers look to have won a campaign to have a ban on weather reports lifted. Imposed at a time when the UK was under constant threat of daylight bombing, the weather gag infuriated farmers.

By **11 July** some 41,000 mothers and children have been evacuated from London in the face of the V1 offensive.

By **12 July,** some two months after the breaking of the Gustav Line and the capture of Monte Cassino, the men of the Fifth and Eighth armies are 250 miles north of the start line and are approaching Florence. German resistance begins to harden along their Gothic Line.

A German nightfighter based at Deelen in Holland landed at RAF Woodbridge in Suffolk on **13 July** after an apparent

navigational error. The Ju88G carried three different radar sets, all designed to negate the RAF's sophisticated electronic counter-measures equipment. British scientists are surprised to see how up-to-date the German devices are.

14 July: Bastille Day in those parts of France that are liberated is marked by the settling of old scores against many Frenchmen and women who collaborated with the Germans.

By **15 July** it becomes clear that U-Boats pose no threat to the Allied supply ship lifeline across the Channel. The vessels of Admiral Dönitz are being sunk on an almost daily basis in the Atlantic, North Sea and Bay of Biscay.

On **16 July** US troops continue to inch their way towards St Lô and are within sight of the town's outskirts.

17 July: Field Marshal Erwin Rommel fell victim to the RAF today when a fighter flown by Squadron Leader J J Le Roux of 602 Squadron strafed the staff car carrying the legendary German commander near Bernay. The incident has left Rommel seriously injured and unconscious in hospital. Ironically, Rommel is fortunate to have been attacked by conventional weapons. Elsewhere in Normandy US aircraft drop napalm for the first time.

On **18 July** VHF radio equipment is introduced into Sherman tanks to provide a direct ground-air link between British armour and rocket-firing Typhoons of the Second Tactical Air Force.

19 July: In London it's estimated that so far 200,000 homes have been damaged by the doodlebugs. Daring fighter pilots have been developing a technique for 'tipping' the doodlebugs off course. This involves the hazardous operation of diving down and alongside one of the pilotless rocket devices and then close enough to cause it to veer off through slipstream turbulence.

Hitler survives an assassination attempt today **(20 July)** when a briefcase bomb explodes in his Rastenburg HQ during a briefing. A table shielded Hitler from the full force of the blast.

21 July: In Italy some 100,000 troops are being pulled out of the front line and sent back to Naples in preparation for the invasion of Southern France.

Today in the South Pacific **(22 July)** US marines reinforce their beachheads on Guam following yesterday's initial landings.

23 July: General Henry Crerar's First Canadian Army becomes operational.

On **24 July** the Red Army is advancing into Poland. Yesterday the cities of Lublin and Pskov were captured. Today the Russians come across the first of Hitler's rumoured concentration camps and liberate the inmates.

25 July: In the Indian Ocean the British Eastern Fleet has been attacking Japanese installations at Sabang.

26 July: In Germany a massive hunt for the Hitler bomb plot conspirators and sympathisers is underway and some 7000 suspects have been rounded up by the Gestapo.

27 July: A succession of key positions held by the Germans are falling to the Soviets. Today Lwow and Bialystok are liberated.

28 July: Japanese defences at Ibdi on Biak, New Guinea, have been crushed by US forces.

By **29 July** the Russian advance into Poland has covered some 450 miles in just five weeks of combat. The Polish capital Warsaw lies just a few score miles from the Red Army tank spearheads.

30 July: US forces have landed on Middleburg and Amsterdam islands in the Far East.

31 July: US Naval commanders back General Douglas MacArthur's plan for the liberation of the Philippines as a priority rather than bypassing the islands and invading Formosa or Okinawa.

Smiles ahead!

...as the Allies advance in France

AUGUST 1944

Normandy

Man and beast get a respite from the fighting in Normandy in August 1944. The photograph above shows cows ambling leisurely past a British field gun on their way to the milking shed. Thousands of farm animals died in the fighting but the plentiful fresh milk was appreciated by the Allied and German forces.

In the photograph below, after taking a shower, British soldiers line up for an issue of fresh underwear from a mobile laundry. The sign in the foreground reads: 'Brighton. Grand August by the Sea. Bank Holiday attraction. Baths will be free. Bring your tanks and bulldozers.'

...in the summer of '44

BREAKOUT

At last a war of movement is open to the Allies in France. A stubborn Hitler fails to see the danger.

On 7 August 1944 the 117th Regiment of the 30th American Division near Mortain in the extreme west of Normandy, saw, clanking through the morning mist, the vague outlines of German tanks. They at once engaged the enemy with bazookas and 57mm guns but with limited effect. The panzers ground their way forward, the vanguard of some 400 others. On Hitler's personal orders the Wehrmacht was mounting a desperate counter-attack aimed at cutting off Patton's rampant Third Army, now charging into Britanny and beyond.

With the situation critical by noon, the sun came to the aid of the Allies. As the last of the mist burnt off, British Typhoons of the Second Tactical Air Force appeared overhead. Between 12.30 hours and dusk they flew

Above: Frank Wootton's famous painting 'Falaise Gap, August 1944' depicts rocket-firing Typhoons wreaking havoc on a German column of tanks and trucks. Reproduced by kind permission of Mrs Virginia Wootton.

294 sorties and knocked the stuffing out of the German armour. 'Suddenly the fighter bombers swooped out of the sky' reported panzer commander General von Luttwitz later, 'they came down in hundreds, firing their rockets at concentrated tanks and vehicles. We could do nothing against them and could make no further progress. By 9 August, the Division was back where it started, having lost 30 tanks and 800 men.'

It was a similar story for all the German units involved in the counterattack. Five years later the Wehrmacht's General Speidel stated: 'The armoured operation was completely wrecked exclusively by the Allied air forces, supported by a highly trained ground wireless organisation.' There's a measure of truth in Speidel's words but they do seem today to be largely grounded in a desire to blame the Wehrmacht's reverse on circumstances beyond their control. In other words, Allied soldiers had nothing to do with

the defeat of the German Army – it was all down to the dreaded jabos, the fighter-bombers.

On the same day that the Mortain attack was blunted, American tanks were in Le Mans. Back in Normandy, General Pat Crerar's Canadians were moving slowly on Falaise which they reached and cleared by 17 August despite a bloody check north of the River Laison. Meanwhile, General Omar Bradley's US forces had turned north. In consequence a pocket had been formed of which the northern side, ending in Falaise, was held by the British and Canadians, and the southern, ending at Argentan, by the Americans.

In the pocket were the remnants of 16 German divisions, including nine panzer divisions. Not until 13 August had Hitler given permission for them to retreat across the River Seine. By then for most it was already far too late to escape. Soon the mouth of the pocket was just 25 miles wide and shrinking almost by the hour.

Fierce action near Chamois

Those outside the pocket were intent on headlong retreat while the Germans caught inside seemed made of sterner stuff. They could have surrendered but instead fought on. On 18 August a fierce action developed near Chamois – a place swiftly dubbed 'Shambles' by the Tommies – when the Germans brought up their few fresh troops in a bid to allow the remaining panzers to escape. Around 48 hours later the Polish Armoured Brigade found itself under pressure from an encircled enemy tank force greater in numbers than themselves. Timely air support decided the issue.

Air Marshal Sir Arthur Coningham's team had brought the air force to the highest pitch. From dusty air strips just a few miles from the Normandy shores the Typhoons and Spitfires with their eager pilots went about their deadly business. No doubt Hitler failed to appreciate the irony that what he had begun in crowing triumph in Warsaw and Rotterdam back in 1939-40 was now being

> *The rockets coming from the British planes looked like shooting stars rushing upon the earth...*

visited on his Wehrmacht many times over in this little corner of Normandy.

The retreating Germans found themselves trapped in a scene from Dante's Inferno. In vain they took to the woods. These became death traps into which bombs, rockets and shells were poured. 'When an air attack developed' recounted a French farmer, caught in the maelstrom, 'and it seemed to me that there was one every half hour at least, the Germans would run from their vehicles looking for any kind of cover to escape the eyes of the pilots. The rockets coming from the British fighters looked from the ground as though shooting stars were rushing upon the earth. A vehicle hit by any burst into instant flame.

Doors of vehicles removed

'In order to leave their vehicles as quickly as possible, the German soldiers had removed the doors and one of their number always lay on one of the front mudguards looking upwards and scanning the sky.'

Away from the main road there were many deep-cut lanes.They remain today where great stretches of beeches and other trees form funnels of green overhead. In the summer of 1944 the Germans attempted to hide beneath these same canopies of foliage, to little avail. The slightest glint of metal glimpsed through a vehicle's additional camouflage of fresh-cut branches would bring down death and destruction from above.

When it was all over, a witness who toured

the Pocket wrote: 'I soon abandoned my jeep for it was impossible to make progress on the secondary roads. Where the retreating Germans had been caught in the open, they lay in irregular swathes mostly in shallow ditches. Their transport was mixed. Cars of every description, many of them Citroens, Renaults and other French makes, strewed the fields, mingled with horses dead in the shafts of stolen carts.

'I noticed one modern limousine painted with the stippled green and brown camouflage effected by the Germans. It contained on the back seat a colonel and his smartly dressed mistress. Each had been shot through the chest with cannon shells. At the entrance to the next leafy lane a tank, its gun pointing skywards, straddled the road. From the turret hung a dead German.

'In the sunken lane under the semi-darkness of the arching trees in full August leaf the picture of destruction was complete and terrible to the last detail. It was obvious what had happened. Typhoons had spotted the column and destroyed the leading and end vehicles, in this case two armoured cars. They had then passed up and down the lane using rockets and cannons. The vehicles were jammed bumper to bumper and each bore the signature of the Second Tactical Air Force – a gaping hole in side or turret. Grey-clad, dust-powdered bodies were sprawled everywhere. I gave up trying to walk over this mile of utter destruction and made a wide detour only to find another lane equally impassable.'

On the original *Operation Overlord* timetable, Paris was to be liberated well over four months after D-Day. Now, suddenly, Allied advances of breathtaking magnitude looked imminent. Paris? Brussels? The borders of the Reich itself? Nothing seemed impossible.

'The Great Swan' was taking flight.

The statue of Wiiliam the Conqueror in Falaise with two British soldiers in front of it in 1944.

Mont St Michel, Normandy, in 1944 and as it is today.

THE SECOND D-DAY

INVASION OF THE SOUTH OF FRANCE

The Mediterranean coast of France was a popular posting for the men of the Wehrmacht. Even in early August 1944 it was a world away from the grim realities of war in Italy, on the Eastern Front and in Northern France, although the 250,000 men of the German 19th Army surely knew their enemy must one day come their way.

Yet if Winston Churchill could have had his way that day would have been put off for quite some time. The British premier wanted the husbanded forces in the Mediterranean to strike instead in the Balkans in a campaign that might have seen the Western Allies first into the capitals of countries like Austria and Hungary before the Red Army arrived to impose Stalin's will.

At this time the Americans were far less suspicious of Russian intentions than were the British. Dismissive of Churchill's 'adventurism', they, along with General de Gaulle and his resurgent French forces, backed *Operation Anvil*, the southern arm of a giant pincer movement to crush the Nazi forces in France.

Out of the darkness

The US view prevailed. So it was that two months and nine days after the Normandy landings came the invasion of the South of France (with a change of codename to *Operation Dragoon*) on Tuesday 15 August 1944. Out of the darkness of a warm Mediterranean night steamed 250 fighting ships (including many Royal Navy vessels such as *HMS Black Prince* and *HMS Ajax*) escorting 1000 transport vessels carrying close to 300,000 Allied soldiers, mainly Americans but also French, Canadian and British. Thousands more men floated down by parachute or were glider-borne to land amidst the fields and vineyards of Provence and the Côte d'Azur.

The main landings were concentrated on the coast between Cannes and Hyeres with the normally quiet fishing port of St Tropez being right in the centre of the action. The light German defences along the resort's now famous Pampelonne and Tahiti beaches and those further west at Cavalaire were softened up by naval gunfire before a phalanx of landing craft and amphibious DUKWs brought the fighting men ashore. Progress was swift in most places; only at Frejus and St Raphael did the Germans put up a stubborn but ultimately futile fight.

A section of a 1947 Michelin Map depicting the landings in the South of France is reproduced below. In the picture above note the St Raphael town sign. The resort of Croix Valmer featured in the plaque (below left) is just north of Cavalaire at the bottom of the map.

Shower of grenades

The defenders were in the main a ragbag army. As in Normandy, many were volunteers from places like Armenia, Georgia and the Ukraine, all at one time glad to be freed from Stalin's tyranny but now finding themselves subject to the whim of another dictator – and worse, expected to fight for a country that was clearly losing the war. The understrength 11th Panzer Division was the only tank force still in the south. But it was in the wrong place around Albi and Languedoc and also came under Hitler's private control.

SUR CETTE PLAGE
LE 15 AOUT 1944 A 6 HRES
DEBARQUERENT LES ARMEES
ALLIEES LIBERATRICES QUI
DELIVRERENT CROIX VALMER

> ## "Aboard *HMS Kimberley* as she closed in on the South of France coast that morning was Winston Churchill, seeing for himself how the invasion fared..."

There were some tragedies. A group of French African Commandos found themselves at the foot of the 350 feet high cliffs of Cap Negre which was topped by a German strongpoint. Sentries spotted their assailants and broke up the attack with a shower of grenades and bullets before it could even get started. Another 700 French Commandos landed to block the highway between Cavalaire and Le Lavandou. Others attacked pillboxes at Rayol and La Canadel.

Douglas Fairbanks Jr's war

Hollywood screen star Lt Commander Douglas Fairbanks Jr led a diversionary attack near Cannes to the east of the real invasion zone where the British gunboats *Aphis* and *Scarab* went close inshore to lob shells at the coastal highway.

Large numbers of the 5000 paratroopers involved landed around Le Muy and Draguignan amidst an eerie low-lying fog covering the valleys and plains; hills and even some houses protruded through the murk. Others were scattered all over the hills of the Maures and Esterel ranges but sowed chaos and confusion in the enemy. At 5.10am a substantial detachment of the British Second Independent Parachute Brigade touched down in the hills of Le Rouet. Eighty of them missed the target but nevertheless managed to destroy a German motorised column with the aid of bazookas and light weapons.

Aboard *HMS Kimberley* as she closed in on the French coast that morning was Winston Churchill, seeing for himself how the invasion fared.

Jaque Robichon's excellent book, *The Second D-Day*, (first published in the UK by Arthur Barker in 1969) tells a story which echoes the old joke about one Scotsman being worth 10 of any other nation's soldiers. He recounts how a jeepload of seven Scots turned up in the nick of time to ambush a German column of reinforcements on the road between Callas and Le Muy. Stripped to the waist in the searing heat of a Provencal August, the Scots blasted away with sten guns and killed 60 of the enemy before piling back into their vehicle and driving off. The whole scene was witnessed by a French farmer. He had his home burnt down in retaliation and livestock slaughtered but he did, at least, live to tell the tale.

St Tropez liberated

Apart from the odd sniper, St Tropez was liberated by late afternoon with the aid of the local French Resistance. The nearby hilltop towns of Gassin and Ramatuelle were also captured. It was an unequal battle. Aix-en-Provence fell on 21 August and three days later the Allies were as far north as Grenoble in the French Alps. Marseille and Toulon surrendered on 28 August. With the whole of the South of France clear of the enemy, the Allies set off in pursuit of the fleeing Germans as they retreated up the Rhone Valley, past Lyon.

Background illustration: Allied warships in St Tropez harbour fire at Luftwaffe raiders shortly after the town was liberated.
Inset: A US soldier standing on the deck of a French warship that had been scuttled in Toulon harbour in November 1942 following the German takeover of the previously Vichy controlled South of France.

NAPOLEON'S BIRTHDAY!

15 August

Was it coincidence that 15 August was also Napoleon's birthday? The French Maquis obviously knew it - their local codename for the landings was that of France's most famous leader. The South of France was where Napoleon came ashore from exile in 1815. Winding northwards through the mountains lies the famous Route Napoleon, passing through Grasse, Sisteron and Gap on the road taken by his fast-growing army which would eventually enter Paris in triumph. In 1944 Allied troops followed north in Napoleon's footsteps. We wonder if patriotic Frenchmen seven decades ago would have appreciated the irony in Mr Bonaparte's fate - a crushing defeat at Waterloo by a combined army of British, Belgians and ... Prussians!

St Tropez AT WAR

Commander Stanley A Nettle was a Royal Navy Beachmaster for Delta Force during the invasion of Southern France. He landed on 15 August 1944 on Pampelonne beach to the west of St Tropez. This is his story.

My original role in *Operation Dragoon* was a planning one as I was Assistant Staff Officer, Operations, at GHQ in Italy. The ships were already in their loading ports when I was told I was to go with them as a Beachmaster. The British transport vessels involved in the landings comprised 17 troop carriers and 42 store ships. I was on board the *Dunera*, a passenger ship with landing craft slung from stem to stern on both sides. We were to land soon after H-Hour on D-Day itself and quickly learnt that there were 12 hospital ships also detailed to rendezvous in the target area, ready to be called forward as necessary. Perhaps it was the knowledge of those hospital ships that made me suddenly very much aware of my white naval cap cover. I thought it would make a tempting target for snipers and so, just before arrival off the coast, I dyed it with the aid of a cup of coffee!

Orange flashes

We were lying quite close to the beach and just before dawn the bombardment of the coast from the warships began. It was a most impressive spectacle to see the orange flashes of the naval guns, feel the swoosh of the shells as they passed overhead and then to see and hear the crash as they exploded on the beaches and beyond. We prayed that none would fall short.

The LCAs (Landing Craft Assault) had been lowered and then the first wave went ashore to clear any minefields and place white tapes to show the safe passages. Once ashore, I hitched a lift to St Tropez in a jeep with an American Lieutenant. On a country road en route there were half a dozen soldiers lying in a ditch. The Lieutenant stopped and asked what was going on. 'There's snipers in them there trees, Sir' said one of them in a real Southern accent. On hearing this the Lieutenant shouted, 'Then what are we waiting for? Get goin'!' and we rushed off. I was glad about my inconspicuous coffee-dyed hat.

I joined up with fellow staff at our HQ and we were allotted an empty farmhouse as a Mess. Next day we started organising the ships for discharge over the beaches according to requirements for the different sorts of cargo. My sector was between St Tropez and St Raphael and I had to thumb my way out to the ships in DUKWs or landing craft. Then the French requisitioned some fishing boats for us to use as boarding vessels which made things a lot easier.

Cross of Lorraine

In 1940 after Dunkirk I had signed up as a supporter of General de Gaulle's Free French Forces and I wore the Free French brooch with the Cross of Lorraine on the lapel of my uniform. This made quite a difference when I met the Mayor of St Tropez, Monsieur Rene Girard. A leader of the local Resistance force, he had been advised in advance of the landings by messengers landed from a submarine. He and his men of the FFI (*Forces Francaises de l'Interieur*) with their armbands and assorted weaponry were out from 4am on D-Day to warn the Allies of German concentrations and any mined roads.

His daughter, Mimi, a charming girl, had been one of the couriers passing messages to the different Resistance cells. Messages were put inside the tyre of her bicycle which she then rode to a prearranged spot in a village where she would leave it whilst she visited someone or called in the shops. In the meantime a Resistance man would take her bicycle, remove the message and insert a response before returning it. Later, Mimi would simply ride it home.

The German troops in this area had been a mixture of admin units and soldiers on leave from the Normandy Front for rest and recuperation. This, together with the information from the Resistance forces, made the Allied advance quicker in my sector than in other parts of the coast. Intelligence passed on by the FFI not only included the locations of fighting troops, but also pinpointed innocent looking houses near main roads which had been turned into well-defended strongholds.

Snipers in St Tropez

Even though St Tropez was captured quite quickly, there were snipers still around and it was dangerous to be alone in the town, particularly at night. The speed of our advance also required us to change the priority of discharge from the ships to the beaches. Now, instead of ammunition, they needed fuel for the vehicles to maintain the chase.

Above: *An American paratrooper pictured with St Tropez Resistance leader Marc Rainaut. The girl in the centre, Mademoiselle Nicola Celebonovitch, warned the Americans of the location of a group of Germans waiting to ambush them.*

I went out to one ship loaded with ammunition to tell him to move further out to sea as we didn't need his cargo straight away. The Captain was more than a little upset and said he wanted his cargo discharged at once as it was unsafe. They had loaded it in Naples without sealing the bulkhead between No 3 hold and the engine room. He'd protested, but had got the standard reply of 'don't you know there's a war on!'. I finally persuaded him to anchor further offshore and I brought in the ships with the fuel. There were German air raids mainly at night and although some ships were hit, none were sunk.

Alpha Beach closed at D+25, but my beach at St Tropez and the others to the east stayed 'in business' until Marseilles was captured. Soon after this I learned that I had been promoted to Lieutenant Commander. As the pressure eased in Marseilles, the Resistance took their revenge on those deemed to have collaborated with the Nazis. Men simply disappeared from circulation. Women were sat in a chair in a public place surrounded by armed Resistance fighters while they had their heads shaved and not too gently either.

Our landing at Pampelonne had been relatively quiet and it was not until later that we heard of the intense fighting and loss of life at the landing places to the east of us where navigational errors in the dark put some of our Allies on to heavily defended points. Altogether though, *Dragoon* was a satisfactory effort leading to the army from the Mediterranean being able to join up with the forces from Northern France in a very short space of time.

LIBERATION
of Paris

As the sultry days of August came to the French capital, all Parisians were aware that the Germans were losing the fight in Normandy. Convoys of ambulances full of Wehrmacht wounded flowed over the Seine bridges and through the city along with trucks towing artillery pieces and hundreds of horse-drawn vehicles and carts. It was in stark contrast to the weeks following D-Day when an endless stream of reinforcements passed through in the opposite direction heading for the '*Zur Normandie Front*'.

The Allies spared the city centre from bombing. Hitler had other plans. His orders to the Commandant of Gros-Paris, General Dietrich von Choltitz, were unequivocal: 'Paris must not fall to the enemy – or the enemy must find it reduced to rubble.'

On 10 August, railway workers came out on a patriotic strike. Three days later the nervous Germans began disarming the city's 20,000 policemen. Posters urging insurrection began to appear on walls. The Germans countered with stickers of their own: 'Achtung! Be warned. The fate of Paris is in your hands.'

Patriotic uprising

Despite the strong words, the German response was muted by their ruthless standards. For one thing, they were anxious to keep the Paris bridges open and intact for their retreating forces and for another, von Choltitz seemed to be wavering in the face of orders to destroy such a beautiful city. The Swedish Consul, Raoul Nordling, was also making strenuous efforts to broker a truce.

On 19 August a call went out for all male Parisians between 18 and 55 to take up arms. Incredibly, many Germans were taken by surprise as Wehrmacht transport was stopped and weapons seized. Public buildings were occupied by the Resistance and more and more policemen cast their lot with the Free French. The Tricolore was hoisted over the Prefecture near Notre Dame and people sang *the Marseillaise*. For the first time in the history of Paris – a city famous for popular uprisings – police and insurgents found themselves fighting on the same side.

Resistance newspapers were published openly on 21 August with big bold headlines urging 'Mort aux Boches et aux Traitres'. Even so, the Germans in the main stayed in their strongpoints and it was clear to rebel leaders that the Liberation of Paris needed help from outside.

Messages were sent to the Allies pleading for intervention. Eisenhower and his commanders had intended bypassing the city but now minds were changed and Maj-Gen Philippe LeClerc's Free French 2nd Armoured Division with 200 tanks and 15,000 men began the race to Paris. In just 40 hours the huge motorised column covered 150 miles. On the evening of 24 August the first armoured vehicles nosed through the Porte d'Orleans and made their way to the Place de l'Hotel de Ville.

Death and gunpowder

SS men in the Luxembourg Garden put up the fiercest resistance but by the afternoon of 25 August the Germans were surrendering in large numbers to the regular French troops rather than the Resistance who had many a score to settle. Von Choltitz kept his dignity and gave up after a two-hour siege of his Hotel Meurice HQ. He would tell his captors that he'd lost faith in the Nazi system since the attempt, albeit failed, on Hitler's life on 20 June.

The fight for Paris cost LeClerc 901 dead while the German losses were estimated at around 2000. In addition some 1000 insurgents and 600 non-combatant Parisians died.

Gilles Perrault was a youngster in Paris during those heady August days of 1944. He remembers: 'We had lumps in our throats as we contemplated the tank drivers who smiled at our show of feeling. Then their radios crackled and we were calmly advised to move away a little by a tank commander. Ten seconds later he opened fire on a German armoured car that loomed up in front of us. It managed to get away, leaving a trail of blood. That night Paris smelled of death and gunpowder. Four years and 46 days had gone by since the Germans had marched into the city.'

On 26 August Perrault, part of an enormous crowd, watched de Gaulle's triumphant parade: 'We were drunk with emotion, drowning in happiness...Night fell and I took a walk along the banks of the Seine under the Tuileries where LeClerc's troops were bivouacked, and heard a strange refrain. The melody was interwoven with a profusion of long sighs, brief moanings and stifled cries. It took me a little while to understand that hundreds of men and women were up there in bed together. Transfixed with near-religious feeling, I spent a long moment there listening to Paris make love.'

Top Left: *A tank from the Free French forces under General LeClerc's command pictured outside Notre Dame.*
Above: *The present-day view of Paris from the top of the famous church.*

WAR DIARY
August 1944

1 August: Kovno in Lithuania has been taken by the Russians, effectively isolating the Baltic States from East Prussia. Evacuation by sea and air is the only escape route open to Germans trapped in the north.

2 August: Half of the island of Guam has now been captured by US forces. Tinian in the Marianas has also been taken at a cost of 394 American dead and 1961 wounded.

In the English Channel mini-submarines piloted by German volunteers are being used against the invasion fleet off the Normandy coast. Called *Marders,* the craft weigh some three tons, have a top speed of less than three knots and carry a single torpedo slung below the hull. Attempts to use them at Anzio earlier in the year ended in failure but today (**3 August**) a success is recorded when the destroyer *HMS Quorn* is hit and sunk.

On **4 August** in Amsterdam, following a tip-off Gestapo agents raid a house and arrest the Frank family who have been hiding in an attic since 1942. The Jewish family includes 14-year-old Anne who has been keeping a diary of her thoughts and experiences.

5 August: In Australia over 1000 Japanese POWs have staged a mass breakout at Cowra camp just before dawn. Wielding improvised weapons, they rushed the compound wire. Three guards were killed but the Japanese lost 234 killed and 108 wounded. Over 300 prisoners succeeded in escaping and a big effort is being mounted to capture them.

South African troops entered Florence today after the retreating Germans declared it an 'open city'.

6 August: Montgomery issues orders for the destruction of the German Army west of the Seine and north of the Loire. Field Marshal von Kluge opens a German counter-attack in the direction of Avranches, Normandy.

7 August: Eisenhower transfers his headquarters from London to Granville, France.

8 August sees the climax of an eight-week struggle by the Japanese to capture the important rail junction at Hengyang, China.

9 August: St Malo and Angers are liberated as the Allies spread out regardless of the threat posed by von Kluge's counter-attack in their rear. Meanwhile the Free French under de Gaulle have declared the Vichy Government null and void in a proclamation issued from Algiers.

10 August: In Paris rail workers have gone on strike at the urging of communist

> **" In Australia 234 Japanese POWs are killed when over 1000 of them stage a mass break-out from their prison camp at Cowra. "**

Resistance leaders. The effect is one of almost total paralysis of the rail network. Hitler is determined that the city should not be spared destruction in the way Rome was.

11 August: The Germans are sending heavily armed units into the Polish capital, Warsaw, to crush an insurrection by the lightly armed men and women of the Home Army.

By **12 August** Patton's Third Army has captured Le Mans and Alencon and bottled up German garrisons in the Brittany ports of Brest, Lorient and St Nazaire.

On **13 August** the American XV Corps halts at Argentan and waits for the Canadian push southwards to start. The area around Falaise is the centre of a pocket through which runs the only escape route for a large number of German units who were previously containing the Allied bridgehead.

The following day (**14 August**) sees the French police join the strikes now crippling Paris. With the Allies clearly winning the police have decided to throw their lot in with the Resistance.

15 August: The French Riviera is the scene of 'The Second D-Day' today when *Operation Dragoon* commences. Troops of the US Seventh Army and French Army B storm ashore on beaches between Cannes and Cavalaire. A large naval force backed up the

The Germans tried to recruit Dutchmen in Occupied Holland into their SS forces. The poster on the right says that the fight is against Bolshevism. Though some Dutch did join up many, many more fought with the Allies. The poster below was distributed in Britain and praised the contribution of the Dutch naval forces.

THE DUTCH

FIGHT ON TO VICTORY

NEDERLANDERS

VOOR UW EER EN GEWETEN OP ! - TEGEN HET BOLSJEWISME DE WAFFEN **SS** ROEPT U !

WAR DIARY
August 1944

landings with a terrific barrage aimed at German gun emplacements. Paratroopers have been dropped behind the coast as far inland as Draguignan.

16 August: Resistance groups in the Savoy region have launched a general uprising in support of the landings in the South of France. American and Free French forces are making rapid progress in all directions under clear blue August skies.

On **17 August** the Canadian's new push results in the capture of Falaise. The Germans are in a trap – the 'Falaise Pocket' – and there is just one route of escape. Roads congested with vehicles, horse-drawn carts, tanks and men present easy targets for the 'cab ranks' of Typhoons in the Normandy skies.

18 August: The Red Army reaches the border of the Fatherland in East Prussia.

19 August: In Paris the prospect of liberation is causing growing excitement. At 7am this morning a large force of gendarmes took control of the Prefecture of Police and fought off a German counter-attack. Paris commander General von Choltitz has been ordered to turn the city into a 'field of ruins' by Hitler.

20 August: Japanese resistance ends on the island of Biak, New Guinea. The US has suffered 2550 casualties whilst the enemy dead are estimated at 4700.

21 August: The Battle of Normandy is almost at an end with the sealing of the Falaise Pocket today. Although 30,000 of the enemy are thought to have escaped across the Seine at least 50,000 Germans have been captured. The air power of the Allies was a key factor in victory. It's now all-out for Paris where the Resistance and police are leading a popular uprising.

22 August: Allied forces from Southern France have advanced northwards through the Maritime Alps against minimal German resistance and have now entered Grenoble unopposed.

23 August: The Battle of the Flying Bombs is being won but at a terrible price. A single V1 impact in East Barnet today kills 211 civilians.

24 August: France rejoices as Sherman tanks and mobile units of General Leclerc's 2nd Armoured Division roll into Paris this evening, to be greeted by delirious crowds. De Gaulle's decision to send Leclerc's forces in against the advice of Eisenhower is about to pay off.

The following day (**25 August**) Paris is officially liberated when General Choltitz surrenders. Today also sees Roumania quit the Axis and the King's new Government declare war on Germany.

26 August: In Southern France, Marseille and Toulon continue to hold out but the Germans have been chased out of Avignon and now the Allies are set for a swift advance up the Rhône valley.

27 August: RAF Bomber Command undertake their first major daylight raid over Germany since August 1941. The synthetic oil refinery at Meerbeck near Homberg is the target of 243 assorted Halifaxes, Lancasters and Mosquitos. The Nazi war machine is running out of fuel – the Luftwaffe alone requires 160,000 tons of aviation fuel each month but is lucky to receive 10,000 tons these days.

28 August: Marseille surrenders to Free French forces following the fall of Toulon yesterday. In the north Rheims and Soissons have been liberated by US forces.

29 August: Partisans in Slovakia have issued a general call to arms and today declared the formation of a free Czechoslovak republic. Great swathes of Occupied Europe are rising up against the Germans.

On **30 August** in Northern Italy the British V and Canadian I Corp crossed the Foglia river this morning to begin their attack on the Gothic Line. The Russians have captured the Romanian oilfields at Ploesti to deny the Germans their major source of oil.

31 August: Allied spearheads and Resistance fighters capture all the bridges over the Somme. The Romanian capital falls to the Russians.

The Allied supply chain via Normandy is too long to permit offensive operations for all units and Eisenhower wants to keep the momentum of Patton's Third Army thrust going at all costs. Montgomery favours a single concentrated push on the left through Belgium and Holland, across the Rhine and into the Ruhr, Germany's industrial heart. Monty believes his plan could end the war before Christmas.

Above: Allied artillery on the move as the breakout gathers pace. As can be seen from the graveyard, many Germans will never leave Normandy.

Into the Night

Ron McGill salutes the Pathfinders of Bomber Command.

A few years ago, when travelling south on the M1, I heard warnings on the radio about multiple accidents in the Luton area. I had to divert and stopped near Bedford to check the map when I noticed a name – Graveley. On the spur of the moment I headed for this village, for I knew it has a special place in the history of Bomber Command; during World War II it was the home of 35 Squadron, one of the original four units that eventually formed the famous Pathfinder Force in August 1942, six months or so after Graveley became operational.

There were many Pathfinder units, but the main one was concentrated into No 8 Group under the command of Air Vice Marshal Donald Bennett. The Pathfinder crews were all volunteers who had agreed to fly further 'tours'. Their navigational skills became legendary and they perfected target marking techniques and used their new equipment to great effect. Their aircrew were allowed to use a quite unique emblem, a gilt RAF Eagle badge proudly worn below any medal ribbons.

It was about 6 o'clock on a beautifully warm and peaceful Saturday evening as I drove into Graveley village. I stopped at the only public house, the Three Horseshoes and mine host, a Mr Barrett, proudly showed me the many photographs of the Pathfinders that adorned the walls of the bar. I mentioned that I was visiting Graveley and explained a connection with two of the Pathfinders, one of which was Ron Wheatley – a Navigator friend

of Don Charlwood, the Bomber Command author of *No Moon Tonight*. The other was Desmond Lander, the late father of a female colleague from my working days. Ron was shot down and killed in mid-1943 and Desmond was also shot down at the same period, but survived the war as a POW and went on to enjoy a long civilian life.

I was directed up the hill to the old airfield and told to look out for a small memorial stone that marked the original entrance to the RAF base. This poignant memorial by the hedgerow was quite obvious and looked well cared for. I turned into an avenue of now mature trees on either side that led to a group of buildings among some trees. Walking

Above: *King George and Queen Elizabeth at Graveley with the men of the Pathfinders Force in early 1943.*
Below: *The Lancaster of the Battle of Britain Memorial Flight.*

down this dusty avenue I noticed that one or two of the original stones lining the roadway carried traces of white. These were the remnants of the white stone pathways, so beloved of the Commanders of RAF bases for their usefulness at night, as well as being neat and tidy.

Blood Wagons

I walked around the derelict buildings that were probably the station HQ and knocked at a large and unusually shaped house. Apologising for the intrusion, I asked whether the original Control Tower existed? What a surprise when the farmer said, 'this is it – we built our house around the Control Tower,' – truly a triumph of original and constructive thought.

The owner (a Mr Evans) was very helpful and showed me the brick built building that once housed the station fire engines (or 'Blood Wagons' as they were known!). He also showed me the wooden outhouse that was the original radar equipment store room. It's now a stable with fine looking horses in occupation.

Mr Evans told me that following its closure in 1968 the wartime hangars had been demolished and the concrete runways dug up and removed. The airfield was then completely given over to cereal farming, although the original perimeter trackways remained around the extensive cornfields. I drove around part of the perimeter track and

BOMBER COMMAND

noted the concrete areas where aircraft would have turned. Some were still darkened with aircraft oil from decades ago.

From the cornfield I could see the hedgerows alongside the Control Tower/House where the WAAFs and airmen would wait for the loaded bombers to get their 'green' and give the aircrews a wave or salute as they began their long take off run. The noise of the whole of the Squadron's aircraft getting ready must have been quite deafening and made for a strange and unreal scene at dusk in the lovely English countryside.

In this same location by the Control Tower photographs have been obtained from the Imperial War Museum showing the whole Squadron personnel lined up for a visit and inspection by King George and his Queen, dated as early 1943. The royal couple held a real affection for the crews of Bomber Command.

Perilous flights

The bombers' regular route out was over Cambridge, then Newmarket and the coast by Southwold for the perilous trip across the North Sea to Nazi-occupied Europe. Their return journeys were very hazardous as they approached Graveley either damaged or almost out of fuel. It was common for a stricken aircraft to literally put down where they could in the darkened countryside and pray for a successful forced landing in a field without trees!

As I walked back to my car near the avenue of trees I thought I could hear the rumble of Merlin engines coughing and then the unmistakeable sound of Lancaster engines pulsing into life. I was transfixed for the moment until I realised that what I was actually hearing was a giant lorry slowly passing by on the nearby roadway.

As I left the waving corn with the many Skylarks I pondered over the total Pathfinder

Force effort of over 50,000 individual sorties flown with 3700 members killed on operations plus many hundreds more wounded or disabled. Graveley initially hosted Halifaxes then Lancasters from March 1944, the latter for a total of 202 raids that cost 33 aircraft. It must have been a fearful, demanding and traumatic time for the aircrews and one during which they lived life to the full as best they could.

As I drove out of the avenue of trees and the airfield entrance the words of the late Roger Freeman, the well known air historian, came back to me. Speaking at a lecture at Shoreham Airport, he said that our old airfields are indeed hallowed ground, but that we are too near in time to fully appreciate them. After my visit to Graveley I could feel how true his words were.

There is a strange footnote to my story of the 35 Squadron Pathfinders that dates back to the 1970s when I had called at my local garage in Worplesdon in Surrey. The elderly garagehand was filling my car with petrol when I mentioned how quiet and peaceful the countryside was in our area.... 'Yes,' he replied, 'but there was a time in the War when it was anything but!'

He went on to tell me the story of an RAF bomber coming down in flames one night that plunged into the fields behind the garage. He said that most of the crew were killed but some parachuted to safety – all this he thought in early 1941 and he recalled the RAF recovery units removing most of the aircraft at that time.

The story progresses to the early 1990s when an article in the local newspapers asked for any information about the crash of

Above: *In truth it was a very dangerous and deadly game for the men of Bomber Command.*
Around 55,000 RAF aircrew were killed in the course of the bombing offensive that sought to cripple the Axis ability to wage war.

a bomber in Worplesdon in 1941? I contacted the air historian contact and described my conversation with the local garagehand and I was able to indicate the crash site in the field at the side of a copse. This was confirmed by other reports and digging eventually recovered most of the aircraft and two of the engines. The aircraft proved to be a Halifax Mark 1, number L.9489, from the famous 35 Squadron that was on it's first operational sortie on the night of 10 March 1941. Four of the crew were killed and two survived to fly again with the squadron (Sqd Leader Gilchrist DFC and Sgt Aedy).

The great sadness of this incident was that the Halifax had completed its operation over France and was returning safely when it was caught over my Puttenham golf course near the Hog's Back, by one of our own nightfighters who sent it down in flames across the nearby hamlets of Wanborough and Normandy before crashing in Worplesdon. The flaming Halifax was seen and remembered apparently by several villagers who were not aware at the time that the falling aircraft was a victim of so called 'friendly fire'.

The site of the crash is now a part of Merrist Wood golf course and there is a poignant memorial on their 14th hole nowadays that records this sad incident and the names of the 35 Squadron crew who lost their lives that tragic night.

'The Scharnhorst doesn't look so Gneisenau'

The dramatic painting by Roy Nockolds on the opposite page formed the front and back cover of the Air Ministry account of Bomber Command's offensive against the Axis from September 1939 to July 1941. It's almost a carbon copy of the photograph of German bombers over London that is reproduced here and in larger format on page 55 of this book. The booklet was published by Her Majesty's Stationery Office and issued for the Air Ministry by the Ministry of Information. Though the publication has a very serious intent, there is room for humour, hence the painful pun about attacks on two of Germany's capital warships contained in the booklet and reproduced as the heading to this piece. Two other quotes it carries are: 'The natives appear to be hostile' and 'The carrier pigeon we carried laid an egg during the attack'.

GOOD PALS

H aving suffered from the problems caused by my father's unemployment in the Thirties, my mother was keen to ensure that her three sons should obtain secure employment. To her, this meant getting a job in the Civil Service or joining the Armed Forces. The latter seemed ideal as, not only would we be paid but we would be housed, clothed and fed as well. Excellent!

My two older brothers enlisted in the RAF, so it was natural that I should follow them. My first two attempts to join as an Apprentice failed due to my defective eyesight – merely common or garden myopia! Then, as the RAF was enlarged due to the deteriorating situation in Europe, medical standards were relaxed and I was accepted in October 1938 to become a Wireless Operator. After training at Cranwell and Yatesbury, I was posted to No 2 (Army Co-operation) Squadron at Hawkinge a month before war was declared on 3 September 1939.

The Squadron went to France and during the next few months, applications were invited from Wireless Operators to train as Air Gunners. Several of us applied, as a more exciting role with immediate promotion to Sergeant, better living conditions and much higher pay was very attractive. At 19 years of age or so, possible consequences didn't figure much in our thinking. Applicants whose eyesight was below standard and who wore spectacles, as I did, were understandably unsuccessful. Though disappointed, were we rejects perhaps fortunate?

I was among a small number from the Squadron who were evacuated from Boulogne on 20 May 1940 – the day before the Germans got there. After detachment to various Army units with a mobile Wireless Tender, I was posted in August 1941 in charge of the RAF Signals Section at the Army's Eastern Command HQ; this was at Luton Hoo, the stately home and estate of Sir Harold and Lady Zia Wernher. I had a staff of several Wireless Operators and we all got on very well with each other. Among them was LAC

Above: *This photograph appeared in the* Worksop Guardian and Ollerton Echo *of 25 June 1943. It is of the crew of a Halifax bomber who had carried out many successful operations, including attacks on Essen, Duisberg, Dortmund, Kiel and Bochum. Most of the men lost their lives in January 1944 on an operation to bomb Stettin. Lawrence 'Vic' Getgood had a pal in the crew, F/Sgt Ivor C Redfearn, who is pictured standing on the right. In June 2007, whilst sailing home from a Baltic cruise, Mr Getgood was able to drop a bouquet of remembrance over the approximate position in the North Sea where the Halifax went down.*

Ivor Redfearn, a lad about my own age from Woodseats, Sheffield. We became good pals.

Again there were occasional invitations from the Air Ministry for airmen to apply for aircrew training. Several of us did so but, once again, I was rejected. Four of my pals were accepted; one to be trained as a Pilot and the others, including Ivor, as Air Gunners. In June 1942 I took them one by one to RAF Bassingbourne to collect their flying kit when they were posted for training. This intermittent departure of my pals was depressing.

Letter from the Padre

After they had left for training and posting elsewhere, some of them kept in touch, albeit spasmodically. Ivor and I exchanged letters now and then while he served with No 35 Squadron (Halifaxes) at Lissett (near Driffield) and Graveley (Cambs). In the summer of 1943 I received a photo from him; possibly a copy was given to all the crew by the pilot skipper, R G Appleby, who came from Ollerton.

By the spring of 1944 I had become a Flying Control Officer at Prestwick, near Ayr. Having heard nothing from Ivor for a long time, I asked the Padre there if he could get any news from his opposite number at Graveley. The reply came in a letter dated 6 June (D-Day) with the devastating news that Ivor's aircraft was lost. Confirming the death

of the pilot and rear gunner, the Graveley Padre ended the letter with the words: '...news just trickles through. There is a chance that the others are somewhere and it often happens that they are home in England before we have the slightest clue.'

Relatively recently I have been in touch with a nephew of one of the crew shown in the photo. From him, I learnt that their Halifax took off from Graveley at 23:59 on 5 January 1944 on an operation to Stettin. The last known position of the aircraft was 50° North and 0320° East which is over the North Sea about 200 miles off Sunderland. It was then operating on only three engines but I believe that, even so, crews would in some circumstances expect to carry on. Also, I understand that this Pathfinder crew was very near to completing a full tour of operations and may have been influenced by that.

Anyway, the aircraft must subsequently have been brought down or crashed and all of the crew killed except one, Plt Off Emery who became a POW at Stalag Luft 3.

The crew in January 1944 comprised: Flt Lt (Pilot) R G Appleby DFC, Plt Off E C Nixon, F/Sgt (Air Gunner) D S James, F/Sgt (Air Gunner) C G Bromham, F/Sgt (Flight Engn'r) B L Robinson DFM, Plt Off (Nav) N G Emery, F/Sgt (W Op/Air Gnr) and I C Redfearn DFM.
LAWRENCE 'VIC' GETGOOD

Halifax Bombers taking off from Graveley.

Epic
of the Sky
Troops

SEPTEMBER 1944

John Cross from Newmarket recalls: 'One night we heard this unusual sounding engine which suddenly stopped. I looked out of the window, and this 'thing' went down the middle of the road somehow missing the houses. I believe it hit our school because I only had lessons for one afternoon a week after that in somebody's front room. Another time I was talking to a neighbour when we heard two cut out together; one landed in playing fields 200 yards away, but we lost sight of the other.

A neighbour, Mr Towner, jumped into his fish pond and I hid behind our dustbins! Sirens often didn't sound for Doodlebugs and I used to stand on top of the Anderson shelter and shout a warning to the neighbours if I heard one cut out.'

Obviously, many of our recollections come from those who were only schoolchildren or teenagers in 1944. David Hollamby from St Leonards-on-Sea remembers staying with his grandparents in Hastings, right in 'Doodlebug Alley': 'My grandfather would take me upstairs into his bedroom from where we could see these evil machines, with their tails ablaze, soaring directly over the house. I had no concept of the fact that immediately their engines stopped they fell to earth with loud explosions, doing untold damage. To minimise the damage to my young mind, my grandfather told me they were fireworks going off.'

Tears at a wedding

John Newcomb from Orpington also recalls the first night of the flying bombs: 'A totally different sound emanated from their crude jet engines. In the morning we could see the things clearly and the word soon got around - 'only duck if the engine cuts out' became the watchwords. And then came the V2s, one fell a few miles away and we found a long length of thin, oily, wire on the driveway.
It came in very useful for the raspberry plants.'

A R Coulter from Bury St Edmunds was awaiting the opportunity to get married in 1944. As an army signals analyst, he was still based in England passing intelligence to Bletchley Park: 'Fortunately I was still around on 17 June, so I set off in the OC's car to catch a train to Liverpool Street. Unfortunately the first Doodlebug to reach London had struck the rail bridge at Bow so I only just managed to make the church by the deadline of 2pm. My kid sister got blast concussion from the same bomb, so we had a smiling bridesmaid apologising for her uncontrolled constant tears.'

Although the bombs themselves destroyed hundreds of houses and other buildings, there were other hazards. Bill Beazley from Bexley Heath was a 16-year-old trainee Post Office engineer: 'Barrage balloons sometimes needed to be lowered very quickly. If a storm developed, lightning could strike one balloon and travel to adjacent ones, bringing the whole lot down. Falling cables could drape across high voltage power lines, which in turn could fuse telephone lines into people's homes. I was

working on a control box at Longfield Hill and a wheatfield lay several feet lower by the pavement. A Doodlebug came over and I knew there were several balloon sites in the vicinity. I dived into the field in case the bomb hit a cable. It sailed through them and I am sorry to say I waved it on its way!'

Bernard Goodsall was a schoolboy at the time. He writes:

'At long last it arrived. The Allies stormed ashore on the Normandy beaches to begin the liberation of German-occupied Europe. D-Day 6 June 1944 is a date that everyone remembers. The folks at home rejoiced; we went to church to give thanks and were convinced that the fighting was coming to a rapid end.

'Our jubilation was short-lived, however, for within days of the landings the Germans unleashed a deadly secret weapon. The Doodlebug was a pilot-less jet-propelled flying bomb with a peculiar engine retort, packed with high explosives.

I was 13 at the time and for us schoolboys it was extremely frightening as we watched them fly over South East Essex on their way to the capital, wondering if the motor would cut out over us. We knew the engine sound of the Heinkels and Junkers 88, but the ominous V1 noise was different; a sort of grunting growl, deep-throated rattle coupled with stammering and coughing with flame spitting from its exhaust.

'Then came a poppity pop-pop popping like a badly tuned two-stroke engine, indicating it was running out of fuel. Silence followed as it fell to earth. Then came a deafening explosion, loud enough to stop the birds singing. My mates and I used to go up to a local picnic site called One Tree Hill, an odd name as there were hundreds of trees there. It gave us a wonderful view as on occasion the Spitfires would 'flip' the wings of the V1s to send them crashing to earth before they could reach London.

'Had D-Day not happened when it did, it would have been catastrophic for Bristol and the West Country, as plans were afoot to launch these weapons from Brittany putting this area well within range of their destructive power. As the launch sites fell to the Allied advance, sometimes the V1s were launched from the belly of a Heinkel 111 to give these abominable little beasts greater penetration into the hinterland.

'Just as we were getting used to the V1s, out of the stratosphere another terrifying weapon arrived to scare the living daylights out of us - the V2 rocket. They flew at four times the speed of sound and if you heard it coming, and we heard plenty, you had been spared, because it had already taken its toll with its massive high explosive payload. Windows for miles around would shatter.

'The V2 was a nasty weapon that could have easily won the war for Hitler had it been operational earlier. No doubt about it, these V2s dented our morale, hopefulness was turned into hopelessness. People prayed a lot and rosaries were much in evidence.

'Yet it could have been worse. The Germans were far more advanced with these types of weapons than the Allies were; on the drawing board were the V3 and V4 and concorde-type wings were due to be fitted to the V2. Had such devices seen service, New York across the Atlantic could have been reached along with many other US eastern seaboard cities.

Cheers in the cinema

'By this time I was 14 years old and my friends and I were working. I was a trainee cinema projectionist and remember well the booing when German troops were shown and the deafening cheering when any of the Allied

Flying Bombs

More memories of the 'Doodlebug Summer' of 1944.

forces came up on the newsreel. So popular were these 'tonics' that the newsreel was shown again after the 'King'.'

The main onslaught of the V1s lasted approximately 80 days during which time fighter aircraft claimed 1850 (the New Zealand squadrons alone accounted for 249), AA fire and rockets 1878, and 232 fell to the barrage balloon defences. After the launch sites in the North of France and along the Belgium coast were overrun by the advancing Allies, the resourceful Germans continued the offensive with bombs launched from Heinkel 111 aircraft. This tactic proved to be too costly in aircraft and pilots and was soon abandoned.

A short campaign using long range V1s was mounted from 3 to 29 March 1945, but by this time the British defences had got their measure, and only 13 bombs succeeded in reaching London. It is not always realised that some 6500 bombs were launched against Allied controlled areas in Europe from October 1944 onwards.

Background: The silhouettes on the left are taken from an amazing photograph of a Spitfire flying alongside a Doodlebug in an attempt to deflect the Flying Bomb off course.

THE GREAT SWAN

The very end of August and first week of September 1944 saw an Allied advance of astonishing rapidity across France and into Belgium. For a few euphoric days it seemed to the British and Canadians in Montgomery's 21st Army Group that the end of the war was in sight.

'The August battles (in Normandy) have done it,' stated one senior intelligence officer reporting at the time to General Eisenhower, 'and the enemy in the West has had it... The end of the war is within sight, almost within reach.'

The grim realisation imposed in the post-D-Day weeks of June and July, when the war in the Normandy hedgerows had settled into a deadly slogging match, was quickly changed into a mood of expectation for the Allies following the crushing defeat of the Germans at Falaise. Paris was liberated on 25 August; the city was at the centre of a broad front of advance by the US 12th Army Group under General Omar Bradley. His forces included Patton's Third Army. 'The man with the ball' - as Montgomery described him - was racing eastwards towards Metz and the Saar Valley.

On an 80-mile front spread in the direction of Paris from south of the Seine Estuary in the area of Honfleur and the present-day Pont de Normandie and Tancarville bridges, the British 21st Army Group was poised to set off in pursuit of the Germans. The latter had salvaged what they could from the battle at Falaise; it was estimated that some 20,000 troops, two dozen tanks and just 60 guns escaped across the Seine.

Over the Seine

Military historians still argue over the Allied strategy at this point in the war. Montgomery wanted an advance on a narrow front through Northern France and Belgium to be sustained all the way into Germany where a 'knock-out' blow would be delivered in the vital Ruhr industrial region. Eisenhower - conscious of the political requirement that the US forces too should play an offensive role - allowed a broad front policy to prevail. The repercussions of this on the rapidly extending supply lines would be felt all too soon. Losing the argument perhaps also influenced Monty to later push so hard for the Arnhem air landings, a high-risk operation of a kind anathema to his character. Some would claim that Britain's top general was determined to have his own way regardless of the changed circumstances.

Perhaps. But on 26 August 1944, when Sir Brian Horrocks took command, if anyone had

told the men of the 21st Army Group's XXX Corps that within three weeks they would be on the Dutch border and little more than 30 miles from Germany, they would have laughed out loud. Then came the Great Swan.

For the men of the famous 11th Armoured 'Black Bull' Division, the chase began early on 28 August at Vernon where, a few days earlier, 43rd Division had forced a crossing to create a bridgehead on the north bank of the Seine. The tankmen and their supporting infantry had experienced a hard time in the grinding attrition of the Normandy battles but were now rejuvenated and ready to roll.

'We motored in blinding dust and crossed the Seine at Vernon over a Class 9 pontoon bridge in total darkness - a strange experience - and then wondered where the hell to go next,' wrote W Steele Brownlie, a Troop Leader with the 2nd Fife and Forfarshire Yeomanry, 'We passed two burning scout cars and then a burning Tiger before eventually we found the regimental harbour. Our orders were to move north at first light with all speed.'

By the second day the advance was gathering momentum with 3 RTR (Royal Tank Regiment) 'swanning' an amazing 60 miles northwards from Tilley. Pockets of German resistance at this stage proved troublesome in places but elsewhere the Allied tanks revelled in the open country, fairly belting along.

Above: *After winning the grinding battle of attrition in the Normandy countryside in the summer of 1944, Montgomery was keen to pursue an attack on a narrow front parallel to the French and Belgium Channel coast with the aim of punching into the German heartland as quickly as possible.*

'Amiens tonight'

As dusk fell on the third day, 11th Armoured forward units were within 20 miles of Amiens, having been greeted by joyous local populations in towns and villages throughout the day. The only unhappy faces belonged to the collaborators who had failed to leave when the Germans quit - instances of summary justice were commonplace, often carried out in full view of the liberators.

'Drinks of all sorts were pressed on us' tankman Roland Jefferson recalled, 'The French called us Tommy and we realised that we were now into the battlezone of the First World War which our fathers had known so well. A common joke was: "Come away from her, she's probably your sister".'

11th Armoured commander, General 'Pip' Roberts, was told to seize the Somme bridges in Amiens in the course of a night dash. 'It was quite simple,' he recalled, 'Ike said to Monty "Amiens tonight"; Monty said to Bimbo (Dempsey) "Amiens tonight"; Bimbo said to Jorrocks (Horrocks)

"Amiens tonight" and Jorrocks said to 'Pip' Roberts "Amiens tonight"; and then the planning started.'

The subsequent daring attack started at 2300hrs in pouring rain. Occasional German vehicles joined the convoy in error and were despatched with thoroughness, although some tagged on oblivious and unobserved for quite a few miles. The Division's Shermans navigated in the main by simply following the dull red exhaust of the tank in front.

Amiens was approached just before dawn and much German vehicle movement throughout the town was observed. Civilians warned the British that around 5000 of the enemy were still around and lots of small individual actions ensued. A King Tiger and 15 ack-ack guns were destroyed in one battle and prisoners came in by the hundred. More importantly, the main bridge and a couple of smaller ones over the Somme were captured intact and the way ahead remained open.

Hail of flowers

Arras, Vimy and Lens were liberated and once more the tankmen were subjected to a hail of flowers, fruit, biscuits and assorted 'friendly' missiles - as the latter might include bottles of wine and beer, the wearing of steel helmets was a sound precaution! Greeting the Local Resistance could also be hazardous to health. The historian of the 23rd Hussars recorded how, 'They would advance in the most friendly manner to shake hands, while in the left hand a fully loaded rifle pointed at one's stomach. In their enthusiasm they were the most dangerous individuals we met.'

Many Germans were anxious to surrender. Patrick Delaforce tells the story of 'Ginger' Wilson, a young Lieutenant in the RAMC who was summoned by an excitable French farmer who asked him to sort out some Germans hiding in his haystacks. Despite being technically non-combatants, Wilson and some of his men armed themselves and set off in pouring rain across the fields to a spot where eight sorry-looking members of the Wehrmacht were discovered, all of whom seemed relieved to be made prisoners.

'A cynical name for the RAMC,' writes Delaforce in his book *The Black Bull*, 'was Rob All My Comrades. On this occasion the enemy were relieved of a pair of jack-boots, a camera, a compass and a pair of scissors.'

For XXX Corps, the days of the Swan were unforgettable. It was a time when a tank or jeep taking a wrong turning might end the day being hailed as liberators by the occupants of a village or even a whole town. Girls would fling themselves at the soldiers, many obviously willing to consummate freedom with the ultimate act of joy. Following a sharp encounter with German 88s at Seclin, Black Bull tankmen relieved the enemy of a large stock of looted wine and spirits; the advance continued with crates of brandy or champagne stowed behind the turrets of the Shermans.

Target Antwerp

Roland Jefferson remembers passing four huge cemeteries from the 1914-1918 war - 'They all looked so neat and tidy even though they had been under German occupation for over four years. There was an air of stillness and reverence as we passed them.'

By the fifth day of The Great Swan it became clear that the site of a British airborne drop on Tournai planned for 3 September was now actually behind the new Allied lines; accordingly the operation was cancelled. US troops moved into the area very early on this same day on the assumption that the British hadn't advanced as quickly as the Americans. In fact the Guards Armoured Division would be in Brussels, 40 miles further on, at almost the exact same time!

The largest surrender of German troops also occurred on 3 September when 25,000 went 'in the bag' around the same Belgian town where, 30 years earlier, British Tommies were reported in their exhaustion to have seen the 'Guardian Angel of Mons.'

The 11th Armoured's progress in leaps and bounds led them to believe Brussels was their objective. Now they learnt that the fleshpots of the Belgian capital were the preserve of the rival Guards Armoured. They soberly contemplated their own target Antwerp, far more important in strategic terms than the Belgian capital, but ringed by forts all likely to be heavily defended.

Torture and interrogation

The columns raced over the border, the welcome as rapturous as ever. The flags changed from red, white and blue to the red, yellow and black of Belgium. Patrick Delaforce tells how at 3am on 4 September after an 87-mile surge forward, 2nd Fife and Forfarshire 'avoiding flying plums, jet-propelled apples and rocket-projected pears, reached Aalst, 20 miles north-west of Brussels. All the cafes were open and Corporal Vallance's Sherman had run out of petrol in the town square where he was observed to be getting on very well with the natives.'

The Germans were falling back but still found time for reprisals. Delaforce went through Breendonk, seven miles east of Malines. Here armed civilians begged him to have a look in a large sinister grey fortress. He discovered that 50 members of the Belgian White Army had been handed over to the Gestapo here for torture and interrogation. The bodies, the blood and the smell of horrible death were still all too real on the morning of 4 September.

At about this same time the spearhead of

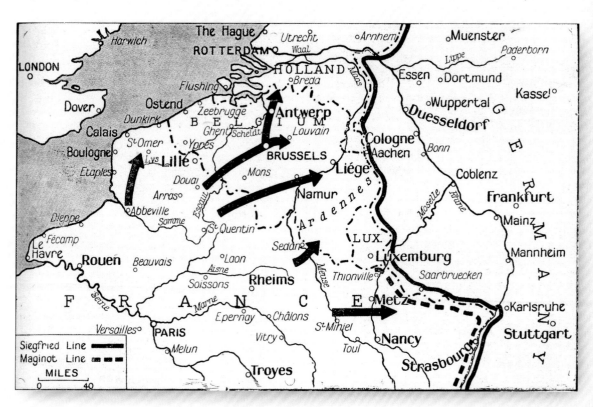

This contemporary map illustrates the directions of the Allied thrusts in September 1944. The Canadians came up the Channel coast whilst British spearheads can be seen liberating Brussels and Antwerp in the course of the 'The Great Swan'. The Americans and Free French forces fanned out across the rest of France and closed on the Siegfried Line beyond Liege, the Ardennes, Metz and Nancy. The Dutch city of Arnhem can be seen at the top of the map and it can be seen as a logical point of advance for the Allies seeking to enter the industrial centre of the Reich.

the 11th Armoured Division was moving into Antwerp having made a fighting advance of 230 miles in the six days since crossing the Seine at Vernon. The city and environs were defended by 15,000 Germans widely scattered, poorly equipped and all shocked to find the Allies closing in so quickly. Even so, many were determined to mount a defence.

Major Noel Bell MC in his *Beaches to the Baltic* book recalls arriving in the city to the sound of rifle fire. 'Germans began throwing grenades at us from a window of a high building nearby. Then 20mm guns opened up and we knew we should have to fight for it. The main streets were densely packed with crowds waiting for us. Our vehicles were unable to move and were smothered with people; we were overwhelmed by flowers, bottles and kisses. Everyone had gone mad. We had to get to the docks at all costs to save them from being destroyed by the Germans who might now be getting organised.'

Glasses of wine

The mixture of euphoric crowds and German sniper and panzerfaust (bazooka) fire was bewildering. Fellow tankman John Dunlop is quoted by Patrick Delaforce: 'We never closed the lids of our turrets, because we then became so blind and so deaf that we felt too vulnerable. We felt a lot safer with them open. But that afternoon I seriously considered closing down. Sporadic firing from upper windows, bursts of small arms fire and an occasional grenade would scatter the civilians climbing over our tanks.'

Colonel Ivor Rees entered Antwerp on the same day to find, '...this mass of populace crowding around, still kissing you, asking you to post a letter to America, to give them some petrol, some more arms for the White Brigade, holding a baby under your nose to be kissed, trying to give you a drink, inviting you to their house, trying to carry you away, offering information about the enemy, just had to be seen to be understood.'

Even in combat the civilians were often present. Two tanks busily blasting the SS HQ earned the attention of celebrating Belgian civilians. 'Each time an empty shell case was pushed out of the tank's open port, a hand would come in bearing a large glass of wine!' records Delaforce.

Out in the River Scheldt a small steamer of fleeing Germans ran aground in a cloud of steam after being hit by armour-piercing shells from a troop of Shermans.

A German column of horse-drawn vehicles was attacked; later the dead horse were hung, skinned and quartered by a local butcher. 'It was unrestrained joy - mad and crazy', said Captain CKO Spence of the Ayrshire Yeomanry, 'and all the time sporadic firing against the stubborn remnants of resisting Germans.' His own effort to 'liberate' a beautiful Mercedes staff car was thwarted when the Belgians got there first.

Collaborators in cages

That night a Bren carrier painted white roared around a district in the city. Manned by Resistance, the vehicle had been hidden but

British units crossing the River Seine on pontoon bridges at Vernon.

kept in working order since the day it had been abandoned by the BEF in 1940! Café parties and dancing in the streets went on until dawn, punctuated by sniper fire and explosions.

The city zoo was turned into a prison. Patrick Delaforce was able to visit the lion house where he watched two pretty Belgian girls checking in the new arrivals. Each cage had a different category of prisoners ranging from German officers through to important Belgian traitors. A large crowd outside the zoo jeered the new inmates. A German officer explained that the Germans (who numbered some 6000 by the 5th) would be handed over to the British in due course; as for the collaborators, they were to be shot that night, 'after a fair trial'. Military historian Alan Moorehead also saw the zoo and recorded that the scenes there must compare with the Colosseum in Rome at the time of Emperor Caligula.

In the chaos and confusion a serious planning error had come to light. The Albert Canal was thought to run through the city centre but in fact it was located to the north. It was important to get across this 60 yards wide waterway before the Germans could put a defensive line along it. There was no way on land around to the north bank of the Scheldt without crossing the canal and until the Allies controlled both the north and south banks of the river there would be no access for shipping to the huge Antwerp docks. 'Pip' Roberts got news that the main bridge over the canal had been blown up at 9am on 5 September. This same day three companies of the King's Shropshire Light Infantry got across by boat to form a bridgehead in the northern suburb of Merxem. But they were too lightly armed to mount an effective

defence against the panzers and heavy weapons mustered by the Germans and on 7 September the decision was made to bring the survivors back, a mission accomplished within 15 minutes without a single casualty. In the previous 48 hours the KSLI had taken 150 casualties including 31 killed and their Colonel Ivor Reeves seriously wounded. The fight for the Merxem bridgehead is a significant KSLI battle honour.

Cointreau and heartburn

For 11th Armoured Division the Great Swan was now definitely ended. German resistance was hardening as their own supply lines shortened whilst those of the Allies stretched longer and longer. More than this, with the borders of the Reich itself just a few score miles away from the British and Americans, the Germans seemed to have rekindled the will to fight.

Though the tankmen and their infantry support had won the battle for Antwerp, the battle for the city's port would continue until November before the Scheldt estuary and the islands of Walcheren and South Beveland were captured at great cost by the Canadians.

A final bright spot for the Division before leaving the city was their occupation of Antwerp Customs House and the liberation of the spoils of war within. Each regiment received 800 bottles of wine and 8000 cigars - enough for a bottle and 10 cigars per man. Patrick Delaforce remembers how his half track crew all stood five inches taller when they left Antwerp than when they went in as they were all standing on cases of Cointreau - '...a delicious liqueur, but taken in abundance it produces heartburn.'

Above: A German gun fires across the Straits of Dover at England. Over 3500 shells fell on Dover and the Kent countryside in the time from 12 August 1940 to mid-September 1944 when the enemy guns fell silent.

ROLLING UP
'La Manche'

The Canadian First Army was tasked with reducing the German defences in the various ports and towns along the Channel coast from the mouth of the Seine to the border with Belgium.

They were assisted by the English 49th Division and the 51st Highland Division, the latter two units being given the thankless task of reducing the fortress of Le Havre in which 11,000 Germans had sought refuge. Seven heavy bomber raids were made on the town; on 5 September alone 348 Lancasters, Stirlings and Mosquitos dropped 1812 tons of bombs. As many as 3000 civilians died before the Germans surrendered on 12 September. The welcome given by the inhabitants to their British liberators was understandably muted.

Where the fighting wasn't light and war damage limited, it was a different story. At Etretat where the famous chalk arch is still a major landmark on this part of the Norman coast, the Scots had been greeted with joyful scenes on 2 September. At St Valery en Caux the arrival of the 51st Highland Division was especially poignant. In 1940 the Division had made a historic stand around the tiny port before being forced to surrender to the victorious panzer forces of the then unknown General Erwin Rommel. Now in these early September days of 1944 the Scots were returning in triumph.

For the Canadians there was a turning of the tables too. At Dieppe on 19 August 1942 they had lost thousands of men killed or captured in the 'reconnaissance in force' raid on this Upper Normandy port. On 1 September 1944 they took the surrender of the port and town. Following the 1942 attack Hitler had ordered an immense ring of concrete bunkers and gun emplacements to be built around Dieppe but in the event the German garrison lacked the will to fight.

Calais and Boulogne proved tougher nuts to crack. September 1944 saw the firing of the last rounds across the Channel by the big German guns on the cliffs in the Pas de Calais area. Dover and the surrounding Kentish towns and the countryside had borne the brunt to the barrage that had begun on 12 August 1940 and continued right through the war years. The casualty toll from the 3514 shells fired in total included 400 civilians injured and 100 killed.

On 1 September a German flotilla of small vessels sailed out of Boulogne carrying personnel not required for the port's defence. Giving covering fire, the German batteries opened up on the sites of Britain's own big guns on the Dover cliffs. A cross-Channel duel resulted which lasted – on and off – until the middle of the month when the Canadians closed in after a series of heavy bomber attacks on the ring of concrete bunkers around the town.

The last shots were fired by the British batteries on 19 September after which barrel wear made further accurate shooting impossible. A German battery that emerged unscathed from the attention of the Allied bombers continued firing for a few days more. On 29 September an attack by Canadian infantry and tanks, including the 'Crocodile' flamethrower variety, finally forced the surrender of the Boulogne garrison.

The Germans in Calais surrendered the next day, 30 September. In the end, holding on to the Channel ports cost Hitler 120,000 men. Thousands more found themselves surrounded in a number of ports in Brittany and on the Atlantic Coast of France. The Allies were in no hurry to storm these fortresses; with time and the tide of war on their side they were content to play the waiting game.

Right: The painting depicts 'British Coastal Artillery'. It is the work of the artist and illustrator Terence Cuneo who went on to find post-war fame as a brilliant painter of trains, racing cars, jet aircraft and action scenes of all kinds. His trademark was the inclusion of a tiny mouse in many of his paintings. The work reproduced here pre-dates 1944 and shows the crew of a coastal artillery piece loading their gun. In the background another gun engages the unseen enemy – most likely a ship or E-Boat as the weapon does not look big enough to fire all the way across the Channel to Occupied France. The white cliffs are presumably those of Dover. The piece was used in a campaign titled 'Help Britain Finish the Job' that was aimed at the USA and the Dominions (National Archives – Art of War). Terence Cuneo died in 1996.

COASTAL ARTILLERY
A PAINTING BY TERENCE CUNEO

> ' *Villages began to slip by. Most of the inhabitants realised that the British were across the Seine and on their way forward, but none imagined they could be arriving so soon and in the middle of the night. They believed that the Germans were still passing through and not many stirred from their beds. But occasionally a keen-eared patriot would detect a different sound of fleeing enemy transport and the more sustained roar of the pursuing British armoured cars and then he knew that it must be 'Les Anglais'. We saw them stir, silhouetted figures pulled back the curtains, flung open their bedroom windows and shouted their heartfelt feelings.* '

Above: A British tank advances into the Belgian capital.
Right: Grand Place, Brussels. Montgomery made a triumphant appearance here on 7 September 1944.

The quote on the opposite page are the words of a participant in the astonishing Allied dash from the Seine to the Belgian capital Brussels and beyond accomplished in a matter of days late in the summer of 1944. The British Second Army of General Miles Dempsey was on the move.

Suddenly territorial advances in leaps and bounds unimaginable just a month before became commonplace. Starring role in the liberation of Brussels went to the Guards Armoured Division, part of General Horrock's XXX Corps. On 31 August he'd told the Guards he wanted them in the Belgian capital within four days. On the evening of 2 September in Douai he reiterated his order – they were to make Brussels the very next day, traversing the intervening 70 miles or so.

Horrocks clearly gave the advance all the trappings of a madcap race by setting his two brigades (5th and 32nd) with Grenadier and Welsh Guards respectively, different routes but a common 'winning post' at their appointed junction spot before the capital.

Madcap race

But the race had deadly handicaps. Pockets of the enemy would stand and fight, usually just long enough to inflict casualties amongst the men in the 'point' vehicles. Then the Germans either surrendered or ran. The Grenadiers initially took the lead and looked all over the likely winners. But at Lessines they had to first crack a German strongpoint and then were held up on the outskirts of Brussels by fighting and the need for fuel for their Shermans. Meanwhile the Welsh Guards, their faster Cromwell tanks bowling along at up to 50mph, ate up the miles to make it to the 'winning post' just ahead of their rivals.

An armoured car of the Household Cavalry commanded by Lance-Corporal I W Dewar, was the first Allied vehicle to nose into the heart of the city. Initially hesitant in case it turned out to contain more retreating Germans, the population soon broke into open rejoicing and quickly swarmed all over the car, grabbing any part of it which could be prised off or removed.

The scene was visited on other liberators a thousand times over. Flowers and even pots of geraniums decorated the mobile weapons of war and Brussels drank deep of the heady draught of freedom. Unbridled joy filled the air; men, women and children cried with happiness. But the Germans were still around and occasional outbreaks of firing scattered the crowds. When the first Welsh Guards tanks entered the city, the Cromwell of Lt John A Dent came across a Panzer Mk IV in the Rue de la Loi and a German bus which was promptly set on fire. Other British tanks in the Rue des Colonies and Rue Royale made for the Cinqauntenaire, where, guns blazing, they took on the enemy.

Battles in the darkness

With nightfall came rumours of a German counter-attack – in fact one was planned but stalled through lack of transport. But small-scale battles erupted all through the hours of darkness as Resistants hunted for Germans to fight. The crowds grew bolder and even

Brussels is Free!

attempted to pillage a warehouse still occupied by the enemy. Firing by the latter and the explosion of train wagons filled with munitions killed some 30 civilians – other Resistants died in clashes with retreating Germans. The British – impeded by the crowds – had still not arrived in strength and had hardly more than 30 tanks in the city by 1am.

Next day the celebrations picked up where they left off with seemingly even more people out on the streets. Horrocks himself hurried to Brussels and Piron's men also moved in. The Belgian Roger Dewandre and his tanks arrived at Laeken via the Bourse, escorting General Horrocks. Here they were received by Queen Elizabeth, the only member of the Belgian Royal Family remaining in the capital.

Champagne campaign

Brussels airfield was still under shellfire but the city was fairly bursting with joy. On the outskirts, a huge cache of champagne and liquor was 'liberated' by a special detail aptly led by Major Hennessy of the famous cognac

family. Also in the 'drinks' party was the future Lord Carrington.

Meanwhile in the city the inevitable retribution began as collaborators and suspected traitors were apprehended.

Another spontaneous wave of enthusiasm broke on 7 September when Montgomery in person was welcomed to Brussels; he made a public appearance in the Grand Place.

The liberation of Brussels and the resulting celebrations swiftly took on a legendary status within the British Army. From humble private to high-ranking officer, the freeing of the Belgian capital was an indelible event in their lives. As General Sir Brian Horrocks went on record in his memoirs: 'There were flowers, fruit, champagne and girls all over our vehicles and kissing such as never before seen. We had become connoisseurs of Liberation, with all the towns and villages we had come through since we crossed the Seine.

'But everyone agreed that the welcome offered by the citizens of Brussels was unparalleled...'

Rocket Science

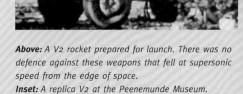

September 1944. London comes under attack from space.

Following on from the V1 Flying Bomb, Hitler's second 'vengeance' rocket, the V2, was the world's first ballistic missile to make a sub-orbital spaceflight.

The V2 campaign began in September 1944 and the last missile fell on Orpington on 27 March 1945. The previous month had seen a hail of 71 rockets striking their random targets in a single week.

Each hit was devastating as the 13-ton rocket impacted at over 3000 miles per hour. There was no warning; the missile descended faster than the speed of sound and survivors would only hear the approach and sonic booms after the blast.

John Clarke was six years old when the first V2 rocket to hit the capital landed outside his house in Chiswick on 8 September. His sister, Rosemary Ann, was killed that Friday in 1944. She was just three. In 2004 John recalled, 'Our house was badly damaged but there wasn't a mark on Rosemary. The blast goes up and comes down in a mushroom or umbrella shape, but in the process of that, my sister's lungs collapsed.'

A needle in the sunlight

R F Payne was also a youngster at the time: 'I remember people talking in the summer about a rocket the Germans were supposed to be developing. They said it was as tall as a telegraph pole and weighed over 10 tons.

'One bright evening in September 1944, I was on Putney Common watching some lads playing football when I noticed high in the sky a puff of smoke and from the smoke a vapour trail appeared at the end of something that looked like a needle glinting in the sunlight.

'Just moments later came a huge explosion some way away. I am sure I had just seen the first V2 to fall on this country.'

The Chiswick rocket took just five minutes to travel there from its launch site in the Netherlands but it would be the spring of 1945 before Allied forces over-ran the last of the sites. In that time some 1400 rockets were fired at this country killing 2724 people and seriously injuring another 6000. South and East London took the brunt of the onslaught, with Woolwich, Ilford, Barking, Greenwich and West Ham each receiving over 20 hits. Some did make it into the central areas; V2 explosions devastated Selfridges in Oxford Street, Speakers' Corner at Hyde Park and Holborn. A rocket hit a packed market building in Farringdon on 8 March 1945 and killed 110. The worst death toll of all came on 25 November 1944, when 168 people lost their lives after a direct hit on Woolworths in New Cross.

Above: A V2 rocket prepared for launch. There was no defence against these weapons that fell at supersonic speed from the edge of space.
Inset: A replica V2 at the Peenemunde Museum.

RAF bomb Peenemunde

The onslaught would have been worse if it had begun sooner. On 18-19 August 1943, the RAF had conducted a bombing raid on the A4 (as the V2 was originally designated) facility at Peenemunde on Usedom Island off Germany's Baltic coast. The raid seriously delayed the rocket's development and prompted production to be moved to an underground facility in central Germany that became known as Mittelwerk. Slave labour from the nearby Dora Concentration Camp was mobilized in the manufacturing process. It wasn't just England that suffered V2 attacks. The vital port of Antwerp in Belgium was struck by 1265 rockets and hundreds more fell on Paris. But the V2 was not to be the war-winning weapon the Nazis hoped for. Ironically, when the war ended, many of the German scientists involved – including Dr Werner von Braun – moved to America to form the core of the American NASA manned space programme.

The background image to this page is an astonishing photograph taken by US pilot Lt Charles Crane. It shows the vapour trail of a V2 in the top left corner. The rocket flashed past his aircraft when he was flying over Germany at 30,000 feet. The Lockheed P-38 Lightning aircraft of fellow pilot Lt Donald Schultz can be seen in the bottom right of same photograph. The P-38's distinctive twin boom tail is visible. The aircraft was widely-used on photo-reconnaissance missions.

MARKET GARDEN
Monty's plan to end the war by Christmas

Vital though it was for the Allied advance upon Germany to clear the Scheldt estuary and get the port of Antwerp working, both Eisenhower and Montgomery agreed to give priority to securing a bridgehead across the great natural barrier of the Rhine. But the move had to be made quickly, before the Germans had the chance to recover from their summer of dramatic reversals on the battlefield.

Montgomery was ready with a plan, an unusually bold and audacious one and, uncharacteristically for this commander who had hitherto frowned on military gambles, one that was clearly dependent on a large helping of good fortune. It involved the British 21st Army Group together with the Allied First Airborne Army which consisted of two American airborne divisions, the British 1st Airborne Division and a Polish airborne brigade.

Airborne carpet

The British 'sky men' had been thirsting for action since long before D-Day when the Division discovered that they didn't figure in the *Overlord* plans - the British airborne role in Normandy going to the 'rival' 6th Airborne. During July, August and early September the Division had been readied for a whole series of mooted drops on objectives just ahead of the advancing Allied armies. Each operation was cancelled in the face of the astonishing progress by the ground forces.

But now the 1st Airborne were being given the key role in Montgomery's plan, *Operation Market Garden*. They would be the spearhead of a 'carpet' of airborne troops landing across Holland. The British paratroopers, later to be reinforced by the Poles, were to descend on the Arnhem area, more than 60 miles from the British front-line troops east of Antwerp. While the British and Polish airborne forces held the bridge over the Lower Rhine (the river was also erroneously referred to as the Lek in some accounts written at the time), the British XXX Corps would drive northwards up a narrow 'corridor' through Belgium and Holland to link up with them and cut off all German troops of the Fifteenth Army to the west.

From their salient north of the Rhine the Allies would then push on into Germany before swinging south into the vital industrial region of the Ruhr, heart of Hitler's faltering war machine. Capturing the Ruhr must hasten the end of the war, perhaps even securing

Gliders on their way to Arnhem, September 1944.

victory before Christmas. In also liberating the rest of the Netherlands the Allies would capture the German V1 and V2 launch sites on the Dutch North Sea coast and put an end to the barrage of rockets falling on England.

To help British ground troops in their advance through the difficult network of canals and rivers between the British front and Arnhem, the American 82nd Airborne Division would land and seize the bridges over the Rivers Waal and Maas near Nijmegen, while the 101st Airborne were detailed to capture and hold bridges over the canals near Eindhoven.

British spearhead

The operation began on 17 September. The British 1st Airborne landed some six - eight miles from the bridge at Arnhem, while the two American divisions dropped much nearer their objectives. The Guards Armoured Division were the spearhead of the northward drive by the British XXX Corps.
In the first few hours things seemed to be going well.

The good news didn't last. The weather turned bad; for many days supplies and follow-up forces could not be flown to Arnhem. Meanwhile the troops there discovered that the Germans were in the area in force and were able to quickly bring tanks and self-propelled guns into action against the lightly armed airborne. Soon the British sky men were cut into two separated groups; a single besieged battalion holding on to the north end of the Arnhem bridge with the rest of the Division trapped in a horseshoe-

shaped enclave around the small town of Oosterbeek, a half a dozen miles away on the north bank of the Rhine.

Both the Germans and the Allies fought hard and desperately. The two American divisions that held the bridges at Nijmegen and Eindhoven suffered heavy losses in the face of German counter-attacks, while the British paratroopers of the 1st Airborne Division held out for nearly five days at the bridge before the survivors were forced to surrender. Four days later the remaining men within the Oosterbeek perimeter - the latter called *Der Kessel* (The Cauldron) by the Germans - withdrew as best they could across the fast flowing Rhine to the relative safety of the southern bank.

Of the 10,000 men who had gone in, just over 2000 came back in the course of the overnight evacuation. Many hundreds more would make their way back into Allied hands during the following weeks and months, thanks in large part to the bravery of the Dutch people who aided them. But at least 1500 dead would never return and for over 6000 others, many of them wounded, the rest of the war would be sat out in POW camps.

Grievous losses

To the grievous losses of British and Polish sky men and RAF crews must be added to the toll of American paratroopers and the tankmen and infantry of XXX Corps. The Americans, indeed, were left in the line until November and suffered a further 3400 casualties in this period in addition to the 3542 dead and wounded during the time of *Market Garden*. It's estimated that something like 10,000 Dutch civilians died during the fighting in mid-September or in the bitter winter of starvation that followed.

Montgomery's plan had not been a complete failure but neither could it be called a success. A deep wedge had been driven into the German line, but that line had not been broken. Allied attention shifted westward to concentrate on a step-by-step advance along the River Scheldt aimed at prising open the approaches to Antwerp.

On 28 September 1944 the Field Marshal ordered a letter to be read out to the survivors of the 1st Airborne as they reassembled in England. The letter included the lines: 'In the years to come it will be a great thing for a man to be able to say, "I fought at Arnhem".'

Arnhem Bridge, 5pm, the Second Day

Celebrated artist David Shepherd writes: 'My painting of Arnhem Bridge at the height of the battle was commissioned by the Second Battalion, The Parachute Regiment.

'We decided right at the beginning that we would endeavour to portray an actual moment of the battle. We discovered that an RAF Mosquito had flown over the bridge, just as a column of German trucks and tanks was coming over it, and had taken a photograph. This was on the second day, at five in the evening. The Germans didn't see the men of the Second Battalion dug in on the ramparts of the bridge and the whole column was 'brewed up'.

'We enlarged the photograph taken by the Mosquito and an amazing amount of detail came to life that had not been previously deciphered. For example, what had been just a blur turned out to be a knocked-out German truck below the bridge, so this detail went into the painting.

'I tried to portray those incredible hours where hand-to-hand fighting was taking place on and below the bridge, with the British on one side of the approach road and the Germans on the other. The painting is so accurate because Colonel (later Major-General) John Frost was in the studio with me and was watching every detail of the painting as it progressed and making sure I got it right because he had been there at the bridge with his men.'

THE FROST REPORT

Major-General John Frost CB, DSO, MC achieved lasting fame at Arnhem. As a colonel in the 1st Airborne Division he led 400 men of the Second Battalion when they captured the northern end of the road bridge over the Rhine. For Frost it really was a 'Bridge Too Far' as he was captured and spent the remainder of the war in a POW camp.

Arnhem aside, Frost experienced a remarkable career in soldiering. At the time of the outbreak of war in 1939 he was commanding the Iraq Levies, a force of Assyrian, Kurdish and Arab tribesmen in the Middle East. Within two years he was back in 'blighty' and a Major in the Parachute Regiment. On 27 February 1942 Major John Frost led the Regiment's Second Battalion on a daring raid on the coast of France. His mission was to capture a working example of the German Wurzburg radar-tracking device, located on a cliff top position at Bruneval, near Le Havre in Normandy. Frost and his men parachuted in, seized vital radar components, took six prisoners and were then transported back across the Channel, courtesy of the Royal Navy.

Soon after, Frost and his paras were sent to North Africa and went into action against the Italians and Afrika Korps. Later, with the Germans kicked out of Tunisia, Frost went with the 1st Parachute Brigade of the 1st Airborne Division and took part in the invasion of Sicily in July 1943, where they distinguished themselves in hard fighting for the Primo Sole Bridge, south of Catania.

Abuse for Customs & Excise

Frost followed Montgomery's Eighth Army onto the Italian mainland where he experienced the 'short days and cold nights of November' giving a foretaste of what an Italian winter could be like. In his autobiography of his war years – *A Drop Too Many* – Frost says of Italy: 'The Germans were fighting hard for every inch and the rain was no friend to offensive mobile operations ... we knew we were being saved for the coming battle in north-west Europe so when we were finally ordered back to Taranto on the first stage of our journey back to the UK there were no regrets.'

Frost later recounted the bliss of leaning over the rail of a troopship newly docked at a British port in wartime. This was just before Christmas 1943: 'The quay was deserted to start with. Then cat-calls and groans marked the arrival of a couple of Military Police who stood, imperturbably, affecting to take no notice. In contrast, members of HM Customs & Excise were very annoyed at the volume of abuse they drew.

Cries of joy and cheers of derision

'There were cries of joy for some very smart WRAC ladies or ATS as they were then called. It was nice to think of them as part of our army. Finally cheers of derision for a Flag car bearing a general from the War Office, whose task it was to make a welcoming speech over a tannoy to all of us on our return to the homeland.'

Frost had some fascinating comments on the austere UK he'd come back to: 'The newspapers were even smaller, cigarettes scarcer, beer even weaker, spirits almost unobtainable. But on the other hand skirts were shorter and we again had good solid silver coins to buy things with.'

Frost and his men were based south of Grantham in Lincolnshire for the first few months of 1944. Each company took over a large country house or its equivalent. Frost's headquarters were initially at Hungerton Hall and a little later, Stoke Rochford Hall.

When they got into action at Arnhem, Frost marched his Second Battalion into the town where they seized the northern end of the road bridge and held out for four days against an overwhelming German force ranged against the lightly-armed paras.

Major General John Dutton 'Johnny' Frost died on 21 May 1993 aged 80.

PRIORITY TELEGRAM

Ron McGill was a spectator of the Arnhem air armada and later witnessed first hand the awful consequences of war.

On Sunday morning 17 September 1944 I was a young teenage helper for our local milkman, delivering and collecting milk bottles in the Doverhouse Road area of Roehampton in SW London.

As we clattered and scurried around doorways at the top of the hill we suddenly became aware of thunder in the bright sky and the ground seemed to begin to shake. We were quite transfixed to suddenly see formation after formation of C47/Dakotas passing fairly low and flying in an easterly direction. Young lads at this time of the war were fascinated by the constant air activity in the English skies and we were all experts in aircraft recognition. The D-Day formations earlier in June were still fresh in our minds – but this vast panorama of comparatively slow and drab coloured aircraft was clearly something different – taking many minutes to pass over us with the sound of their engines throbbing on for a long time.

Grim battle

The noise bought people from their homes and they quietly gathered in the streets; few had any doubts it was yet another stage in the battle against Nazi Germany and that young men would be lost during the day. If I recall correctly, it was not until the evening that we heard on the radio an Allied Airborne Force had parachuted into Holland, at a place we had never heard of – Arnhem – in an attempt to bring the dreadful war to a close. At school the next morning our teacher, a Great War veteran with a bad limp, called us all to attention and quietly asked us to stand and think for a few minutes about the young men fighting a grim battle that very day, deep in Occupied Holland.

I remember it was difficult to concentrate for the rest of that day and I think in the end we were all sent home early – alive to the excitement of it all.

Now move forward to the last day, but one, of December 1944. It is tucked away in my memory for an incident of pure misery that brought home to me the tragic impact of war.

On reaching my 14th birthday in October, I joined the Post Office as a Boy Messenger (or Telegram Boy as they were known) and I was appointed to the busy office at Hammersmith Broadway. Out in all weathers, pushing heavy red bikes around for long hours, always alert for the staggering explosions of the German V2 rockets and literally swamped with the volume of wartime telegrams, it was not that easy a job for less than £1 per week.

The incident in question came in the afternoon of that December day when I happened to be the first boy back in from delivery when yet another of the Priority 'war casualty' telegrams was brought down from the Instrument Room by the lady telegraphist. It was the sensible practice to hand these to the older boys to try and seek neighbourly help prior to the actual delivery, but as I was the only one there, I had the briefing and left for the first of my Priority calls without delay.

An Arnhem casualty

The address was in a small row of 19th century houses on the left-hand side of the Hammersmith Bridge Road, very near to the bridge itself. The house had the usual flight of concrete steps up and over the basement flat to a front door and two further flats above. I propped my heavy bike against the gateway of the house I wanted and before I could do any more, the door opened to show a pretty young woman with a small child hanging on to her dress. She took one look at me, slumped back hard against the wall and slowly crumpled down to the floor in a dead faint.

I rushed up the steps and somehow righted her against the wall, moved the baby back further into the hallway and ran for help. I was able to bring an older woman from another house and together we managed to get the stricken lady to a chair where she finally came round and opened the most anguished of blue eyes that I had ever seen in my young life. The neighbour opened the telegram and confirmed to me the death in action of her Airborne husband who had, apparently, been missing since the Arnhem drop back in September. She also told me that the young woman was going to have a second baby and she asked me to stay while she made urgent arrangements for her care.

Feeling of guilt

I stayed with the young woman for about 20 minutes and she never took her eyes off me and quite pitifully, was unable to speak or cry. Then other ladies came in and I was able to leave and cycle back to the office, quite shattered by this contact with the grief that I had brought to this household.

I had a dreadful feeling of guilt and that evening, after telling my father about the episode, I suggested this first-hand misery was not for me and perhaps I should seek factory work? He simply said, 'Somebody has to do it son,' and persuaded me to stay. This I did and greatly enjoyed the humour and companionship of the other 20 boys, some of whom have remained friends to this day.

In later years, I could never pass that small terrraced house without a twinge, particularly if the young children were playing on the steps. Then came a moment in the late 1960s when I was driving back through Hammersmith and gave my usual glance at the house... only to see that the whole row had gone, cleared in the redevelopment of Hammersmith Bridge and its approaches.

It is nearly 70 years ago now, but I can still recall the pure misery of those unforgettable blue eyes and the delivery of my first Priority Telegram.

Gerald Levy may well have been the youngest of the 'Sky Troops' to parachute into battle.

HALF PINT PARA

Gerald Levy volunteered for the Army just three months after his 17th birthday in 1944. He was admitted to the ranks under a special scheme for War Office-recognised members of the Army Cadet Force. Posted to a recruit depot in Hamilton, Scotland, he and his fellows were kitted out and the next day marched to the railway station with a pipe band at their head. In full marching order he says they looked like a parade of heroes even though they had been in uniform for just 24 hours.

Posted to barracks set up in a disused dye works at Alexandria near Dumbarton, Gerald was one of 90 volunteers known initially as the 'Milk Boys' because, being under 18 years, at mid-morning NAAFI break they were marched to the cookhouse for milk and buns.

Parachute Regiment

After competing the recruit training (volunteers did six weeks and conscripts eight), Gerald volunteered for the Parachute Regiment and was posted first to Aldershot and then to Newark for jump training. They had not seen anyone as short as 5ft 4ins but he was allowed in provided he passed all the physical and mental tests. Eventually he was posted to the Third Battalion The Parachute Regiment in time to take part in the airborne assault to capture the road and rail bridges at Arnhem in Holland in the course of *Operation Market Garden*.

On Sunday 17 September 1944 Gerald dropped onto the heathland at Wolfhezen (DZ X), quite a few miles west of Arnhem. Gerald remembers it as a good drop and the First, Second and Third Battalions duly formed up and made for the Arnhem bridges, each meant to follow a different route. The Germans blew up the railway bridge early in the battle. The Second Battalion under Colonel John Frost made it to the north side of the road bridge and held on tenaciously for

four days under heavy tank and artillery bombardment until they were over-run.

The Third Battalion advanced to the outskirts of Arnhem where the lightly-armed paras were driven back by strong German panzer units backed by seasoned infantry. The Battalion was decimated to the point where it had to be merged with other troops to form 'Lonsdale Force' under Major Dickie Lonsdale.

Oosterbeek perimeter

Their task from then on was to hold the south-east corner of the horseshoe-shaped perimeter around the small town of Oosterbeek in which the remaining 1st Airborne soldiers and their glider pilots found themselves trapped by the Ninth and Tenth SS Panzer Divisions who were armed with tanks, artillery and flame-throwers. The 1st Airborne had been told to expect relief within a couple of days at most. It held out for nine. Life inside the perimeter was hellish. Incessant shelling, mortaring and raking small-arms fire poured in at all hours. The Germans called it *Der Kessel* (The Cauldron).

Eventually, on the dark, rainy night of 25/26 September, an evacuation was put in train. From all around the enclave into which the remnants of the Division had been squeezed, men were assigned to marked routes leading to the banks of the Rhine to

the south. Those to the north, farthest from the river, were evacuated first, so Gerald's unit was one of the last to leave its position.

At the river the men slid down the bank into the mud to await their turn to board the small boats. The latter diminished in alarming numbers as dawn approached and German fire and the swift current exacted their toll. Gerald had sustained a bad head injury during the battle and was brought out by comrades who had looked after him for three days; he was lucky – most of the seriously wounded had to be left behind.

Gerald spent some weeks recovering in hospital. No longer fit for airborne duty, he was transferred to the Royal Army Service Corps where eventually he was appointed Divisional Chief Clerk 1. But that, as Gerald says, is another story.

Above: The 60th anniversary of the Arnhem drop was marked by a series of poignant commemorative events in Holland in September 2004. But of course, the many veterans who made the trip found time for some fun. Enjoying a refreshing beer in the Kleyn Hartenstein Restaurant in Oosterbeek are (left to right): Arthur Sobey, Norman Jones, Ronald Hare, Gerald Levy and Len Wilson. Seventy Years On Editor David Arnold has accompanied Gerald back to Arnhem for the battle anniversaries of 1994, 2004 and 2008.

Left: Gerald and his grand-daughter Nina pictured at the John Frost Bridge in September 2004.

We Met Again!

in her autobiography *Some Sunny Day*, a book that headed the best-sellers list in 2009 along with an album of her music that topped the charts. Here are some excerpts from the book:

'The first show we gave along the Arakan Road was at a hospital. Then we put on a performance for some 4000 of the lads at a rest camp. That was how it went; you just performed your best to whoever was in front of you. The largest audience I had was 6000, the smallest was just two.

'I met a lot of high-ranking officers during this trip and strange to say I was less in awe of them then than I would be today. Then, everybody was doing a tough job of work, and they were just soldiers or airmen to me. I met Brigadier Lentaigne. He had succeeded Brigadier Wingate, the man who organised the Special Force that operated in unbelievable danger behind Japanese lines in the jungle. Wingate christened his men 'Chindits', after a fabulous Burmese lion.

Chindits in the jungle

'I never met Wingate because he'd been killed in an air crash the day after I left England. But I did meet some of his Chindits, who emerged from a spell in the jungle while I was in Comilla. I was told I was to go and see them – 'but not today,' the message added, 'because they have to be de-loused and cleaned'. I didn't sing to them that time. For them, having been out of touch with even army-style civilization for months at a stretch, it was enough to know that the Fourteenth Army they were part of was not completely forgotten, so we just talked.

'In Dimapur, near the front line, I saw some Japanese prisoners. They were sitting on the ground and had obviously just been captured. They gave me a very curious look as if to say 'what is that woman doing here?' I didn't stop to tell them.

'On the way home our aircraft passed very low over El Alamein in Egypt's Western Desert so that we could see where the battle had been fought. It was at Djerba, in Tunisia, that the rumours were confirmed. Tomorrow would be 6 June – D-Day. I returned to England after the greatest adventure of my life, to find that my country and its allies had embarked on their own greatest adventure.'
David Arnold

*Sadly the veterans Leslie, John and Stanley have all passed on since 2005 but their families will never forget that they really did meet again with Dame Vera after all those years.

Vera Lynn famously flew out to Burma in 1944 to boost the morale of the men of the 'Forgotten' Fourteenth Army engaged in a bitter struggle against the Japanese who were then bent on invading India.

Vera featured in a number of photographs with the troops at their jungle camps and airfields, one of the best-known being the one seen at the top of this page. Fast forward 60 years and I'm pleased to say that I was instrumental in bringing together three of the men in the original photograph to once more meet with Vera who, of course, had in the interim been made a Dame in recognition of her iconic status in British showbiz history.

Leslie Sumption, John Ashby and Stanley Johnson went on stage with Dame Vera at a concert simply titled *We'll Meet Again* held at beautiful Glynde Place near Lewes, East Sussex, on 28 May 2005. Accompanied by the 70-strong Pendyrus Male Voice Choir, the three veterans joined Dame Vera in singing *that* song. There wasn't a dry eye amongst the 8000 people in the audience.

Dame Vera has written about her Burma trip

WAR DIARY
September 1944

By **1 September** 'The Great Swan' has been underway for four days. It's the name given by the British – notably the men of the 11th Armoured 'Black Bull' Division – to their rapid advance through Northern France in pursuit of the retreating Germans. The Allied progress since the breakout from the Normandy bridgehead a month ago has been astonishing. Some units are covering 60 miles or more in a day and are close to the Belgian border.

The following day the Finns finally accept Stalin's peace terms. Marshall Mannerheim believes that to delay an armistice any longer can only result in even more stringent Russian demands.

3 September: German troops have quit Brussels ahead of the arrival of the Guards Armoured Division. British units crossed the border in force over the last 24 hours to be welcomed by cheering crowds waving the red, yellow and black flag of Belgium.

The British 11th Armoured Division enters the port of Antwerp today **(4 September)**. Crowds of joyful civilians are out on the streets despite the presence of a large German garrison determined to make a stand. Bullets, shells and grenades fly in some parts of the city whilst close by, Allied fighting vehicles and their crews are mobbed by people offering flowers, bottles and kisses to their liberators. The Allies are desperate to secure a large port on the North Sea in order to shorten their supply lines which now stretch all the way back to Normandy.

5 September: In London the Government has decided that all Soviet citizens captured by British forces are to be repatriated to the USSR whether they want to go or not. Some 12,000 are currently being held in camps in the UK and hundreds more are being captured daily. Many of these Russians volunteered to fight with the *Wehrmacht* but the majority simply wanted to get out of the German POW camps where they had been starved and treated terribly. Thousands manned Hitler's Atlantic Wall but when the Allied invasion came most gave themselves up as quickly as they could.

On **6 September** blackout conditions in towns and cities across Britain have been relaxed and the Home Guard are told to partially stand down. German aircraft are no longer a threat and the blackout is no deterrent to the V1s.

7 September: Sedan is captured and the Moselle river crossed by the Allies. The town was the scene of the *Wehrmacht's* breakthrough in May 1940 when Hitler unleashed Blitzkrieg on France and Belgium. Now it is the Germans who are on the

This illustration by Leslie Ashwell-Wood depicts the fighting abilities of the M4 Sherman tank optimistically suggesting it could destroy the heavily armoured German Tiger and Panther tanks (National Archives – Art of War).

receiving end of 'Lightning War'.

A new type of German rocket – the V2 – plunged out of the early evening sky above Chiswick, West London, today **(8 September)**. Despite the resulting massive explosion, which left an enormous crater, just three people were killed. The noise of the blast was terrific – witnesses described it as like 'double thunderclaps followed by the rush of an express train'. These new weapons take just minutes to reach their targets hundreds of miles away. Unlike the V1, the V2 is a true rocket which ascends to the edge of space before hurtling back to earth.

On **9 September** the Allies enter Dutch territory when US forces drive into Maastricht. Further south in Lorraine there are supply problems for Patton's Third Army. There is no fuel for the tanks, which have halted on the banks of the Moselle, a tantalisingly short distance from the German border.

10 September: The first Allied vehicle, a US jeep crosses into German territory. The following day 20,000 surrounded Germans in Orleans surrender to the 83rd US Infantry Division.

11 September: Churchill and Roosevelt begin the 'Octagon' conference in Quebec. An important item on the agenda is the development of the top-secret atomic bomb.

On this day **(12 September)**, three months and one week after the first Allied soldier had set foot on French soil, the historic junction takes place of *Operation Overlord* and *Operation Dragoon* when soldiers from the Normandy beaches meet with soldiers from the South of France landings. The meeting takes place at Nod-sur-Seine, 150 miles south of Paris.

13 September: The British Eighth Army is hampered by the weather and terrain in their attacks on the Gothic Line in Italy.

Today **(14 September)** a daring underwater raid on Bergen, by a midget submarine, succeeded in destroying a huge floating dock. X24 commanded by Lt H P Westmacott negotiated 30 miles of offshore islands and mine fields before slipping into the Norwegian harbour.

The following day the *Arundel Castle* docks at Liverpool with over 1000 repatriated POWs returning home after, in some cases, four years of captivity.

16 September: After an 11-day lull the doodlebugs are back in southern England. This time they are being launched from aircraft flying from airfields in Holland.

On **17 September** *Operation Market Garden* is launched. In a bid to deliver a decisive blow to Germany and end the war early, Allied paratroopers drop into Holland to secure a series of bridges and waterways which form a corridor to the German border. Along it, according to Montgomery, will pour Allied

WAR DIARY
september 1944

Florence was freed from German oppression by 22 August 1944. Here we see men of the Eighth Army marching through the city. In the background is Il Duomo, fourth largest church in the world, dating from 1298. Largely spared destruction, the famous city quickly became a popular destination for Allied soldiers on leave. In September the Allies continued to make progress in breaking down the Gothic Line north of Florence and by the end of the month bridgeheads had been forced across the River Uso – the famous Rubicon of Julius Caesar. Rimini on the Adriatic coast was liberated and the Fifth Army had closed to within 15 miles of Bologna.

German self-propelled gun parked outside.

19 September: In New York Churchill and Roosevelt have been discussing the military applications for atomic energy and have agreed on full collaboration between their two countries. A decision is secretly made to use the atomic bomb on Japan as quickly as possible after the detonation of a test device.

By **20 September** US airborne troops have taken Eindhoven and Nijmegen. The 'corridor' is now in place but its narrowness is causing problems for the British armour advancing along it. The one main road is extremely vulnerable to attack from the flanks and a single tank or field gun can hold up an entire army.

There is now no hope of relief for Frost's men at Arnhem Bridge. Although Urquhart has escaped from his bolthole all he can do is form a defensive horseshoe around the village of Oosterbeek. German tanks are now pressing in on the lightly armed 'Red Devils'

On **21 September** British tanks cross the Waal bridge at Nijmegen but it is too late for 2nd Battalion at Arnhem bridge, who have been forced to surrender – Frost himself is amongst the wounded.

22 September: In the Pacific, Admiral Halsey's Third Fleet claims 205 Japanese aircraft destroyed both on the ground and in the air against 15 American losses.

23 September: Supreme Allied Commanders HQ is being moved from Normandy to Versailles. Since the invasion of France the Germans have lost upwards of a million men, over half of them captured.

On **24 September,** in the Pacific the Japanese launch a determined attack on US positions on Peleliu. Meanwhile in the Caroline Islands, on the atoll of Ulithi, the Americans are constructing a port in the safe haven of an enormous lagoon.

25 September: Montgomery authorises the withdrawal of British and Polish paratroops from the north bank of the Rhine.

The following day in Italy the Eighth Army crosses the **Rubicon**, the legendary river known to Caesar's legionnaires. The British are heading in the opposite direction to Caesar but hope their action will prove as decisive in ending a war.

On **27 September** the remaining British and Polish troops, many of them wounded, trapped on the north bank of the Rhine surrendered in the last hours of the nine-day battle to hold the bridgehead around Oosterbeek and Arnhem. Only 2400 of the 10,000 who took part in the operation escaped by boat or by swimming the river.

By **28 September** British troops are based on the Dalmatian islands in the Adriatic and are supporting Tito's partisans in preparation for an invasion of mainland Yugoslavia.

29 September: Dover need fear the 'big guns' of the Germans no more as Canadian troops capture the great batteries in the Cap Gris Nez area near Calais. Since 1940 the Germans have been able to hurl shells at the harbours and towns around Kent's white cliffs.

On **30 September** the surviving 7000 Germans of the Calais garrison surrender, despite brave displays of resistance which suggested they would fight on to the last man. Almost all of France is now free.

armies into Germany's lightly defended interior. The swift capture of the Ruhr industrial area will cripple German military capabilities and topple the Nazis.

The operation begins well as American paratroopers attack and secure bridges across the Maas and Waal rivers. At the northern end of the corridor 1st Airborne Division land against light opposition some eight miles from their target, the bridges at Arnhem. However jeep-carrying gliders fail to arrive and those that do are caught in an ambush. As Lt Col John Frost's Second Battalion nears the northern end of the road bridge at twilight there are ominous signs that a German reaction will not be long in making itself felt.

18 September: Lt Col Frost and Second Battalion have formed defensive positions overnight. Radio contact is erratic and reinforcements have failed to reach them, the Germans are approaching from the north and also have a tight grip on the southern end of the bridge. The commanding officer Maj-Gen Urquhart is currently hiding in the attic of a Dutch house with a

Two examples of the work of German war artist Walter Gotschke depicting panzers in action on the Russian Front. They appeared in Signal magazine in 1944 with the comment: 'Signal's photographers have often published colour photographs of burning villages. Scarcely one of these photographs, however, is so thrilling in its grimness as the artist's impressions of tanks shown here.

The photographer does not take such photographs because they offer him too few details. The artist's eye, on the other hand, wide open in terror, preserves the memory of the journey through the sea of flames.'

WARSAW'S AGONY

October 1944. Polish dreams of freedom crushed as the Red Army looks on...

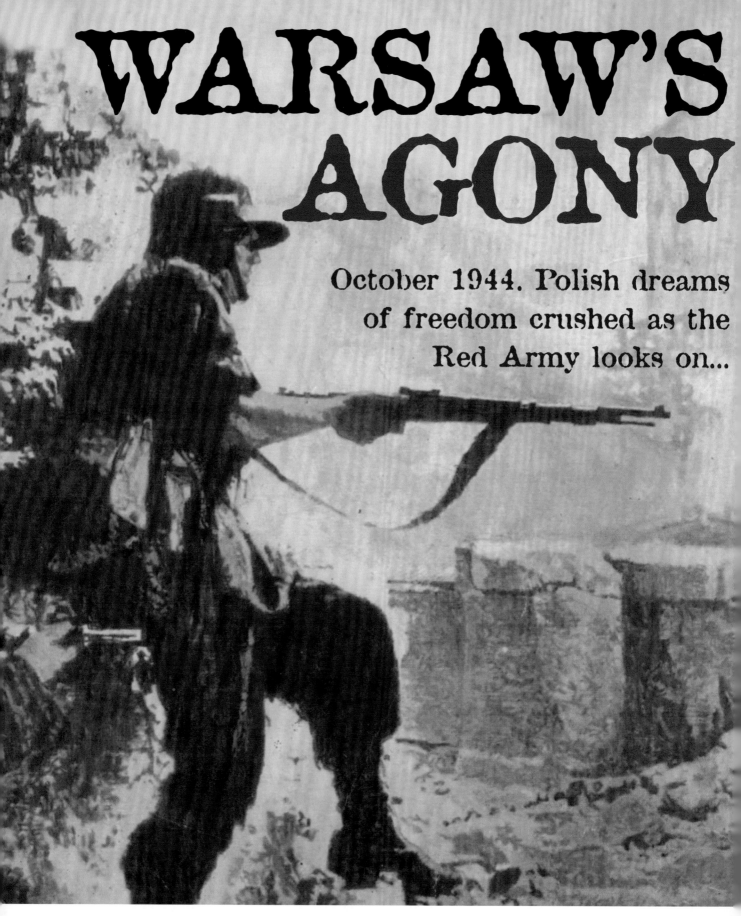

General Bor-Komorowski, Commander-in-Chief of the Polish Home Army, signalled the start of the Warsaw Uprising on 1 August 1944. A little over two months later, on 2 October, this same leader, with a sad and heavy heart, ordered his remaining fighters to lay down their arms and submit to the Germans. In the intervening period the beautiful Polish capital had been transformed into a desolate heap of rubble.

And around 250,000 people, including at least 40,000 civilians, had lost their lives.

Even as part of a world war full of numbing brutality and mindless destruction, the crucifixion of Warsaw must be considered the most pointless exercise in violence. After all, by the end of July 1944 the guns over the ever-advancing Red Army could be heard by the Poles even from the banks of the Vistula and a broad sweep of Polish territory was

already free of the hated Nazi occupiers. Surely all the freedom fighters of the Home Army needed to do was wait a few weeks more for liberation from the East? Why did they risk needless confrontation with a ruthless and unpredictable German enemy who had no apparent choice but to retreat in the face of Stalin's limitless legions?

The key to the tragedy lay in divided loyalties. General Bor and the Home Army owed allegiance to the Polish Government-in-Exile based in London since the occupation of their country by the Germans (and until Hitler turned on them too, in part by the Russians) in 1939. By 1944 however, Stalin had built up a large army of Polish Communists who had appointed their own political leadership. Bor and the London Poles had good grounds for suspecting that Stalin's intentions for post-war Poland did not allow for democracy.

Notoriously cruel

Churchill and other Western leaders shared their suspicions but geography alone ruled out any hope of large-scale assistance for the Home Army. The latter perceived that their only hope of asserting independence lay in freeing themselves from Nazi rule before the Russians and Communist Poles were able to. An uprising was inevitable.

In the first week the lightly armed Poles – buoyed up by enthusiasm and the knowledge that the Russians were close by – were successful. Key points and buildings all over the city were captured and much of the German garrison fled or was captured. But once the Germans had recovered from their surprise they reacted strongly. Hitler gave priority to the crushing of the rebellion. He allowed Himmler to divert precious land and air forces to carry out the task. Amongst the units selected by the SS supremo were SS police units, a brigade of Russian ex-POWs and a brigade of ex-convicts, all of whom were already notorious for their cruelty and excesses to soldiers and civilians alike. With relish this well-armed army, backed by powerful artillery and panzer support, set about reducing Warsaw to ruins.

Just as the German guns began to pound the city, block by block, so the guns of the Red Army close by fell silent. The Russians would make no attempt to support Bor's uprising. Indeed, for some time they even refused to allow British and American aircraft engaged in supplying arms to Warsaw to make emergency landings – let alone stops to refuel – in Russian-held territory.

Cry for help

Beleaguered Bor and the London Poles could only plead with the Western Allies. Three of their demands were simply not feasible – Allied bombing of the Warsaw area, the despatch of Polish fighter squadrons from France to the Warsaw area and the dropping of the Polish parachute brigade into the capital, even though in the latter case the men were anxious to go to the aid of their fellow countrymen.

A fourth request, a considerable increase in the air supply of arms and ammunition, was scarcely less formidable but was undertaken. The task fell upon the Allied air forces in Italy and the 1,759 mile round trips were probably the most hazardous of any made by Allied aircraft during the war in Europe. On five nights between 12 – 17 August out of 93 aircraft despatched, 17 failed to return.

The introduction of delayed-drop parachutes later enabled containers to be released above the range of the considerable light flak in position in and around the city. Bad weather meant many cancelled flights. When, six weeks after the uprising began the Russians finally permitted aircraft to land in their territory it was a case of too little too late despite a large-scale escorted operation by US aircraft flying a 'supply shuttle' out of UK bases and the start of nightly arms drops by planes of the Red Air Force.

> **"** Soldiers of the capital! I have today issued the order which you desire, for open warfare against Poland's age-old enemy, the German invader. After nearly five years of ceaseless struggle, carried on in secret, you stand today openly with arms in your hand, to restore freedom to our country, and to mete out fitting punishment to the German criminals for the terror and crimes committed by them on Polish soil. **"**

General Bor-Komorowski in a radio address to the Polish Home Army on 1 August 1944.

On the ground the Poles fought desperately against an enemy who brought Tiger and Panther tanks and flame-throwers to bear on houses and strongpoints where the defenders often only had rifles and pistols with which to defend themselves. Warsaw's Old Town – preserved since medieval times – was obliterated. Himmler wanted the fate of the city to be a terrifying warning to the rest of Europe.

Polish messenger women and children – the sole means of communication for the Home Army – took to the sewers. These same tunnels had become the distribution route for the dwindling supplies of food and ammunition. But the Poles never lacked courage in the face of the daunting odds and thousands died manning their street barricades to the very end. Blizzards of artillery fire followed by Stuka dive-bombing would be concentrated on different districts day after day. Remote-controlled Goliath mini-tanks packed with explosives were deployed against Home Army strongpoints.

Massacres of captured insurgents and civilians alike were reported. Early in the Uprising a young woman named Wanda was seized while taking shelter with others in the Ministry of Commerce building in Elektoralna Street. Narrowly escaping rape, she was driven with a procession of mostly young women with children towards the district of Wola. At one point German troops ordered them all to lie down from one side of the street to the other to form a human barricade against insurgent fire.

'We were all prepared to die' she later told George Bruce, author of *The Warsaw Uprising* (Rupert Hart-Davis Ltd, 1972), 'Bullets whistled over our heads or past our ears. As if by some miracle they only hit the Germans... They were bewildered by the fact that only they were falling and we thought that they would most certainly take their revenge on us. Stupefied and astonished they looked towards the insurgent posts and then at our quiet, resigned attitude, and the children clinging to their mothers. At last they let us go.'

Others were not so fortunate. It's estimated that as part of a deliberate plan based on Himmler's orders nearly 40,000 civilians were killed in the uprising.

Rights of combatants

The end was not far away. On 1 October General Bor declared in a message to the London Government, 'I have decided to enter into negotiations for surrender with full combatant rights, which the Germans fully recognise.'

Astonishingly, the latter part was true. The heroic resistance had forced their enemy to confer Geneva Convention statutes upon the Poles, fighters and civilians alike. German General von dem Bach praised the valour and courage of the Home Army. Of course the Germans also knew that very soon the Russian offensive must resume whereupon besieged Warsaw would be relieved. The eyes of the world would then see a victory for an enslaved people over their one-time masters.

The next day the Poles began marching out of Warsaw to lay down their arms outside of the city. By 6 October the whole place had been evacuated. Now the wholesale destruction of those parts not already razed in the fighting began. It only ended once Warsaw had been destroyed as no city had ever been destroyed before.

Yet Warsaw was destined to be no Carthage. Within a year work commenced on reconstruction of this one-time city of life and light astride the Vistula. The project turned into a national saga with the entire Old Town being re-erected street by street and house by house, even to the carvings and mural designs.

Today, Poland is a democracy once more. More than six decades on, Warsaw must count as the embodiment of this proud nation's will to survive and go forward.

'By the end of the war some 30,248 British merchant seamen had lost their lives with another 11,000 either injured or taken prisoner. These men, or their bereaved dependents, would not be entitled to any compensation, nor would they receive a war pension. Merchant seamen were "civilians" according to the War Ministry.'

Thus reads the preface to a 2004 book of wartime memories by Ron Tubb – *Red Duster Recollections – A Merchant Seaman's Experiences in World War II.*

Born in Bridgend in 1916, the sea was very much Ron's destiny as soon as he enrolled at a Nautical Training School at the age of 12. Ron's experience of war included witnessing the Liverpool Blitz, the U-Boat menace and attacks by enemy aircraft. By 1942 he had gained his Master Mariner's Certificate and subsequently served on troop ships and tankers. He sailed to Australia and the Far East, North America and the Caribbean, gradually rising in rank along the way.

On one crossing of the Atlantic he recalls his convoy being three days in dense fog: 'Even though ships were within a couple of cables of each other, none could be seen. At one point a passenger liner was on our port side and we could hear children laughing and shouting, but the liner was invisible. Eventually we came out of the fog at an angle and saw ship after ship eerily emerging. The fog bank resembled a vertical wall.'

To Curacao for diesel

Ron also wrote: 'Promoted to First Officer, in March 1944 I signed on the *MV Dipladon*, sailing for the West Indies, to load diesel in Curacao. We were then ordered to proceed to the Mediterranean. As Gibraltar was full of naval ships, we anchored off Oran in North Africa before proceeding to Marseille to discharge part of our cargo.

'At recently-liberated Toulon, we tied up alongside a French warship, one of many scuttled earlier in the war to deny their use by the Germans. I was told that some German forces had been cut off and trapped on Toulon Island and a fierce battle had ensued with Senegalese troops, under French command. No Germans left the island alive.

'I went ashore, to find the area honeycombed with tunnels and the oil tanks housed underground. In one tunnel were four large, high-speed diesel engines, the type

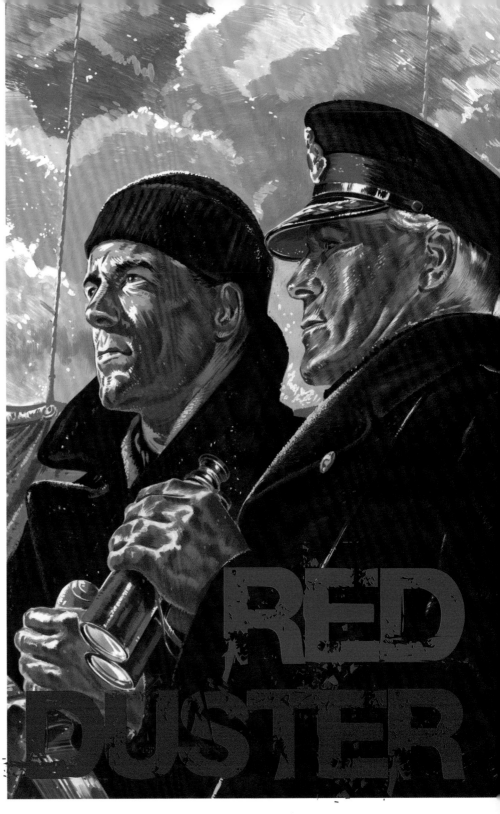

used in E-Boats. They were all booby-trapped. One had to tread very gingerly, as there were piles of ammunition and guns everywhere and signs warning of mines.

Massive bomb blast

"We next sailed along the South of France coast, oiling various British and US men-of-war. Following an air raid warning we sighted some planes. I recall nothing of what happened next. I apparently lost consciousness for a while and was told later that the ship had been caught in the massive blast of a bomb.

'Having discharged all our cargo we headed back across the Atlantic to Galveston, Texas. I became unwell during this passage and needed to return to Britain for an operation.

Above: *The Life-Line is Firm. This painting by Charles Wood was incorporated into a 1942 window poster that supported the vital role of Britain's Merchant Navy.*

Left: *Roy Nockolds painted this Hawker Hurricane approaching an Escort Carrier. These ships were usually converted merchantmen with a rudimentary flight deck that could take a small number of aircraft.*

'My journey homeward was by Pullman train to New York where I joined the *MV Amastra*, as acting Master. Our voyage was without incident and we arrived safely in Liverpool. I soon underwent an operation in Bridgend Hospital and, after three months convalescence, was told by a Ministry of Transport doctor that he would not recommend me for further sea duties. This was devastating news.'

GREEK TRAGEDY

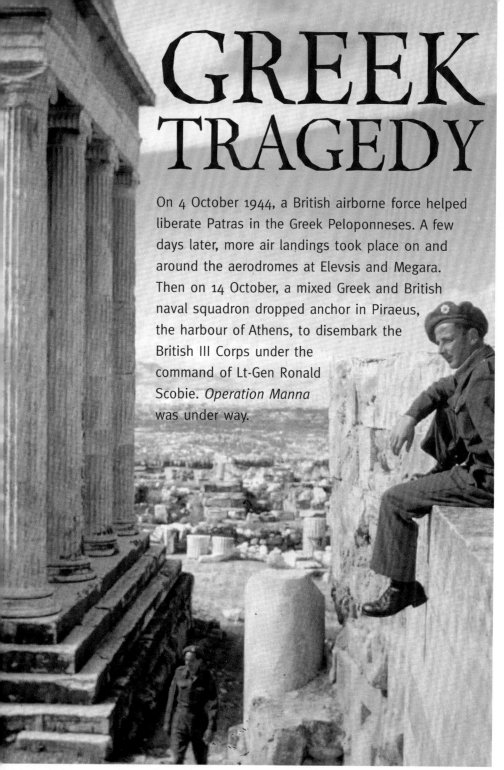

On 4 October 1944, a British airborne force helped liberate Patras in the Greek Peloponneses. A few days later, more air landings took place on and around the aerodromes at Elevsis and Megara. Then on 14 October, a mixed Greek and British naval squadron dropped anchor in Piraeus, the harbour of Athens, to disembark the British III Corps under the command of Lt-Gen Ronald Scobie. *Operation Manna* was under way.

The undertaking had two aims. Firstly, to be sure that once the Germans were chased out, Greece's borders with Albania, Yugoslavia and Bulgaria, especially, would be respected. Churchill feared that the Communist regimes now rising to power in these countries must inevitably have designs on northern Greek provinces such as Eastern Macedonia.

Secondly, General Scobie was ordered to prevent, by force if necessary, the Greek Peoples' Liberation Army (ELAS) from usurping the established political system by unconstitutional means. George Papandreou headed up the de facto Greek Government at this point. He struck a liberal and democratic posture and his appointment earlier in the year seemed enough to bring together opposing factions in the Greek political spectrum. At one time, a mutiny by pro-Communist Greek sailors on a warship in Alexandria had led to bloodshed.

But now the danger of subversion was growing daily. In answer to a call by the EAM (a left-wing Liberation Committee), units of ELAS converged on Athens, en route passing large numbers of retreating Wehrmacht soldiers without seeking battle.

Churchill under fire

A call by Papandreou for the demobilisation of all guerilla groups of both the Left and the Right on 1 December was refuted by the EAM. Within days fighting flared on the streets of Athens between police and rebel ELAS supporters. On 5 December, Churchill ordered Scobie to restore order. At the same time as the general declared a state of martial law, ELAS fighters moved in to seize key points in the Greek capital. The British seemed inextricably caught up in someone else's civil war.

Early successes for ELAS included the capture of the rear RAF headquarters at Kifissia where around 500 British military personnel were trapped in a wrecked hotel and taken captive. After protracted negotiations they were released.

However, it was not long before the trained and disciplined British army gained the upper hand, even though the ELAS threat could not be entirely extinguished. Over the Christmas period, Churchill himself went to Athens, basing himself aboard the cruiser *HMS Ajax* in Piraeus and meeting representatives from all sides of the conflict to a background of intermittent gunfire in the city. Shells were even lobbed at his ship, which responded in kind on the Prime Minister's orders.

Within a week of Churchill's departure, full-scale talks began to find a peaceful solution. A new Greek premier, General Plastiras, assured both sides of a role in the political future of the country and urged a return to duty for 'all who have been misled and turned their arms against their country'.

On 12 February 1945, Harold McMillan, British Minister Resident in the Mediterranean, could report to London that the Civil War in Greece was, for the time being, over.

EYE WITNESS Tom Dean served in the 46th RTR (Royal Tank Regiment) which was sent to Greece to combat the EAM and ELAS communist rebels. He records:

We learnt the hard way soon after our arrival in the Greek capital that tanks were not the right answer for house to house fighting. Consequently we tankmen were often used as infantry. It was a messy business, made more so because we didn't know who we could trust in this virtual civil war.

A group of us were guarding the wireless station in the hills at Pellini, some miles outside Athens. After the street fighting it seemed a cushy billet. Supplies came in via RAF parachute drops and one canister was found to contain a bazooka and ammunition.

A loyalist Greek told us that three members of our Regiment together with two infantrymen were being held captive by ELAS in a nearby village. Our officer decide on a night raid and so, at 1am, he plus one sergeant, one corporal (myself) and four troopers set off with our friendly guide.

Luck was with us and we were almost out of the village with our freed prisoners before the alarm was raised and indiscriminate firing began. At this point we split into pairs and legged it smartly back to the station.

Within a few days we learned that ELAS

A leaflet from the communist rebels aimed at demoralising the British forces trying to keep the peace in Greece.

were planning a retaliatory raid. Sure enough, a couple nights later they opened up with machine-gun fire from three sides. Next we heard the roar of an armoured car coming up the road towards the main gate. It turned out that ELAS had acquired the vehicle in an earlier raid on an RAF aerodrome.

Fortunately for us, we had two infantrymen, armed with the bazooka, in a slit trench near the gate. They loosed off a missile and scored a direct hit on the armoured car which promptly blew up in a tremendous explosion. The enemy immediately withdrew and didn't come back. It seems that the rebels had stored a box of dynamite in the vehicle and had planned to wreck the wireless station.

As a consequence of the raid on the village, our officer was awarded the Military Cross and the sergeant got the Military Medal. What the outcome would have been for us if we hadn't had the bazooka and the two infantry lads who knew how to use it, I wouldn't like to speculate!

This poster from early in the war points out that there are Free Greeks fighting on against the Nazis.

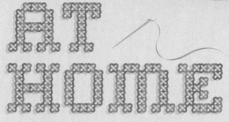

AT HOME

By the early spring of 1945 things were improving in the kitchens of British housewives. At the end of February, fresh supplies reached London greengrocers, a fact noted in the *Daily Telegraph*:

'… dwarf runner beans of the French variety are in the West End shops. Grown in Cornish and Devon hot-houses, they cost 30s per lb. Grapefruits from the Middle East have also arrived. They will be distributed in the same way as oranges and lemons at a controlled price of 8d a lb.'

Even so, there was still rationing of meat and shortages encouraged alternatives. Rabbit was widely used and sausages often contained interesting substitutes for meat. A very popular film of the period, *Millions Like Us*, memorably includes a character observing: 'It's a mystery what's in these sausages… and I hope it's not solved in my time!'

Tinned meat was imported in huge quantities from the United States and in this way Spam (chopped luncheon meat) entered the national diet. Corned beef too was regularly on the menu. Whalemeat become widely available in 1945 but was generally disliked because of its fishy, oily taste.

Further strain on the food front came with the need to feed the millions of newly liberated peoples of Europe, many of them displaced or living in areas devastated by the fighting. As a consequence of the shortages most British people who had access to a garden or allotment continued to grow as many vegetables as they could.

Britain's war effort was sustained by the efforts of countless women workers, who had replaced men sent off to serve in the Forces. Women were involved in just about every light and heavy industry as well as in such occupations as ferry pilots delivering new aircraft to RAF bases. An exception was

The Kitchen Front
122 WARTIME RECIPES
broadcast by Frederick Grisewood, Mabel Constanduros and others, specially selected by the Ministry of Food.

" It's a mystery what's in these sausages… and I hope it's not solved in my time! "

the mines. In the pits the Bevin Boys toiled to keep up with Britain's insatiable need for energy from coal to drive the manufacturing machines and heat homes.

Following an announcement by Minister of Labour, Ernest Bevin in December 1943, boys of 18 had been conscripted to work in the mines. It was a tough business. One youngster – T Buckland – working down Glapwell Colliery in Nottinghamshire told a newspaper: 'I travel five miles by bus to get there. Then I drop down the shaft in a cage at about 60mph, with the draught through the holes blowing right up our legs, and it's cold!

'It is roughly four miles from the pit bottom to the point where I work, which makes it nine miles from my home. We're making a new roadway and work in 70 degrees of heat. Halfway through my shift I have generally drunk my four pints of water and then have to go thirsty. It makes you value water.'

'We fill between 12 and 16 tubs of rock in a shift and a tub holds about one ton. Twelve to 16 tubs a night isn't bad, is it?'

Art Direction

Evolution of a Wartime Poster Painting

Clive Uptton painted the two pictures displayed on these pages. His first version *(above)* was the one reproduced in a smaller size to the other. Dating from mid-1944 it shows three British soldiers, dressed in jungle fatigues and carrying Thompson sub machine guns, wading through a jungle swamp that's almost certainly in Burma.

Mr W Embleton of the Ministry of Information has written some notes for the artist on the painting to the effect: 'Dear Uptton. This looks very promising indeed - thanks a lot. My only comments are that the leading figure should look more "urgent" - at present he looks a little unreal and is asking to be shot at. Could he not be clambering forward like the chaps following him? Also watch carefully the position of the gun which should be held under his right arm surely? As title is to be overprinted in black I think we doctor the background a little don't you? Otherwise fine - Embleton.'

Clive Uptton took on board the Man from the Ministry's suggestions (or, rather, his polite directions!) and produced the second version seen on the page opposite *(National Archives - The Art of War)*.

CHOCOLATE STAIRCASE
AND THE
VALLEY OF DEATH

In September and October 1944 the importance of Allied air power in helping the troops on the ground defeat the Japanese in Burma was demonstrated forcefully on the Tiddim Road and Kabaw valley. The latter name means 'Valley of Death' and the area is said to be one of the most highly malarial places in the world as well as being home to the scrub typhus mite.

Throughout the two months in question, 11th East African Division made steady progress against a retreating enemy. Appalling weather brought mud and floods and the potential for epidemics amongst the troops was enormous. However, a combination of good hygiene discipline and the fact that the whole length of the road was sprayed with DDT from the air by fighter-bombers, kept Allied casualties from both malaria and typhus to a minimum. The Japanese, on the other hand, perished in their hundreds from these diseases.

Supplied by air

Parallel to this advance, Fifth Indian Division was advancing south down the Tiddim Road. After crossing the Manipur River in mid-September, continuous landslides on the road behind made re-supply by road impossible and the Division had to be supplied entirely by air – even down to spare jeep engines. Everything came down by parachute as there were no landing strips and in the monsoon conditions it was impossible to construct any.

At the beginning of October the battle for Tiddim began. The final approach to the town from the north was very difficult especially once the road leaves the valley of the Manipur River and climbs 3700 feet in 10 miles, the first six consisting of 36 steep hairpin bends known as the 'Chocolate Staircase'. Tiddim itself is 162 miles from Imphal and lies 5600 feet above sea level.

Having failed to hold the river line it quickly became clear that the Japanese thought they stood a good chance of holding Tiddim and their troops constructed strong positions at just about every milestone in the road. Hurricane fighter-bombers intervened at every opportunity – when not blasting the enemy with bombs the noise of the low-flying aircraft helped hide the rumble of advancing tanks. Heartened by such effective support, the Indian Division pressed their attack with great vigour with the result that Tiddim was occupied on 18 October.

British soldiers of the Fourteenth Army enjoy a game of cards just 300 yards from the Japanese positions.

Battle for Walcheren

A s the autumn of 1944 gave way to winter on the Dutch - German border the weather became cold and damp. In the low-lying Peel Country, troops on both sides found their slit trenches quickly filling up with water. Lots of small but nonetheless deadly dangerous operations took place as the British felt their way forward to the strong points and bunkers of the Siegfried Line.

One important battle was the British assault on Walcheren Island that began on 1 November at dawn in atrocious weather. The island was important because it commanded the Scheldt and so long as the Germans held it the Allies could not use the river to gain access to the vital port of Antwerp.

An eight day struggle ensued before the last of the German defences were overcome. Minesweeping of the Scheldt began on 4 November and the first convoy sailed into Antwerp on 28 November.

Along the whole Western Front the Germans fought hard though a steady stream of prisoners came in. Very often these men proved not to be German at all. In his book *Churchill's Desert Rats – from Normandy to Berlin with the 7th Armoured Division* (Alan Sutton Publishing, 1994) Patrick Delaforce quotes one tankman's view of a batch: 'This lot were a rabble and included a couple of Mongolians, ex-Russians who were used as stooges and general dogsbodies of *Wehrmacht* men who were themselves a more contemptible shower. One skinny 12-year-old Hitler *Jugend* from the Langemark Division, blubbered and writhed when captured yet this dangerous lad had a Schmeisser machine pistol, a Luger, three potato masher grenades and a wicked paratrooper knife.

The culprit received a damned good spanking and was sent off to a POW cage.'

Hurtgen Forest

To the south in late October, Aachen had been the first German city to fall in the west. Its capture also involved the first breaching of the Siegfried Line, Hitler's last major defensive bastion before the River Rhine itself. But beyond Aachen the Americans became embroiled in bloody fighting in the Hurtgen Forest. So fierce and gruelling was the conflict that a number of units were withdrawn and sent south to the quiet Ardennes sector for rest and recuperation.

In Alsace the US Seventh Army and First French Army had closed on the Siegfried Line in a number of places in November and December. The city of Strasbourg on the River Rhine itself was captured by General Leclerc's men on 23 November. Around the town of Bitche, the Germans had taken over a section of the old French Maginot Line, which had been designed to afford all-round defence.

Shermans outgunned

A large pocket of Germans remained on French territory in the area of Colmar and southwards to the border with Switzerland. The Vosges Mountains around here – today so popular with tourists and famous for wines

produced on the gentle slopes facing the Rhine – made it easy to defend the roads leading to Germany. Hitler was determined to hold on to Alsace – a region which had long been a cause of strife between the French and Germans. He sent in powerful Panther and Jagdpanther tanks which outgunned the Shermans of the French First Army. Progress was slow and costly; it took to the end of 1944 to liberate most of Alsace and even then parts of the Colmar pocket remained in German hands.

Meanwhile, in the approximate centre of the Western Front, below Luxembourg, Patton's third US Army was driving towards the Saar region of Germany. In his way lay the French city of Metz, fortified and garrisoned under the command of a tough Nazi who was determined to obey Hitler's order to fight to the last man. It was not until 18 November that the first Americans entered Metz; it took another four days before the Germans finally surrendered.

A British General (almost certainly Alexander) observes forward while Sherman tanks advance (National Archives).

WAR DIARY
October 1944

The first day of **October 1944** sees the US 7th Armoured Division getting a bloody nose in the course of an attack around Overloon and Venray in Holland. The Americans are fighting in the same area as the British 11th Armoured but lack the latter's combat experience and progress is less than three miles in a week.

On **2 October** at 10pm the guns stop firing in Warsaw, 63 days after the uprising began. The Polish Home Army is out of ammunition and food and without hope of Russian relief. Some 15,000 Polish fighters have died along with an estimated 200,000 civilians and 10,000 SS and Wehrmacht troops. Surrendering Polish fighters are being treated as prisoners of war rather than rebels.

3 October: Fighting on the Channel coast continues. In Dunkirk the Germans agree to a truce to allow the civilian population to be evacuated. In Italy the US Fifth Army is nearing Bologna but casualties are high, 550 killed or wounded a day.

4 October: Britain is still under bombardment from V2 rockets. It was hoped that *Operation Market Garden* would remove or at least restrict this threat. It is believed they are being launched from Denmark.

5 October: Today the British landed on mainland Greece by sea. It seems the Germans are evacuating the country as fast as possible; the British are moving quickly to trap the 10,000-strong German garrison in Athens. It will be another two days before Hitler gives the order for his men to pull out.

6 October: In Burma the battle for Tiddim continues with tanks and air support proving to be the Allied 'ace' as the 5th Indian Division advances. The men of the Japanese 15th Army are resolutely defending every bend in the road.

7 October: The inmates of Auschwitz-Birkenau Concentration Camp stage a mass revolt against their tormentors today. With hammers and pickaxes for weapons they managed to overpower some guards and the revolt quickly spreads. SS reinforcements are quickly on the scene and set about ruthlessly crushing the revolt. Few of those involved in the uprising will live to tell the tale.

8 October: US forces are moving on Aachen in Germany in a pincer movement.

By next day advance parties of Land Forces, Adriatic, are within sight of Megara airfield, 20 miles west of Athens. In the next two days convoys from Italy and the Middle East will put to sea, heading for the Greek capital.

10 October: The Dumbarton Oaks conference in Washington has not fully resolved the deep differences of opinions between the US, USSR and Britain.

Today **(11 October)**, four Gloster Meteors of No 616 Sqdn are carrying out a week-long programme of fighter affiliation exercises with Eighth USAAF to give the bomber crews experience of jet fighter attacks. This is in response to the activation of the first operational German jet fighter unit.

12 October: In the East China Sea, Admiral Halsey's Third US Fleet is attacking Formosa with carrier-based aircraft.

On **13 October** King George VI visits VIII Corps HQ in the Netherlands and meets General 'Pip' Roberts of 11th Armoured Division and other commanding officers.

14 October: Germany's greatest military hero of the war, Field Marshall Erwin Rommel, dies. He was visited at his home by two senior officers sent personally by Hitler. They told the 'Desert Fox' that he could either take his own life at once or be arrested for implication in the 20 July bomb plot against Hitler. He was able to say farewell to his family before taking poison.

Athens and the Greek capital's port, Piraeus are occupied by British troops.

15 October: The industrial heartland of Germany, the Ruhr, has been the target for a massive bombing campaign over the last few days. Duisburg was hit by 1013 RAF Lancasters and Halifaxes and 1251 USAAF Flying Fortresses and Liberators.

With the Russians already inside his country, Hungarian Regent, 73-year-old Admiral Nikolaus Horthy von Nagybanya, announces on the radio his intention to seek an armistice with Stalin. Within hours he is in the custody of German commandos led by SS Colonel Otto 'Scarface' Skorzeny. The Nazis appoint an 'Acting Regent' who orders Hungarian forces to fight on against the Red Army.

In the Netherlands the Churchill tanks of the Guards take Overloon on **16 October.** A Victoria Cross has been won by Sgt George Eardley of the King's Shropshire Light Infantry for undertaking under heavy fire three brave actions against enemy machine-gun posts.

17 October - Norway. Grand Admiral Dönitz is determined to resurrect the U-Boat threat to Allied shipping by utilising new technology. A new and improved version of the Schnorkel allows submarines to replenish their air supply whilst remaining

Still the Best!

BIRD'S CUSTARD

BIRD'S CUSTARD AND JELLIES

Right: A 1944 advertisement for a popular brand of custard.

WAR DIARY
October 1944

submerged and out of sight of vigilant Allied aircraft.

18 October: In Germany all able-bodied men between 16 and 60 are being called-up for the *Volkssturm* (People's Front) home guard in defence of the Reich.

Today **(19 October)** the start of a major Russian push into East Prussia is reported. In Burma Indian troops of the Fourteenth Army have taken Tiddim.

20 October: In early 1942 General MacArthur vowed 'I shall return' when forced to leave the Philippines. Today he fulfilled that vow when at noon he walked through the surf onto the beach at Leyte. The 600-ship US invasion force was not due to attack for another two months but when large gaps in the Japanese defences were noticed it was decided to go in early. By the end of the day 100,000 US troops will be ashore.

21 October: Belgrade is still celebrating after the entry into the city of the First Proletarian Division of Tito's Army of National Liberation 24 hours ago. The escape route out of Yugoslavia for German Army Group E is threatened.

On **22 October** the Red Army invading Prussia stops just 45 miles short of Hitler's Rastenburg 'Wolf's Lair' Headquarters. Meanwhile Second Tactical Air Force is conducting a bombing campaign against known launch sites for V2 rockets in the Netherlands.

The following day **(23 October)** the Battle of Leyte Gulf opened with the sinking of two Japanese heavy cruisers and a light cruiser by US submarines waiting in ambush.

Moscow reports making further gains in Northern Transylvania, Hungary, Czechoslovakia and Yugoslavia.

24 October: In what may turn out to be the greatest naval battle ever fought, a total of 282 American and Japanese vessels are locked in combat today. The US Navy have superior numbers but sustain an early setback with the loss of the carrier USS *Princeton*, sunk by dive-bombers. Over 1000 Japanese sailors perish as their battleship *Musashi* goes down.

25 October: In the Netherlands the Germans are counting the cost of a low-level bombing raid carried out by RAF Typhoons on a building housing a conference of high-ranking officers. Two generals and 92 German officers and other ranks died.

Soviet forces advancing from Lapland have crossed into German-occupied Norway to seize the port of Kirkenes in the far north of the country.

On **26 October** the Battle of Leyte Gulf ends in a crushing defeat for the Imperial Japanese Navy - they have lost 28 ships including their last four carriers against a toll of four US vessels sunk. It puts an end to Japanese hopes of stemming the US advance on the home islands. The battle produced an ominous portent for the Americans when suicide pilots - Kamikaze (Divine Wind) - claim their first victim, the escort carrier *St Lo*.

27 October: It seems the Allies must spend another winter in Italy as the bad weather has scuppered the offensive plans of the Eighth and Fifth Armies on either side of the Apennines.

The next day Bulgaria and the Russians sign an armistice giving control of the country's armed forces to the Red Army.

29 October: The battleship *Tirpitz*, moored in Norway, is once again the target of an RAF airstrike. Even though 32 massive 12,00lb Tallboy bombs are dropped, poor visibility prevents any hits being scored.

The Hungarian Third Army has disintegrated in the face of a powerful assault by Russia's 6th Guards Tank Army leaving the road to Budapest wide open. But even as the Russians approach the capital, the SS - organised by the notorious Adolf Eichmann - continue the deportation of Hungarian Jews destined for the death camps in Germany.

On **30 October** US ground forces on Leyte capture Dagami. Out at sea the Kamikaze have been attacking US aircraft carriers. In the last two days the *Intrepid*, *Franklin* and *Belleau Wood* have all been hit.

31 October: The Japanese prepare to release 9000 balloons, each carrying an explosive charge, in the hope that the prevailing wind will carry them 6000 miles across the Pacific to detonate in the USA. The vast majority of the balloons will never make it but a few will cause minor casualties.

Below: The Gestapo HQ at Aarhus in Denmark actually under attack on 31 October 1944 by 25 Mosquito fighter-bombers of RAF No 12 Group. The raid destroyed Gestapo records and enabled a young pastor, Harald Sandbaek, to escape from a torture chamber. The aircraft flew so low that one of them hit the roof of the building, losing its tail wheel and the port half of the tail plane. Even so, the sturdy machine managed to make it back to base.

Beverly Hills stamp dealer Marshall Goldberg served with General George S Patton's Third Army as it advanced through France in 1944.

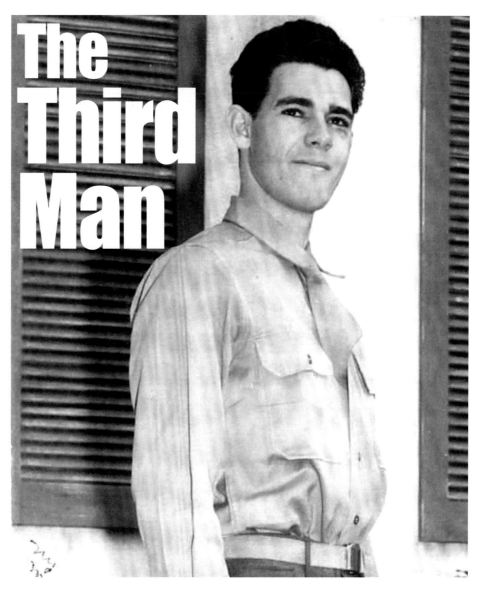

The Third Man

Friends of mine – Peter Betts and Pat Silver-Lasky – moved to California in 2009, *writes David Arnold*. We have stayed in touch and one day they suggested I might like to hear some of the wartime experiences of an American acquaintance. I was intrigued, not least because *Seventy Years On* is, in the main, a repository of British wartime memories and to have an American take would be interesting.

Marshall Goldberg lives in Beverly Hills and at a time when most folk of his age would be retired he is still active in the family's stamp dealing business. In 1944 Marshall was a soldier in the 134th Infantry Regiment, destined to be part of General George S Patton's famous Third Army. The 134th arrived on the front lines just outside St Lo, Normandy, on 8 July 1944 having come ashore a short time before on Omaha Beach.

The unit motto was 'All Hell Can't Stop Us' and the men soon went into action in the hedgerow country known as the bocage. The hedgerows – ancient property dividers used by local landowners – made highly effective defensive barriers and the Germans quickly found that as little as a single machine-gun mounted in the right position could hold up the advance of any number of men. Early in the battle, Company C had advanced farther than any other unit in the assault on St Lo, but it had suffered 60% casualties on the way. The company persevered across the sunken roads and hedgerows for three days at the end of which the Allies claimed the city.

SS Das Reich Division

For its bravery in the action near St Lo, the 1st Battalion of the 134th Infantry Regiment, including Company C, was cited for 'extraordinary heroism and outstanding performance of duty'. A letter was published in the *Daily Sun* in the town of Beatrice, Nebraska, on 22 August 1944. Staff Sergeant Charles Young wrote: 'We took the town, but, oh, the price we had to pay. I cannot tell the names of the boys; they will be in *The Sun* before long. There are so few of us left you would never know it was Company C.'

After a few days in St Lo, the regiment next moved south, to the Vire River. By 5 August, only 22 days into the battle, the 134th Infantry had broken through the German lines. The company was transferred farther south near the Mortain area, where they came into contact with the SS Das Reich Division, a crack unit leading a desperate counter-attack against the threatened American breakout. After seven days

of constant fighting and pushing forward, the Germans were defeated, Mortain was liberated and the 134th became the spearhead of the right flank for Patton's Third Army.

Marshall remembers incidents from the advance through France: 'One morning we were near the River Moselle and it was raining. We were riding on tanks through an open field when suddenly we were attacked. I jumped off the tank and cowered behind it in a deep rut made by our tracks. The rut was about two feet deep – deep enough to give me shelter from the deadly flying shrapnel from bursting German shells. I lay there for some time. Then the shelling stopped. I heard a soldier approaching from behind. He

tried to remove my helmet and my rifle. He thought I was dead. I yelled, "I'm alive!"

Across the Blies River

'Early in December we crossed the Saar River in Lorraine and moved into the town of Saareguemines. By now the artillery was able to lob shells into Germany. On 12 December 1944 I crossed the small but fast-flowing and deep Blies River with half a dozen other soldiers from my Company in a boat because all the bridges were blown out. I do believe that in this action the 134th Infantry Division became the first Allied unit to move on to German soil, or at least soil that was considered German by Adolf Hitler.

'We occupied the first large house we came across, about 200 yards from the river, at around 8am. We found 12 German soldiers in the three-storey brick house; they surrendered. There was high ground right up ahead so we put a machine-gun group in front of the house to cover it. We mainly stayed in the basement throughout the day and my partner and I stood guard on the second floor from midnight. In the early hours of 13 December the Germans came

Above: Marshall Goldberg pictured before he shipped out for Europe in 1944.
Left: An American bazooka team watches a road near the German border wary of the approach of enemy armour.

over the hill and attacked us with panzerfaust (bazooka) rockets and an 88mm gun; a heavy shell crashed into the house and threw the pair of us into the hallway where we were showered with bricks. My partner had both eyes severely damaged. I was not so badly injured and began pulling bricks off him. By now the house was on fire and I told him we had to get away. The nearest door had been blown out and I began moving him to relative safety where his wounds could be treated. Unfortunately a German sniper must have been observing our movement for very quickly I received a bullet wound and collapsed to the floor.

Rockets and grenades

'I remained conscious and could hear the Germans yelling close by and the explosions of the grenades they were throwing into the basements and windows of neighbouring houses. I remained on the floor until our boys drove the Germans back. It was daylight before I was picked up and put on a stretcher. The first aid men wanted to take me back to the river along with many other soldiers wounded in the attack. However, even though a Red Cross flag was plainly visible, the Germans continued to throw shells at us. After two aborted attempts we finally made it across the river.

'I spent many weeks in hospital and was eventually sent back to England in the middle of January 1945 where I spent some time kicking my heels at a military warehouse somewhere in southern England. I did find time to visit members of my Mother's family in Towton, Yorkshire.

'Oddly enough, Towton in 1461 was the location of what is believed to have been the biggest and bloodiest battle ever fought on British soil. It occurred during the Wars of the Roses and up to 28,000 men died in the conflict, as many as one in a hundred of the population of England at the time.

'Eventually I returned to the US aboard the troopship liner *Queen Mary*.'

Above: A jeep passes a trailer carrying a rubber pontoon for a bridge for Patton's Third Army.

*Company C of the 135th Infantry Regiment was awarded a Distinguished Unit Citation for the action near Habkirchen, Germany, on 12–21 December 1944. According to the citation, after crossing the River Blies 'the unit then established a holding position and, during the course of the day, repulsed a number of enemy counterattacks,' with a 'marked exhibition of courage and determination after a three-hour period of fierce fighting, during the course of which engineers were able to establish a footbridge across the river'. Nine out of 10 of Company C soldiers sustained wounds in action in 1944-45.

1944 STAMP DUTY

I was very keen to learn Marshall's story not least because of his interest in stamps. Another of my contributors to *Seventy Years On*, Bernard Brind, is an avid stamp collector and has over 11,000 in albums in his Lewes, East Sussex, home. Some examples relevant to the Second World War are reproduced here. Bernard's story starts on page 150.

Marshall recounts an amusing tale concerning stamps: 'My brother ran our stamp business in Los Angeles while I was fighting overseas. French stamps were much in demand by collectors at the time because of the German Occupation so I sought examples to send home. Before each battle we were given K-rations, ammunition and cigarettes. Since I never smoked, one day I went into a store in a small town and offered to trade my cigarettes with the shop owner in return for French stamps. He willingly agreed.

Sugar Loaf Hill, Nancy

'My problem now was that I had to find a way to get my stamps back to the USA. I asked my lieutenant what would be the best way to get them to my brother. He said that if I mailed them they would most likely be confiscated and instead recommended that I carry them with me in my pack wrapped in paper and powder so they wouldn't stick together.

'We were riding tanks near the city of Nancy in October 1944. When we reached Sugar Loaf Hill (Pain du Sucre) the Germans counterattacked. All of us riding on the tanks jumped off and at once began digging slit trenches in the hillside. I was in such a hurry that I left my pack with my stamps on the tank. Everyone in my squad yelled out, 'Marshall! Get your

stamps! They'll be ruined!' I said, 'To Hell with the stamps, my life is more important!'

'I never recovered the stamps but here I am alive today in 2010 and still in the stamp business nearly seven decades later.'

Below: A poster urges US civilians to invest in War Bonds.

ZIG-ZAG

Tom Howard tells the extraordinary tale of Eddie Chapman, the only Englishman ever to be awarded Germany's highest military honour, the Iron Cross.

Above: *The de Havilland factory at Hatfield where Mosquito aircraft were built. Eddie Chapman (pictured left) was ordered by his German spymasters to sabotage the plant.*

The name of Eddie Chapman first came into my life in 1978. I was living in a house called Apes Hall in the pleasant fenland town of Littleport. One day, over a cup of tea, a neighbour, Bill Shaw, asked me if I'd heard about the German spy who'd parachuted into the grounds of Apes Hall during the war.

Bill continued: 'He wasn't actually a German, he was an English fellow, called Chapman, sort of a double agent. Funny thing, we never found his parachute.'

By now I was highly intrigued but frustrated because Bill couldn't tell me any more. It was many months later before the mysterious parachute man took on a less hazy identity. I saw a film called *Triple Cross* and in it Christopher Plummer starred as Eddie Chapman while Yul Brynner played his German spymaster.

Gradually I built up a clearer picture. Eddie Chapman was born in County Durham in November 1914. As a grown-up he moved to London. Eddie was self confident to the point of daring. I believe his cockney associates would have described him as 'having more front than Selfridges!' Times were hard, it was the Depression and Eddie was drawn to the criminal underworld. He formed the 'Jelly Gang' – a group of burglars whose speciality was blowing open safes with gelignite in Odeon cinemas.

Sought by the mainland police, Eddie fled to Jersey where he was caught while burgling a nightclub and sentenced to two years in Jersey Prison. He was still incarcerated when the Germans occupied the island in June 1940.

Sabotage an aircraft factory

The Germans interrogated him thoroughly in the course of which Eddie boldly convinced them that he had a grievance against the British authorities and that his only allegiance was to money. Very cheekily, he offered to work for the Nazis. Soon he was shipped to Germany for further interrogation and was given basic military training. Eddie was a quick learner and quickly picked up the language.

Desperate for agents, the Germans had decided that Chapman was an ideal candidate. Next he undertook intensive training in sabotage, wireless telegraphy and parachuting. His first mission was to carry out sabotage at the de Havilland aircraft factory near Hatfield in Hertfordshire. He was given a

> Eddie told me how he would rather be interrogated 50 times by the Germans than once by those British bastards from Oxford and Cambridge..

detailed escape route that would return him to Germany via neutral Portugal.

In October 1942 a fast Luftwaffe aircraft transported Eddie to England where he parachuted down near Wisbech in Lincolnshire. Upon landing he went straight to the police and was very soon in the hands of British Intelligence. As it happened, the British knew an agent was coming because they had already broken the German codes. Even so they were both surprised and suspicious when Eddie first told his story. They had a department that was expert at 'turning' German agents. It was named MI 20. This was in fact, not a number as such, but a pseudonym for the number in Roman numerals: XX – double cross. Although Eddie had 'turned' already, they still gave him a very hard time. Later he would tell me how he 'would rather be interrogated 50 times by the Germans than once by those bastards from Oxford and Cambridge!'

Agent codename 'Zig-Zag'

Finally, Eddie was designated as British agent 'Zig-Zag'. It was decided that the Germans must be made to believe that Eddie's mission was a success. The 'attack' on the de Havilland factory was one of the most remarkable deception operations of the Second World War. During the night of 29/30 January 1943, an elaborate system of camouflage was installed at the factory to make it appear to German reconnaissance aircraft that a very large bomb had exploded inside the factory's power plant. Bomb-damaged transformers were created out of wood and papier-mache, and buildings were disguised with tarpaulins and corrugated iron sheets painted to appear from the air as if they were the half-demolished remains of walls and roofs. Rubble and debris was spread around the power plant by an explosion. Separately, MI5 arranged for a fake story to be planted in the *Daily Express* reporting 'an explosion at a factory on the outskirts of London.'

The ruse was a complete success, even deceiving most of the factory's own staff. Chapman radioed the Germans to inform them of the successful 'demolition'. In March 1943 Eddie returned to Germany via Portugal and was de-briefed by his delighted German 'handlers'. For his exploit he was awarded the Iron Cross, the only Englishman to ever receive one. He was not to return to England on another mission until December 1944 when he parachuted down at Apes Hall.

Fast forward several decades. Life is full of strange coincidences and our lives sometimes cross other peoples' lives in an odd fashion. My friend from childhood, Elizabeth Ashley, was in the habit of going to health farms. One day she told me she'd found a place called Shenley Lodge in Hertfordshire and remarked that the boxer John Conteh trained there. She said it was more like to an army training camp than a beauty farm and the owner who took them in the gym for exercise was akin to a sergeant major. In a later conversation she told me the owner's name was Eddie Chapman and his wife was Betty. Just on a hunch I asked her to ask him if he was the real Zig-Zag. He was! He was also most interested to learn that I was residing at Apes Hall and he invited Lizzie and myself to meet him at Shenley Lodge.

Stream of Flying Bombs

Eddie was very forthcoming with facts about his remarkable story. For his second mission his brief was to monitor the accuracy of the V1 Flying Bombs and V2 Rockets falling on London and to report back their effect on public morale. The mission began at 2.30am on 16 December 1944 when Eddie took off from a Luftwaffe airfield in Holland in a fast fighter modified so that he could drop through an open 'trapdoor' in the fuselage floor at his feet. The aircraft flew in the midst of a major Flying Bomb attack and, at a given point, broke off and headed north over East Anglia. It did not escape detection, however, and was picked up by an RAF night-fighter not far from the planned drop zone. The aircraft climbed to gain height and at the same time flew an evasive pattern, desperately trying to shake off the attacker. The signal came to bale out and Eddie scrambled through the hole in the floor.

As he drifted down, Eddie was witness to a drama above as the British night-fighter pressed home its attack. He saw the aircraft he had just left burst into flames and plunge to earth,

> "The agent ended up in London once more where he was able to feed back to the Germans false information about the fall of their V-weapons... "

exploding in a fireball as it hit the ground. It is likely that the British plane was a Mosquito, ironically a product of de Havilland. Seconds later Eddie landed heavily on a narrow strip of hard road and suffered a severe wrench to the back from which he experienced problems for the rest of his life. He dumped his parachute by the side of the road and walked towards a big house he could vaguely make out in the gloom. This was Apes Hall.

His loud banging on the door brought the house to life; lights came on in windows and the door was opened by George Convine, the farm foreman, who asked 'what the hell was going on?'. Eddie was allowed in after he told him he was a British airman who had baled out. This was not disbelieved as his civilian clothes were covered up with a flying suit.

Mysterious and enigmatic man

Eddie told me that his everlasting memory of being in Apes Hall was of the three small daughters of George Convine sitting on the stairs and staring at him with wide eyes through the banisters. He asked George to call the police and soon three officers arrived. He remembered the policemen being large and the car being small and it being a somewhat cramped ride to Cambridge after they'd stopped to pick up his parachute.

Eventually he ended up in London again

where his British handlers instructed him to follow his German orders. For a few months, until all the launch sites were over-run by the Allies, he was able to feed back false information about the fall of the V-weapons in the hope that the Germans would misdirect them into open countryside rather than onto London.

I found Eddie Chapman to be a mysterious and enigmatic character who obviously enjoyed recounting his story. Parts of his life were shady but there is no doubt that his efforts after landing at Apes Hall saved lives. I lost contact with him in the Eighties and last saw him on a television show about the Costa del Sol or Costa del Crime as it was known for a while. He was talking about some of the notorious criminals he had known, including the Krays and 'Mad' Frankie Fraser.

Eddie Chapman died in 1997. MI5's files on him were released to the National Archives in 2001. By the time I knew Eddie, Bill Shaw had retired and I'd lost touch with him also, so I was never able to tell him what happened to the parachute.

* Tom Howard has written a book about Apes Hall in which he speculates on the origin of the house's name. He concluded that it came from the Latin word for an arched or curved configuration, Apse or Apsis, reflecting the site's location in a large arched bend of the Old Croft River, now dry. Tom lived in Apes Hall for 18 years; today he resides in Ireland.

Tottenham Grammar School's V2 Victims

Learning how Eddie Chapman had helped deflect the rain of V1 and V2 rockets was particularly poignant to me as I had been a schoolboy in London throughout the war, had suffered the Blitz of 1940-41 and had

A V-weapon victim is helped to safety.

been subjected to the Vengeance weapon attacks of 1944-45. Indeed I'd had school friends who'd been casualties of the Doodlebugs and two of my closest pals, Harry Poulten and Peter Goodman, were killed when a V2 missile fell about 50 yards away from our school in White Hart Lane, Tottenham, North London. They were both just 14. The incident happened at lunchtime on 15 March 1945 and another lad, Norman Burns, lost his arm. If it had come down half an hour later then a whole school year would have been walking by the impact site on their way to the school playing fields. Pupils helped the National Fire Service with clearing up and some Form 5 boys were commended for their rescue work in damaged houses opposite. Within two weeks of this incident the terror weapon assault ceased.

ALL DOWN TO LUCK

Don Feesey recalls some cruel twists and turns of fate for air crews.

In the last years of the war I was a navigator in a four-engined Lancaster bomber, following 24 months of concentrated training in classrooms and in the air taking in astro navigation, meteorology, armaments, photography, aircraft recognition and engines. To qualify required tough study.

There were seven airmen in a Lancaster crew – pilot, engineer, bomb-aimer, navigator, wireless operator, mid-upper gunner and rear gunner. Our squadron was located in a desolate part of North Lincolnshire, where the wintry weather of 1944/45 consisted of frequent fogs, frost and snow. It all added to the strain of the constant night operations over Germany. For navigators there was a great deal of pre-flight preparation to be done, and often these efforts were wasted when a raid was 'scrubbed' at the last minute due to weather conditions locally or over Germany.

Once in the air, the navigator was constantly checking the aircraft's position, revising the wind speeds and direction and changing course and air speed in order to be at the various turning points and at the target on time. There was no visual navigation as we flew in darkness and usually in dense cloud. Oh – and it was cold. On one occasion, I poured hot tea from my thermos into my plastic cup, which split open with the temperature at minus 40ºC. The tea immediately froze to my maps preventing me from plotting courses or winds and it also froze to my lap and thighs.

Our crew completed 311 operations. We were the lucky ones as enemy night fighters, searchlights and flak were terrifying and many new crews on the squadron perished due to bad luck or inexperience early on. Once, all four of our engines packed up and the pilot gave the order 'abandon aircraft'. We had been losing height for some time and now we were falling rapidly. The pilot and I were the last to leave and as I was preparing to fall through the hatch by the pilot's feet I felt him pulling at my shoulder. I guessed that he was probably caught up somewhere and needed my help to get free. I went back, fearing that we were then so low that we should both die when the plane crashed. It transpired that an engine had come back to life and he wanted me to help him fly back to England.

We kept losing height and over the Channel we were only just above the waves and lower than the cliffs ahead. I had been desperately operating the throttles and petrol cocks and miraculously a second engine burst into life and we were able to clear the cliffs and make an emergency landing at Manston near Margate.

By April 1945 we had nearly completed our tour of 30 operations. So too, had our Flight Commander and his crew and they finished before us. The navigator had been at school with me in the 1930s. He was married and his pregnant wife came up to stay in the local pub to celebrate the end of the crew's tour. Within a day or two the length of a tour was raised to 32 and although the Flight Commander had officially completed he elected to do the extra two. At the briefing for the 32nd, the air gunners were warned to be particularly vigilant as the bomb aimer's wife was also pregnant and due to give birth that night. It would never do to shoot down the stork! Sadly the plane was shot down and all the crew died. The joy of the poor girl at the pub was cruelly destroyed and two new babies were to be fatherless.

Survival or death on each raid was just down to luck.

WAR DIARY
November 1944

The beginning of **November 1944** sees fuel shortages bringing the advance of General Patton's Third Army to a virtual standstill along the Moselle River. In the Vosges Mountains on the Franco-German border north of Switzerland, the French First Army is closing on Strasbourg.

2 November: The Eighth Army's main enemy is now the Italian winter. Since July they have sustained over 20,000 casualties and every infantry battalion has required reorganisation. Around 400 tanks have been lost in action or simply worn out.

3 November: The Allies finally secure both sides of the Scheldt Estuary. Canadian troops on the south bank take the surrender of 12,500 Germans around the town of Breskens. Within a few hours minesweepers will begin clearing the waterway to the vital port of Antwerp.

On **4 November** the Russians are halted 40 miles from Budapest by a combination of rain, extended supply lines and stiffening German resistance.

The following day Zionist extremists demanding a Jewish homeland in Palestine assassinate Lord Moyne, British Minister-Resident in the Middle East, outside his home in Cairo.

6 November: The town of Middleburg in the centre of Walcheren island is liberated.

Tokyo **7 November:** The spy Richard Sorge is executed in Sugamo prison. Over a period of eight years, Sorge supplied the Kremlin with secret Axis political and military plans. His greatest coup was assuring Stalin that the Japanese had no plans to attack the USSR. Stalin was able to move large numbers of troops from the Far East to join the fight against Hitler.

On **8 November** the famous German air ace Major Walter Nowotny dies when his Me262 jet fighter crashes. He was credited with 258 'kills' made mainly on the Eastern Front.

9 November: Patton's Third Army crosses the Moselle on a broad front and is heading for the German border just a few miles away.

10 November: In Poland a Red Cross party has been allowed access to the concentration camp of Auschwitz-Birkenau. The camp authorities carefully conceal areas where mass murder has been turned into a production line industry.

Winston Churchill is in Paris for the Armistice Day celebrations **(11 November)** and is buoyed up by the warm welcome from the populace.

On **12 November** in Norway the biggest single menace to Allied shipping in northern waters is eliminated when the *Tirpitz* is sunk by 12,000lb 'Tallboy' bombs in a raid by 30 Lancasters.

13 November: In Yugoslavia the *Wehrmacht* have pulled out of Skopje, site of their headquarters for the southern province of Macedonia.

French Alps **14 November:** Air Chief Marshall Sir Trafford Leigh-Mallory and his wife die in an air crash en route to Ceylon.

15 November: A general strike by workers is underway in Turin and attacks by Italian partisans fighters are increasing.

16 November: Antwerp has become a major target for Hitler's V-Weapons. Ten flying bombs crashed down onto the streets and houses today, killing 263 civilians.

On **17 November** the last few Germans in the Albanian capital, Tirana, surrender as the city awaits the arrival of Communist Partisan leader Enver Hoxha.

19 November: During an air raid on the bridge at Venlo on the Dutch-German border an RAF Mitchell bomber is hit by flak causing the tail-plane and turret to break off. Inside it the rear gunner, Warrant Officer Cote, a French Canadian, 'fluttered down to earth like a leaf', and miraculously suffered no worse injury than a broken leg. He is made a PoW.

The US Treasury estimates that waging world war is costing the country $250m for each day of conflict.

20 November: After five years, the blackout ends tonight with the switching on of streetlights in Piccadilly and the Strand and various other thoroughfares and squares in the capital.

21 November: In Italy General Alexander stands the Allied armies down for the winter. Air sorties, artillery duels and fighting patrols will be the pattern of the war here until the spring.

22 November: Today the men of Patton's Third Army liberate the ancient capital of Alsace-Lorraine, Metz.

23 November: In a surprise attack, Free French troops, under the command of Generals Leclerc and de Lattre, enter Strasbourg today. Around 3000 Germans are captured whilst many more hastily retreat across the Rhine.

On **24 November** American B-29 Superfortresses out of Saipan bomb Tokyo in daylight for the first time. Just 24 out of 111 participating aircraft found the target.

The following day a V2 rocket brings carnage to New Cross Road in South London when it crashes down on a busy Woolworth's store killing 160 people and injuring 135 others.

26 November: General Sir Harold Alexander, top Allied commander in Italy, is promoted to Field Marshal. The appointment has been backdated to 4 June so that he is now technically senior in rank to Montgomery.

27 November: A German ship sailing from Norway is sunk by British aircraft from the Fleet Air Arm. Unknown to the airmen, the vessel was transporting 2248 Russian prisoners. Just 415 survive.

28 November: The first Allied convoy will dock in the port of Antwerp today. Supplies can now be landed within 60 miles of the British forces facing the Germans along the River Maas.

29 November: A US submarine torpedoes Japan's 'unsinkable' aircraft carrier, *Shinano*, in the Kumano Sea off Japan.

RAF bombers are in action in the early hours of **30 November** over Dortmund. UK munitions factories are finding it hard to keep up with the demand for bombs to smash the Nazi war machine.

In 1944 the Allies ran an air transport service from India to China in support of the Chinese forces fighting the Japanese. There were also a number of US airfields on Chinese territory. The supply flights had to cross the Himalayan Mountains - known as 'The Hump' to the pilots. For loading and unloading the aircraft, elephants were found to be faster and more efficient than men. Here an elephant loads 55-gallon drums of petrol from a truck to a C-46 in India.

Flying Start to Life

I was just 10 when war broke out in 1939. As a youngster in Fairfield, Buxton, 1000 feet up in the Peak District of Derbyshire and seemingly far from any action, I found to my excitement that all sorts of new things were going on.

All manner of interesting equipment appeared in print and for real; strange new shapes in the skies and lots of activity on the ground. I remember a Tiger Moth flying overhead with a somewhat spluttering engine. It appeared to be approaching Combs Edge, the top of which was higher than the plane was flying! Its engine spluttered and stopped and the craft started to glide down steeply and disappeared.

I grabbed my bike and took off helter skelter until I ran out of track, abandoned my steed and hot-footed it over gates, walls and rough grass until I could just see the top of a yellow wing beyond a stone wall – success! In my mind I was already telling my friends about how I had been the first on the scene and had rescued a dazed pilot from the wreckage of his aircraft when, to my dismay, I saw a policeman standing importantly beside the apparently undamaged fuselage embedded in the bog with no pilot to be seen. How he got there so quickly I never knew. I was told in no uncertain terms to scarper. Deflation!

Parade twice weekly

I soon joined the Buxton College Air Training Corps № 1504 Squadron and proudly paraded twice weekly in my smart new uniform. I was learning how to be an airman, especially on how to recognise aircraft from all angles. It was exciting to watch a Westland Lysander cruising slowly over the town so that the anti-aircraft troops could practice aiming at it – no real ammunition allowed.

Once I saw something I could not identify, flying not too far away, near Loughborough. It looked like a Boston, but was much more angular. I quickly sketched it. That evening two Observer Corps men gave the ATC a lecture on aircraft recognition. After it finished I produced my sketch and asked one of the men for help identifying it. He whispered, 'I'll get shot if someone finds out, because it's still on the secret list; but I'll tell you if you promise to keep quiet.' I had seen my first Douglas Invader.

I had a collection of model aircraft, all built to a 1:72nd scale, constructed from bits of scrounged wood and cellophane – the wheels and dope [paint] were the only bits that I bought. When building them I referred constantly to my most treasured possessions; the *Aircraft of the Fighting Powers* volumes published annually throughout the war.

Wings for Victory Week

One year I was invited by local toy shop, Elliots, to produce a window display to mark the Wings for Victory Week (a week every year when people were encouraged to save funds to help the war effort). It was of a British airfield and overhead was a Heinkel 111 falling steeply with a tuft of pink cotton wool tinged with red and black at the rear of an engine, closely followed by a Westland Whirlwind which had shot it down. A crew member was descending by parachute.

I had suspended 140-odd home-made black silhouette-sized models of aircraft at various angles from my bedroom ceiling, so that I could memorise them at all angles. When my cousin Ronald came to stay we lay in bed and tried to shoot the aircraft down with dried peas.

Another year it was the turn of the Army to benefit from a savings campaign, and a local playing field was used for a demonstration by the Parachute Regiment. They had some tiny motor bikes for dropping from aircraft and we youngsters were allowed to sit on them. When my turn came my friend said, 'bet you can't start it!' What a challenge! I zoomed towards the audience, but mercifully a burly paratrooper grabbed hold of me before I hit anyone.

Spot them in the Air! PUBLISHED BY THE DAILY MIRROR 3D 3D

Later we ATC Cadets were treated to our first weekend camp at RAF Ashbourne, an airfield just south of Buxton. We were promised our first flight – in an Anson. However, as it was a few days after D-Day every available flying machine was being used to carry supplies to the south of England and beyond so you can imagine our disappointment.

In the summer of 1945 our camp was at RAF Syerston between Newark and Leicester, a Lancaster base where we did indeed achieve our first flight (mother had bravely signed the 'blood chit' allowing her plane-mad – and only child – to fly with the RAF). I will never forget being strapped in to the mid-upper turret of a real Lancaster complete with guns; I can still see the runway dropping away below us. We set off westwards at a few hundred feet altitude and saw the familiar ground of Dovedale guarded by Thorpe Cloud where the river turned west, and the famous stepping stones where we had often crossed the river.

We traversed Cardigan Bay and flew out into the Irish Sea. Our mission was to carry 'weeping' bombs, too dangerous to transport by land, and dump them into the sea where they were deemed to be out of harm's way. Imagine that today; the RAF taking schoolchildren on a low-level flight with unstable explosives on board. Thank goodness mother knew nothing of this. After dropping our dangerous cargo the co-pilot reported that one of the bombs had exploded as it entered the water, a fair measure of the instability of the contents.

Aircraft awaiting disposal

The following year the camp was again at Syerston, but by then it had become a Dakota station, stacked with unwanted aircraft awaiting disposal. One day we were flown to RAF Silloth on the Solway coast where dozens of old Dakotas were lined up prior to dismantling. On board on the return journey were the crews of several now-dumped Dakotas, who were returning to Syerston.

The following day, the end of our camp, we were all flown in a Dakota to Ringway (now Manchester Airport) so that we could be driven home, whilst some of our ATC flight who lived nearer to Syerston than Ringway were to be returned to Syerston by plane. We sat at Ringway in a bus, waiting until our chums took off before departing ourselves. However, to our horror just after the Dakota became airborne one engine cut out and the pilot made a split-second decision to abort the take-off and came to an abrupt stop off the end of the runway. Our hearts were in our mouths at seeing the near demise of our chums but, thankfully, all ended well.

Even in Northern England later in the war we too were subjected to bombardment by V1s. They were air-launched over the North Sea from Heinkel 111 bombers. We heard and saw several going overhead on Boxing Day night 1944 and, although we were 25 miles from Manchester, we heard one engine cut out followed by the crump as it crashed harmlessly on the moors just to our west – obviously filled with too little fuel or released much too early.

To a schoolboy the war was an interesting and exciting time, although it was badly tinged in the early days by the knowledge that my favourite woodwork teacher had been killed in North Africa, not by enemy action but in a road accident.

The war, even to a youngster, had its ghastly side.
Laurence Draper

WAR DIARY
December 1944

By **1 December** most of the Western Front is now situated on the territory of the Reich. Patton's Third Army has moved up to the main German defensive line along the Saar River.

Laurence Olivier's *Henry V* is drawing huge audiences in the West End even though the critics have not been universal in their praise of Shakespeare on celluloid.

2 December: General de Gaulle is in Moscow for talks with Stalin. The French leader is keen to re-establish his country's political role as a major power.

On **3 December** Home Guard units from all over the country held a final parade in the centre of London, marching past King George who was giving their farewell salute.

4 December: In a rare winter attack, the Eighth Army makes a forward movement into Ravenna on Italy's Adriatic coast.

5 December: All German women over 18 are asked to volunteer as auxiliaries for the armed forces in order to free up men for front line duty. Reich women's leader Gertrud Scholtz-Klink makes the appeal.

Queen Elizabeth singles out the women of Britain for praise in a speech on **6 December,** citing their war work as a major factor in making possible the Allied victories to date.

The following day US forces extend their grip on the Philippines with successful landings at Ormoc Bay on Leyte in the face of *Kamikaze* air attacks.

8 December: US warships and aircraft are targeting a new 'stepping stone' to the Japanese homeland. Iwo Jima – halfway between the Marianas and Japan – is to be invaded.

Hungary - **9 December:** The Red Army has penetrated to the banks of the Danube north of Budapest where the city garrison is preparing for a siege.

10 December: In a superb feat of engineering, men of General Slim's Fourteenth Army in Burma have built the world's largest Bailey Bridge. At 1154ft, the structure spans the Chindwin River.

On **11 December,** senior German officers are shocked at Hitler's exhausted appearance and uncontrollable trembling as he unveils plans for a surprise offensive out of the Belgian Ardennes.

12 December: After a remarkable four month voyage half-way around the world, a German transport U-Boat has reached the Japanese-held port of Djakarta in the East Indies. The crew are stretching their legs on dry land for the first time since sailing from besieged Bordeaux in late August.

13 December: Kamikaze attacks in the Philippines damage a US destroyer and the cruiser *Nashville*. Nature too, adds to the toll when a tropical storm producing 75-foot waves sinks three destroyers with the loss of 719 men.

London - **14 December:** Post-war planning for the capital is aired with the publication of the Greater London Plan which supports the creation of a 'green belt' around the city and the setting up of 10 new towns to absorb the expected population boom.

15 December: In the thick Ardennes forests the *Wehrmacht* have secretly assembled a large army including hundreds of panzers and a vast array of artillery.

16 December: Just before dawn sees the start of the Ardennes Offensive. The Allies are caught by complete surprise as strong German forces erupt out of the forest heading west.

Antwerp is the ultimate goal of the attack. Today that city is the target of a V2 rocket that falls on a packed cinema, killing 567 people including 296 Allied servicemen and women.

In Athens fighting continues in the area of the Acropolis between British paratroopers and communist ELAS rebels.

17 December: A top secret US unit at Wendover Air Force base, Utah, continues training flights over the Great Salt Lake. The airmen know only that they will most likely eventually be dropping a bomb of exceptional power on a target in Japan.

Belgium: 125 captured GIs have been massacred by SS troops under the command of Lt-Col Joachim Peiper near the town of Malmedy.

18 December: In the Baltic, RAF bombers sink eight enemy ships and damage a ninth. The vessels were carrying German evacuees from East Prussia - thousands of civilians die.

19 December: Panic over German infiltration behind the Allied lines spreads as far to the rear as Eisenhower's Versailles HQ where the Supreme Allied Commander is confined to his office.

In the Schnee Eifel area of the Ardennes, 6000 American soldiers are surrendering to encircling German forces.

Next day **(20 December)** the Germans reach the important crossroads town of Bastogne and begin to surround the American 101st Airborne and 10th Armoured Divisions.

21 December: Snow is falling over large parts of the Ardennes as bad weather keeps the powerful Allied air forces grounded.

22 December: Britain's Home Front war effort is being aided by the efforts of carefully selected German POWs who are being paid up to six shillings a week to dig potatoes and harvest sugar-beet.

23 December: German forces together with two Italian Divisions still loyal to Mussolini launch a surprise counter-attack in the direction of Pisa and the port of Leghorn on Italy's north west coast as Allied aircraft are grounded by bad weather.

24 December: A swarm of doodlebugs are launched in mid-air from modified Heinkel bombers over the North Sea. Just 17 out of 31 of the V1 weapons reach their Manchester target, killing 32 civilians and injuring 49 others.

Clearing skies over the Ardennes allows the Allied air forces to decisively intervene in the Battle of the Bulge. For the Luftwaffe, Arado 234 'Blitz' jet bombers make two successful raids on rail yards at Liege.

25 December: British units are helping contain the Germans in the 'Bulge'. Near Neuville in Belgium, 'A' Squadron 23rd Hussars, enjoy a Christmas dinner consisting of 'iced bully beef and frozen cheese sandwiches'.

26 December: German Field Marshal Gerd von Rundstedt responds to the Fuhrer's refusal to call off the Ardennes Offensive with the remark, 'This is Stalingrad Number Two'.

27 December: Winston Churchill has spent Christmas in the Greek capital trying to broker a ceasefire in the civil war. In one incident when ELAS sniper fire hit the British Embassy whilst Churchill was inside, the statesman exclaimed, 'Cheek!'.

28 December: Bastogne is the focus of renewed attacks by the encircling German forces.

29 December: The Russian-sponsored Committee of National Liberation in Lublin has declared itself to be the Provisional Government of Poland. Free Poles in London protest that the Lublin move is illegal.

30 December: Newspapers report on a domestic fuel crisis predicted to last until at least the end of February 1945. Mainly caused by the very cold weather, consumers are warned they 'must cut down or be cut out'. Ironically, it has only been six weeks since the blackout rules were relaxed.

On **New Year's Eve** 1944, the British inhabitants of the Channel Islands are about to enter a fifth year under Nazi Occupation. The Allies are reluctant to bomb or invade because of the risk to civilians. Besides which, the islands have been turned into formidable fortresses bristling with concrete gun emplacements. With food in short supply, Christmas was a cheerless time and with the news of the Ardennes Offensive, the islanders must wonder whether deliverance will ever come. The very first Red Cross supply ship, the *Vega*, from Portugal has just arrived.

STAND DOWN

DAD *Bless him!*

EYE WITNESS

Cyril Beavor represented C Company, 46th West Riding Battalion, in the last parade of the Home Guard before the King in London on 3 December 1944. Here are his memories of the occasion.

I was on the 'Stand Down' parade of the Home Guard on 3 December 1944 and remember it well. My role was as representative of the 46th West Riding Battalion of the King's Own Yorkshire Light Infantry and I had been given the honour of 'Private most worthy of the honour of representing the Battalion.'

At least that is what it said in the letter I received from its Adjutant. The Battalion had been given a quota of one Second Lieutenant, one Lower Corporal and one Private. We, at least, had decided that the personnel to be duly honoured to parade in the capital in front of a crowd of many thousands should be chosen from men of existing ranks. However, I later met men on the parade who had been demoted from officer rank to private, just so they could have a place in history!

Each company made its recommendations to a committee of senior officers. I was told by my Company Commander that the choice of Private had finally come down to one of two men. I was one and the other was a man well known to like his liquor. I learned later that what tipped the balance in my favour was my being teetotal; I was therefore unlikely to besmirch the honour of the regiment, whereas the other private was very likely to get drunk if let loose in London.

Three events during the parade itself stick out in my memory. The first was that we did not know who would take the salute, so it was a surprise when on the command 'eyes left' for the salute I saw that the King himself was taking it and that he was accompanied by the Queen and the two Princesses. I am not an ardent royalist but my step certainly became lighter.

The second memory was of nearly losing my footing on wet wooden flooring laid down, I believe, near Piccadilly Circus. The third was the wheeling column receiving the sharp edge of a Regular Sergeant of the Guard's tongue, as it drifted out of line.

I recall while I was in London that I slept two nights in the cavalry barracks in Knightsbridge and heard at least one V2 rocket land.

In the evening of the parade there was a concert in the Albert Hall for which I was lucky enough to get a seat.

The concert cast included Tommy Trinder, Vera Lynn and Cicely Courtnedge. I was right up in the back row of the 'gods'.

On the printed programme was a poem written by a member of the Home Guard who had heard the news that a German General had just inspected a parade of the Volkssturm, the German Home Guard. It was reported that his car had driven up, he had got out, taken one look at the men on parade and promptly suffered a nervous breakdown!

Above: Private Cyril John Beavor in 1944.

Left: Cyril's copy of the 'Stand Down' Concert Souvenir Programme is reproduced here.

Below: The Doncaster Sector Detachment about to entrain for London at Doncaster Station on 2 December 1944. Private Beavor is fourth from the right.

SOUVENIR of the HOME GUARD STAND DOWN CONCERT

Given by the DAILY MAIL, SUNDAY DISPATCH AND LONDON EVENING NEWS

at THE ROYAL ALBERT HALL DEC. 3rd, 1944

Manager : C. S. TAYLOR

Glenn Miller's last waltz

Left: Mrs Sibyl Windsor pictured in wartime and as she is today. Sibyl danced with Major Glenn Miller (on trombone) shortly before his aircraft was lost somewhere over the English Channel in December 1944.

Ron McGill reveals a little piece of musical history concerning the famous Bandleader and a Hertfordshire lass.

It is strange sometimes when conversations between friends suddenly unearth nuggets of information that have never been mentioned before. I was visiting Corfe Castle in Dorset to see Mrs Sibyl Windsor, a dear friend and a well known lady in the community life and activities of Corfe Castle.

Sibyl, now a bright and bubbly lady in her early 80s, had seen a feature about Major Glenn Miller that commented on the sad loss of this legend in December 1944. Her eyes brightened (even twinkled) as she said, 'Do you know, I was the last girl to dance with Glenn Miller before he was lost.'

To say there was a stunned silence is an understatement and, of course, we all wanted to know more – it was a bit like the popular song in the 1940s: 'That I had danced with a man who had danced with a girl who had danced with the Prince of Wales.'

Our dear Sibyl explained that

Major Glenn Miller was 40 years old in 1944 and a hugely successful bandleader. He joined the US Army to 'put a little more spring into the step of marching men'. His timeless hits include Moonlight Serenade *and* Chattanooga Choo Choo.

she had become a WAAF during the war and in late 1942 had qualified as a fully fledged Signals Officer after intensive training in the West Country. In 1944, with her mother seriously ill, she had been released on compassionate home leave to nurse her mother at their home in Hitchin, in Hertfordshire.

Towards the end of 1944 one of the Hitchin ladies took it upon herself to 'round up' the local girls, make sure they wore civilian dresses etc and then coach them off to the Squadron dance nights in the area, usually to Bassingbourn or Alconbury where they invariably had a great time dancing with the US aircrews.

By this time the V1 Doodlebug attacks on London and the South East were quite devastating and Glenn Miller and his group had moved out from 25 Sloane Street in London to a location in Bedford. This move was more than timely as a V1 did strike their original billet the very next day with, sadly, extensive loss of life.

Miller's magical sound

Major Miller was determined to play as much as he could and made many air base visits as well as performed concerts in popular venues. His last public performance was at the Queensbury Hall All Services Club in Old Compton Street in London's West End before returning to Bedford. It seems he made a few more 'Orchestra Stops' for Squadrons in that area and that is where our dear Sibyl's path crossed with Glenn Miller.

Sibyl believes that this time they were

coached off to Bassingbourn for the usual lively night of wonderful music in a crowded hangar. The evening drew to a close and what a surprise for Sibyl when Glenn announced to the crowd that it was time for the last waltz; he stepped purposefully down from the stage and, from the bevy of Hitchin beauties, selected Sibyl for his dance partner. She remembers she was in a daze, quite overwhelmed with the charm of this tall languid Bandleader and she floated round in his arms knowing full well that the eyes of all the Hitchin beauties were watching her in obvious envy.

The dance ended and the orchestra closed the proceedings with Glenn politely returning her to her friends – drawling his thanks for a nice ending to the evening.

As we all know, this story then took a very poignant turn indeed with the wretched news that Glenn Miller's aircraft went missing. It had taken off from the Twinwood Farm, Bedford, airbase on 15 December 1944 bound for Paris but was lost somewhere over the English Channel. Down the years there has been much speculation surrounding the sad loss of this popular musician and well loved personality. The most likely scenario is that his aircraft flew beneath a returning Allied bomber fleet that had been unable to identify their target on the German-occupied European mainland that night. As was common practice in such circumstances they jettisoned their bombs into the sea and one of these bombs struck Glenn Miller's aircraft.

Clearly our dear friend Sibyl Windsor has her own special niche in the history of the Second World War.

UNFORGETTABLE

J Jenkins shares memories of wartime in far-flung places.

March 1942: After training as a wireless mechanic in the RAF, I embarked with about 3000 other men on the Belgian ship *Leopoldville*. The convoy assembled off Gourock and I recall one of the other ships as the *Arbosso*. Conditions were cramped with hammocks slung jammed together. Later in the hot latitudes the foetid atmosphere became unbearable, making it imperative to find a bed space out in the open decks, crowded though they were.

We made it undamaged to Freetown, Sierra Leone, from where we sailed unaccompanied to Capetown. This was Paradise! I was entertained by a middle-aged couple who lived in an opulent house on the lower slopes of Table Mountain. Unfortunately, the idyll had to end and all too soon it was back at sea again for a fast solo run up the east coast of Africa to Egypt on the *Niew Amsterdam*, a large Dutch liner. Once in Egypt I was posted to Aden and so it wasn't long before I was re-tracing my passage back south down the Red Sea, a comfortable trip on a ship carrying a large number of Italian POWs who foregathered each evening and sang excerpts from various operas.

East and West Link

Unfortunately for me, my destination was not the well established and well endowed Aden HQ, but was a tiny unit out on the lonely isthmus connecting the base to the mainland. My new home consisted of a couple of parallel bungalow buildings, one housing the technical staff of about a dozen men, the other the sergeant in charge, the cook and the cookhouse. Transport amounted to a single open three ton truck and a driver. About a quarter of a mile away across the sand was the purpose of the unit's existence. A three foot thick stone wall surrounded a half buried wholly enclosed building, which housed the transmitting hall and associated workshop. About a dozen large transmitters were ranged around the hall. Their purpose was to transmit signals sent by landline from Aden HQ on one side and RAF Khormaksar on the mainland on the other side. The function of the staff was to attend these transmitters 24 hours a day, re-tuning and repairing as necessary. The station worked Karachi in India (now Pakistan) on one side and Asmara in Eritrea and Cairo in Egypt on the other, making a link between East and West. On one occasion, sleepily re-tuning a transmitter in the middle

of the night, I didn't follow the proper procedure and was knocked unconscious with 3500 volts across the chest.

I left Aden in April 1943 for another trip up the Red Sea to a unit near Haifa in what was then Palestine. We were ordered to take a Commando training course, soon learning that it was in preparation for the invasion of Sicily. For a few weeks it was all cross country runs, physical jerks, bayonet charges and other toughening up exercises. The pervading smell of orange blossom in the fresh springtime air was a compensation and I had some evenings off in Haifa and also visited Nazareth before the powers that were decided we would be better employed on the technical jobs we were trained for. So then it was back across the Sinai wilderness and into Egypt, a journey illuminated by a silvery moon.

I was next kept busy preparing 15cwt vans housing radio gear. These vehicles were allegedly waterproofed to enable them to ascend a beach covered by two or three feet of water, but I doubted whether they would stand the strain. I never did find out if they could because I was posted off the unit and never got to Sicily. Instead I kicked my heels for some months in a transit camp near Helwan, south of Cairo. The compensations here were a visit to the Pyramids and a

number of trips into Cairo where there were various forms of entertainment. The camp was on the edge of the desert but it might as well have been in the middle of it given the heat, the flies and the sandstorms.

A curious phenomenon I noticed was that any individual or group walking across a wide, empty stretch of sand would start off in the right direction, but would slowly veer round, always clockwise, until they were walking at right angles to the route they should have been taking. Whenever this was pointed out to them they expressed surprised. I'm sure this natural human tendency must account for many people getting lost in the desert.

Tour of Pompeii

After an eternity of waiting, in March 1944 I was very relieved to be posted to a unit on the Adriatic coast of Italy, a new establishment conducting operations over Yugoslavia in support of Tito's partisans battling the occupying Germans. Our transmitters were housed in cabins mounted on the backs of trucks parked at a distance from the living quarters and the metal airstrip laid down like a carpet. Leave allowed me to visit Sorrento from where I went on a tour of Pompei – doubtless escorted by the same guides who had earlier showed German soldiers around – and I also

EVE OF DESTRUCTION

J Jenkins (story above) opens with his sailing off to war on the Belgian troopship *Leopoldville*. Nearly three years later, on Christmas Eve 1944, the same vessel was torpedoed and sunk by a U-Boat just a few miles off the port of Cherbourg. As a result nearly 800 US soldiers drowned in the freezing cold waters of the English Channel.

German submarines had not made much impression in hindering the vast naval and merchant ship traffic between British ports and Normandy in the months following D-Day. RAF Coastal Command and the British and US navies were vigilant and increasingly successful in steadily reducing the number of enemy U-Boats in the Western Approaches.

Few dared come close to the shore. An exception occurred on that fateful Christmas Eve. The US 66th Infantry Division – 'The Black Panthers' – were on their way to back up the Allied forces engaged in the Battle of the Bulge. The only vessel available to

transport them was the *Leopoldville*, not the fastest or most modern of ships. She was still crewed by Belgians.

It was early evening at 5.45pm about six miles away from Cherbourg and the safety of land when the torpedo struck. The *Leopoldville* began to sink quite slowly at first. Though the soldiers lined up on deck it appears that no orders were initially forthcoming to take to the boats. Nor had any lifeboat drill been held prior to sailing. By the time it became clear that they would have to abandon ship the men found that many of the lifeboats had fitments that were rusty and impossible to move.

The destroyer *HMS Brilliant* came alongside and soldiers began leaping from one ship to the other. Many fell into the sea. Thousands of men were rescued but almost 800 perished.

To this day there is no reference to this disaster either in the Royal Navy history or in US military records.

wandered through the streets of Naples where the Black Market was rife. Later in Rome I had another guided tour round a virtually empty Vatican – a very different experience from when I visited it years afterwards as a holidaymaker, when the madding crowd destroyed all the beauties of the place. I attended an audience given by the Pope, but did not join those who went up to receive the Papal blessing. My final spell out of camp was on a course in the beautiful baroque town of Lecce, in the south, where it was delight enough just to wander round the streets.

The winter of 1944-45 was bitterly cold. Tents collapsed under the weight of snow and the wooden boards which made our improvised beds developed a tendency to float out of the tent. Gumboots did nothing to keep feet warm in the icy slush. It was best to go on the overnight shift well flushed with wine, which we tended to try to consume in the quantities in which we had swigged beer in North Africa, usually with disastrous results. I recall one of the big five ton trucks sank up to its haunches in the mud.

Strange aircraft

Early in 1945 I was posted to Malta and switched from working on heavy ground-based transmitters to those on aircraft of great variety. Malta was an important staging post between Europe and the Middle and Far East. It was common to go on duty in the evening and be faced with up to 40 aeroplanes requiring servicing by morning. I remember one time when a very large aircraft appeared over the airfield of a type no one on the ground had seen before. It was an American Skymaster, one of the ambitiously large experimental aeroplanes that were being produced at that time, post-war soon to be overtaken by jet propelled airliners. The buzz went round that it was stopping only to refuel. Sighs of relief all round. But when it finally came to a halt, a head popped out of a window up in the lofty fuselage and an American voice called out: 'Any wireless people down there?' Thus I was faced with a repair job in a totally strange aircraft, a task I accomplished in fear and trembling lest I should do something wrong and flop the Colossus down on its belly or something equally dire.

Off duty, Malta had considerable compensations. At that time, long before the island was covered in holiday hotels, there were many beauty spots, wonderful swimming and animated life to enjoy. The war ended in the summer of 1945 but for me duty and leisure on Malta went on in the same way until October when my tour of duty abroad came to an end and I returned home. I was demobbed in June 1946, going with that sense of being cast adrift in an unknown world. I suppose it was a common experience. Looking back, I had a safe and a relatively comfortable war but it remains an unforgettable episode in my life.

BATTLE OF THE BULGE

Hitler's last gamble with a major offensive in the West meets with initial success but ultimate failure in the face of stubborn Allied resistance.

On the foggy and wintry dawn of 16 December 1944, in the rugged and heavily forested Belgian Ardennes region, Hitler began a massive gamble that hinged on history repeating itself. For it was from this same area in 1940 that he launched his Blitzkrieg on the West, a campaign that crushed the armies of France, Belgium and Holland in a matter of weeks and had bundled the British Expeditionary Force in total disarray off the bomb blasted beaches of Dunkirk by the beginning of June.

Now the Fuhrer was determined to make it happen again. Against all Allied expectations he'd succeeded in putting together a mighty new Panzer army with orders to break through the lightly-held Ardennes front, cross the River Meuse and drive for Antwerp, splitting the British and American forces asunder in the process. Backing the assault would be a rain of V1 flying bombs and V2 rockets directed against London and Antwerp, the latter a vital supply port for the Allies.

The German units included seasoned, crack troops, equipped with powerful tanks and the latest weaponry. In the skies, pilots of the new jet fighters were confident they would soon win back air superiority for the Luftwaffe.

Earlier triumph

But now it was a vastly different Europe, over four years on from the earlier triumph of German arms. Vast Allied armies and air forces were encamped before the German line of defence that stretched from the North Sea to the Swiss frontier. From positions in Holland, Belgium and France they were poised to roll over Germany's last bastions before the Rhine – the fortifications of the Siegfried Line. Around Aachen, the Americans had already breached this Westwall and were fighting on German soil.

Yet the Allies couldn't be strong everywhere and the inhospitable Ardennes was one part of the Allied line where their forces were spread thinly. Ironically, though the Germans did not know it, the Ardennes was also the main storage area for the Allied fuel supplies for the Western Front; fuel was a commodity the Wehrmacht was desperately short of. Indeed, the panzers would run dry within days of the offensive starting unless they could capture large quantities.

In places green and inexperienced American units reacted in bewilderment and confusion to the surprise assault by panzers and infantry erupting out of the quiet forests. But in key sectors, the Americans recovered quickly and stubbornly held their ground. The attack by Sixth Panzer Army was the first to be blunted as, in the centre, Fifth Panzer Army made the greatest progress but at the critical price of leaving the town of Bastogne in the hands of the US 101st Airborne Division and a scratch force of defenders.

Bastogne beseiged

Glaring newspaper headlines in Britain and America stirred up much public apprehension but there was much less alarm amongst the Allied fighting troops. Eisenhower, Montgomery and the other Allied commanders reacted coolly and efficiently in the face of initial confusion and rumour. The Germans soon found themselves vainly pushing at the shoulders of the 'Bulge'; thus their advance was funnelled through a relatively narrow base. The British XXX Corp moved south to guard the Meuse crossings. Hitler refused to reinforce the partially successful Fifth Panzer's advance at the expense of the stalled Sixth. Meanwhile the commander of the American stronghold at Bastogne, sustained by airdrops, turned down a German surrender ultimatum with one contemptuous word: 'Nuts!'

Patton's Third Army then struck a powerful blow against the Bulge from the south and on the day after Christmas one of his armoured

divisions drove through ice and snow to break the lines around the 101st Division. Hitler's last great offensive in the west was doomed, a fate confirmed when, with improving weather, the Allied air forces joined in the attack with a vengeance.

Now the Fatherland's radio and newspapers prepared their audience for the worst. On 28 December the German News Agency issued a statement: 'The Allied High Command has now concentrated 24 tank divisions and heavily armed shock formations in the Ardennes.

'Among them are the 51st (Highland) British Infantry Division, renowned as a crack unit since the Africa campaign. They have gone in to the line east of Dinant.

'General Eisenhower has considerably reinforced the firepower of the First and Third Armies by supplying them with additional batteries of the biggest calibre. This strength, in conjunction with close-range air support, has caused the battle to become stationary.

'The German spearheads have been taken back according to plan...to avoid unnecessary losses and enable us to meet the American counter-attacks with compact strength. German forces found themselves forced to give up some ground in the face of ferocious battles against Americans attacking in masses all along the far-flung southern shoulder of the German salient. A policy of elastic defence is being followed between Bastogne and Echternach.'

Back to the start line

The battle continued into the New Year with undiminished intensity. But now it was the Americans, supported by British units including the Sixth Airborne Division, who were attacking while the enemy grimly tried to hold on to what they had won. Slowly the Germans fell back.

By 16 January 1945, after a month of bitter fighting in the grip of a winter far colder than usual, the Germans found themselves once more lined up more or less on their own frontier, almost the original start line for the offensive. The planned Allied drive into Germany was delayed by perhaps six weeks or so but the Ardennes Offensive had cost Hitler dearly in scores of thousands of irreplaceable men; even more significantly, Germany's panzer forces in the West had been decimated.

Above: At the start of the offensive, morale was high in the German ranks.

Above: This 30-ton Sherman tank is on display in the town of Bastogne, a key defence position for the US forces who blunted the German attack.

Above: At the end of the battle, thousands of German soldiers surrendered to the Allies.

The Wehrmacht had received large numbers of new 45 ton Panther tanks (illustrated here) with superior firepower to any Allied tank.

THE BRITISH ROLE

> **Belgian population very scared. It was cold and pouring with rain. Vls were passing overhead. Very depressing.**

At the time the British did not refer to it as 'The Bulge'. They knew it as the Battle of the Ardennes. In the early days of the German offensive it was the Americans who bore the brunt of the fighting. Indeed, in the House of Commons on 18 January 1945, Premier Winston Churchill referred to the episode as 'the greatest American battle of the war'. There were around 40 US troops involved for each British soldier and the Americans lost around 70 men for each British casualty.

Nevertheless, as the battle progressed, the British arrived in numbers to play an important role. On the following pages we publish the stories of some of the British soldiers involved in that bitter winter battle, beginning with this account by A C Jenkins of Ilford, Essex: In early December 1944, I was serving in A Company, 7th Battalion, Argyll & Sutherland Highlanders, a posting I reckon amounted to one of the toughest jobs around at the time. We were part of the 51st Highland Division (although a hell of a lot of us were actually English!) and were comfortably billeted in a seminary in the south of Holland.

Above: 'Roll of Honour' memorial erected at La Roche-en-Ardennes to the memory of the 54 Scots killed during the Battle of the Ardennes.

Although not aware of it at the time, we were undergoing training for the forthcoming Reichswald offensive. Against regulations, I kept a diary and this records that on 16 December, on the very day that the German attack in the Ardennes opened, we all attended a performance by the Divisional Concert Party – 'The Balmorals' – and, of possibly more significance, that a large number of V1 flying bombs were observed flying overhead.

At 11pm on the following night, after a quiet day, we suddenly found ourselves on the move. Over the next couple of days we went into Belgium, passing over the 1815 battlefield of Waterloo, then back into Holland, finally ending up at the small town of Valkenburg where we were supposed to relieve a US outfit. They, however, had other ideas and refused to give way to a bunch of Limeys. Notwithstanding, it looked as if we were to be there for some time and so laid plans for a slap-up sit-down Christmas Dinner.

Alas for the best-laid plans; on Christmas morning we were put on an hour's notice to move out, fully kitted up. Thus we ended up eating our dinner out of mess tins, standing up in the open air. Merry Christmas! We eventually moved on to a suburb of Liege, where several of us were billeted with a family. It was touching to read the hand-written banner strung up in their living room - 'Welcome to our Liberators. Welcome to brave English soldiers'. If similar banners were hung in all the houses,

I'm not sure what the true Highlanders would of made of the sentiments!

Meuse bridge guard

On 29 December we moved to the western side of the city to guard a bridge over the River Meuse. Our new billet was with another family in a farmhouse of the kind common in that area of Belgium; it had a cow and a few pigs in winter housing in one part of the building and living quarters in the rest. We duly passed our compo rations onto 'Mum' who promptly responded that this kind of fare might be alright for the pigs, but wasn't fit for humans. For the rest of our stay she fed us, Lord knows how, on her own supplies. Perhaps her husband being in the Resistance helped. We had a memorable New Year's Eve with them. On 7 January we were ordered to move. The lady of the house couldn't understand why we were leaving and my last memory is of her refusing to let our successors - some Seaforths - into the house in our place!

Prolonged snowfalls caused drifts that made it difficult to follow the roads. Our destination was the village of Grimbiemont, where we relieved an East Lancs battalion. The place had seen some hard fighting and was still subject to shelling. Taking shelter in a ruined house we discovered the bodies of three unfortunate East Lancs boys; next day, despite the ground being frozen, we managed to give them some sort of burial in the churchyard.

Expecting an attack

It was cold, so much so that the oil on our rifle bolts froze and orders came down to wipe every trace of the substance from our weapons. It was the second time in the war that I'd received such a command, the first being at Blackpool when I was in the Essex Regiment and the sand used to jam our rifles.

Within 24 hours we were told to expect an attack from German infantry and tanks. We anticipated an assault by the terrible King Tigers of awesome reputation but all that happened was that a press-ganged Pole from the 116th Panzer Division crossed the lines to surrender. We heard movement from the general direction of the enemy but that was all.

After a miserable freezing night spent trying to keep warm, we were relieved (on 10 January) by units of the Sixth Airborne Division and withdrew to Hotton for a night's rest in a barn. Sheer luxury!

The plan next day was for a Black Watch battalion in our own 154 Brigade to take La Roche-en-Ardennes and for us to then pass through them. But the Black Watch were held up and we spent the entire day on the road. Tragedy almost intervened when the three tonner carrying 9 Platoon skidded off the icy road and landed up on its side. How we 30 men in that truck escaped injury I shall never understand.

Another night, another barn and more gentle snowfall; in the morning we were driven to the outskirts of La Roche, by now taken by the Black Watch, and then marched down a winding river valley towards Hives, several miles south of La Roche. I remember the pine tree branches, blasted down by shellfire, and the pine needles and debris frozen such that it felt like walking over ball bearings.

Panther tanks

Amidst sporadic shelling, we reached a crossroads where there was yet another barn to afford shelter from the biting wind and cold. Our first

section headed on down the road, descending into a shallow valley with a stone hut at the bottom. As the leading man reached this, there was a burst of machine gun fire and the crump of exploding shells which between them claimed several killed and wounded amongst our men. Some of the latter somehow struggled back, despite being badly hit. Perhaps the cold served to dull the pain.

Another section went down only to meet the same fierce reception. By now a scout car from the Derbyshire Yeomanry had spotted the source of the firing; two dug-in Panther tanks on the high ground ahead. Our own turn to advance was coming up and our Company Commander, Major Samwell MC, decided to accompany us with two Shermans of the Northants Yeomanry also lending support. Somewhat reluctantly we all moved out. Just a few yards later, seconds after Major Samwell had ducked behind the lead tank to report back via the telephone link carried at the Sherman's rear for just that purpose, there was a blinding flash and a shower of sparks and metal fragments, some of which must also have hit L/Cpl McCormick just in front of me. An 'old soldier' in the best and worst meaning of the word, McCormick was the bane of the Sergeant Major's life and at 33 years of age he seemed almost a grandfather to we mere 19 year olds. With a wife and several children back in Glasgow, he should never have been serving in a rifle company.

Understandably, the rest of us legged it back to the barn as fast as we could. For their part, the Panthers and our own tanks backed off. By this time the powers that be realised that there was no way forward down our road; B Company later advanced via a different route. We were withdrawn to the village for another miserable night with no blankets and only a can of self-heating soup for comfort. In a nearby outhouse lay the body of a poor old Belgian woman killed by shellfire. Jaundice had been stalking me for several days and on the following morning, I reported sick. Before departing for the 25th British General Hospital in Brussels, I just had time to bid a hardly fond farewell to the Ardennes.'

Brussels in turmoil

On the night of 23 December lead elements of three British divisions were moving up to their allotted positions. Troop Leader W S Brownlie of the 11th Armoured 'Black Bull' Division remembered: We were to move to the Ardennes soonest. Forget waiting for the new Comet tanks, leave all heavy kit behind, pick up old Shermans in Brussels, get to the Meuse and help stop the Jerries. Cups of coffee in Aalst; Brussels in turmoil, population very scared. It was cold and pouring with rain, V1s were passing overhead, very depressing.

Defence of Dinant

Ken Baldwin writes of an incident at Dinant on the Meuse in which his father, Sgt G W 'Tiny' Baldwin figured: My father was with G Company, 8th Rifle Brigade, 11th Armoured. He was involved in the push through Belgium and Germany and was among the first troops to arrive at the Baltic.

One night an incident occurred which did nothing to reduce the tension. On the far bank of the Meuse there was a road running alongside the river. This road passed through a hole carved out of the rock through which a Sherman tank could just squeeze its way. Sergeant Baldwin's carrier section manned a post at the rock whose function it was to stop all passers-by and vehicles and examine their papers. The sentries doing the checking had a Very-light pistol which they were to fire if any vehicle would not stop, whereupon Sergeant Baldwin was to pull a string of mines across the road at the exit to the hole in the rock. It was an arrangement of which any Boy Scout might well have been proud.

At about midnight a Very-light went up. The mines were set off and there was a deafening explosion which all asleep in the neighbourhood took to be the bridge itself. When the smoke and dust had cleared away the remains of a shattered jeep were found and by it the bodies of three dead Germans. They had been travelling in a captured American jeep and were wearing American greatcoats over their German uniforms, in the pockets of which were found very detailed plans of our defences. When challenged they had refused to stop. In one respect the episode was less fortunate, for Sergeant Baldwin's mines had gone up with such a bang that an American standing some considerable distance away had had his jaw broken.

And so another one comes round. This time – for luck – we refuse to say 'the last behind the wire'... Some of us have said it too often.

These are the opening words to *The Flywheel* 'Xmas Number' of December 1944, a remarkable hand-written magazine produced by British POWs in Stalag IVB in the period from May 1944 to March 1945.

It was the product of the 'Muhlberg Motor Club', who comprised several hundred motoring enthusiasts incarcerated in the camp which was situated near Muhlberg-on-Elbe, Germany, some 80 miles south of Berlin. Built to house 15,000 prisoners, at times nearer 30,000 Allied servicemen were crammed in the cold, filthy and verminous wooden huts of the camp.

Thomas Swallow, who was captured near Tobruk in 1942, was the co-editor. He remembered how it was virtually impossible to escape from the camp so the inmates had to make their own entertainment.

'There was a passion for motorbikes and motorcars so we set up the club. It was our way of saying to the Germans, we can beat you. We had classes for everything imaginable – musical appreciation, business methods. We even had German lessons.'

The Flywheel was produced entirely by hand including all the wonderful illustrations of machines and landscapes. Many were drawn from memory but there were also outside sources. Tom's mum, for instance, regularly sent cuttings from home of current magazines with reports of wartime motoring events that helped the club keep track of the outside world.

All the paper and materials used in the production of the magazine was obtained through a system of 'beg, borrow, buy or barter – stealing from Jerry was taken for granted'.

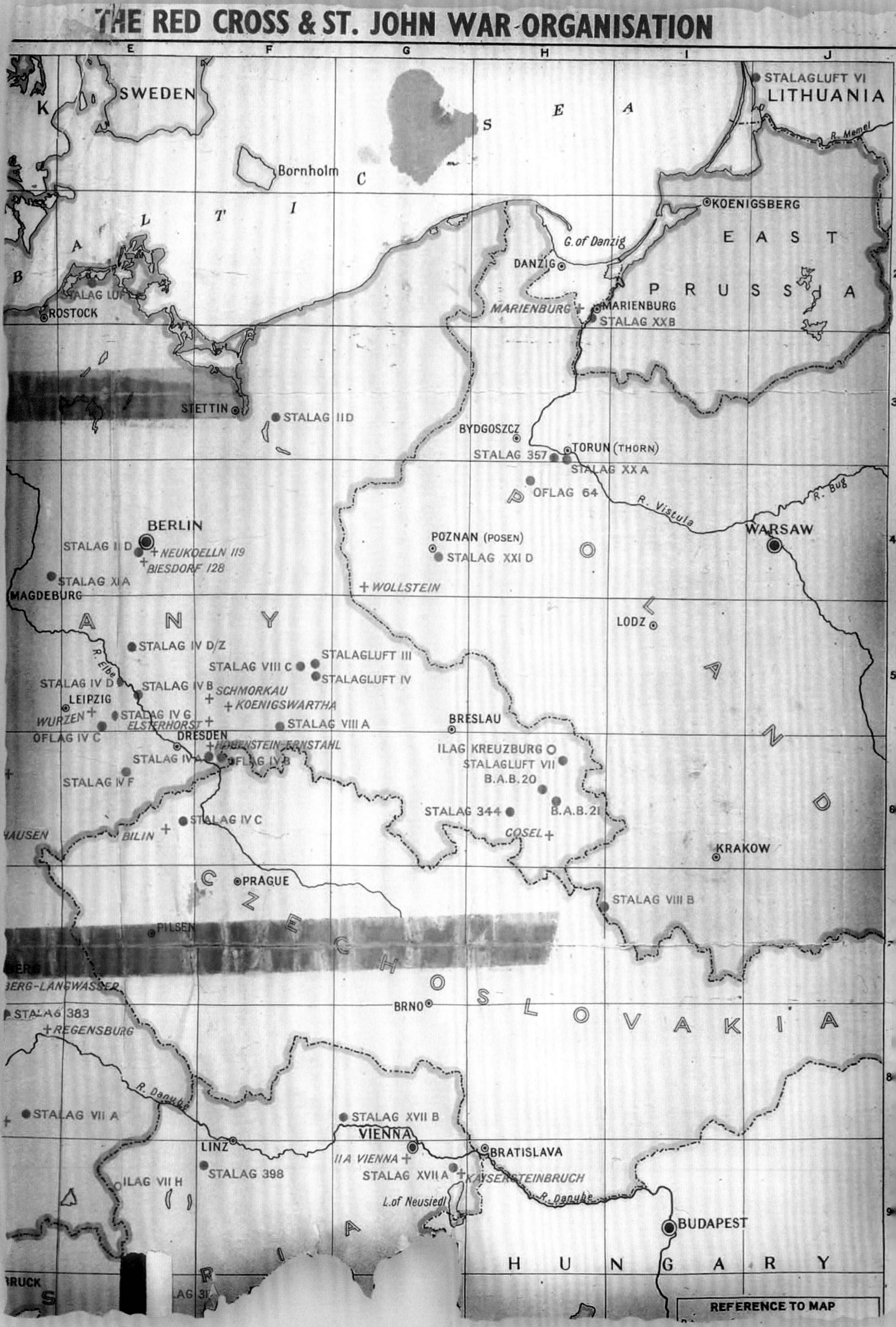

THE RED CROSS & ST. JOHN WAR-ORGANISATION

SWEDEN

Bornholm

BALTIC SEA

STALAGLUFT VI

LITHUANIA

R. Memel

KOENIGSBERG

EAST

G. of Danzig

DANZIG

PRUSSIA

MARIENBURG + MARIENBURG
STALAG XXB

STALAG LUFT
ROSTOCK

STETTIN

STALAG II D

BYDGOSZCZ

TORUN (THORN)
STALAG 357 STALAG XX A

OFLAG 64

R. Vistula

R. Bug

WARSAW

BERLIN
STALAG II D + NEUKOELLN 119
+ BIESDORF 128

POZNAN (POSEN)
STALAG XXI D

STALAG XI A
MAGDEBURG

+ WOLLSTEIN

LODZ

POLAND

GERMANY

R. Elbe

STALAG IV D/Z

STALAGLUFT III
STALAG VIII C
STALAGLUFT IV

STALAG IV D STALAG IV B
+ SCHMORKAU
+ KOENIGSWARTHA

LEIPZIG
WURZEN + STALAG IV G.
+ ELSTERHORST
OFLAG IV C DRESDEN +
STALAG VIII A

BRESLAU

STALAG IV A + HOHENSTEIN-ERNSTAHL
OFLAG IV B

ILAG KREUZBURG
STALAGLUFT VII
B.A.B.20

STALAG IV F

STALAG 344 B.A.B.21

HAUSEN
BILIN + STALAG IV C

COSEL +

KRAKOW

CZECHOSLOVAKIA

PRAGUE

STALAG VIII B

PILSEN

BRNO

...BERG
...BERG-LANGWASSER
... STALAG 383
+ REGENSBURG

R. Danube

STALAG VII A

STALAG XVII B
VIENNA

LINZ

II A VIENNA +
STALAG XVII A + KAYSERSTEINBRUCH

ILAG VII H

STALAG 398

L. of Neusiedl

R. Danube

BUDAPEST

BRUCK

...LAG 3...

AUSTRIA

HUNGARY

REFERENCE TO MAP

Five years 'In the Bag'

As a Youth in Training in the Post Office Engineering Department in 1939 I was conscripted into the Royal Corps of Signals as Signalman 2364104 and spent the next six months training in Hampshire and Yorkshire.  Subsequently I was attached to the 30th Infantry Brigade formed as a diversionary force for the defence of Calais and the evacuation of the BEF from Dunkirk.

Captured at the fall of Calais on 26 May 1940, myself and other survivors of that battle were taken to Stalag XXA at Thorn in Poland where I was designated *Kriegsgefanganen* 11870. We spent the next 18 months working in various POW Camps around that city undertaking house demolition work, road and sewer construction and other labouring tasks.

In the autumn of 1941 I was one of about 250 British POWs transferred to Stalag XXB at Marienberg in East Prussia. After a short stay there I was 'posted' along with 22 other POWs and two German guards, to a 5000 acre State Farm in a small village called Faulen in East Prussia near the Lithuanian border.

The next three years were spent on a variety of farming activities, but all this came to a sudden end in January 1945 when the entire farm, POWs and civilians, was evacuated in front of the Russian winter offensive. All British POWs were marched westwards (crossing the frozen River Vistula over the ice) and traversed northern Germany under pretty atrocious winter conditions living off meagre Wehrmacht army rations and what we could scrounge from a partially evacuated countryside.

After a cross-country march of about 700 miles, crossing the Rivers Oder and Elbe in the process, we eventually reached the town of Lehrte in West Germany midway between Brunswick and Hanover, an area under attack by the advancing American forces. Our stay in Lehrte in a

A workparty of 27 British POWs at Faulen, East Prussia. They were employed on a State Farm from October 1942 to January 1945. Robert Marks is one of the party. He's also featured left in later years.

displaced persons camp was comparatively short; the town was captured by the Americans and we were freed.

Looked after by the Americans and enjoying their hospitality fully, after about 10 days all British POWs were loaded into Lancaster bombers returning from missions over South East Germany and we finally reached home after being away from our families' and loved ones for almost six long years.

In conclusion one must always remember the Red Cross who helped us to survive those years in captivity with gifts of food parcels and clothing, through some very difficult and never to be forgotten times.

Robert M Marks

*The various camps which held Mr Marks can be seen on the map.

The POW Camps

Maps prepared by the Red Cross and St John War Organisation were provided to ensure that the whereabouts of British and Commonwealth prisoners-of-war were known throughout the conflict. Red Cross officials visited all camps to ensure that the terms of the Geneva Convention were being honoured. The Red Cross also provided food parcels which were a vital supplement to the sparse rations provided by the Germans.

Letters sent by loved ones back home were, of course, treasured by those 'In the Bag' as were messages sent in reply. The comfort of knowing the location of POWs was a boost for morale.

The map reproduced here is shown without the legend as the original is now very fragile. It's dated 30 June 1944 and was made available for publication by Diana Gant. Her father, Private Edward Thompson, was captured in the North African desert on 20 June 1942. Private Thompson was in the Royal Artillery and was in the process of changing a lorry tyre when the sudden appearance of the enemy changed his life instead. He spent the rest of the war in Stalag XVIIA, east of Vienna in Austria.

Stalag Luft III (scene of 'The Great Escape' in March 1944) can be seen in the centre of the map midway between Berlin and Breslau. Colditz Castle is actually designated as Oflag IV C and features on the map between Leipzig and Dresden.

Tony Graves

British soldiers captured in 1940 around the Pas de Calais region of Northern France.

"UP HOUSEWIVES AND AT 'EM!"

PUT OUT YOUR
PAPER · METAL · BONES
THEY MAKE PLANES. GUNS. TANKS. SHIPS. & AMMUNITION

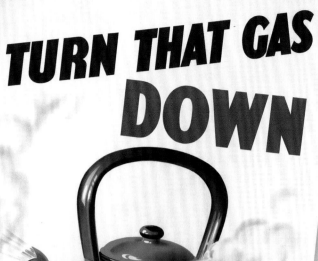

TURN THAT GAS DOWN

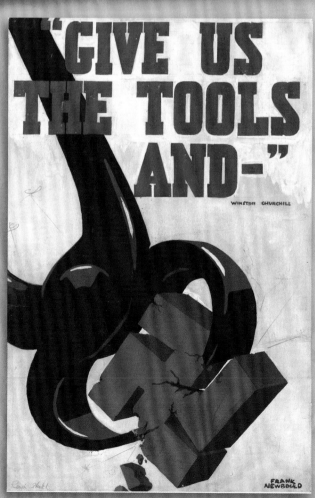

"GIVE US THE TOOLS AND-"

WINSTON CHURCHILL

FRANK NEWBOULD

DOES
IT ~~DOESN'T~~ MATTER:
COUNTRY
THE ~~FIRM~~ PAYS FOR IT

Don't waste
HERE -
the Fuel you save
AT HOME!

SPICE ISLANDS HELL

The prison camp letters of a young British RAF serviceman doomed to die in Japanese captivity in the Far East echo down the years with a message of faith and love of family, records David Arnold.

When looking for stories of the courage, stoicism and endurance ordinary people have experienced during times of conflict and war, I have found it amazing just how close to home you can uncover the most astonishing tales. In the case of our late, dear neighbour Felicity Reed, it is the story of the heartbreaking waste of her brother's young life. Dennis George Moppett was a Leading Aircraftman in the RAF Volunteer Reserve who hailed from Lewes in East Sussex. In 1940 he was posted to France and, when the Germans over-ran that country, he managed to get safely back to England. Later he was posted to the Far East and sailed there via South Africa. He served in Malaya and, when the Japanese invaded, his unit first fell back on Singapore and was soon evacuated to the island of Java.

The Japanese then invaded Java and the Dutch East Indies. In the ensuing chaos and confusion, some British and Commonwealth forces escaped by boat but, for Dennis, there was no third successful evacuation and his fate to become a Prisoner of War was sealed with the capitulation of the Dutch forces. Along with over 5000 of fellow RAF personnel, Dennis was ordered to surrender by his commanders. Imprisoned on Java, where the conditions were at least tolerable by the standards of what happened later, he was one of several thousand men who sailed from Surabaya in the *Amagi Maru* and *Matsukawa Maru* on 22 April 1943, bound for Ambon where they were to be employed as slave labour in the construction of airfields.

Concealed inside bamboo tube

Unlike most of his fellow prisoners, from early on, Dennis determined to keep a record of his captivity. Using a forbidden supply of paper and ink, he wrote a long series of letters addressed to his Mother and Father and two

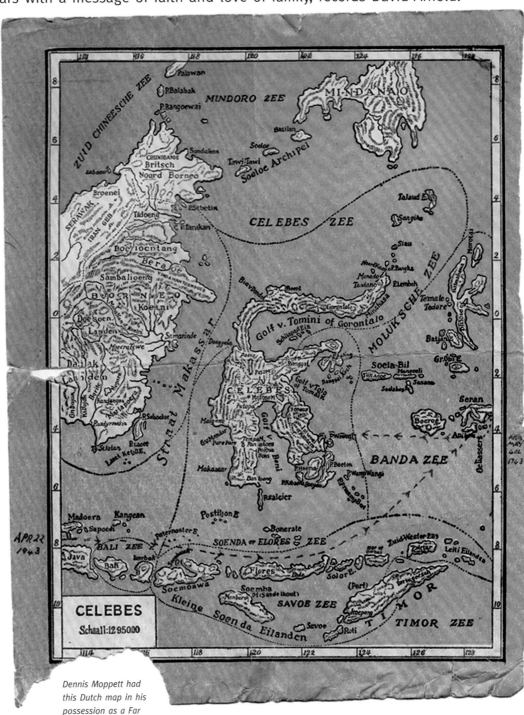

Dennis Moppett had this Dutch map in his possession as a Far East POW. It was kept hidden in the bamboo container pictured overleaf. On it he recorded the sea routes he and his fellow prisoners followed when being transported from island camp to island camp. It is almost certainly the map obtained by his friend Bob Lee and referrred to in the letter dated 17 October 1943.

sisters, Sheila and little 'Fifi', as Felicity was affectionately known. The letters, of course, could never be posted and Dennis stored them rolled up and concealed inside a bamboo container. They are unusual in that they were

written almost at the same time as the events they record unfolded, rather than being retrospective accounts written years later.

Dennis never made it home. He died on 6 January

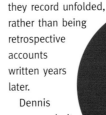
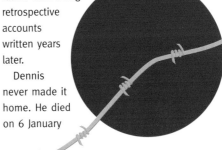

At the top of this montage can be seen the bamboo container that preserved the letters of Dennis Moppett. Note how he carved his home address on it. A sample letter appears in the background. The photographs are from the Moppett family album and feature Dennis in his RAF uniform, his mother and father on a picnic with his sisters Sheila and baby Fifi (Felicity). Dennis is also pictured holding Fifi in the back garden of their Lewes home.

1945, one of the thousands of victims of the horrendous treatment meted out by the Japanese to their prisoners of all nationalities during the Second World War. A comrade of Dennis who did survive and was finally liberated after the surrender of Japan late in 1945, brought the letters back to England and presented them to the family. They make sad and poignant reading, but they give a compelling insight into what the prisoners went through in the Far East. It is likely that the contents of the letters were 'self-censored' by Dennis because he would have been in serious trouble if the documents had fallen into the hands of his captors. Even so, the horror of the situation he and his comrades found themselves in as the war went on comes through clearly. To add to

their agony, the growing Allied superiority in the air and at sea posed further grave danger to the POWs who were transported between islands on boats vulnerable to submarine attack. They were also forced to work in docks and on airfields that were all targets of the bombers and fighters of their own side.

Starvation and disease

What kept Dennis going was his love for family and faith in God, a faith that must have been sorely tested in the midst of privations and so much suffering and death. As a long-time resident of Lewes (his hometown) myself, I find his memories of happy days spent at Sussex locations that are almost on my doorstep particularly poignant. Yet, amidst the sad catalogue of

disease and starvation, some pages feature a cheerful sense of humour. There is even an intriguing mention of a certain Joan, clearly a girl who had caught the young man's eye before he went off to war. Sadly, there would never be a romance and one can only imagine the despair Dennis fought to keep at bay as the days, months and years of captivity racked up.

His sister Felicity – little Fifi – passed away in the summer of 2009. She was happy for me to tell the story of Dennis and carry many of his letters in *Seventy Years On*. Her three sons, Tim, Matthew and Daniel have been very helpful in making a transcript of the letters available from which I have drawn the following edited highlights.

David Arnold

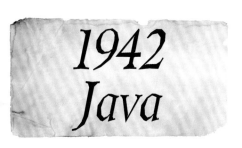

1942 Java

Wednesday 6 May: My dearest Mum and Dad – what an age it seems since I was writing to you. This is only the second letter I have written to you since I was a prisoner, as we have been told that the first ones have not yet left. The postal arrangements seem to have broken down. It seems pretty useless writing at the moment, I know, but I feel I must just 'speak' to you and even if I can't send it, I shall have put my thoughts on paper and feel near to you.

At the last camp, it was just the same as an RAF camp with plenty of fatigues, but here, where we arrived on Good Friday, we are under Japanese command. Our first greeting was a bit gruff, but they have gradually discovered we are not such a bad crowd after all. Some of them can speak a few English words. We are all in a big hangar and are dry which counts for a lot.

We get up and parade for roll call at 7.30am, just as the sun is rising. At 8am we breakfast and at 9am we start work which takes the form of varieties of manual work. At 1pm we have tiffin and start work again at 2.30. We knock off for the day at 4.30, so you can see it's not all bad. There is not a lot of room for us all to bath at once so we are marched down to the village wells where we get a good cooler. At 5.30pm we come back for dinner, which is usually stew and rice. We still have a bit of money left and can sometimes get eggs, fruit and bread from the natives.

At the last camp we had a Padre and were able to go to Communion Service. Here we have nothing like that, but the first Sunday we were here was Easter Sunday and our old CO gave a sort of service and we had the 121st Psalm. I still have some of your letters, Mum, and have just been reading some. It is

> **The birds are singing beautifully, small yellow butterflies are flitting all over the field in front of me and the sun is shining brightly. There is a very high mountain we can see from here. It's supposed to be an extinct volcano and the top is nearly always covered in cloud.**

comforting just to see your writing.

Bits of news get passed around and some of it we know definitely is real news and it does buck us up. At the moment it only looks a matter of weeks or a couple of months, if everything goes well, before we are free.

Friday 8 May: This morning for some reason we are not working. I am sitting in the shade round the back of one of the hangars and it is very pleasant and cool. The birds are singing beautifully, small yellow butterflies are flitting all over the field in front of me and the sun is shining brightly. There is a very high mountain we can see from here. It's supposed to be an extinct volcano and the top is nearly always covered in cloud. The rumours going round are still good ones and when the kites go over we look for the day when they will have 'stars' on the wings and not red circles.

Saturday 9 May: Well, another afternoon 'at ease'. Something must be wrong for us to have all this time off – it almost seems as though they can't be bothered with us. For tiffin we had fried rice and onions and vegetables chopped up – it made quite a change. Our own cooks do the cooking but I think some of us wonder whether that's an advantage or not!

I wonder how you all are and what you are doing now? I believe we are seven hours ahead of you so it's not 8am with you yet. I suppose, Dad, you are at work; Fifi is just waking up, Mum and Sheila sound asleep. Do you still call her 'Fifi', or is it Felicity Ann now? I still think of her as 'Baby' but she will be five years old next month. I wish we could all be together – just for a few minutes. I dream of home at nights and think of you all day and read all your letters through again and again.

I do hope you have heard something by now and are not worrying. This is a bit different from France. It was not a case of being taken prisoner – the whole of the RAF was just ordered to sit down and wait like a lot of sheep for their captors to come. It was little use trying to get to the coast as you can't swim 1000 miles. Some tried to get away but couldn't and just came back and waited. Before the Dutch capitulated we were making for a boat and but for one or two of the usual blunders that get made, we should probably be sailing back to Blighty now.

Wednesday 13 May: For some reason reveille was early this morning. It was still dark and (to us) a bit cold. The cookhouse fire was blazing away and I pictured a winter morning at home with the fire crackling up the chimney and egg and bacon frying. The dish I long for is pork chop in a casserole with baked potatoes, beans and lashings of rich brown gravy. I can almost taste it. I do hope the food position isn't any worse for you because of the Battle of the Atlantic.

> **This is a bit different from France. It was not a case of being taken prisoner – the whole of the RAF was just ordered to sit down and wait like a lot of sheep for their captors to come. It was little use trying to get to the coast as you can't swim 1000 miles.**

Wednesday 20 May: I've been waiting all week for this little chat with you but we have been busy loading railway trucks. Pushing them up and down the railway line just suits me – never thought I'd have a full-sized railway to play with.

My friend Bob is very confident that we shall be free by Christmas. I hope he is right but I just wait from day to day. There is a rumour that we are moving from here soon. I do not like any mention of a move in case we leave this country – although I wouldn't mind moving from this particular spot in case we see some kites with stars and stripes come over and blow the place to smithereens.

Friday 22 May: I'm lying on my bed, the lights are on and it has just got dark. I'm not sure of the exact time because only one or two of the chaps are left with watches. The rest have sold them to the Japanese over the last three days. The Japanese now want to buy all of our cigarette cases and wallets etc, all of which they are paying for in Java-Japanese money. We think they want to be rid of their money in case they leave here soon. My pen is the only thing of any value I have left. I lost my watch on the train. My camera I gave to a native.

The rumour of us moving is true and it is also exactly 12 months ago today that I sailed from Scotland. It was 6pm when we slipped out and everyone was singing 'Ay, ay, yippee, yippee aye' and it seemed to echo all around the bay. I little thought then that I would be in this pickle by this time, this year. Do you remember, Dad, how we mentioned the possibility of being taken prisoner, just before the train drew out of Lewes Station – the last time I said goodbye to you? Such a lot has happened in a year. Fancy! I have sailed half way round the world, taken part in two evacuations, just missed the third and am now hoping for the best.

Wednesday 27 May: We are moving on Sunday and a train is coming up here to fetch us – we were told we would have to march the 10 kilometres to the station.

Yesterday was the first anniversary of Bob's wedding day. He was married a week before he left England. To celebrate it we had egg and bread fried in dripping and, oh boy, did we enjoy it.

Monday 1 June: We have arrived at the new camp and it is a proper prison camp. Lorries had taken us to the station. Before we left many of the Japanese came round shaking hands with us and saying goodbye.

Sunday 14 June: On Friday I was working in the fields making hay – the sun was bright and the field was near the sea. The hay smelt rich and I can just remember – like a dream – playing in the hay at Floods Bottom when I was small. Do you remember the truss of hay you carried on your back, Dad, when we were camping at Barcombe and all the spiders and beetles we found in it? Under several of the piles of hay we moved today we found snakes coiled up and in all we killed eight.

Today, one of our chaps has cut my hair and I've had the weekly shave and feel much better. I never told you how I lost my kit on the train. We were on our way to a port that was destroyed before we got there. We were put on a special troop train that we hoped was going to another port. Bob and I were lying together on the floor of a goods wagon when the train was ambushed and set on fire. We hadn't a rifle between us and the Officers ordered us to get out and walk along a road. I got hold of a tommy-gun but it wasn't much use. The front of our party were crossing a bridge when it blew up; it had been mined. As many as it was possible to rescue from the river were brought back and then we crossed and walked about 25 miles. Next day at noon we were picked up by another special train and after travelling all night and half the next day arrived at a station where we were told the Dutch had capitulated and so here we are today.

Bob has just come in with a rumour that Singapore has been re-taken. If we could believe all the stories passed around here in a day, well, we should be free in a few weeks. The day before yesterday, I was boiling my towel over a fire, just outside when something landed with a thud behind me.

> **Our train was ambushed. We hadn't a rifle between us. I got hold of a tommy-gun but it wasn't much use. The front of our party were crossing a bridge when it blew up; it had been mined. As many as it was possible to rescue from the river were brought back.**

I turned round and someone had slung a kitten over the wall. It landed on its back and didn't move, so we thought it was dead. After a while it crawled up to the fire that seemed to revive it a bit. I took it in and made a bed of straw for it. I managed to get a little soup into it but really it was too young to be taken from its mother. In the night it mewed pitifully. Yesterday evening I was trying to feed it with soup again and it was mewing hard when a cat miaowed on the wall. A duet followed between the cat and the kitten until I put the kitten on the wall and the cat ran off. It soon came back though and snatched its 'little 'un' up in its mouth and made off with it. Exit me minus one kitten! It was not much more than a fortnight old and its eyes were just open. I wished Fifi could have seen it, she'd have loved it.

Wednesday 1 July: When we are on working parties now, we get two rolls at breakfast and an extra ration of dinner at night, especially meat. On the days we work we get 10 cents, that's just over a farthing. I'm cheaper to run than an electric fire! Bob, George and I are making ourselves a bit more comfortable and have even managed to acquire three chairs and a small table. There is an RAF Padre in the camp and Bob and I hope to go to Communion next Sunday.

This time last year I was nearing the end of my fortnight in South Africa and what memories I still have of it; it seemed to be a land of plenty where there was wealth, good food and entertainment – oh and lights in abundance. Then when we arrived at Singapore there was no blackout until December and Java had only semi blackness. It seems difficult to realise that you have had a blackout at home for nearly three years without a break.

I don't think I shall ever forget how I stayed away from school to hear 'Moonlight Sonata' with you at the Odeon, Mum. At one of the concerts we had a week or two ago, one of the sergeants played it and my thoughts flew home.

Sunday 12 July: We have had a bit of excitement here in the last few days. Wednesday was the seventh month since the war with Japan began and to 'celebrate' it, the wives of the interned Dutchmen in the camp were allowed to visit them. The Parade ground had a rough bamboo fence put round it and the visitors were not allowed beyond this but the prisoners were allowed to go into the arena to see their wives and friends. To begin the proceedings a 'Rising Sun' flag was hoisted on a pole in the middle while we were on parade. A small Nipponese guard presented arms and then what I suppose was their national anthem was played on an accordion. After that the Japanese Camp Commander, who speaks quite good English, made a speech that said that on 8 December

> **The stars were bright last night, especially the Southern Cross. I look up at that and think of the old Plough shining down on you. I am praying hard that you may have heard some news by now. If only you hear something, just to know we are fine – or even have a "feeling" that we're OK.**

last year, England and America had declared war on Japan and thus forced her into a war she had sought to avoid. Since entering it she had made it her resolve to unite the peoples of Eastern Asia and free them from our dominance. Today saw the completion of that as the Emperor proclaimed himself 'Rajah of Asia'.

Well, as soon as the gates were opened, the Dutch wives, sweethearts and friends came trooping in bowed down with hampers and suitcases. Many of them had no relations to visit and had come especially to see the British prisoners. We were not allowed inside the fence but could walk round and round the outside, where food and clothing was speedily handed out to us. A boy called to the crowd and just gave out money and Bob and I each received a five-guilder note (12/6d). We were absolutely amazed. It was the same all afternoon. We had coffee, soup, cigarettes, biscuits, fruit and sweets and all things like that which make such a difference.

Sunday 19 July: Exactly a year ago today, I landed in Singapore at the end of our two-month trip over three oceans. It is now 19 weeks since we were taken prisoner. The stars were bright last night, especially the Southern Cross. I look up at that and think of the old Plough shining down on you. I am praying hard that you may have heard some news by now, although we have been told that our names have been sent off. If only you hear something, just to know we are fine – or even have a 'feeling' that we're OK. Sheila has sat for her Oxford by now, I expect, and perhaps my 'Little Fifi' is a big Felicity just starting school. Good night for now. God bless you and watch over you all.

Sunday 26 July: I was working yesterday for the first time in a fortnight. We were at a hospital pulling down air-raid shelters and digging blast walls away. It wasn't really hard but it made me very tired and I got sunburnt! It is strange but if I am not continually in the sun my body loses its tan and I burn again next time. At tiffin time the guards brought out a big block of ice and smashed it with a rifle butt. Some of them are using old Ross rifles. One of them got his jammed the other day when he was loading it and was going to push a piece of bent rusty iron rod down the spout to clear it! It makes you wonder why ever did we have to leave Malaya?

We have now all been numbered and wear little red labels with our numbers in black. Mine is 827. The Dutch wear white labels, the Chinese yellow and the Americans blue. We are getting eggs from someone who gets them to us whenever he can. He got some chillies the other day and for tiffin we have been making 'nasi goreng' with pieces of ginger and onion in it.

This morning it has been raining hard and it is very muddy here. Using only an axe I have made a pair of wooden sandals from a piece of thick wood and a strip of rubber.

Sunday 9 August: As you will have noticed there is a big break in my letters. There has been a very strict tightening up of things in this camp, our kits have been searched and we ourselves are searched at odd times. The main object seems to be to prevent communications passing. Last Wednesday night I was sitting adding my weekly contribution to this when a Nipponese guard came stealthily in and took the page from me. I tried to explain it was a letter but he couldn't understand me and must have thought I was writing a message. However, I have heard nothing about it since.

I was working last Thursday but we do not get 'paid' now and do not get the extra roll of bread. Fires are now forbidden so we are not able to make our 'nasi goreng' for tiffin. I have started Dutch classes again. I still get the pronunciation of the 'g' and 'k' wrong but I know I shall never get a better opportunity to learn than at present.

When we pass a Nipponese sentry, we have to bow, or salute, and when they come into our billets we have to stand to attention. In the last half hour I think we have stood up six or seven times. You may find now, that I am writing this in rather a 'precise' manner but if they should read this I should not like it to be misunderstood.

Constantly my thoughts and prayers are that you are not worrying about me and that, although you have not been informed about us, you may feel we are safe. Somehow I feel like the Irishman in Tipperary, telling you that if you don't receive this you'll know it has been taken off me!

Thursday 27 August: I am now working in the hospital. It should give me the opportunity to practise speaking Dutch. I have made good friends with a Dutchman called Dolf who got me the job.

On Sunday we had a Communion Service in the morning and the evening service was especially good as we now have a harmonium. Our last hymn was 'Lead Kindly Light' and it reminded me of the first time I went to St Andrew's Cathedral in Singapore. The words 'the night is dark and I am far

from home' really struck me. The other day I looked at the bottom of my kit bag and realised the few things there were the total of all I now possess in the world.

Sunday 30 August: George, Bob and I have built a sort of 'lean-to' shelter. There is bamboo fencing around it and along the bottom of the fence I have planted some beans and they seem to be coming on fine. A sudden gardening craze has gripped the whole camp and on every spare piece of ground someone has 'staked their claim' – it looks as if a gold rush is on!

At the moment I have a mixture of prickly heat and nettle-rash and do so itch. Yesterday an Ambonese soldier died. He had been sent out of the camp to the town hospital. His is the fifth death since the camp opened.

I wonder what you will be doing this

> **❝The flowers here bloom and die without season. The evenings have no twilight or dusk. I long for the English dusk and dawn – dawn here startles you into action, too suddenly. I often think of the dawns we watched when doing Home Guard duties and I long for the crispness of the English air.❞**

afternoon? I don't suppose it's possible to go to the sea now. Perhaps you have gone over to Telscombe - but of course I had forgotten that you do not have the car out now, have you? Maybe you have all gone over the Race Hill instead – I do hope you still have these outings together and can go out and enjoy yourselves. I remember we had some good picnics together. There was one at Telscombe when Baby had a ride on the groundsheet and Dad pulled her along. From the cliffs we saw a Hospital ship come in from France to Newhaven. Right from the first, Fifi enjoyed a game or a joke, didn't she? I've never forgotten how she gurgled and cooed at three months, when I came back from Auntie Doris in 1937.

Well I see by our sundial that the time is getting on so I think I'll have just a few minutes on my bed and have a shower before I go back to the kitchen.

Sunday 6 September: Yesterday we were rather suddenly moved to another camp, about half the size of the previous one and not far from it. Here we have at last met a lot of our old pals, but there many of whom we have still not heard. I was very sorry to leave the last camp. Dolf had been a wonderful companion to me and parting was like losing a very old friend. He is 28 and has

a wife and child of eight months. When he was taken prisoner, she was only two months old, but he has seen them since on a visiting day. When I left the camp several of the Dutch gave me presents of soap and similar necessities that we cannot get. There was even a tin of butter and it seemed a miracle to us that there could have been any butter left in the camp!

At this new camp it is horribly crowded. George, Bob and I and two other lads were looking for somewhere to sleep when an RAF Officer came up and detailed us for permanent work in the cookhouse. We have had one day of it and found it has several advantages such as a clean billet and shower and it is a little quieter than the rest of the camp.

Sunday 27 September: Just over a week ago there was a bit of an upheaval in the cookhouse. The Ambonese native troops who are in this camp with us complained to the Nipponese that the cookhouse was not treating them fairly. The accusation was quite unfair, as they are now finding out, but the result was that there are now representatives in the galley of all the nationalities imprisoned here and we now have 10 English, five Australians, five Americans, five Chinese and 10 Ambonese. George, Bob and I are still staying in the same billets as a permanent fatigue party.

From where I am sitting now on the steps of the verandah of the billet, the trees are waving about and rustling overhead. There is a warm breeze blowing and the sandy ground in front of the house is baking in the sun. Some papers of mine blew away just now and I ran after them in bare feet – to say I was like a cat on hot bricks would be to put it mildly!

The fine weather must be coming to an end at home now and the leaves will be beginning to fall. Here the flowers keep blooming and dying without season. The evenings have no twilight or dusk. I do long for the English dusk and dawn – dawn here startles you into action, too suddenly. I often think of the dawns we watched when doing Home Guard duties and I long for the crispness of the English air.

Sunday 4 October: There has been a whisper that the Red Cross is to be recognised and that our names are to be sent. I hope this is true. About a week ago a lot of fresh milk, butter and eggs were sent in by the Red Cross. This was the first time they have been able to work in any big way. Everything went to the sick-bay where there are men badly in need of sustenance.

Monday 12 October: Yesterday afternoon I looked at all my photos of home. They give me such a longing to be with you, although they also bring to mind such happy thoughts and memories of when and how they were taken. I have the photo of Fifi with all her Christmas toys in the dining room when she was 18 months old and I have the photos taken at Piltdown and Telscombe in 1940. I have just been reading the last letter I had from you, Mum, written on 17 October last year. It is falling to pieces as it has been almost through fire and water and has mould over it but it is very precious to me.

The physical conditions here could be far worse and we are reminding one another of the plight of our prisoners in Germany where cold must be one of the biggest things to contend with. I did intend to write more of the daily life here in the camp but just lately I am not in the mood to want to remember Java at all.

Saturday 17 October: The RAF Dental Officer here has given me two temporary fillings. I am glad now of the care you took over my teeth, Mum, as it is at a time like this that one reaps the benefit. I am feeling pretty fit even now (thankfully) and that must be due to the good food I've had in previous years.

Wednesday 4 November: This ink is pretty tarry stuff but it is all I can scrounge. We have had four deaths in about three weeks from dysentery. There is no nourishment in the food. It just about keeps you going but you have no resistance to any illness. The Medical Officers have been complaining about the weak state of the men (there are several cases of beri-beri) and some special food is coming in that includes peas that counteract the disease. The Red Cross have sent in bottles of fruit, condensed milk, chocolate, cocoa powder, brown sugar and dried fish. Unfortunately I ate a few raw onions about five days ago and they upset my stomach badly.

Friday 13 November: The good food lasted exactly seven days and was then stopped by the Nipponese and even goods from the Red Cross have been prevented from coming in. Another order was for us to have all of our

> In the last four days there have been four more deaths from dysentery.
> Chaps are saying that it's a one-way journey to the hospital outside, as the cases go out one day and are dead the next.
> It's awful to see how thin the fellows have gone.

hair cut off. Bob, George and I had it done together and now – what with our numbers – we all look like a crowd of convicts.

The rain is almost continuous and the whole camp has become a sea of mud. I expect the temperature has only dropped a few degrees but it feels to me as if it is going to snow and I go about with a shirt and Dutch tunic on. Our job here includes cleaning tubs out in the rain. We say it will get us used to the weather we'll have when we get back to Blighty. I have a cold and my nose keeps running – it's a job to get even pieces of rag and paper, of course, is even more scarce.

Friday 20 November: I dreamt of little Fifi all night long and dreamt she was a baby again. It gave me such a longing to see you again.

In the last four days there have been four more deaths from dysentery. Chaps are saying that it's a one-way journey to the hospital outside, as the cases go out one day and are dead the next. It's awful to see how thin the fellows have gone and in the last few weeks it is more and more noticeable as all our reserves have been used up.

Some months ago some Dutch tunics, trousers and boots were available but now there is no attempt to clothe us. Fellows are walking around in rags and wooden clogs and in some cases, bare feet. It is very over-crowded here. Imagine Lewes Secondary School with every room full. At night it is impossible to step between the sleeping men. Imagine every corridor full, the gym in the same state and even the bicycle shed outside full of men and when it rains the mud becomes inches thick everywhere. I shouldn't be complaining because we do have many things for which to be thankful – but thankful only to Providence and no one else. But when I stop to think of the men I do feel that some record should be made of them. Three days ago a chap from our unit died. He'd been in the same station as me in Malaya and Java. He was a big chap but had gone horribly thin in the last few months.

Friday 4 December: I am now 22, so I can say, at least, that the whole of my 21st year has been wasted. A Japanese officer has made a speech to us in which he regretted our condition in this camp but stated he could not do anything about it.

On Wednesday we had a bombshell when half the camp was moved away and George had to go with them. We expected to join them the next day but the order was cancelled. I do hope we shall be together again soon – we three have been together since I landed in Singapore and we've been fortunate in keeping together so far.

The other day we were pulling a barrel of rice out for dinner and I cut my foot, which has turned septic and is swollen. It is a bit painful to walk on but there is an MO attached to the cookhouse and he is looking after it well.

> I am now 22, so I can say, at least, that the whole of my 21st year has been wasted. A Japanese officer has made a speech to us in which he regretted our condition in this camp but stated he could not do anything about it.

Nine months ago today was the capitulation. A few weeks before that I sent you a cable and a letter from Batavia. I often wonder if you got them. All I put was 'Safe – Java'. It seems a bit ironical now, but it seemed right at the time.

Wednesday 16 December: Yesterday a sentry called me to sweep the platform around the sentry box. We don't mind doing that as we get a glimpse of the road outside. When I was doing it I saw a white Dutch girl with fair hair, in a light blue frock, riding a bicycle! It was the first girl I had seen for over three months.

The sentry asked me my name but couldn't quite pronounce it so called me 'Moppay'. In Malay he asked me if I knew anyone who had a watch to sell. I found a fellow but he wanted too much for it. Even so the sentry gave me three cigarettes. Manufactured cigarettes are almost a thing of the past. Everyone rolls their own from tobacco and papers. Cigarettes used to cost five cents for 20 but can now be sold for two guilders a packet (to the officers, in the main).

Friday 18 December: I had a wonderfully vivid dream last night. I was a Prisoner of War home on one day's leave in England and I was walking from Newhaven to Lewes with Sheila and passed along the road that goes past Glynde. I met you both and told you all about the life out here and the fact especially of the 14 men who have died from dysentery. In the evening, after I had been sitting talking to you all day, Sheila and I and you both got on a steamer at Newhaven to go back to Java. But I fell asleep and when I awoke there was only Sheila with me and we were on our way to the island.

Tuesday 28 December: We had a good dinner on Christmas Day, considering we are prisoners. I do hope you had a good Christmas at home and were happy. The best Christmas present I had was that I could send you a postcard. We were allowed 20 words and three set phrases. Mine said: 'Dear Mum and Dad, I am constantly thinking of you. It will be wonderful when we meet again. The Nipponese treat us well so don't worry about me and never feel uneasy. I am quite well and whole. Keep trusting, God bless you, I am waiting for a reply earnestly.'

1943 Haruku

29 January: On 4 January we moved back to the camp I was at before, with the Dutch. The other half of the English who had been separated from us a couple of months ago, joined us in a few days. Dolf was still there and we were very pleased to see each other again. He offered me my job again in the hospital which I was glad to take up.

Saturday 6 February: About a week ago we had an issue of Dutch tunics and shorts – all of which are too small for anyone to wear without alteration. I did not get a pair as I have a pair of gym shorts and some khaki shorts. The khaki shorts I have patched so much and the material is so rotten that the stitches will not hold so I have handed them in for 'repair'. Meanwhile I am wearing a pair of shorts I found in a dustbin.

Brian now works with me at the hospital and I am glad he has the job as the food is so good and I like to know he is getting it. Every scene in this life is familiar to us now, but even our billet would seem very strange to you, built as it is of bamboo and rushes.

Yesterday the rumour was running around that Germany had capitulated. About a week ago it was stated in the Nipponese newspaper that the German Sixth Army had surrendered at Stalingrad but the report said that the event was of no real importance.

All I live for each day is to see you all again. Whenever I dream (and it is often), I dream of you all at home, in the past, in the present and in the future, in hundreds of different scenes. But the time is surely coming when it will not be dreams.

Monday 8 March: Twelve months ago today, Bob and I were trying to make up our minds whether to make a dash for the coast in the hope of finding a boat and getting away.

I have had three library books in succession

> **Yesterday a sentry called me to sweep the platform around the sentry box. We don't mind doing that as we get a glimpse of the road outside. When I was doing it I saw a white Dutch girl with fair hair, in a light blue frock, riding a bicycle! It was the first girl I had seen for over three months.**

that I have not read. In the first the wife is already dead and the husband spends the whole book dying of stomach trouble. In the second, the wife finishes by divorcing the husband and in the third the heroine dies of pneumonia. The book I have now is not so cheerful either!

Wednesday 24 March: Eight months ago the hospital had a maximum of 60 patients, now we have 260, with several hundred 'sick in quarters' as we have no space for more. I had a small piece of yeast given me and have been making a very tasty drink from bananas, very like cider. Last night we opened the first bottles as a special treat.

Tuesday 25 May: We have all been moved off the island. We left Surabaya, Java, on 22 April packed literally like sardines, head to foot on shelves in the ship's hold. Much to our surprise we sailed eastward until we arrived at Ambon on 28 April. Here the things we unloaded included anti-aircraft shells. The next morning we discovered the need for these when five Allied bombers came over, the first we had seen for 13 months!

On 30 April we sailed to Ceram (Seram) where we unloaded the bulk of our cargo – bombs and petrol. I think we left about 1000 men, mostly Dutch, there, presumably to build an aerodrome. The remaining 2000 of us were crammed on a small ship that took us to Haruku (Haroekoe) where we are now in a camp of rush huts, in semi jungle, near a native village. We were brought to build an aerodrome but after about a fortnight it was necessary to stop work as we could not raise 800 fit men out of 2000. Over 1400 men are now sick with dysentery and there have been more than 30 deaths. Medical supplies are scarce, food is poor and sanitation is practically non-existent. Now that it is almost too late, today we had an inoculation. Deaths are increasing by four or five a day. We have no padre with us and victims are buried just outside the camp in a small clearing. All our water from a stream has to be boiled. I am still working in the cookhouse.

You all seem to me to be in a far away world, a sort of paradise where this place is forgotten and everything is just the opposite to the way it is here. There is hardly a night goes by that I am not in that world with you and often it is the one thing to long for in the day time – to dream all night!

Saturday 29 May: I was speaking to an Officer last night and he said that most of the cases are dying from depression and starvation. On Thursday Stan Edwards died. He was a little Welshman and I had only heard the day before that he was ill. That is how it is – so many are ill that you don't know much about them until you hear of their death. There's nothing much more for me to write as everything seems too trivial with this all around us.

Tuesday 15 June: The Nips here have started a rumour that Germany capitulated on 21

> **There was a slight breeze blowing as I walked back to the billet just now and it made me long to be striding along the South Downs with the wind whistling in my ears.**

April but I don't believe it – I think the story is only being repeated to cheer our chaps up a bit. Before we were prisoners we used to wonder where the war would end but now you ask yourself 'how will all this end?' But still there's a mightier power working things out than we imagine and the only thing to do is to trust for the best and pray for that time when I shall see your happy faces again. The mind reaches that dull state, when all you long for is to meet again and feel that love between one another whether in this world or another.

Saturday 26 June: It's half past four and 'tenko' (roll-call parade) is in an hour. I have just been reading one of your letters written exactly two years ago. I now feel very homesick but have gained a lot of confidence. It's a dreary afternoon again and threatens to rain. Last night I had a nightmare and was yelling away for dear life. Afterwards I went to sleep again and dreamed of you all at home, but we were still prisoners and all going to be shot. So you, Dad, were going to blow us all up. But still, I was enjoying the dream all the same because I was with you.

Thursday 8 July: Today has been lovely and bright and the sun has been shining all day. There was a slight breeze blowing as I walked back to the billet just now and it made me long to be striding along The Downs with the wind whistling in my ears. As I stood in the river washing the rice boxes and soup bins this morning, 'Run Rabbit Run' was running through my head. The tune makes me think of the way Fifi always used to call a rabbit 'Diddle-iddle' – how I'd love to hear her dear little voice again.

Some 213 men have now died and hundreds are sick with beri-beri and complaints from lack of vitamins.

Saturday 10 July: My 'Yasame' afternoon again and I have been to the hospital seeing Brian and the rest. 'Yasame' is the Nippon word for 'stand at ease'. I was up twice in the night as my stomach has been upset the last couple of days. I hope it gets better today as stomach-ache is the last thing you need to get in this camp.

Wednesday 21 July: The Nip Medical Officer is supposed to have said that out of 1500 prisoners in Rangoon, 650 have died. It sounds a horrible proportion but now that we have been in contact with the Nips for 16 months it is easy to understand their mentality and their callousness. Whatever depths the European countries have sunk to, they still have Christian instincts deep in them or their ancestors but these animals are heathens and it is a fact that we, here, often leave out of our reckoning when trying to fathom them.

Thursday 29 July: Yesterday a Nip soldier shot himself and we have been warned to be very correct in our behaviour towards them as they are upset over it. Several weeks ago a Nip ran away but was recaptured and brought back. The Nips also suspect that the cookhouse night watch have passed food out to men in the camp (the 'food' being brown beans and sugar which we never have and wouldn't be able to get). If this happens again they are going to shoot all the kitchen staff (100 of us!) so I hope it doesn't. We have heard a rumour that Sicily has been taken by the Allies.

Ever since we have been prisoners a popular tune with us has been 'I'll Be With You, In Apple Blossom Time'. I suppose the apple blossom has been looking lovely the last few weeks at home – well we're too late this year but we can always hope for the future.

Sunday 1 August: Yesterday I had to go on a working party to the aerodrome. I was with Georgie Hunter all day and the sun shone brightly. The hard compressed core that has to be dug away is very much like chalk and has a thin layer of soil on top and then short grass very much like we have on the Downs. All the time I was thinking of the happy picnics we'd have on the hills and I told Georgie about them. I got very sunburnt as it is a long time since I worked outside. I came back feeling as if I have had a day by the sea and even today I feel as though I have had a day out somewhere and feel happier for it. August Bank Holiday four years ago (1939) we were just starting our camp at Barcombe. I believe you all went to Eastbourne on the Sunday and left Sheila and me to look after the tent.

Left: More photographs from the Moppett family album. Thoughts of family illuminated the prison camp life endured by Dennis. He was particularly fond of little Fifi who is seen in four photographs here. Dennis records how he came across a Lilliput annual in his prison camp and how it featured a photograph of his home town, Lewes. David Arnold writes: 'I discovered a copy of Lilliput magazine in the Needlemakers, a utopia for nostalgia addicts in Lewes. By strange coincidence, the building can be seen in the bottom right of bomb-damaged West Street, Lewes, in the 1943 photograph on page 345. Strange, too, that the Lilliput should have a snow scene on the cover. The winter of 1939-40 was exceptionally severe as can be seen from the picture of Fifi in her igloo. As I was putting this poignant story together in December 2009, Lewes fell under the heaviest blanket of snow the town had seen in many years!'

> **Owing to the increase in dysentery cases, this morning 30 men who are 'sick in quarters' were sent to the 'drome. The Nips are working us to death, literally.**

In the evening it looked like a bad storm was coming so we went home and Dad took Sheila to her Girl Guide camp at Rodmell – or did that happen on the Monday? I know we went out later to see her and I remember how keenly we listened to the wireless for international news and came home in a hurry when it looked as if war would break out.

Wednesday 4 August: I have just been reading the 91st Psalm, Mum, and it has wonderful promises in it. God can most certainly bring us all back together again safely, if it is His will. He is a God of love and we have such love in our little family that it hurts. You say that in one of your letters that you sent me when I was at Yatesbury. And perhaps God in his love will let us continue that life together. Otherwise without God's help it looks as if we here must all die unless human help comes in a matter of weeks. How hopeless we should all be here without something Divine to put our trust in.

Friday 20 August: On the night of 11–12 last, Harold Mutter died. He had been in hospital since a few weeks after we arrived here. He was a very good friend of Bob Bird, Georgie Fisher and George Hunter and all the old Singapore crowd. We were on the same station at Malaya. He was 30 and married and always made the best of the news, whatever it was. He was terribly thin before he went into 'hospital' and just wasted away as 250 men have already done and many more will. Every day 400 men are required for working parties on the 'drome, but this morning, owing to the increase in dysentery cases, 30 men who are 'sick in quarters' were sent up there. The Nips are working us to death, literally, and if we all should die it will be 2000 less mouths to feed and they can fetch more prisoners from Java to work for them.

Friday 3 September: Four years ago today war broke out. I can remember how we all sat in the dining room listening to the wireless and then at the end the sirens went and we went down to the cellar as we expected the sky to be black with aircraft – at least I did – as the 'blitzing' began. Now we are starting the fifth year! But I wonder if it will run a full five years.

On Wednesday afternoon I borrowed a Red-Cross armlet and went into the isolated part of the 'hospital' to see Brian. He is very bad with beri-beri and his face is swollen and his legs are twice their size. They have no treatment here for it but the cure is simple – just good food, a few eggs, milk, cheese and meat.

Monday 6 September: I can't imagine what my big sister of 18 looks like now. She must be a fine young lady and how I wish I could see you, Sheila. I wonder if you still go to school, perhaps you are married – but I hope not, because I do want to go to your wedding. The weather here is lovely and bright. I remember how lovely the weather can be at home in September. We moved to Abinger Place on your birthday.

Tuesday 14 September: On Sunday there was a ship in and they called for a working party from the kitchen to unload rice and beans. When we arrived we had to unload drums of petrol, timber and 50 250-kilo bombs. I didn't know the Nips used such heavy ones as all we have handled up to now have been much lighter. For the last week on the 'drome they have not been using dynamite for blasting but burying bombs and detonating them. There was an air raid alarm last night and we heard bombs dropped in the distance and kites over. Rumour has it that New Guinea and the Solomons are in Allied hands, Italy is on the point of capitulation and we have invaded the Netherlands and France.

I may not have mentioned before, but about three weeks ago we had a crocodile sent in as our meat ration. I was very surprised to find that it was whitish meat and tasted lovely – a cross between rabbit and chicken. We've also had four water buffalo that were bought with our own funds for £5 each. They are very large boned animals and have very little fat on them.

Monday 20 September: Frank Mase told me yesterday that he had seen Dr Springer about Brian and that he has said we shall lose him, perhaps in a few days. I went to see him in the afternoon and he was very weak. He talked cheerfully about what he would do when he got out of here but really I think he knows.

The doctor summed it up by saying that there is maybe one chance in a hundred of Brian making a surprising recovery. I can't believe it. His is such a valuable life and God could make such use of him now and after the war. Why does he take the good away like this? Or is it because some are too good for such wickedness to surround them?

Down the sides of our huts are a kind of shelf made of slats of bamboo about five or six feet in width from the wall and a couple of feet off the ground. These 'shelves' are our beds and get full of dirt, bugs and lice. It is just the same in the hospital. You can imagine there is little air or comfort especially when you have to lie on the 'shelf' all day and all night. There are no medical conveniences, no medicines, no soap or water and no lights at night. The food is the same as for the rest of the camp – rice and porridge for breakfast, steamed rice and a few leaves floating in floury water (soup) at midday and at night more steamed rice and soup. If we are lucky the soup is made from tapioca roots – we get a ration of half a pint, the same size as a Heinz Baked Beans tin. Sometimes we get green fruit and two or three figs. The Japs expect men to live and work on this day after day and they also expect poor bodies that are weak and lacking in every vitamin to recover on it. It is a matter of time as to how many will come through this for soon we shall all be suffering from beri-beri. Our only hope is that we can have a quick release, as there is no likelihood of any improvement in food and they intend keep us here to maintain the aerodrome when it is bombed.

Wednesday 22 September: We heard a drone in the sky this morning and saw a formation of 12 big bombers fly over at something like 24,000 feet absolutely without opposition. About five minutes later we heard a terrific rumble in the distance and knew that once again the Allies had done a good job. You have no idea how it made our spirits soar.

Monday 27 September: There is a rumour of a big naval battle going on between here and New Guinea. I hope it is true as every bit of action in these parts brings the Allies nearer to us. The need for the Allies to come and free us is urgent for we have a definite 'expiry limit' and can only hold out so long. What few vegetables the Nips have been supplying to us have decreased in quality in the last few days.

Day by day my thoughts are constantly with you and my prayers are for your safety. We had our short weekly Service last night and though they are very simple they do bring me so near to home. Do you remember, Mum, what a glorious Christmas morning it was the first time we went to Communion and how the sun shone? But it was to be a very sad one for us later when Grandpa died.

> **There is little air or comfort in the hospital. You lie on bamboo slats all day and all night. There are no medicines, no soap or water and no lights at night. The food is the same as for the rest of the camp.**

I always wished he could have lived another year to see Fifi. He would have loved her so. I long to see you all so much but just lately I have dreamt a lot of Sheila. We used to quarrel a lot but we didn't mean it and I think now that all brothers and sisters do if they have any 'go' in them.

Friday 1 October: Bob Lee has always talked of the possibility of a get-away ever since we have been prisoners. Even before we were officially prisoners we wondered what our chances were of getting away from Java. Now that we have been here, so much nearer the Allies but with conditions grimmer, he has talked of it all the more. In the last few days we have been trying find out a bit about distances and the possibilities of getting a boat and so on. I think if we can get a boat we shall go.

Wednesday 13 October: Brian is still getting weaker and is very tired but he can hold a perfectly normal conversation with us and still talks of his recovery. I feel so very helpless as there is very little we can do; even to try to make him a bit more comfortable is rather hopeless when you see the dirt and filth around. I will see him this afternoon and I know he will be pleased with some tobacco that Bob has got for him. Little things like that cheer him up a bit and it's good to do something, however small.

Sunday 17 October: Frank brought me some good news of Brian on Thursday. Dr Springer had decided to operate on him to try and drain the water out. They did it and Frank says he is doing all right.

About a fortnight ago 200 letters arrived from England but 200 don't go far among all of us. They were about a year old. Last night I dreamt Fifi was a baby again and Sheila and I were taking her to see the 'gnome' who kept the woodwork shop in Station Street. We couldn't find him in the shop so went upstairs and there at the end of a long room he was sitting treadling away at his fretwork machine. I wonder whatever made me dream of that?

Monday 25 October: It is now nine days since Brian had his operation. He is looking terribly thin and there is very little flesh on him but at least the water is not collecting again. Bob

has managed to get hold of a map the other day on a fairly large scale of this part of the world. We have heard that two Dutchmen who tried to escape from Amahi have been beheaded – but you might as well be shot or beheaded as die a lingering, painful and miserable death from starvation.

Sunday 31 October: It may have been the weather but for the last couple of days I have not felt so cheerful. At times I feel like chucking it up and legging, or rather, swimming it home. I'm feeling better today and realise how ungrateful I am, for certainly I get a lot more privileges and little comforts than the majority who are deprived and there's no cause for me to grumble. I need to think of Brian's continual remark, even when he was most ill, the RAF slang, 'we'll cope'. In other words, we'll get through somehow.

Saturday 6 November: In peacetime, I suppose we should just be getting over Bonfire Night now. Rumour has it that there is revolution in Germany. Yesterday I met a Dutch doctor who gave me a lot of information about making yeast and has promised me two rations of yeast in water for Brian every day. Yeast is our most valuable source of Vitamin B here and it's the anti beri-beri vitamin we are badly lacking in our rice diet. I hope now to make enough every day for four or five of us.

Thursday 18 November: There are several signs in the camp that we shall all be moving somewhere in a few weeks – but why and whether it will be back to Java, I don't know. I went to the dentist last Monday and had what was called a 'root filling' that involved sticking needles right into the nerve. It left me with a bad headache and I went to bed in the afternoon.

On Saturday we were rather misbehaving on 'tenko' and all the cookhouse staff were bashed about a bit by the Nip Gueno and accused of laughing at the Nip soldiers. The Gueno said he was going to send us all to the aerodrome and get a new cookhouse staff. After a few days in suspense I think we were forgiven, for he seems to have let the matter drop. Well I think we can't be prisoners much longer as I have only two more pages left for my notes and after that have no more paper.

Sunday 21 November: A few days ago we were given permission to use the canoe from the shore to fish but it was stated that if we were to paddle out of range of the guards' rifles we would be fired upon. My stomach has been very upset for over a week now and nothing seems to put it right.

Tuesday 23 November: Around 750 sick men and 50 'fit' will be moving during the night or tomorrow morning. Brian and Frank Mase will be among them along with Gordon Riddle and Roger Collins. They have been told they are going to Java, but I rather doubt this, as there are only supplies for a four-day journey. The

remainder of us will not be going yet. I do not think that we (the so-called 'fit') will go to Java, in any case. More likely we will go to Celebes or Borneo to build another runway.

In the middle of Sunday night, I was awakened by a kite flying around and shortly afterwards the air-raid bugle was blown and a few minutes later there were loud explosions from about five miles away. The kite then flew straight over the camp heading eastwards. I thought they were going to drop a few on us, but evidently the pilot was anxious to get back in time for breakfast!

Monday 29 November: The last load of sick men sailed on Thursday. They were crowded on board, worse than when we came. The same morning at about 11am four Allied kites were over and bombed the port but according to rumours our boat was not touched.

I was 23 yesterday but I don't feel any older than when I joined the RAF at 19.

Sunday 5 December: All the Nips yesterday were saying 'Germany tida begnose' (Germany no good). The same story came from every guard – that there was no war between Germany and England. I do hope it is true. It would be wonderful for you to have a Christmas with the lights full on and real Peace ringing through the air. I would love to be going to Communion with you on Christmas morning, Mum, but at any rate I think we can hope for that next year.

Tuesday 7 December: At about 11.30 this morning nine big bombers came over and bombed the aerodrome and the Nips' barracks here. There was no opposition and they came in at about 7000 feet. Ten or so incendiaries fell all round the kitchen but that was all that fell in the camp. Every day 1100 men go on working party up to the 'drome. I am anxious to see Bob and George come home safely tonight. Leaflets were dropped to the effect that the 'Rising Sun' was beginning to set and the Yanks dared the Nips to go and bomb Pearl Harbor again as they did two years ago.

One of the fellows in the kitchen was hit in the side by an incendiary and when he came to, it was burning his leg but he is not too bad now. Well it's fine to see four-engined kites go over as long as they don't drop anything. We are nearly at the end of our

338

> **How wonderful to have a Christmas with the lights full on and real Peace ringing through the air. I would love to be going to Communion with you on Christmas morning, Mum. We can hope for that for next year.**

prisoner of war days, surely we are not going to be exterminated by our own people?

Thursday 9 December: An Englishman has died from a leg wound and we have heard that 60 natives were killed by the bombing in the village. The natives are all moving to another village. They are lucky – we must stay here and all that is intended for the Nips, we shall get too. Bob and Georgie were working there yesterday, clearing away the dead and the debris – a pretty gruesome job. The small stores around the jetty were hit, the Nips' wireless stations, the petrol dump was just missed and two dispersal points on the 'drome were hit. I hope the pilots know we are in this camp as it must show up very plainly from the air, especially the large parade ground.

Monday 20 December: I expect everything at home is rush and bustle now preparing for Christmas and I bet Fifi is getting excited, bless her little heart. If only I could pop home for a few hours as I did the Christmas before I came overseas. I have just been shown a photo of Lewes in a *Lilliput* annual. It shows Southover Church from the Cockshut with Cliffe Hill in the background.

Wednesday 29 December: On Christmas Eve we had community carol singing in the evening followed by popular songs round a piano which had been brought in for the occasion. Bob, George and I enjoyed it, especially as we had a bottle of my homemade banana wine to keep us company.

Friday 31 December: Tomorrow is a big feast day for the Nips and a holiday for us also. I have one bottle of banana wine left and Bob, George and I will drink the health, tonight, of all of you in Blighty.

1944 Freedom?

Tuesday 4 January: Just eight months ago today, 2000 of us landed on this island. In that time almost 400 have died from diseases – mainly starvation and dysentery – and 500 sick men have been sent back to Java, many

of whom will not have survived the journey. With the New Year, a great wave of optimism seemed to roll over the camp and everyone is convinced that this is the year of our release.

Sunday 9 January: At last I have managed to get hold of a mosquito net and the last few nights I have been sleeping well. Our new billet is quite pleasant and I am sitting now with my back against the 'window' and can see the guards' pet monkey playing outside. He gets up to all sorts of mischief. Fifi would be delighted with him.

Saturday 5 February: Last Sunday night a sailing boat came at about 10pm with rice and other Nip food stores aboard. We were working a couple of hours backwards and forwards in the water unloading it.

At 8.30pm last night there was an air raid over Port Amboina (Ambon). We heard five lots of bombs drop and five kites came over, one at a time. We saw one go past the moon which was at its highest and very nearly full and another as it went overhead flashed a red light on and off several times. Many like to think it was a friendly signal from the crew as much as to say 'OK chaps, don't worry. We know you're there.'

Friday 10 March: I was on an outside working party a few days ago and worked with Bob and George all day. I managed to get some coconuts, nutmegs, clove leaves and a root like ginger to bring back. I dreamt I was in a Revolution in South America last night and I was fighting with cutthroat razors with two girls and had my left wrist cut open and blood shot everywhere. It must have healed up very quickly for the next I knew I was walking arm in arm with you, Mum, and Joan. I am always thinking of Joan and often wish I could have had a few months longer in England, to have seen her more. By this time she could be married but I never think of that for long.

Friday 19 March: I found a small turtle yesterday and we had turtle soup for supper. There were two eggs in it which I fried and had for tiffin. All day I am thinking of you and longing to see you all, but sometimes it gets worse like a wound that won't heal. I have all the photos I brought out with me, but if only they could talk. I read your letters again and again and get a fresh memory each time.

> **A fellow was hit in the side by an incendiary. It's fine to see four-engined kites go over as long as they don't drop anything on us. We are nearly at the end of our prisoner of war days, surely we are not going to be exterminated by our own people?**

> **I dreamt I was walking arm in arm with you, Mum and Joan. I am always thinking of Joan and often wish I could have spent a few months more in England, to have seen more of her. By now she could be married but I never think of that for long.**

Friday 21 April: We have moved into a new billet where is not so easy to write without being seen. I have 'pal'd up' with Pat Hunt in the last few weeks and we do our bits of cooking together. He has been in the Navy for about four years and comes from Hove and has a brother-in-law living in Lewes. It's nice to be with a few chaps from Sussex as we can talk about so many things in common. When one of Pat's friends from Brighton was talking the other night, he said something about a 'twitten' and nobody, but Sussex men, knew the word. George (from Newcastle) had never heard of 'Conkers'.

Tuesday 16 May: The camp is situated right by the sea and when I went down to the shore just now thoughts of home struck across my mind. The sky was a clear blue and the sea just a little darker, sparkling and rippling in the sunshine. Out in the bay were four or five native sailing boats and, just offshore, canoes were gliding across the water. I thought of the happy days we have had at Newhaven and how, after the walk from the station, you top the beach and the salt air and sparkling sea greets you. This morning I have a happy feeling that God is caring for us and blessing the love between our little family. Even though I am in a prison camp and separated in body by thousands of miles, I feel this morning how good it is to be alive and enjoy this love and sunshine. As I sit here and write I can hear the pitiful bleatings of our goat. Some months ago, it had a young one and the two were inseparable. I have often watched them and taken bundles of greenery to them, every time thinking of the young lambs we took Baby to see at Glynde. Now the young one has died in the night and the mother is crying for it all the time. I should not be surprised if she pined away.

Sunday 11 June: The sun is shining brightly and it makes me think of June sunshine in England. I have just been reading some of your letters of June 1941; three years old but

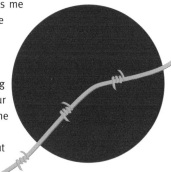

still as bright as ever in their news and memories. Around 500 letters have arrived here but there were none for me. They ranged from Christmas 1941 to January 1943.

Monday 19 June: I wonder what sort of birthday dear little Fifi had. I was thinking of her so much all day and we made a 'cake' to celebrate it. Seven years old – she must be a big girl and Sheila will soon be 19 – what a young lady, I wonder if she is seriously courting? I have had no shoes for some months now; a large part of the camp is like it and I have got used to it. But the rain has left very sharp stones sticking up and they are so hard to walk on. There are some large trees here and when I go past them first thing in the morning they have a strong scent like May blossom, which makes me think so much of home.

Monday 31 July: In the last two days a lot has happened. We have moved from Haruku (Haroekoe) in parties of 15 or 20. Yesterday morning 12 sick men (including six stretcher cases) were crammed on a sampan (small native sailing boat). Another 20 of us were put on a sort of pontoon effort that consisted of a wooden platform on two sampans side by side that were towed by a motor boat. Going along by the island was OK but when we caught the open sea between the islands, the sampans shipped water and the whole lot sank. The two Nip guards leapt aboard the motorboat that came alongside and then it broke down, leaving 20 of us swimming about in the water. We collected the large timber and tied it together to make a raft and sat on it singing and shivering until the motorboat started up and picked us up after about an hour. I lost none of my kit but some lost everything

This morning there was a further raid on the 'drome and five waves of bombers came over. We had 100 men working there and there were 47 injured with one man killed.

Friday 11 August: On Wednesday there was another raid on the 'drome and three waves each of five Liberators came over and plastered the place. There were still dozens of useless kites there from a previous raid but they managed to make a mess of it again. Lockheed Lightnings came down to sea-level and machine-gunned sampans. This is not surprising as sampans are now the only

means of communications between the islands. Pat was down there in a shelter on the side of one of the dispersals when a bomb burst about six feet away. He was pretty shaken but unhurt.

Monday 21 August: On 12 August 100 of us left Liang for Ambon where we were put in a church. In the following two days 500 men came to the church and 400 more went to a school up the road. The confusion that exists reminds me of the way we were moved about by our people in Java before the capitulation. They say we are waiting for a boat, but I hope it will not turn up and that we will be released here. I cannot describe the optimism among the fellows; everyone says it will be months but I believe that secretly everyone thinks it will be only a few weeks. There is hope in me that it may be just a few days. Since we left Liang it has been subject to very heavy raids and the camp was showered with shrapnel. This information came from 10 prisoners who were left behind to chop wood. When we left Liang there was not one single machine gun defending the 'drome.

Tuesday 22 August: Rumour has it that the Yanks will invade on the 25th and will free these islands by the 28th. Fantastic as this rumour sounds, I think it could be true. The Yanks have done a lot of shouting in the past and have not lived up to it. Now they have the opportunity to save face it is possible they mean to do it in real Yank fashion. There is no defence here and the kites come over just as they please and do aerobatics in the sky.

Saturday 26 August: Two days ago we were suddenly moved from Ambon town to the camp across the bay; Lehat – the worse camp of the lot. For two nights our new party have slept in the open, but owing to a move round we are now under cover with 12 inches of bed space per man. I find I am not putting so much hope now into an early release. Whilst unloading some small ships, some of our lads have been able to knock off tinned salmon, milk and dried fish and this has been a great help as our food is only rice and boiled leaves. Latest gen is that Germany is retreating on all fronts, Paris is in our hands and we are making for the German frontier.

Monday 28 August: A lot of my photos did not survive the ducking they got when the sampans sunk. The cover of my Bible also came unstuck. But still we must hope that I shall have the real thing with me soon and not photos. It does not seem possible that Sheila will very shortly be 19. I look at her photos and think what a lovely girl she must be. I'm sure the boys go mad after her. And Fifi too, seven years old but three when I last saw her. Roll on the Yanks and we may be home before she is eight.

Tuesday 29 August: I concluded yesterday with 'Roll on the Yanks'. They rolled on quicker than I expected. Half an hour later Lockheed Lightnings were over, strafing

shipping in the bay and dive-bombing. We tried to get our heads down but we had very few trenches. In half an hour they were back with wave after wave of Liberators at about 10,000 feet. In all over 120 kites passed over and bombed Amboina on the other side of the bay, which we left on the 24th. Thirty of our lads were working in the town and two of them were killed, one RAF and one Army. Bob Lee was among 20 men in a trench that was hit. He is a bit scratched and shaken but is otherwise OK.

Saturday 2 September: Yesterday 500 men embarked on a ship bound, we believe, for Java. Bob Lee and Clive Penn were among them. The night before it sailed, one of the Nip sergeants asked Clive if he could get a few of his Christian friends together to pray for a safe passage. This morning I have been working inside the camp making an air-raid shelter for the Nips. Another small ship has come in similar to the one that took the last draft away and the fellows are in hope of another move. A real Red Cross ship properly marked came into the jetty on the other side of the bay this morning but I don't think it will be for us but for the Nip wounded.

Sunday 3 September: Five years ago today war broke out. I little thought at the time it would land me here and last as long as this. Conditions are getting worse. Food is poor. Sanitation is bad. There is a lot of fever; Georgie Hunter has been down with it for four days now and can eat nothing. Dysentery is on the increase and there are now 80 cases. More people have beri-beri than have not.

Sunday 19 September: On Saturday 150 men moved and Georgie Hunter went with them. There was an air raid this morning and afternoon and the ammo and petrol dumps were set on fire.

Monday 25 September: I have had fever. It is mostly over but I can't eat and I can't keep my balance when I walk. Yet if this was in Blighty, a few mugs of tea, some eggs and milk would put us right in a day or two. Out of 4000 prisoners who came to these islands, 700 have died here, the rest have gone away somewhere on ships, supposedly to Java. We are 250 left here with 150 on the other side of the bay. There is precious little defence here. We are getting kites over every day making raids and strafing. The Yanks could walk in. We haven't been fighting for our own people in the trenches in slime and filth like in the last war but I don't think many British troops have endured two and a half years in the same conditions as we have in the course of this war. It was bad enough being bombed and shelled when you were on the right side but to be mass bombed as we are now is far worse because we know how really effective they are at the job. I wonder if they have told you I'm dead, or have you given me up as dead? No, Mum, never do that, don't think I'm dead, or ever give up praying we shall all be together again.

Wednesday 27 September: All the Asian prisoners expect the Yanks to invade this moon. I should like it to be so but I think the Yank intention is to bomb every Nip out of these parts and let them get out and take us with them. Then when the Yanks do come they will not be hampered by having to take hundreds of Nip prisoners or be troubled with sick ex-POWs. The Asian prisoners are guarded by Nip Marines. We are under mostly Korean prison guards who are supposed to be non-combatants.

Thursday 28 September: Something today suddenly made me think of the time, Mum, when you and I went to Clarke's Café for tea. How guilty we felt for being extravagant enough to dine out in Lewes! I think it was during the holiday that Dad and Sheila had in Darwen. We also saw 'Jill Darling' at the Hippodrome. And later in the week went to a Good Friday lantern lecture in Southover Church. Oh, I am glad to have these things to look back on, but they do make me long and pray for the future when we shall be able to make happier times together.

Monday 2 October: I am just snatching a few minutes between raids. Since 7.30am we have had bombing raids with Liberators wheeling about the sky like in an air display and Lightnings ripping in and out of the trees machine-gunning against not a scrap of opposition. Leaflets in Malay that were dropped yesterday say the Allies will bring plenty of food and medical supplies when they come and that 'it won't be long now'!

They have not actually attacked the camp yet but they have come unhealthily close as there is a boatyard just a short way down the road from here. I pray now that no boat will get in to take us away as it is not safe even for a canoe on these waters now. To have come so near to freedom and then have it snatched away would be too disappointing.

Friday 6 October: We have had five deaths in three days from dysentery, beri-beri and jaundice. The Yanks were over all of last night and we are getting very little sleep. They have already been over this morning, bombing and strafing. I am still feeling weak and it is difficult to eat the food but you have to force it down somehow.

Saturday 7 October: At midnight last night we were told to get our kit packed. We had breakfast at 2am and moved off to the jetty in the pouring rain. At about 5am after three hours of bedlam we got on a barge and crossed the bay to a jetty near Ambon where we were 'dispersed' to the trees.

Saturday 21 October: At 3.30pm in the afternoon of 7 October we set sail from Ambon in an overcrowded old wooden boat of about 400 tons and proceeded as fast as we could (six knots) to get as far away from Ambon as possible in daylight in the hope that we should not be seen and strafed by Lightnings. The hold was packed and all the sick men were lying on deck to get more air. Next morning half the hold was unusable because the bilge pumps were not working and we had to bale out with buckets. I was feeling shaky when we boarded but strangely enough picked up on the boat. Others began to go down and down. A dysentery patient died and was buried at sea. We arrived at Muna (in the south of the Celebes Islands) on the 13th with three less men than we started off with. The boat had to be unloaded not just in a hurry but in a panic. The Nips do everything like that with sticks in their hands and they drive and shout at you like we are cattle and then land up in a mess and don't know where anything is. Since we have been here (seven days), 15 men have died from general weakness, beri-beri and fevers.

The next day another ship arrived bringing the last 200 prisoners from Ambon. They had not been so lucky as we for they were first bombed by a Liberator (it missed) and then dive-bombed and machine-gunned by two twin-engined kites despite the fact that everyone was waving, plus a white sheet was flying from the mast and the letters POW were painted on the hatch covers in white. In their stupidity, however, the Nips had continued firing their machine guns. After the first attack two kites passed over, fired a burst out to sea and rocked their wings. Most on board took it as a sign of recognition.

Sunday 22 October: Seven men died last night and more will continue to die if the Nips do not improve the food. There is plenty of all that we need on this island of Muna but the Nips do not seem to be making much effort to get anything in. The MOs have asked that we be allowed to buy eggs and bananas but that is as far as it goes – yet eggs – unobtainable on Ambon – cost just two cents here. We have been out of Java 18 months and for the first time we are surrounded by plenty but men are dying from lack of it.

Monday 23 October: I think the fever has completely left me now for a while, although it rears up at intervals. My feet have begun to swell slightly, like your bad ankle, Mum, and when I press it in it stays in, like a dent. If it is not checked, it spreads and the whole body swells. In our weak state, when the swelling grows around the heart and lungs, they cease

> **Since 7.30am we have had bombing raids with Liberators wheeling about the sky like in an air display and Lockheed Lightnings ripping in and out of the trees machine-gunning against not a scrap of opposition.**

to operate and this is the cause of the deaths we are getting now. The fellows speculate on how much longer this war can last and whether the Yanks or beri-beri will arrive first.

Friday 27 October: We have been here a fortnight today and 43 men have died in that time.

Sunday 29 October: Yesterday was 'Yasame' day (day off – if such a thing exists in a POW camp). We were able to go to a clean part of the river where we could bathe and wash our clothes. We collected some green leaves; although cooking is forbidden we try to get a lot of leaves to eat raw, to keep the beri-beri down. There are practically no vegetables or greens of any sort coming into the camp, although yesterday everyone was able to buy three bananas for five cents.

Wednesday 1 November: I hope that my beri-beri is going as the swelling in my feet and ankles is very slowly going down and this morning I can actually feel my ankles. There were five deaths last night. We are between the devil and the deep blue sea. The sea voyage to Java is treacherous and unsafe owing to the bombing (I doubt if any ships are getting through), but on the other hand, if deaths here continue at this rate there will be only 50 or so of us left by Christmas!

Tuesday 14 November: In the last fortnight a disaster has overtaken our little crowd here. A boatload of 100 men who left here for Java was machine-gunned and sank with the loss of 27 lives. I was on an extra draft of 30 sick men who should have been on that boat but we were turned back when it was found that there were oil drums in the hold and the ship couldn't hold any more. Three Lightnings attacked at 11am the day after the boat set off. The survivors got back to the camp and were well looked after by those who were left.

I have been suffering from pain in the stomach for about a week. I reported sick and had some opium and creosote tablets given me to ease the pain. The next day I was put on an outside working party, pulling a bullock cart

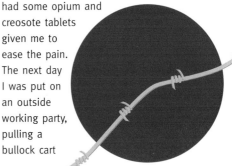

> **"We are slowly starving. It's funny though how often I have lain down and thought of all sorts of food and especially of all the missed opportunities for eating that civvy life offered. I can quite see Billy Bunter's point of view all the time now."**

along with 11 others. It upset my stomach and at midday the MO diagnosed it as dysentery and I came in sick. I'm allowed nothing but tea and was given a dose of salts. Though I'm dreadfully hungry my stomach has been quiet today and I hope I shall have a little rice porridge tomorrow and that they have driven the dysentery out.

Wednesday 15 November: The doctor has been around this morning and has put me on 'pap' which is at least a beginning of getting back to what food the camp offers. Mum, do you remember whenever I was sick at home, you put it down all the time to a 'foreign body' in me – a Japanese lady, you said. I wonder what made you say Japanese?

Saturday 18 November: On Thursday the doctor put me back on normal food and I have moved out of 'hospital' to a more convalescent part known as 'Sick in Quarters'. My tummy is quite OK now. The other day a large kite flew over escorted by four Lightnings. I don't think it was a bomber on operations as they don't bother with escorts. I hope it was a 'big cheese' on his way to peace talks somewhere.

Friday 24 November: Last Saturday I came out of SIQ and came back to the company, feeling OK and the next day I started work in the 'yeast factory' again. We get 200gms of 'yeast

water' a day as our chief source of Vitamin B. On Tuesday six Liberators came over the village at about 500 feet, machine gunning all the way. They fired from their rear guns mostly, but fortunately the camp was not touched.

Yesterday morning I suddenly had dreadful pain in my back and down the right side of my stomach. The MO gave me morphine after deciding I had colic. I think it is the worse pain I have ever experienced but the morphine sent me to sleep and had deadened the pain by the time I woke up.

Food is getting shorter and complaints have been made to the Nip CO who said he would see that something was done. However, yesterday he said that owing to the actions of the Yanks around the ports, strafing the villages and the fishing boats, the Natives are all against the English and will not supply food. The Yanks do come and attack anything and I think they will have a go at the camp one of these days.

Tuesday 28 November: Well, 24 today. It's bad enough spending a birthday in a prison camp, but to be in 'hospital' as well! It must be getting cold in Blighty now but it's difficult to imagine it with the sun here 110 degrees and over in the shade, day after day.

The day before yesterday we had an inspection by the Nip Camp Commander who finished up with a bit of a speech in which he said they were unable to get us back to Java as the Allies were attacking even small ships (don't we know it!).

Wednesday 29 November: I lay awake last night thinking of the preparation of all the things we have at Christmas time – making the puddings and cakes and then the marzipan and icing them. I do wonder how you all are and if you are safe and keeping healthy. At this end I must be thankful that God has brought me along safely all

this time and I feel it will not be very much longer now.

Monday 4 December: We had a reconnaissance kite over this morning so the war cannot be over yet. I am back on 'normal' food today which means I am allowed steamed rice and have just finished my five days of 'nasi goreng' – which seems to have gone nowhere! I have a few more days to go on quinine but my feet are still coming up and my legs are very shaky with beri-beri. We cannot go very long on this food. It is slow starvation. It's funny though how often I have lain down and thought of all sorts of food and especially of all the opportunities for eating that civvy life offered but which were neglected. I can quite see Billy Bunter's point of view all the time now.

Saturday 9 December: Last night we had an impromptu concert for an hour with a bit of a band the lads had got together. The Nips too were holidaying and most of them were drunk. The band had just struck up 'There'll always be an England' when the 'Shobong' (Nip Duty Officer) came out and stood listening. At the end he clapped with the rest of us and when they played a few swing tunes, he broke into a jitterbug. When the band was playing the other night, they played a few tunes and then suddenly started to swing a tune that must have shaken the Nips; it was their anti-Allies propaganda song that the Nips have taught the Natives, except that our chaps hotted it up and really swung it.

The final preserved letter (above) written by Dennis Moppett was dated Saturday, 9 December 1944. It is assumed that he would have had some pages with him when he re-entered the camp hospital and that these would have been confiscated subsequent to his death.

To the Memory of Far East POWs

On Remembrance Sunday 2009, my wife Barbara and I visited the National Memorial Arboretum at Alrewas, near Lichfield in Staffordshire. There we found the Far East Prisoners of War Memorial Building, a hugely impressive permanent exhibition dedicated to telling the story of the death and suffering endured by Allied prisoners in the years 1942 – 45. It has been created through the efforts of COFEPOW, an organisation comprising Children and Families of Far East Prisoners of War. COFEPOW members are today, in the main, siblings and relatives of those who laboured on both Burma and Sumatra railways, on the Sandakan (Borneo) Death Marches, down mines in Formosa, in factories in Japan, building roads in Burma, in prisons in Hong Kong, on air strips on a host of Far East islands and were incarcerated on the 'Hellships' that transported them. Civilian Internees suffered badly and the horrific plight and terrible death toll that befell many of the indigenous populations in the region is also recognised.

The names of all the British victims are recorded in the Memorial Building. We tapped Dennis George Moppett into the computer and up came his name along with his RAF service number, 1281149, and rank of Leading Aircraftman. It was good to find that he is fittingly remembered with honour in his own country.

Above: A former Japanese POW clearly happy to have survived but who also makes sure the unlucky ones who didn't make it are not forgotten.

The Dolf Unger Story

The Dutchman who befriended Dennis Moppett in the Internee and POW camp established in the Jaarmarkt (Annual Fair Market) in Surabaya, Java, was fortunate to survive the war. In October 1943, Dolf was one of 3000 captives crammed into a ship meant to hold 900 that sailed to Singapore where they were incarcerated in Changi Prison Camp.

Writing his own account of prisoner life after the war, Dolf recalled an incident during his time at Changi: 'There were German navy ships in Singapore. On one occasion some Japanese guards were beating a British POW. Some German sailors intervened and pulled the Japanese away. They then gave the POW cigarettes and chocolate bars. It was simply a matter of German racial superiorities surfacing when they saw a blond man beaten up by yellow Japanese.'

Despite fearing a transfer to the horror railroad camps in Burma, on 6 November 1943, along with 3000 fellow prisoners, Dolf entered the hold of another packed transport ship, *Hawaii Maru*, and set off on a terrifying 30-day voyage to Japan. On the way the ship got caught up in a typhoon near Saigon before calling at Taipei on the island of Formosa (Taiwan). Nearing Japan, the convoy was attacked by US aircraft. Through the portholes, Dolf and many of the men could see the ship next to them get hit by a bomb that caused a huge explosion. It listed badly and lifeboats were launched. Dolf's vessel became even more crowded as surviving POWs were taken aboard. Next morning there were no other ships to be seen; Dolf feared they had all been sunk.

Despair tempered by hope

Ashore in Japan, Dolf and 338 fellow prisoners were taken to Tsumori Camp at Osaka where temperatures of 20 degrees below zero made life even more miserable. Pneumonia became prevalent and the Dutchman almost died of it before receiving a life-saving dose of sulphonamide. Many of his companions succumbed to illness and malnutrition: 'The Jaarmarkt camp on Java was a bad camp but it was fairly heaven compared to the winter, the darkness, the polluted air in the harbour district of Osaka. It was our saddest Christmas ever. There was too much death, hunger, hopelessness.' Yet the deeply religious Dolf attended a Christmas service where he remembered: 'At our moment of despair there was a moment too of singing, praying for our loved ones, of hope, though there was little to hope for.'

American bombing raids intensified in 1944 and odd bombs fell in and around the camp. Then in 1945 a new fear tormented the

> The Jaarmarkt camp on Java was a bad camp but it was fairly heaven compared to the winter, the darkness, the polluted air in the harbour district of Osaka, Japan.

prisoners when the Japanese vowed to shoot all their captives should the Americans invade the mainland. Dolf recalled how extra machine guns were mounted on the sentry towers and trained to cover every corner of the enclosure.

On 15 May 1945 the Tsumori Camp was closed because the neighbouring factories, where the prisoners worked alongside Japanese civilians, had all been bombed out. With their not having been exposed to the brutalizing Japanese military code, Dolf sensed that the civilians were heartily sick of the war. They were also suffering great loss of life from the Allied bombing as well as enduring chronic food shortages. Dolf was next moved to Nagaoka Camp and set to work in a carbide and carbon factory with acrid fumes all around him. At one time the men were reduced to eating locusts.

Contemptuous laughter

On 27 August Dolf and his surviving companions learned that the war was over. The Allied ranking officer announced: 'The Japanese Camp Commander has told us that the Emperor, out of the goodness of his heart has called the war off.' Dolf remembers ripples of contemptuous laughter greeting this statement before the officer went on: 'The truth is that the Americans have beaten the hell out of them. We are free. Can you believe it? In time we will go home and see our families again.'

It was 23 December before Dolf was joyfully reunited in Singapore with his wife, Irene, and daughter, Reneetje. He had not seen the pair for three and a half years. Dolf had made part of the journey on the deck of a British aircraft carrier while his wife and daughter arrived from Java on a Royal Navy destroyer.

Java had become a dangerous place for Dutch colonists; the people of the Dutch East Indies wanted independence and, under their leader, Sukarno, were prepared to fight to get it. Dolf and his family went to Holland and would later emigrate to the United States. But he never forgot the months he knew Dennis Moppett in the Jaarmarkt Camp. In 1946 he wrote a letter addressed to Dennis at his Lewes home. The RAF man's mother responded to say that her son had not returned. In 1948 Dolf visited the Moppett household and would do so at intervals for many years to come. On that first visit, Dolf read the collection of letters written by Dennis and kept hidden and intact in the bamboo tube.

In 1983 Dolf concluded writing his own personal memoirs of wartime and a copy of them is in the possession of the Moppett family. In 1986 Felicity, Sheila and their mother sent Dolf a copy of the Dennis diaries that had by then been typed out by Felicity's son, Matthew.

Friendship formed with Dennis

In response Dolf wrote a letter in which he said: 'Dennis and I met in June 1942 at the Jaarmarkt Concentration Camp. There was an Anglican service and Holy Communion. After the service I noticed a young Englishman standing there and I simply said "Hallo!" We walked to our bamboo huts and the roots of friendship germinated in the context of our both being young Christians.

'I invited him to work in our sickbay where we shared our thoughts, doubts and hopes. When he left in September on a transport we felt like we were giving up something which could not be replaced. In January 1943 he returned and we had another four months in companionship. When he was sent with all of the English and most of the Dutch soldiers to one of the most horrible camps in the entire Pacific War Theatre (unknown to us at the time of departure), we had no gifts to share, but our military insignia* which we promised to exchange again after the war.

'His diaries portray him as he was. They show courage and the radiance of his optimistic character. His Anglican background, his splendid family background, all contributed to a faith that was much stronger than mine when we met. Most of all, his faith had a radiance which I keep tracing all through his diaries. These are a personal witness of a youth who had no boundaries of dogma, nationality or race relationships. Dennis was truly a youth for all seasons.'

David Arnold

*Post-war, Dolf presented the Moppett family with the RAF badge that Dennis had given him.

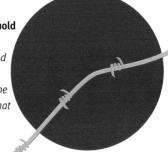

A Cruel Irony

Dennis George Moppett died on 6 January 1945 on the island of Muna (Moena) in the Celebes. His body is today interred in Ambon War Cemetery, along with some 2000 other victims of Japanese aggression. Ambon is one of a group of islands once known as the Spice Islands (now called the Maluku or Moluccos Islands) located south of Ceram (Seram) in the Banda Sea of the Far East. The tragic fate of so many Allied POWs in Asia is well documented. The letters written by Dennis seem to understate the terrible conditions endured by the prisoners and this is most certainly due to the punishment he would have received if incriminating missives fell into the hands of his captors. The Doctor Springer, mentioned by Dennis in connection with a sick friend, was well known (along with others) for the great work they did in helping men survive. In particular they identified yeast as a major ally in the fight against the scourge of beri-beri.

As the war progressed, the Allies all but destroyed the once-powerful Japanese navy. The poster above was aimed at occupied peoples of the Far East and depicts a British Special Forces soldier sabotaging a Japanese submarine (National Archives). Sadly, thousands of Allied POWs lost their lives when Japanese transport ships were sunk in relentless attacks made by sea and air.

Australians killed in cold blood

As it was, hundreds of prisoners were murdered by the Japanese rather than let them live to tell of the awful circumstances of their lives as slaves of the Empire of the Sun. In 1942 hundreds of Australians were killed in cold blood by the Japanese on Ambon and three quarters of the Australians captured in the area died from maltreatment or murder.

It is also a cruel and sad irony of war that many POWs died as a result of Allied bombing and submarine torpedo attacks. The Japanese generally did not mark POW ships with a Red Cross and the Allies had also broken the naval codes so knew where Japanese shipping could best be intercepted. One of the worst incidents occurred on 29 November 1943 when the transport ship *Suez Maru* was sunk by the US submarine *Bonefish*. On the Moluccas, with Allied prisoners dying daily through starvation, disease and beatings by their guards, the Japanese decided to send the sickest prisoners back to Java. A total of 640 men, including a number of Japanese sick patients, were taken on board the passenger-cargo ship, *Suez Maru*. In two holds, 422 British (including 221 RAF servicemen) and 127 Dutch prisoners were accommodated. Japanese patients filled the other two holds.

Survivors shot in the water

Escorted by a minesweeper W-12, the *Suez Maru* set sail from Ambon but while entering the Java Sea the vessel was torpedoed by *USS Bonefish*. The ship started to list as water poured into the holds; hundreds of Allied and Japanese men escaped into the water. The Japanese mine sweeper started to pick up survivors, but only their own nationals, leaving the British behind. As many as 250 men were left struggling in the sea. The minesweeper then made several slow circles around them and minutes later machine-gun and rifle fire were directed at the defenceless survivors. Empty rafts and lifeboats were then rammed and sunk before the minesweeper made off towards Batavia (Jakarta). Of the 547 British and Dutch prisoners, there was only one survivor, a British soldier, Kenneth Thomas, who was picked up a day later by an Australian minesweeper.

The *Suez Maru* must be the ship mentioned in Dennis Moppett's letter of 29 November 1943. The rumour that 'our boat was not touched' seems sadly unfounded. More than one in 10 of POW deaths at sea were the result of 'friendly fire'.

USS Bonefish was sunk off Honshu, Japan, on 18 June 1945. All 86 crew were lost. The *Bonefish* was the last Allied submarine to be sunk in World War II.

Fifi and the Lewes Bombs

While her big brother Dennis was in captivity on the Spice Islands of the Far East, enduring the cruel regime of his Japanese captors, little Fifi herself faced mortal danger in the heart of the Moppett family's home town of Lewes in Sussex.

While terminally ill in hospital in the summer of 2009, Felicity (Fifi) spoke to my wife Barbara about her memories of the only serious air raid that befell the county town during the war. It occurred at around 50 minutes past noon on 20 January 1943.

Felicity, then aged five, was having lunch at her grandmother's house at 199 High Street, Lewes, on the day of the bombing. The school she attended, Broughton House, was at the bottom of the street and, because her mother had a severe bout of flu, grandma was providing lunch. Felicity remembered being in the basement kitchen when the bombing started and was fairly well protected from the terrific noise of the onslaught.

Safe in the basement

Soon after the bombing had finished, Felicity's mother burst through the door evidently terrified as to what may have happened to her mother and daughter. She found Felicity and her grandmother quietly tucking into their lunch and for her trouble got a good telling off from her own mum for leaving her sick bed when the pair were quite safe where they were in the basement.

Felicity's mother's anxiety was quite understandable. Most of the houses and buildings anywhere near the vicinity of the bombing had their windows blown out and glass had been showered everywhere. Yet not a single window in the grandmother's house was broken.

The reason for this fortuitous escape from harm emerged later. Prior to the onset of the bombing, Grandma's dog, Laddie, had been let out for his constitutional in the back garden; the door was deliberately left open

very low over the town – low enough for the pilot to be clearly visible (indeed, one person was adamant that the German had bright blue eyes). The enemy aircraft was pursued by several Spitfires that went on to shoot down the German aircraft; the pilot died in the impact.

Errand boy killed

Bombs fell in several places in the town, the most serious damage being caused in and around West Street. A young RAF officer, home on leave, was killed in one of the houses nearby and a seven-year-old boy who had gone to fetch a loaf of bread for his mother was also killed.

Lewes resident John Armitage was just five years old and living in nearby St John Street at the time. He recalls: 'The police made us move away from our houses. My mum cried "But I've got a rice pudding in the oven." When we eventually got home it was covered in soot.'

John Armitage today lives in Sun Street, Lewes, close to where the Moppett family lived during the war. Barbara and myself have lived in St John Street, 100 yards from West Street, since 1973.

In 1943 one of the West Street buildings caught in the bomb blast housed the Co-op. The impressive clock hanging from the building

Top: The scene of devastation in West Street, Lewes, after the German raid of 20 January 1943.
Above: The clock in the top picture still hangs on the same building today.
Left: Little Fifi dressed up in fun as a Local Defence Volunteer before the grim reality of war visited her home town.

for him to wander back in as and when. Because the door was open, when the bombs fell there was no vacuum that could cause the aftershock of the explosions to shatter the windows.

The bombing was attributed to a Luftwaffe fighter-bomber. Eyewitnesses said it passed

stopped at 12.50pm on the day of the attack. The clock still hangs there today. It doesn't show 12.50pm but nor does it work. Ironically, the building is now the home of Wallis & Wallis, specialists in military memorabilia!

David Arnold

A GERMAN CHRISTMAS & NEW YEAR

Anita Birch recalls her childhood in wartime on the Baltic coast of Germany and remembers the kindness of the British POWs who shared their Red Cross parcels with her family.

In 1944 I was a four-year-old German girl, living with my parents, auntie and two small brothers in the town of Elbing, in what was then West Prussia, way up on the Baltic Coast. Today it is part of Poland. That year for us children seemed free from danger; the sound of gunfire and the bombing was a million miles away in the western part of Germany, although like all wartime families we felt the effects of food rationing and the wartime restrictions etc.

During the summer of 1944 a small group of British POWs on a work party were billeted in our back yard, working for our landlord. The POWs had their own wooden hut, but my mother allowed the men to use the facilities of her kitchen to brew their tea and coffee or to make drinking chocolate. In return, quite often some cocoa powder would mysteriously appear on top of the kitchen cupboard, a treat we children had never known.

Red Cross parcels

As the summer wore on the relationship between the family and the POWs was maintained in a polite and friendly way. As small children, we were the bond between all. I am sure that many of the men had families and children of their own back home and they must have missed them terribly. As in all such cases language was a problem, as neither side could understand much of what was said, but a smile and a thank you was adequate.

As Christmas 1944 approached the POWs put up a Christmas tree and decorated it with sweets and chocolates received in their Red Cross parcels. On Christmas Day we small children were invited into the hut. To our delight we were taken to the Christmas tree and allowed to pick off some of the sweets and chocolates. We put these into a colourful brocade pouch, which must have been sent to one of the POWs in a parcel from Britain. I kept that pouch well into my teenage years. In mid-January 1945, however, everything changed. The Russians were advancing swiftly from the east and our POWs were returned to their camp in Elbing. History tells us that they were joined by thousands of other POWs and forced to march to the western part of Germany. For my family, as well as other Elbing families, we were given one hour to evacuate the city. We left our home with what we could carry and made our way westwards, joining countless other people on the same trek – a journey made in deep snow which was to last for six days.

Wounded soldiers

Cold and hungry we eventually arrived at a railway station that was still operational. Many people were hoping to catch a train west. Fortunately my father knew the train driver and managed to get us on the last train. We were all huddled together at the end of the carriage

Above: Anita pictured in the summer of 1944 in the North of Germany with her two brothers.

near the door. This was the only space available as it was a hospital train packed with wounded soldiers from the Russian front. Whilst the nurses tended the injured troops my mother assisted by holding candles (these were among the few items we brought with us), giving the only light available. They did not allow children to come into the compartment, but through the open door we often caught a glimpse of the soldiers. Although at the tender age of four I never knew the significance of my adventure, the sight of those wounded soldiers heavily bandaged and in pain still remain, as do the images of nurses brushing their teeth with snow.

Arduous journey

The journey was long and arduous. Every so often the train would have to stop to avoid the bombing and on these occasions every opportunity was taken by all the able-bodied men (including my father) to search for food. After many days on the train we eventually arrived at the hospital town of Hamelin, in what was to be known as West Germany.

I spent my childhood and my teenage years in that area. Then in 1962 I married an Englishman, John, and moved to England where I have lived ever since.

1945: YEAR OF VICTORY

A BALTIC TRAGEDY

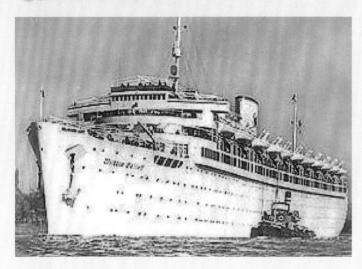

The world's largest-ever loss of life from a single ship sinking occurred early in 1945.

At approximately 9.10pm on 30 January 1945, the German liner *mv Wilhelm Gustloff* was sunk in the Baltic Sea by torpedoes fired from the Russian submarine S-13.

Nothing very remarkable about that, you might think; just another victim to add to the thousands of tons of shipping already lying on the seabed as a result of the war. But this sinking was different. Firstly, it was some years before the real scale of the tragedy became clear. Secondly, to this day, no one knows exactly how many men, women and children perished in the icy Baltic waters that night, but the most reasoned estimates suggest that it was in the region of 7700, making it the most horrific single ship sinking disaster in maritime history, far larger in scale than that of the *Titanic* or *Lusitania*.

Because the liner was grossly overcrowded with desperate refugees, wounded troops, U-Boat cadets and military personnel, no proper passenger manifest was ever recorded – hence the uncertainty over numbers.

Wilhelm Gustloff was launched in 1937 as a 'one class' cruise liner for the Nazi 'Strength through Joy' propaganda programme and was designed to accommodate 1465 passengers on cheap holidays to Mediterranean resorts. Early in the war the vessel was noted as being suitable for transporting troops for *Operation Sealion,* the German invasion of Britain that never happened. Next she went to Norway to serve as a hospital ship. Poorly maintained, by 1945 the ship's speed was diminished to around a maximum of 15 knots which added to her vulnerability when she made her fateful voyage of escape from Gotenhafen

Terrified refugees

With the Russians swarming across Poland and East Prussia, ships sailing from the Gulf of Danzig represented one of the last escape routes for tens of thousands of terrified refugees seeking to move west towards unoccupied Germany. Hundreds of thousands of frantic people were desperate to find places on the few remaining evacuation ships, some even scrambling up boarding nets after the *Wilhelm Gustloff* had cast off.

The night was icy cold with snow showers and poor visibility. The ship sailed with two small escort vessels, one of which had to return to port with a leak. The captain of the *Gustloff* decided to keep the ship fully illuminated as a protection against possible collision and this proved the undoing of the vessel. Torpedoes from the Russian submarine struck with terrible force and the liner immediately began to list to port, so much so that the starboard lifeboats were rendered

unusable. The escort vessel *Lowe* was alongside within 15 minutes and her crew soon became exhausted from pulling passengers from the freezing sea. The water was so cold that many people had died within minutes of immersion.

Hope was re-kindled with the appearance of the battle cruiser *Admiral Hipper*, herself already laden with 1500 refugees. But after assessing the situation, Captain Henigst decided that it would be too great a risk to stop his vessel and present another target to the lurking submarine. Signalling the rescue vessels 'success and good luck', the warship resumed her course and swept away at 32 knots, leaving the stranded survivors with a sense of bewilderment and betrayal.

Bout of heavy drinking

By an irony of war, the S-13's captain, Alexander Marinescu, had sailed from his base port of Hango (on Finnish territory occupied by the Russians) ahead of schedule, allegedly to escape the shore patrol who wanted to arrest him for unruly behaviour after a bout of heavy drinking. In spite of the declared aim of Stalin to utterly destroy Hitler's Third Reich, Marinescu failed to receive any sort of official recognition for his exploits in the Baltic, which included the sinking of the *General Steuben* on 10 February in the course of the same voyage with the loss of over 4000 lives. Indeed, after the war he was sent to a Gulag labour camp and later worked in a motor factory.

Today, the liner rests at the bottom of the Baltic, about 50 miles from the wreck of the *Steuben* and some 70 miles from the *Goya*, another ship crammed with refugees sunk whilst fleeing the Russian advance. The watery graves have been designated permanent war memorial sites, off limits to divers and salvage crews but, nevertheless, many artefacts have been removed from the wreck by souvenir-hunters. On Polish navigation charts, the wreck of the *Wilhelm Gustloff* is described simply as 'Obstacle No 73'.

Top left: The Wilhelm Gustloff *in peacetime.*
Top right: The ship with its pennant.
Above (clockwise from top left): Wording from the ship's menu. Two recent views of the wreckage lying on the Baltic's seabed.

WAR DIARY
January 1945

1 January: The 1948th day of the war opens with a surprise German attack along a 50-mile front between Saarbrucken and Strasbourg. *Operation North Wind* is directed against a section of the Allied frontline weakened by the redeployment of the US 6th Army to counter the earlier German offensive in the Ardennes. A further attack from the air, *Operation Bodenplatt*, is mounted by hundreds of aircraft and concentrates on Allied airfields in Holland and Belgium.

In the Pacific, American naval forces are suffering increasing losses from 'Kamikaze' aircraft. The Japanese also have a number of explosive-filled submarines with crews who have vowed to die in attempts to close in on US warships.

2 January: Admiral Sir Bertram Ramsay, naval chief of the Allied Expeditionary Force, is killed when his aircraft crashes in Paris. Ramsay was a key figure in planning the Dunkirk evacuation and the Allied invasions of North Africa and Sicily. He was also in charge of naval operations in support of the D-Day landings

In Copenhagen, resistance fighters destroy a factory making parts for V2 rockets. In the Atlantic, a new weapon of war is introduced to the Allied arsenal as the Sikorsky helicopter is used for convoy escort duties for the first time.

3 January: The strategically important Burmese port of Akyab is liberated by a single British artillery officer after the Japanese had pulled out of the town 48 hours previously.

Canadian forces are being augmented through conscription. Today the first draftees set sail for Europe from Halifax. A Nazi concentration camp is liberated at Breendonck in Holland – it is one of the first of Hitler's death camps to be revealed to the outside world.

4 January: Intense naval actions are taking place in the East China Sea, off the Philippines and in the Indian Ocean. A 'Kamikaze' pilot slams his aircraft into US carrier *Ommaney Bay* causing it to sink with the loss of 93 lives.

The US press is speculating on an alarming warning from Admiral Jonas Ingram that New York may soon be attacked by flying bombs launched from German submarines. The Kriegsmarine are thought to have at least 300 U-Boats still operational and they have been noticeably more active in the North Atlantic of late.

5 January: In Greece the new premier General Pastiras has formed a moderate cabinet in a bid to resolve the bitter civil war blighting the country. In the Ardennes, the weather again intervenes to bog down a major American offensive in the snow.
Air support is denied by low cloud. On the home front construction begins on the first of Britain's 'prefab' houses.

6 January: On the Philippine island of Luzon the Japanese continue with their 'Kamikaze' air campaign. Today 150 US naval crewmen die. By the end of the day, the Japanese have less than 100 aircraft left. Meanwhile, American bombers continue their relentless raids on Tokyo.

7 January: In Burma, Japanese forces are retreating towards Mandalay whilst Royal Marine Commandos attempt to block their path. The general advance of British and Commonwealth troops is supported by naval bombardment. Heavily-armed motor launches are harrying enemy vessels in the maze of coastal inlets in this part of Burma.

Meanwhile, in Moscow, Stalin agrees to step up operations on the Eastern Front in order to relieve the pressure on the British and the Americans. Meanwhile, during a press conference, Field Marshal Montgomery upsets the Americans by apparently playing down their contribution to stemming the German advance in the Ardennes.

8 January: The US 7th army is engaged in fierce fighting to repulse a determined German attack at Rimling.

9 January: General Heinz Guderian, Chief of the General Staff, warns a disinterested Hitler that the Russians are planning a major Eastern Front offensive.

In the Philippines, the US 6th Army, supported by heavy naval bombardments has landed at Lingayen Gulf, 110 miles north of the Phillipines capital, Manila.

10 January: A Hitler decree issued in Berlin sanctions the death penalty for anyone found guilty of diverting essential supplies from the military.

In the Malacca Strait, on **11 January**, the British submarine *Tally Ho* sinks the Japanese cruiser *Kuma*. On the same day, in the Ardennes, troops of the

Left: These captured German soldiers are just 14 years old.

WAR DIARY
January 1945

US 3rd Army link up with men of the British XXX Corps at St Hubert. At a conference in Versailles, Allied air force commanders determine to step up attacks on Germany's dwindling sources of fuel.

General Guderian's warning to Hitler three days ago is vindicated when, on **12 January,** the Russians hurl 163 divisions at German positions in Poland and East Prussia. The Germans resist from well prepared defences, but are outnumbered by five tanks to one.

14 January: General Slim's army in Burma commences crossing the Irrawaddy in force. This day also sees the Red Army cut the important railway line south of Crakow as its headlong advance across Poland gains momentum.

15 January: More good news comes from the Far East as two Chinese armies link up and the famous 'Burma Road' is reopened under Allied control. In London, the boat train service to the Continent starts again after a five year break.

16 January: Russian troops capture Radom and move to encircle Warsaw which finally falls on **17 January** to an assault masterminded by Marshal Zhukov. It is a city largely in ruins and destined for a bleak future after a Soviet-sponsored 'puppet' government is installed on **18 January** under President Bierut. He denounces the Polish Home Army who led the uprising against the Germans last August as 'irresponsible' and 'murderers who are provoking civil strife'. It is clear he intends a purge of all those who do not follow the communist line.

In the concentration camp Auschwitz-Birkenau, the Nazis order the immediate evacuation of 20,000 inmates considered fit enough to travel.

20 January: The Germans advance to within eight miles of Strasbourg causing panic in the city. *Operation North Wind* has proved a brilliant German counter-stroke and has stretched the forces of the American/French 6th Army Group to near breaking point.

In Washington, Franklin D Roosevelt is inaugurated for a fourth term as President Harry S Truman becomes his Vice-President. In Budapest, the provisional government agrees to pay $300 million reparations to the Allies and join them in the fight against Germany.

21 January: Indian troops have landed on Ramree Island in Burma and attack Kangaw.

On **22 January** in Berlin Hitler agrees a major ship building programme utilising slave labour. It's a strange decision but typical of the air of unrealism pervading around the Führer and his Nazi acolytes.

Next day **(23 January)** Hitler appoints Heinrich Himmler as C in C of Army Group Vistula. Himmler has no experience of operational command.

24 January: French forces halt the German advance on Strasbourg at the last bridge before the city. One of the Wehrmacht's top generals – Heinz Guderian - meets von Ribbentrop, the Nazi Foreign Minister, to tell him bluntly that 'the war is lost'. Guderian's outspokenness has put him out of favour with Hitler.

25 January: The Pacific island of Iwo Jima is heavily bombarded by the US navy who are anxious to break down the Japanese defences ahead of landings planned for next month.

26 January: The Red Army closes to within 100 miles of Berlin where old men, officer cadets and young boys have been recruited into the Volkssturm defence force and ordered to defend the capital to the last man.

27 January: The world is waking up to the existence of the dreadful Nazi concentration camps. Today, four young Red Army soldiers

Right: A monument to 61 British officers and men of the 13th (Lancashire) Battalion The Parachute Regiment who died in a battle for the village of Bure in the Belgian Ardennes between 3 and 5 January 1945.
Below: Sherman tanks in the snow during the Ardenne fighting in January 1945.
Inset: A Sherman on display in the region today.

advance into Auschwitz-Birkenau to be greeted by a host of 'living skeletons' moving slowly in a landscape of corpses sprawled in the snow.

28 January: Despite the persistence of the Arctic winter, the liberation of northern Norway – an area known as Finmark – continues. The Red Army has the largest number of men engaged in this snowy theatre of war, but now there are also Norwegian troops, sent from Britain after five years of waiting and training, keen to play a role in ending the Nazi occupation. The retreating Germans operate a 'scorched earth' policy and are destroying towns and villages. Over 40,000 civilians have been deported from Finmark in recent months; around 20,000 remain to greet their liberators.

29 January: In Burma, the Fourteenth Army continues to tighten its grip around the important city of Mandalay and is steadily pressing in on the Japanese who have little hope of reinforcement or major re-supply.

30 January: In the Baltic, Russian submarines are taking a heavy toll of German shipping and thousands of refugees are drowning in the freezing waters.

31 January: Russia's top commander, Marshal Zhukov, crosses the German frontier as Soviet forces advance to the River Oder and cut the rail link between Berlin and Danzig in East Prussia. They now pose a real threat to the city of Frankfurt, just 45 miles from Berlin.

THE WESTERN FRONT

'In this, the twilight of their gods, the defenders of the Reich displayed the recklessness of fanaticism and the courage of despair...'

A t 0500 hours on 8 February 1945, 1400 guns of the Canadian 1st Army opened fire on German positions along a seven-mile front between the Maas and Waal rivers close to the Dutch-German frontier. At 10.30 hours, Montgomery's XXX Corps, under the command of General Pat Crerar, moved into the attack with three divisions of British troops and two of Canadians. In reserve was the British 43rd Division and the tanks of the Guards Armoured Division.

The German position was heavily mined and included a flooded area and the thickly-wooded Reichswald Forest on one flank. Hitler and his commanders had viewed the risk of an attack in this sector as unlikely and Crerar's men had a good first day, taking in 1300 prisoners by nightfall.

On 10 February, the US Ninth Army were due to launch an offensive aimed at Dusseldorf on the Rhine but were frustrated in a landscape purposely flooded by the Germans. The flooding was also hampering the British advance and the enforced delay allowed the Germans to bring up paratrooper and panzer reinforcements.

The middle of February saw much bitter fighting. The Canadian Army official history records show the Germans seemed to have lost none of their morale: 'In this, the twilight of their gods, the defenders of the Reich displayed the recklessness of fanaticism and the courage of despair. In the contests west of the Rhine, in particular, they fought with special ferocity and resolution, rendering the battles in the Reichswald and Hochwald forests grimly memorable in the annals of this war.'

The Canadians secured the Reichswald and took the little town of Cleve before being reinforced across the Maas by the British 52nd Division and 11th Armoured. But in 11 days of fighting they had only advanced some 15 miles.

A *Daily Express* reporter recorded: 'So wet is this battle that the troops now call their commander Admiral Crerar. He often directs the fighting wearing fisherman's waders. The men mainly sing the Bing Crosby ditty, "..or would you rather be a fish?". The wounded come back from battle riding high in "ducks" across the floods.

'At any hour you are likely to meet Field-Marshal Montgomery... suddenly along the sodden road marked "Cleared of mines only to verges" comes a busy little jeep with a great red light flashing on and off by the radiator. Two grim MPs with red caps ride the bumps with stiff backs. Behind them comes the biggest car I ever saw, shining black and silver, with an outsized Union Jack fluttering at the bonnet. And inside alone sits Monty, who never misses a salute.'

Even so, the Allies were winning the war of attrition. Now the weather improved and Montgomery fixed 23 February for the start of a renewed attack (joint Operations *Veritable* and *Grenade*). In his order of the day to the men of the 21st Army Group, Monty assured them that this was to be the beginning of the last round against Germany.

The intended 'knock-out' blow was preceded by the biggest Allied air attack of the war with 10,000 bombers and fighter-bombers smashing the Third Reich's remaining communications network.

By the last day of February the Allies had broken through in a number of places. The Germans now saw that their only hope of staving off defeat in the west was to retreat behind the Rhine. Harried by the Allied air forces, thousands of men and vehicles escaped over the river. As the Allies closed up, the Germans ordered the demolition of all the Rhine bridges, to leave their enemy frustrated before this immense natural barrier. Getting across the river in strength would clearly be a daunting task.

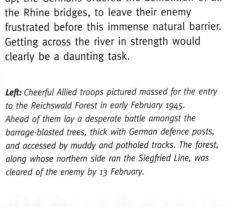

Left: Cheerful Allied troops pictured massed for the entry to the Reichswald Forest in early February 1945. Ahead of them lay a desperate battle amongst the barrage-blasted trees, thick with German defence posts, and accessed by muddy and potholed tracks. The forest, along whose northern side ran the Siegfried Line, was cleared of the enemy by 13 February.

WAR DIARY
February 1945

The month opens with the Red Army spreading out across Poland as the German retreat continues. Fighting alongside the Russians is a considerable force of Polish soldiers who have embraced the communist doctrine, either through willingness or political expediency. On **1 February** the town of Torun falls. However, the weather does not favour the attackers and Marshal Zhukov's tanks massing along the River Oder are bogged down in a sea of mud.

1 February Far East: A massive 50,000 ton floating dry dock at Singapore is sunk by US Super-Fortresses. The dock had been constructed in Britain and towed the 8000 miles to the island prior to the outbreak of war. Ironically, it is the second time the dock has been sunk; the British scuttled it in the face of the Japanese invasion early in 1942.

2 February: The Hungarian capital Budapest remains under siege by Russian forces. Troops of the 1st French Army, together with US troops, today enter Colmar, south of Strasbourg in Alsace. This far south, Germany's Siegfried Line is on the eastern bank of the Rhine.

On **3 February** USAAF bombers drop 3000 tons of ordnance on Berlin. Five square miles of the city are set ablaze. Ecuador declares war on Germany and is soon to be joined by Venezuela, Chile and landlocked Paraquay. All these countries seek invitations to the planned post-war United Nations conference.

4 February: Stalin, Roosevelt and Churchill are meeting at Yalta on the Black Sea for a conference to discuss the post-war shape of Europe. They will agree on the division of Germany into four zones of occupation.
In Wales Rudolf Hess tries to commit suicide with a bread knife whilst under guard in a mental hospital. Hess, at one time Hitler's chosen successor, flew alone to Scotland in 1941 on a 'peace' mission clouded in secrecy.

All of the territory of Belgium is now free of the Nazi invaders.

5 February: The Red Army is crossing the River Oder and has secured a small salient on the other bank. On the same day, Greek communist insurgents give up their arms as the government agrees an amnesty. Weary diplomat Harold Macmillan is able to report to London that the civil war in Greece is over.

6 February: In the Philippines, General Douglas MacArthur announces the imminent liberation of the capital, Manila. House to house fighting continues in the downtown business area and the old city.

7 February: Russian forces continue to clear the east bank of the Oder of the relatively small numbers of Germans who still offer resistance. RAF bombers make night attacks on enemy troop concentrations around Cleve and Goch, between the Maas and Rhine rivers.

8 February: RAF Lancasters raid a synthetic oil plant at Politz near Stettin, Germany. The Nazi war machine is rapidly running out of fuel. Lancasters also drop 12,000lb bombs on concrete pens sheltering E-Boats at Ijmuiden, Holland. Two days later the RAF will return to hammer nearby U-Boat pens.

The German navy still has a considerable submarine force. The latest vessels incorporate ingenious devices to avoid detection by sea and air. The 'Schnorkel' is a tube or funnel device fitted aboard a U-Boat, enabling the latter to draw down fresh air from the surface and discharge exhaust gases from the engine. In this way, it can stay submerged for extended periods of time. Other U-Boats carry a gyro-plane in a special container on deck. The gyro-plane can lift an observer several hundred feet into the air and hover while he makes a reconnaissance for enemy warships or merchantmen. There is also the 'water donkey', a dummy U-Boat hauled behind a real submarine. The dummy boat creates a wake near the surface and attracts the attention of prowling Allied aircraft. Hit by bombs, the 'water donkey' releases oil and wreckage to convince the attackers they have destroyed a real U-Boat.

9 February: British and Canadian troops are pushing through a gap in the Siegfried Line following a bombardment by 1000 guns and a heavy bomber attack. The Canadians use amphibious vehicles to cross flooded lowlands and reach the Rhine.

Round-the-clock Allied bombing continues over German-held Europe throughout the early days of February.

10 February: The Nakajima aircraft works at Ota near Tokyo is the target of a raid by Super-Fortresses. Long range carrier-based

The 'Big Three' pictured at the Yalta Conference in February 1945, where plans for the post-war occupation of Germany and settlement of Europe's borders were discussed. Churchill, Roosevelt and Stalin and their advisers decided that British, American and Russian forces would each control a separate zone of Germany. France would also be invited to take a zone of occupation. A Central Control Commission representing the three major powers was to have its HQ in Berlin. The Nazi leaders would learn of the fate of their country only after agreeing to unconditional surrender to the Allies.

Mustang fighters also struck at Japanese positions in the Chinese seaport of Tsingtao.

The important port of Elbing on the Vistula river is captured by Russian Marshal Rokossovsky's army, cutting the rail link between Berlin and Konigsberg in East Prussia.

11 February: Scottish troops enter the town of Cleve in Germany while Canadians occupy Millingen on the Rhine.

Burma: British and American bombers raid Rangoon today.

12 February: At Yalta in the Crimea, US President Roosevelt, Russian leader Stalin and British Premier Churchill issue a statement on joint plans for the defeat of Germany of the post-war settlement of Europe. They also agree that a Conference of United Nations should be called to meet at San Francisco on 25 April 1945.

After a bloody 50-day siege, Budapest falls to the Russians on **13 February**. The Austrian capital, Vienna, is next in the Soviet sights.

14 February: The historic German city of Dresden, an important rail and communication centre for the Wehrmacht in their struggle to stem the Russian advance, is raided by around 800 Lancaster bombers who virtually obliterate the city. Over 50,000 people die in the resulting firestorm.

In New York, a pair of captured German spies - William Colepaugh and Erich Gimpel - who landed from a U-Boat last November, are sentenced to death.

15 February: Soviet forces encircle Breslau, where martial law is declared, and in Burma, Indian troops capture Pagan.

16 February: After a massive air and sea bombardment, American paratroops and seaborne forces assault on the island fortress of Corregidor that dominates the entrance to Manila Bay. The 5200 Japanese defenders, fighting from a maze of caves and tunnels, put up a fanatical defence. In early 1942, General McArthur left the doomed island garrison by fast torpedo boat in the face of overwhelming Japanese forces, vowing: 'I will return'. Now he is fulfilling his promise.

17 February: US carriers are into the second day of mounting big air raids on Tokyo and Yokohama. They will also complete the final wave of bombardments of Iwo Jima, ahead of the invasion. Four days of intensive ground fighting will follow before the Stars and Stripes are raised on Mount Suribachi, boosting the morale of the sorely tested marines.

18 February: German women are being drafted into the Volkssturm to support the armed forces – previously the call was for female volunteers. At the same time, the Soviet advance forces missile expert Wernher von Braun and other scientists to abandon the rocket establishment at Peenemunde on the Baltic coast.

On **19 February**, Heinrich Himmler meets Red Cross representative Count Folke Bernadotte to make overtures for peace talks with the western Allies.

In the Pacific US Marines land on the island of Iwo Jima in the Volcano Islands, less than 1000 miles from the Japanese mainland. Bitter fighting lies ahead.

The German garrison in cut-off Konigsberg stages a counter-attack to clear the road to Pillau.

20 February: En route from Yalta, US President Roosevelt and British Premier Winston Churchill meet for four hours in Cairo to discuss the war against Japan, in the aftermath of the certain defeat of Germany. Churchill confirms Britain is determined 'to throw everything it has against the Japanese'.

21 February: Japanese resistance ends on Luzon but fierce fighting continues on Corregidor and around Manila. Kamikaze aircraft sink the carrier *Bismarck Sea* and damage the *USS Saratoga*. The next day around 2000 Japanese soldiers die when a vast ammunition store on Corregidor blows up.

22 February: US troops cross the Saar river. Eisenhower claims that to date the Allies are holding 900,000 prisoners from the European campaign. Uruguay declares war on Germany and Japan.

23 February: The German garrison in Poznan has held out for a month against the Russians. Around 100 miles behind the front line, the survivors today surrender to the Russians. Its rail network will greatly assist him in the final assault on Berlin.

Turkey today declares war on Germany and its remaining Axis partners. The country can now claim a place at the UN Security Conference in San Francisco in April.

24 February: Egypt's premier, Ahmed Maher Pasha is assassinated by gunmen from a pro-Axis group.

Thirty of the latest design U-Boats have been launched in German shipyards this month in the face of the tremendous Allied bombing campaign. By the end of February, the Kriegsmarine will have lost 19 submarines in action. The German navy's big problem is the attrition in experienced crew.

25 February: A raid by 172 B-29 bombers sees 450 tons of incendiaries drop on the centre of Tokyo, gutting around 28,000 buildings. At the same time, Berlin is the target for another massive 100-bomber daylight raid by the USAAF. Follow up attacks by RAF Mosquito fighter-bombers rekindle the fires as soon as they are extinguished. All over eastern Germany millions of refugees are making their way westwards, desperate to escape the advancing Russians.

28 February: In the Rhineland, on a 150 mile front from Trier in the south to Udem in the north, US, Canadian and British forces drive the Germans back towards the Rhine. The American Ninth Army is two miles from Munchen-Gladbach, the gateway to Düsseldorf. The famous city of Cologne with its distinctive cathedral is only 10 miles from the front and in range of US 150mm 'Long Tom' howitzers.

In Burma, after an 80 mile advance from the Irrawaddy, the 17th Indian Division and 255th Indian Tank Brigade encircle picturesque Meiktila. If Major General 'Punch' Cowan's column can take the town, the bulk of the Japanese army in Burma will be captured or killed.

On Iwo Jima, the Americans still face fierce pockets of resistance but have now taken the central airfield to facilitate fighter support for B-29 raids on Japan. In the Philippines, after the capture of Manila and Corregidor, the Americans land virtually unopposed on the island of Palawan, only 800 miles from the Chinese mainland and 250 miles from Japanese-held oilfields in North Borneo. Deep water anchorages will allow naval units to harass enemy shipping en route to Japan.

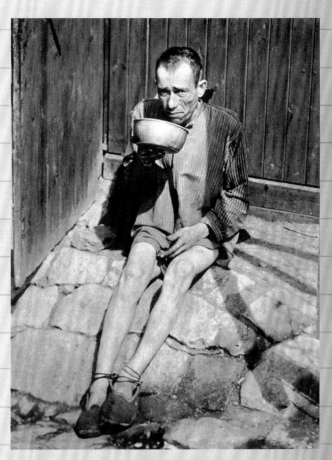

As the Allies advance closer to the heart of Germany more and more evidence of the Nazi genocide programme is uncovered with the discovery of concentration camps where millions of men, women and children - mainly of Jewish origin - have been murdered. A few inmates - such as this man - survive to bear witness to the horror.

BRIDGEWORK

March 1945. The Allies surge across the Rhine into Germany's heartland.

The Allied crossing of the Rhine was the big story of March 1945. For the British it would be the start of their last big offensive in the north of Europe; Monty saw to it that the preparations were thorough, involving boats, airborne landings and masses of tanks and artillery.

It was expected that all the Rhine bridges

Left: A dramatic depiction of Cologne being bombed by the RAF earlier in the war (National Archives – Art of War).

Above: A view from the top of Cologne Cathedral taken by an Allied cameraman after the Rhine crossing of March 1945. Note the Hohenzollern Bridge collapsed in the river. Cologne's distinctive twin-spired cathedral led a charmed life; like St Paul's in London it was surrounded by rubble and broken buildings yet miraculously remained largely intact.

would be down. However, late in the day on 8 March the astonishing news broke that US troops had seized a crossing intact. The Germans had delayed blowing the Ludendorff Bridge at Remagen, between the cities of Bonn and Coblenz, until the last possible moment at which point their demolition charges failed to ignite properly, leaving the bridge weakened but still standing. US troops rushed across to establish a salient. Despite German shellfire, the bridgehead was rapidly reinforced under the cover of a powerful air umbrella and US columns were soon probing deeper into Germany. Despite the attention of Luftwaffe bombers and enemy frogmen seeking to plant explosives on the structure, the bridge remained in use until the middle of the month when it partially collapsed.

British attack in the north

In the absence of a bridge further north, Montgomery devised *Operation Plunder*, a plan to secure a bridgehead on the east bank of the Rhine from where the Allied armies could break out, encircle the industrial Ruhr and thrust into the northern plains of Germany. The demarcation line between the assaulting formations – the British Second and US Ninth Armies – was the town of Wesel. The British were to assault in the north. Boats would ferry men and machines across the river until engineers could construct new bridges.

Backing up *Plunder* was *Operation Varsity*, an air assault by the men of the 17th US and British Sixth Airborne Divisions. The waterborne assault was to begin on the evening of 23 March. Air landings from the air up to eight miles beyond the east bank of the Rhine would commence next morning.

For two days before the attack went in, the Germans were heavily bombed and subjected to an immense artillery barrage fired by some 2000 heavy and medium guns. At 21.00 hours on 23 March, the Black Watch began crossing the river under cover of a heavy smoke screen. Soon the word came back from the Jocks that they were safely ashore on the east bank.

The 1st Commando Brigade had been given the task of capturing Wesel itself. They crossed a couple of miles north of the town, waited while the RAF carried out a raid and then entered the smoking ruins. The Commandos encountered pockets of resistance but by morning had secured a large part of the town.

Above: The Ludendorff Bridge over the Rhine at Remagen.

Jeeps and men falling out

Now came the air assault contained in a mighty procession of 1500 planes and 1300 gliders. In near perfect weather, the Allied airborne forces came down. Johnny Johnson of the 2nd Ox and Bucks had his LZ beyond the town of Hamminkeln. He recalled: 'My glider held a jeep and six men. We were hit twice in the air, once in the tail and then right underneath where the two pilots sat. They were screaming their heads off with pain but managed to crash-land the aircraft. We came down right on top of German positions. As the other gliders were landing, Jerry had machine guns trained on them and 88mm guns. I saw gliders hit in the air and jeeps and men falling out. It was terrible. Nearby were some power lines with six US paratroops, drooped wide, hanging on them, electrocuted.'

Despite the losses, by mid-afternoon the first Allied ground troops had reached the airborne forces. Over the next few days the British and US bridgeheads linked up and by 28 March the Allies were over 20 miles beyond the Rhine. *Varsity* was a success, albeit an expensive one. On the first day the Sixth Airborne suffered 1078 casualties and lost 50 aircraft and 11 gliders to German ground fire. Coupled with *Operation Plunder*, it paved the way for a rapid advance across Germany.

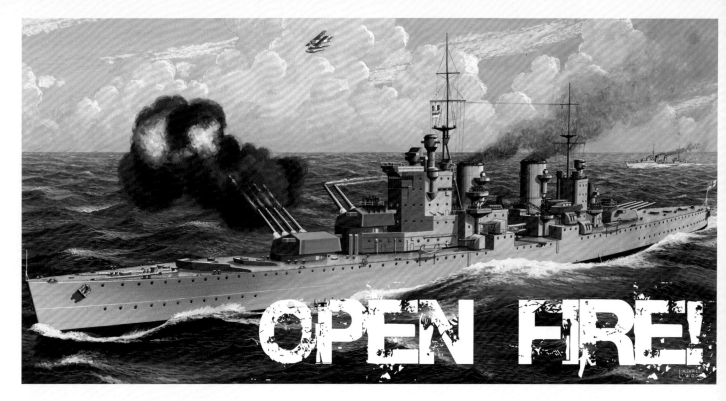

OPEN FIRE!

March 1945: Royal Navy sailor C J Thorpe took part in the Med's last major surface battle of the war.

The British destroyers *Lookout* and *Meteor*, together with the French destroyers *Tempete* and *Basque*, were patrolling several miles apart to the westward of Cape Corse, the northern-most point of Cassino. The night was calm and by midnight the new crescent moon had long since set behind dark clouds. At 2am on the morning of 18 March information was suddenly received that three enemy warships were at sea and somewhere near Cape Corse.

After days and weeks of patrolling on the part of the Allied destroyers the news was almost too good to be true. The enemy was some 70 miles from his nearest bases at Genoa and Spezia. There was a reasonable chance that he might be intercepted before reaching the protection of his minefields and coastal batteries and without waiting for further orders, the *Meteor* and *Lookout* increased to full speed and steamed to north-eastward. The *Lookout*, which was nearest, steered directly towards the enemy, while the *Meteor*, considerably to the westward, headed to cut him off if he retired north. The *Tempete* and *Basque*, further west still, moved to cover a convoy in the vicinity and later joined in the chase.

Glimmering wakes

One can imagine the scenes on board these ships at the prospect of action – the men in the engine and boiler rooms using every effort and artifice to obey the sudden order for full speed; the watch below tumbling out of their hammocks at the pipe 'Action

Stations!'; the gun and torpedo tubes' crews mustering round their weapons and making them ready; the Captains and personnel on the bridges checking the relative positions of their own ships and the enemy and peering out through the darkness for a first glimpse of black shapes with their glimmering wakes and low waves.

The *Lookout* was alone. Her Captain, D H F Hetherington DSC, knew there were three enemy vessels and that the odds were against him. But acting in the best Service tradition he did not hesitate. He went in to attack, and his temerity was rewarded.

At two minutes past 3am the enemy was sighted – three ships in line ahead steaming at high speed for their bases and seemingly oblivious to any prospect of trouble. Sweeping down upon them the *Lookout* opened up a heavy fire at point blank range and fired torpedoes when the sights came on. The first few salvoes brought an ill-directed and confused reply from the enemy, though as the action proceeded it became accurate enough, the *Lookout* frequently passing through the spray flung up by falling shell.

Tongues of flame

Presently the second ship in the enemy line showed signs of distress. She turned out of the line and came to a standstill, with tongues of flame and dense clouds of smoke from fires between decks. Her crew abandoned ship, throwing rafts into the sea and themselves after them. The other two enemy ships, repeatedly hit by the *Lookout's* guns, made off to the northward at top speed, firing wildly back as they strove to make good their escape. In spite of the fire that had been poured upon her, the *Lookout* was entirely undamaged.

The *Meteor* made contact with the two

Above: A painting of a British warship in action (National Archives – Art of War).

fleeing enemy ships at 3.52pm, some 13 miles to the northward of where their consort had been sunk. Closing in the *Meteor* poured in a devastating fire and also fired torpedoes, one of which went home in a pillar of flame and smoke on the second ship in the enemy line, which finished her. The solitary survivor sought safety in flight and managed to escape into the enemy minefields and coastal batteries.

The *Meteor* rescued 120 men from her victim, all of them being Germans. When daylight came, no trace could be seen of the *Lookout's* opponent, but another 125 of her survivors were later rescued from rafts by coastal craft sent out to the scene of the action. The vessels sunk were ex-Italian warships each of about 1000 tons.

The *Meteor* and *Lookout* were both congratulated by the Commander-in-Chief, Mediterranean, Admiral Sir John Cunningham, on their most satisfactory night's work that still further reduced the small numbers of enemy warships now remaining in the ports of the Gulf of Genoa.

Right: C J Thorpe pictured aboard HMS Lookout late in the war. His account of the naval encounter off Cape Corse in which he participated as a Seaman Torpedo man is based on a contemporary report published in The Times of Malta dated 3 April 1945.

DIVISION KANADA

The German garrison in the Channel Islands called themselves 'Division Kanada' as they believed that country to be their eventual destination as POWs. However, in the spring of 1945 they proved that as far as they were concerned the war was far from over.

On 9 March 1945, the day that the American 9th Armoured Division famously captured the Remagen Bridge across the Rhine, Admiral Huffmeier, commander of the German forces on the Channel Islands, 500 miles behind the front, launched one of the most audacious commando raids of the war; he had sent his men to capture the French port of Granville, once Eisenhower's first HQ in France, and now a quiet backwater of the war.

Lt-Commander Sandel in the US torpedo boat PC 564 had been the first to spot the German convoy. The young naval officer had only taken over command a few days before and his crew was a scratch one, recruited mainly from US port offices in England. But he didn't hesitate. As soon as the first suspicious green blobs appeared on the radar screen, he set course for the Germans.

He saw them when they were three miles away. Immediately he ordered three flares to be shot into the air for identification purposes. But almost simultaneously, a German flare burst directly above his ship, bathing it in an icy white light. His response was immediate.

'Open fire!' he yelled to the gun crew. The 76mm cracked into action. The little ship shuddered. But the shell hit the water 200 yards away from the leading enemy ship. The crew went to fire again. Nothing happened – the brand new artillery piece had jammed after the first round!

Complete surprise

The torpedo boat didn't get a second chance. With a roar a more powerful German 88mm gun opened up. The shell hit the bridge, killing or wounding everyone on it. Three more rounds punched into PC 564; drifting helplessly, its steering gone, its radio knocked out, the little ship disappeared into the night, leaving the Germans elated at the first success in their daring venture.

The Germans took the port by complete surprise. A French infantry company, alarmed by the noise, got out of their bunks. But their CO Captain Amand ordered them back to their quarters. Later, when asked why, the Frenchman shrugged and said, 'I thought the Americans were out on night manoeuvres and everybody knows that they do things completely different to the rest of the world.'

The Germans swarmed ashore. The US port

Above: An 88mm anti-aircraft gun in Jersey with its Luftwaffe crew. The 'kills' ringed on the barrel were obtained prior to the gun coming to the island.

commander ran for help but could find none. The German engineers, working against time as they wanted to be at sea again before the dawn, blew up installations throughout the supply port, cheering every time a crane or loading device came crashing down.

Meanwhile, the infantry of Division Kanada swept through the town freeing their own men who were working for the Allies in the docks, jubilantly herding Allied officers, some still in their night clothes, out of their hotels at bayonet point and everywhere cramming anything edible down their starved throats. The audacious raid went without a hitch. The Germans took scores of prisoners, released 55 of their own men, blew up four ships and captured one British coaler complete with crew. When the first American Sherman crawled cautiously into the port just before dawn, it found the birds flown and the docks a smouldering shambles.

Besieged Dunkirk

A few days later Admiral Huffmeier held a parade at which he awarded the Iron Cross to several members of the raiding party. This he followed up with something more welcome than the piece of metal – a packet of cigarettes and a jar of looted jam for each man.

Huffmeier's example caught on. In besieged Dunkirk, Admiral Frisius headed a 12,000 strong garrison. He sent a force to attack the mainly Czech troops surrounding the port. The Germans caught the Allies completely off guard. While British tanks rolled into Lübeck in Germany, British engineers at Gravelines, 10 miles south of Dunkirk, blew the bridge across the River Aa in the face of the surprise attack. Over 89 Czech soldiers wandered into the triumphant Germans' POW cage!

All along the coastline Allied troops reported attacks by German forces, real or imaginary, and while in Germany itself the front-line Allied soldiers celebrated their imminent victory, their second-line comrades dug themselves in, fearful of further German commando attacks.

ESCAPE!

Around 2000 German POWs were housed in Island Farm Camp 98 at Bridgend, South Wales, in the opening months of 1945. A year previously, the camp had held US troops awaiting the invasion of Europe and General Eisenhower once paid a visit. Despite the fact that the war was clearly going very badly for their country, German morale was very high, although it was greatly influenced by a large number of pro-Nazi officers who held sway over the camp. Local civilians were subjected to loud singing of military songs and said the noise from the camp often resembled that of a 'bad tempered football crowd'.

On the night of 10/11 March 1945, a mass escape took place when some 70 prisoners

made their way through a tunnel under the wire. For many the resulting freedom was short-lived and most were quickly rounded up. At Laleston, two miles from the camp, church bells were rung as an alarm for the first time since Churchill had ruled in 1940 that they were only to be sounded in the event of a German invasion.

However, four of the escapees – who included U-Boat commander Oswald Prior – managed to steal an Austin 10 car that belonged to Dr R Baird Milne. Intent on getting to the big airport at Croydon, they only made it as far as the Forest of Dean before running out of petrol. They next stowed away on a goods train and were finally caught near Castle Bromwich, about 110 miles from Bridgend.

Back in captivity, when one of the Germans learnt they'd taken a doctor's car, he apologised and offered to pay for the petrol!

The Bax Factor

Spitfire pilot Raymond Baxter took part in an unusual operation over Occupied Holland in March 1945.

In the spring of 1945 602 (City of Glasgow) Squadron were flying their socks off in Operation Big Ben – the anti-V2 campaign. On several occasions during those ops pilots reported seeing the white trails of V2 rockets arcing up at incredible speed and height towards their indiscriminate targets. Raymond Baxter said it made them even more determined to strike back as hard as they could. Equipped with Spitfire XVIs they were dive-bombing every reported or suspected launch site and skip-bombing and strafing interdiction targets throughout Occupied Holland. Four sorties per pilot per day were not uncommon.

One day the Squadron Leader, Max Sutherland DFC, proposed a special mission. He said he believed that five Spitfires flying low and fast could take out the HQ of the German V1 and V2 operations, located just outside The Hague in the pre-war offices of Shell-Mex. Baxter thought it was a 'dodgy' order not least because of the well-manned heavy and light flak known to be in the flightpath they must follow.

Max was not one to be daunted. He arranged for the Australian Squadron 453 to lay on a diversion and said that the five Spits must fly 'flat and low' and in close formation to make the attack. After a disappointing abort, because cloud obscured the target, the attack was delivered precisely according to plan on 18 March. Baxter recalled how the five aircraft flattened out at about 100 feet with the building dead ahead and square in their gyro-sights: 'At about 300 yards we let go with our two 20mm cannon and 0.5in machine guns and then released our single 500lb and 250lb, 11-second delay bombs.'

As he cleared the roof of the building at near enough 400mph, to his horror Baxter saw ahead at eye-level 'this black cockerel atop the weather vane on the church spire across the road'. The pilots knew the church was there but not the height of its spire. Fortunately, Baxter's Spitfire missed the cockerel and ensured that the pilot would live on to enjoy a highly successful career as a radio broadcaster and popular presenter of the BBC *Tomorrow's World* programme.

The mission was a complete success; Max got a Bar to his DFC and the other pilots got a 'Collective Mention'. The BBC news at 9pm the same night reported, 'During the day, RAF fighter bombers continued their attacks on selected ground targets in Occupied Holland.'

In the book *Tales of My Time*, Raymond Baxter recounted to his good friend Tony Dron a fascinating postscript to the story: 'Years later the distinguished aviation artist, Michael Turner, read about my cockerel and said he'd like to paint a picture of it. I managed to find the original PRU (Photographic Reconnaissance Unit) print on which our attack had been based.

'Some time after the painting was completed Michael received a letter from a total stranger in Holland requesting my address. It transpired that, totally by chance, Aad Devisser had visited an exhibition of Second World War aviation art, seen Michael's painting and realised that he too was there on 18 March 1945.

'As a 16-year-old, he was doing his best to avoid deportation to a labour camp. With his parents he lived in caretaker quarters in the Shell-Mex building. As he described it, "I heard you coming...and looked into your eyes."

'Mercifully, although we destroyed their home, he and his family survived, including the dog. My late friend, Aad Devisser, wrote of "the admiration and gratitude he and his fellow Dutch men and women felt for the RAF pilots who were risking their lives for us".'
*Raymond Baxter died on 15 September 2006, aged 84.

Left: *Raymond with Lt Sylvia K Johnson of the US Army Nursing Corps at her Bridport hospital on the eve of D-Day. The pair later married.*

WAR DIARY

On **1 March**, US troops capture München-Gladbach and approach the town of Neuss. The Western Front now runs in almost a straight line from Holland in the north to France's border with Switzerland in the south. The River Rhine – swollen from the winter rain is the biggest obstacle in the way of the Allies.

2 March: Bucharest falls to the Red Army and the Kremlin will waste no time in installing a client communist regime. The people of Rumania have suffered ruination through the reckless gamble of their leaders when they joined Hitler in making war on their feared neighbour, Russia.

Cologne suffers an attack by 858 RAF bombers who leave much of the city in ruins. Miraculously, the 13th Century Gothic cathedral is hardly damaged and regular services continue to be held in the vestry.

3 March: The last pockets of resistance in Manila are mopped up by US forces. Over 20,000 Japanese soldiers have died defending the capital of the Philippines. Also in the Far East, Meiktila, south of Mandalay in Burma, is declared free of the enemy.

Meanwhile, in Holland over 500 civilians die in The Hague when an RAF attack on a V2 rocket site misses the target.

For the first time since June 1944, Luftwaffe piloted aircraft bomb random targets in southern and northern England. Around 70 fighter-bombers and Heinkel 188s are involved; up to eight of the raiders are believed shot down.

4 March: German bombers again target England, but in smaller numbers than last night. Luftwaffe night fighters shoot down 20 British bombers returning from a raid on the Dortmund-Ems canal.

On the same day, Finland joins the list of nations formally declaring war on Germany and American armour reaches the Rhine between Cologne and Düsseldorf.

5 March: Desperate to bolster their fighting strength, Germany is conscripting 16-year-old boys to do battle against the advancing Allies. Some have already been awarded the Iron Cross for destroying Allied tanks with *panzerfaust* (bazooka) rounds. Today US troops are entering the suburbs of Cologne on the west bank of the Rhine.

Buckingham Palace reveals that the King has granted to Her Royal Highness the Princess Elizabeth a commission with honorary rank of second subaltern in the Auxiliary Territorial Service. At present the Princess is attending a driver training course at a centre in the south of England.

6 March: Dutch resistance fighters who today ambush SS General Hans Rauter planned to execute him for 'crimes against the people of Holland'. The attempt fails and 17 Dutchmen will be executed in reprisal.

7 March: US troops are amazed to find a bridge over the Rhine intact at Remagen when demolition charges fail to explode. Soldiers make it to the eastern side of the Ludendorff Bridge and form a perimeter. General Omar Bradley tells his commanders to 'shove everything you can across it'.

In the Far East, Chinese forces capture Lashio, terminus of the Burma Road supply line from India to China.

British newspapers report that the milk ration for non-priority adult consumers is to be increased from two pints to two and half pints a week later this month.

8 March: Late tonight, and with great audacity, the Germans launch a surprise attack from the Channel Islands against the port of Granville in Normandy, around 500 miles behind the Allied armies on the Western Front.

9 March: The Red Cross supply ship *Vega* berths in Jersey, bringing more provisions for the civilian population and a small quantity of petrol for the island's ambulance.

In Indo-China, the Japanese go on the offensive against French troops who seek to re-impose colonial rule by Paris.

10 March: Tokyo suffers the single most destructive air raid of the war so far when hit by US B-29 Super-Fortresses flying from the Marianas Islands. Around 16 square miles of the industrial area of the city are destroyed and around 83,000 people die.

11 March: Nagoya in Japan is bombed by 285 Super-Fortresses.

Europe also racks up a record raid in the same 24-hour period when 1108 RAF bombers drop 4851 tons of ordnance on Dortmund. Another 1079 Allied planes shatter the vital Krupp works at Essen. U-Boat yards and oil refineries at Hamburg, Kiel and Bremen are also attacked.

In Wales, German prisoners stage their own 'Great Escape' when 66 men exit their camp via a 45ft-long tunnel under the barbed wire. By nightfall 43 have been recaptured, some by Land Girls armed with pitchforks.

12 March: The bridgehead at Remagen is now over 10 miles wide and four miles deep. The Germans have tried to bomb the bridge and have also sent frogmen down the Rhine with explosive charges, but all attacks fail.

13 March: A young girl dies of typhus in the Bergen-Belsen concentration camp. Her name is Anne Frank. Although she is just one of millions to perish without trace in the Holocaust, the diary of her wartime experiences – not found by the Nazis when they discovered her family's Amsterdam hiding place – will become an icon of how the human spirit can shine through in the midst of evil.

Anne Frank.

14 March: The supply of oil from Hungary to Germany is further curtailed after Allied bombers strike refineries just 35 miles away from the advancing Russians.

15 March: *The Daily Telegraph* reports how last night RAF 617 Squadron – The Dambusters – scored a direct hit on the Bielefeld viaduct using an enormous 22,000lb Grand Slam bomb designed by Barnes Wallis. The viaduct carried the last intact double track rail line out of the armaments manufacturing Ruhr region of Germany. Though factories will continue to build tanks and aircraft, the means to transport them to the front lines in east and west has been all but destroyed.

16 March: Rudolf Hoess, former commandant of the death camp at Auschwitz, admits he had two million inmates murdered – mainly gassed – between June 1941 and the end of 1943 on the express orders of Hitler's cohort, Himmler.

The V2 offensive against England is all but over. Although some of the elusive mobile launch sites in Holland have evaded Allied air attacks, lack of fuel and the inability to transport newly-built rockets is curtailing the campaign. One of the last blasts hits Smithfield Market in London, where 110 people are killed and 123 seriously injured.

17 March: Supreme Allied Commander Dwight D Eisenhower reins in General 'Blood and Guts' Patton and orders a halt to any advance towards the Czech border, now less than 100 miles away, even though the Germans have little to stop the

359

WAR DIARY
March 1945

Americans from reaching Prague before the Russians.

The bridge at Remagen collapses today, causing the death of 28 US soldiers.

In Tokyo, the Japanese leadership order children over the age of seven to give up school and assist in the war effort.

18 March: The Polish First Army captures Kolberg as Russian forces close in on the Baltic ports of Danzig and Gdynia.

In the Pacific, US warships bombard enemy positions on the Kurile Islands, north of the Japanese mainland.

19 March: Hitler issues the 'Nero Command,' demanding that Germans choose the utter destruction of the Fatherland over surrendering to the Allies. 'If the war is lost, the nation will also perish,' he declares.

German jet aircraft works are attacked in the south of Germany.

The British Government says that peace will signal a two-year period of frantic house-building. With 750,000 new dwellings required, hundreds of thousands of building workers will be given priority release from the services.

20 March: In Burma, the 19th Indian Division under Major General Peter Rees capture Fort Dufferin in Mandalay. The city is finally secured after 10 days of close quarter fighting, much of it with swords, bayonets and kukris.

Overshadowed by events in North West Europe, in Italy the Allies are preparing a major offensive to trap the German army in the Po Valley. Shortages of ammunition and the transfer of units to the Western Front are made up for by the arrival of new flame-throwing tanks and 400 amphibious troop carriers, ideally suited to river crossings.

21 March: General Heinz Guderian fails to persuade Himmler to accompany him to Berlin to help persuade Hitler to seek an armistice.

Denmark: RAF Mosquito aircraft bomb the Gestapo HQ in Copenhagen.

22 March: General Patton sends his Third Army troops across the Rhine at Oppenheim, south of Mainz. Montgomery is disappointed that Patton's move pre-empts his own major Rhine crossing further north, planned for tomorrow.

23 March: Monty's army of British, Canadian and US forces cross the Rhine in the Wesel Sector. The British general promises to 'chase the enemy from pillar to post,' across the North German plain.

A *Daily Telegraph* report from US war correspondent Cornelius Ryan describes the last stand of German forces on the west bank of the Rhine in the Mainz-Wurz area. The Germans are desperate to cross the river, but are caught between General Patton's Third Army and the Seventh Army of General Patch. Ryan observes: 'It is a hopeless venture for the Germans. They cannot hope to hold out very long because of the terrific weight of men and material that threatens them from either side.'

24 March: The German Ninth Army commanded by General Busse has mounted unsuccessful attacks twice in recent days in attempts to relieve the encircled defenders of Kustrin. Hitler orders Busse to prepare for another attack.

25 March: Many American generals believe they can make it to Berlin before the Russians get there. Major-General Isaac D White,

commander of the Second Armoured 'Hell on Wheels' Division has detailed orders and map overlays completed today. His plan is to advance to Magdeburg on the Elbe, 80 miles away.

Once across the river his men will dash up the autobahn and he believes they could make it to Berlin within 48 hours.

26 March: Carrier-based planes of the British Pacific Fleet carry out attacks on airfields on Okinawa, Formosa and neighbouring islands. Taking Okinawa will be the final step before an assault on the Japanese home islands. A vast invasion force of 1400 ships carrying 182,000 troops is *en route*.

Hitler's deputy, Martin Bormann, calls for volunteers to become 'Werewolf' guerillas who will strike at the enemy from any direction in the Fatherland.

27 March: The last V2 to fall on Britain strikes Orpington in Kent today. Since early September 1944 it is reckoned that 1050 rockets have targeted Britain, killing 2754 people and injuring another 6523.

US troops land on the island of Cebu in the Philippines.

Soviet forces break into Danzig and Gydnia in East Prussia. General Busse mounts another attempt to relieve the German forces trapped in Kustrin. Although some of his Ninth Army panzers break through to the city, the main attack is smashed by an overwhelming massive Russian artillery barrage. Busse reports he has lost 8000 men in the fruitless fighting.

28 March: Berlin is the target of wave after wave of Russian fighter planes who rake the city with machine gun fire. The German capital is just 50 miles from the Red Army's leading tank spearheads. They are meeting fierce resistance. Western forces are nearly 200 miles from the Nazi capital, but face light opposition. Churchill has advised the Americans that, 'we should shake hands with the Russians as far to the east as possible.'

29 March: Montgomery's armour reports a significant advance out of their bridgehead on the east bank of the Rhine. British and Canadian troops clear Emmerich and cross from Holland into Germany.

30 March: The famous German university town of Heidelberg falls to the US Seventh Army. General Tolbukin's Russian forces cross into Austria from Hungary. General Slim's Fourteenth Army reports the capture of the important town of Kyaukse in Burma. Grapefruit from the Middle East has been arriving in British shops recently costing 8d per lb.

31 March: Allied HQ issue a bulletin claiming the Allies are poised for the final attack on Germany. The ultimate goal of Montgomery's 21st Army Group is Germany's Baltic ports. Patton is about to link up with the US First Army at Kassel while the French First Army is over the Rhine between Mannheim and Karlsruhe and swinging south towards the Swiss border.

In Japan, US Super-Fortresses bomb airfields in Kyushu and the aircraft factories at Nagoya are hit again.

Right: British armour lined up to bombard German defences in preparation for an Allied advance.

ITALY
The Final Push

Above: Two Spitfires on patrol over Northern Italy.

Below: A British officer surveys the distant Alps in the direction of Austria. Ten months after marching into Rome on 5 June 1944, the hard slog up the boot of Italy is almost complete.

April 1945 saw the Allies achieve victory in the Italian Campaign.

Nine days into the month, the Eighth Army launched a powerful assault against German defences on the Senio River. Flame-throwers played a big part in the initial attack, which had been preceded by a tremendous artillery barrage.

By midday on 10 April over 1200 prisoners had been taken and the advance was going well. Allied air support dropped 350,000 fragmentation bombs on German troops and fortifications. Some Italian fascist supporters – Blackshirts – still fought alongside the Germans, but many more Italians were engaged on the Allied side, either as regular troops or partisans.

Though fierce fighting continued for several days, good progress was reported by both the Eighth and Fifth Armies. Argenta, a key defence town, was liberated on 17 April and after Bologna fell on 21 April it became clear that the enemy was close to collapse, as they hastily retreated to the River Po. Eighth Army men crossed the river on 24 April and on the same day took Ferrara. On 26 April Verona was taken and the next day US troops entered Genoa. Popular uprisings against the Germans and Blackshirts took place in many towns and cities. At the same time Tito's Yugoslav patriots – having liberated their own country – were moving into Italian territory, determined to reclaim the city of Trieste ceded to Italy after the Great War.

In about 20 days, the remaining German armies in Italy were virtually eliminated as a fighting force opening the way for an Allied thrust northwards into Austria, always the goal since the landings on Sicily. The unconditional surrender of nearly one million German soldiers, sailors and Luftwaffe personnel in Italy and Southern Austria was signed at Caserta on 29 April, after the Allies had completed their swift advance across the North Italian plain. However, the surrender would not come into official effect until 2 May when Field-Marshal Alexander issued a declaration to the men of the Eighth and Fifth Armies: 'After nearly two years of hard and continuous fighting you stand today as victors in the Italian Campaign. You may well be proud of this great campaign, which will long live in history as one of the greatest and most successful ever waged.'

WAR DIARY

April 1945

1 April: It's the 2038th day of the war. The Red Army captures Sopron close to the Austria-Hungary frontier and threatens Vienna. In Italy, the Allies are preparing a massive assault on the German forces south of the River Po. Will this be the last big battle of the gruelling Italian Campaign? Eighth Army commander, Lt-Gen Richard McCreery, leads a force that includes British and Americans (many of Japanese origin), Brazilians, Italians, New Zealanders, Poles, Indians, Gurkhas and a Jewish Brigade. British commandos began their attack east of Lake Comacchio on the Adriatic coast tonight.

In Paris the famous landmarks of Notre Dame and the Arc de Triomphe are floodlit for the first time since the outbreak of war in 1939.

In the Pacific, the largest amphibious landing of the Pacific campaign is taking place. Over half a million US personnel are involved as troops land on the island of Okinawa.

2 April: In Berlin Hitler's favoured deputy, Martin Bormann calls for 'victory or death' from the German people. British and US troops occupy the town of Munster.

Moscow announces the capture of Hungary's oil centre at Nagy Kaniisza.

Italy: Eighth Army forces land on a spit of land separating Lake Comacchio from the Adriatic, north of Ravenna.

Germany: Men of the British 6th Guards' Tank Brigade liberate 9000 Russian POWs from Stalag 326 at Eselheide, between Munster and Hamm.

3 April: U-Boat yards at Kiel are bombed by US Flying Fortresses while RAF Lancasters attack German troop concentrations at Nordhausen, north east of Cassel.

Canadian First Army troops advance in Holland and cross the Twenthe Canal between Zutphen and Hengelo.

Far East: Super-Fortresses attack aircraft works on Japan's Honshu island.

4 April: The *Schwarze Korps*, a Nazi propaganda publication controlled by SS leader Heinrich Himmler, concedes that Germany is 'on the verge of absolute collapse'.

In Germany French forces enter Karlsruhe and the towns of Cassel, Gotha and Aschaffenburg are reported clear of the enemy by other Allied armies.

U-Boat yards at Kiel and Hamburg are again the target of US heavy bombers.

The Russian army led by Marshal Malinovsky takes Bratislava, capital of Slovakia, by storm. The Red Army also announces further territorial gains in Austria.

RAF Coastal Command Mosquitoes attack German shipping in the heavily defended anchorage of Sande Fjoord in Norway.

5 April: The Kremlin announces the Soviet Union's scrapping of the five year neutrality pact with Japan. Already reeling from the devastating US bombing attacks on her cities and industries, Japan now faces the certainty of a new front opening up against her along the Soviet Far East border with Manchuria and the eastern Pacific seaboard as soon Stalin feels the time is right. Moscow's denunciation of the pact coincides with the resignation of General Koiso's cabinet in Tokyo. The new prime minister is Admiral Suzuki. Advisers at the court of the Emperor urge the premier to end the war quickly.

In Germany, the British First Commando Brigade clear Osnabruck of the enemy, while Minden is secured by men of the Sixth Airborne.

6 April: Red Army troops break into the suburbs of Vienna where street fighting takes place.

Over 100,000 prisoners are rounded up in the German

" **The Eighth Army's ranks now include British and Americans (many of Japanese origin), Brazilians, Italians, New Zealanders, Poles, Indians, Gurkhas and a Jewish Brigade.** "

industrial heartland of the Ruhr.

Minister of Labour, Ernest Bevin, says that the wartime coalition government led by Churchill will be dissolved at the earliest opportunity to pave the way for a general election.

In the Balkans, Yugoslav partisans under the command of Marshal Tito moved in to take control of the town of Sarajevo after the Germans had largely withdrawn.

Far East: Three US destroyers reported sunk by Japanese aircraft off Okinawa.

7 April: The 72,000 ton Japanese battleship *Yamato* is sunk by carrier-based US aircraft off Kyushu. With little fuel left, the ship's hopeless mission was to draw US aircraft and naval units away from the Okinawa battle and into the range of kamikaze pilots flying from the Japanese home islands. Two Japanese cruisers and three destroyers are also destroyed in the same action. US bombers attack Tokyo and Nagoya.

RAF Mosquitoes, flying from Continental bases for the first time, attack targets in Berlin. At night Allied parachutists land in Holland, east of the Zuider Zee.

In Germany, soldiers of the US First Army seize 13 rail wagons loaded with V2 rockets destined for launch sites on the Dutch coast. It is the first time any of the missiles have been captured intact. The train was held up because in all parts of the Netherlands still occupied by the Germans, the Dutch rail workforce remains on strike with many key personnel in hiding. The 30,000 rail workers first failed to turn up for duty on 18 September 1944 following an appeal broadcast by the free Dutch government after consultation with the Allied High Command. Since then the country's rail service has been greatly incapacitated. A number of the strikers have been executed and families taken hostage. Thousands of others remain in hiding. A Dutch transport official later describes the situation: 'One half of occupied Holland was in hiding – the other half kept it hidden.'

8 April: General Patton's troops discover art treasures and what appears to be the entire Reichsbank gold reserves hidden 700 yards inside a salt mine at Merkers, 30 miles south of Mulhausen. There are also millions of pounds worth of various foreign currencies.

Denmark: A flotilla of 21 small vessels crammed with Danish patriots escaping from the German occupiers of their country is heading across the Baltic for the safety of neutral Sweden.

9 April: The Third Reich's one-time 'spymaster', Admiral Canaris, is hanged for treason. The former head of the *Abwehr* (military intelligence) was suspected of involvement in the plot to assassinate Hitler in July 1944 and of making peace overtures to the Allies.

The US Ninth Army takes over the Krupp plant in Essen, a major source of German armaments. RAF bombers damage one of Kriegsmarine's two remaining pocket battleships, the *Admiral Scheer*, and inflict serious harm on the heavy cruiser *Admiral Hipper*.

In Italy, the Eighth Army reports the crossing of the River Senio

WAR DIARY
April 1945

after a heavy bombardment of German positions from the air.

10 April: One by one Germany's major cities are falling to the Allies. US Ninth Army troops today capture Hanover where they liberate 60,000 slave workers and 300 British POWs. The road to Bremen is now blocked and the Allies have also occupied Essen. US bombers are in action attacking jet aircraft bases in the Berlin area and claim to have destroyed 305 enemy planes. RAF bombers hit railway yards at Leipzig. These attacks are just two of 5600 Allied sorties flown today; 40 aircraft are reported lost, mainly due to German flak.

11 April: Soldiers of the US Ninth Army reach the Elbe near Magdeburg and enter Brunswick. Tomorrow US troops will cross the river, but will not advance much further east in strength; they expect to rendezvous with Red Army forces at any time.

The surviving 21,000 emaciated and disease-ridden inmates of Buchenwald Concentration Camp are liberated by the US Third Army. Over 1000 German civilians from Weimar will be marched the six miles to the camp to observe the horrors inflicted on victims of the Nazi system.

Vichy police chief and enthusiastic collaborator with the Nazis, Lucien Rottée, is sentenced to death in Paris.

In Germany, US troops capture an intact V-weapons plant at Nordhausen. They race to remove material relating to rocket science ahead of the arrival of the Red Army. The latter will have post-war control of the region. Franz Von Papen is captured in the Ruhr region.

Norway: RAF Coastal Command set on fire five German merchants ships off the coast.

Off Okinawa, the US carrier *Enterprise* is crippled and the battleship *Missouri* seriously damaged in kamikaze attacks. On shore, progress is painfully slow in the face of the fanatical Japanese defence.

12 April: The world is stunned by the sudden death of US President Franklin Delano Roosevelt. The only president ever elected four times, 63-year-old Roosevelt, a polio sufferer for 20 years, was a good friend to Churchill and a staunch supporter of the British stand against the Nazis – even when America was still neutral. Roosevelt is succeeded by Harry S Truman, the son of a Missouri farmer.

The Eighth Army are advancing in Italy and today units cross the Santerno River.

Tokyo and Koriyama aircraft works bombed by USAAF Super-Fortresses.

13 April: Seven years and one month since the *Anschluss* – when Hitler forcibly joined Austria to Germany – Vienna has a new master as Marshal Tolbukhin's men take complete control of the city, making 130,000 Germans prisoner in the process. Despite the fighting, most of the principal buildings have survived major damage.

Unimaginable scenes of death and suffering greet US troops at Ohrdruf and Buchenwald. The latter was one of Hitler's first concentration camps, created in 1938. Battle hardened commanders Bradley, Patton and Eisenhower are moved to tears at the sight of piles of rotting corpses and mass graves.

Carrier aircraft of the British Pacific Fleet attack Japanese airfields on the island of Formosa (Taiwan).

14 April: Now only 40 miles from Berlin, victorious Red Army marshals Zhukov, Koniev and Rokossovsky are poised with massed strength for the final assault on the German capital. Elsewhere the Luftwaffe reel from non-stop attacks on airfields. In a 48 hour period 1738 aircraft are destroyed on the ground and another 332 shot down in combat.

British troops are set to liberate Arnhem in Holland. The town with its bridge over the Rhine was the target of *Operation Market Garden* in September 1944. Just a single battalion of lightly armed British skytroops got to the bridge and held it for a few days before being over-run by superior German forces backed by panzers and artillery.

15 April: Allied attention is turning to German garrisons besieged in towns and ports on the country's Atlantic coast since the previous summer. Yesterday, 1350 US aircraft bombed German positions in the Gironde estuary, not far from Bordeaux. Over 1300 aircraft hit the same area today dropping 7000 bombs and incendiaries and 460,000 gallons of a new inflammable liquid. The liquid is held in containers that burst and splash their contents over 60 square yards. Following the air attacks, French forces mount land and sea attacks and it is reported that their Second Armoured Division has entered Royan.

Canadian units reach the North Sea coast of Holland; tomorrow they will liberate the town of Groningen. Die-hard Nazis set fire to the already badly battered centre of Arnhem as they retreat from

The enormous Zeppelin Stadium in Nuremberg fell to the US Seventh Army on 16 April 1945. Once the scene of Hitler's ranting speeches to hundreds of thousands of Germans, now the concourse is empty except for a knocked-out US tank and a couple of jeeps.

WAR DIARY
April 1945

the Dutch town. With the famous Arnhem 'Bridge Too Far' now collapsed in the Rhine, British troops cross the river in landing craft.

British troops enter the concentration camp at Belsen. They find one Englishman among the 60,000 inmates.

16 April: Burma: Rangoon is now firmly in General Slim's sights and the Japanese are in retreat throughout Burma. Taungup, the last coastal Japanese supply base in Burma's Arakan region, is captured by the Fourteenth Army. The Imperial Army in the country now has no hope of outside aid reaching them.

On Okinawa, the Americans still battle against an estimated 80,000 die-hard Japanese who are concealed in a vast maze of tunnels and caves. In two days of vicious fighting the US forces have advanced just 1800 yards.

Berlin: Hitler retreats to his bunker under the Reich Chancellery accompanied by his mistress Eva Braun. The besieged population also seek shelter in cellars and trenches and await the arrival of the Russians with dread. Deserters and 'defeatists' are hunted down and summarily executed by roving SS squads. Food supplies are dwindling and many people wish only to surrender.

A small force of RAF Lancasters with 12,000lb bombs sink the pocket battleship *Lutzow* at Swinemunde. So far in April the Allies claim to have destroyed 3599 German aircraft, 3214 of them on the ground. In one single day US bombers and fighters raided 55 airfields in Germany, Austria and Czechoslovakia.

17 April: Germany: Fierce fighting continues in the city of Nuremberg following the entry yesterday of armoured spearheads of the US Seventh Army.

Denmark: RAF Mosquitoes make a low-level attack on the Gestapo HQ at Odense. Another 832 German aircraft are reported destroyed today, most of them on the ground.

Austria: Soviet troops capture the oil centre of Zistersdorf.

18 April: Field Marshal Walter Model commits suicide in a forest outside Dusseldorf. Only a few months ago he assumed command of German forces in the West and issued a ringing call to arms. Now the battle for the Ruhr has ended and there are 325,000 German prisoners in Allied hands.

In Holland, the Canadian First Army approaches the Zuider Zee in the face of stiffening opposition. Today the Germans breach dykes and cause flooding that will further delay progress. The Dutch in the north of the country have been waiting nearly 10 months for liberation after the failure of *Market Garden* and destruction of the Rhine bridges deflected the Allies into a different direction of attack.

Madrid: Hoping to appease the Allies, Generalissimo Franco prohibits all German aircraft from landing on Spanish territory. The fascist dictator kept his country neutral in the war and fears that western governments will press for 'regime change' in Spain after the defeat of Germany.

Nearly 1000 RAF bombers pound German defences and an airfield on the tiny North Sea island of Heligoland. They will return to finish the job with 12,000lb bombs tomorrow.

The Eighth Army capture Argenta in Italy.

19 April: Leipzig is captured by the US First Army. Polish troops serving with the Red Army capture the German city of Rothenburg. Russian units report the establishment of a bridgehead over the River Oder, west of Kustrin.

Long-range Mustang fighters flying the 1500 mile round trip from Iwo Jima make a first attack on Atsugi Airfield, south west of Tokyo. They report 85 Japanese aircraft destroyed.

Burma: The last of the country's main oilfields will fall into Allied hands over the next few days as the Fourteenth Army advances up to 50 miles a day.

20 April: Berlin: Hitler spends his 56th birthday listening to the rumble of Russian artillery coming ever-closer to his capital. The

Fuhrer emerges from his bunker just once to decorate members of the Hitler Jugend. Tonight RAF Mosquito fighter-bombers and Red Air Force aircraft will range over the city.

All organised German resistance in Nuremberg has ended.

Italy: Fifth Army units have entered the Po Valley west of Bologna. Operating with Eighth Army assistance they will liberate that city tomorrow.

21 April: Berlin is now virtually surrounded by Russian armour, artillery and soldiers; Zhukov's men are probing into the city suburbs. Allied bombing raids on German targets continue; today railway yards in the Munich area are hit by US aircraft flying from airfields in Britain and Italy.

Patton's Third Army captures the town of Asch in Czechoslovakia.

The USSR announces the signing of a 20-year pact of mutual assistance with the Polish (Lublin) Government. The pact effectively consigns post-war Poland to the Soviet sphere of influence.

Burma: With the capture today of the major centre of production at Yenangyaung, almost all of the country's oilfields are in Allied hands.

22 April: Himmler meets Swedish Count Folke Bernadotte representing the International Red Cross in secret at the Baltic port of Lubeck and offers to cease fighting the Western Allies but not the Russian enemy in the East.

RAF Lancasters bomb the great port of Bremen in the north of Germany. French forces occupy Stuttgart and Freiburg and advance down the eastern bank of the Rhine to the Swiss frontier.

The US Seventh Army troops under General Patch capture a bridge over the Danube at Dillengen unopposed. They are heading for Munich.

French leader General de Gaulle goes in person to congratulate his troops who have cleared the Gironde pockets on the Atlantic coast of France at Royan and Pointe de Grave of German resistance.

Russian assault troops report being less than three miles from the Unter den Linden in the centre of Berlin.

Soviet Foreign Minister Molotov arrives in Washington on his way to a conference in San Francisco.

23 April: Marshal Koniev's forces join in the battle for Berlin when they attack from the south. RAF Mosquitoes twice bomb Kiel and German shipping at Travemunde on the North Sea coast.

Japan: US Super-Fortresses raid an aircraft works at Tashikawa, west of Tokyo.

On the Home Front, the authorities remove lighting restrictions over most of Britain.

The Czech Government-in-Exile calls for a popular uprising.

24 April: Goering sends Hitler a telegram offering to take over command of the Reich in view of the fact the Fuhrer is trapped in Berlin. A furious Hitler promptly orders the arrest of his one-time highly favoured crony from the earliest days of National Socialism.

In Italy Ferrara is occupied by the Eighth Army; Modena and Spezia by the Fifth. Allied troops are across the River Po.

London: At sunset tonight the Speaker of the House of Commons switches on the lamps in the famous Clock Tower housing Big Ben, an action he describes as lighting, 'a beacon of fresh hope in a sadly torn and distracted world'.

The ferocious fighting on Okinawa continues. On the west coast of the island, the Americans re-occupy the town of Kakuzu, captured in a Japanese counter-attack two days earlier.

25 April: Churchill and President Truman discuss Himmler's offer of a German surrender on the Western Front. The pair agree that nothing less than unconditional surrender on all fronts is required to end the war in Europe.

Berlin is now completely encircled by the Red Army and there is no way out for the defenders and no way in for relief forces. In fact, the latter only exist as figments of Hitler's imagination.

The flags of 46 countries hang as a backdrop at the opening of the historic Allied Nations Conference in the Opera House, San Francisco.

Okinawa: 21,000 Japanese have been killed so far in the battle for this island, while just 400 have been captured.

26 April: US troops advancing from the west meet with Red Army soldiers from the east at Torgau on the River Elbe. The historic rendezvous is sealed with handshakes. Second Lt William D

Robertson from Los Angeles is credited with being the first American to greet a soldier of Marshal Koniev's First Ukrainian Army.

A month after the last V2 rocket fell on England, the authorities release details of the very first one to crash to the ground in 1944. The explosion occurred in Chiswick, West London, at precisely 6.49pm on 8 September; three houses were destroyed, three people killed and 20 injured. The authorities add that 1050 rockets came down in total, killing 2754 people and seriously injuring another 6523.

27 April: General Sir Miles Dempsey's British Second Army announces that Bremen has been cleared of enemy resistance. In the port's Deschimag shipyards, 16 almost completed U-Boats were discovered.

Russian and American troops make contact on the River Elbe north east of Leipzig and Germany is cut in two.

A British Parliamentary deputation of two peers and eight MPs which visited Buchenwald concentration camp has issued its report detailing the horrors inflicted on thousands of prisoners.

28 April: 'Il Duce' – Benito Mussolini – deposed dictator of Italy, is discovered and detained by partisans as he and an entrourage attempt to escape to Switzerland. He is executed at Dongo, Lake Como. Later his body is suspended ignominiously upside down from a garage roof in Milan. His mistress, Clara Petacci, and other Italian fascist leaders meet the same fate. All organised resistance in the Genoa area has ended. In the north east of Italy, Eighth Army soldiers are just 30 miles from Venice. Overnight they will enter the city.

American and Russian forces link up on a 50-mile front along the Elbe, north and south of Torgau.

29 April: After three weeks of negotiations, representatives of the German army in Italy sign a document agreeing to unconditional surrender at Caserta. More than one million German and Italian fascist soldiers are preparing to lay down their arms and march off to prison camps, although the surrender will not come into effect until 2 May.

Royal Marine Commandos of the British No 1 Commando Brigade cross the River Elbe to establish a broad bridgehead and capture Lauenburg.

Netherlands: Unescorted Lancasters of RAF Bomber Command drop sackloads of food to the starving civilian population in the German-occupied cities of The Hague, Rotterdam and Leyden. Before the drop, a radio broadcast assures the Dutch, 'Allied aircraft are on their way. The next aircraft you hear overhead will be carrying food, not bombs.' The International Red Cross had previously secured agreement with the Germans not to attack the British relief effort. Elsewhere in Holland, at Amersfort, a Dutch unit of the German SS is fighting against the British 49th Division.

30 April: Berlin: The ruined Reichstag is captured by the Russians, effectively signalling the end of the bloody battle for Berlin. In his bunker, Adolf Hitler takes a last lunch and then shoots himself at 3.30pm. Eva Braun, the Fuhrer's long-time mistress who became his bride just 36 hours previously, takes poison. Their bodies are taken into the grounds of the Chancellery and cremated in a shell hole. The vaunted 'Thousand Year Reich' has lasted little more than 12 years. Hitler's successor is nominated as Grand Admiral Karl Donitz, the mastermind of Germany's deadly U-Boat campaign, which accounted for the loss of 15 million tons of Allied shipping. Donitz is in the north of the country. He realises Germany faces certain defeat, but knows that his duty is to secure the most advantageous terms he can for an armistice. Some of his staff hold out hope that hostilities might cease on the Western Front allowing Germany and the Western Allies to join forces against the Soviet armies now pouring into Eastern Europe in vast numbers.

Italy: Turin is liberated and New Zealand troops cross the River Piave.

Burma: Fourteenth Army troops are at Pegu and have driven the Japanese from a defile which was their last natural defensive position before Rangoon.

Main picture: *May 1945. Happy Russians and Americans exchange greetings in Germany.*

Inset: *This sign was erected near the spot at Torgau on the River Elbe where the first official rendezvous between the Red Army and US forces occurred on the afternoon of 25 April 1945. The encounter – around 75 miles south of Berlin – signaled that the Third Reich was split in two.*

VICTORY! THE RED ARMY RAISE THEIR FLAG OVER THE REICHSTAG BUILDING IN BERLIN

Adolf Hitler and Benito Mussolini in their time of power.

DEATH OF THE DICTATORS

As April opened there was cheering news for the Allies from every theatre of war. In Burma Lord Louis Mountbatten declared that the Japanese forces in the country had been decisively defeated and no longer existed as an effective fighting force. In the Pacific the Americans were grinding down the Japanese ability to wage war. On the Chinese mainland, Nationalist and Communist forces were attacking the Japanese.

But it was events in Northern Europe that most occupied the attention of the British press and radio. On the Western Front prisoners were coming in at a rate of 25,000 a day and British, Canadian, US and French formations reported daily gains. The Red Army too was rampant, clearing Hungary of the Germans and taking the centre of Vienna on 9 April. The Russians were also inexorably closing in on Berlin. Only diehard Nazis refused to believe that utter defeat was inevitable.

Hitler's cohorts were briefly cheered on 12 April when they heard the news of US President Roosevelt's death. Propaganda Minister Josef

Goebbels congratulated his Fuhrer and assured him it was the turning point of the war, citing astrological predictions as evidence. However, when Harry Truman was sworn in as the new President and the Allies remained clearly resolute in their aim of inflicting total defeat on Germany, a cloud of depression again descended on Hitler's bunker in the heart of Berlin.

The German leader was 56 on 20 April, by which date the rumble of Russian artillery was clearly audible in Berlin. Two days later the battle for the city began, an eight day fight of apocalyptic proportions that cost the lives of hundreds of thousands of German soldiers, civilians and Red Army men and further devastated the already bomb-blasted capital.

Hitler held out hope of a last-gasp relief of Berlin by one of his few remaining cohesive forces. But when Russian forces got within a few hundred yards of his bunker, the Dictator knew his time was up. At 3.30pm on 30 April 1945, Hitler shot himself; his bride of just a few hours, Eva Braun, took poison. Both bodies were dumped in a shell hole, doused in petrol and set alight.

On the same day that Hitler died, the symbolic Reichstag building fell to the Russians. The vaunted 'Thousand Year Reich' was all but ended.

In Italy, two days earlier, another Dictator with much blood on his hands came to a gruesome end. Benito Mussolini, his mistress Clara Petacci and a dozen supporters were captured by partisans at Dongo on Lake Como as they fled towards Switzerland. Executed by firing squad, their bodies were hung upside down on a garage forecourt in Milan and reviled by a jeering crowd.

Daily Mail

NO. 15,285   ONE PENNY   ⋆ ⋆   FOR KING AND EMPIRE   WEDNESDAY, MAY 2, 1945

HITLER DEAD, GERMAN RADIO TELLS WORLD

Admiral Doenitz is new Führer:
'The battle goes on'

DAY
The full official

ADOLF HITLER is dead. Grand Admiral Doenitz, Commander-in-Chief of the German Navy, has been appointed his successor. The German radio gave this news to the world at 10.25 last night in the following words: "It is reported from the Führer's headquarters that our ...

NO NEWS FROM HIMMLER, BUT
Surrender begins on three fronts

REPORTS received in London late last night indicated ...

CHANNEL ISLANDS FREE

O n 8 May 1945 the destroyers *HMS Bulldog* and *HMS Beagle* left Plymouth to rendezvous with the Germans four miles off Guernsey. After tense negotiations, the German commander of the Channel Islands agreed to a full surrender with effect from the next day, 9 May.

This was in fact the day after VE Day was celebrated in the rest of the British Isles. Indeed, the last Channel Island to be freed was Alderney on 16 May. All civilians had been evacuated from this island and it was not until December that they were permitted to return.

The pictures and illustrations on this page reflect aspects of the Occupation and Liberation. Tope left is Jersey schoolgirl Patricia Bullock (later Mrs Patricia Foster). She spent the war on the island with her family. The Red Cross document was sent by her Aunt Mimie from the mainland in 1944 and expresses sympathy that Patricia didn't pass an exam.

Top right are pictures of the Red Cross ship *SS Vega* that brought desperately needed food supplies for the islanders in the first few days of January 1945.

Below appear a couple of pages from autograph books signed for islanders by the Royal Navy seamen who liberated the islands. The food parcel and autograph books are in the possession of the late Mrs Foster's family. Under the autographs is a picture of the German garrison awaiting transport to camps on the mainland.

Finally at bottom left there are views of peaceful present-day Jersey and Guernsey.

A Cosby Show!

Brian Jones was a sailor on *HMS Cosby* when the ship was part of Force 135 that sailed to liberate the Channel Islands.

When we first heard of the job, we were not at all keen on it. The war in Europe had ended, but the Germans in the Channel Islands had not surrendered. We had three-inch guns, but it was known that the islands were heavily fortified, and as we approached we expected to get blown out of water.

However, all went well and we (ourselves and one LST) arrived quite safely in St Aubin Bay, Jersey. We had barely anchored before we were surrounded by hosts of small boats and rafts loaded with the local population. The natives appeared friendly; in fact they cheered us and shouted 'up the Navy'. That was Wednesday.

There were thousands of Germans wandering around on the island, but they were not openly hostile. Within a very short time many of the locals clambered up the ship's side, and as 'Jack' opened his heart and pocket, out poured chocolate and cigarettes. In exchange they gave us souvenirs of the Occupation and related tales of life under German rule.

The next three days were absolutely terrific. We were the first British Forces the people of Jersey had seen for five years, and they certainly let us know it. Our first blokes ashore (motor-boat crew) didn't even touch the ground, as they were chaired and cheered round St Helier. On Thursday we had a ships' concert and some of the local girls sang too. We provided many with supper by the simple means of giving them our own. But to see the pleasure on their faces as they tucked into their first square meal for five years was well worth our slight sacrifice.

Each night we could see the fireworks and hear the sounds of revelry ashore. On Friday came leave, which was what we were waiting for. The people had had a very thin time, but look remarkably fit, despite the fact that since the start of the year, they'd been existing on Red Cross parcels weighing nine pounds each, but which had to last a month. The canteen was nearly bought out. Believe me, you could have bought a house with a pound of tobacco, but no one took advantage.

I was 'Watch' so stayed on the ship, but spent another very pleasant evening with the islanders who came aboard. By now they had just about the run of the *Cosby*. I made some very good friends whom I met the following day, and still more suppers were given away. Indeed we crew hardly ate whilst we were there, except for breakfasts. And even then, some of the islanders were aboard.

Next day was our turn. My 'oppo' (Ken) and I were to meet Martin (one of the local lads) by a well-known hotel. Martin hoped to have his car out, but he couldn't get a battery; frustrating because petrol 'borrowed' from the Germans was plentiful.

The party we were with were all from Victoria College. There were four chaps, Hugh, Martin, Eric and Dick, and three girls (sisters) Jean, Nora and Ruth (I think their surname was Mossop).

We thoroughly enjoyed ourselves. The food parcel we got ashore was greatly welcomed and they gave us tea from their Red Cross supplies. Jean was a nurse, Ruth and Nora were teaching. All the boys had been in prison for having wireless sets and/or trying to escape. Martin had only got out of prison on our arrival, and Hugh's name was in the *Daily Express* as one of the leaders of the island's resistance movement.

Girls who had been with the Germans were called 'Jerry-bags' and they were having a pretty rough time. We had been warned not to get involved. Our friends showed us all round St Helier. We saw the houses of the 'Jerry-bags' tarred with the swastika, but the thing that really struck one was the abundance of British flags and ribbons that appeared. Many had been saved since the Coronation and had been hidden away from the Germans for five years.

Another amazing thing was the large number of Germans wandering around, though they were quite docile. I know, now, what a film star feels like – if I signed my autograph once that day, I signed it a hundred times. One of my treasured souvenirs is a Jersey note with all the autographs of all of our party of friends on the back.

The day was sweltering but that didn't stop a soccer match between the ship and the island. We lost 4-1. But considering they had about 18,000 potential players (to our 180) to choose from that's not surprising. The local boy scouts were very much to the fore, acting as messengers and guides to the relieving troops. They'd hidden their uniforms during the Occupation.

When it was time to go, we were very sorry to leave Jersey and its people.

Right: Brian Jones with crewmates in wartime.

Image from the Deep...

Brian Jones served as a seaman from 1943 to 1946. Most of the time he was on the full commission of *HMS Cosby*, a US-built Destroyer Escort classified as a frigate in the Royal Navy and one of 78 transferred to the RN. The ships played a significant role in the war at sea but their importance has been overshadowed by more glamourous vessels. Brian says that *HMS Cosby* served mainly escorting convoys on the Atlantic, North Sea and English Channel, 'having a fairly unexciting time until participating in the Liberation of Jersey'.

In August 1945, he was witness to an extraordinary incident that led to the revealing of a sad and poignant story. It was reported at length in the William Hickey column in the *Daily Express* (reproduced in part here).

Brian was on board *HMS Cosby* in Falmouth Harbour, Cornwall, when a shipmate hooked a large fish that was promptly sent down to the galley. There the cook gutted it and, inside the fish, discovered, wrapped in tinfoil, a photograph of a lady. The *Express* carried the story on a Monday, written up in slightly tongue-in-cheek vein. By the weekend the mystery had been solved. The lady was Mrs Bianca Dault of the George Hotel, Largs, Ayrshire. Her husband was Captain Georges Dault of the French Mercantile Marine. His ship, *Villa de Tamatave,* had been torpedoed and sunk in the Atlantic en route to New York on 23 January 1943. Captain Dault was officially posted missing.

On her husband's last leave home, Mrs Dault had given him the photograph. She told the *Express*: 'I wrote a message in Italian on the back: "My love, I love you so much." He said he would carry it with him everywhere. I never saw him again.'

The Daily Express, August 1945.

WILLIAM HICKEY

But it was true

LAUGHTER is very near to tears.

A fish story was published in this column on Monday —how a sailor, fishing from the frigate Cosby in Falmouth harbour, caught a fish with a snapshot inside it. On the back, in Italian, "My love, I love you so much. Your ——" Signature illegible; looked like "Beatrice."

Frankly, I suspected it was a fo'c'sle yarn; offered a guinea for the most ingenious story of how the portrait got into the fish.

Shoals of stories arrived by first post yesterday — tales of mystery and imagination; pulls full of laughs. And the true story, which is a theme for

SOMEONE snowed Mrs Bianca Dault the picture

Victory in Europe: Britain goes Crackers!

At one minute past midnight on 9 May 1945 peace in Europe was officially declared. But the celebrations were already well under way across Britain. Premier Winston Churchill's 3pm broadcast on 8 May was the signal for the Victory festivities to begin. Over 50,000 people poured onto the streets of central London. The King and Queen and Churchill, together with the Princesses Elizabeth and Margaret, made no less than eight appearances on the royal balcony, each time to a rapturous welcome by the adoring crowd.

Outburst of pure joy

Licensing laws were suspended and as night fell the population partied on in an unbridled outburst of pure joy. The crowds on the streets on the day following VE Day were just as excited and were out in huge numbers from early morning.

Queen's corgi greets the crowds

Soon after midnight at Buckingham Palace when the lights had been turned down, a door was seen to open and a servant appeared in the forecourt with a dog. It was Crackers, the Queen's Corgi, out much later than usual for his nightly airing.

On this exceptional occasion, and much to their delight, Crackers was introduced through the railings to the multitude of people who were still present outside the Palace. 'Where does he sleep?' a woman asked. With admirable discretion the servant courteously replied, 'I wouldn't like to tell you that, madam.'

Quite what Crackers made of it all is not recorded.

All pictures: Getty Images

In the rest of the month of May, many thousands of street parties were held all over the country. On Sunday 13 May the King and Queen went to St Paul's Cathedral for a service of thanksgiving and prayers for a swift final end to the war in the Far East. It would be another three months before Japan surrendered on 14 August 1945 when more unrestrained celebrations took place. The war had lasted just 20 days short of six years.

Above: *St Paul's Cathedral pictured floodlit during victory celebrations in London on 9 May 1945.*
Far left: *A happy group marches down a London street on 8 May.*
Left: *Children at a Victory Tea Party and Concert held in Wimbledon, South London.*

RETURN TO VAUXHALL

Even now, looking back at that period of 1945 I can still feel the incredible joy and feelings of relief that my family had come through despite losing our home at Vauxhall in South London in April 1941 and being 'bombed out' of our second home at Roehampton in July 1944.

Now well into my 70's I still have those summer of '45 thoughts and how vivid they are to me. On a train journey a few years ago, from my home in Guildford to London, the train made an unspecified stop at Vauxhall. On impulse I jumped out and spent an hour in that neighbourhood before travelling on to the City for my meeting. I walked along the Vauxhall platform and remembered how in September 1939 we schoolchildren had waved goodbye to the line of distraught and tearful parents on the opposite pavement – but most of us were excited at the adventure of the forthcoming journey to the countryside. We were happy with our lunch packs and enjoyed being with our classmates and kindly familiar teachers from our school.

Sense of loss

Having arrived in Berkshire and been deposited around various homes about half of us gave up by Christmas and had returned home to be with our parents once more. They were more than relieved for they had found the impact of silent streets and childless homes more than they could bear... a sense of loss that is rarely mentioned. I remember the start of the Battle of Britain. At Vauxhall, we had a grandstand view being so near one of the Luftwaffe's aiming points, Waterloo Station.

On my recent return trip I walked along the side of our old school at Lawn Lane, then a Victorian structure but nowadays one with many modern additions. At Vauxhall Park nearby I listened and could hear again the laughter and cries of the WAAF Barrage Balloon girls raising and lowering their billowing charges as quickly as they could. They were all so kind and would offer us sweets and apples

etc whenever they could. I turned into Vauxhall Grove and paused outside No 71, the house where we had lived in the middle flat of three during the 1930's. There used to be a small brick shelter in the roadway here and I recalled sheltering there after an air raid warning and popping my head out to see the vast formation of German bombers overhead, twinkling in the September sunlight and curving round in superb formation to follow the Thames en route to the London Docks. This was the famous raid of 7 September that destroyed much of London's dockland area.

I recalled once more the time of the Dornier that crashed on to Victoria Station and the sight of the mortally wounded pilot parachuting across the people in Harleyford Road and over the Oval Cricket Ground to land and die by the nearby Underground Station. Although he was the enemy this was a sad and wretched incident for he was attacked by some bombed-out survivors living in a nearby Community Centre.

> **Nazi Germany had another go at us in July 1944 with a V1 Flying Bomb. Our house was left without a roof...**

Very soon we were into the Blitz period when London was attacked for 57 consecutive nights. On my walk I looked up at the top window of our old house and remembered the massive attack on the City of London by the Luftwaffe at Christmas 1940. This attack was on a Sunday night when we had chanced it and stayed at home. My father had lifted me from the safe place under the stairs and took me to the window, placing me on his shoulders to look over the rooftops to the burning City of London saying, 'Have a look, son, at a sight you will never forget'. How true, that awful sea of red flames and smoke seemed to be the end of our world in London and of course for many citizens it was.

I remembered now how life in the Vauxhall shelter changed for us with an air raid in April 1941. This was a widespread attack on London and we somehow lived through the nearby explosions, the clouds of dirt and dust, to find in the morning that the outside wall of our house had collapsed, caught by blast from a parachute mine that had landed and exploded on the nearby Milk Depot.

Like so many with their homes gone we then spent two weeks in a Church Hall before further evacuation, this time as a family but minus belongings and a home, back to the Berkshire countryside on the western outskirts of Reading. We never returned to Vauxhall as

we were eventually re-homed in 1943 to a small house at Roehampton, also in South London. Nazi Germany had another go at us in July 1944 with a V1 Flying Bomb that left us roofless and despatched us on the move again to Blackpool in Lancashire, until our roof was repaired and the house made habitable again.

From this time onwards for me it was a case of leaving school and working as a Telegram Boy for the GPO at Hammersmith. This was a difficult time for all Londoners with the V1's still arriving and exploding and then the dreaded V2 rockets with their silent approach and ear-splitting explosions that stretched so many to breaking point.

Children killed

As I walked back to Vauxhall Station on my recent visit I thought again of my mates in Class 2 at Lawn Lane School. We were all evacuated together, drifted back to London, went through the day and night bombing of the Blitz, shared our boxes of bomb splinters and shrapnel and limited classes at school and were deeply saddened to hear that some children had been killed and injured.

The War had of course brought massive upheavals to millions of people in Europe with death and destruction on an extensive and unforgettable scale. Even so, and on a much lesser scale of upheaval in South London, I remember pondering in the weeks following VE Day that I had never seen or heard any news of my 1939 classmates and sadly, nothing has been known to the present day.

As I travelled away from Vauxhall Station and on to the City I said a quiet 'goodbye dear friends' to all my young classmates in Class 2 at Lawn Lane School in 1939 with the sincere hope that some had made it through to that Victory summer of 1945.

Ron McGill

*Above left: A young Ron McGill is in the centre next to the classroom wall in this pre-war photograph taken at Lawn Lane School. **Inset:** Ron today. **Below:** Crowds gathered in Trafalgar Square on VE Day 1945.*

Many thousands of British and Commonwealth prisoners of war liberated by the Allied victory were flown home to Britain in Lancaster bombers converted into troop carriers. Newly arrived POWs are seen in the picture above. The picture below shows a group of delighted British soldiers enjoying their freedom. They are displaying a number of trophies seized from their former guards.

Released prisoners ran a gamut of emotions from guilt at being made captive in the first place, to deep depression, to unbridled joy. For some, their liberation heralded a time when they would meet their families and friends for the first time in nearly six years. It was not unusual that some fathers would be seeing sons or daughters for the first time ever, their offspring having been conceived before they marched off to war and born when 'Dad' was overseas or already a captive of the enemy.

The first garden party to be held at Buckingham Palace since pre-war days took place on 24 May, when the King and Queen were hosts to nearly 2000 former prisoners-of-war, men who had served with the army, navy and air force. The picture (above) shows the King chatting to some RAF officers with Princess Elizabeth on the right.

WAR DIARY
May 1945

1 May: On the 2068th day of the war Field Marshal Gerd Von Rundstedt – one of the Wehrmacht's top commanders – is captured by US forces.

Tito's Yugoslav partisans have pushed into the port of Trieste just ahead of New Zealand troops in Britain's Eighth Army. The two forces meet at Monfalcone, west of the city. Trieste and the Istrian peninsula have been in Italian possession since the break-up of the old Austrian Empire in 1918. It will now become a focus of dispute between Tito, who says that the non-inclusion of Trieste in post-war Yugoslavia is 'unthinkable', and the Italians who want to retain it. One suggestion is for the city to become a freeport.

All of Munich, the city that played a prominent role in the rise of Hitler and the Nazis, is now in the hands of US forces.

Pacific: Australian and Dutch East Indies troops land on Tarakan Island off Borneo.

2 May: After 17 days of bitter house-to-house fighting, Berlin finally capitulates to Marshals Zhukov and Koniev. In the afternoon the garrison laid down its arms, and by evening more than 70,000 German soldiers are in captivity. British troops capture the Baltic ports of Lubeck and Wismar.

In Italy, the negotiated surrender of all Axis forces is formalised. The Wehrmacht in Trieste surrender to New Zealand troops of the Eighth Army, but other German units fight on against Tito's partisans.

3 May: Burma: Following parachute landings by Gurkha troops at the mouth of the Rangoon river two days ago, an amphibious assault is now underway. But the Japanese have already evacuated the area after destroying the oilfields and most of the city infrastructure. The Japanese retreat is confirmed by an Allied pilot who sees a message painted on the roof of the gaol by POWs: 'Japs gone. Exdigitate.'

Europe: Hitler's chosen successor Admiral Donitz moves his seat of government to Denmark. Portugal observes an official day of mourning for Hitler. Irish Free State Prime Minister Eamonn de Valera calls on the German Embassy in Dublin to express his regrets at the Fuhrer's death.

Baltic Sea: Three liners carrying survivors from two concentration camps are sunk in Neustadt Bay by rocket-firing Typhoons with the loss of an estimated 8000 lives. The RAF pilots believed the vessels were German troopships. Nazi officers had forced the inmates onto the ships rather than allow the Red Cross to discover them in their camps.

British troops move in to occupy Hamburg.

4 May: Germany: Luneburg Heath is the scene of the signing of the official surrender to Monty's 21st Army Group of all German armed forces in North West Germany, the Netherlands and Denmark with effect from 8am tomorrow. More than 500,000 troops will join the 500,000 already taken prisoner in the past 24 hours. Montgomery turns down a request that German civilians fleeing the Russian advance be allowed to pass through British lines.

Japan: As the bitter battle for Okinawa goes on, the aircraft carrier *HMS Formidable* is damaged by Kamikaze attack and a further 17 US ships are sunk. Over 130 Japanese aircraft are destroyed.

After occupying Innsbruck and Salzburg in Austria, soldiers of the Seventh Army drove through the Brenner Pass to link up with Fifth Army troops at Vipiteno in Italy.

5 May: In Prague, Czech patriots have started an armed rising against the German garrison still occupying the city. General

> **"Three unmarked German liners carrying over 8000 concentration camp inmates are sunk by rocket-firing RAF Typhoons."**

Patton is within reach of the capital, but the Russians insist it is their 'prize'.

Red Army units capture Swinemunde and Peenemunde on Germany's Baltic coast. The latter was the site of a key research and manufacturing plant for Germany's secret V-weapons programme. On 17 August 1943 a force of 596 RAF Lancaster bombers largely destroyed the plant.

Austria: Mauthausen concentration camp and satellite camps at Gunskirchen and Ebensee are the last such centres to be liberated. There are 110,000 survivors of whom 28,000 are Jews; 3000 emaciated inmates will die from disease and the effects of privation even after liberation. The bodies of 10,000 prisoners are discovered in a single communal grave.

Just 24 hours after Admiral Donitz ordered all remaining U-Boats at sea to return to base, five vessels are sunk by an Allied air strike in the Kattegat. The Kriegsmarine have now lost 784 of 1162 U-Boats employed in the course of the war.

Denmark: Allied troops enter Copenhagen.

Hitler's mountaintop eyrie at Berchtesgaden is captured by French Chad Territory forces. Much of the building was destroyed in an RAF raid several weeks ago.

Oregon, USA: Elsie Mitchell and five children in the town of Lakeview are killed by a bomb attached to a balloon that has floated across the Pacific from Japan.

6 May: Donitz dismisses Heinrich Himmler from all German Government offices.

Portugal severs diplomatic relations with Germany.

The important Czech arms centre of Pilsen is captured by the US Third Army as they advance on a broad front towards Prague.

7 May: In an undistinguished schoolroom in the city of Rheims, General Jodl, on behalf of Admiral Donitz signs an agreement for the unconditional surrender of all German land, sea and air forces in Europe. He states: 'With this signature, the German people and the German armed forces are, for better or for worse, delivered into the victor's hands.' General Walter Bedell Smith, Eisenhower's Chief of Staff, signs for the Allies. The surrender will come into effect at 23.01 hours tomorrow and includes German forces still fighting the Red Army. Today the garrison of Breslau capitulated to the Russians after an 82-day siege.

Troops of the Eighth Army cross the Italian frontier and enter Austria.

British and Canadian troops are moving into northern Holland and Denmark in force.

Norway: General Boehme broadcasts a 'cease fire' order to the 400,000 German service personnel occupying the country.

Firth of Forth: The last casualties of the Third Reich's war at sea are sustained when U-2336 sinks two Allied merchant ships off the coast of Scotland.

8 May: In Berlin the ratification of the surrender is signed by Chief of the German High Command, Field-Marshal Keitel, Marshal Zhukov for the Russians and Air Chief Marshal Tedder for the Western Allies. At 3pm, British Premier Winston Churchill, speaking in the House of Commons, proclaims the end of the war in Europe. Top Nazi Herman Goering – disgraced by Hitler in the last days of

WAR DIARY
May 1945

the war – is arrested by US troops in Fischhorn. The last large German city yet to fall under Allied control, Dresden, is occupied by the Red Army at the end of a two day battle.

Fighting between German and Russian forces continues in parts of Czechoslovakia, although the German commander in Bohemia today ends the conflict in Prague when he surrenders the capital.

German Army Group Kurland – long cut off in this peninsula in Latvia - surrenders to the Red Army.

Croatian capital Zagreb is liberated.

Oslo: Eleven Allied officers arrive with Norwegian troops and Crown Prince Olav to declare the liberation of Norway.

9 May: The cruisers *Nurnberg* and *Prinz Eugen*, the only major German warships to survive the war intact, surrenders in Copenhagen harbour along with the last remnants of the Kriegsmarine surface fleet.

The Channel Islands are finally freed when the German occupiers sign an unconditional surrender aboard *HMS Bulldog* at 7.14am. A token force of 22 men of the Royal Artillery go ashore on Guernsey to take custody of the 10,000-strong island garrison.

Prague: Red Army troops finally secure the city after four days of hard fighting.

10 May: Norwegian patriots arrest Vidkun Quisling. The invader Nazis installed Quisling as head of a puppet administration. The name Quisling will remain synonymous with betrayal and treachery.

The first U-Boat to give itself up under the terms of the surrender arrives in Weymouth Bay, Dorset. The crew of U-249 line up on deck under the watchful eyes of a party of Polish naval ratings. Another U-Boat flying the black flag of surrender is sighted from the air off the coast of Scotland.

Field-Marshal Von Kesselring surrenders to the Americans at Hitler's Berchtesgaden retreat in Bavaria. Kesselring had led the German defence of Italy which held up the Allies for so long.

Burma: The Japanese retreat continues. It is announced that a Burma Star medal will be struck for issue to men who have fought in this campaign. On the northern coast of New Guinea Australian troops are within two miles of Wewak.

11 May: Still more German forces surrender, this time in Czechoslovakia and in the Aegean Islands.

In New Guinea, Australian forces attack Wewak where they seize the area occupied by the Japanese Eighteenth Army after a gruelling six month campaign in steamy jungle conditions. General MacArthur's 'leap-frog' policy of by-passing Japanese strongholds has left the Australians with the arduous and costly task of defeating a stubborn enemy who is more often prepared to die than surrender. MacArthur, meanwhile, has his hands full with the desperate struggle for Okinawa and the gradual liberation of the vast archipelago of the Philippines. Fresh landings of US forces on Mindanao are announced today.

Oslo: British airborne troops arrive at Gardemoen airfield. The 300 men march through the Norwegian capital's crowded streets while armed Germans remain on street duty.

12 May: Field-Marshal Montgomery is cheered by thousands of Danes lining a six-mile route in Copenhagen. Monty later lunches with King Christian and Queen Alexandrine at Amalienborg Castle where he is invested with the Grand Cross of the Order of Dannebrog with Diamond Star as a mark of the Danish people's gratitude for their liberation.

Guernsey: A convoy with 2000 tons of foodstuff is unloaded.

Crete: The unconditional surrender of the island's German garrison is signed in Heraklion.

Okinawa: Japanese reinforcements come ashore behind the American front line but are successfully repelled.

13 May: Germany: The 51st Highland Division make a ceremonial Victory Parade in the port of Bremerhaven. Kilts are in evidence along with skirling bagpipes. German civilians are confined to their homes during the period of the parade. British troops, including Scots Guards, occupy the North Sea island of Heligoland.

Suffolk: Two E-Boats put into Felixstowe Harbour bringing the German E-Boat fleet commander, Admiral Bruening, to surrender.

London: Churchill makes a broadcast to mark the Allied triumph in Europe but warns people that, 'all our toils and trouble are not yet over.' Today King George and Queen Elizabeth drive through the capital to a Thanksgiving Service at St Paul's. Elsewhere in Britain, 4407 freed POWs are flown in from the Continent by No 46 Group RAF Transport Command.

Russian troops who landed on the Danish island of Bornholm in the Baltic two days ago are in the process of rounding up the 25,000-strong German garrison which had refused to surrender. In all the operation will take five days. British troops occupy the German island of Heligoland.

14 May: On Okinawa US forces capture the important airfield at Yonabaru. In attacks on US warships the Japanese lose 21 aircraft and succeed in damaging just one vessel. In Luzon (Philippines) the Americans capture the important Balete Pass. The Allies mount constant bombing raids against Japan's home islands; today they also hit enemy airfields in China.

London: Work is about to commence on the removal of 80,000 sandbags that have successfully protected Westminster Abbey from air-raid damage for well over half a decade.

A British warship visits Gothenburg now that Sweden has declared her ports open again.

15 May: The last pockets of German resistance surrender in Yugoslavia. Nearly a million and a half Yugoslav civilians (including 55,000 Jews) and 305,000 soldiers have perished out of a pre-war population of 15 million. Partisan leader Tito is determined to keep his country united and has accepted royalists into a provisional government while making it clear that Yugoslavia will be a communist state.

Oslo: Crown Prince Olaf of Norway, wearing British battledress, arrives from exile in England aboard a Royal Navy destroyer. He is welcomed by Maj-Gen Robert Urquhart, commander of the British First Airborne Division, who are in the vanguard of the Allied liberation forces. Urquhart led the First Airborne at the ill-fated 'Bridge Too Far' battle at Arnhem in September 1944.

Okinawa: In the face of fierce resistance US troops inch their way into the island capital, Naha. The Japanese war cabinet announces the abrogation of all treaties with Germany and other European nations.

16 May: The last major surface action of the war takes place in the Mallaca Straits west of Penang in Malaya and ends with the sinking of the Japanese cruiser *Haguro* by aircraft and destroyers of the Royal Navy's East Indies Fleet.

A British naval and military expedition re-occupies Alderney, the last of the Channel Islands to be freed, and takes 3200 Germans prisoner.

17 May: In London the Minister of Fuel and Power announces a basic petrol ration for civilians as from 1 June.

Indian Ocean: Allied heavy bombers attack Japanese strongholds on the Andaman Islands.

18 May: US casualties on Okinawa approach 20,000 – more than those sustained in the conquest of Iwo Jima. Though the capital Naha was entered yesterday, the campaign has been bogged down, with average daily forward movement of just 133 yards.

Japan withdraws garrisons from the Chinese ports of Foochow, Amoy and Swatow and transfers them to Hong Kong. Chinese troops will enter the Treaty port of Foochow later today.

Trieste: Marshal Tito and his partisans refuse to leave this disputed territory and claim they have the right to make the city part of Yugoslavia.

London: In a radio broadcast, Clement Atlee MP says: 'I have just returned from San Francisco. There the delegates of nearly 50 nations have been meeting in order to try to construct the framework for the preservation of peace.'

19 May: The unceasing daily round of air strikes by US Fortresses and Super-Fortresses against Japan continue. Targets today include Hamamatsu, near Nagoya, and the island of Formosa.

DAS BOOT!

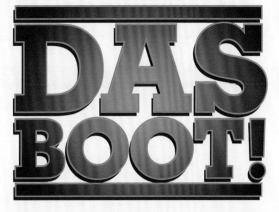

A tale of two submariners – one British, one German – who both sailed in U-Boats after the war had ended.

Roy Holley had just turned 20 when he was 'called up' in February 1940. This is his story:

It has never ceased to amaze me that on mobilisation, all sorts and all trades ranging from lorry drivers, bank clerks, postmen, shop assistants etc, were simply thrown together and told they were going to become soldiers, sailors or airmen. It's even more amazing that by and large the system worked.

I opted for the Royal Navy and served for over five years in various parts of the world in a variety of ships ranging from frigates to cruisers. In that time, you can imagine my experiences covered the good, the bad and, sometimes, the hilarious. However, my strangest experience was reserved for my very last ship. This was HMS Philante, a private steam yacht converted for wartime service.

The war in Europe ended in May 1945 and as part of the surrender terms, the German U-Boat fleet was ordered to stay on the surface and fly white flags while awaiting a Royal Navy vessel to escort them to the UK.

We met 'our' U-Boat somewhere off the coast of Norway and I, as a Signalman, together with a Sub-Lieutenant and four Able Seamen, comprised the escort party. I can remember trying to clamber up the seaweed-encrusted hull of the U-Boat in a choppy sea. Indeed, so slippery was it that one of our men fell into the water and had to be pulled out by a German crewman.

Upon going aboard we did wonder what sort of reception we'd get, having been fed all the propaganda about this arrogant 'master race'. In fact it was all very amicable. The German submariners were for the most part young lads like ourselves, in our early to mid-Twenties, who like us had been called up willy-nilly. They were soon showing us photographs of their girlfriends. We'd taken emergency rations with us and I swopped my Spam for some salami-type sausage and all participants enjoyed the exchange.

Our destination was Loch Eriboll in the far north of Scotland and on the way we ran into a Force 10 gale. The Kapitan, who spoke good English, wanted to submerge as it would make for more comfortable progress. We told him to remain on the surface, our decision influenced by the events of the Great War when the German Grand Fleet scuppered itself in Scapa Flow; we didn't want to take the chance of the Kapitan himself being a 'death or glory' boy.

We took a pasting from the storm but made it to Loch Eriboll where we handed the submarine and crew on to higher authorities. Upon reflection, I must say that when I joined the Royal Navy I could never have imagined for a moment that I'd end up serving on a German U-Boat

Several U-Boats failed to heed the call to give themselves up. This is the story of U-977:

On 2 May 1945 U-977 left a Norwegian fjord and headed out to sea on its first-ever combat mission. But even as the U-Boat searched for ships to sink, the order came for the entire German submarine fleet to surrender. Dismayed at the prospect of captivity, Kapitan Heinz Schaeffer then made an extraordinary proposal to his crew; meekly surrender to the Allies or stay with him in the U-Boat and escape to South America.

Over 100 days later the U-Boat arrived in the Argentinian port of Mar del Plata, Her arrival caused a huge stir and there was much speculation about the voyage. Was she carrying gold or even high level Nazi fugitives? Indeed,

Above: *The view from a U-Boat as it closes in on a merchant ship it has already torpedoed.*

three months after the German surrender, South American newspapers were asserting that Hitler and Eva Braun had been passengers aboard U-977 and were now in hiding in Patagonia.

It was some six decades later before the true story came out. It was told by a pensioner living with his wife Heather in a quiet little town in Worcestershire. In 1945 Helmut Maros had been the wireless operator aboard U-977. He told the *Daily Mail*: 'I have never laid eyes on so much as an ingot of gold in all of my life. Nor did I ever meet Adolf Hitler and it would be hard not to if he'd been on board that very cramped boat!'

Helmut remembered the Kapitan's offer: 'He said we could either accept the bitter bread of captivity or we could try to escape to Argentina. Our heads were spinning at the quandary we were in. Schaeffer calculated we had just enough fuel for the voyage but we would have to sail at a snail's pace underwater and sometimes very deep for at least two months in our creaky vessel.

'But what prospect was there for us in Germany? We were all worried sick about our families; we didn't even know if they were alive. We knew the Russians would exact a terrible revenge.'

Thirty two men decided to take the gamble. The rest of the crew were dropped off in Norway. The U-Boat set off and stayed submerged until almost at the Equator. 'We had to keep very quiet,' said Helmut. 'Every so often we would hear the throbbing of an approaching ship. You knew if it had found us. There would be the repeated "ping" of the sonar rays, then a series of distant "whooshes" as the depth-charges hit the water. Then came the explosions that would knock the boat sideways. Fortunately we were never holed.'

The U-Boat started out well provisioned. Giant hams hung down from the middle of the ship: 'With so many fumes we had the best smoked meats in the navy,' said Helmut. But it was not long before the meat went rotten and maggots and flies appeared everywhere. The faces of the crew took on a green pallor and their vision began to suffer.

Then on 14 July 1945, Schaeffer gave the order to surface. Just as he predicted they had reached the Cape Verde Islands. For the next 40 days they sailed on the surface until they finally reached Argentina. Their goal in sight, the crew found themselves in another dilemma. Should they give themselves up to the Argentine authorities or go ashore in a quiet bay and lose themselves in the local population? Helmut said: 'In the end there was really no option. Where would we go? How would we survive?'

On 17 August U-977 nosed into Mar del Plata. The crew were handed over to the Allies. Schaeffer was flown to the US for six months of interrogation. Ironically, he would eventually return to Argentina and go into business.

Helmut was sent to a POW camp in Britain, first at Bury St Edmunds and later at Boxmoor Station. At the latter he was allowed to go out. One day he spotted a pretty girl on a bus, holding a basket of freshly picked fruit. Her name was Heather Bisley and she offered the young German an apple. From this chance encounter, romance blossomed and the pair married in 1951.

Above: Helmut with English bride Heather Bisley in February 1951. Inset: Helmut in 2005.

Making Britain his home country was an easy decision for Helmut: 'Germany had been smashed to pieces and I had lost a brother who was a pilot in the Luftwaffe. My sister's husband was also killed along with their three children who died when their school was bombed.'

Helmut remembered meeting Heinz Schaeffer by chance near Marble Arch a few years after the war. The pair had a drink at a nearby pub. 'He talked endlessly about the opportunities in South America,' said Helmut. 'He was full of optimism as he always had been. I'll always be grateful to him because if he hadn't led to me to Argentina I would never had met Heather and lived to lead a wonderful life over here.'
At least one other U-Boat escaped to Argentina. U-530 arrived at Mar del Plata on 10 July and was handed over to the Allies a week later. Helmut's vessel, U-977, was acquired by the US Navy. She was torpedoed and sunk by USS Atule in a naval exercise off Cape Cod on 13 November 1946.

Sea of SECRETS

May 1945. Some incidents at sea kept secret from earlier in the war are being disclosed. One concerns a naval disaster off the coast of Donegal on 2 October 1942. The *Queen Mary* – with 15,000 US troops on board – was travelling all-out for the Clyde with an escort of two cruisers. The *Queen Mary* was steering the usual zig-zag course so as not to present an easy target for torpedoes.

Travelling at 30 knots, she crashed full tilt into *HMS Curacao*, which, cut in half, sank in five minutes, taking 338 of her crew with her. *Queen Mary* sustained a huge dent in her bow and was forbidden to stop to aid survivors because of the danger posed by any lurking U-Boats.

Sister ship *Queen Elizabeth* came close to grief in April 1945 when, two days out from New York, an enormous 'rogue' wave almost overwhelmed her. Thousands of tons of water cascaded onto her decks and for a second or two the entire vessel was immersed. Fortunately, the ship righted herself; there were no casualties although the material damage was extensive.

Bombs smuggled aboard
Two years previously, *Queen Elizabeth* had been involved in a serious breach of security while berthed in New York. Despite a guard of 750 security personnel, two small bombs were somehow smuggled aboard the ship, presumably by Nazi agents or sympathisers. Upon being discovered, the devices were thrown into the harbour.

Figures released on 19 May 1945 show that the two Queens between them since the spring of 1940 had transported 1,250,000

Main picture: US sailors heading for home excitedly view the skyline of New York.

Inset: A postcard showing the Queen Elizabeth in peacetime paintwork. New York was the most frequent destination of both this vessel and her sister ship, the Queen Mary.

Allied troops across 95,000 miles of the world's oceans. In fact the *Queen Mary* still holds the record for the most people on board a single ship at one time – 16,683. Hitler offered a bounty equivalent of £50,000 to any of his U-Boat crews that sank one of the Queens. But the Grey Ghosts, as they were known, remained unmolested in their high-speed zig-zag dashes across the Atlantic throughout the war even though Nazi propaganda chief Goebbels once announced to the world that the *Queen Elizabeth* had been torpedoed.

Churchill's tribute to the Queens
After VJ Day, the *Queen Mary*, while still primarily in her wartime grey, had her funnels repainted back to Cunard red and black. It was with this appearance that she made 11 more crossings to the United States and Canada on these occasions carrying British 'GI Brides.'

Winston Churchill crossed the Atlantic three times aboard *Queen Mary* during his wartime premiership. It is fitting then to let his eloquency pay tribute to the war service of the two great Monarchs of the Atlantic: 'Built for the arts of peace and to link the Old World and the New, the Queens challenged the fury of Hitlerism in the Battle of the Atlantic. Without their aid the day of final victory must unquestionably have been postponed.'

WAR DIARY
May 1945

19 May: Burma: Around 66,000 Japanese soldiers remain in Burma boxed into three areas. Around 40,000 are in the eastern sector and this is the only place where organised resistance goes on as the enemy seeks to keep open an escape route to Siam and Moulmein. It is estimated that Japanese casualties in Burma total 105,328 since 1 February 1945.

20 May: Okinawa: Japanese soldiers in US Marine uniforms make a desperate counter-attack, but are bloodily repulsed.

China: Rail installations along the River Yangtse near Nanking are attacked by Allied bombers.

21 May: On the orders of the British, the last hut of the infamous Belsen concentration camp is burned to the ground. Allied troops hold an outdoor dance on the site of the camp; the men's partners are Yugoslav girls held in Belsen and now awaiting repatriation

Chief architect of the Nazi terror policy, Heinrich Himmler, is caught by the British. He was found disguised as a rural policeman. Admiral Donitz is also arrested in Denmark, along with leading members of his short-lived government.

Middle East: The Government of Syria and the Lebanon protest at the presence of French troops and call for the withdrawal of all foreign forces, 'now that the war is over'.

A French poster celebrates the fiery death of the Nazi eagle.

22 May: Copenhagen: The cruisers *Prince Eugen* and *Nurnberg* are handed over to the Senior British Naval Officer in Denmark, Rear-Admiral Reginald Holt.

On the 1262nd day of the war against Japan, the US War Department makes public for the first time the existence of the enemy's balloon bomb campaign that has caused casualties along the western seaboard of the USA and Canada.

23 May: British Second Army HQ, Luneburg: Despite stringent security measures, Gestapo and SS chief Himmler manages to commit suicide by biting on a cyanide capsule concealed in his mouth. Yet another top Nazi prepared to betray Hitler in the last desperate days of the Reich, Himmler chooses suicide over the ignominy of a war crimes trial by the Allies.

At home, Winston Churchill visits the King to resign as Prime Minister, thus ending the wartime coalition government. He is invited to form a new administration ahead of a general election to be held on 5 July.

24 May: Australian troops have been fighting hard in the jungles of New Guinea for the first five months of this year. Cape Moem, the last enemy stronghold in Wewak, falls to the 6th Australian Division today.

Okinawa: The Japanese mount another desperate attempt to turn the tide of battle when aircraft carrying assault troops crash land on US airfields. The Americans are on permanent high alert in anticipation of surprise attacks and kill all of the enemy.

Burma: Fourteenth Army troops reach the inland port of Bassein.

25 May: In Tokyo, Emperor Hirohito and his family barely escape with their lives as part of the Imperial Palace is destroyed by B-29 bombers flying from the Marianas; 464 aircraft have dropped 4000 tons of bombs on the capital in the past two days. The Japanese retaliate with even more Kamikaze attacks on Okinawa and Allied shipping; 111 Japanese aircraft and pilots are lost. The US Navy announces the sinking of the destroyer *Little* and four small vessels.

Burma: Fourteenth Army units occupy the inland port of Bassein, 88 miles west of Rangoon.

26 May: A round-the-world RAF Lancaster completes experimental flights over the Magnetic and Geographic North Poles to test radio and radar, compass and other navigational equipment. Today the aircraft, codename Aries, touched down at the Empire Air Navigation School at Shawbury, Shropshire.

Middle East: Tension between French troops and Syrian forces grows and shooting is reported in the city of Aleppo.

27 May: Okinawa: Part of the capital Naha is declared secured. Chinese troops entered Nanning, capital of Kwansi province.

The rail link between Berlin and Moscow is operating once more. Carriages and engines must change at the River Vistula due to the different rail gauges.

28 May: The seaport of Yokohama, Japan, suffers a first air raid by 500 US Super-Forts which drop 2500 tons of bombs. Earlier, Mustangs from Iwo Jima neutralised the city's fighter defences. It is estimated that 60,000 homes are destroyed and 250,000 civilians made homeless. Units of the British Pacific Fleet arrive at Apra Harbour, Guam.

Germany: The British traitor William 'Lord Haw-Haw' Joyce is captured by the British Second Army. Joyce broadcast pro-German propaganda from Berlin for most of the war.

Middle East: Syrian workers go on strike in Damascus and Aleppo. French guns shell the Syrian local administrative office at Homs and three French soldiers are killed by tribesmen at Hama.

29 May: Air Force chiefs still believe the non-stop aerial assault on Japan will prove to be the decisive factor in preventing a long drawn out infantry invasion. Thousands of civilians have abandoned urban areas and blitzed factories producing war supplies and armaments. Domestic morale has slumped profoundly. Additional B-29 aircraft have been ordered to the Far East from India to intensify the onslaught. Today the Allies announce that 51 square miles of Tokyo have been destroyed in Super-Fortress firebomb attacks.

30 May: Over 100,000 US troops went ashore on Okinawa in the landings which commenced on 1 April. Just 325 miles from the Japanese mainland, the enemy has mounted a fanatical defence of the 34-mile long island. The US claim that the Japanese death toll up to today is 61,519; just 1353 soldiers of the Emperor have been made prisoner.

Damascus: A truce has been arranged between the French and Syrian nationalists to allow the evacuation of British and US civilians caught up in the fighting in the city.

Tehran: The Persian Foreign Minister demands the withdrawal of British, US and Russian troops from oil-rich Persia.

31 May: England is gradually returning to normal life. The last air raid shelter bunks are removed from South Wimbledon Underground station. On beaches along the South and East coasts, civilian casualties still occur from incidents involving mines and unexploded ordnance. Royal Engineers and navy divers are tackling the long and dangerous task of clearing minefields on beaches identified as possible invasion routes for the Germans in the danger years 1940-41. Unfortunately, some maps identifying mine locations have been lost and coastal erosion has added to the problems of locating the mines. In cities and towns other teams work on defusing unexploded bombs discovered buried in rubble. It is a task that will go on for many years.

The Admiralty announce that between 3 September 1939 and 8 May 1945, 730 Royal Navy ships have been lost.

Levant: Intervention by the British diplomats leads to a cease-fire in Syria and the Lebanon.

Eric White's war saw him shooting at Doodlebugs over Kent and being shot at on a latrine in Meiktila, Burma.

I was called up at the start of 1940. I chose the RAF because my mother had brought home from one of her cleaning jobs copies of *War Illustrated* that told the story of the Great War (1914 to 1918). Although I was very young, I learned to read from these publications and the experience made me never want to end up in a trench; that's why it was the RAF for me!

After several gunnery courses at Douglas and Ronaldsway on the Isle of Man, I became a Ground Gunner manning all kinds of guns on various airfields. Later we became the RAF Regiment. When the Flying Bombs came we formed part of the 'Diver Belt' across Kent meant to prevent Hitler's rockets from reaching London. First we were based at Dungeness then at Sandgate, right in the path of their fixed course. The Flying Bombs had the unmistakable sound

BURMA VICTORY

of a two-stroke motor bike and were coming over continually. Behind us were heavy guns. Any rocket that was hit usually came down on or near us. I was also bemused to find myself in a trench for the first time!

We were near the beach and on one occasion, when swimming amidst the barbed wire, we were strafed by a ME109. I saw the bullets ripping up the water.

Over 'The Hump'

When this was over I joined an RAF Regiment Squadron that was going overseas 'to guard the Khyber Pass.' Great I thought. We sailed from

Ace aviation artist, Frank Wootton, was in Meiktila , Burma, in 1945. The capture of the airfield there in February was the key to victory. The painting at top left depicts Dakota supply planes. Seven of these were lost on 29 March to enemy fire. The RAF Regiment drove back two companies of Japanese, killing 48 of them.

Middle left: *Frank Wootton photographed while at work on what became the finished painting reproduced at bottom left. It features No 607 Squadron Spitfires at Mingladon, Rangoon, in the monsoon period of 1945. This squadron fought in France in May 1940 and in the Battle of Britain before finishing the war in India and Burma. Frank's own wartime story appears on pages 249 to 252 of this book.*

Liverpool on the Queen of Bermuda. In India we went by train to Agartala to do a battle course after which my CO asked me to go on a three-inch mortar course with the Army. This was a new weapon for us. I was to take four corporals and 14 men. We also had a young officer who promptly went sick and was never seen again. I was left in full charge.

At the end of the course our depot gave me two of the latest three-inch mortars with reinforced base plate and barrel to take better bombs. The mortar is a simple weapon; the barrel has a fixed firing pin and provided you're handed the bomb right way round you drop it down the barrel and if the angle of barrel and compass bearing etc are all lined up you usually get the mortar bomb on target. 'Keep them well oiled in their wooden boxes. Being RAF you will never use them,' was the advice. Next minute we (me and my team) are sat on forms along both sides of this American aircraft with our mortars and bombs lined along the centre in front of us. We took off and flew over 'The Hump'. This was the name given to the range of hills or mountains separating India and Burma. There were lots of air pockets. Though we didn't know it at the time, Meiktila airstrip was below us and all around us puffs of smoke appeared. We were being fired upon by Japanese anti-aircraft guns. The thought occurred that we had no parachutes. The American pilot skillfully avoided getting hit and we landed.

We were still under fire and all our gear was more or less thrown off. 'Handle high explosive mortar bombs with care' didn't apply. An army major with jeep and trailer appeared (he had been expecting us) and I tried to tell him we were RAF Regiment. 'You're in the ******** 17th Indian Division now!' he exclaimed.

Rock hard ground

We were ordered to dig a pair of mortar pits with a communicating trench and issued with a field telephone and a list of 16 local targets. The OP (Observation Post) would watch for any enemy in any of these places. Digging in was difficult as the ground was rock hard but we were well exposed and spurred on by enemy fire. By evening we were almost ready. The field telephone rang with the instruction to line up on target 'Nagpur', as none of our patrols would be in the area that night. Both mortars were lined up but both were not pointing the same way. We had to sort it out. Eventually we became very good at it. Nor did the irony escape me that I was in a trench again!

In order to prevent disease we had two latrines. One for night and one for day. It was preferable to use the day one even though it was outside the wire. One day a Sgt Major

asked if I was going to the day latrine. We both put a full magazine in our Sten guns and set off for the toilet, which was two oil drums dug into the ground with holes in the top to sit on and very hot with the sun. We were sat talking and suddenly – ping ping; bullets were hitting our drums! Understandably, we got away pretty smartish.

Back in relative safety, the Sgt Major got his cigarettes out. His Sten gun sling was over his shoulder as he lit his cigarette. The sling slid off his shoulder and the butt of the gun hit the floor, whereupon the bolt of the gun recoiled and fired a 9mm bullet into his person. The Sgt Major was evacuated by air. I was glad I didn't smoke.

We were in Rangoon making preparations to attack heavily-mined Japanese-held islands when the atomic bombs were dropped that ended the war.

The photograph above features Eric and pals in a trench at Meiktila in the spring of 1945. It was first published in The Yorkshire Post *of 11 August 1945 with the headline, 'Yorkshiremen in Burma'. When the photograph was released by the Air Ministry on 27 April 1945 the full caption read: 'After defending the Meiktila airstrip in Central Burma in conjunction with other ground forces against the crack Japanese Imperial Guards Regiment for nearly four weeks, the men of the RAF Regiment are now having a few days rest by the side of Lake Meiktila. The Japanese suffered very heavy losses and casualties were sustained by the Regiment.*

'These Regiment gunners were photographed in a Japanese foxhole and come from the Yorkshire area. Left to right they are: Sergeant 'Chalky' White of 30 Church Lane, Crossgates, Leeds; Leading Aircraftman William Thompson of 20 Regent Place, Keighley; Leading Aircraftman Norman Wingfield of 12 North Bridge Road, Doncaster and Leading Aircraftman Walter Priestley of 185 Granville Street, Park, Sheffield.'

The photograph is inset on the actual mortar target co-ordinates issued to Eric and his men at Meiktila. On the co-ordinates document is an example of a Japanese Occupation banknote.

There's something very comforting in these scenes of London life after the war in Europe has ended. The message seems to be that things can get back to normality very soon. Even so, for Britain many years of post-war austerity lie ahead (National Archives).

FAR EAST FINALE

A Victory Parade was held in Rangoon on 15 June when the Red Ensign of the Port Commissioner was once again flown over the city. The flag had been found by US forces on the island of Attu in the Aleutians.

Allied bombers were active against the remaining Japanese dispositions in Borneo, dropping many tons of ordnance. On 24 June British aircraft also destroyed a bridge over the River Kwai in Siam (Thailand). The structure had been built at a cost of many thousands of British, Commonwealth, Chinese and Thai lives.

Meanwhile, Chinese forces were steadily pushing the Japanese back in China and also in Indo-China. The latter was a colony of France until seized by the Japanese; in June 1945, despite American reservations, the French in Europe were putting together an expeditionary force that aimed to restore the rule of Paris in Hanoi.

On 29 June Tokyo radio announced that the country had begun moving her war factories to Manchuria, out of the range of Allied aircraft. The Japanese also claimed that around five million of their civilians had been injured or killed in air attacks so far. On the same day, President Truman approved a plan for the invasion of Japan, an operation that could involve up to five million US servicemen. Landings on Kyushu could begin on 1 November followed by landings on the main island of Honshu on 1 March 1946.

The bombing of Japan's cities was relentless. In just two days (2 – 3 July), 1100 Super-Fortresses dropped 8000 tons of bombs on Kure, Shimonoseki, Ube and Kumamoto, places with names largely unknown outside of the country.

British carriers attacked

On 4 July, speaking from Manila, General MacArthur announced the complete liberation of the Philippines. It was known, however, that there were thousands of Japanese soldiers still hiding out in the dense forests and on remote islands. Some would still be there over 30 years after the end of the war.

On 7 July British warships bombarded enemy positions on the Nicobar Islands in the Indian Ocean. Next day in the Pacific, three British aircraft carriers were damaged by kamikaze attacks. A few days later British carrier-borne aircraft were in action against targets in Sumatra. The Japanese were also becomingly increasingly alarmed at the prospect of an attack by the Red Army; though sorely short of fighter planes, Tokyo sent precious squadrons off to reinforce bases in Manchuria and Korea.

By the middle of the month, Allied warships were confident enough to close in at night on the shores of Japan to bombard ports and cities on the island of Hokkaido. On 18 July the US fleet fired 2000 tons of shells at the city of Hitachi in the space of just 50 minutes while US and British aircraft destroyed the remnants of the Japanese navy at the Yokosuka naval base. Ships sunk included their most powerful battleship, the Nagato.

Monsoon rains and endless mud

In Burma, Japanese forces fleeing Rangoon attempted to break out over the Pegu Yomas mountains. Although monsoon rains and endless mud had so far prevented the British from finally crushing the enemy, more than 10,000 Japanese soldiers had perished before the beginning of August.

On 22 July the first peace overtures emanated from Tokyo when a statement was issued to the effect that the Government was open to negotiations but would not give in to threats. That same night saw US destroyers enter Tokyo Bay for the first time to torpedo enemy shipping. A few days later British warships carried out minesweeping operations off the Malayan island of Phuket. On 26 July, Britain, China and the US issued the 'Potsdam Declaration' that threatened the 'prompt and utter destruction' of Japan if she did not surrender unconditionally. Within two days the Japanese rejected the ultimatum, apparently mostly because of concerns about the

Great Britain will pursue the WAR AGAINST JAPAN to the very end. WINSTON CHURCHILL

Above: A promise that's nearly fulfilled. In July of 1945 the Japanese were in retreat everywhere and their homeland was under relentless air attack. British land, air and naval forces were leaving Europe to join in the Far East war effort. Even so, Allied landings on Japan itself were expected to be fiercely contested and heavy losses were anticipated.

Emperor's future status.

On 31 July British frogmen used limpet mines to destroy the Japanese cruiser *Takeo* at anchor in Singapore harbour. Next night, in another daring attack, the British midget submarine XE4 penetrated the Japanese-controlled Saigon River in Indo-China. Three frogmen from the submarine then cut the Saigon – Singapore and Saigon – Hong Kong communication cables. Leaflets were also dropped on numerous Japanese cities warning of imminent fire-bomb attacks. Targets included Hiroshima and Nagasaki. But when these two cities were attacked in the course of the first 10 days of August, the weapons used were massively more powerful and destructive than any conventional fire-bomb attack could ever have achieved. The age of atomic warfare was here.

ATOM

" At 8.15am on 6 August 1945, the city of Hiroshima became the victim of of the first atomic bomb to be used in anger. It is believed that around a third of the population of 290,000 perished instantly. "

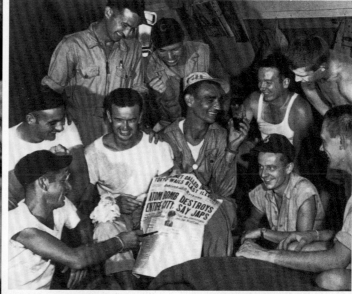

Main picture: Hiroshima after the blast. The dome structure was all that remained recognisable as having been a building.

Inset top: Colonel Paul Tibbets in the cockpit of Enola Gay before the mission.

Inset right: Some of the crew of Enola Gay read the newspaper headlines announcing the first-ever detonation of an atomic bomb.

AGE ARRIVES

The potential power of atomic weapons was well known to the scientists of many develkoped countries including Germany. Fortunately for the Allies, Hitler's haste to go to war meant that his scientists never really entered the race to build an atomic bomb. Instead their energies were channeled into developing other super-weapons such as the fearsome V1 and V2 terror rockets and even these programmes were severely disrupted by the growing Allied air offensive.

It was a different story on the other side of the Atlantic. The US was able to put limitless money and resource into the effort to make the world's first atomic bomb. The top secret Manhattan Project gathered together top scientific brains and in a remarkably short time a prototype bomb was built. On 16 July 1945 at Alamogordo in the remote New Mexico desert, the first device was successfully tested when it exploded with a force equivalent to 20,000 tons of TNT. Following a flash that could be seen 125 miles away, the blast sent an ominous mushroom cloud 40,000 feet into the air.

Three days later at the Potsdam Conference in Germany, British Premier Winston Churchill and the US President, Harry Truman, agreed privately that the atomic bomb would be employed against Japan if the country refused to surrender unconditionally. The pair were unsure whether Stalin was aware of the awesome new weapon.

Japanese submarine strike

The vital uranium – 235 needed to construct atomic bombs was dispatched to the Pacific island of Tinian on board the *USS Indianapolis*. Mission completed, the ship was returning home when it was sunk by one of the few remaining operational Japanese submarines. Just 316 survivors were eventually picked up from the shark-infested Philippine Sea where 880 of her crew perished.

On 5 August 1945, seven US B-29 aircraft took off to raid Hiroshima on Japan's Honshu Island. One of the aircraft was the *Enola Gay* under the command of Colonel Paul Tibbets. It was carrying an atomic bomb. At 8.15am next morning, the city of Hiroshima became the victim of the first atomic bomb ever to be used in anger. In a blinding flash, the lightweight structures of the city centre were vapourised. Only a few concrete structures survived the blast. The exact number of casualties will never be known but it is thought that around a third

of the population of 290,000 perished instantly. 'This is the greatest thing in history,' declared President Truman as he made his way home from Potsdam.

Shocked though they were at reports of the terrifying power of the new weapon possessed by the Allies, Tokyo did not immediately give in. Even a declaration of war on Japan by the Russians, delivered at Stalin's behest on 8 August, was not enough to force a surrender. Next day a second atomic bomb was dropped on the shipbuilding port of Nagasaki; the results were equally devastating as at Hiroshima.

Tokyo offers to surrender

On 10 August a broadcast was made from Tokyo offering to surrender, providing the 'prerogatives of the Emperor' were not prejudiced. But fighting still continued wherever Allied air, sea and land forces were in contact with the Japanese. The Russians had already advanced 120 miles into Manchuria. Three days later, Outer Mongolia declared war on Japan on the same day that British and US aircraft hit the Tokyo area with a hail of conventional bombs.

On Tuesday 14 August 1945 – 1346 days after their infamous attack on Pearl Harbor in December 1941 – the Japanese Government at last accepted the inevitable and agreed to surrender. The Second World War was almost over after nearly six years of conflict. The news was announced simultaneously in London, Washington and Moscow. General Douglas MacArthur was authorized to accept the surrender while Emperor Hirohito would broadcast to the Japanese people in what would be the first time anyone outside of court circles would hear the voice of the man considered a living divinity.

At dawn on 15 August, Avenger aircraft made what was the war's last British bombing raid when they attacked a factory near Kamohaura. In Tokyo, military fanatics attacked the royal palace to urge the Emperor to persist with the fight. When it became clear the attempt had failed the coup leader committed hara kiri.

Last shots fired in Burma

On 16 August Hirohito ordered all Japanese servicemen to lay down their arms and a new Government was formed under Prince Higashikuni. Despite the broadcast, many Japanese fought on, particularly in Manchuria

and outlying areas of the Pacific where communications were difficult or non-existent. British warships off Tokyo were ordered to cease fire from 11.15am. Even then, some Japanese aircraft continued to attack; five were shot down, as allowed in the Allied rules of engagement. In Burma, the last shots were exchanged between men of General Slim's Fourteenth Army and tattered remnants of the Japanese trapped in the bend of the Sittang River, east of Pegu.

Over the next two weeks or so Japanese forces gradually surrendered all over the Far East and Pacific. The Russians continued to move swiftly and occupied the whole of Manchuria, Korea and the Kurile Islands, a part of the Japanese homeland.

On 29 August a British fleet sailed into Hong Kong to reclaim the colony while the Japanese in Singapore surrendered to Lord Louis Mountbatten. On 31 August, General MacArthur became the first foreigner in authority over Japan in 1000 years when he established the Supreme Allied Command in Yokohama. The greatest and most destructive conflict the world has ever known had now ended, although the formal surrender of Japan did not take place for two more days.

Above: The Japanese surrender delegation on board USS Missouri in Tokyo Bay on 2 September 1945.

Saved by the Bomb

Ron McGill relates how a British POW held captive near Hiroshima in August 1945 survived the terrifying advent of the Atom Bomb.

Left: *A sailor from* HMIS Sutlej *(an Indian Navy vessel) surveys the devastation in Hiroshima.*

Back in August 1985 I remember a lunchtime conversation with colleagues at the Wimbledon HQ of BT in South West London. It was the 40th anniversary of the dropping of the atomic bomb and we were discussing the rights and wrongs of the decision.

The talk seemed to be drifting towards a concensus that humanity should have dictated against the use of such a devastating weapon at a time when Japan was obviously losing the war. Suddenly, a quiet voice piped up: 'I do not agree with you. The atomic bomb saved my life and that of many otherwise doomed friends of mine.'

We looked astonished at this obviously truthful and sincere statement. It had been made by one of my engineering colleagues, Ted Harker. Ted, a cheerful person, was stockily built with grey thinning hair. He was one who normally kept his own counsel but on this day we all wanted to hear him out and we pressed him for his story.

Captured at Singapore
And what a story – for Ted was one of the thousands of our soldiers captured at the fall of Singapore in February 1942. There followed for Ted and his friends much hard work on construction and railway sites for the Japanese, always hungry and suffering constant disease and malnutrition that gradually eroded their numbers as many died in captivity.

When the New Year of 1945 dawned the Japanese authorities sifted some of the hardiest of the survivors and shipped them to Japan and a city facing an extensive bay that led to the open sea. The new job (good for only as long as their poor wretched bodies would last) consisted of loading and unloading goods and engineering work of many kinds in a shipyard in

a place they learnt was called Hiroshima.

Ted had about 50 soldier colleagues with him and, with the poor food and frequent beatings, they felt they could not last long in their weakened state and life looked more than bleak during those months of 1945. They did not have the luxury of huts or barracks and they were placed in deep caves in the foothills about 10 miles away that surrounded Hiroshima. Contact with Japanese citizens was almost nil for they were 'trucked in' to the dockyards and brought back to their caves at the end of the working day. They were given just enough food and drink to keep them working effectively by the Japanese guards who lived in rough quarters at the entrances to their caves.

Earth-shattering experience
That fateful morning of 6 August dawned and the B29 (Enola Gay) arrived high over Hiroshima and dropped the first Atom Bomb to be used in anger at 8.16am. This was equal to about 20,000 tons of TNT and we now know that 80,000 citizens were killed immediately and that four square miles of the city was turned into a burning wasteland. For Ted and his colleagues down in the caves all they could hear and feel was the earth-

> " All that Ted and his fellow prisoners down in the caves could hear and feel was the effects of what appeared to be an earthquake, a phenomenon not uncommon in Japan. "

shattering experience of what appeared to be an earthquake, not uncommon in Japan.

Weakened as they were the prisoners remained resting in their caves waiting for the usual call to the trucks by their guards. This call never came and at noon some of the men checked the entrance and were astounded to find that their guards had gone and their quarters were abandoned. They then made a decision that probably saved their lives from the then unknown dangers of deadly radiation. They stayed resting in their caves and shared out what food and drink they could find in the deserted guards' quarters. They treated this break as a luxury rest and recovery period for by now there were only 35 of them left alive and able to walk and work.

Skeletal soldiers
After about two weeks a small group of Japanese civilians passed nearby and stopped briefly at the caves to be amazed at the sight of the almost skeletal soldiers coming slowly out into the daylight. A few of the POWs understood the Japanese language and they told the others that a massive disaster had overcome Hiroshima and they all agreed again to stay where they were, out of the possible earthquake chaos and hopefully safer where they were – although by now their stock of food was diminishing rapidly.

The world soon knew of the Japanese surrender that was signed on 2 September and subsequently, various US military units began to arrive to study the complete devastation of Hiroshima. They in turn somehow learned of the presence of Allied prisoners somewhere in the nearby foothills and they came and searched the area and the caves and discovered some of the soldier prisoners still alive. Needless to say the surviving POWs found it all a miracle; liberation at last.

Miracle of liberation
A US officer later told my friend Ted that they had found some of their missing guards who admitted that they knew the prisoners could not last much longer. They said that the plan was to execute their captives in the next few weeks as the guards were being withdrawn to help reinforce the coastal defence of Japan against the expected Allied invasion of the mainland. Instead of that fate it was time to receive medical care and attention and proper food and drink to see them on the slow but sure recovery road after their three hard years of captivity.

After he had explained this dramatic tale some four decades on in our BT restaurant Ted would only say dryly, 'it was rather a close run thing.' Clearly, he and his colleagues were forever grateful for the Atom Bomb which gave them many extra years of life after they had come to terms with the fact that they had seemed surely doomed to die in Japan in 1945.

A Kind of Peace

The Second World War may have ended but in the coming decades there would be plenty of occasions when Britain's armed forces were called into action in locations right around the globe.

The sudden surrender of Japan in the summer of 1945 left a large number of occupied European colonies in the Far East without effective government. In many cases they also had burgeoning nationalist movements with leaders who were anxious to seize territory and power and resist the return of British, Dutch and French colonial rule.

Britain had made contingency plans for a swift return to Malaya, Singapore and Hong Kong and military and civilian personnel quickly moved back and assumed a governing role. However, as neither the French nor the Dutch had the necessary forces in the Far East, their colonies posed problems. The Anglo-American Joint Chiefs of Staff decided that whatever Allied troops were available should be used in these areas to disarm and repatriate the Japanese and restore civilian administration.

As a result, British and Indian forces became involved in policing the Netherlands East Indies (NEI) and the southern part of French Indochina (later known as South Vietnam). Unfortunately both territories contained strong nationalist movements and the British found themselves in the midst of bitter confrontations as the Dutch and French governments sought to re-impose their authority.

The first British landings in the NEI took place on 29 September at Batavia (now the Indonesian capital, Jakarta) on the island of Java. Early hope that the local people would accept the British presence was quickly dashed; the Indonesian nationalists, led by Ahmed Sukarno, had already formed a government and had achieved a semblance of political control over most of the island. The Japanese garrisons had encouraged the nationalist movement and even provided them with arms and training.

Japanese assistance

As well as dealing with the nationalist threat, the British troops also had to restore law and order in many areas where looting and murder held sway in the absence of authority. Ironically, local British commanders used armed Japanese soldiers to aid them in this task, a measure allowed in accordance with

Exhausted! Here's a picture that sums up how the members of Britain's armed forces must have felt at the end of the titanic world-wide war that raged from September 1939 to August 1945, *writes David Arnold*. I found it in an album of wartime photographs put together by my wife's late uncle Jimmy Kane and now in her possession. That's Jimmy on the left and you can see the clear likeness to his brother Geordie Kane who was killed at Anzio in April 1944 (see page 225). I never had the opportunity to ask Jimmy about his experiences in the Royal Navy but it is clear from the album that he served all over the world including highly dangerous Malta convoys, off the coast of Normandy on D-Day and in the Far East in the summer of 1945. At that time he was aboard the aircraft carrier *HMS Indomitable*. The ship took part in the liberation of Hong Kong at the end of August and her aircraft were in action against Japanese explosive motor boats in Lamma Bay almost on the last day of the war. A few weeks earlier the vessel had been hit by a kamikaze attack but was saved from serious damage due to her armoured deck.

the terms of the Japanese surrender.

Even though Dutch forces were arriving, it would not be until November 1946 that the last British and Indian troops were able to withdraw. It had been a difficult operation and one which the British had not expected to undertake. The fact that they did so in an unfamiliar country against armed opposition is very much to their credit.

British in Saigon

In September 1945, at the same time as the operations on Java were underway, British and Indian forces moved into southern Indochina. Their arrival in Saigon was part of an Allied move to clear the former French possessions of Vietnam, Laos and Cambodia.

A communist-controlled group known as the Viet Minh had already picked up the reins of power and set up a revolutionary government in the northern city of Hanoi. Nationalist Chinese troops who moved into

the north of the country to disarm the Japanese did not interfere with the Viet Minh, who presumed from this that the French were unlikely to return.

In fact the French were intent on resuming their pre-war status, using the British presence as a preliminary move. The British, on the other hand, were going in under orders that they were to merely supervise the Japanese surrender in the south of Vietnam and restore law and order up to the 16th parallel. It was another recipe for trouble.

The first British troops landed by air near Saigon on 8 September. By the middle of October all three brigades of Major General D D Gracey's 20th Indian Division were present and facing a very tense situation. Armed resistance broke out in many places, usually taking the form of attacks on individual soldiers and convoys of vehicles. Gracey quickly recognised that he had insufficient resources to secure the whole of the south.

Instead he opted to concentrate his forces in and around Saigon, holding the city until the French could take over. To exert control over Saigon, Gracey had to enlist the support of the surrendered Japanese, who were re-armed and joined the British and Indian troops on the streets. It was a tough few months with the men facing raids, sabotage of utilities, bombs, sniping and a resentful population generally set against a return of the French.

Clamour for independence

The first major French military units arrived in October. They were under the command of General Leclerc, who had led the Free French liberators of Paris in August 1944. But in Saigon and Hanoi, Leclerc was not viewed as a liberator but rather was seen as an enemy of a people eager for independence. By the end of 1945 most of the British forces had been withdrawn.

In this same period, far more serious trouble had been brewing in India, where the clamour for independence had developed during the Second World War and had been encouraged by British promises that it would be granted in the long term. In the winter of 1945 – 46 there were mutinies in the ranks of the Indian Army and British battalions were called into action to put them down.

There was also bitter religious strife between the Hindu Congress Party and the Moslem League. It would be several years before Partition would see the setting up of a mainly Hindu India state and Moslem Pakistan. The last British troops withdrew from the sub-continent in February 1948.

Problems in Palestine

The British had other problem areas to look after in the immediate aftermath of the war. In Greece, there was simmering violence between monarchists and communists in which the British were caught up in offering support to the existing anti-communist government. The British were not to leave Greece until 1948 when their role was passed on to US forces.

Palestine, too, posed problems. At the end of the war the First Infantry Division was the only British formation in Palestine. It was charged with keeping the peace there and also stabilising neighbouring Lebanon and Syria. In the autumn of 1945 the Sixth Airborne Division was released from service with the British Army On the Rhine (BAOR) and sent to Palestine.

Opposition to continued British rule came mainly from the Jews, angry at official policies that restricted the flow of refugees who had survived the Holocaust in Europe only to be denied access to a Jewish homeland. During the war, Jewish units had fought for the Allies; a Jewish Brigade Group fought in Italy with the British Eighth Army. The British Officer Orde Wingate, famous as the leader of the Chindits in Burma in 1943 – 44, helped train the first Jewish fighters in the late 1930s. Unfortunately,

Above: Sabah, August 1964. A British soldier is winched up into a Royal Navy Wessex helicopter. Britain sent forces to aid the former British colonies on the island of Borneo face up to the threat of an invasion by Indonesia. Successfully defended, Sabah and Sarawak went on to join the Malaysian Federation while oil-rich Brunei remained an independent Sultanate.

once the war in Europe ended, many of these well-trained men enlisted in Jewish militant bands such as the *Haganah* and *Stern Gang*.

It was a very messy situation, not eased by Arab fears of an impending Jewish state likely to emerge in the near future. In September 1947 the British Government acknowledged that the Palestine issue was one they could not resolve and accordingly announced they would be relinquishing the Mandate on 15 May the following year, handing the question over to the United Nations.

By the time the British withdrew in 1948, the lives of 338 British soldiers, police and civilians had been lost.

Cold War confrontation

June 1948 also saw the first major Cold War confrontation in the Berlin Airlift, a massive and sustained operation that saw the people of West Berlin solely but successfully supplied by air for around a year after the Soviet Union cut off land access.

Eleven months after the end of the Berlin blockade, the Cold War killing ground moved out of Europe into Asia. On 25 June 1950 the communist North Korean army erupted across the de facto 38th parallel border and invaded the Western-backed Republic of Korea in the south of the country. A long and bitter see-saw struggle ensued in which Britain lost 686 men killed before a niggling and unsatisfactory cease-fire came into effect on 25 July 1953.

From 1948 until 1960, Britain was also caught up in a number of military campaigns where her forces had to confront large-scale guerrilla activities in territories that had been or were still colonies of the Empire. The major ones took place in Malaya, Kenya and Cyprus. None of these conflicts were described as

'wars'; typically the hostilities in Malaya were termed an 'Emergency' even though the fighting lasted some 12 years. A main reason for not calling it a 'war' was because the term would have invalidated the insurance cover for the rubber plantations.

In Malaya the insurgency had the general support of about half a million non-Muslim Chinese immigrants who lived on the edges of the jungle. Thousands of British national servicemen fought in Malaya and their obvious youth learned them the sobriquet of the 'Virgin Soldiers'; 446 British soldiers lost their lives but eventually by 1960 Malaya emerged as an independent and stable country.

Mau Mau insurgency

British forces were also involved in the so-called Indonesian Confrontation that took place on the giant island of Borneo between 1962 and 1966 when Indonesia attempted to de-rail the states of Sabah and Sarawak who had joined the Malaysian Federation. When it was over, the then Defence Secretary Dennis Healey said of the campaign: 'Borneo saw one of the most efficient uses of military forces in the history of the world.'

In 1952 Britain's colony of Kenya suffered the Mau Mau insurgency. It was tribal-based, with most of the rebels coming from the Kikuyu people. It took until 1960 to fully suppress the uprising by which time around 12,000 Mau Mau fighters had been killed for the loss of 600 members of the security forces. In the early Sixties British troops successfully intervened to help quell mutinies in several East African countries recently granted independence.

Cyprus was one colony the British were keen to retain owing to its important strategic position in the Eastern Mediterranean. Some 80% of the population were Greek with the remaining almost all Turkish. In 1954, encouraged by Cypriot leader Archbishop Makarios, a movement called EOKA began actively campaigning for *Enosis* – union with Greece. The Turkish Cypriots were alarmed and Britain became caught up in a vicious struggle that ultimately led to Cyprus becoming an independent, though effectively partitioned, state in 1959. Over 100 British soldiers and 50 policemen were killed during the Cyprus troubles. As a consolation Britain was able to keep her military bases on the island.

On a number of other occasions, Britain's armed forces acted as 'policemen' or served in UN peace-keeping forces on just about every continent. In 1961 the oil-rich state of Kuwait was threatened with invasion by Iraq; warnings of British intervention were enough to deter Baghdad. Throughout all this time Britain had also maintained her obligations as an important member of NATO and had strong forces, based mainly in West Germany, to counter the threat of an invasion by the Soviet Union and her Eastern Bloc allies.

THE BERLIN AIRLIFT

Stan Rendell MBE served with the RAF in post-war Germany in 1948 at a time when the Soviets blockaded Berlin's road and rail links with the West.

The Berlin Airlift was an operation which, for more than a year, kept two million Germans supplied with food and other necessities – albeit at a cost of nearly 80 lives. Certainly it was at times hectic, exciting, and dangerous, but it also had its lighter moments, and as one of the large number of RAF ground crew involved I well remember the many small children we helped off the Dakotas when they landed back at RAF Lübeck.

Initially the returning passengers from Berlin had been mainly adults, including visitors trapped by Russia's sudden blockading of all road and rail access from the Western zones. The organised aerial evacuation of literally thousands of children from West Berlin began later, the older children often being deputed to look after the younger ones. The aircrews did their best for them but these were military cargo-carrying aircraft with no creature comforts. They were loaded up at Lübeck in the morning with essential supplies and, during a quick turnaround at Berlin for unloading and any necessary servicing, canvas bench seating normally used for paratroopers was re-fixed in position along the sides of the cabin. The next day the same aircraft might be carrying sacks of coal into the city on another shuttle run.

The evacuation of children and some sick or elderly folk was an aside to the main task of keeping West Berlin's inhabitants supplied and independent of Russian control. In the end-of-war partition of Germany it had been agreed that, despite Berlin being in the Russian zone, all the occupying powers should have occupation rights over a part of that important city. Now, by closing the land links to the Western zones, Russia was blatantly trying to force the Western powers out of Berlin.

Dakotas shifted to Fassberg

At RAF Lübeck we were close to the edge of the Russian Zone of Germany and aircraft making an instrument approach to the east end of the runway had to fly over Russian controlled territory. In air miles the RAF station at Fassberg was a little farther from Berlin with RAF Wunstorf a little farther again. But it was to Wunstorf that the Dakotas and their personnel were hurriedly despatched from England in June 1948 and from there they started the airlift. Very quickly they were joined by four-engined Avro York aircraft (a cargo/passenger development of the Lancaster bomber). Accommodation at Wunstorf soon became over-stretched and three or four weeks later, the Dakotas were shifted to Fassberg.

Fassberg was a former Luftwaffe base and numerous damaged Focke Wulf FW190 fighters were still scattered around the airfield, half hidden in the surrounding woods. Nearer the runways the relative peace was shattered by the noise of round-the-clock revving engines, for the Dakotas were now joined by the four-engined Douglas Skymasters of the Americans. Interlocking steel planking was used to extend runway and aircraft parking areas and the movement of the aeroplanes on these strips added to the cacophony. The

Above: There were lots of accidents. In this incident a pilot braked too hard and pitched the aircraft on its nose.

aerodrome was crowded, but Anglo-American relationships were good, and the food provided for us in the American mess was far better than RAF rations. We tucked into huge beef steaks! With aircraft being operated all day and all night, the work pressure was immense.

In September 1948, as the airfield became overcrowded, I was on board one of the last Dakotas to pull out of Fassberg en-route to RAF Lübeck. The aircraft was loaded with stores and heavy equipment; and with its door removed to accommodate one of the big three-bladed spare propellers, one blade projected slightly into the slipstream. When we ran into a severe storm the flight became rather exciting. The heavy aircraft was tossed about; rain and hailstones came through the

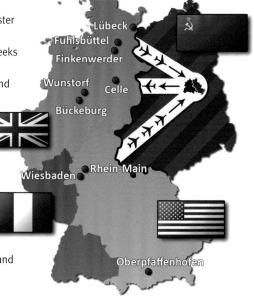

GET SOME IN!

Derek Askew's National Service saw him in Cyprus in 1955.

The first attack by EOKA occurred just before midnight on Thursday 31 March 1955 when they threw a couple of bombs over the fence at GHQ Nicosia destroying the sergeant major's bicycle. All regiments in the area were mobilised to defend British army establishments, including ourselves the Royal Signal Regiment – so it had to be serious.

Unfortunately Thursday in the British Army was pay day, and the custom was to get blind drunk. So you can imagine the reception the duty sergeant got when he burst into our tent at half past midnight in hysterical frenzy to announce that the bloody Greeks were attacking us and to report to the armoury to draw weapons. We made an appropriate reply – which cannot be repeated here – and went back to sleep. Five minutes later he was back. This time he was not to be denied. Overturning beds and kicking anything that didn't move, we were soon at a great speed running towards the armoury, clad only in our pyjamas (or not clad, as the case may be).

Weapons issued to drunks

When I arrived, the queue resembled a bonding convention between the Rip Van Winkle Society and the local nudist club, except nobody wanted an inebriated nudist standing behind him. At the front of the queue weapons were being handed to drunks – never a good idea. Worst still the lads were being dispatched immediately to protect the camp perimeter 'as they stood'. Thank God the RAF camp alongside ours was not aroused. As the rest of us inched towards the armoury door the inevitable happened – they ran out of guns. Undaunted, our demented sergeant told us to find anything we could use as a weapon. Tent pegs seemed like a good idea, so we quickly moved to the nearest tent and very quickly had all eight pegs out of the ground. As the canvas collapsed to the ground loud swearing was heard from underneath it. For a while the life form inside appeared to move around in circles. When it eventually crawled out from beneath, we recognised it to be the guard commander sergeant minus his teeth; he obviously couldn't find them. As he was clearly going to kill us we quickly informed him that the other sergeant had told us to do it. Now we had two demented sergeants close to exchanging blows.

At this point the duty officer made a brief appearance from the latrines and ordered us to report to motor transport – as we stood – for dispatch to the transmitter site at Ayii Trimithiias. In next to no time 16 of us were climbing on to the back of a three ton Bedford truck, eight of us with guns and eight with tent pegs.

It is important to know at this point that army drivers only have two speeds – ramming and kamikaze, and tend to drive as the crow flies. It wasn't long after leaving the camp during our fifth off-road excursion that we ran over some large rocks. Two of the lads who had been happily sitting on the tail board firing at passing strangers were catapulted into the air off the back of the truck – but they kept firing.

Sten gun goes off

A pyjama-clad Praetorian concerned at their departure tried to get the driver to stop by banging on the roof of the cab with the butt of his Sten gun; unfortunately the safety catch was off and, being a recoil weapon, 30 rounds were unleashed from the muzzle destroying a perfectly good canvas roof (luckily it wasn't raining).

Reacting to the banging and automatic gun fire, our driver decided terrorists must be in hot pursuit and put his foot flat to the floor, inventing a third mode of driving now known as 'low level flying'.

On arrival at the transmitter site we had an enormous problem trying to get in because we couldn't wake them up, despite repeated blowing of the lorry horn.

Eventually a bleary eyed corporal appeared at the gate. Seeing a bunch of half naked drunken renegades wielding guns and tent pegs he made a hasty retreat to the control cabin where he rang the Squadron Office back in Nicosia to tell them he was under attack. The duty officer told him to defend his position with all possible means and that reinforcements had already been dispatched.

As we stood at the gate shivering and absolutely peed off, it occurred to us that we might be a bit vulnerable. One of our motley crew (known affectionately as Henry-etta; excused boots – light duties – and of a different persuasion), suggested we all got back onto the truck and cuddled up for warmth. Fearing friendly fire we decided his option was the lesser of two evils, so we moved off about half a mile and parked in a nearby vineyard to wait for dawn. Sleep was virtually impossible so by the time dawn broke we were feeling like a bunch of zombies after our all-night bonding session. At this moment a face appeared above the tail gate of the lorry – it was a Greek Cypriot shepherd. At first his expression was one of disbelief, but quickly it changed to a knowing grin. He wagged his finger at us and said something in Greek; a translation was not required. At this moment I never needed my mother more.

It would take some five decades before a Cyprus campaign medal was issued.

Far left: British soldiers prepare for potential rioting during a 24-hour strike planned by Greek Cypriots late in 1955.
Left: Men of 45 Commando use detectors as they search for EOKA mines in the village of Akanthou in September 1955.

THE SUEZ CRISIS

November 1956. Britain and France make a successful assault to regain control of the Suez Canal but have to give it up again under superpower pressure from Washington and Moscow.

The British withdrawal from India in February 1948 soon called into question the need for Britain to police the Suez Canal. The traumatic birth of the independent states of mostly Hindu India and majority Muslim Pakistan cut at the heart of the declining British Empire and the imperial trading system and thus the reasoning for maintaining a strong military presence in the Middle East.

Egypt was key to the future ownership of the Canal. Already deemed to be independent, Egypt accepted British troops as 'guests' under the terms of a 1936 treaty. Following various coups and a series of anti-British riots and terror campaigns, an agreement was reached with Egyptian leader Colonel Gamal Abdul Nasser in October 1954 that gave the British 20 months in which to withdraw their forces. A proviso to the agreement was the right of the British to return should the use of the Canal be threatened by an external power.

Suez Canal nationalised

Unfortunately Nasser quickly lost favour with most Western countries through his strident pan-Arab rhetoric, support of Algerian rebels waging a bloody anti-colonial war against France and implacable objection to the existence of the State of Israel. He also refused to join the West-leaning Baghdad Pact of Middle East states. Faced with a Western arms embargo, Nasser turned to the communist Eastern Bloc where he found a ready supply of armaments and aircraft. Then on 26 July 1956 Nasser nationalised the Suez Canal Company, cutting off at once the lucrative flow of tolls to the Paris-based Anglo-French consortium that hitherto operated the waterway.

The pride of Britain and France was severely wounded and the two countries shared the view that Nasser was a provocative and dangerous 'loose cannon' in the Middle East. Secret preparations began for joint military action aimed at regaining control of the Suez Canal. Despite a clear lack of support from the USA and outright warnings of 'grave consequences' by the Soviet Union, invasion planning continued through the summer but

was subject to various delays. Eventually France brought Israel into the equation and in secret talks invited the Israelis to participate in an attack on Egypt that would precipitate the Anglo-French seizure of the Canal.

Hungarian uprising crushed

The Israeli assault began on 29 October. British involvement in the affair began on 1 November when the cruiser *HMS Newfoundland* sank an Egyptian frigate in the Gulf of Suez. Successful and well-executed Anglo-French air and sea landings took place in the following days. However, at the same time intense diplomatic pressure to halt hostilities had been building not only at the UN but also in Washington and in Moscow. The latter two superpowers literally called the shots. Britain was particularly vulnerable to financial pressures brought to bear by the USA. In consequence a ceasefire was declared to come into effect at midnight on 6 November 1956 and a UN peacekeeping force began arriving in Egypt on 14 November.

The cost in Western casualties was light – just 22 British dead. But the price paid in lost prestige was enormous. Britain's world status was greatly diminished. Ironically, in part it was the fall-out from the Suez political reverse and the US failure to lend support that influenced Britain's decision not to get involved with America's anti-communist crusade in Vietnam that began just a few years later.

Another irony was that even as the Suez Crisis was making world headlines, the Soviet Union was ruthlessly suppressing a popular anti-communist uprising in Hungary. Suez provided a timely smokescreen to mask the brutal goings on taking place behind the Iron Curtain.

British forces were stationed in Libya at the time of the Suez Crisis. A regular newsletter – *Tripoli News* – was prepared by the Royal Army Educational Corps (RAEC) and issued by the Commander of the Tripolitania District. The contents of the first newsletter (Volume 1, Number 6) to appear within hours of the ceasefire between the British, French and Israeli forces and the Egyptians coming into effect at midnight on Tuesday 6 November 1956 are reproduced here. They give a fascinating insight into how the British authorities viewed their conduct and accomplishments at Suez.

Eisenhower re-elected

At 06.30 (GMT) this morning Mr Adlai Stevenson, the Democratic candidate conceded the US election to Mr Eisenhower. At that time Mr Eisenhower was leading by 42 states (470 electoral votes) to 6 (61 votes).

Above: *Soldiers of 40 Commando, Royal Marines, raise the White Ensign in Port Said on 6 November 1956.*

TRIPOLI NEWS

Egypt: Ceasefire

Orders to British and French troops to cease fire became effective at midnight last night. Announcing this in the House of Commons last night, Sir Anthony Eden said that Egypt had accepted an unconditional ceasefire, and that the British and French governments had communicated with Mr (Dag) Hammarskjold (at the United Nations), asking him to confirm that this was so, and that the (UN) force which would be set up would be competent to perform its task. President Eisenhower said that he was delighted at the news.

A French spokesman stated that the Egyptian ground forces had been scattered before the ceasefire was ordered. It has also been announced that for the first time in British military history, helicopters have been used to land troops on foreign soil. A whole Royal Marine Commando was landed by this means. Naval divers have already begun work on the clearing of obstacles from the Canal.

Shortly before the ceasefire came into effect, Saudi Arabia informed the UN that she had broken off diplomatic relations with Britain, and will stop all oil supplies to Britain and France.

UN meeting postponed

The meeting of the General Assembly to discuss the Middle East situation has been postponed until this afternoon, when the Afro-Asian resolution will be debated. This calls for the immediate withdrawal of British, French and Israeli troops from Egypt. The situation in Hungary will be discussed this evening.

Eleven countries – Canada, Ceylon, Colombia, Czecheslovakia, Denmark, Finland, India, Norway, Pakistan, Rumania, and Sweden – have offered to contribute troops to the International Force.

Hungary

Reports reaching London indicate that resistance is continuing in many places and fighting still carries on in Budapest. Many countries are preparing aid and relief for Hungarian refugees. Belgium, France, Switzerland, Sweden and the Netherlands have offered temporary asylum to refugees. A protest march has been held in Bonn, and a three minutes silence throughout Western Germany. There have been demonstrations in Paris, Madrid, Luxembourg, Lisbon and Stockholm. Spain and the Netherlands have announced that they are withdrawing from the Olympic Games as a protest.

Above: Royal Marine Commandos on HMS Theseus about to fly to Port Said, Suez, in November 1956.
Background below: Port Said seafront soon after the H-Hour bombardment on 6 November.

Replies to Soviet Union

Sir Anthony Eden said last night that it was only because of the extreme gravity of the situation that he had not rejected Marshal Bulganin's note as unacceptable. In his reply he had said that it ill became the Russians to speak of barbarity (concerning Suez) at a time when Soviet forces were viciously crushing the heroic resistance of a truly national movement in Hungary. The fact that he had asked the UN to take over in Egypt refuted the false and baseless accusations of Russia.

Today's celebrations in Moscow of the anniversary of the Russian Revolution will be boycotted by the British, French and American ambassadors.

Syrian oil pipeline

The Syrian Government has denied the British statement that the Syrian army was responsible for the damage to the Iraq Petroleum Company's pipeline. Nevertheless it has undertaken to see that the damage is repaired.

Tripoli News of 9 November:

Israel accepts terms

At a midnight conference of the UN, the Secretary General announced that Israel is willing to withdraw her troops from Egypt. In Tel Aviv it was said that Israel's conditions are that an effective international force should move in and that Egypt should stop sending murder gangs across the frontier.

In a broadcast, Mr Ben Gurion said that his answer to Mr Bulganin's note included a photostat copy of a general order issued last February to the commander of the Egyptian Third Division saying that the Egyptian army must be prepared to eliminate Israel quickly and by the cruellest means.

Reply to Baghdad Pact

The Foreign Office state that a note has been received from the four other countries of the Baghdad Pact – Turkey, Pakistan, Iraq and Persia – asking Britain to withdraw her forces from Egypt. The reply said that Britain had taken the only action open to her to stop a general conflagration in the Middle East. The friendly and constructive advice of these powers agreed with our own views, and had weighed heavily with us in bringing about a ceasefire. The time is now right for the settlement of these issues and all members of the Baghdad Pact can play a great part in the restoring of order to the Middle East.

Opposition vote defeated

In the House of Commons yesterday, a motion of censure on the Government for not calling a meeting of Commonwealth Premiers was defeated by 58 votes. Mr Thorneycroft said there had been no time for such a meeting but talks had been going on at the highest level. Russia was dismayed at the failure of her plans. She had armed Egypt to the teeth and, through Colonel Nasser, hoped to gain control in the Middle East. The action of Britain and France in Egypt could not be compared with that of Russia in Hungary; they had started a war, we had entered to stop a war. We had gone in just in time to stop the Egyptian airforce from running amok. Otherwise, not only Budapest, but also Tel Aviv and Cairo would have been in flames.

US Resolutions on Hungary

The United States has tabled UN Resolutions. One calls for the Russians to cease their aggressions against Hungary which violates all laws of justice and morality. Communist Yugoslavia has also called upon Russia to withdraw.

President Eisenhower has said that few events had ever so stirred the indignation of the American people.

Local News

A warrant has been issued for the arrest of Colonel Sadik, Egyptian Military Attache, who has taken refuge in the Egyptian Embassy, now ringed by Libyan Police. He is accused of organising disturbances and reported to be very full of himself, having received news from Cairo that five or six MiGs had bombed Cyprus! This news would appear to be exclusive to the Egyptian Information Service.

Airlift of families

The evacuation of (British) families from the Tripoli area is almost complete. Between 0830 and 1905 yesterday, 522 passengers left Idris Airport in light aircraft, including three Britannias. The total lifted so far is 1590. The remaining 55 people are due to leave this morning.

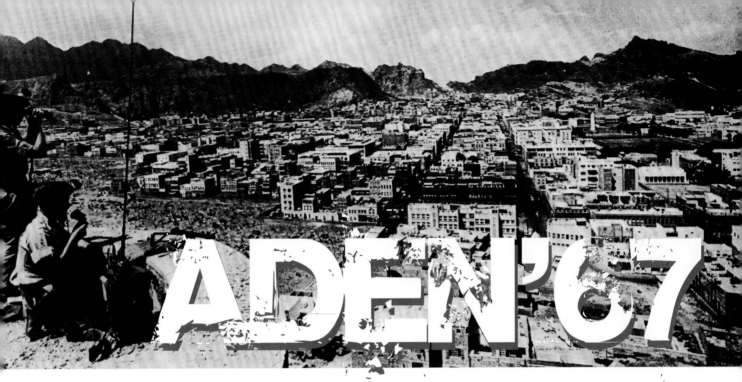

ADEN '67

The deep-water harbour of Aden on the Arabian peninsula had been under British control since 1839 and ruled from Britain as a Crown colony since 1937. Aden's geographic position made it an important staging post on the route to India. In February 1959, six emirates, sheikhdoms and sultanates of the Western and Eastern Aden Protectorates came together to form the Federation of South Arabia (FSA) under the auspices of Britain. By the end of 1963, Aden, along with another 10, had joined.

The members of the Federation had banded together on the understanding that a British presence in the region would be maintained even after full independence was granted some time before 1968. However, by the early 1960s, there had emerged a swathe of nationalist movements opposed to the states' traditional rulers and their British backers. The earliest threat to the FSA came from Yemen which had claims to some of its territory. After 1962, the Yemen began to openly support the two main rebel groups, the National Liberation Front (NLF) and the Front for the Liberation of South Yemen (FLOSY). In December 1963 the FSA declared a state of emergency and called on the Britain for military aid.

At first the insurrection was confined to the hinterland but late in 1964 a campaign of terror began to make itself felt in Aden.

The hotspot of trouble was the district of Crater. Surrounded by the jagged cliffs of an extinct volcano – the Jebel Shamson – on all but the seaward side, Crater was a nightmare for the British Army to patrol. There were just two main routes in and out and within the town's myriad narrow backstreets, insurgents found it easy to mount ambushes using grenades, small arms, mortars and mines. Even though 1967 was to be the last year of a British presence, rebel activities did not abate. On 20 June the British forces suffered their heaviest losses of the whole campaign when they lost 22 men killed

and 31 wounded in several ambushes. The trouble began with two mutinies by local security forces both of whom mistakenly believed that British troops had turned on them.

The first incident occurred when members of the South Arabian Police ambushed a passing truck, killing eight and wounding eight other men, all from the Royal Corps of Transport. Later, members of the Aden Armed Police opened fire on two Land Rovers carrying nine British soldiers; eight of them were killed. Four soldiers sent to find out what had happened were never seen or heard from again.

Rebel flags raised

The British were forced to withdraw from the immediate area. Next day Crater was sealed off and over the next 10 days pressure was mounted on the rebels. From the heights of the Jebel Shamsan, snipers killed 10 insurgents who were found to be armed with captured British weapons. Even so, it was a galling time for the troops who were forced to witness the terrorists running up rebel flags in the heart of the city.

Newly arrived in Aden at this time were a battalion of the Argyle and Sutherland Highlanders under the command of Lt-Colonel Colin Mitchell, soon to earn the sobriquet 'Mad Mitch'. Three of his men in an advance party were amongst the British killed on 20 June and Mitchell was determined to stamp his authority on the situation as quickly as possible. His view that a surprise night attack by his men would swiftly overcome the enemy finally prevailed.

The assault began at 7pm on 3 July and was preceded by the pipers playing *Monymusk*, the traditional tune that has heralded an Argyll attack for centuries past. In a tribute to their comrades killed on 20 June, an Argyll officer carried with him a cromach, a shepherd's crook which had belonged to one of the victims. The wireless

Above: The Crater district in Aden sits in an extinct volcano. Soldiers of the Royal Northumberland Fusiliers are seen here on an observation post above the town.

Below: Lieutenant-Colonel Colin 'Mad Mitch' Mitchell at the wheel of a jeep carrying soldiers of the Argyll and Sutherland Highlanders on 4 July 1967. The unhappy passenger sat next to Mitchell is Aden Police Chief Mohammed Ibrahim who has just been ordered to surrender his men or face dire consequences.

aerials of the armoured cars of the Queen's Dragoon Guards sported the red and white hackle of the Northumberland Fusiliers, the unit that had lost most men to the rebel ambushes.

'Hackles fly again in Crater'

The attack was a success and met little resistance. The Queen's Dragoon Guards sent a message to the Northumberland Fusiliers: 'Your hackles fly again in Crater.'

That evening Mitchell confronted the Superintendent of the Aden Armed Police and calmly informed him that unless his men surrendered at once, the 'wild hillmen' that were the Argyll and Sutherland Highlanders would wipe them out. Soon the police were out and about collecting weapons they had earlier distributed to the rebels and re-arresting criminals they had freed at the time of their mutiny.

Crater was the scene of no further serious trouble until the British left Aden for good at the end of November 1967.

Crater Crash

Martin Forde was an Army Air Corps helicopter pilot with the Queens Dragoon Guards in Aden at the height of the Aden insurrection. When his aircraft was disabled over Crater by rebel gunfire on 20 June 1967, he managed to get it down on the steep and rugged side of the extinct volcano despite having a kneecap smashed to pieces by a bullet. It was a very hard landing; a soldier of the Northumberland Fusiliers being transported in a pannier slung alongside the Bell 47 lost both legs when they were severed by one of the helicopter's skids.

Martin remembers the long wait for rescuers to arrive. 'I had a .38 Smith & Wesson revolver and wondered who would get to us first. Friend or foe?' In the event it was 45 minutes before a Wessex helicopter arrived with some Royal Marines to effect a rescue.

Though Martin made a good enough recovery to enable him to carry on flying for another three decades, now, some 43 years after the incident, he is still having operations on that same damaged knee. The soldier who lost both legs – Jim Keighley – also survived and gets around today on artificial carbon fibre legs.

Rugged Radfan Mountains

It was inevitable that Martin Forde would join the Queen's Dragoon Guards for he was the son of RSM Martin Forde of the King's Dragoon Guards and the younger Martin had practically lived with the Regiment since he was nine. He joined up as a volunteer on 1 January 1959 at the age of 17 on the very day the QDG was formed.

Martin's military career initially saw him serving in Saladin Armoured Cars. In 1962 he volunteered to join the Army Air Corps who were keen to take on men who had experience of how the army functioned on the ground. Martin

and helicopters hit it off from the start. After qualifying as a pilot he saw service in Northern Ireland and Germany.

In 1966 he was posted to the British Protectorate of Aden where trouble had been brewing for some time. Martin spent six months in the rugged and inhospitable Radfan Mountains along what was then the border with Yemen. Then, just as the Six Day Arab-Israeli war broke out, Martin was seconded to the Argyll & Sutherland Highlanders who were due to replace the Royal Northumberland Fusiliers in Aden. Martin took Lt-Col 'Mad Mitch' Mitchell on a recce flight over the city and he recalls the officer was outspoken about what he was going to do to tame the rebels.

After the Israeli victory, Algeria called for a General Strike throughout the Arab world on 20 June. It was anticipated that trouble could flare up in the Crater District. In the morning Martin was tasked with lifting a picket of Northumberland Fusiliers up to a sandbagged look-out post on the caldera heights some 250 feet above Crater. This was achieved by carrying the soldiers in panniers attached to the outside of the helicopter; it enabled Martin to touch ground for the briefest time to allow the soldiers to jump in or out.

Army Land Rovers on fire

At noon Martin flew back to the look-out to retrieve the four Fusiliers who had come under fire from the mutinous police and a number of terrorists on the Crater rooftops. Back at base with the last two men, an Argyll officer counter-manded Martin's orders and said he must take the soldiers back to the look-out. Flying over Crater again, Martin could see roads blocked off and, even more ominously, two Army Land Rovers on fire with a number of bodies around them. Martin circled the scene three times but could not establish any radio contact.

By now aware that fire was being directed at his Bell 47 helicopter, Martin slowed down to 40 knots and prepared to touch down near the look-out. This is when his machine was hit and in his own words, 'my knee exploded and ended up looking like a horrible pink cauliflower'. A second bullet knocked his leg off the pedal causing the helicopter to go into a spin, lose lift and drop out of the sky. Martin managed instinctively to level the Bell out just before it hit hard on the side of the steep cliffs that surround Crater.

Though he recalls feeling little pain in his knee, Martin was unable to get out. Luckily the second Fusilier, John Duffey, had escaped unscathed and he was able to release Martin and extricate him and also get badly injured Fusilier Keithley to relative safety. Just before the helicopter's fuel tanks blew up, Duffey also retrieved a radio. John Duffey's actions that day earned him a Distinguished Conduct Medal.

Another 31 years of flying

Fifteen minutes after a radio call for help was made, a Bell 47 appeared but almost immediately flew off. Thirty minutes later the much larger Wessex machine came in to land some way above the crash scene. It was a further 45 minutes before the two injured servicemen could be brought up the steep and slippery slope to the rescue helicopter.

Martin was in hospital until March 1968 before going to Saighton Camp in Chester for rehabilitation. 'The place was fantastic but it was just unfortunate that at the time there wasn't the technology to replace kneecaps. Even so I carried on flying for another 31 years, until I retired from Bristow Helicopters, Redhill, in 1999. In my time I've flown over the jungle in Indonesia, the desert in Iran and the South China Sea.'

Martin Forde is the current Chairman of the Royal British Legion, Sussex County. He has a stated aim: 'I do believe it is vital to educate people so they understand that the Legion is not just about remembering the two world wars. It is there for those who serve their country now and all those who have served previously.'

NORTHERN IRELAND

Former British soldier Ken Wharton is determined to ensure that the events in Northern Ireland from 1969 up until the present day will not be forgotten. For the British troops stationed there over three decades, Ulster could be a hellish place full of hate where it was hard to comprehend how they were just 30 minutes flying time away from their homes and loved ones on the mainland.

On Thursday 14 August 1969 I was a young soldier, just 19, with so little experience of this great big world. I was watching a television set in a NAAFI club at a barracks in the deep south of England. When you are a Leeds born and bred Yorkshire boy who, prior to taking a train to Aldershot to join up in early 1967, had only left the confines of God's own county three times, then Hampshire was the deep south. The TV showed scenes – in black and white, of course – of a drama being played out in a country so close you could spit across the Irish Sea and hit it, and yet, it was a country of which I had never really heard. That was, until it thrust itself into our newspapers, our televisions, our radios and soon enough and surely enough, into our collective psyches.

That country was Northern Ireland. A place which was to have a personal effect on my life for several years; an effect on all our lives for almost 30 and it will, sadly, for many, be a name synonymous with violence, tragedy, intolerance, suffering and sudden death. Did I say that it had a personal effect on my life for a few years? No – it is much more than that; I will be haunted forever by the suffering of my comrades and the wonderful, innocent people of Northern Ireland who neither sought nor supported terrorism.

The British Army was sent into Northern Ireland by the Labour Government of Harold Wilson in response to a breakdown of law and order in the face of increasingly savage sectarian violence between Protestant and Catholic factions. Initially welcomed by both sides, the British troops soon found themselves in an impossible position, caught between the two communities and increasingly the target of extremist paramilitary groups, especially that of the Irish Republican Army (IRA) and various breakaway factions.

Appalling civilian tragedy

Over the following three decades some 300,000 British troops served in Northern Ireland. The net result upon the lives of the people living in both the British mainland and Ulster was the loss of over 1300 Military personnel, over 300 Police lives, and well over 4000 lives in total. It also cost billions of pounds in destroyed property and exacted an emotional and psychological cost that can never be measured. The change that was won over those near 30 years of struggle with the IRA and the other paramilitaries was paid for with the blood of British troops and Ulster policemen. That same blood which stained the streets of the Ballymurphy Estate, the Turf Lodge, Twinbrook, the Ardoyne, the Creggan, the Bogside and the fields of Ulster, ultimately paved the way for freedom, the removal of fear and the ever-present threat of terrorist violence which, thankfully, an entire new generation of Northern Irish no longer have to face, at least not on anything like the scale

A tracker dog, trained to sniff out explosives, assists a Royal Wesh Fusilier in the Strabane countryside.

experienced during the Troubles.

Let us not forget either, that the other circa 3000 deaths represented an appalling civilian tragedy, as the great majority of the fatalities were not the paramilitaries. That majority of innocent bystanders included those caught in the crossfire of the bullets or the indiscriminate terrorist bombs, or those slaughtered because they gave the wrong answer to that most perverted, most evil of all questions: 'Are you a Protestant or a Catholic?' The events of that period of time from 1969 through to 1998 (and in some cases, beyond those arbitrary 'parameters') will forever haunt Northern Ireland.

Not so long ago I visited Northern Ireland for the first time in over 30 years as I had many ghosts to lay. I am pleased to report that, although the Black Mountain continues to dominate Belfast and will for millions more years, some things have changed. There are more cars; the houses are newer, with many of the old blackened terraces of the Lower Falls replaced by newer dwellings. Indeed, the dump that was the 'Murph is changed beyond all recognition; the gardens are tidier, there

> **Innocent victims included those caught in the crossfire of the bullets or the indiscriminate terrorist bombs, or those slaughtered because they gave the wrong answer to that most perverted, most evil of all questions: "Are you a Protestant or a Catholic?"**

are no old fridges or cookers sitting in the front gardens, and no rusting Vauxhall Vivas or Ford Anglias, propped up on bricks. The houses are cleaner – exterior wise – and the ubiquitous packs of stray dogs which chased our PIGs around the 'Murph, or Turf Lodge or Andersonstown now appear to have gone to that great doggie Heaven in the sky. However, when I walked around the Creggan heights in Londonderry, or Derry or 'stroke' city whilst the yellow paint now gleams and covers up the scruffily scrawled 'We stand by the IRA' slogans, the underlying menace and threat seemed to me to be still there. Moreover, one does feel that one is in a foreign country and the green painted post boxes, sand stores and the plethora of Irish Tricolour flags give the impression that one is actually in the Irish Republic and not on a British street.

The British Army had to go in

Perhaps when the arbitrary borders – some say historical – of Northern Ireland were drawn up, some of the six counties should have stayed within the Irish 'Free State', and certainly there is a case for Co Armagh within this hypothesis. Whatever the rights and wrongs of this delineation of countries, by 1969, it clearly wasn't working and, whether or not the popularly held views about discrimination were fact or naively held belief, the Army had to go in. On that wonderfully hot August day in 1969, British squaddies in their shiny tin helmets, denim uniforms, SLRs with fixed bayonets at the ready, were deployed onto the streets of the Falls, the Divis, the New Lodge, the Ardoyne, the Gobnascale, the Waterside, the Bogside and the aforementioned Creggan. Their only knowledge of civil unrest was a brief exposure to an Army training film 'Keeping the Peace' which came in two parts. Who would have guessed, who could have guessed, that three decades and more later, those same soldiers or their successors would still be on those same streets, still fighting by now, a second generation of terrorists?

By the end of that first day's deployment, five people, including nine year old Patrick Rooney – killed by a stray (possibly) RUC round would be lying dead and the following evening, the first of nearly 1300 British troops would be killed as he visited the home of his parents in Whitehall Row in the Divis Flats area. Trooper Hugh McCabe, aged 20, was on home leave from the Queen's Irish Hussars based in the then West Germany, when he too, was killed by a 'stray' round. After that, it never really stopped and even after the 'final' ceasefire, the so-called Real IRA saw fit to butcher another 29 innocents in the sleepy market town of Omagh in Co Tyrone.

Atrocity piled upon atrocity

The IRA and INLA took their terror war further afield and British blood – military and civilian alike – was spilled in Belgium, Holland and

Germany. It stained the streets and roads of London, Deal, Derby, Litchfield, Yorkshire, Eastbourne, Northumberland, Warrington, Guildford, Birmingham and Tadcaster. There was never a let up as the terror gangs sought to sicken the British public into putting pressure on their Government to withdraw from Ulster. I do not class myself as a particularly intelligent person, but I confess my inability to understand how the bombers of the 'Mulberry Bush' in Birmingham or the 'Horse and Groom' in Guildford could sit and drink amongst the revelers and then walk out, having planted a bomb, fully cognisant of the death and maiming which would be caused amongst those happy, smiling faces. As each atrocity outdid the previous atrocity, as outrage after outrage followed, the terrorists felt that they could push the British over the emotional edge and pressurise their Government to pull out of the North. What they forgot and what an invaluable historical lesson they overlooked was the willingness of the British to stoically bear anguish. After all, a certain Austrian house painter had tried much harder than them in 1939 and had, as posterity has recorded, failed spectacularly. Most people would agree, particularly those who survived the Blitz during those dark days of 1940 and 1941, that the Luftwaffe was a much more terrifying enemy.

Over the long and tortuous course of the Troubles which dragged on for almost three decades, the decent people of Ulster – Protestant and Catholic alike – had to contend with the almost daily mayhem and death. Those of us fortunate to be on the mainland saw only what the Government of the day allowed us to see. At the announcement of the death of a soldier or a policeman, most of us shrugged and thought 'that's a pity' and then moved on. For the people of the Province and those who had lost a loved one, there was no moving on and Wilson, Callaghan, Heath, Thatcher, Major and Blair continued to send out more soldiers to the 'twilight zone' of Northern Ireland and they were quickly forgotten. I made an oath to myself, that through my writing, I would never allow that to happen.

Ken Wharton is the author of *A Long Long War*. The book tells the story of the Troubles in Northern Ireland from the perspective of the British soldiers who served there between 1969 and 1998. The book received much critical acclaim. Patrick Bishop, bestselling author of *3 Para* and *Bomber Boys* wrote of it: 'Here at last is the authentic voice of the veterans of a grueling and thankless campaign. Powerful, revealing and moving.' *A Long Long War* was first published in 2008 by Helion & Company Ltd. A second book of Northern Ireland memories – *Bullets, Bombs and Cups of Tea* – was published in 2009.

UDR: THE DRIVE HOME

Regular British Army soldiers faced extreme danger when serving in Northern Ireland. But at least, if they survived unscathed, they would eventually go home and leave the Troubles behind them. For the men and women of the Ulster Defence Regiment (UDR) it was different. Northern Ireland was home.

As Ken Wharton puts it: 'These UDR personnel wore the same uniforms, used the same weapons and their bodies were equally vulnerable to a 9mm or 5.56mm bullet or landmine or a mortar attack as were the regular soldiers. The only difference was that they didn't have the relative 'security' of the mainland or the Regimental depot.

'The UDR men and women lived, ate and drank in the communities they had to patrol; they had to shop and relax amongst the very people they might have arrested or questioned or were actively seeking. For the UDR soldier there was no escape into the community, knowing that their every move was very likely being observed by the enemy within. IRA intelligence gathering on the domestic and working arrangements of these part-time soldiers was so good and so thorough that over 80% of UDR personnel killed were in one of these situations.

This is a typical journey home in the life of a UDR man: 'Most of us commute to and from work; some by rail, most by car, but I used to drive back and forth to work in the time I was part-time UDR, starting at 1930 and finishing at 0400. I had a 20-mile drive, through some areas of "interest".

'When leaving I would go through the usual routine; beret, INIBA, webbing and combat jacket would all go into the boot. Cover with blanket. Take out baggy boiler suit and squeeze it over your uniform. Gloves on – smaller size, with the pad cut off the knuckles. Fit like pilot's gloves. Save your hands getting cut to ribbons if the windscreen comes in. Start up, seat belt on.

'OK, here we go; out the gate, give gate sentry the fingers, speed bumps, top of the road, no slowing, fast as she can take it, anyone could be waiting. Left? No, straight on, don't set a pattern; through the lights – red or not, stop for no man. Over the bridge, through the "ville", keep going, no stopping, go, go, out into the country. Past the County Hall, floor it down the long straight; did a VCP here just a couple of hours ago. Through the "hog hill" – a type of chicane in the middle of the village – and then change down and speed through. Real country now, no street lights, eyes get used slowly to the dark; now there are bumpy culverts, rutted, shadowy, too fast to dwell on them.

'Down the long hill, try not to slow for the corner at the bottom and then fly down the long sloped straight; tight corner and then down to

third; look around for following lights; picked anyone up? Big wall on the left, roadside monastery, tight left at the top; careful now. Past the cop shop, yellow sodium lights; did a LURK on a house near here last week. Change down and then left into "their" patch. Now my antenna switches on and past the pub at the crossroads; the villages here are in "enemy" territory. Good men have died in them. Through the village – VCP here earlier too – down the hill, into the dark again with narrow roads, tension notches up a tad, past the corner, high hedges and then down to second for the last one, wait, wait for it, and then out into the open road, back up the gears, long straight, check the mirrors for lights. None; up to 75, 80, foot off gas for "S" bends, crossroads; mirror again; bad road here, culverts again, close to their area again.

> " During the Regiment's lifetime, 203 serving members of the UDR were killed; 40 of these brave men and women were killed on duty while 163 were murdered in their homes, outside their homes, at work, driving to work or driving home from work or UDR service. "

'Stretch of concrete road, it dips into dead ground with blind corners, over the crest and ****! Jam on brakes, fishtail to a stop, just short of a car on its roof; heart going 19 to the dozen; there's room to pass. Sneak a look into the car; no-one in it, caused by some young lad with slower reactions than you. Phew! Up the hill and then floor it past the "T" junction then left, no slowing, past bingo hall, over the crossroads and as fast as possible into the dark again. Now it's the fun part; road narrows and as it dips, turn off the headlights; that should confuse the bastards. If they are waiting, they'll still hear me but won't see me straight off; buy some time. Then I'm through and nearly home.

'Houses in a clump to the left; a few street lights cast a weak light; sharp left and then pull up at the door. I switch off the engine and listen to the silence then get out and listen again and enjoy the cooling wind. I find the keys, open the door – quietly, you noisy git. Boots off, sweating in the boiler suit. Sit in the chair and she finds you still there, three hours later.'

The Terrible Toll

Between 14 August 1969 and today over 300,000 British troops have served in Northern Ireland. Statistics compiled for the period 1968 to 2003 record that 47,541 people were injured as a direct consequence of the Troubles. Of these 6262 were soldiers of the British Army and the UDR and 11,212 were members of the RUC (now known as the Northern Ireland Police Force). These figures exclude the death toll, which is generally reckoned to be around 3700, although Ken Wharton believes the true figure to be over 4000.

Wharton has pointed out the enormity of these statistics, made even more horrific given the geographical size of Northern Ireland and small population of around one and a half million people. He has calculated that if the total figures were applied pro-rata to a similar conflict on mainland Britain then the number of dead and injured in the population of around 59 million would total over two million people. He says, 'Put another way, there would be more casualties, civilian and military, than Britain suffered in the entire Second World War.'

As it is, the author – after working with a number of members of the Northern Ireland Veterans Association (NIVETS) – also firmly believes that the British Army and UDA fatalities incurred in the Troubles actually are

> " If a similar conflict to that in Northern Ireland had engulfed all of mainland Britain, there would have been more casualties, civilian and military, than this country suffered in the entire Second World War.. "

in excess of 1000, several hundred more than the 'official' figure.

Towards the end of his book, *A Long Long War*, Ken quotes the words of an anonymous former British soldier who served in Northern Ireland in the early Seventies:

'My name doesn't matter, enough just to say that I am one of the 300,000 British soldiers that served in Northern Ireland between 1969 and the present day. We are the faceless ones, ignored and ridiculed by all sides in the conflict, including our own masters, and yet, without our involvement, one of the worst civil wars that the world may have seen would have ravaged not only the Six Counties, but would, I believe,

have spread far into the Republic.

'It is so easy to forget the facts with relation to the British Army and the Troubles, depending of course on which side of the fence you sit. My aim is to broaden that fence into a triangle, so that the facts about the Army are also taken into account. It may hurt those whose doctrine has always been to believe the fables of the 1916 Easter uprising, or likewise those whose misguided love of King Billy rules their lives. Tough.

'The British Army never asked, nor wanted, to become involved in the day-to-day security of Northern Ireland. Senior officers fought tooth and nail to keep us out. Political intrigues forced the issue onto a weak and foolish British Government.

'The majority of British troops were pulled out of Germany to serve in Northern Ireland. These included many from the "province", from both sides of the political divide, whose homes were there, and whose parents lived there. The make-up of the rank and file was a strange one, at the time. Many soldiers came from broken homes, many from the inner city slums of Salford, Birmingham, Liverpool and London. They were streetwise, having themselves been on the wrong side of the law before taking the Queen's Shilling.

'We went as an army to protect the Catholic minority from being wiped from the face of the map. Without the British Army, that would have been the outcome. Troops were welcomed in both Catholic and Republican areas with open arms. Not something that Gerry Adams now likes to admit.'

ANZIO TO BELFAST: AN AWFUL LINK IN TIME

In January 1971 I first met Barbara, the girl who was later to become my wife. She lived in a little village deep in the Sussex countryside and at the time I lived in South East London. We wrote to each other a lot in those early days. In March of that year one of her letters contained the news that two distant cousins from Scotland had been killed whilst serving with the Army in Northern Ireland.

It was sad to read but I must admit I did not dwell on the matter for too long. Barbara hadn't ever met the pair and Northern Ireland was already escalating into a very messy problem that was difficult to understand.

It was many years later, following the visit of Barbara and I to Anzio to see the grave of her mother's brother, Royal Scots Fusilier Geordie Kane, killed there in April 1944, before it dawned on me that, of course, my wife's cousins must have been related to him. I pondered how sad it was that a family should lose someone in the Second World War and then lose two more young men just over a quarter of a century later. Further, it could be argued that Geordie had, at least, died in a just war against the wickedest tyrant in history.

But Northern Ireland was part of our own country yet seemed to be little more than a fragmented, embittered and bigoted place full of people who hated each other.

Then, in putting together *Seventy Years On*, I made contact with Ken Wharton, author of *A Long Long War* and a champion of the ordinary British soldiers caught up as helpless pawns in Northern Ireland's political quagmire. I mentioned about Barbara's cousins and Ken immediately knew who the lads must be.

Anzio casualty 'Geordie' Kane.

Youngest Army victim

As the story came out I was shocked and horrified to discover the full facts. Barbara's two cousins had been brothers, John and Joseph McCaig, aged 17 and 18 respectively and were soldiers in the Royal Highland Fusiliers. Murdered with them was a cousin of theirs, 23 year-old Dougal McCaughey.

Whilst off-duty on the night of 10 March 1971

in a bar in Belfast City Centre, the trio were offered a lift to a party where, no doubt, they were told there would be young ladies galore. The bodies of the three young men were discovered in the morning by the side of a narrow country lane. Geoff Smith was a soldier at the scene following the murders. He told Ken Wharton: 'The Civvy Police reckoned that had been just two murderers. I was going to say at this point gunmen... but these people were not gunmen or terrorists or freedom fighters – they were just cold blooded, evil minded, bloody murderers. Two of the young unarmed men had been shot in the back of the head while the third had evidently turned around and been shot in the chest.'

At 17 John McCaig was the youngest soldier to die in the Troubles. After this incident, soldiers under the age of 18 were not allowed on the Northern Ireland streets. The Belfast coroner described the murders as one of the '...vilest crimes heard of in living memory...'

The three soldiers are remembered with their names on trees growing in the National Memorial Arboretum, Staffordshire.

DAVID ARNOLD

Vinny

Marie Scott remembers her soldier son, Vincent.

I have a brother, Derek, who lives in Liverpool with his wife Trisha, **writes David Arnold**. Just as my wife Barbara's Scottish relations have suffered trauma through the British army's imperative to keep the peace in Northern Ireland, so did pointless tragedy visit Trisha's family on 24 October 1990 when her nephew Vincent Scott was one of the victims of a devastating IRA bomb. Vincent died along with four other soldiers and a kidnapped civilian.

I met with Vincent's mother Marie in November 2009 having earlier promised her that he and his murdered colleagues would be remembered in this book. The terrible circumstances of the incident moved the Catholic Bishop of Londonderry to describe the IRA act as 'crossing a new threshold of evil' that marked a new low in the history of the Troubles.

Marie Scott and her sister Trisha have had their lives blighted by what happened to Vincent as have his brother, Michael, and sisters, Annette and Julie. My brother Derek remembers the 21-year-old as a lovely lad, kind and generous of heart.

Football in Belfast

'Vinny really lived for football' said Marie. 'But he only ever wanted to play for Liverpool. He actually got into the Liverpool Boys Team and when he was 14 once went to play a friendly in Belfast. When he came back he told me he'd had a great time and the people had been really good to them.

'In his time at Liverpool he met Kevin Keegan – in fact he once brought Kevin's shirt home and I stuck it in the wash with everything else not realising how important it was. Vinny almost made it as a pro footballer

and could have got a place in the Chester team. But he'd set his heart on Liverpool and when it was clear he wouldn't make it at Anfield he decided to join the local Lancashire regiment, the Kingsmen.'

Marie told me that Vinny hadn't seen the army as a long-term career. In fact he was due to leave the Kingsmen before the end of 1990. Then the tragedy struck. On the day of the bombing Vinny had actually swopped duty with a colleague.

In 1993 Marie and around 20 other bereaved relatives went to the location where the Kingsmen died. She said it was noticeable how the local people – many of whom were injured in the explosion – showed great respect for the visitors: 'Workmen downed tools,' she told me.

Kingsmen remembered

Northern Ireland's Troubles have sometimes embarrassed mainland politicians and it has been a struggle to have the sacrifices made by so many soldiers recognised in the form of memorials. Marie and her family take some comfort from the fact that there is now a plaque in the city dedicated to the men of the King's Regiment who have given their lives. Vincent Scott's name is on that plaque.

The family also make regular visits to the National Memorial Arboretum in Staffordshire. My wife Barbara and I went with Marie, Trisha, Derek, Julie and her partner, Ed, on Remembrance Sunday 2009. Vinny Scott's name appears on the hugely impressive Armed Forces Memorial and is also attached to a tree in the Arboretum as are the names of all the members of the British armed forces who have died in the service of their country since the end of World War II.

Ken Wharton in his book *A Long Long War* describes the incident in which Vinny was murdered: 'It took place at a Vehicle Control Point in Buncrana Road, Coshquin outside Londonderry. The Provisional IRA used a 'proxy

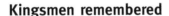

Left to right: Marie with her daughter Julie and sister Trisha at the National Arboretum.

Above: Vinny Scott in Northern Ireland. He was killed in an IRA bomb outrage on 24 October 1990. This photograph was developed after his camera and personal effects were returned to his mother, Marie. The 21-year-old Liverpool lad never saw the picture.

bomb' for the first time when they abducted and held hostage the family of a local man, Patsy Gillespie. He was tied into a car and told to drive to the VCP or his family would all be killed. Patsy was 42 and worked on an army base in the area and it is thought the IRA used this to sickeningly justify their appalling actions.

Warning shout in vain

'The bomb detonated as the van arrived at the checkpoint and despite bravely shouting out a warning to the soldiers, the bomb went off and Patsy and five soldiers of the King's Regiment were killed. Seconds after the explosion, IRA gunmen opened fire on the devastated position from the Republican side of the border.

'The soldiers were Kingsman Stephen Beacham (20) from Warrington; Lance Corporal Stephen Burrows (30) from Blackpool; Kingsman Vincent Scott (21) from Liverpool; Kingsman David Sweeney (19) from Widnes and Kingsman Paul Worrall who was 23 and from Runcorn.

'Patsy Gillespie was a 42-year-old man who lived at Galliagh near Shantallow and worked on the Fort George base. He was married with three children and a testimony must be paid to his bravery in trying to warn the soldiers who were manning the VCP.

'Three soldiers' children and Mr Gillespie's three children were left fatherless by the outrage.'

Concorde and the Bear

Barry Mayner recalls a miles high Cold War encounter.

At 0830hrs on Saturday 5 September 1985, I was the navigator taking over the Q1 aircraft XV579 'R', a Phantom FG1 of No 43 Squadron based at RAF Leuchars in Fife. Together with Phantom Q2 we were on standby for the Northern QRA (Quick Reaction Alert). My pilot was Flying Officer Tony Andrew and this was his first day on duty at the Alert Sheds.

It wasn't long before the Alert Klaxon sounded, closely followed by the ground crew and the Q2 aircrew tumbling out of the adjoining accommodation. We were airborne at 0920hrs and started to climb to 28,000ft. The QRA Controller at RAF Buchan told us that a Victor tanker from RAF Marham was 100 miles behind us in support.

We proceeded out over Western Scotland and into the Atlantic where we were vectored towards two Russian aircraft that had come from the Murmansk area and were by now about halfway between Iceland and the Faroe Islands. Quite a start to a weekend on duty!

Successful intervention

We carried out a successful intervention and identified the Soviet planes as Tu95 Bear 'D' aircraft, door numbers 19 and 25. We were by now heading south west and the Victor tanker was 'cutting the corner' to join up with us. As soon as it arrived we refueled to full and awaited developments. The Bears headed out into the Atlantic and we were instructed to fly with them until PLE (Prudent Limit of Endurance). Since we had a tanker to ourselves this was obviously going to be a long trip.

One of our routine tasks on QRA sorties

Above: Barry's photograph of a Russian Bear long-range reconnaissance aircraft. Note the moon obscured by the right wing and the vapour trail made by Concorde flying some 30,000ft higher en route to New York.

was to photograph intercepted aircraft. Out came the camera. I was doing my MGM bit with the lens when I noticed that the moon was nicely positioned by the nearest Bear's wingtip. Then to my utter amazement I saw supersonic Concorde enter the viewfinder. She was some 30,000ft above us flying at Mach 2.

RAF Lightning scrambled

The remainder of the sortie took us to a point out in the Atlantic where we were closer to the Azores than to the nearest RAF UK base, St Mawgan in Cornwall. Returning home, we first asked to fly a holding pattern off the Isles of Scilly and await the arrival of another Victor tanker. To relieve us from task, a Southern QRA aircraft, a Lightning from RAF Binbrook, was scrambled and we were able to fly up the Irish Channel and return to Leuchars after being airborne for seven hours and 35 minutes. In the course of his inaugural sortie as a QRA pilot, Tony had intercepted his first Russians, been over flown by Concorde (a unique experience, I believe, in Cold War history) plus he had taken the Phantom on a huge loop right around Ireland before landing back at our point of departure.

Some weeks later we found out that the Russian Bears had flown over the newest US Navy 'supercarrier' *Dwight D Eisenhower*, which was carrying out its first sea trials, and had then gone on to land in Cuba.

Inset above: Sqd Ldr John Nevill (left) and Flt Lt Barry Mayner pictured in 1970 celebrating the completion of a 15-hour sortie around Britain in their RAF Phantom F4M fighter, XV409. The epic flight took place on 23/24 April in order to prove that the aircraft was capable of flying from a UK base non-stop all the way to Singapore. Britain was withdrawing from her Far East air bases but wanted to reassure Malaysia and Singapore that RAF air power could be despatched immediately should these former colonies be threatened by an unfriendly neighbour.

The flight of XV409 was deemed a success and at the time was thought to be the longest jet fighter sortie ever flown. It paved the way for four Phantom F4Ms from No 54 Squadron to attempt the flight non-stop to Singapore on 18 May in order to take part in the SEATO Exercise Bersata Padu. Barry Mayner was the navigator in one of the Phantoms along with his pilot, Flt Lt John Armstrong. Their aircraft had to divert to Gan air base in the Indian Ocean when a Victor tanker was unable to make the planned mid-air refuel rendezvous.

The deployment to Singapore was a great success and all aircraft and personnel were recovered to home base RAF Coningsby on 30 June / 2 July 1970.

Major Cain

Major Robert Henry Cain VC was born on 2 January in the Isle of Man. He was 35 years old and attached to the South Staffordshire Regiment in 1944 when he carried out the actions that would merit the Victoria Cross. During the fighting that followed the air landings around Arnhem from 17 to 25 September, Major Cain's company was closely engaged with panzers, self-propelled guns and infantry. The Major was everywhere danger threatened, moving among his men and encouraging them to hold out. By his leadership he not only halted the enemy attacks but clearly demoralized the Germans. Although he was suffering from a perforated ear-drum and multiple wounds, he refused medical attention.

In November 1944 Major Cain was staying at RAF Manston in Kent where he met fighter pilot Peter Ayerst DFC. The pair enjoyed a drink at the Three Compasses pub in Canterbury. Peter's wartime experiences are related in detail in the story 'The Decoy' that starts on page 30 of *Seventy Years On*.

At the end of the war Major Cain he oversaw the German surrender in Norway. After leaving the army Cain returned to his pre-war job at Royal Dutch Shell. He died of cancer on 2 May 1974.

His daughter, Frances Catherine Cain is the agent for and is married to British television presenter and journalist Jeremy Clarkson who presented a documentary on him and other VC winners. The young Ms Cain remained unaware of her father's VC until after he died. Apparently he'd never thought to mention it.

Around 20 years ago I was privileged to view the Oosterbeek battlefield with Sergeant Henry McAnelly, an Arnhem veteran who had settled in the town post-war to become an official guide. Sergeant McAnelly showed me slit trenches in the woods and pointed out rusty ration cans. He also related the tale of how he had once given a tour to a visiting Soviet general in the Cold War years: 'I told the Russian the story of Captain Robert Cain and added that a total of five VC medals were won at Arnhem. I added mischievously the fact that the VC was fashioned from metal from Russian cannons captured by the British at Sevastopol during the Crimean War.

'The general looked straight at me. Then with a twinkle in his eye he said, "Sergeant, you may have the cannon. But we still have Sevastopol." '

Private Beharry

Johnson Gideon Beharry was born in Grenada in 1979. He joined the British Army in 2001, serving in the 1st Battalion Princess of Wales's Royal Regiment. He was deployed to Kosovo and Northern Ireland before being sent to Iraq in April 2004. Following his heroic actions on 1 May and 11 June of that year, he was awarded the VC in 2005. It was the first VC given out since the Falklands War of 1982. Johnson's honour was bestowed upon him for 'two separate acts of outstanding gallantry of the highest order' while he was based in Al Amarah, Maysan. The soldier's first show of bravery occurred when he drove his injured colleagues to safety under heavy Iraqi fire, before putting his own life at risk to get the wounded men out of the armoured vehicle and to safety.

Pte Beharry was again driving a similar vehicle through hostile territory in June, when the Warrior was ambushed by Iraqis. Enemy rocket propelled grenades hit the vehicle and left Pte Beharry with serious head injuries. Despite these injuries, the soldier drove the vehicle out of the ambush area and to safety before losing consciousness.

His citation reads: 'For his repeated extreme gallantry and unquestioned valour, despite intense direct attacks, personal injury and damage to his vehicle in the face of relentless enemy action, Private Beharry deserves the highest possible recognition.'

At the time of receiving the award, Lieutenant Colonel Matt Maer, Pte Beharry's commanding officer, described how his troops were in action every day for five months, more than 800 times in all. It was the longest period of continuous combat experienced by the British army since the Korean War 50 years before. The soldiers were repeatedly attacked by Mahdi militia, supporters of the radical Shia cleric, Moqtada al-Sadr.

The Victoria Cross is Britain's highest military honour awarded for exceptional examples of bravery. David Arnold highlights three awards spanning seven decades.

Corporal Budd

'It is with deep regret that the MoD must confirm the death of Corporal Bryan James Budd of 3rd Battalion, The Parachute Regiment in Sangin, Helmand Province, Afghanistan, on 20 August 2006. Cpl Budd, 29, died as a result of injuries sustained during a fire-fight with Taliban forces in Sangin, Helmand Province, southern Afghanistan. The incident occurred whilst on a routine patrol close to the District Centre.'

Thus read the initial announcement of Corporal Budd's death. But what was hidden behind the words 'routine patrol' was a story of exceptional bravery on not one but two occasions that led to Corporal Budd being awarded the Victoria Cross.

During the summer of 2006, Corporal Budd's 'A' Company were deployed in the District Centre at Sangin under constant attack from Taliban small arms, rocket-propelled grenades, mortar and rocket fire. On 27 July, whilst on patrol, Corporal Bryan Budd's section engaged two enemy gunmen on the roof of a building. During the ensuing fierce fire-fight, two of Corporal Budd's section were hit. One was seriously injured and collapsed in the open ground, where he remained exposed to heavy enemy fire, with rounds striking the ground around him. Budd personally led the attack on the building where the enemy fire was heaviest, forcing the remaining fighters to flee. This prompt action proved decisive in breaking the enemy and allowed his wounded colleague to be evacuated to safety.

A month later Corporal Budd was leading his section on another patrol. Another section was advancing with a Land Rover fitted with a .50 calibre heavy machine gun on the patrol's left flank. Pushing through thick vegetation, Corporal Budd spotted a number of enemy fighters 30 metres ahead. Unfortunately the enemy saw the Land Rover and the element of surprise was lost for the whole platoon. At this point Corporal Budd decided to assault the enemy and ordered his men to follow him. They quickly came under a withering fire that wounded three men and forced the section to take cover. Though wounded, Corporal Budd continued to move forward, attacking and killing the enemy. Inspired by Corporal Budd's example, the rest of the platoon resumed their attack, eliminating more of the enemy and forcing their withdrawal. Corporal Budd subsequently died of his wounds; when his body was later recovered it was found surrounded by three dead Taliban.

Corporal Budd's VC was announced in the *London Gazette* of 14 December 2006.

1982 FALKLANDS WAR

On this page are two more examples of Frank Wootton's brilliant aviation art that we have been fortunate to have illuminate the pages of *Seventy Years On*. At the top we see 'The Last Scramble' featuring three Vulcan bombers (one is very tiny on the runway in the bottom left-hand corner). This was painted early in 1982, the year of the Falklands War but actually before the war commenced. The title refers to the fact that the mighty delta-wing strategic bomber was due to be withdrawn from service later that year. History records, of course, that the aircraft had a final mission in anger to undertaken in bombing Stanley Airfield. Frank also painted scenes depicting the in-air refueling necessary to enable the aircraft to fly all the way from Ascension Island in the mid-Atlantic to the Falklands and back.

The second Frank Wootton painting (right) depicts a Harrier GR 3 and Sea Harrier over *HMS Hermes*. During the Falklands War the carrier was the flagship of the Task Force. Both paintings have been reproduced with the kind permission of the late Mrs Virginia Wootton.

In the centre of the page we have a photograph of the aircraft carriers *HMS Hermes* and *HMS Illustrious*. It's one of a number of pictures of the Task Force in the possession of Falklands War Royal Navy veteran Steve Wells who now lives in Lewes in East Sussex just two doors from *Seventy Years On* Editor, David Arnold.

A trio of 1982 South Atlantic war veterans now all serve with the Lewes, East Sussex, Fire Service. David Arnold tells their story.

Steve Wells was born in Malta to Royal Navy parents so it was almost inevitable that he would join the Senior Service. In 1982 he was a member of the crew of *HMS Birmingham*, a Type 42 destroyer. He worked in the blacked-out radar room as an operator. He remembers that a big black identification was painted on the ship because the Argentine Navy had purchased two vessels of the same design as the Type 42 so it was important to be able to identify which was which.

Steve recalls that when the ship got down to the Falklands and went on picket duty in the 250 mile exclusion zone, a terrific storm brewed up and rather than run with the tempest the ship stayed in position. The storm got so bad that the ship was in danger of breaking in half. In the end it had to make for shelter off West Falkland for emergency welding repairs.

In preparation for the conflict most of the ship's lifeboats had been taken away to make

Firefighters Three

room for short-range weapons and positions for small arms. In the event, *HMS Birmingham* was not attacked and survived the conflict undamaged. The ship went on to attend the Battle of the Atlantic 50th Anniversary in 1993. She was decommissioned on 20 October 2000.

South Atlantic picket duty

Steve has an unusual tale to tell of his relations with the Argentines: 'Before the Falklands we were tied up for a year in Portsmouth. One day I met an Argentine sailor at the end of the jetty. He was going home and had a car to sell. I bought it. At a bargain price.'

As well as serving on *Birmingham* during the actual Falklands War, Steve went on to do several more tours in the South Atlantic when the *Birmingham* was selected for further picket duty in 1983-84, an assignment he found very tedious for such a long period of time.

Early in 2008 Steve renewed an old friendship with a Navy chum, John Arrowsmith, who visited him at his Lewes home, two doors from my own house. Back in the early Eighties John had been a loader for the ship's Oerlikon anti-aircraft guns that were of World War II vintage. John told me he was at his mother-in-law's home on leave when he saw on TV that the Task Force was being put together to recover the Falklands

from the Argentine invaders. At the time he was planning to get married. The nuptials were at once put back six months. In the event his wife-to-be Karen saw him for just 13 days in the whole of the following year.

Guide on HMS Victory

John still resents not being able to communicate regularly with Karen: 'It was all the fault of a couple our lads putting out an appeal for pen pals in *The Sun*. There were thousands of responses and it was impossible to fit all the letters in the postal helicopters. It meant that genuine family letters were hugely delayed.' John's Royal Navy career was completed when he served as a guide on

Top: Steve Wells, Rob Martin (without moustache) and Dave Swayne pictured in Lewes Fire Station. All three served in the forces in the Falklands War but didn't know each other then.
Far left and centre: *Steve and Rob in the early 1980s. The other photograph is of John Arrowsmith and was taken in the Falklands.*

Rob saw overseas service in the one-time British colony of Belize on the east coast of Central America at a time when neighbouring Guatemala was threatening to invade. Then in the first Gulf War he was stationed in Daran, Saudi Arabia, at a time when Saddam Hussein was sending Scud rockets in anger at the coalition air base and at Israel. His most exciting moment there came when a Patriot missile was fired off at what was thought to be an incoming Scud: 'I had some bottles of wine I'd been keeping safe but the incredible noise of the Patriot shattered all of them.'

Based at Bomb Alley

Dave Swayne is a retained fire fighter at Lewes. He spent five years in the Royal Marines and served with B Company 40 Commando based at Plymouth. His journey to the Falklands began with a berth aboard the liner *Canberra*. Down in the South Atlantic he transferred to the assault ship *Fearless* – best described as a 'Landing Platform Dock' that can transport men and equipment and get them ashore in locations where there are no harbour facilities.

Landing craft took Dave and his colleagues ashore in San Carlos Water, the inlet that soon earned a very different name – 'Bomb Alley'. He spent most of his time in the Falklands at this location and witnessed many Argentine bombing raids. At the end of the war Dave was sent to West Falkland where it was known there were Argentine forces although no one could be sure they would give themselves up. As it happened, upon the approach of the Marines the enemy surrendered at once.

Nelson's ship, *HMS Victory* in Portsmouth.

Lewes fireman Rob Martin clocked up nine years as an Armourer with the RAF. He left for the Falklands on 17 May 1982 aboard the Task Force Replenishment vessel *St Edmund*, a requisitioned ferry. At Ascension Island he transferred to the *Contender Bezant*, a container ship leased by the British Government. She carried two sorely-needed Chinook helicopters and a mass of supplies (in 1984 the ship was purchased outright by the Royal Navy and re-christened *RFA Argus*. She is due to remain in service until at least 2020).

Rob's extensive photo collection includes pictures taken in the Tropics showing locals in canoes alongside the ship offering fruit and souvenirs for sale. They are scenes that would be familiar to British servicemen heading south past the Equator at any time in the last three centuries.

Rob arrived in the Falklands about four days before the Argentines gave up; he went ashore in Port Stanley 24 hours after the surrender. He remembers a Stanley Airfield littered with abandoned weapons and grenades. One of the jobs he and his mates had to contend with was the dismantling of booby traps. He told me of one incident involving a captured Pucara. They cleared it by firing the aircraft's ejector seats via the employment of what Rob describes as an 'ingenious detachable rope'. With evident pride, Rob says that the Navy boys tried to do a similar job on another aircraft but they didn't know about the 'rope trick' with the result that the debris from the explosion went all over the place.

Inset: Robert Fox (third form left) in 1982.

Former RAF 'Erk' Rob Martin also has a copy of *The Penguin News* dated 30 June 1982 that celebrates the surrender of all Argentine forces in the Islands and includes a memoir written by the BBC correspondent Robert Fox, quoted in part here:

'Reporting the campaign and the plight of the Islanders has been most rewarding in my experience but the business of actually getting the stuff back has been sheer hell. The Marisatt satellite link can give you a clearer phone call to London from the Falklands than one can get from Brighton or Bognor. The trouble was actually getting to the ship to broadcast. After Goose Green, I hopped on a helicopter at dusk with the pilot announcing cheerily, "I haven't got an observer, so watch out for Pucaras, mate."

'Sometimes links with London were as strange as when 45 Commando were marching to Teal Inlet. "Air raid warning red" came the order from the front of the two mile column. When it reached the end of the line the boys could be seen jumping and throwing their rifles in the air as the echoes of "Galtieri's dead" came back to the leading companies.

'Finally I would just like to say this. Many fine young men have died and been maimed in mind and body in this campaign... many of you have suffered losses of loved ones, injuries and desecration of your homes... I salute all of you for the way you have come through the last three months. Goodbye and God bless every one of you.'

CHINOOK!

Falklands veteran Tom Jones once landed in an RAF Chinook helicopter in Dame Vera Lynn's back garden in the sleepy village of Ditchling, East Sussex. It was an event that led to romance and his marriage to Dame Vera's daughter, Virginia, in 1986. In the Falklands Tom served in the only Chinook helicopter that escaped the sinking by Argentine Exocet missile of the *Atlantic Conveyor*. Astonishingly, that same helicopter, Bravo November, is still in service today and has been in action in Afghanistan. Joey Clark recounts the whole incredible tale.

Tom Jones joined the RAF in 1958 and by 1962 was flying on Handley Page Hastings transport aircraft. In 1968 he went on to helicopters, serving with Search & Rescue. He received a commission in 1970 and went to work as an instructor. In 1980 he became part of the team given the task of introducing the twin-blade Chinook into RAF service and Tom trained crew in all aspects of the helicopter.

Tom recalls: 'Having seen the first full-term training course through, I joined 18 Squadron in 1981 when I was a Flight Lieutenant. At the time the Argentine military junta leader General Galtieri was becoming more and more unpopular with his people and was also losing the respect of the country's armed forces. There was also a border dispute with Chile.

'Soon there was a lot of sabre-rattling going on in respect of the Falkland Islands as the junta looked for a way to win over the support of the Argentine people. The country did indeed have a long-standing claim to the Malvinas, as they called the Falklands. The British didn't really respond to the increasingly aggressive rhetoric. Nor did they take the situation seriously when Argentine 'civilians' landed on several uninhabited islands that were also British possessions in the South Atlantic. With hindsight it can be seen that the Argentinean leaders came to truly believe they could seize the Falklands by force with no fear of a military response emanating from faraway Britain.'

The war began on Friday 2 April 1982 with the Argentine invasion of the Falklands and the Southern Ocean island of South Georgia. Tom was in 18 Squadron that was assigned to the British Task Force charged with recapturing the islands. The unit sailed aboard *Norland*, a requisitioned ferry more used to plying the North Sea between Hull and Holland. Their companions on the ship were men of the Parachute Regiment. First stop was Ascension Island, a few hundred miles south of the Equator in the middle of the Atlantic. At the same time, the four Chinooks of 18 Squadron, along with eight Wessex helicopters and eight Sea Harrier aircraft, were transported aboard the *Atlantic Conveyor*, one of a number of merchant navy ships requisitioned by the Royal Navy that were termed STUFT – 'Ships Taken Up From Trade'.

Ferry to the South Atlantic

Tom recalled: 'With us being on a different ship to our machines, it meant we had no actual Chinooks to train on. However, we made the most of our time at sea and took the opportunity to practice drills. We also mapped out an outline of the Chinook, to scale, on the *Norland's* deck. Once we tested how many men we could fit in and came up with the precise figure of 82.'

He went on: 'Once in the vicinity of the Falklands, 18 Squadron transferred to the assault ship *HMS Fearless*, a vessel destined to be the Royal Navy's last steam-powered warship. In our time on *Fearless* it

Helicopter Bravo November: From the Falklands 1982 to Helmand Province, Afghanistan, today.

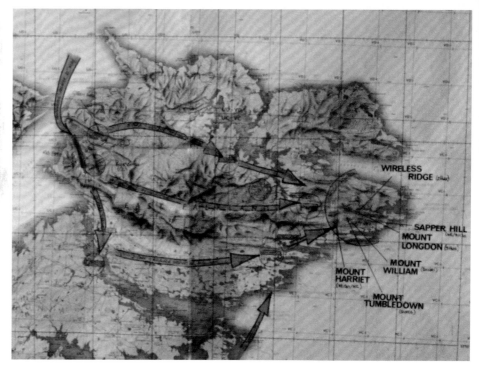

came under regular attack from the Argentine air force. Being battened down on a ship in action where you are not part of the crew is no place to be as there is really nowhere to go. On one occasion a call came over the tannoy for anyone with search and rescue experience. I had the required experience so I answered the call and learnt that *HMS Coventry* had been hit and casualties needed to be evacuated. I was able to assist.

Exocet missile attack

'We were, of course. on *Fearless* waiting for our Chinooks to arrive. In fact, only my machine, Bravo November, made it.'

On 25 May *Atlantic Conveyor* was sailing with other ships east of the Falklands when a pair of Argentine Super Etendard aircraft carrying Exocet missiles attacked. One missile was directed at a frigate. The ship detected the weapon's approach and fired off a shower of metal strips known as 'chaff'. This deflected the missile off-course. Unfortunately it and a second missile then locked on to the *Atlantic Conveyor* which was hit by both weapons that caused huge fires to break out; 12 crew, including the ship's Captain, Ian North, lost their lives. Eventually the ship was abandoned with the loss of invaluable helicopters and a vast quantity of equipment. Fortunately, all of the aircraft had already been off-loaded. Even so, the incident would seriously handicap the mobility and resupply logistics of British land forces once they were ashore on the Falklands.

A single Chinook escaped the disaster. Tom's aircraft, Bravo November, had been up on a test flight at the time when the Exocet struck and was able to fly to safety aboard the aircraft carrier, *HMS Hermes*. He recalled: 'Our helicopter wasn't welcome on *Hermes* as it was seriously in the way of the Harriers. There was even talk of bunging it overboard. Eventually a decision was made to fly it to St Carlos instead with top cover provided by the Harriers.'

Of the conflict he says: 'We never knew how long a flying day would be or where we might be tasked to go. Living conditions on the ground were pretty basic, made more so by the loss of so much equipment in the *Atlantic Conveyor*. At first our 27-man detachment was co-located with 845 Royal Naval Air Squadron who flew Wessex helicopters. Rations and water were in short supply. For accommodation our ground crew made two-man shelters by hanging poncho capes across clumps of bracken whilst us aircrew sheltered in the remnants of tents purloined from the Royal Navy.

'By contrast to our rough and ready

Above: A map of the British assault on Port Stanley (from the private collection of Tom Jones).

Previous page: Bravo November lifts a captured Argentine Pucaro aircraft.

existence on the Falklands, whenever we set down on *SS Uganda*, the hospital ship, they would, without fail, bring coffee out to us on a silver tray and served in china cups.'

Tom never doubted that the conflict would end in favour of the British: 'The airfield at Pebble Island was disabled early on and the Argentine Navy didn't put to sea again after the *Belgrano* was sunk. This and the Vulcan bombing of Stanley Airport enhanced the British resolve.

'I can remember the prisoners of war we carried. Many were just 18 or 19 and you could see in their expressions as they trudged aboard our Chinook that they really had no concept of what was going on. Then from the air they could see the extent of our forces, the huge ammo dumps and field hospitals. And there was no mistaking the burial grounds.'

The battle for the Falklands ended with the Argentine surrender on 14 June 1982. By this time Bravo November had notched up 109 flying hours. Four days earlier, on 10 June, four replacement Chinooks had arrived in the islands.

SS Uganda in the South Atlantic.

Extracts from 18 Squadron Operations Record Book

San Carlos Water, East Falkland, 27 May 1982

Two 18 Sqn crews and supporting personnel were flown ashore at first light from *HMS Fearless* to set up camp at Look-out Hill in Saint Carlos Water. As a result of *Atlantic Conveyor* being sunk, the detachment was lacking tents, aircraft spares, oils, tools and communications equipment.

Extreme care had to be exercised in positioning our defence posts and shell scrapes as the Royal Navy had so arranged their own arcs of fire that they traversed our own position.

The detachment's first flying task was to carry 40 tons of ammunition from Ajax Bay to several Royal Artillery batteries positioned around San Carlos Water. One hour after completion of the task, Ajax Bay was bombed by four Argentine A4 Skyhawks resulting in a large quantity of ammunition being destroyed.

Bravo November was utilised taking casualties to *SS Uganda*, the hospital ship, and to the field hospital in Port St Carlos.

We could only land across the back of *SS Uganda*, which was never designed to carry a Chinook.

San Carlos Water 28 May 1982

The detachment dug deeper shell-scrapes as a result of numerous bomb attacks in San Carlos Water during the afternoon. In order to carry out oil replenishment on Bravo November, unofficial oil grades supplied by the Royal Navy were used.

As a result of the previous night's bombing of Ajax Bay, two casevac sorties were flown to *SS Uganda* positioned 50nm (nautical miles) northwest of Fanning Head. The casualties included in the main, stretcher cases and a few walking wounded, many with leg or arm amputations. The sea state was extremely rough causing *Uganda's* aft landing deck to pitch some 30 feet between waves. The operation called for a high degree of crew co-operation and taxed to the utmost the flying skills of the pilot. On the final return journey the low cloud, which had hitherto provided cover from enemy aircraft, broke, revealing a clear blue sunny sky and a Red Alert indicating enemy aircraft within 10 miles. Hugging the waves and at maximum speed, Bravo November made the comparative safe haven of San Carlos Water without encountering the enemy.

San Carlos Water 29 May 1982

The detachment is still camping out amidst the 'diddle dee' (Falklands heather). An Argentine naval officer on forward reconnaissance duties was caught by marines during the night one kilometer from the detachment's location. Rations and water continue to be scarce as does the prospect of obtaining adequate tentage for the groundcrew. In addition, communications with *HMS Fearless* and hence the tasking cell are unreliable.

No 3 Para were moved by Bravo November from Port San Carlos to Teal Inlet which was captured earlier in the day.

30 May 1982

The Detachment moved to Port San Carlos to occupy three garages and a conservatory, the property of Mr Alan Miller, Farm Manager. The new accommodation provides protection from the elements and reliable communications.

The day time sorties involved taking ammunition to 2 Para at Camilla Creek House, Goose Green and the Teal Creek House.

31 May 1982

Another day of red alerts and living in slit trenches.

The first day's entry in the squadron operations book.

1 June 1982

5 Brigade arrived in San Carlos Water during the night and 7th Gurkha Rifles were assembled on Blue Beach ready to be flown by Bravo November to Darwin and Goose Green, Argentine casualties, blown up own landmines, flown to Ajax Bay for medical treatment.

2-3 June 1982

Remaining Gurkhas moved from Blue Beach to Darwin and Goose Green. Commencement of transporting 1200 prisoners, also from Goose Green to Ajax Bay; 60 POWs carried on each flight.

29 Battery Royal Artillery transferred from Blue Beach to Bluff Cove in the first move to place a ring of artillery and infantry around Stanley.

4 June 1982

Numerous Argentine Canberras overflying Port San Carlos. Argentine Chinook fuel ferry tanks located at Goose Green.

Move of 7th Ghurkas Rifles from Blue Beach to Darwin, returning with POWs from

HMS Antelope *in San Carlos Water.*

Goose Green to Ajax Bay. No 2 Para who were lifted into Fitzroy and Bluff Cove on 2 June were finally reunited with their bergens and personal equipment.

5 June 1982

Several red alerts necessitating a day of slit trench blues. Today saw the beginning of 'Sunday School Outings' for the Royal Navy; over 50 RN personnel were taken by Bravo November to Goose Green in what transpired to be a hunting expedition for souvenirs – helmets, bayonets, weapons and the like. One Surgeon Captain remonstrated with a Chinook crew member for not saluting him – until the dangers of saluting officers in such an environment were pointed out to him.

Bravo November completed 50 flying hours.

6 June 1982

Tasked at first light to lift a downed Sea King from Fanning Head. As it is known to have been unguarded for five days in an area where Argentine troops are known to have been the Royal Navy requested to declare it safe from booby traps before we carry it to a secure area.

More POWs moved from Goose Green to Ajax Bay and 97 Battery were positioned at Bluff Cove.

7 June 1982

A red alert at first light saw San Carlos being attacked by Canberras, one of which was downed by a Rapier missile. The slit trenches are full of water so that if the Argie bombs didn't get you one stood a good chance of drowning.

8 June 1982

The bombing of *Sir Galahad* and *Sir Tristram* involved Bravo November in two casevac sorties in which 57 walking wounded and seven stretcher cases were taken to Ajax Bay.

10 June 1982

First light insertion of 30 marines to Elephant Beach House to bring in Argentine stragglers. More fuel from Port San Carlos to Teal and ammunition from Teal to the Mount Kent gun batteries.

12 June 1982

Second phase push for Stanley scheduled for today; consequently Bravo November was tasked to carry more fuel forward to Fitzroy to keep the remaining task force helicopters airborne. Task successfully executed.

14 June 1982

The final push for Stanley began in the early hours with Bravo November carrying the largest tonnage in a single day since she began flying on 27 May.

At 1600 hours news came through at 2359 Zulu time the surrender of the Falklands would take place.

Wing Commander A J Stables, OC of 19 Squadron, wrote in conclusion in the Operations Record Book: 'The one Chinook (Bravo November) carried a greater weight of freight than an entire squadron of Sea Kings.'

In Harm's Way

Perhaps the most dangerous moments for Bravo November and her crew in the Falklands came on the night of 30 May 1982 when the aircraft positioned at Green Beach in preparation for a planned series of sorties to Mount Kent where a force of SAS soldiers required reinforcements, heavier weapons and ammunition. Tom Jones was one of the crew along with Sqd Ldr Dick Langworthy, Flt Lt Andrew Lawless and Sgt Gary Rogan. Night vision goggles would be worn.

For the first sortie, the Chinook transported three light guns (one underslung), plus 21 troops with their equipment. The aircraft set off at 2030hrs in excellent weather and took a route that avoided enemy positions at Top and Lower Malo House and Estancia House. Argentine forces were also known to be in the vicinity of Mount Kent.

After a 30-minute flight, flashes from a torch indicated the drop point for the underslung load which was duly delivered, an operation carried out in darkness as no lights could be used in case they drew the attention of the enemy. The other two guns were to be placed 50 metres on either side of the first gun. Despite being assured by SAS Commander, Lt Col Michael Rose, that the landing site was flat and secure, the terrain was actually boggy and rough and unfortunately, upon landing, the rear wheels sank into the soft ground and prevented the ramp from being lowered. The aircraft re-positioned until the ramp could be opened sufficiently to allow the first of the internal guns to be off-loaded together with the troops. As the process was being repeated for the second gun there were problems with the winch cable and winch hook and damage was sustained to the ramp. The gun had to be manhandled off the helicopter. Tom's written record of the incident states: As a consequence '...the unloading took 35 minutes during which time rising tension married with exchanges of gunfire on the ridge 200 metres away fostered an electric atmosphere within the aircraft.'

Incoming artillery rounds

Many years later, Flt Lt Lawless recalled of the night: 'The fog of war intervened – the ground was not flat and was covered in boulders. We couldn't find anywhere to land. I can distinctly remember troops moving under the rotor disc firing their guns – this was not part of the plan. There were incoming artillery rounds. Finally, just as the guns were about to be unloaded the SAS, covering the landing area, engaged a company of Argentine troops to the north-east.'

Bravo November headed back to San Carlos but the crew soon found they were flying into a snowstorm. Then their night vision goggles began to fail. Due to a faulty altimeter and lack of visibility, the Chinook hit the sea about

> " I can distinctly remember troops moving under the rotor disc firing their guns – this was not part of the plan. There were incoming artillery rounds. Finally, just as the guns were about to be unloaded the SAS, covering the landing area, engaged a company of Argentine troops to the north-east.
> **Flt Lt Andrew Lawless, Bravo November** "

two miles north west of Estancia House. 'We were lucky, because if we had hit solid ground we would have been dead', said Lawless. 'We hit at 100 knots. The bow-wave came over the cockpit window as we settled and the engines partially flamed out. I knew we had ditched, but I was not sure if we had been hit. Dick (the pilot) said he thought we had been hit by ground fire. As the helicopter settled, the bow wave reduced. We had the collective still up and the engine wound up. We came out of the water like a cork out of a bottle. We were climbing!'

In the back of the helicopter, Tom Jones had lost his helmet in the impact and had been about to jump out, believing the helicopter to be breaking up. A crewman beckoned him to put on another helmet and by the time he was on the intercom he learnt that the helicopter was climbing and passing 1500 feet!

Cockpit door missing

ZA718 had held together although its radio antenna had been ripped off, the autopilot had failed, there were holes in the fuselage and the cockpit door was missing after it had been jettisoned by the co-pilot.

The crew noticed a cluster of lights and flew towards them; it was SS Uganda at anchor in Foul Bay. Having established their approximate position, Bravo November headed south. By now the aircraft was 65 minutes late and returning to base from a direction and height not previously briefed. To avoid the risk of being shot down by friendly forces all the aircraft lights were switched on; in addition a radio call was made although the aircraft's radio receiver was not functioning so they had no way of knowing if their message was picked up.

As they approached base they could see the lights of Port San Carlos. Tom recorded: 'It was discovered later that the radio call had been received and the blackout broken to provide sufficient lighting for a landing. Apart from the ramp, no other damage to the aircraft was detected. However, the remaining three sorties were abandoned until a more detailed damage inspection could be carried out.'

That time spent on the Norland discovering just how many troops could be packed into a Chinook proved to have been usefully employed when, on 2 June, the crew were tasked by Brigadier Wilson to transport a company of 2 Para from Goose Green to Fitzroy and Bluff Cove – both locations having been vacated by the Argentine forces one hour previously. Tom wrote in the Operations Record Book: 'The remaining daylight hours would only permit two sorties in which to transport 154 paratroops, each man carrying personal weapons, additional ammunition and four mortar rounds. This amounted to double the normal permitted load.

'Although the operation was completed without incident in the failing light and poor visibility, it was subsequently discovered that

Flight of Fancy!

In August that year Dame Vera Lynn accepted an invitation to open a fete in Dorchester. The TV presenter Noel Edmonds offered to collect Dame Vera in his helicopter. Unfortunately it broke down.

The RAF stepped in and offered the services of a Chinook. It so happened that Bravo November was the only one available with Tom Jones aboard as crewman. The Chinook duly landed in Dame Vera Lynn's garden in the village of Ditchling, West Sussex, and flew the great lady off to her appointment.

Accompanying Dame Vera was her daughter, Virginia. From this chance encounter, a romance blossomed between Tom and Virginia with the couple eventually marrying. You could say that 'fete' moves in mysterious ways! Tom Jones rose to the rank of Squadron Leader before retiring from the RAF in 1993.

Top: Dame Vera Lynn waves goodbye to onlookers from the doorway of Bravo November as it lifts from a Dorchester field.

Below: Vera with her daughter Virginia, late husband Harry Lewis and the 1992 crew of this remarkable Chinook. Tom Jones is kneeling just in front of Virginia.

the SAS in the mountains above Fitzroy very nearly "took out" Bravo November with a Striker missile, thinking it to be an Argentine Chinook. This was a result of them not being informed that the helicopter was flying to a location 45 miles from its known position of operation.'

Another lucky escape

Fortunately, the SAS held their fire when they spotted that the tell-tale door was missing on the left hand side of the cockpit. It was another very lucky escape for Bravo November.

By the time the Argentines surrendered, Bravo November had notched up over a hundred flying hours, carried some 1500 troops, 95 casualties, 650 POWs and 550 tons of cargo. Sqn Ldr Langworthy was awarded a DFC for his bravery at the controls of ZA718 during the campaign – sadly, almost a year later, he died of a heart attack after returning to the Falklands to lead the Chinook detachment. By chance this included Bravo November and, in a unique honour, the Air Force Board approved the placing of a plaque commemorating his DFC in the helicopter's cockpit.

Bravo November: Still flying after all these years

Twenty years after the Falklands campaign, Bravo November was back with 18 Squadron as the unit was preparing to send a detachment to the Middle East on board *HMS Ark Royal* in the build-up to the invasion of Iraq. During the liberation of Iraq, Bravo November spearheaded the assault on the Al Faw peninsula, the site of a major oil refinery, being the first British helicopter to land Royal Marines ashore in Iraq. The mission was to pre-empt any attempt by the Iraqis to sabotage the oil refineries.

Squadron Leader Steve Carr was nominated to plan and lead the first wave of five Chinooks that were to land the commandos, and he chose ZA718 to lead the mission. They overcame adverse weather conditions with visibility reduced by dust and smoke, all while dodging relentless opposition fire. 'I was flying Bravo November on the first wave,' recalled Carr. 'Visibility was down to 1000 to 1500 metres – it was very dark, there was low cloud and the air was full of dust thrown up by American tank columns and artillery fire. Our night vision goggles were not much use. We went down to 50 feet when we entered Iraq.

Each aircraft had 42 Marines on board plus their rucksacks, each weighing around 60 kilograms. We had removed all the seats, so the troops were all stood up, holding on to ropes that we had strung across the cabin roof. Once we'd been cleared in to the landing site, the aircraft went in three waves, two pairs and a singleton, each element about one minute apart. The Marines must have been pretty pumped up as they were out of my aircraft in 12 seconds. Within two minutes over 200 Marines were on the ground.

'Tracer all over the place'

'On the second run we were in a fire-fight, with tracer all over the place. Fortunately, all of it seemed to be outgoing.'

The Chinooks were not the only aircraft in the air over Al Faw and the 18 Squadron pilots had to carefully co-ordinate their missions to prevent accidents. 'You know it's for real when you are talking on the radio to two American AC-130 Spectre gunships in orbit above you, engaging some Iraqis who are firing at the Marines from entrenched positions,' said Carr. 'It was quite exciting. It was a busy piece of air space.'

During a three-day period, the aircraft averaged 19 flight-hours per day, delivering combat vehicles, artillery and troops. The mission was the first opposed UK helicopter assault since the Suez Crisis in 1956 and the largest in UK military helicopter history.

Over the next three weeks, 18 Squadron flew support missions for British troops operating around Basra, before returning home early in the summer. The squadron's contribution to the success of the Al Faw operation was recognised with Carr being awarded the Distinguished Flying Cross for his role in the operation.

Three years later on the night of 11 June 2006 Flight Lieutenant Craig Wilson, captain of Bravo November in Afghanistan, was

Above: A Chinook in action in Afghanistan. After the Falklands, Chinook ZA718 – Bravo November – went on to serve in Lebanon, Germany, Northern Ireland, Kurdistan and Iraq. It is still in service today and has flown on active duty in Afghanistan. Over the course of a decade, the veteran HC1 Chinook was subject to a myriad of minor modifications and refinements resulting in no two airframes being the same. In May 1993, Bravo November became the first RAF Chinook to be converted to Chinook HC2 standard, work being completed a year later. It was this conversion that has granted Bravo November such remarkable longevity – that and a healthy combination of expert crews and good old-fashioned luck!

tasked to recover a casualty from a landing site in Helmand Province. In difficult and dangerous conditions, despite having done little night flying in that country, he flew at 150ft and made a precision landing to extract the casualty.

Making helicopter history

A few hours later he was tasked with a further casevac, but had to hold off while an Apache gunship suppressed Taliban fire. Wilson accomplished another difficult landing before returning to base with just enough fuel to remain airborne. Despite having been on duty for over 22 hours he then volunteered to deliver reinforcements to help British troops caught up in a threatening situation on the ground. His extreme and persistent courage also ensured the recovery of two badly wounded soldiers and played a vital role in saving their lives.

Flight Lieutenant Wilson received the DFC for 'exceptional courage and outstanding airmanship' while operating in Helmand Province. He said it was a team effort, adding: 'I suppose really it's sort of bitter sweet, as it's very nice to receive an award, but it's for everybody. You can't do it on your own, but it just happened to be my name that was put forward. It takes four people to fly a Chinook.'

This is Lewes artist Bob Mayston's depiction of the famous Carolyn Grace Spitfire that can also be seen in an aerial photograph on page 221. This aircraft actually flew in action in World War II and is credited with downing the first enemy fighter to be destroyed on D-Day 6 June 1944. It is still flown regularly at air shows and events. As such, Spitfire ML 407 truly symbolises the spirit of this book. It's a flying icon that's still with us – Seventy Years On!

Below: Bob Mayston has also painted HMS Daring, the Royal Navy's newest and most powerful Type 45 Destroyer. The ship was formally commissioned in July 2009 and is based in Portsmouth. The painting was presented to Captain Paddy McAlpine OBE in July 2010 and now hangs in the Captain's Cabin of HMS Daring.

ACKNOWLEDGEMENTS

I have had a great deal of assistance over the years in putting together first, *Fifty Years On*, then *Sixty Years On* and now this new edition, *Seventy Years On*.

It is impossible to name everybody but in particular in respect of this new book I would like to thank Dame Vera Lynn DBE, LLD, her daughter Virginia and son-in-law, Tom Jones for their gracious help. It is very pleasing to be able to include Tom's own astonishing story about the Chinook helicopter, Bravo November. Tom was a member of the crew of this machine that saw action in the Falklands War in 1982 and, nearly three decades later, was still flying on active service supporting British forces in Afghanistan.

That Dame Vera herself has flown in Bravo November is in itself amazing but it is also doubly delightful that her flight was the key to Tom and Virginia meeting and later marrying.

My grateful thanks must also go to the National Archives who gave me access to the original artwork of a range of dramatic wartime posters and paintings. They greatly enhance this book as they did for *Sixty Years On*.

Virginia and Frank Wootton OBE

My friend Mrs Virginia Wootton has made an immense contribution in generously allowing me to reproduce a number of the works of her late artist husband Frank Wootton OBE, along with some of his own wartime experiences as recounted in his own words. Sadly, Ginny has not lived to see this second book published; she passed away on 23 March 2010.

I am very grateful to another celebrated artist, David Shepherd CBE, for making

SEVENTY YEARS ON

available two of his most evocative paintings of wartime – 'Arnhem Bridge, 5pm' and 'Winter of 1943 – Somewhere in England'. By the way, I do apologise to David for digging up the somewhat disturbing implication that there may two unexploded German bombs buried somewhere on his Sussex property. For certain, I do not recommend any other kind of digging up!

The photographic contents of *Seventy Years On* have come from many sources, the main one being the men and women who have contributed so much to the content of this book. These people either experienced the war years and subsequent post-war conflicts or knew individuals who did and took the time to write up their stories. I thank them all and am only sorry that despite the length of this book I could not include all of the fascinating tales that came my way. It is my intention to quickly develop a *Seventy Years On* website to feature many more real life stories.

Travels to Italy, France and Holland

The Imperial War Museum have kindly furnished me with a number of photographs over the years and much other material has been collected by me in my many travels to Italy, Normandy, Holland and farther afield. A significant number of unique photographs and documents have been furnished by friends and family, not least that of my wife, Barbara.

In any event, if I have inadvertently failed to acknowledge a picture source, I apologise and give my assurance that the omission was not intentional.

I must also thank all my former magazine colleagues from my days as Editor of *Motoring & Leisure* who gave me great support in putting together the previous book, *Sixty Years On*. They all have wished me well with this latest project. I greatly appreciated their many offers of help, some of which I took up, but more often I just needed to press on, not least because my book designer Marion Hughes was always more aware of looming deadlines than ever I was.

Finally, in closing I would like to dedicate *Seventy Years On* to two people. One is my little brother Jimmy Arnold (1955–1966) in memory of the many happy hours we spent playing with our army of little soldiers. The other is the late Margaret Simpson, the much-loved sister of my wife, Barbara. She died aged just 62 in January 2009; a devastating blow to her husband Tony and the whole family.

Margaret was a very good friend to me and always very supportive of my efforts to weave her family's history into a much broader tapestry of our times. If I have succeeded with *Seventy Years On* then I know that Margaret would most certainly have approved and I will be a happier man for that.

David Arnold, July 2010

Left: Frank Wootton is best known for his paintings of aircraft but he also enjoyed painting the Sussex landscapes to be found close to the home he shared with his wife Ginny near Alfriston in the shadow of the rolling South Downs. With quite a few of the stories in Seventy Years On *originating in my home town of Lewes it seems appropriate to acknowledge this rich seam of history by reproducing this work by Frank. It depicts Hamsey Church, a 10th century Saxon building, set on a slight rise in the valley of the River Ouse just a few miles north of Lewes. In fact I can clearly see the chalk pit on the hillside from my bedroom window in St John Street in the town centre. The sight would also have been very familiar to Dennis Moppett and his sister Felicity. Dennis had the misfortune to be captured by the Japanese on Java early in 1942. Along with thousands of fellow prisoners, he endured years of hardship and malnourishment before succumbing to disease and dying on 6 January 1945. Dennis kept a large stash of letters hidden from his captors and they miraculously survived the war and were given to his family. Full of references to places in and around Lewes, they make very poignant reading. Felicity's sons gave me permission to print some of the contents of the letters and the story starts on page 329 of* Seventy Years On. *As peaceful as the scene seems, on the river bank and in the fields around Hamsey Church remain a whole array of pillboxes, hurriedly built in 1940 when the threat of a German invasion was high. The pillboxes are still in place seven decades later.*

LEST WE FORGET

INDEX

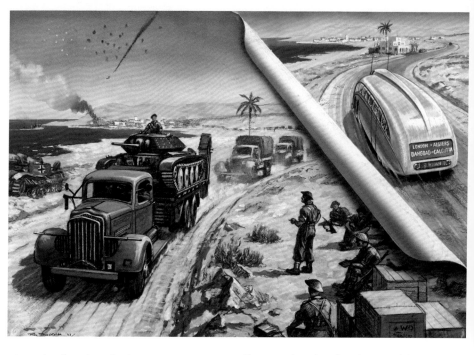

The poster above dates from the years of the North African desert campaign, soon after the decisive Eighth Army victory at El Alamein. The military image (which includes enemy bombers in the background) peels back to show the same location in a peaceful future secured by our forces. It looks ahead to when luxury coaches will speed passengers from London to Algiers and along the North African shore to Baghdad (incorrectly spelt as Bahgdad), Calcutta being the ultimate destination. Artist Roy Nockolds could not have imagined how air travel would eclipse the joys of the long-distance coach, nor that Algiers, Baghdad and Calcutta would not be on most people's ideal holiday destination list, seven decades on!

To view more such fascinating pieces of artwork held by the National Archives, visit:
wwwnationalarchives.gov.uk/theartofwar

Seventy Years On is published by Crown Publishing Ltd, 14 St John Street, Lewes, East Sussex BN7 2QE.

Enquiries regarding the book can be sent by email to: david.arnold@me.com

www.seventyyearson.com